# 1001 GREAT
## FAMILY DAYS OUT

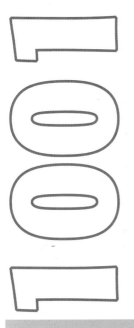

Produced by AA Publishing
Reprinted 2009
© Automobile Association Developments Limited 2007 All rights reserved.

Editorial: lifestyleguides@theAA.com

All images are from AA World Travel Library:

Front cover – all images are from AA World Travel Library:

cl AA/P Baker; c AA/K Doran; cr AA; bl AA/S L Day; bc AA/W Voysey; br AA/J A Tims

p1tl AA/P Baker; p1tc AA/K Doran; p1tr AA; p1b AA/J A Tims; p4-5 AA/M Moody; p46b AA/M Moody; p47 AA/R Coulam; p105 AA/L Whitman; p207 AA/S McBride; p208-9 AA/M Jourdan; p255 AA/R Elliot; p308 AA/J Smith; p309 AA/G Matthews; p340-1 AA/S Day; p349b S Whitehorne

Printed in Italy by Printer Trento SRL, Trento

Published by AA Publishing, which is a trading name of Automobile Association Developments Limited whose registered office is Fanum House, Basingstoke, Hampshire, RG21 4EA

CIP catalogue record for this book is available from the British Library Registered number 1878835.

ISBN-10: 0-7495-4853-3
ISBN-13: 978-0-7495-4853-7

A04074

# How to use the guide

**①** CARLISLE

**②** **Tullie House Museum & Art Gallery**

**③** Castle Street CA3 8TP
☎ 01228 534781 ▤ 01228 810249
**Email:** enquiries@tulliehouse.co.uk
**Web:** www.tulliehouse.co.uk

**④** **Dir:** *M6 junct 42, 43 or 44 follow signs to city centre. Car park in Devonshire Walk*

**⑤** Dramatic audio-visual displays, striking recreations of long vanished scenes and imaginative hands-on displays. There is something for everyone, no matter what age - the stunning underground Millennium Gallery or Border River pathway linking to Carlisle Castle.

**⑥** **Times:** *Open: Nov-Mar, Mon-Sat 10-4, Sun 12-4; Apr-Jun & Sep-Oct, Mon-Sat 10-5, Sun 12-5; Jul-Aug, Mon-Sat 10-5, Sun 11-5. Closed 25-26 Dec & 1 Jan.

**⑦** **Fee:** *Ground floor (including Art Gallery & Old Tullie House) - Free. Upper floors & Millennium Gallery - £5.20 (ch £2.60 concessions £3.60) Family ticket (2ad+3ch) £14.50

**⑧** **Facilities:** ℗ (5mins walk - disabled parking on site by request) ⦿ (Licensed) 🗐 ♿ (chair lift, ramped access, lifts to all floors, toilets), shop ⊗ (ex guide dogs) 🚌

---

This guide is divided into regions. Within each region counties are listed alphabetically. To find a particular county refer to the page opposite. Locations and attractions names are listed alphabetically.

**①** **Town name**

**②** **Establishment name**

**③** **Contact details:**
The STD code is shown before the telephone number. (if dialing Northern Ireland from England, Scotland or Wales, use the STD code, but for the Republic of Ireland you need to prefix the number with 00353, and drop the first zero from the Irish area code)

**④** **Directions:**
Where shown these have been provided by the places of interest themselves. Please telephone for directions where these are not supplied.

**⑤** **Description**

**⑥** **Times:**
Times quoted in the guide are inclusive - for instance, where you see Apr-Oct, that place will be open from the beginning of April to the end of October. An asterisk * before the times means they are not confirmed for 2007.

**⑦** **Fees:**
Prices for most entries are current. An asterisk * before the prices means they are not confirmed for 2007. If no price is quoted, please contact the attraction for information.

**⑧** **Facilities:**
This section includes information on parking, refreshments, gift shops, accessibility and whether dogs are allowed admission. Visitors with mobility disabilities should look for the wheelchair symbol. We strongly recommend that you telephone in advance of your visit to check exact details, particularly regarding access to toilets and refreshment facilties. Assist dogs are usually accepted where attractions show the 'no dogs' symbol unless otherwise stated. *Please note: Opening times and admission prices are subject to change.*

| Keys to symbols and abbreviations | | | |
|---|---|---|---|
| Telephone | ☎ | Coaches | 🚌 |
| Fax Number | ▤ | English Heritage | ⚏ |
| Suitable for visitors in wheelchairs | ♿ | National Trust | 🌿 |
| Parking at Establishments | ℗ | National Trust for Scotland | 🗝 |
| Parking nearby | ℗ | Historic Scotland | 🏛 |
| Refreshments | ⬚ | Cadw (Welsh Historic Monuments) | ⬧ |
| Restaurant | ⦿ | No credit cards accepted | 🈺 |
| Picnic Area | ⚠ | Bank holidays | BH |
| Worksheets Available | 🗐 | Prices/Times not confirmed for 2007 | * |
| No dogs | ⊗ | | |

# Contents

**3**

# Central England

Iron Age hill fort in the Malvern Hills

## CHESTER
### Chester Zoo
Upton-by-Chester CH2 1LH
☎ 01244 380280 📠 01244 371273
**Email:** marketing@chesterzoo.co.uk
**Web:** www.chesterzoo.org
**Dir:** *2m N of city centre off A41 & M53 junct 10 southbound, junct 12 all other directions*
The largest zoological gardens in the UK, with more than 7,000 animals of more than 500 species. Catch feeding time on Sealion Beach, visit Islands in Danger with the Komodo Dragons, feel the Spirit of the Jaguar and the awesome Tsavo-the Black Rhino Experience. Take to the treetops in the Zoofari overhead railway.
**Times:** *Open all year, daily from 10. Last admission varies with season from 5.30pm high summer to 3.30pm winter. (Closed 25-26 Dec).
**Fee:** *£14.50 (ch £10.50). Family ticket £47.50.
**Facilities:** 🅿 ⓟ (next door) 🍴 (Licensed) ⛽ ♿ (electric scooters, audio guide, induction loop, Braille, toilets) shop, ⊗ (ex guide & sensory dogs) 🚌

## CHESTER
### Dewa Roman Experience
Pierpoint Lane (off Bridge St) CH1 1NL
☎ 01244 343407 📠 01244 347737
**Email:** info@dewaromanexperience.co.uk
**Web:** www.dewaromanexperience.co.uk
**Dir:** *city centre*
Stroll along reconstructed streets experiencing the sights, sounds and smells of Dewa (the Roman name for Chester). Starting with a roman galley the tour includes a reconstructed street giving a flavour of life inside a Roman fort. You return to the present day via an extensive archaeological 'dig', where you can discover the substantial Roman, Saxon and medieval remains that lie beneath modern Chester. Roman soldier patrols are available as guides.
**Times:** Open all year,  daily Feb-Nov 9-5, Dec-Jan 10-4 . (Closed 25-26 Dec & 1st Jan).
**Fee:** *£4.25 (ch £2.50, under 5's free, concessions £3.75). Family ticket £12. Party £3.25 (10 or more)
**Facilities:** ⓟ (200yds) ♿ shop, guided tours ⊗ (ex guide dogs) 🚌 🚲

## ELLESMERE PORT
### Blue Planet Aquarium
Cheshire Oaks CH65 9LF
☎ 0151 357 8804 📠 0151 356 7288
**Email:** info@blueplanetaquarium.co.uk
**Web:** www.blueplanetaquarium.com
**Dir:** *off M53 junct 10 at Cheshire Oaks. Follow signs for aquarium*
A voyage of discovery on the longest moving walkway in the world. Beneath the waters of the Carribean Reef, see giant rays and menacing sharks pass inches from your face, stroke some favourite fish in the special rock pools, or pay a visit to the incredible world of poisonous frogs. Divers hand feed the fish and sharks throughout the day and can answer questions via state of the art communication systems.
**Times:** Open all year, daily from 10. (Closed Xmas). Seasonal variations in closing times, please call to confirm.
**Fee:** *£9.95 (ch (3-15) £7.50, under 3's free, concessions £7.50). Family ticket from £34.
**Facilities:** 🅿 ⓟ (100 yds) ⛽ 📕 £2.95 for guide book ♿ (wheelchair hire, lifts, hearing loop, toilets) shop, guided tours ⊗ (ex guide dogs) 🚌 (group rates, must book in advance)

## ELLESMERE PORT
### Boat Museum
South Pier Road CH65 4FW
☎ 0151 355 5017
📠 0151 355 4079
**Email:** bookings@thewaterwaystrust.org
**Web:** www.boatmuseum.org.uk
**Dir:** *M53 junct 9*
Occupying a historic dock complex at the junction of the Shropshire Union and Manchester Ship Canals, this museum has the world's largest collection of floating canal craft, from a small weedcutter to a 300-ton coaster. Boat trips are also available. There are indoor exhibitions on canal life and local history, together with period worker's cottages, a blacksmith's forge and working engines.

**Times:** *Open Summer daily 10-5. Winter daily 10-4. (Closed 25 & 26 Dec).
**Fee:** *£6.45 (ch £4.75, concessions £5.25). Family ticket £18.50, senior family ticket £17.75.
**Facilities:** 🅿 ☕ (Opening times as museum) 🪑 📱 ♿ (tactile map for blind, free wheelchair use, toilets) shop, guided tours ⊗ ex guide dogs 🚌 Pre-booking preferred

## JODRELL BANK
### Jodrell Bank Visitor Centre & Arboretum
Macclesfield SK11 9DL
☎ 01477 571339 📠 01477 571695
**Web:** www.manchester.ac.uk/jodrellbank
**Dir:** *M6 junct 18, A535 Holmes Chapel to Chelford road*
Set within the splendid 35-acre Granada Arboretum with its National collections of Malus and Sorbus, the observatory at Jodrell Bank Visitor Centre, has a scientific and engineering wonder – the magnificent Lovell telescope, one of the largest radio telescopes in the world. The new Observational Pathway leads you 180 degrees around the telescope. Within the complex there is a 3D-theatre, shop, café and a small exhibition area as well as the Environmental Discovery Centre. The Planetarium is currently under re-development.

**Times:** *Open daily Nov-mid Mar 10.30-3, wknds 11-4; mid Mar-end Oct 10.30-5.30
**Fee:** *£1.50 (ch 4-16yrs £1) 3D theatre £1
**Facilities:** 🅿 🪑 ♿ (wheelchair loan, toilets) shop, ⊗ (ex guide dogs) 🚌 (pre-booking required)

## KNUTSFORD
### Tatton Park
WA16 6QN
☎ 01625 534400
📠 01625 534403
**Email:** tatton@cheshire.gov.uk
**Web:** www.tattonpark.org.uk
**Dir:** *5m from M6 junct 19, or M56 junct 7. Signed on A556, 4m S of Altrincham. Entrance to Tatton Park on Ashley Rd, 1.5m NE of junct A5034 with A50*
Tatton is one of England's most complete historic estates, with gardens and a 1000-acre country park. The centrepiece is the Georgian mansion, with gardens laid out by Humphry Repton and Sir Joseph Paxton. More recently, a Japanese garden with a Shinto temple was created. The Tudor Old Hall is the original manor house,
where a guided tour is available. There is also a 1930s working farm and a children's adventure playground. Special events most weekends include the RHS flower show and open air concerts.
**Times:** Open mid Mar-early Oct, Tue-Sun & BH 1-5; Gardens & parkland all year Tue-Sun & BH.
**Fee:** *Mansion, £3.50 (ch £2), family £9, groups 12+ £2.80 (ch £1.60) Saver tickets available
**Facilities:** 🅿 (charged) 🍴 (Licensed) 🪑 ♿ (old hall & areas of farm not accessible, Braille guides, toilets) shop, garden centre, guided tours ⊗ (ex in parkland) 🚌 🐾

**CHESHIRE**

**CHESHIRE**

## MACCLESFIELD
### Macclesfield Silk Museum
Heritage Centre Roe Street SK11 6UT
☎ 01625 613210 ▤ 01625 617880
**Email:** info@macclesfield.silk.museum
**Web:** www.macclesfield.silk.museum
**Dir:** *Turn off A523 & follow brown signs in town centre*
The development of the silk industry in Macclesfield is told through a colourful and award-winning audio-visual programme. For over 200 years Macclesfield was the leading producer of silk in Britain. Displays of silk costumes and textiles further illustrate the importance of silk to the textile industry. The Silk Museum is part of the Macclesfield Heritage Centre which also runs a full and varied programme of exhibitions, musical and artistic events throughout the year.

**Times:** Open all year, Mon-Sat 11-5, Sun & BH Mon 1-5. Closed 25-26 Dec, 1 Jan & Good Fri.
Please ring for winter Opening times.
**Fee:** *£3.60 (concessions £2.95). Joint ticket with Paradise Mill £7.25 (concessions £5.95). Accompanied ch free
**Facilities:** Ⓟ (50mtrs) †◎¶ (Licensed) 🍴 ♿ (ramps, chairlift, audio guides, induction loop, toilets) shop ⊗ (ex guide dogs) 🚌 (pre-booking)

## MACCLESFIELD
### Paradise Mill & Silk Industry Museum
Park Lane SK11 6TJ
☎ 01625 612045 ▤ 01625 612048
**Email:** info@macclesfield.silk.museum
**Web:** www.macclesfield.silk.museum
**Dir:** *turn off A523 'The Silk Rd' & follow brown signs*
A working silk mill until 1981, with restored jacquard hand looms in their original location. Knowledgeable guides, many of them former silk mill workers, illustrate the silk production process with the help of demonstrations from weavers. Exhibitions and room settings give an impression of working conditions at the mill during the 1930s. Adjacent Silk Industry Museum opened in 2001 and focuses on the design and manufacturing processes.

**Times:** Open all year, BH Mon & Mon-Sat from 11-5 (Closed Sun, 25-26 Dec & 1 Jan, Good Fri)
**Fee:** *£4.10 (concessions £3.45), family £10.80, joint ticket with Silk Museum £7.25 (concessions £5.95)
**Facilities:** Ⓟ (100yds) ♿ (care needed on uneven floors in Paradise Mill, toilets) shop, guided tours ⊗ (ex guide dogs) 🚌 (pre-booked)

## MOULDSWORTH
### Mouldsworth Motor Museum
Smithy Lane CH3 8AR
☎ 01928 731781
**Web:** www.mouldsworthmotormuseum.com
**Dir:** *6m E of Chester, off B5393, signposted. Or M56 junct 12 into Frodsham then B5393 into Mouldsworth, follow brown heritage signs in village*
Housed in a 1937 Art Deco building close to Delamere Forest, this is a superb collection of over 60 motor cars, motorcycles and bicycles. There is also a massive collection of automobilia – old signs, pumps, tools, mascots and badges, as well as old motoring toys, Dinky cars and pedal cars all complemented by a motoring art gallery, that has posters and advertising material. School parties are encouraged for a guided tour and structured talk. Motoring clubs visit on Sundays. There is also a Harry Potter car for children to sit in. Also holds a collection of early teapots, many from 1920s and 30s.
**Times:** *Open Feb-Nov (Sun only), Etr wknd, early May BH Mon, Spring BH Sun-Mon & Aug BH wknd; Sun, Feb-Nov; also Wed, Jul-Aug, noon-5.
**Fee:** £4 (ch £2, including free quiz with prizes)
**Facilities:** Ⓟ Ⓟ (100yds) 🍴 ♿ (hands on items) shop, guided tours 🚌 2 coaches at any one time ⊚

## NANTWICH
### Stapeley Water Gardens
London Road Stapeley CW5 7LH
☎ 01270 623868 & 628628 🖷 01270 624919
**Email:** info@stapeleywg.com
**Web:** www.stapeleywg.com
**Dir:** *off M6 junct 16, 1m S of Nantwich on A51*
Stapeley Water Gardens consists of three main areas.
The Palms Tropical Oasis is a glass pavilion which is
home to sharks, piranhas, parrots, skunks and exotic
flowers. The two-acre Water Garden Centre houses the
national collection of water-lilies, as well as Koi carp and
other water features. There is also a garden centre with a
children's play area.
**Times:** Open Summer: Mon-Sat 9-6, BHs 10-6, Sun 10-
4, Wed 9-8; Winter: Mon-Sat 9-5, BHs 10-5, Sun 10-4,
(Wed 9-8 Angling dept only). The Palms Tropical Oasis
Open from 10
**Fee:** The Palms Tropical Oasis £4.45 (ch £2.60,
concessions £3.95). Family ticket (2 ad & 2 ch) £12.10
(2 ad & 3 ch) £14.30.
**Facilities:** 🅿 †◎¹ (Licensed) 🗒 ⅊ (free wheelchair loan,
toilets) shop, garden centre ⊗ (ex guide dogs) 🚌

## NESTON
### Liverpool University Botanic Gardens
### (Ness Gardens)
Ness Gardens South Wirral CH64 4AY
☎ 0151 353 0123 🖷 0151 353 1004
**Email:** nessgdns@liv.ac.uk
**Web:** www.nessgardens.org.uk
**Dir:** *off A540 near Ness-on-Wirral, follow signs*
A long association with plant collectors ensures a wide
range of plants, providing interest for academics,
horticulturists and amateurs alike. There are tree and
shrub collections, water and rock gardens, herbaceous
borders and glasshouses. A regular programme of
lectures, courses and special events take place
throughout the year for which tickets must be obtained in
advance. A new visitor centre offers meeting and
conference facilities, and weekly exhibitions by local
artists.
**Times:** Open all year, Nov-Feb, daily 9.30-4; Mar-Oct,
daily 9.30-5. (Closed 25 Dec).
**Fee:** *£4.70 (ch free admission when accompanied with
an adult, concessions £4.30)
**Facilities:** 🅿 🅟 (250mtrs – reserved grass field) 🍴
⅊ (wheelchair route, induction loop in lecture theatre,
toilets) shop, garden centre ⊗ (ex guide dogs)
🚌 (please book in advance)

## NORTHWICH
### Arley Hall & Gardens
CW9 6NA
☎ 01565 777353 & 777284 🖷 01565 777465
**Email:** enquiries@arleyhallandgardens.com
**Web:** www.arleyhallandgardens.com
**Dir:** *5m N of Northwich on B5075. 5m NW of Knutsford
A556*
Owned by the same family since medieval times, the
present Arley Hall was rebuilt in early Victorian times in
the style of a Jacobean stately home and contains fine
furniture, plasterwork, panelling and family portraits. The
gardens include a walled garden, unique clipped Ilex
avenue, herb garden, scented garden and a woodland
garden with rhododendrons, azaleas and exotic trees as
well as the double herbaceous borders, one of the
earliest to be established in England (1846). Special
events for 2007 include:- Country Fair 26-27 May,
Garden Festival 23-24 June, outdoor concerts and plays,
ring for details.
**Times:** Gardens, grounds & chapel: Open Etr-end Sep,
Tue-Sun & BH 11-5. Hall dates TBC
**Fee:** *Gardens, Grounds & Chapel £4.70 (ch 6-16 £2,
concessions £4.20) Family ticket £11.80 Hall £2.50 (ch
6-16 £1, concessions £2). Party 15+.
**Facilities:** 🅿 †◎¹ (Licensed) 🍴 🗒 ⅊ (ramps, parking by
entrance, toilets) shop, garden centre, guided tours
⊗ (ex in gardens on lead) 🚌 (min 15 people)

**CHESHIRE**

## NORTHWICH

### Salt Museum

162 London Road CW9 8AB

☎ 01606 41331 🖷 01606 350420

**Email:** cheshiremuseums@cheshire.gov.uk

**Web:** www.saltmuseum.org.uk

**Dir:** on A533 0.5m S of town centre and 0.5m N of
A556. Well signposted from A556

Britain's only Salt Museum tells the fascinating story
of Cheshire's oldest industry which dates back over
2,000 years. With the aid of models, reconstructions,
photographs, original artefacts and audio-visual
rogrammes the museum throws a new light on the
production of something we all take for granted.

**Times:** Open Tue-Fri 10-5, wknds 2-5 (Sun 12-5 in Aug)
Open BH & Mons in Aug 10-5.

**Fee:** *£2.50 (ch £1.20, concessions £2) Family ticket (2
ad + 2 ch) £6

**Facilities:** 🅿 🍴 (No hot food) 📖 ♿ (introductory video
with induction loop facilities, toilets) shop ⊗ (ex guide
dogs) 🚌 (advance bookings preferred)

## STYAL

### Quarry Bank Mill & Styal Estate

Wilmslow SK9 4LA

☎ 01625 527468 🖷 01625 539267

**Email:** quarrybankmill@nationaltrust.org.uk

**Web:** www.quarrybankhill.org.uk

**Dir:** 1.5m N of Wilmslow off B5166, 2.5m from M56
junct 5, 10m S of Manchester. Heritage signs from A34
and M56

Founded in 1784, Quarry Bank Mill is one of the finest
surviving cotton mills of the period. Inside the water and
steam-powered mill there are hands-on exhibits and
demonstrations that show how traditional spinning and
weaving was transformed through the ingenuity of early
textile engineers. Using the most powerful working
waterwheel in Europe, two mill engineers bring the past
to life. At the Apprentice House you can discover what
home life was like for the pauper children who worked
in the mill in the 1830s. After all this history take a walk
through surrounding wood and farmland along the River
Bollin.

**Times:** Apr-Sep daily 11-5 (last admission 4); Oct-Mar,
Wed-Sun 11-4. Last admission 3. Apprentice House &
Garden, Tue-Sun, Oct-Mar Wed-Sun: Timed tours

**Fee:** Mill & Apprentice House £9 (ch £4.70). Family ticket
£20. Mill only £6 (ch £3.70). Family ticket £16.

**Facilities:** 🅿 (charged) 🍴 (Licensed) 🚻 ♿ (wheelchairs,
chairlift, ramps, Braille & large print guide, toilets) shop,
⊗ (ex in park) 🚌 (usually not on Sun) 💐

## WIDNES

### Catalyst Science Discovery Centre

Mersey Road WA8 0DF

☎ 0151 420 1121 🖷 0151 495 2030

**Email:** info@catalyst.org.uk

**Web:** www.catalyst.org.uk

**Dir:** signed from M62 junct 7 and M56 junct 12

Enter a colourful world of science and technology in
interactive galleries, and experience an amazing journey
of discovery in the interactive theatre. Take a trip in an
all-glass external lift to the Observatory, 100 feet above
the River Mersey. A range of special events is planned
throughout the year. Please ring for details.

**Times:** *Open all year, Tue-Fri daily & BH Mon 10-5,
wknds 11-5. (Closed Mon ex BH's, 24-26 & 31 Dec &
1 Jan).

**Fee:** *£4.95 (ch 5-16, concessions £3.95). Family ticket
(2+2, 1+3) £15.95, (2+3) £17.95.

**Facilities:** 🅿 🅿 (200yds) ♿ (toilets) shop ⊗ (ex guide
dogs) 🚌 (advance booking)

## BOLSOVER
### Bolsover Castle
Castle Street S44 6PR
☎ 01246 822844 📠 01246 241569
**Web:** www.english-heritage.org.uk
**Dir:** *on A632*
This award-winning property has the air of a romantic storybook castle, with its turrets and battlements rising from a wooded hilltop. See the stunning Venus garden with its beautiful statuary and fountain. State-of-the-art audio tours are available.
**Times:** Open all year, Apr, Oct, Thu-Mon 10-5 (4 on Sat); May-Sep, daily 10-6 (4 on Sat); Aug, daily 10-7; Nov-Mar, Thu-Mon 10-4. Closed 24-26 Dec & 1 Jan. May also close early for evening events

**Fee:** £6.60 (ch £3.30, concessions £5). Family £16.50. Prices and opening times are subject to change from Spring 2007. Please check web site or call 0870 333 1181 for the most up to date prices and opening times when planning your visit.
**Facilities:** 🅿 ⛽ ♿ (keep not accessible) shop, 🚫 🚐 ⊞ ♻

## BUXTON
### Poole's Cavern (Buxton Country Park)
Green Lane SK17 9DH
☎ 01298 26978 📠 01298 73563
**Email:** info@poolescavern.co.uk
**Web:** www.poolescavern.co.uk
**Dir:** *1m from Buxton town centre, off A6 and A515*
Limestone rock, water, and millions of years created this natural cavern containing thousands of crystal formations. A 45-minute guided tour leads the visitor through chambers used as a shelter by Bronze-Age cave dwellers, Roman metal workers and as a hideout by the infamous robber Poole. Attractions include the underground source of the River Wye, the 'Poached Egg Chamber', Mary, Queen of Scots' Pillar, the Grand Cascade and underground sculpture formations.

**Times:** *Open Mar-Oct, daily 10-5. (Open in winter for groups only).
**Fee:** *£6.20 (ch £3.50)
**Facilities:** 🅿 ⛽ 📷 ♿ (audio loops, ramps, controllable underground cameras, toilets) shop, guided tours 🚫 (ex guide dogs or in park) 🚐 (pre-booking required)

## CASTLETON
### Blue-John Cavern & Mine
Buxton Road Hope Valley S33 8WP
☎ 01433 620638 & 620642 📠 01433 621586
**Email:** lesley@bluejohn.gemsoft.co.uk
**Web:** www.bluejohn.gemsoft.co.uk
**Dir:** *follow brown Blue-John Cavern signs from Castleton*
A remarkable example of a water-worn cave, over a third of a mile long, with chambers 200ft high. It contains 8 of the 14 veins of Blue John stone. The major source of this unique form of fluorspar for nearly 300 years, it is still mined in the winter months.
**Times:** Open all year, daily, 9.30-5 (or dusk). Guided tours of approx 1hr every 10 mins.
**Fee:** *£7 (ch £3.50, pen & student £5) Family ticket £19. Party rates on request.

**Facilities:** 🅿 Ⓟ (100yds) 📷 ♿ (not suitable for disabled visitors) shop 🚐

DERBYSHIRE

DERBYSHIRE

## CASTLETON
### Peak Cavern
Hope Valley S33 8WS
☎ 01433 620285
**Email:** info@peakcavern.co.uk
**Web:** www.devilsarse.com
**Dir:** *on A6187, in centre of Castleton*
One of the most spectacular natural limestone caves in the Peak District, with an electrically-lit underground walk of about half a mile. Ropes have been made for over 500 years in the 'Grand Entrance Hall', and traces of a row of cottages can be seen. Rope-making demonstrations are included on every tour.
**Times:** *Open all year, daily 10-5. Closed 25 Dec
**Fee:** *£6.25 (ch £4.25, other concessions £5.25). Family ticket £18.50.

**Facilities:** 🅿 (charged) Ⓟ (300mtrs) 🚻 📷 £2.95 shop, guided tours 🚌

## CASTLETON
### Speedwell Cavern
Winnats Pass Hope Valley S33 8WA
☎ 01433 620512 📠 01433 621888
**Email:** info@speedwellcavern.co.uk
**Web:** www.speedwellcavern.co.uk
**Dir:** *A625 becomes A6187 at Hathersage. 0.5m W of Castleton*
Descend 105 steps to a boat that takes you on a one-mile underground exploration of floodlit caverns part of which was once a lead mine. The hand-carved tunnels open out into a network of natural caverns and underground rivers. See the Bottomless Pit, a huge subterranean lake in a huge, cathedral-like cavern.
**Times:** Open all year, daily 10-5.30 (Closed 25 Dec). Phone to check Winter opening times due to weather.

Last boat 4
**Fee:** *£6.75 (ch £4.75).
**Facilities:** 🅿 (charged) Ⓟ (200yds – pay & display on roadside) 📷 £2.95 shop, guided tours ⊗ (ex assist dogs) 🚌 (ex weekends or school hols)

## CASTLETON
### Treak Cliff Cavern
Hope Valley S33 8WP
☎ 01433 620571 📠 01433 620519
**Email:** treakcliff@bluejohnstone.com
**Web:** www.bluejohnstone.com
**Dir:** *0.75m W of Castleton on A6187*
An underground world of stalactites, stalagmites, rock and cave formations, minerals and fossils. There are rich deposits of the rare and beautiful Blue John Stone, including The Pillar, the largest piece ever found. Show caves include the Witch's Cave, Aladdin's Cave, Dream Cave and Fairyland Grotto. Visitors can also polish their own Blue John Stone and purchase Blue John Stone jewellery and ornaments in the Castleton Gift Shop.
**Times:** *Open all year, Mar-Oct, daily 10-last tour 4.20,

Nov-Feb daily 10-last tour at 3.20. Tours are 40 mins and guided. Enquire for last tour of day & possible closures. Closed 24-26 & 31 Dec & 1 Jan
**Fee:** *£6.50 (ch 5-15 £3.50). Family ticket (2 ad & 2 ch) £18.
**Facilities:** 🅿 Ⓟ (roadside, charged at wknds & BHs) 🚻 ♿ (walking disabled only) shop, guided tours 🚌

## CHATSWORTH
### Chatsworth

Bakewell DE45 1PP

☎ 01246 582204 📠 01246 583536

**Email:** visit@chatsworth.org

**Web:** www.chatsworth.org

**Dir:** *8m N of Matlock off B6012. 16m from M1 junct 29, signposted via Chesterfield, follow brown signs*

Home of the Duke and Duchess of Devonshire, Chatsworth contains a massive private collection of fine and decorative arts. There is a splendid painted hall, and a great staircase leads to the chapel, decorated with statues and paintings. There are pictures, furniture and porcelain, and a trompe l'oeil painting of a violin on the music room door. The park was laid out by 'Capability' Brown, but is most famous for the work of Joseph Paxton, head gardener in the 19th century. The park is also home to the Duke and Duchess personal collection of contemporary sculpture.

**Times:** *Open 15 Mar-23 Dec, House & Garden 11-5.30, Farmyard 10.30-5.30.

**Fee:** House & Garden: £9.75 (ch £3.50, concessions £7.75). Family ticket £23. Pre-booked group discounts available. Garden only: £6 (ch £2.75, concessions £4). Family ticket £14.50. Farmyard & Adventure Playground: £4.50 (ch under 3 free, pen £3). Groups 5+ £3

**Facilities:** ❷ (charged) 🍽 (Licensed) ♿ (3 electric wheelchairs available for garden, toilets) shop, garden centre, guided tours and audio commentaries (charged) ⊗ (ex park & gardens on lead) 🚌 (pre-booking preferred)

## CRESWELL
### Creswell Crags Museum & Education Centre

Crags Road Welbeck S80 3LH

☎ 01909 720378 📠 01909 724726

**Email:** info@creswell-crags.org.uk

**Web:** www.creswell-crags.org.uk

**Dir:** *off the B6042, Crags Road, between A616 and A60, 1m E of Creswell village*

Creswell Crags, a picturesque limestone gorge with lakes and caves, is one of Britain's most important archaeological sites. The many caves on the site have yielded Ice Age remains, including bones of woolly mammoth, reindeer, hyena and bison, stone tools of Ice Age hunters from over 10,000 years ago and new research has revealed the only Ice Age rock art in Britain (about 13,000 years old). Visit the Museum and Education Centre to learn more about your Ice Age ancestors through an exhibition, touch-screen computers and video. Join a 'Virtually the Ice Age' cave tour, picnic in Crags Meadow, or try the new activity trail. Plenty of special events year round, contact for details.

**Times:** Open all year, Feb-Oct, daily, 10.30-4.30; Nov-Jan, Sun only 10.30-4.30.

**Fee:** *Museum & site free. Ice Age tour £3.90, (£2.50 ch); Rock Art tour £6 adults, (£3 ch) no under 5's on tours. £2 parking donation requested.

**Facilities:** ❷ 🍴 📱 ♿ (mobility scooter, tour may be unsuitable due to steps, toilets) shop, guided tours ⊗ (only assist dogs in museum) 🚌 (pre-booking advised)

## CRICH
### Crich Tramway Village

Matlock DE4 5DP

☎ 01773 854321 📠 01773 852326

**Email:** enquiry@tramway.co.uk

**Web:** www.tramway.co.uk

**Dir:** *off B5035, 8m from M1 junct 28*

A mile-long scenic journey through a period street and open countryside with panoramic views. You can enjoy unlimited vintage tram rides, and the exhibition hall houses the largest collection of electric trams in Britain. The nostalgic village street contains the village pub, a restaurant, tearooms, a sweet shop, an ice cream shop, and even a Police sentry box. For children there is also an indoor Discovery Depot and an outdoor adventure playground. Ring in advance for details of special events.

**Times:** *Open Apr-Oct, daily 10-5.30 (6.30 wknds Jun-Aug & BH wknds). Nov-Dec wknds 10.30-4

**Fee:** *£9 (ch 3-15 £4.50, pen £8). Family ticket (2ad+3ch) £24

**Facilities:** ❷ 🍽 (Licensed) 🍴 📱 ♿ (Braille guidebooks, converted tram, talktype facility, toilets) shop, guided tours 🚌

## CROMFORD
### Arkwright's Cromford Mill
Mill Lane DE4 3RQ
☎ 01629 823256 📄 01629 823256
**Email:** info@cromfordmill.co.uk
**Web:** www.cromfordmill.co.uk
**Dir:** *off A6, 3m S of Matlock*
Sir Richard Arkwright established the world's first successful water-powered cotton spinning mill at Cromford in 1771. The Arkwright Society are involved in a major restoration to create a lasting monument to an extraordinary genius. Guided tours are available, and there is a programme of lectures and visits – ring for details. The Mill site is part of the Derwent Valley Mill World Heritage site.
**Times:** *Open all year, daily 9-5 (Closed 25 Dec).

**Fee:** *Guided tour & exhibitions £2 (ch & pen £1.50). Mill site free.
**Facilities:** 🅿 🍽 ♿ (ramps, toilets) shop, guided tours (charged) 🚌 (booking essential)

## DENBY
### Denby Pottery Visitor Centre
Derby Road DE5 8NX
☎ 01773 740799 📄 01773 740749
**Email:** visitor.centre@denby.co.uk
**Web:** www.denbyvisitorcentre.co.uk
**Dir:** *8m N of Derby off A38, on B6179, 2m S of Ripley*
Situated around a cobbled courtyard with shops and a restaurant. Pottery tours are available daily including hands on activities such as paint-a-plate and make a clay souvenir. There are lots of bargains on Denby seconds in the factory shop, hand-made blown glass from the Glass Studio, Dartington Crystal Shop, gift shop, gallery, garden shop, and hand painted Denby.
**Times:** Open all year. Factory tours, Mon-Thu 10.30 & 1. Craftroom tour, daily 11-3. Visitor Centre Mon-Sat 9.30-5, Sun 10-5. Closed 25-26 Dec.
**Fee:** Free. Factory tour £4.95 (ch £3.95). Craftroom tour £3.50 (ch £2.50)
**Facilities:** 🅿 🍽 (Licensed) 🚻 ♿ (lift, toilets) shop, garden centre, guided tours ⊗ (outside only, ex guide dogs) 🚌 (pre-book for tour visit)

## EYAM
### Eyam Hall
Hope Valley S32 5QW
☎ 01433 631976 📄 01433 631603
**Email:** nicola@eyamhall.com
**Web:** www.eyamhall.com
**Dir:** *Turn off A623 just after Calver Crossroads & Stoney Middleton. Left at top of hill. Eyam Hall village centre.*
An intimate 17th-century manor house in the heart of the famous plague village. Home to the Wright family since 1671, the Hall offers a glimpse of domestic history through the eyes of one family, in portraits, furniture, tapestries, costumes and memorabilia. Converted farm buildings house the Eyam Hall Craft Centre. Please telephone for details of musical and theatrical events throughout the season.

**Times:** Open House & Garden: Etr Sun & Mon, Spring Bank Hol Sun & Mon, Jul & Aug: Wed, Thu, Sun, BH Mon 12-4. Craft Centre year round Tue-Sun 11-5
**Fee:** House £6.25 (ch £4, concessions £5.75). Family ticket £19. Craft centre free admission.
**Facilities:** 🅿 🅿 (0.25m) 🍽 (Licensed) 🚻 📷 ♿ (disabled entrance via special gate, ramps, toilets) shop, guided tours ,audio commentaries (charged) ⊗ (ex guide & dogs in grounds) 🚌

## HARDWICK HALL
### Hardwick Hall
Doe Lea S44 5QJ

☎ 01246 850430 📄 01246 858424

**Email:** hardwickhall@nationaltrust.org.uk

**Web:** www.nationaltrust.org.uk

**Dir:** *2m S M1 junct 29 via A6175. Access by Stainsby Mill entrance only*

An outstanding example of Elizabethan architecture, described as more glass than wall, Hardwick Hall was built by Bess of Hardwick between 1590 and 1597, and is surrounded by 300 acres of historic parkland. Other attractions on the estate include Stainsby Mill, a fully functioning water-powered mill with 17-foot waterwheel; the Stone Centre where visitors can learn about the art of stonemasonry; and the Park Centre which details local wildlife. Lots of talks and special events. Contact for details.

**Times:** *Open 25 Mar-29 Oct, Wed-Thu, Sat-Sun, BH Mon, 12-4. (Last admission 30mins before closing). Garden Wed-Sun, 11-5. Old Hall Wed, Thu, Sat & Sun 10-6. Parkland gates all year 8-6 (5.30 in winter).

**Fee:** *House & Garden £7.80 (ch £3.90). Family ticket £19.50. Garden only £4 (ch £2). Family £10.

**Facilities:** 🅿 🍽 (Licensed) 🪑 ♿ (large print & Braille guide, wheelchair pre-book, toilets) shop ⊗ (ex in park on leads) 🚌 (advance booking) 🌺 ♻

## ILKESTON
### The American Adventure Theme Park
DE7 5SX

☎ 0845 330 2929 📄 01773 716140

**Email:** sales@americanadventure.co.uk

**Web:** www.americanadventure.co.uk

**Dir:** *off M1 junct 26, signed, take A610 to A608 then A6007*

This is one of Britain's few fully themed parks, based on the legend of the whole continent of America. Take a cruise on the Harleys Angels bikes or the wheel of a New York Dodger. Pick up the pace on the Mini Mine Rush coaster or enjoy a unique 4D cinema experience in the Motion Master. All this as well as favourites like the Buffalo Stampede, Digger Depot, Yankee Clipper and The Runaway Train. At weekends there's a Live Shootout with Sheriff Rocky Raccoon, and keep an eye out for Miss Hugsy Bear.

**Times:** *Open 8 Apr-5 Sep & 21-29 Oct, daily from 10.30; 9 Sep-15 Oct wknds only from 10.30

Fee: *£12.50 ad and ch 1.05metres and above, below 1.04metres £4.99

**Facilities:** 🅿 🍽 🪑 ♿ (free wheelchair hire, must pre book, call 0845 330 2929, toilets) shop, ⊗ (ex guide dogs) 🚌 (pre-book for discounted rates)

## MATLOCK BATH
### Peak District Mining Museum
The Pavilion DE4 3NR

☎: 01629 583834

**Email:** mail@peakmines.co.uk

**Web:** www.peakmines.co.uk

**Dir:** *On A6 alongside River Derwent*

A large display explains the history of the Derbyshire lead industry from Roman times to the present day. The geology of the area, mining and smelting processes, the quarrying and the people who worked in the industry, are illustrated by a series of static and moving exhibits. The museum also features an early 19th-century water pressure pumping engine. In the Pump Room there is a large and informative exhibition on recycling.

**Times:** Open all year, daily Apr-end Sep 10-5, Oct-end Mar 11-3. Closed 25 Dec.

**Fee:** Museum & Mine: £5 (ch £3, concessions £4.50). Family £11.50. Museum only or mine only £3 (ch £2, concessions £2.50). Family £8.50. Party rates.

**Facilities:** 🅿 (charged) 🅿 (Pay & Display) 🍵 (seating for 8-10) 📋 ♿ (chair lift to mezzanine) shop, guided tours ⊗ (ex guide dogs) 🚌 ♻

**DERBYSHIRE**

## MATLOCK BATH
**Temple Mine**
Temple Road DE4 3NR
☎: 01629 583834
**Email:** mail@peakmines.co.uk
**Web:** www.peakmines.co.uk
**Dir:** *off A6. Telephone for directions.*
A typical Derbyshire mine which was worked from the early 1920s until the mid 1950s for fluorspar and associated minerals. The museum exhibits bring the mining processes and methods to life and provides a real insight into underground working conditions in the mid-20th century.
**Times:** Apr-end Sep timed visits 12noon and 2 daily, Oct-end Mar timed visits 12noon & 2 weekends only
**Fee:** Museum & Mine: £5 (concessions £4.50, ch £3),

Family ticket £11.50. Museum only or mine only: £3 (concessions £2.50, ch £2), Family £8.50.
**Facilities:** Ⓟ (Pay & Display) guided tours (charged) ⊗ (ex guide dogs) 🚌 ♿

## MATLOCK BATH
**The Heights of Abraham Cable Cars, Caverns & Hilltop Park**
Derby DE4 3PD
☎ 01629 582365 🖷 01629 581128
**Email:** enquiries@h-of-a.co.uk
**Web:** www.heights-of-abraham.co.uk
**Dir:** *on A6, signed from M1 junct 28 & A6.*
The visit begins with a spectacular cable car journey across the Derwent Valley to the summit of the hill top country park. There are the two show caverns with exciting tours to the underground world within the hillside. The 'Miners Tale', in the Great Rutland Cavern; Nestus Mine and the 'Story of the Rock' at the Masson Cavern Pavilion, an Explorer's Challenge, woodland walks and the Victoria Prospect Tower.

**Times:** *Open daily 14-22 Feb & Etr-Oct 10-5 (later in high season), 28 Feb-26 Mar wknds only, for Autumn & Winter Opening telephone for details.
**Fee:** *£8.50 (ch £5.50, pen £6.50)
**Facilities:** Ⓟ (300mtrs) ⦿ (Licensed) ⏃ ♿ (ring for details, toilets) shop, ⊗ (ex in grounds & cable car) 🚌

## RIPLEY
**Midland Railway Butterley**
Butterley Station DE5 3QZ
☎ 01773 747674 & 749788 🖷 01773 570721
**Email:** mrc@rapidial.co.uk
**Web:** www.midlandrailwaycentre.co.uk
**Dir:** *M1 junct 28, A38 towards Derby, then signposted*
A regular steam-train passenger service runs here, to the centre where the aim is to depict every aspect of the golden days of the Midland Railway and its successors. Exhibits range from the steam locomotives of 1866 to an electric locomotive, with a large section of rolling stock spanning the last 100 years. Also a farm and country park, along with narrow gauge, miniature and model railways. Regular rail-related special events throughout the year. Contact for details.

**Times:** Open all year, trains run wknds Feb-Dec & most school holidays
**Fee:** *£9.95 (ch 5-16 £5.50, pen £8.95) children under 5 free. Party 15+.
**Facilities:** ❶ Ⓟ (200yds) ⛉ (at Butterley Station & museum site) ⏃ 🗋 ♿ (special accommodation on trains, toilets) shop, guided tours 🚌

## WIRKSWORTH
**Wirksworth Heritage Centre**
Crown Yard DE4 4ET
☎ 01629 825225
**Email:** heritage@heritagecentre.wanadoo.co.uk
**Web:** www.storyofwirksworth.co.uk
**Dir:** *on B5023 off A6 in centre of Wirksworth*
The Centre has been created in an old silk and velvet mill. The three floors of the mill have interpretative displays of the town's past history as a prosperous lead-mining centre. Each floor offers many features of interest including a computer game called 'Rescue the injured lead-miner', a mock-up of a natural cavern, and a Quarryman's House. During the Spring Bank Holiday you can also see the famous Well Dressings. Newly renovated exhibits on the top floor include one on quarrying, information about local girl round-the-world yachtswoman Ellen MacArthur, and local memories from the Second World War. There's also a small art gallery carrying local works.
**Times:** *Open Etr-Sep, Wed-Sun & BHs 10.30-4.30
**Fee:** *£3 (ch £1, pen £2). Party 20+ 10% discount
**Facilities:** ℗ (80yds – pay & display) ☕ (daily 9-5, except Mon) 🍴 (Licensed) shop, guided tours ⊗ (ex guide dogs) 🚌 (must book in advance) ♿

## BROCKHAMPTON
**Brockhampton Estate**
Bringsty WR6 5TB
☎ 01885 482077 & 488099 📄 01885 482151
**Email:** brockhampton@nationaltrust.org.uk
**Web:** www.nationaltrust.org.uk
**Dir:** *2m E of Bromyard on A44*
This traditionally formed 1700 acre estate has extensive areas of wood and parkland, with a rich variety of wildlife and over 5 miles of walks. At the heart of the estate lies Lower Brockhampton House, a late 14th-century moated manor house with a beautiful timber-framed gatehouse and ruined chapel.
**Times:** *Open Apr-Oct daily (ex Mon & Tue) but open BH Mons Apr-Oct 12-5 (12-4 in Oct). Mar weekends only, 12-4. Woodland walks open to dusk throughout the year.
**Fee:** *Lower Brockhampton £4 (ch £2) Family £10.
**Facilities:** ℗ 🍴 📷 (voluntary donation) ♿ (special parking, ramps, Braille guide, toilets) shop, guided tours ⊗ (no dogs in house ex assist) 🚌 (pre booking) 🌿 ♿

## HEREFORD
**Hereford Cathedral**
HR1 2NG
☎ 01432 374200 📄 01432 374220
**Email:** office@herefordcathedral.org
**Web:** www.herefordcathedral.org
**Dir:** *A49 signed from city inner ring roads*
Built on the site of a place of worship that dated back to Saxon times, Hereford Cathedral contains some of the finest examples of architecture from the Norman era to the present day, including the 13th-century Shrine of St Thomas of Hereford, the recently restored 14th-century Lady Chapel, and the award-winning new library building. The Mappa Mundi and Chained Library exhibition tells the stories of these famous national treasures through models, artefacts and changing exhibitions.
**Times:** Cathedral Open daily 7.30-Evensong; Mappa Mundi & Chained Library Exhibition Summer: Mon-Sat 10-4.30, Sun 11-3.30. Winter: Mon-Sat 11-3.30 (closed Sun).
**Fee:** *Cathedral admission free (donation invited). Mappa Mundi & Chained Library Exhibition £4.50 (concessions £3.50). Family ticket £6-£10. Party 10+.
**Facilities:** ℗ (0.25m) 🍴 📷 ♿ (touch facility for blind, Braille & large print info, toilets) shop, guided tours ⊗ (ex guide dogs) 🚌 (Pre-booking essential)

**DERBYSHIRE / HEREFORDSHIRE**

HEREFORDSHIRE / LEICESTERSHIRE

## LEDBURY
**Eastnor Castle**
Eastnor HR8 1RL
☎ 01531 633160 🖷 01531 631776
**Email:** enquiries@eastnorcastle.com
**Web:** www.eastnorcastle.com
**Dir:** *the castle is 2.5m E of Ledbury on the A438 Tewkesbury road*

This magnificent Norman Revival castle was started in 1832 and completed a generation or two later. The house is well-placed in a lovely setting, with a deer park, arboretum and lake. Inside are tapestries, fine art and armour, and the Italianate and Gothic interiors have been beautifully restored. There's an adventure playground, nature trails and lakeside walks. Events take place throughout the year.

**Times:** Open 5-9 Apr, every Sun & BH from 15 Apr-Sep, daily 16 Jul-Aug (ex Sat ) 11-4.30 (last admission 4).
**Fee:** Castle & grounds £7.50 (ch £4.50, pen £6.50) Family £19.50. Grounds only £3.50 (ch £1.50, pen £2.50). Family £8.50.
**Facilities:** ❷ ⛱ 🗐 50p ♿ (wheelchair climber, lift) shop, guided tours 🚌

## BELVOIR
**Belvoir Castle**
Grantham NG32 1PD
☎ 01476 871002 🖷 01476 871018
**Email:** info@belvoircastle.com
**Web:** www.belvoircastle.com
**Dir:** *between A52 & A607, follow the brown heritage signs from A1, A52, A607 & A46*

Although Belvoir Castle has been the home of the Dukes of Rutland for many centuries, the turrets, battlements, towers and pinnacles of the house are a 19th-century fantasy. Amongst the many treasures to be seen inside are paintings by Murillo, Holbein and other famous artists. Within the castle there is also the Museum of the Queens Royal Lancers. The lovingly restored gardens are open to visitors. Special events planned every weekend throughout the season, phone for details.

**Times:** *Open Apr-Sep, closed Mon & Fri
**Fee:** *£10 (ch £5, pen £9).
**Facilities:** ❷ ⓟ 🍴 (Licensed) ⛱ 🗐 £1 ♿ (permitted to be driven/drive right up to castle entrance, toilets) shop, guided tours  audio commentaries  (charged) 🚫 (ex guide dogs) 🚌 (not Mon or Fri)

## COALVILLE
**Snibston Discovery Park**
Ashby Road LE67 3LN
☎ 01530 278444 🖷 01530 813301
**Email:** snibston@leics.gov.uk
**Web:** www.snibston.com
**Dir:** *4.5m from M1 junct 22 or from A42/M42 junct 13 on A511 on W side of Coalville*

Snibston has recently had a major makeover, making it an even more up-to-date all-weather science centre. In the Extra Ordinary hands-on gallery visitors can see how technology has affected everyday life. The Fashion Gallery has a wide selection of historic and modern costumes, while the underground life of a miner can be explored in the colliery tour. There are also rides on a diesel locomotive, or fun in the adventure play area.

**Times:** Open daily, Apr-Oct 10-5; Nov-Mar 10-3. School hols & wknds 10-5. Closed 2 weeks in Jan for maintainence.
**Fee:** £6 (ch £4, concessions £4.20). Family ticket £18
**Facilities:** ❷ ⓟ ⛱ 🗐 ♿ (Braille labels, touch tables, parking available, toilets) shop, guided tours (charged) 🚫 (ex guide dogs) 🚌

## DONINGTON LE HEATH
### Donington le Heath Manor House
Manor Road Coalville LE67 2FW
☎ 01530 831259 📄 01530 831259
Email: museum@leics.gov.uk
Web: www.leics.gov.uk/museums
Dir: *S of Coalville*

This is a rare example of a medieval manor house, tracing its history back to about 1280. The house was heavily modernised around 1618 and was then tenanted as a farm from 1670 to 1960, remaining virtually unchanged. It has now been carefully restored and contains some fine oak furnishings. The surrounding grounds have also been restored to reflect the plants available in the 17th-century and include flower and herb gardens. The adjoining stone barn houses a restaurant.

Times: Open Mar-Nov 11-4 daily, Dec-Feb Sat-Sun 11-4
Fee: *Free
Facilities: 🅿 🍴 (Licensed) ⋒ ♿ (toilets) shop, guided tours audio commentaries ⊗ (ex guide dogs) 🚌 (max 50) ♻

## LEICESTER
### National Space Centre
Exploration Drive LE4 5NS
☎ 0870 607 7223 📄 0116 258 2100
Email: info@spacecentre.co.uk
Web: www.spacecentre.co.uk
Dir: *off A6, 2m N of city centre midway between Leicester's central & outer ring roads. Follow brown rocket signs from M1 junct 21, 21a or 22 & all arterial routes*

The award-winning National Space Centre offers a great family day out, with six interactive galleries, a full-domed Space Theatre, a 42-metre high Rocket Tower, and the new Human Spaceflight Experience with 3D SIM ride. Explore the universe, orbit Earth, join the crew on the lunar base, and take the astronaut fitness tests – and all without leaving Leicester!

Times: *Open during school term: Tue-Sun, 10-5 (last entry 3.30). During school hols: daily, 10-5 (last entry 3.30)
Fee: £11 (ch 4-16yrs & concessions £9). Family of 4 £34, of 5 £42
Facilities: 🅿 (charged) ⋒ 🍴 Free-£2.95 ♿ (induction loop, large text, wheelchairs, lifts, toilets) shop, ⊗ (ex guide dogs) 🚌 (must be pre-booked)

## LEICESTER
### New Walk Museum & Art Gallery
53 New Walk LE1 7EA
☎ 0116 225 4900 📄 0116 225 4927
Web: www.leicester.gov.uk/museums
Dir: *On New Walk. Access by car from A6 onto Waterloo Way at Railway Stn. Right into Regent Rd, right onto West St, right onto Princess Rd which leads to car park*

This major regional venue houses local and national collections. There's an internationally famous collection of German Expressionism and other displays include the Rutland Dinosaur and the Egyptian Gallery. An Extensive Natural History collection augmented by art from the renaissance to contemporary.

Times: *Open all year, Apr-Sep, Mon-Sat 10-5, Sun 1-5. Oct-Mar, Mon-Sat 10-4, Sun 1-4. Closed 24-26 & 31 Dec & 1 Jan)
Fee: *Donations welcome. Small charge for some events.
Facilities: 🅿 ♿ (wheelchairs for loan, minicom, induction loop, toilets) shop, ⊗ (ex guide dogs) 🚌

## LOUGHBOROUGH
### Great Central Railway
Great Central Road LE11 1RW
☎ 01509 230726 ▤ 01509 239791
**Email:** booking_office@gcrailway.co.uk
**Web:** www.gcrailway.co.uk
**Dir:** *signed from A6*
This private steam railway runs over eight miles from Loughborough Central to Leicester North, with all trains calling at Quorn & Woodhouse and Rothley. The locomotive depot and museum are at Loughborough Central. A buffet car runs on most trains.
**Times:** *Open all year daily, trains run daily Jun-Aug & school hols; Sep-May, Sat, Sun & BHs
**Fee:** *Runabout (all day unlimited travel) £12 (ch & pen £8). Family ticket (2ad+3ch) £30 (1ad+3ch) £20

**Facilities:** ℗ ⊑ (refreshments available at Loughborough) ⚭ (Licensed) ⚸ ♿ (disabled coach available on most trains, (check beforehand), toilets) shop ⇛

## MARKET BOSWORTH
### Bosworth Battlefield Visitor Centre & Country Park
Ambion Hill Sutton Cheney Nuneaton CV13 0AD
☎ 01455 290429 ▤ 01455 292841
**Email:** bosworth@leics.gov.uk
**Web:** www.leics.gov.uk
**Dir:** *follow brown tourist signs from A447, A444 & A5*
The Battle of Bosworth Field was fought in 1485 between the armies of Richard III and the future Henry VII. The visitor centre offers a comprehensive interpretation of the battle, with exhibitions, models and a film theatre. Special medieval attractions are held in the summer months.
**Times:** *Open: Country Park and Battle Trails all year. Visitor Centre Open Apr-Oct, daily, 11-5; Nov-Dec, Sun 11-4; Mar, wknds 11-5. Parties all year by arrangement.

**Fee:** *Visitor Centre £3 (concessions £2). Family ticket £8.50. Special charges apply on event days. Subject to review.
**Facilities:** ℗ (charged) ℗ (0.5m) ⚭ (Licensed) ⚸ ▦ £2.99 ♿ (wheelchair & electric scooter hire, tactile exhibits, toilets) shop, guided tours ⇛ (booked in advance)

## MOIRA
### Conkers
Millennium Avenue Rawdon Road Swadlincote DE12 6GA
☎ 01283 216633 ▤ 01283 210321
**Email:** info@visitconkers.com
**Web:** www.visitconkers.com
**Dir:** *on B5003 in Moira, signed from A444 and M42*
Located in the heart of the National Forest, Conkers is a unique mix of over one hundred indoor interactive exhibits and activities. There are 4 discovery zones set within 120 acres of woodland with lakeside walks, woodland trails and natural habitats, an assault course, adventure play areas, a miniature train and bike hire facilities. With many events in the covered amphitheatre, and a range of other activities, there is a wide range of opportunities for family fun and entertainment.

**Times:** Open daily, summer 10-6, winter 10-5. Closed 25 Dec.
**Fee:** *£6.50 (ch 3-15yrs £4.50, ch under 3 free, concessions £5.50). Family ticket (2ad+2ch) £18.95
**Facilities:** ℗ ⊑ (Two lakeside cafés) ⚸ ♿ (multi access walks & trails accessible to wheelchairs, toilets) shop, guided tours ⊗ (ex guide dogs) ⇛

## SHACKERSTONE
### Battlefield Line Railway
Shackerstone Station CV13 6NW
☎ 01827 880754 ▤ 01827 881050
**Web:** www.battlefield-line-railway.co.uk
**Dir:** *follow brown signs from A444 & A447.*
The Battlefield Line is the last remaining part of the former Ashby and Nuneaton Joint Railway which was opened in 1873. There is a regular, and mostly steam, railway service from Shackerstone via Market Bosworth to Shenton in Leicestershire which is operated by the Shackerstone Railway Society. Shackerstone Station has been fully restored and accommodates an extensive steam railway museum with a collection of rolling stock. There is also a shop selling souvenirs.
**Times:** *Open all year Sat, 12-5, Sun & BH Mon 10.30-

5.30. Closed Xmas
**Fee:** *£7 (ch £4, pen £5). Family ticket (2ad+2ch) £20
**Facilities:** 🅿 🍴 🗐 ♿ (toilets) shop, guided tours 🚌

## TWYCROSS
### Twycross Zoo Park
Atherstone CV9 3PX
☎ 01827 880250 ▤ 01827 880700
**Web:** www.twycrosszoo.com
**Dir:** *on A444 Burton to Nuneaton road, directly off M42 junct 11*
Set in 50 acres of parkland, the zoo is home to around 1000 animals, most of which are endangered species. Twycross is the only zoo in Britain to house Bonobos – humans' 'closest living relative'. There are also various other animals such as lions, elephants and giraffes, and a pets' corner for younger children. Other attractions include a Penguin Pool with underwater viewing and a Children's Adventure Playground.
**Times:** *Open all year, daily 10-5.30 (4 in winter).

Closed 25 Dec.
**Fee:** *£8.50 (ch £5) pen £6.
**Facilities:** 🅿 🍴 (licensed in summer) 🍴 ♿ (toilets) shop, 🚫 (ex guide dogs) 🚌

## CLEETHORPES
### Pleasure Island Family Theme Park
Kings Road DN35 0PL
☎ 01472 211511 ▤ 01472 211087
**Email:** reception@pleasure-island.co.uk
**Web:** www.pleasure-island.co.uk
**Dir:** *Follow signs from A180*
Pleasure Island is packed with over seventy rides and attractions. Hold on tight as the colossal Wheel of Steel rockets you into the sky at a G-force of 2.5, then hurtles you around 360 degrees, sending riders into orbit and giving the sensation of complete weightlessness. It's not just grown ups and thrill seekers who are catered for at Pleasure Island. For youngsters there's hours of fun in Tinkaboo Town, an indoor themed area full of rides and attractions. New attractions in the park include the

Booster, and the Masai Warrior Show.
**Times:** *Open Apr-3 Sep, daily from 10. Plus wknds during Sep-Oct & daily during half term (23 Oct-29 Oct).
**Fee:** *£14 (ch under 4 free, pen £8.50).
**Facilities:** 🅿 🍴 (Licensed) 🍴 🗐 ♿ (toilets) shop, 🚌

## CONINGSBY
### Battle of Britain Memorial Flight Visitor Centre
LN4 4SY

☎ 01526 344041 📄 01526 342330

**Email:** bbmf@lincolnshire.gov.uk

**Web:** www.lincolnshire.gov.uk/bbmf

**Dir:** *on A153 in Coningsby village – follow heritage signs*

View the aircraft of the Battle of Britain Memorial Flight, comprising the only flying Lancaster in Europe, five Spitfires, two Hurricanes, a Dakota and two Chipmunks. Because of operational commitments, specific aircraft may not always be available. Ring for information before planning a visit.

**Times:** Open Mon-Fri, conducted tours 10.30-3.30; (winter 10.30-3) (Closed 2 wks Xmas).

**Fee:** *£3.80 (concessions £2.50) Family £9.90

**Facilities:** 🅿 🅿 (0.5miles – car park locked at 5pm) 🍴 📄 ♿ (electric wheelchairs not allowed in hangar, toilets) shop, guided tours 🚫 (ex guide dogs) 🚌 (pre-booked)

## GRIMSBY
### National Fishing Heritage Centre
Alexandra Dock DN31 1UZ

☎ 01472 323345 📄 01472 323555

**Web:** www.nelincs.gov.uk

**Dir:** *follow signs off M180*

Sign on as a crew member for a journey of discovery, and experience the harsh reality of life onboard a deep sea trawler recreated inside the Centre. Through a range of interactive games and displays, your challenge is to navigate the icy waters of the Arctic in search of the elusive catch.

**Times:** *Open Etr-Oct, Mon-Fri 10-5, Wknds & BHs 10.30-5.30

**Fee:** *£6 (ch & concessions £4). Family ticket (2ad+5ch) £12. Discounts for group bookings

**Facilities:** 🅿 (charged) 🅿 (100mtrs) ♿ (toilets) shop, guided tours 🚫 (ex guide dogs) 🚌 (prior booking required) ✉

## LINCOLN
### Museum of Lincolnshire Life
Burton Road LN1 3LY

☎ 01522 528448 📄 01522 521264

**Email:** lincolnshirelife.museum@lincolnshire.gov.uk

**Web:** www.lincolnshire.gov.uk/museumoflincolnshirelife

**Dir:** *100mtr walk from Lincoln Castle*

A large and varied social history museum, where two centuries of Lincolnshire life are illustrated by fascinating displays of domestic implements, industrial machinery, agricultural tools, a collection of horse-drawn vehicles and a WW1 tank called FLIRT. A variety of living history events are held throughout the year. The museum also accommodates the exciting and interactive Royal Lincolnshire Regiment Museum which tells the story of the regiment with the aid of videos, an audio tour, and displays that respond to touch screen computers.

**Times:** *Open all year, May-Sep, daily 10-5; Oct-Mar, Mon-Sat 10-5 (last admission 4). Closed 24-26 & 31 Dec, 1 Jan.

**Fee:** *£2.10 (concessions £1.30). Family (2ad+3ch) £5.50.

**Facilities:** 🅿 🅿 (250yds) ♿ (wheelchair available, parking space, toilets) shop, 🚫 (ex assist dogs) 🚌 (pre-booked groups) ✉

## LINCOLN
### Usher Gallery
Lindum Road LN2 1NN
☎ 01522 527980 🖹 01522 560165
Email: usher.gallery@lincolnshire.gov.uk
Web: www.lincolnshire.gov.uk/usher
Dir: *in city centre, signed*
Built as the result of a bequest by Lincoln jeweller James Ward Usher, the Gallery houses his magnificent collection of watches, coins, porcelain and miniatures, as well as topographical works, watercolours by Peter de Wint and Tennyson memorabilia. The gallery has a popular and changing display of contemporary visual arts and crafts. There is also a lively lecture programme and a children's activity diary.

Times: *Open all year, Tue-Sat 10-5 (last entry 4.30), Sun 1-5 (last entry 4.30), from 1 Jun daily 10-5.Open BHs. Closed 24-26 Dec & 1 Jan.
Fee: *Free
Facilities: 🅿 ℗ (150yds) 🛤 ♿ (large print guides, induction loop, parking, toilets) shop, ⊗ (ex guide dogs) 🚌

## SCUNTHORPE
### Normanby Hall Country Park
Normanby DN15 9HU
☎ 01724 720588 🖹 01724 721248
Email: normanby.hall@northlincs.gov.uk
Web: www.northlincs.gov.uk
Dir: *4m N of Scunthorpe off B1430*
A whole host of activities and attractions are offered in the 300 acres of grounds that surround Normanby Hall, including riding, nature trails and a farming museum. Inside the Regency mansion the fine rooms are decorated and furnished in period style. There is a fully restored and working Victorian kitchen garden and also a Victorian walled garden selling a wide range of Victorian and other unusual plants from barrows located at the gift shop, and Farming Museum.

Times: *Open: Park all year, daily, 9-dusk. Walled garden, daily 10.30-5 (4 in winter). Hall & Farming Museum, Apr-Sep, daily 1-5.
Fee: *Mar-Sep £4.40 (ch £2.20, under 5s free, concessions £4). Family season ticket £17.
Facilities: 🅿 (charged) 🍽 (Licensed) 🛤 🗐 ♿ (audio tour, wheelchair/scooter, toilets) shop, garden centre guided tours ⊗ (ex guide dogs, & on leads) 🚌 (pre-booking advised)

## SKEGNESS
### Church Farm Museum
Church Road South PE25 2HF
☎ 01754 766658 🖹 01754 898243
Email: churchfarmmuseum@lincolnshire.gov.uk
Web: www.lincolnshire.gov.uk/churchfarmmuseum
Dir: *follow brown museum signs on entering Skegness*
A farmhouse and outbuildings, restored to show the way of life on a Lincolnshire farm at the end of the 19th century, with farm implements and machinery plus household equipment on display. Temporary exhibitions are held in the barn with special events throughout the season. There is also a restored timber framed 'mud and stud' labourer's cottage on site.
Times: *Open Apr-Oct, daily 10-5 (last entry 4.30)
Fee: *Free admission apart from special events

Facilities: 🅿 ⊡ (during summer) 🛤 🗐 ♿ (wheelchair available, grounds accessible with care, toilets) shop, guided tours ⊗ (ex guide dogs) 🚌 ♻

**LINCOLNSHIRE**

**LINCOLNSHIRE**

## SKEGNESS
### Skegness Natureland Seal Sanctuary
North Parade PE25 1DB
☎ 01754 764345 🖹 01754 764345
**Email:** natureland@fsbdial.co.uk
**Web:** www.skegnessnatureland.co.uk
**Dir:** *N end of seafront*
Natureland Seal Sanctuary accommodates seals, penguins, tropical birds, aquarium, reptiles and includes a pets' corner. It also has free-flight tropical butterflies (May-Oct). Natureland is renowned for its rescue of abandoned seal pups, and has successfully reared and returned to the wild a large number of them. The hospital unit incorporates a public viewing area, and a large seascape seal pool which has with underwater viewing.
**Times:** *Open all year, daily at 10. Closing times vary according to season. Closed 25-26 Dec & 1 Jan.
**Fee:** *£5.50 (ch under 3 free, ch £3.60, pen £4.15). Family ticket £16.40
**Facilities:** ⓟ (100yds) ⌷ (Etr-Sep) 🍴 📗 50p ♿ (low windows on seal pools, toilets) shop, 🚌 (book in advance)

## SPALDING
### Butterfly & Wildlife Park
Long Sutton PE12 9LE
☎ 01406 363833 & 363209 🖹 01406 363182
**Email:** butterflypark@hotmail.com
**Web:** www.butterflyandwildlifepark.co.uk
**Dir:** *off A17 at Long Sutton*
The Park contains one of Britain's largest walk-through tropical houses, in which hundreds of butterflies and birds from all over the world fly freely. Outside are 15 acres of butterfly and bee gardens, wildflower meadows, nature trail, farm animals, a pets' corner and a large adventure playground. Within the Wildlife Park there is the Lincolnshire Birds of Prey Centre, with daily displays of birds of prey, an Ant Room where visitors can observe leaf-cutting ants in their natural habitat, and Reptile Land, home to a variety of crocodiles and snakes.
**Times:** *Open 20 Mar-end Oct, daily 10-5. (Sep & Oct 10-4).
**Fee:** *£5.70 (ch 3-16 £4.20, pen £5.20). Family ticket £17-£20. Party rates on application.
**Facilities:** ⓟ 🍴 📗 ♿ (wheelchairs available, toilets) shop, ⊗ (ex guide dogs) 🚌

## STAMFORD
### Burghley House
PE9 3JY
☎ 01780 752451 🖹 01780 480125
**Email:** burghley@burghley.co.uk
**Web:** www.burghley.co.uk
**Dir:** *1.5m off A1 at Stamford*
This great Elizabethan palace, built by William Cecil, has all the hallmarks of that ostentatious period. The vast house is three storeys high and the roof is a riot of pinnacles, cupolas and paired chimneys in classic Tudor style. However, the interior was restyled in the 17th century, and the state rooms are now Baroque, with silver fireplaces, elaborate plasterwork and painted ceilings. These were painted by Antonio Verrio, whose Heaven Room is quite awe-inspiring. The Sculpture Garden is dedicated to exhibiting the best in contemporary sculpture, in glorious surroundings.
**Times:** *Open end Mar-Oct, daily (ex Fri). Please telephone for details.
**Fee:** *£9 (ch 5-15 £4, pen £8) Family £22
**Facilities:** ⓟ 🍴 (Licensed) 🪑 ♿ (chairlift access, some mobility required, toilets) shop, garden centre, guided tours ⊗ (ex in park & on lead) 🚌 (pre-booking required)

## WOOLSTHORPE
**Woolsthorpe Manor**

23 Newton Way Grantham NG33 5NR

☎ 01476 862826 📄 01476 860338

**Email:** woolsthorpemanor@nationaltrust.org.uk

**Web:** www.nationaltrust.org.uk

**Dir:** *7m S of Grantham, 1m W of A1*

A fine stone-built, 17th-century farmhouse which was the birthplace of the scientist and philosopher Sir Isaac Newton and where he returned during Plague years from 1665-67. The house incorporates the Science Discovery Centre and exhibition and includes an early edition of Newton's Principia Mathematica (1687).

**Times:** *Open 4-26 Mar, Sat & Sun 1-5; 29 Mar-1 Oct, Wed-Sun (open BHs) 1-5; 7-29 Oct, Sat & Sun 1-5

**Fee:** *£4.50 (ch £2.20). Family ticket £11.20

**Facilities:** 🅿 ♿ (Braille & large print guide, wheelchair available, toilets) 🚫 (ex guide dogs) 🚌 (one at a time, book with manager) 🐾 ♻

## ALTHORP
**Althorp**

NN7 4HQ

☎ 01604 770107 & 0870 167 9000 📄 01604 770042

**Email:** mail@althorp.com

**Web:** www.althorp.com

**Dir:** *from S, exit M1 junct 16, & N junct 18, follow signs towards Northampton until directed by brown signs*

Althorp House has been the home of the Spencer family since 1508. The house was built in the 16th century, but has been changed since, most notably by Henry Holland in the 18th century. Recently restored by the present Earl, the house is carefully maintained and in immaculate condition. The award-winning exhibition 'Diana, A Celebration' is located in six rooms and depicts the life and work of Diana, Princess of Wales. There is, in addition, a room which depicts the work of the Diana, Princess of Wales Memorial Fund.

**Times:** *Open Jul-Sep, daily 11-5. Closed 31 Aug.

**Fee:** *£11.50 (ch £5.50 & pen £9.50). Family ticket £28.50. Tickets discounted if pre-booked (not confirmed)

**Facilities:** 🅿 ⛱ ♿ (disabled parking, wheelchairs, audio tour, shuttle, toilets) shop, 🚫 (ex guide dogs) 🚌 pre-booking essential

## EDWINSTOWE
**Sherwood Forest Country Park & Visitor Centre**

Mansfield NG21 9HN

☎ 01623 823202 & 824490 📄 01623 823202

**Email:** sherwood.forest@nottscc.gov.uk

**Web:** www.nottinghamshire.gov.uk/countryparks

**Dir:** *on B6034 N of Edwinstowe between A6075 and A616*

At the heart of the Robin Hood legend is Sherwood Forest. Today it is a country park and visitor centre with 450 acres of ancient oaks and shimmering silver birches. Waymarked pathways guide you through the forest on a number of walks. A year round programme of events includes the spectacular Robin Hood Festival 31 Jul-6 Aug 2007.

**Times:** *Open all year. Country Park: Open daily dawn to dusk. Visitor Centre: Open daily 10-5 (4.30 Nov-Mar)

**Fee:** Free

**Facilities:** 🅿 (charged) 🅿 (0.5m – charges at certain times) ⛱ ♿ (wheelchair and electric buggy loan, toilets) shop 🚌

### FARNSFIELD
**White Post Farm Centre**
Newark NG22 8HL
☎ 01623 882977 & 882026 ▤ 01623 883499
**Email:** admin@whitepostfarmcentre.co.uk
**Web:** www.whitepostfarmcentre.co.uk
**Dir:** *12m N of Nottingham on A614*
With over 25 acres there's lots to see and do at the
White Post Farm Centre. There are more than 3,000
animals including pigs, goats and sheep, along with more
exotic animals such as bats, reptiles and meerkats. The
new indoor play area is ideal for small children, and there
is also a sledge run, trampolines and pedal go-karts.
**Times:** Open daily from 10
**Fee:** *£7.30 (ch 2-16 £6.60, under 2's free)
**Facilities:** ❷ ⓟ (100m) ☕ (child friendly food) ⧎ ♿

(free hire wheelchairs, book if more than 6, toilets) shop,
guided tours ⊗ (ex guide dogs) 🚌 (pre-booking
required)

### NEWARK-ON-TRENT
**Newark Air Museum**
The Airfield Winthorpe NG24 2NY
☎ 01636 707170 ▤ 01636 707170
**Email:** newarkair@onetel.com
**Web:** www.newarkairmuseum.co.uk
**Dir:** *easy access from A1, A46, A17 & Newark relief
road, follow tourist signs, next to county showground.*
Based on a a WWII airfield the Neward Airt Museum is a
diverse collection of transport, training and
reconnaissance aircraft, jet fighters, bombers and
helicopters, now numbering more than seventy aircraft.
Two Undercover Aircraft Display Halls and an Engine Hall
make the museum an all-weather attraction.
**Times:** *Open all year, Mar-Sep daily 10-5; Oct-Feb,
daily 10-4. Closed 24-26 Dec & 1 Jan. Other times by
appointment.
**Fee:** *£6 (ch £3.50, pen £5.50). Family ticket (2ad+2ch)
£16.50. Party 15+.
**Facilities:** ❷ ⓟ (50yds) ☕ (closes 30mins before
museum) ⧎ ▤ from 50p ♿ (toilets) shop, guided tours
🚌

### NEWARK-ON-TRENT
**Newark Millgate Museum**
48 Millgate NG24 4TS
☎ 01636 655730 ▤ 01636 655735
**Email:** museums@nsdc.info
**Web:** www.newark-sherwooddc.gov.uk
**Dir:** *easy access from A1 & A46*
The museum is home to a diverse range of social
collections and fascinating exhibitions including recreated
streets, shops and houses in period settings. There are
also children's activities. The mezzanine gallery, home to
a number of temporary exhibitions, features the work of
many local artists, designers and photographers.
**Times:** Open Apr-Sep: Tue-Sun, 10.30-4.30, Oct-Mar:
Tue-Sun, 10.30-4.Open spring and summer BH Mon,
10.30-4.
**Fee:** Free
**Facilities:** ⓟ (250yds) ☕ (tea and coffee shop) ▤ ♿
(toilets) shop, ⊗ (ex assistance dogs) 🚌 (pre-book) ♿

## NEWARK-ON-TRENT

**Vina Cooke Museum of Dolls & Bygone Childhood**

The Old Rectory Cromwell NG23 6JE

☎ 01636 821364

**Email:** info@vinasdolls.co.uk

**Web:** www.vinasdolls.co.uk

**Dir:** *5m N of Newark off A1*

All kinds of childhood memorabilia are displayed in this 17th-century house: prams, toys, dolls' houses, costumes and a large collection of Victorian and Edwardian dolls including Vina Cooke hand-made character dolls.

**Times:** Open Apr-Sep, Tue, Thu, Sat-Sun & BH 10.30-4.30. Mon, Wed, Fri and Oct-Mar by appointment, please telephone.

**Fee:** £3 (ch £1.50, pen £2.50).

**Facilities:** ❷ ℗ (20yds, roadside) ⏚ shop, guided tours ⊗ 🚌 (pre-book, max 53 people) ♿

## NOTTINGHAM

**Galleries of Justice**

The Shire Hall High Pavement Lace Market NG1 1HN

☎ 0115 952 0555 📠 0115 993 9828

**Email:** info@nccl.org.uk

**Web:** www.nccl.org.uk

**Dir:** *follow signs to city centre, brown heritage signs to Lace Market & Galleries of Justice*

The Galleries of Justice are located on the site of an original Court and County Gaol. New developments include the arrival of the HM Prison Service Collection, which will now be permanently housed in the 1833 wing. Never before seen artefacts from prisons across the country offer visitors the chance to experience some of Britain's most gruesome, yet often touching, reminders of what prison life would have been for inmates and prison staff over the last three centuries. 2007 is the 100th anniversary of the Probation Service.

**Times:** Open all year, Tue-Sun & BH Mon 10-5 (also open Mons in school hols). (Last admission one hour before closing). Contact for Xmas opening times.

**Fee:** *£7.95 (concessions £5.95). Family ticket £22.95 (2ad+2ch).

**Facilities:** ℗ (5 mins walk) ⏚ ♿ (Braille control lifts, induction loop, large print lables, toilets) shop, ⊗ (ex guide dogs) 🚌 (prior booking preferred)

## NOTTINGHAM

**Nottingham Castle**

NG1 6EL

☎ 0115 915 3700 📠 0115 915 3653

**Web:** www.nottinghamcity.gov.uk

**Dir:** *Follow signs to city centre, then signs to castle.*

This 17th-century building is both museum and art gallery, with major visiting exhibitions, by historical and contemporary artists, as well as the permanent collections. There is a 'Story of Nottingham' exhibition and a gallery designed especially to entertain young children. Guided tours of the underground passages take place on most days.

**Times:** Open all year, daily 10-5. Grounds 8-dusk. Closed 24-26 Dec.

**Fee:** Joint ticket with Brenhouse Yard. £3 (ch and concessions £1.50, under 5's free) Family £7 (2 ad up to 3 ch) Group ticket: 1 free ticket for every 10.

**Facilities:** ℗ (400yds – limited disabled spaces, book in advance) 📖 various costs ♿ (parking at castle, for more info call 0115 915 3676, toilets) shop, guided tours ⊗ (ex guide dogs) 🚌 (no coach parking on site)

## NOTTINGHAM
### The Museum of Nottingham Life

Brewhouse Yard Castle Boulevard NG7 1FB

☎ 0115 915 3640 🖹 0115 915 3601

**Email:** anni@ncmg.org.uk

**Web:** www.nottinghamcity.gov.uk

**Dir:** *follow signs to city centre, the museum is a 5 min walk from city centre with easy access from train, tram and bus.*

Nestled in the rock below Nottingham Castle and housed in a row of 17th-century cottages, the museum presents realistic glimpses of life in Nottingham over the last 300 years. Discover the caves behind the museum and peer through 1920s shop windows.

**Times:** Open daily, 10-4.30. Last admission 4. Closed 24-26 Dec, 1-2 Jan.

**Fee:** Joint ticket with castle £3 (concessions £1.50) Family ticket £7.

**Facilities:** Ⓟ (100yds) 🚻 🍴 ♿ (call 0115 915 3600 for info on access, toilets) shop, ⊗ (ex guide dogs) 🚌 No coach park, 30 people max ♨

## NOTTINGHAM
### The Tales of Robin Hood

30-38 Maid Marian Way NG1 6GF

☎ 0115 948 3284 🖹 0115 950 1536

**Email:** robinhoodcentre@mail.com

**Web:** www.robinhood.uk.com

**Dir:** *in city centre, follow brown & white signs. 2min walk from Castle*

Explore the intriguing and mysterious story of the legendary tales of Robin Hood in medieval England. There are film shows, live performances, an adventure ride and falconry to be enjoyed, you can even try your hand at archery. In the evening the centre has banquets and live entertainment.

**Times:** *Open all year, daily 10-5.30. Last admission 4. Closed 25-26 Dec.

**Fee:** *£8.95 (ch £6.95, concessions £7.95) Family £26.95

**Facilities:** Ⓟ (NCP 200yds) 🍴 ♿ (specially adapted 'car', lift, toilets) shop, audio commentaries ⊗ (ex guide dogs) 🚌

## NOTTINGHAM
### Wollaton Hall & Park

Wollaton NG8 2AE

☎ 0115 915 3900 🖹 0115 915 3932

**Email:** info@wollatonhall.org.uk

**Web:** www.wollatonhall.org.uk

**Dir:** *M1 junct 25 signed from A52, A609, A6514, A60 and city centre*

Built in the late 16th century, and extended in the 19th, Wollaton Hall and Park holds Nottingham's Natural History Museum, Nottingham's Industrial Museum, the Wollaton Park Visitor Centre, and the Yard Gallery, which has changing exhibitions exploring art and the environment. The Hall itself is set in 500 acres of deer park, with herds of red and fallow deer roaming wild. There are also formal gardens, a lake, nature trails, adventure playgrounds and a sensory garden. The many events throughout the year include pop concerts, and twilight bat walks.

**Times:** Due to ongoing refurbishment please ring 0115 915 3900 for details, will reopen summer 2007.

**Fee:** *Free wkdays. Ticket for both Hall & Museum £1.50 (ch & concessions £1). Family ticket £4. Charge made at wknds & BHs only. Group rate 1 free for every 10 tickets.

**Facilities:** Ⓟ (charged) 🚻 🍴 ♿ (call 0115 915 3700 for info on access) shop, guided tours ⊗ (ex guide dogs) 🚌

## SOUTHWELL
### The Workhouse
Upton Road NG25 0PT
☎ 01636 817250 📠 01636 817251
**Email:** theworkhouse@nationaltrust.org.uk
**Web:** www.nationaltrust.org.uk
**Dir:** *13m from Nottingham on A612*

Enter this 19th-century brick institution and discover the thought-provoking story of the 'welfare' system of the New Poor Law. The least altered workhouse in existence today, it survives from hundreds that once covered the country. Explore the segregated stairs and rooms, use the audio guide, based on archive records, to bring the 19th-century inhabitants to life in the empty rooms, then try the interactive displays exploring poverty through the years and across the country.

**Times:** *Open 25 Mar-9 Apr, 30 Sep-29 Oct: Sat and Sun 12-5. 10 Apr-1 Sept: Open daily except Tue 12-5. 27 Apr-30 Jul and 2-29 Sep: Thu, Fri, Sat and Sun 12-5.
**Fee:** *£4.90 (ch £2.40). Family ticket £12.20 (2 ad and 3 ch)
**Facilities:** 🅿 Ⓟ ♿ (virtual tour, photo album, wheelchairs available, toilets) guided tours, audio commentaries 🚫 (ex guide dogs) 🚌 (must book in advance) ♨ ♨

---

## SUTTON-CUM-LOUND
### Wetlands Waterfowl Reserve & Exotic Bird Park
Off Loundlow Road Retford DN22 8SB
☎: 01777 818099
**Dir:** *signed on A638*

The Reserve is a 32-acre site with lakes and woodland, providing a home for both wild and exotic waterfowl. Visitors can see a collection of birds of prey, parrots, geese, ducks, and wigeon among others. There are also many animals from around the world including small mammals, farm and wild animals such as llamas, wallabies, emus, monkeys, red squirrels, deer and goats.
**Times:** *Open all year, daily 10-5.30 (or dusk – whichever is earlier). Closed 25 Dec.
**Fee:** *£2.50 (ch & pen £2).

**Facilities:** 🅿 🚻 ♿ (wheelchair available) shop, 🚫 (ex guide dogs) 🚌 ♨

---

## OAKHAM
### Rutland County Museum
Catmos St Rutland LE15 6HW
☎ 01572 758440 📠 01572 758445
**Email:** museum@rutland.gov.uk
**Web:** www.rutland.gov.uk/museum
**Dir:** *on A6003, S of town centre*

Rutland County Museum is the perfect introduction to England's smallest county. The 'Welcome to Rutland' gallery is a guide to its history. The museum includes a shop and study area. On show in the 18th-century Riding School are displays of archaeology, history and and extensive rural life collection.
**Times:** Open all year, Mon-Sat 10.30-5, Sun 2-4. Closed Good Fri, Xmas & 1 Jan.
**Fee:** Free admission

**Facilities:** 🅿 (charged) Ⓟ (adjacent – pay & display, free on Sun) ♿ (induction loop in meeting room, toilets) shop, 🚫 (ex guide dogs) 🚌 (pre-booking preferred) ♨

**NOTTINGHAMSHIRE / RUTLAND**

COSFORD
**The Royal Air Force Museum**
Shifnal TF11 8UP
☎ 01902 376200 📠 01902 376211
**Email:** cosford@rafmuseum.org
**Web:** www.rafmuseum.org
**Dir:** *on A41, 1m S of M54 junct 3*
This is one of the largest aviation collections in the UK. Exhibits include the Victor and Vulcan bombers, the Hastings, York and British Airways airliners, the Belfast freighter and the last airworthy Britannia. The research and development collection includes the notable TSR2, Fairey Delta, a Bristol 188 and many other important aircraft.
**Times:** *Open all year daily, 10-6 (last admission 4). Closed 24-26 Dec & 1 Jan

**Fee:** *Charges made for special events only.
**Facilities:** 🅿 †◯† (Licensed) ⌃ ♿ (free loan of 3 manual w/chairs and 3 motor scooters, toilets) shop, guided tours (charged) ⊗ (ex guide dogs) 🚌 (pre-booked only) ♨

---

CRAVEN ARMS
**The Shropshire Hills Discovery Centre**
School Road SY7 9RS
☎ 01588 676000 📠 01588 676030
**Email:** zoe.griffin@shropshire-cc.gov.uk
**Web:** www.shropshirehillsdiscoverycentre.co.uk
**Dir:** *on A49, on S edge of Craven Arms*
This attraction explores the history, nature and geography of the Shropshire Hills, through a series of interactive displays and simulations. These include Landscape of Contrasts, Ancient Landscape, a simulated Balloon Flight, and Land of Inspiration. The Centre has 23 acres of meadow lands sloping down to the River Onny for all visitors to explore. The Centre also houses the Secret Hills Gallery which features changing displays of craft and artworks.

**Times:** Open all year, daily from 10. (Last admission 3.30 Nov-Mar, 4.30 Apr-Oct).
**Fee:** £4.50 (ch £3, chunder 5 free, pen £4). Family ticket £13.50. Groups 20+ £3.75 each, ch £2.50 each.
**Facilities:** 🅿 Ⓟ (500yds – locked at 5pm Nov-Mar & 6pm Apr-Oct) ⌃ 📖 ♿ (wheelchair available, toilets) shop, guided tours ⊗ (ex guide dogs) 🚌 (pre-booked)

---

IRONBRIDGE
**Ironbridge Gorge Museums**
Coach Road Coalbrookdale Telford TF8 7DQ
☎ 01952 884391 & 0800 590258 📠 01952 884391
**Email:** tic@ironbridge.org.uk
**Web:** www.ironbridge.org.uk
**Dir:** *M54 junct 4, signed*
Ironbridge is the site of the world's first iron bridge and the birth of the industrial revolution. At the end of the 18th century the various industries in this 6 mile gorge represented the most technologically advanced in the world With royal consent, the bridge was cast and built here in 1779, to span a narrow gorge over the River Severn. Now Ironbridge is the site of a remarkable series of museums based on the industries of the past, recreating 19th century industrial life with living history museums which feature social history displays.
**Times:** *Open all year, 10-5. Some small sites closed Nov-Mar. Telephone for exact winter details.
**Fee:** *£13.25 (ch £8.75, pen £11.50). Family £42. Passport to all sites, until all have been visited. It is therefore possible to return to Ironbridge on different days to ensure the whole atmosphere of the museums is captured.
**Facilities:** 🅿 Ⓟ (Pay & Display near – short stay only at visitor centre) †◯† (Licensed) ⌃ ♿ (wheelchairs, potters wheel, Braille guide, hearing loop, toilets) shop, ⊗ (ex Blists Hill & guide dogs) 🚌 (min group 20 for ticket discount)

## LUDLOW
**Ludlow Castle**
Castle Square SY8 1AY
☎ 01584 873355
**Email:** hduce@ludlowcastle.plus.com
**Web:** www.ludlowcastle.com
**Dir:** *A49 to town centre*
Ludlow Castle dates from about 1086. In 1473, Edward IV sent the Prince of Wales and his brother – later to become the Princes in the Tower – to live here, and Ludlow Castle became a seat of government. John Milton's *Comus* was first performed at Ludlow Castle in 1634. Nowadays, contemporary performances of Shakespeare's plays, together with concerts, are staged in the castle grounds during the Ludlow Festival (end June-early July). Please telephone for details of events running throughout the year.
**Times:** Open all year, Jan Sat-Sun 10-4; Feb-Mar & Oct-Dec daily 10-4; Apr-Jul & Sep daily 10-5; Aug daily 10-7; (last admission 30 minutes before closing). Closed 25 Dec.
**Fee:** £4 (ch under 6 free, ch £2, pen £3.50). Family ticket £11.
**Facilities:** Ⓟ (100yds) ⏣ ⦿ (Licensed) ⊼ 🗐 50p-£2 ♿ (toilets) shop, guided tours, audio commentaries (charged) 🚌

## TELFORD
**Hoo Farm Animal Kingdom**
Preston-on-the-Weald Moors TF6 6DJ
☎ 01952 677917 🖷 01952 677944
**Email:** info@hoofarm.com
**Web:** www.hoofarm.com
**Dir:** *M54 junct 6, follow brown tourist signs*
Hoo Farm is a real children's paradise where there is always something happening. A clean, friendly farm that appeals to all ages and offers close contact with a wide variety of animals from fluffy yellow chicks and baby lambs to foxes, llamas, deer and ostriches. A daily programme of events encourages audience participation in the form of bottle feeding lambs, pig feeding and collecting the freshly laid eggs. New for this year is ferret racing! The Craft Area offers the chance to try your hand at candle dipping, glass or pottery painting or even throwing a pot on the potters wheel. There are Junior Quad Bikes and a Rifle Range, Pony Rides, powered mini tractors as well as indoor and outdoor play areas and a new games room. Please telephone for details of special events running throughout the year.
**Times:** Open: 19 Mar-9 Sep, Tue-Sun 10-6. 10 Sep-26 Nov, Tue-Sun, 10-5. 26 Nov-24 Dec, daily 10-5 closes at 1 on 24 Dec. Closed 25 Dec to mid March.
**Fee:** £5.25 (ch £4.75 & pen £4.50). Family ticket (2ad+3ch) £21.
**Facilities:** Ⓟ ⏣ (sandwiches, snacks and drinks) ⊼ ♿ (toilets) shop, ⊗ (ex guide dogs) 🚌 pre-book only

## WELLINGTON
**Sunnycroft**
200 Holyhead Road Telford TF1 2DR
☎: 01952 242884
**Dir:** *3m W of Telford in Wellington off B5061*
A Victorian gentlemans villa, typical of houses built for prosperous business and professional people on the fringe of towns and cities. The house is a time capsule of early 20th century life both above and below stairs, when it was home to the Lander family. Displays of embroidery by Joan Lander can be seen within the house.
**Times:** HouseOpen 23 Mar-29 Oct, Fri, Sun & Mon, 1-5 (last admission 4). Also open Good Fri & BH Mons. Entry by guided tour only.
**Fee:** *House & Garden £5 (ch £2.50). Family £12.50. Garden £2.50 (ch £1.25). Family £6.30
**Facilities:** Ⓟ Ⓟ (0.25m – parking limited) ⊼ 🗐 ♿ (toilets) guided tours ⊗ (ex on leads in grounds) 🚌 (advance booking essential) 🐾 ♿

## WESTON-UNDER-REDCASTLE
### Hawkstone Historic Park & Follies
Shrewsbury SY4 5UY
☎ 01939 200611 📄 01939 200311
**Email:** info@hawkstone.co.uk
**Web:** www.hawkstone.co.uk
**Dir:** *3m from Hodnet off A53, follow brown heritage signs*
Created in the 18th century by the Hill family, Hawkstone was once one of the greatest historic parklands in history. After almost one hundred years of neglect it has now been restored and designated a Grade I historic park. Visitors can once again experience the magical world of intricate pathways, arches and bridges, towering cliffs and follies, and an awesome grotto. The Grand Valley and woodlands have centuries-old oaks, wild rhododendrons and lofty monkey puzzles. The park covers nearly 100 acres of hilly terrain and visitors are advised to wear sensible shoes and clothing and to bring a torch. Allow 3-4 hours for the tour, which is well signposted and a route map is provided in the admission price. Attractions include 'Hear King Arthur' and meeting the Duke of Wellington in the White Tower to discuss the Battle of Waterloo.
**Times:** *Open from 10, Jan-Mar, Sat & Sun; Apr-May, & Sep-Oct, Wed-Sun; Jun-Aug, daily. Closed Nov & Dec.
**Fee:** *Wkdays £5.50 (ch £3.50 pen & students £4.50). Family ticket £15.
**Facilities:** 🅿 🍴 (Licensed) ⛱ ♿ (no access to follies due to terrain, access valley only, toilets) shop, 🚌

## WROXETER
### Wroxeter Roman City
SY5 6PH
☎: 01743 761330
**Web:** www.english-heritage.org.uk
**Dir:** *5m E of Shrewsbury, 1m S of A5*
Discover what urban life was like 2,000 years ago in the forth largest city in Roman Britain. See the remains of the impressive 2nd-century municipal baths and view the excavated treasures in the museum.
**Times:** Open all year, Mar-May & Sep-Oct, daily, 10-5; Jun-Aug, daily, 10-6; Nov-Feb, Wed-Sun, 10-4. Closed 24-26 Dec & 1 Jan.
**Fee:** £4 (ch £2, concessions £3). Family £10. Prices and opening times are subject to change. Please check web site or call 0870 333 1181 for the most up to date prices and opening times when planning your visit.
**Facilities:** 🅿 ♿ shop, 🚌 ♯ ⊚

## ALTON
### Alton Towers
ST10 4DB
☎ 08705 204060 📄 01538 704097
**Email:** info@alton-towers.com
**Web:** www.altontowers.com
**Dir:** *from S: M1 junct 23a or M6 junct 15. From N: M1 junct 28 or M6 junct 16*
Alton Towers is a fantastic day out for all the family. With world-first rides and attractions as well as some beautiful gardens, this is more than just a theme park. Recent additions include the Spinball Whizzer, a spinner coaster, as well as The Flume, in which visitors now travel in red bath tubs, replacing the original rustic logs. There are a number of rides and attractions for younger children too. Alton Towers has more than enough for an action-packed dayout and the site includes several shops and restaurants.
**Times:** *Open daily 12 Mar-30 Oct
**Fee:** Advance book, Adults from £23 (ch from £16)
**Facilities:** 🅿 (charged) 🍴 (Licensed) ⛱ ♿ (disabled guest guide books, toilets) shop, ⊗ (ex guide dogs) 🚌

## CHEDDLETON
### Churnet Valley Railway
The Station near Leek ST13 7EE
☎ 01538 360522 ▤ 01538 361848
**Email:** enquiries@churnetvalleyrailway.co.uk
**Web:** www.churnetvalleyrailway.co.uk
**Dir:** *3m S from Leek, 3m N from Cellarhead along A520. Kingsley & Froghall Station is situated on the Stoke to Ashbourne road, A52*
The Churnet Valley Railway runs through the hidden countryside between Cheddleton, with its Grade II Victorian station, Kingsley and Froghall, with the newly built station and Canal Wharf. The journey incorporates Consall, which has a sleepy rural station and nature reserve, and Leekbrook with one of the longest tunnels on a preserved railway. Special Events: 1940s wknd Apr, Ghost Train Oct, Santa & Steam Dec, Day out with Thomas Feb and Jul.
**Times:** Open every Sun, Mar-Oct; all BHs Wed & Sat, Jun-Aug; Diesel trains every Tue & Thu in Aug and every Sat Mar-Oct.
**Fee:** All day travel: £9 (ch £5, pen £7)
**Facilities:** 🅿 Ⓟ (100 yards) ☕ (Tea rooms at each station) 🚻 ♿ (ramps, toilets) shop, guided tours 🚌 (pre booking necessary)

## LICHFIELD
### Lichfield Heritage Centre
Market Square WS13 6LG
☎ 01543 256611 ▤ 01543 414749
**Email:** info@lichfieldheritage.org.uk
**Web:** www.lichfieldheritage.org.uk
**Dir:** *in city centre*
A colourful new exhibition, 'The Lichfield Story' gives a vivid account of Lichfield's rich and varied history over 2,000 years. It is home to the Staffordshire Millennium Embroideries which are displayed within their own gallery. In addition, the exhibition houses fine examples of City, Diocesan and Regimental silver, ancient charters and archives. Two audio visual presentations, a Family Trail and, for younger children a Mouse Hole Trail, provide interest and fun for all the family.
**Times:** *Open all year, daily 10-5, Sun 10.30-5. (Last admission 4). Closed Xmas & New Year.
**Fee:** *£3.50 (ch 5-15 £1, concessions £2.50, under 5's free). Family ticket (2ad+2ch) £8. Viewing platform (when available) £2 (ch £1, concessions £1.50). Groups and school parties welcome by arrangement, contact the administrator's office for information
**Facilities:** Ⓟ (200yds) ♿ (lift to first floor, toilets) shop, 🚫 (ex guide dogs) 🚌 (by arrangement only)

## SHUGBOROUGH
### Shugborough Estate
Milford Stafford ST17 0XB
☎ 01889 881388 ▤ 01889 881323
**Email:** shugborough.promotions@staffordshire.gov.uk
**Web:** www.shugborough.org.uk
**Dir:** *6m E of Stafford off A513, signed from M6 junct 13*
Set on the edge of Cannock Chase, Shugborough is the magnificent 900-acre seat of the Earls of Lichfield. The 18th-century mansion house contains fine collections of ceramics, silver, paintings and French furniture. Part of the house is still lived in by the Lichfield family. Costumed characters help to recreate the past and there is a varied programme of events each year.
**Times:** *Open 18 Mar-28 Oct, daily 11-5. Site Open all year to pre-booked parties.
**Fee:** *£10 (ch £6, concessions £7). Family Ticket £25. Parking fee (£3) refunded on purchase of all site ticket.
**Facilities:** 🅿 (charged) ☕ (Lady Walk Tearoom) 🍽 (Licensed) 🚻 📷 ♿ (step climber for wheelchairs, 2 Batricars, toilets) shop, guided tours, audio commentaries (charged) 🚫 (ex guide dogs & in parkland) 🚌 🌿

### STOKE-ON-TRENT
**Ceramica**
Market Place Burslem ST6 3DS
☎ 01782 832001 📄 01782 823300
**Email:** info@ceramicauk.com
**Web:** www.ceramicauk.com
**Dir:** *A4527 signposted Tunstall. After 0.5m right onto B5051 for Burslem. Ceramica is in Old Town Hall in centre of town.*
A unique experience for all the family, Ceramica is housed in the Old Town Hall in the centre of Burslem, Mother Town of the Potteries. Explore the hands-on activities in Bizarreland, and learn how clay is transformed into china. Dig into history with the time team and take a magic carpet ride over the town. Discover the past, present and future of ceramics with the interactive displays in the Pavillions. Explore the Memory Bank and read the local news on Ceramica TV.
**Times:** *Open all year Mon-Sat 9.30-5, Sun 10.30-4.30. For Xmas opening please telephone.
**Fee:** *£3.75, (concessions £2.50, under 4's free). Family ticket (2ad+2ch) £10. Group of 12 £2.50 per person.
**Facilities:** 🅿 (charged) Ⓟ (200m) (Vending machines for food and drink) ⛲ ♿ (ramps, lift to all floors, tactile displays, toilets) shop, ⊗ (ex guide dogs) 🚌 (pre-booking is advised)

### STOKE-ON-TRENT
**Gladstone Working Pottery Museum**
Uttoxeter Road Longton ST3 1PQ
☎ 01782 237777 📄 01782 237076
**Email:** gladstone@stoke.gov.uk
**Web:** www.stoke.gov.uk/gladstone
**Dir:** *A50 then follow brown heritage signs*
Located at the heart of the Potteries, Gladstone Pottery Museum is the last remaining Victorian Pottery industry. Whilst touring the original factory building discover what it was like for the men, women and children to live and work in a potbank during the era of the coal firing bottle ovens. In original workshops working potters can be found demonstrating traditional pottery skills. There are also lots of opportunities for you to have a go at pottery making, throw your own pot on the potters wheel, make china flowers and decorate pottery items to take home. Also explore Flushed with Pride, dedicated to the story of the development of the toilet, and The Tile Gallery, a fine collection which traces the development of decorative tiles.
**Times:** *Open all year, daily 10-5 (last admission 4). Limited opening Xmas & New Year.
**Fee:** £5.95 (ch £4.95, concessions £4.95). Family ticket £18 (2ad+2ch).
**Facilities:** 🅿 🍴 (Licensed) ⛲ ♿ (electric buggy available to loan, toilets) shop, ⊗ (ex guide dogs) 🚌 (advance booking for guided tour & food)

### TAMWORTH
**Drayton Manor Theme Park**
B78 3TW
☎ 08708 752252 📄 01827 288916
**Email:** info@draytonmanor.co.uk
**Web:** www.draytonmanor.co.uk
**Dir:** *M42 junct 9/10, on A4091. Exit at T2 of M6 toll*
A popular family theme park with over 100 rides and attractions set in 280 acres of parkland and lakes. Drayton Manor features world-class rides like 'Apocalypse'- the world's first stand-up tower drop, 'Stormforce 10' – the best water ride in the country and 'Shockwave' – Europe's only stand-up rollercoaster. A new rollercoaster sensation is G-Force. Plus a host of family attractions, children's rides, zoo, museum, shops and attractions.
**Times:** Park open end Mar-Oct. Rides from 10.30-5 or 6. Zoo open all year.
**Fee:** Please telephone or visit website for details.
**Facilities:** 🅿 🍴 (Licensed) ⛲ ♿ (ramps or lifts to most rides, some rides limited access, toilets) shop, garden centre ⊗ (ex in park & guide dogs) 🚌

## TAMWORTH
### Tamworth Castle

Tamworth Borough Council Marmion House Lichfield Street Staffs B79 7NA

☎ 01827 709629 & 709626 📄 01827 709630

**Email:** heritage@tamworth.gov.uk

**Web:** www.tamworthcastle.co.uk

**Dir:** *M42 junct 10 & M6 junct 12, access via A5*

The dramatic Norman motte and bailey castle was once the home of England's Royal Champions and today is (reputedly) haunted by two lady ghosts. Special events are held throughout the year and quizzes, dressing-up, brass rubbing and puzzles make it a great family day out. Tamworth Castle was purchased by the town corporation in 1897 and was then opened to the public.

**Times:** *Open mid Feb-Oct: Tue-Sun 12-5.15, (last admission 4.30). Nov-mid Feb: Thu-Sun 12-5.15, (last admission 4.30).

**Fee:** *£4.95 (ch £2.95 & pen £3.95). Family £13. Prices subject to change.

**Facilities:** ℗ (100yds & 400yds) ☕ (Tea,coffee, snacks) ⛱ ♿ (one wheelchair) shop, guided tours (charged) 🚫 (ex guide dogs) 🚌 (limited space)

## WESTON PARK
### Weston Park

Weston-under-Lizard Shifnal TF11 8LE

☎ 01952 852100 📄 01952 850430

**Email:** enquiries@weston-park.com

**Web:** www.weston-park.com

**Dir:** *on A5 at Weston-under-Lizard, 3m off M54 junct 3 and 8m off M6 junct 12.*

Built in 1671, this fine mansion stands in elegant gardens and a vast park designed by 'Capability' Brown. Three lakes, a miniature railway, and a woodland adventure playground are to be found in the grounds, and in the house itself there is a magnificent collection of pictures, furniture and tapestries. There is also an animal centre and Deer Park.

**Times:** Open wknds from 15 April–July, then daily until 3 Sep.

**Fee:** *Park & Gardens £2.50 (ch 3-14 £1.50, pen £2). House, £2.25 (ch 3-14 £1.25, pen £1.75). Family ticket (2 ad & 3 ch) inc house, park & gardens £9.50.

**Facilities:** ℗ ☕ (Coffee Bar 11-5) 🍽 (Licensed) ⛱ 📋 Guide book £4 ♿ (disabled route, access to restaurant & shop, toilets, disabled parking nearby) shop, guided tours 🚌

## ALCESTER
### Ragley Hall

B49 5NJ

☎ 01789 762090 📄 01789 764791

**Email:** info@ragleyhall.com

**Web:** www.ragleyhall.com

**Dir:** *8m SW of Stratford-upon-Avon, off A46/A435, follow brown tourist signs*

Built in 1680, Ragley is the family home of the Marquess and Marchioness of Hertford and houses a superb collection of 18th century paintings, porcelain and furniture. Set in 27 acres of gardens and 400 acres of parkland, The house contains a stunning mural by Graham Rust, *The Temptation,* and England's finest Baroque plasterwork dated 1750. Ticket includes the house, Terrace Tea rooms overlooking the rose garden, gift shop, adventure playground, unique 3D maze, lakeside picnic area, woodland walk and stables containing equestrian memorabilia. Location for the BBC's production of *Scarlet Pimpernel.*

**Times:** *Open mid Apr-end Sep, Thu-Sun & BH Mon. Park & Garden open daily, mid Jul-end Aug.

**Fee:** *House (including garden & park) £6 (ch £4.50, pen £5). £1 entry to state rooms.

**Facilities:** ℗ ☕ (tea room) ⛱ ♿ (lift to first floor, toilets) shop 🚌 20+ must pre book for group rates 🚭

COMPTON VERNEY

**Compton Verney**

CV35 9HZ

☎ 01926 645500 🖷 01926 645501

**Email:** info@comptonverney.org.uk

**Web:** www.comptonverney.org.uk

**Dir:** *7m E of Stratford-upon-Avon on B4086 between Wellesbourne & Kineton*

Warwickshire's largest art gallery, housed in an 18th-century Grade I Robert Adam mansion house and set in 120 acres of glorious 'Capability' parkland. Six permanent collections include; Naples 1600-1800, German 1450-1650, British portraits, china, British Folk Art and the Marx-Lambert collection. There is also a programme of changing exhibitions, special events, tours and workshops.

**Times:** *Open 24 Mar-9 Dec, Tue-Sun, 10-5. Closed Mon except BH.

**Fee:** *£7 (ch under 5's free, 5-16 £2, concessions £4) Family £16 (2+up to 4 ch).

**Facilities:** (w/chairs, large print guides, hearing loop, toilets) shop, guided tours (ex assist dogs)

---

GAYDON

**Heritage Motor Centre**

Banbury Road Warwick CV35 0BJ

☎ 01926 641188 🖷 01926 641555

**Email:** enquiries@heritage-motor-centre.co.uk

**Web:** www.heritage-motor-centre.co.uk

**Dir:** *M40 junct 12 and take B4100. Attraction signed*

Home to the largest collection of historic British cars in the world, the Heritage Motor Centre is set in 65 acres of grounds. Attractions at the Centre include the Time Road, a fascinating journey through Britain's motoring and social history, the motoring cinema, and the 'Get Behind the Wheel' zone, where visitors get the chance to sit in a variety of cars from the collection. Outside features include; Land Rover 4x4 off-roading, go-karting, and children's miniature roadway.

**Times:** *Open all year, daily 10-5. (Closed 24-26 Dec).

**Fee:** *£8 (ch 5-16 £6, under 5 free, & pen £7). Family ticket £25. Additional charges apply to outdoor activities

**Facilities:** (snacks, hot and cold meals) (lift to all floors, limited number of manual wheelchairs, toilets) shop, guided tours (ex guide/hearing dogs)

---

KENILWORTH

**Kenilworth Castle**

CV8 1NE

☎ 01926 852078 🖷 01926 851514

**Web:** www.english-heritage.org.uk

Explore the largest and most extensive castle ruin in England, with a past rich in Kings and Earls and major events in history. Its massive red sandstone towers, keep and wall glow brightly in the sunlight. Kenilworth Castle covers a large area and includes a Tudor garden. Discover the history of Kenilworth through the interactive model in Leicester's Barn.

**Times:** Open all year, Apr-May & Sep-Oct daily, 10-5; Jun-Aug, daily, 10-6; Nov-Feb, daily, 10-4. Closed 24-26 Dec & 1 Jan. Gatehouse may close early Sat for private events

**Fee:** £5.90 (ch £3, concessions £4.40) Family £14.80. Prices and opening times are subject to change. Please check web site or call 0870 333 1181 for the most up to date prices and opening times when planning your visit.

**Facilities:** (open Apr-Oct, daily) shop,

## MIDDLETON
### Ash End House Children's Farm
Middleton Lane Tamworth B78 2BL
☎ 0121 329 3240 📄 0121 329 3240
**Email:** contact@thechildrensfarm.co.uk
**Web:** www.childrensfarm.co.uk
**Dir:** *signed from A4091*
Ideal for young children, this is a small family-owned farm with many friendly animals to feed and stroke, including some rare breeds. Café, new farm shop, stocking local produce, play areas, picnic barns and lots of undercover activities.
**Times:** Open daily 10-5 or dusk in winter. Closed 25 Dec-1 Jan and wkdays in Jan.
**Fee:** £4.50 (ch £4.90 includes animal feed, farm badge & all activities).

**Facilities:** 🅿 ☕ (high chairs available) 🚻 ♿ (toilets) shop, guided tours (charged) 🚫 (ex guide dogs) 🚌 (prior arrangement only)

## SHOTTERY
### Anne Hathaway's Cottage
Cottage Lane Stratford-upon-Avon CV37 9HH
☎ 01789 292100 📄 01789 263138
**Email:** info@shakespeare.org.uk
**Web:** www.shakespeare.org.uk
**Dir:** *House in Shottery Village, 1m from Stratford*
This world-famous thatched cottage was the childhood home of Anne Hathaway, William Shakespeare's wife. The cottage still contains many family items including the beautiful Hathaway Bed. In the stunning grounds there is a quintessential English cottage garden, orchard, sculpture garden, a romantic willow cabin and a maze.
**Times:** *Open Nov-Mar, daily 10-4; Apr-May & Oct-Nov, Mon-Sat 9.30-5, Sun 10-5; Jun-Aug, Mon-Sat 9-5, Sun 9.30-5.

**Fee:** *£5.50 (ch £2, concessions £4.50). Family ticket £13. All five Shakespeare Houses £14 (ch £6.50, concessions £12) Family ticket £29.
**Facilities:** 🅿 ☕ (Mar-Oct only) ♿ (access room with virtual reality tours of cottage, toilets) shop, 🚫 (ex assist dogs) 🚌

## STRATFORD-UPON-AVON
### Shakespeare's Birthplace
Henley Street CV37 6QW
☎ 01789 204016 📄 01789 263138
**Email:** info@shakespeare.org.uk
**Web:** www.shakespeare.org.uk
**Dir:** *in town centre*
Shakespeare was born in this half-timbered house in 1564. Containing original and replica artefacts, it is now presented as it may have been when he was a boy. The ticket price includes entrance to an exhibition of the author's life, including a first edition of his complete works from 1623.
**Times:** *Open Nov-Mar, Mon-Sat 10-4, Sun 10.30-4; Apr-May & Sep-Oct, Mon-Sat 10-5, Sun 10-5; Jun-Aug, Mon-Sat 9-5, Sun 9.30-5.

**Fee:** *£7 (ch £2.75, concessions £6) Family ticket £17. All five Shakespeare Houses £14 (ch £6.50, concessions £12) Family ticket £29. All three Shakespeare Houses £11 (ch £5.50, concessions £9) Family ticket £23.
**Facilities:** 🅿 (coach park 100mtrs – drop off only, max 30 mins) ♿ (computer based virtual reality tour of upper floor, toilets) shop, guided tours 🚫 (ex assist dogs) 🚌

**WARWICKSHIRE**

## STRATFORD-UPON-AVON
### Stratford Butterfly Farm

Tramway Walk Swan's Nest Lane CV37 7LS
☎ 01789 299288 🖷 01789 415878
**Email:** sales@butterflyfarm.co.uk
**Web:** www.butterflyfarm.co.uk
**Dir:** *south bank of River Avon opposite RSC*
Europe's largest live Butterfly and Insect Exhibit.
Hundreds of the world's most spectacular and colourful
butterflies live in the unique setting of a lush tropical
landscape, with splashing waterfalls and fish-filled pools.
See also the strange and fascinating Insect City, a
bustling metropolis of ants, stick insects, beetles and
other remarkable insects. For those brave enough, don't
miss seeing the dangerous and deadly residents in
Arachnoland!

**Times:** Open all year, daily 10-6 (winter 10-dusk).
Closed 25 Dec.
**Fee:** £4.95 (ch £3.95) concessions £4.45. Family
£14.95
**Facilities:** Ⓟ (opposite entrance – site parking orange
badge holders only) 🍴 📷 Free-40p ♿ shop, guided
tours 🚫 🚌

## STRATFORD-UPON-AVON
### The Teddy Bear Museum

19 Greenhill Street CV37 6LF
☎: 01789 293160
**Email:** info@theteddybearmuseum.com
**Web:** www.theteddybearmuseum.com
**Dir:** *M40 junct 15, follow signs to town centre*
Collection of some of the oldest and rarest teddy bears in
the world, displayed in a house once owned by Henry VIII.
Lots of modern teddy bears star too, including the
original Fozzie Bear, the Paddington Bear from the
earliest television series, Mr Bean's bear, and many
more.
**Times:** *Open all year, daily 9.30-5.30 (ex Jan & Feb 10-
4.30). Closed 25-26 Dec.
**Fee:** *£2.95 (ch £1.95, concessions £2.45). Family ticket
£9.50 (2ad+3ch or 1ad+4ch)
**Facilities:** Ⓟ (30yds & 200yds) 📷 ♿ (access to ground
floor shop, only) shop, 🚫 (ex guide dogs)
🚌 (pre-booking required)

## WARWICK
### Warwick Castle

CV34 4QU
☎ 0870 442 2000 🖷 0870 442 2394
**Email:** customer.information@warwick-castle.com
**Web:** www.warwick-castle.co.uk
**Dir:** *2m from M40 junct 15*
From the days of William the Conqueror to the reign of
Queen Victoria, Warwick Castle has provided a backdrop
for many turbulent times. Attractions include Kingmaker,
Death or Glory, and Birds of Prey. Please telephone for
details of events running throughout the year.
**Times:** Open all year, daily 10-6 (5pm Nov-Mar). Closed
25 Dec.
**Fee:** *£13.95-£17.95 (ch 4-16 £8.95-£10.95, pen
£9.95-£12.95, students £10.75-£12.95). Family ticket
(2ad+2ch) £38-£48. Wheelchair bound visitors free.
Group discounts are available if pre-booked.
**Facilities:** Ⓟ (charged) Ⓟ (20 min walk – max 300 cars,
charge varies on area) 🥤 (Takeaway) 🍽️ (Licensed) 🍴
📷 only for booked school visits ♿ (hearing loop, large
print guides, DVD, audio guides, toilets) shop, guided
tours (charged) audio commentaries (charged)
🚫 (ex assistance dogs) 🚌 (must pre-book to qualify
for discounts)

## WILMCOTE
### Mary Arden's House and the Shakespeare Countryside Museum

Station Road CV37 9UN

☎ 01789 293455 🖷 01789 292083

Email: info@shakespeare.org.uk

Web: www.shakespeare.org.uk

**Dir:** *3m NW of Stratford-upon-Avon off A3400*

This picturesque, half-timbered Tudor house was the childhood home of Shakespeare's mother, Mary Arden. The site also includes Palmers Farm – a working farm where visitors can see rare breed farm animals, including Gloucester Old Spot pigs, Cotswold sheep and Longhorn cattle. Falconry displays take place and there is a children's adventure playground .

**Times:** *Open Nov-Mar, Mon-Sun 10-4, Apr-May & Sep-Oct, Mon-Sun 10-5, Jun-Aug, Mon-Sun 9.30-5.

**Fee:** *£6 (ch £2.50, concessions £5) Family ticket £15. All five Shakespeare Houses £14 (ch £6.50, concessions £12) Family ticket £29.

**Facilities:** 🅿 🛱 ♿ (toilets) shop, guided tours ⊗ (ex assist dogs) 🚌

## BIRMINGHAM
### Birmingham Botanical Gardens & Glasshouses

Westbourne Road Edgbaston B15 3TR

☎ 0121 454 1860 🖷 0121 454 7835

Email: admin@birminghambotanicalgardens.org.uk

Web: www.birminghambotanicalgardens.org.uk

**Dir:** *2m W of city centre, follow signs for Edgbaston, then brown heritage signs*

Originally opened in 1832, the gardens include the Tropical House, which has a 24ft-wide lily pool and lush vegetation. The Mediterranean house features a wide variety of citrus fruits and the Arid House has a desert scene with its giant agaves and opuntias.

**Times:** *Open daily, wkdays 9-7 or dusk, Sun 10-7 or dusk. Closed 25 Dec.

**Fee:** *£6.10 (concessions £3.60); £6.40 summer Sun & BHs. Family £18 (£19 summer & BHs) Groups 10+ £5 (concessions £3.20)

**Facilities:** 🅿 Ⓟ 🍴 (hot & cold food and drinks) 🍽 (Licensed) 🛱 ♿ (3 wheelchairs, 2 electric scooters & Braille guides, toilets) shop, garden centre, guided tours ⊗ (ex guide dogs) 🚌 (pre-book)

## BIRMINGHAM
### Museum of the Jewellery Quarter

75-79 Vyse St Hockley B18 6HA

☎ 0121 554 3598 🖷 0121 554 9700

Email: bmag-enquiries@birmingham.gov.uk

Web: www.bmag.org.uk

**Dir:** *off A41 into Vyse St, museum on left after 1st side street*

The Museum tells the story of jewellery making in Birmingham from its origins in the Middle Ages right through to the present day. Discover the skill of the jeweller's craft and enjoy a unique tour of an original jewellery factory frozen in time. For over eighty years the family firm of Smith and Pepper produced jewellery from the factory. This perfectly preserved 'time capsule' workshop has changed little since the beginning of the century. The Jewellery Quarter is still very much at the forefront of jewellery manufacture in Britain and the Museum showcases the work of the city's most exciting new designers.

**Times:** Open Etr-Oct, Tue-Sun 11.30-4. (Closed Mon ex BH Mon)

**Fee:** Free

**Facilities:** Ⓟ (limited 2hr stay/pay & display) ♿ (tours for hearing/visually impaired booked in advance, toilets) shop, ⊗ (ex guide dogs) 🚌 (pre-booked)

## BIRMINGHAM
### RSPB Sandwell Valley Nature Reserve
20 Tanhouse Avenue Great Barr B43 5AG
☎ 0121 357 7395 📠 0121 358 3013
**Web:** www.rspb.org.uk
**Dir:** *off B4167 Hamstead Rd into Tanhouse Ave*
Opened in 1983 on the site of an old colliery, Sandwell Valley is home to hundreds of bird, animal and insect species in five different habitats. Summer is the best time to see the yellow wagtail or reed warblers, while wintertime attracts goosanders, snipe, and redshanks. There are guided walks and bug hunts for children in the summer. The shop, and a visitor centre are open all year round.

**Times:** *Open Tue-Fri 9-5, Sat & Sun 10-5 (closes at dusk in winter). Closed Mon, 24 Dec-2 Jan
**Fee:** *Free
**Facilities:** 🅿 🍴 ♿ (toilets) shop, 🚌 ♿

## BIRMINGHAM
### Thinktank at Millennium Point
Millennium Point Curzon Street B4 7XG
☎ 0121 202 2222 📠 0121 202 2280
**Email:** findout@thinktank.ac
**Web:** www.thinktank.ac
Thinktank is the award winning, Birmingham Museum of Science and Discovery. Four floors with ten themed galleries are packed with interactive exhibits that explore everything from locomotives and aircraft to intestines and taste buds to emotional robots! Themed events, exhibitions, talks and tours run throughout the year.
**Times:** *Open daily 10-5 (last entry 4). Closed 24-26 Dec
**Fee:** *£6.95 (ch £4.95). Family ticket (2ad+2ch) £20, concessions £5 (peak) £3.50 (off peak)

**Facilities:** 🅿 (charged) 🅿 🍵 (hot and cold meals, snacks, beverages) ♿ (induction loop, wheelchair loan, BSL events, parking, toilets) shop, 🚫 (ex guide dogs) 🚌

## BOURNVILLE
### Cadbury World
Linden Rd Birmingham B30 2LU
☎ 0845 450 3599 📠 0121 451 1366
**Email:** cadbury.world@csplc.com
**Web:** www.cadburyworld.co.uk
**Dir:** *1m S of A38 Bristol Rd, on A4040 Ring Rd. Follow brown signs from M5 junct 2 and junct 4*
Cadbury World now has much more to see, do and taste. There are two new attractions: Essence, where visitors can create their own unique product by combining liquid chocolate with different tastes, and Purple Planet, where you can chase a créme egg, grow cocoa beans, and see yourself moulded in chocolate.
**Times:** *Opening times vary throughout the year please contact the information line 0845 450 3599.

**Fee:** *£12.50 (ch 4-15yrs £9.50, concessions £9.95)
**Facilities:** 🅿 🍵 (self service) 🍴 (Licensed) 🍽
♿ (adapted ride & lift to 2nd floor, subtitles, toilets) shop, audio commentaries (charged) 🚫 (ex guide dogs)
🚌 (must book in advance, min 15 paying)

## COVENTRY
### Coventry Cathedral & Visitor Centre
7 Priory Row CV1 5ES
☎ 024 7622 7597 📄 024 7663 1448
**Email:** information@coventrycathedral.org
**Web:** www.coventrycathedral.org
**Dir:** *signposted on all approaches to the city*
Coventry's old cathedral was bombed during an air raid of November 1940 which devastated the city. The remains have been carefully preserved. The new cathedral was designed by Sir Basil Spence and consecrated in May 1962. It contains outstanding works of art by 20th century artists and designers, including a huge tapestry designed by Graham Sutherland, the west screen (a wall of glass engraved with saints and angels) by John Hutton, bronzes by Epstein, and the great baptistry window by John Piper.
**Times:** *Open all year, daily, Etr-Oct 8.30-6, Oct-Etr 8.30-5.30.
**Fee:** *Cathedral £3 donation. Camera charge £2. Video charge £5.
**Facilities:** ℗ (250yds) ⛱ ♿ (lift, touch and hearing centre, paved wheelchair access, toilets) shop, ⊗ (ex guide dogs) 🚌 (booking in advance required) ♨

## COVENTRY
### Herbert Art Gallery & Museum
Jordan Well CV1 5QP
☎ 024 7683 2381 & 2565 📄 024 7683 2410
**Email:** artsandheritage@coventry.gov.uk
**Web:** www.coventrymuseum.org.uk
**Dir:** *in city centre near Cathedral*
Part of the Arts and Heritage service of Coventry, the Herbert is currently undergoing a major redevelopment programme, which is due for completion in 2008. During the time of the redevelopment there will be an active schedule of temporary exhibitions, a number of events and plenty of activities for children.
**Times:** *Open all year, Mon-Sat 10-5.30, Sun 12-5. Closed 24-26, 31 Dec & 1 Jan
**Fee:** Free
**Facilities:** ℗ (500yds) 📗 ♿ (disabled parking, automatic doors, toilets) shop, ⊗ (ex guide/assistance dogs) 🚌 (pre booking preferred) ♨

## COVENTRY
### Lunt Roman Fort
Coventry Rd Baginton CV8 3AJ
☎ 024 7678 5173 & 7683 2565 📄 024 7622 0171
**Email:** info@theherbert.org
**Web:** www.theherbert.org
**Dir:** *S side of city, off Stonebridge highway, A45*
An extension of The Herbert arts complex and located about 3 miles from the city centre. This turf and timber Roman fort from around the end of the 1st century has been faithfully reconstructed. An Interpretation Centre is housed in the granary.
**Times:** *Open 27 Mar-Oct, Sat-Sun & BH Mon 10-5; mid Jul-end Aug, Thu-Tue 10-5; Spring BH wk, Thu-Tue 10-5.
**Fee:** *£2 (concessions £1).
**Facilities:** ♿ ⛱ 📗 ♿ (ramp to Granary Interpretation Centre, toilets) shop, guided tours ⊗ (ex guide/assistance dogs) 🚌 (pre booked) ♨

**WEST MIDLANDS**

# 1001 Great Family Days Out

## DUDLEY
### Black Country Living Museum
Tipton Road DY1 4SQ
☎ 0121 557 9643 & 520 8054 📄 0121 557 4242
**Email:** info@bclm.co.uk
**Web:** www.bclm.co.uk
**Dir:** *on A4037, near Showcase cinema*
On the 26-acre site is a recreated canal-side village, with shops, houses and workplaces. Meet the costumed guides and find out what life was like around 1900. Ride on a tramcar, take a trip down the underground mine, venture into the limestone caverns or visit the olde tyme fairground (additional charge). There are also demonstrations of chainmaking, glass engraving and sweet-making. Watch a silent movie in the Limelight cinema, taste fish and chips cooked on a 1930s range, and finish your visit with a glass of real ale in the Bottle and Glass Inn.
**Times:** *Open all year, Mar-Oct daily 10-5; Nov-Feb, Wed-Sun 10-4. (Telephone for Xmas closing)
**Fee:** *£11 (ch 5-18 £6, pen £9). Family ticket (2ad+3ch) £30.
**Facilities:** 🅿 (charged) ☕ (tea,coffe, cakes) 🍽 (Licensed) 🚻 ♿ (ramps available, toilets) shop, guided tours ⊗ (ex guide dogs) 🚌 (pre-booking advised)

## DUDLEY
### Dudley Zoological Gardens
2 The Broadway DY1 4QB
☎ 01384 215313 📄 01384 456048
**Email:** marketing@dudleyzoo.org.uk
**Web:** www.dudleyzoo.org.uk
**Dir:** *M5 junct 2 towards Wolverhampton/Dudley, signed*
The gardens provide a range of activities for all the family. From lions and tigers to snakes and spiders, enjoy animal encounters and feeding times. Get closer to some furry, and some not so furry creatures, and have fun on the fair rides, land train, and the adventure playground. Step back in time and see history come to life in the castle.
**Times:** *Open all year, Etr-mid Sep, daily 10-4; mid Sep-Etr, daily 10-3. Closed 25 Dec.
**Fee:** *£9.95 (ch 4-15 £6.75, concessions £7.25). Family ticket £31 (2ad+3ch)
**Facilities:** 🅿 (charged) 🅿 (0.25m) 🍽 (Licensed) 🚻 ♿ (land train from gates-castle, w/chair pre book, toilets) shop, guided tours ⊗ (ex guide dogs) 🚌

## SOLIHULL
### National Motorcycle Museum
Coventry Road Bickenhill B92 0EJ
☎ 01675 443311 📄 0121 711 3153
**Web:** www.nationalmotorcyclemuseum.co.uk
**Dir:** *M42 junct 6, off A45 near NEC*
The museum has five exhibition halls displaying British motorcycles built during the Golden Age of motorcycling. Spanning 90 years, the immaculately restored machines are the products of around 150 different factories. There are over 700 machines on show, most of which are owned by the museum, while others are from private collections and private ownership. Restoration work is carried out by enthusiasts and the collection is continuously updated with new additions acquired from all over the world.
**Times:** *Open all year, daily 10-6. Closed 24-26 Dec.
**Fee:** *£6.95 (ch 12 & pen £4.95). Party 20+ £5.95
**Facilities:** 🅿 🍽 (Licensed) ♿ (toilets) shop ⊗ (ex guide dogs) 🚌

## STOURBRIDGE
**The Falconry Centre**
Hurrans Garden Centre Kidderminster Road South Hagley
DY9 0JB
☎ 01562 700014 🖷 01562 700014
**Email:** info@thefalconrycentre.co.uk
**Web:** www.thefalconrycentre.co.uk
**Dir:** *off A456*
The centre houses some 70 birds of prey including owls, hawks and falcons and is also a rehabilitation centre for sick and injured birds of prey. Spectacular flying displays are put on daily from midday. There are picnic areas around the site, a calender of special fun days and training courses are available.
**Times:** *Open all year, daily 10-5 & Sun 11-5. Closed 25, 26 Dec & Etr Sun.

**Fee:** *£3.50 (ch, pen & disabled £2.50). Party 25+ 10% discount.
**Facilities:** ℗ ☕ (light lunches, snacks, afternoon teas) 🍴 ♿ (Ramps in most places, toilets) shop, garden centre ⊗ (ex guide dogs) 🚌 (max 60, pre-booked only)

## WALSALL
**The New Art Gallery Walsall**
Gallery Square WS2 8LG
☎ 01922 654400 🖷 01922 654401
**Email:** info@artatwalsall.org.uk
**Web:** www.artatwalsall.org.uk
**Dir:** *signed from all major routes into town centre*
Opened in 2000, this exciting art gallery has at its core the Garman Ryan Collection, and a Children's Discovery Gallery that offers access to the very best in contemporary art in the only interactive art gallery designed especially for young people.
**Times:** *Open all year, Tue-Sat 10-5, Sun noon-5. Closed Mon ex BH Mon, 25-28 Dec & 1 Jan. Please telephone to confirm.

**Fee:** Free
**Facilities:** ℗ (5 minutes on foot – free on site for disabled) 📱 ♿ (lift access to facilties, induction loop, large print, toilets) shop, guided tours ⊗ (ex guide dogs) 🚌 ♻

## BEWDLEY
**West Midland Safari & Leisure Park**
Spring Grove DY12 1LF
☎ 01299 402114 🖷 01299 404519
**Email:** info@wmsp.co.uk
**Web:** www.wmsp.co.uk
**Dir:** *on A456 between Kidderminster & Bewdley*
Located in the heart of rural Worcestershire, this 200-acre site is home to a drive-through safari amongst an amazing range of exotic animals. Animal attractions include the new Leopard Valley, Twilight Cave, Creepy Crawlies, the Reptile House, Sealion Theatre, and the new buffalo, Boma. There are also a variety of rides, amusements and live shows suitable for all members of the family.

**Times:** Mid Feb-early Nov. Times may change refer to website.
**Fee:** *£8.99 (ch 4 free). Multi-ride wristband £8.75. Ride tickets £4 for three tickets from machines (various no of tickets per ride).
**Facilities:** ℗ 🍽 (Licensed) 🍴 📱 ♿ (most areas accessible slopes/tarmac paths) shop, guided tours ⊗ (ex guide dogs) 🚌

## BROADWAY
### Broadway Tower
WR12 7LB

☎ 01386 852390 📄 01386 858038

**Email:** info@broadwaytower.co.uk

**Web:** www.broadwaytower.co.uk

**Dir:** *off A44, 1m SE of village*

The 65ft tower was designed by James Wyatt for the 6th Earl of Coventry, and built in 1799. The unique building now houses exhibitions depicting its colourful past and various uses such as holiday retreat to artist and designer William Morris. The viewing platform is equipped with a telescope, giving wonderful views over 13 counties.

**Times:** Open Apr-Oct, daily 10.30-5. Nov-Mar (tower only) wknds weather permitting 11-3 or by prior booking.

**Fee:** Tower, £3.80 (ch 4-4 £2.30, concessions £3) Family £10 (2ad+2ch)

**Facilities:** 🅿 🍽 (Licensed) 🏠 ♿ (toilets) shop, 🚌

## BROMSGROVE
### Avoncroft Museum of Historic Buildings
Stoke Heath B60 4JR

☎ 01527 831886 & 831363 📄 01527 876934

**Email:** admin@avoncroft.org.uk

**Web:** www.avoncroft.org.uk

**Dir:** *2m S, off A38*

A visit to Avoncroft takes you through nearly 700 years of history. Here you can see 25 buildings rescued from destruction and authentically restored on a 15 acre rural site. There are 15th and 16th-century timber framed buildings, 18th-century agricultural buildings and a cockpit. There are industrial buildings, a working windmill from the 19th century, and a 20th-century fully furnished pre-fab house.

**Times:** *Open Jul-Aug daily 10.30-5; Apr-Jun, Tue-Fri 10.30-4.30, Sat-Sun 10.30-5; Sep-Oct, Tue-Fri 10.30-4.30, Sat-Sun 10.30-5; Mar, Tue-Thu, Sat-Sun 10.30-4

**Fee:** £6 (ch £3, pen £5). Family ticket £15 (2ad+3ch)

**Facilities:** 🅿 🏠 📄 ♿ (ramps, wheelchair available, toilets) shop, guided tours, audio commentaries (charged) 🚫 (ex on lead) 🚌 contact museum for group bookings

## KIDDERMINSTER
### Bodenham Arboretum & Earth Centre
Wolvesley DY11 5SY

☎ 01562 852444 & 850456 📄 01562 852777

**Web:** www.bodenham-arboretum.co.uk

**Dir:** *follow brown signs W from Wolverley Church island along the B4189*

An award winning arboretum, over 2,700 species of trees and shrubs, attractively landscaped in 156 acres. The arboretum is incorporated into a working farm. There are five miles of paths that lead through the woodland glades and take the visitor around the lakes, pools and grazing fields.

**Times:** *Open Mar-23 Dec, Wed-Sun, 11-5. Oct, daily. Also open Jan-Feb weekends only.

**Fee:** *£5 (ch 5-16 & w/chair users £2)

**Facilities:** 🅿 🏠 📄 ♿ (toilets) shop, guided tours 🚫 (ex on leads) 🚌 (advance booking required)

## KIDDERMINSTER
### Severn Valley Railway
Comberton Hill DY10 1QN
☎ 01299 403816 🖷 01299 400839
**Web:** www.svr.co.uk
**Dir:** *on A448, clearly signed*

The leading standard gauge steam railway, with one of the largest collections of locomotives and rolling stock in the country. Services operate from Kidderminster and Bewdley to Bridgnorth through 16 miles of picturesque scenery along the River Severn. Special steam galas and Day out with Thomas weekends take place during the year along with Santa Specials.
**Times:** * Trains operate wknds throughout year, daily, early May end of Sep, school hols & half terms, Santa Specials, phone for details.

**Fee:** *Subject to Review. (Train fares vary according to journey. Main through ticket £11.80 return, Family ticket £31)
**Facilities:** 🅿 (charged) Ⓟ (200yds) Licensed 🛏 🗒 ♿ (some specially adapted trains, call for details, toilets) shop, 🚌 (pre-booked)

## KIDDERMINSTER
### Worcestershire County Museum
Hartlebury Castle Hartlebury DY11 7XZ
☎ 01299 250416 🖷 01299 251890
**Email:** museum@worcestershire.gov.uk
**Web:** www.worcestershire.gov.uk/museum
**Dir:** *4m S of Kidderminster clearly signed from A449*

Housed in the north wing of Hartlebury Castle, the County Museum contains a delightful display of crafts and industries. There are unique collections of toys and costume, displays on domestic life, period room settings and horse-drawn vehicles. Visitors can also see a reconstructed forge, a schoolroom, a wheelwright's and tailor's shop. Admission to the Museum now includes access to the magnificent State Rooms, where the Bishops of Worcester entertained visitors to the castle.

**Times:** Open Feb-Dec, Tue-Fri 10-5; Sat, Sun & BHs 11-5. Closed Good Fri.
**Fee:** £4 (ch & pen £2). Family ticket £11.
**Facilities:** 🅿 Ⓟ (200 yrds) 🛏 🗒 ♿ (car parking spaces, close to main building, lift, toilets) shop, guided tours 🚫 (ex guide dogs & in grounds) 🚌 (pre-booking essential)

## REDDITCH
### Forge Mill Needle Museum & Bordesley Abbey Visitor Centre
Forge Mill Needle Mill Lane Riverside B98 8HY
☎ 01527 62509
**Email:** museum@redditchbc.gov.uk
**Web:** www.redditchbc.gov.uk
**Dir:** *N side of Redditch, off A441*

The Needle Museum tells the fascinating and sometimes gruesome story of how needles are made. Working, water-powered machinery can be seen in an original needle-scouring mill. The Visitor Centre is an archaeological museum showing finds from excavations at the nearby Bordesley Abbey. Children can become an archaeologist for the day and explore the ruins of this fascinating ancient monument.

**Times:** *Open Etr-Sep, Mon-Fri 11-4.30, Sat-Sun 2-5; Feb-Etr & Oct-Nov, Mon-Thu 11-4 & Sun 2-5. Parties by arrangement.
**Fee:** *£3.70 (ch 60p, pen £2.70). Family ticket £8. Reduced admission charge for holders of a Reddicard.
**Facilities:** 🅿 Ⓟ (150mtrs) 🛏 🗒 ♿ (wheelchair, museum audio tour, Braille guide, hearing loop, toilets) shop, guided tours, audio commentaries 🚫 (ex guide dogs) 🚌 (pre-booking)

WORCESTERSHIRE

WORCESTER
### The Elgar Birthplace Museum
Crown East Lane Lower Broadheath WR2 6RH
☎ 01905 333224 📄 01905 333426
**Email:** birthplace@elgarmuseum.org
**Web:** www.elgarmuseum.org
**Dir:** *3m W of Worcester, signed off A44 to Leominster*
In 2000, the Elgar Centre was opened, to complement
the historic Birthplace Cottage and to provide additional
exhibition space for more treasures from this unique
collection, telling the story of Elgar's musical
development and inspirations. Listen to his music as the
audio tour guides you round the easily accessible
displays. 2007 is the 150th Anniversary of Elgar's birth,
so there will be special events and concerts. Contact the
museum for details.

**Times:** *Open daily, last admission 4.15.
Closed 23 Dec-end Jan.
**Fee:** *£5 (ch £2 & pen £4.50) concessions £3.
**Facilities:** 🅿 Ⓟ (50yds) 🪑 📱 £3.50 ♿ (large print
guides, audio facilities, wheelchair, toilets) shop, audio
commentaries ⊗ (ex guide dogs) 🚌 (must pre-book)

**Worcester Cathedral**

**WORCESTERSHIRE**

# North England

The Millenium and Tyne Bridges, Newcastle upon Tyne

# 1001 Great Family Days Out

## ALSTON
### Nenthead Mines
Nenthead Mines Heritage Centre Nenthead CA9 3PD
☎ 01434 382726 📄 01434 382294
**Email:** info@npht.com
**Web:** www.npht.com
**Dir:** *5m E of Alston, on A689*

Set in 200 acres in the North Pennines, this hands-on heritage centre contains exhibitions and displays on geology, local wildlife, conservation, social history and the story of the Northern Pennine's mining past. Visitors can operate three enormous water wheels, gaze down a 328ft deep brewery shaft, and take an underground trip through the Nenthead mines which were last worked for lead in 1915. Special events take place throughout the year.

**Times:** Open Etr-Oct, daily during school hols & BHs 10.30-5 (last entry to mine 3.30). Closed Mon & Tue in term time.
**Fee:** £4-£6.50 (ch site free, concessions £3.25-5.50, mine £2). Family ticket £15.50
**Facilities:** 🅿 Ⓟ 🅰 🗐 ♿ (ramps & motorised scooter, toilets), shop, guided tours audio commentaries 🚌

## ALSTON
### South Tynedale Railway
The Railway Station Hexham Rd CA9 3JB
☎ 01434 381696
**Web:** www.strps.org.uk
**Dir:** *0.25m N, on A686*

Running along the beautiful South Tyne valley, this narrow-gauge railway follows the route of the former Alston to Haltwhistle branch. At present the line runs between Alston and Kirkhaugh.
**Times:** *Open Apr-Oct & Dec, wknds and BHs; 15 Jul-Aug, daily. Also open school hols & some wknds in Dec. Please enquire for times of trains.
**Fee:** *Return £5 (ch 3-15 £2.50). Single £3 (ch 3-15 £1.50). All day £8 (ch 3-15 £4). Family ticket £14.

**Facilities:** 🅿 Ⓟ (150mtrs) 🅰 🗐 ♿ (railway carriage for wheelchairs, pre-booking required, toilets), shop, guided tours 🚌 (pre-booking essential)

## BASSENTHWAITE
### Trotters World of Animals
Coalbeck Farm Keswick CA12 4RD
☎ 017687 76239 📄 017687 76598
**Email:** info@trottersworld.com
**Web:** www.trottersworld.com
**Dir:** *follow brown signs on A591/A66 from Bassenthwaite Lake*

Home to hundreds of friendly creatures including lemurs, wallabies, zebras, red pandas, otters and other exotic animals along with reptiles and birds of prey and a family of gibbons which will keep families amused for hours. Informative, amusing demonstrations daily bring visitors closer to the animals. Clown About is an indoor play centre with soft play area and ballpools for toddlers upwards.

**Times:** Open all year, except 25 Dec & 1 Jan, 10-5.30 or dusk if earlier.
**Fee:** *£5.95 (ch £4.50, under 3 free)
**Facilities:** 🅿 🅰 🗐 ♿ (toilets), shop, guided tours 🚫 (ex guide dogs) 🚌

## BIRDOSWALD
### Birdoswald Roman Fort
Brampton CA8 7DD
☎ 016977 47602 📄 016977 47605
**Email:** birdoswald@dial.pipex.com
**Web:** www.birdoswaldromanfort.org
**Dir:** *signposted off A69 between Brampton & Hexham*
A visitor centre introduces you to Hadrian's Wall and the Roman Fort. This unique section of Hadrian's Wall overlooks the Irthing Gorge, and is the only point along the Wall where all the components of the Roman frontier system can be found together. Birdoswald isn't just about the Romans, though, it's also about border raids in the Middle Ages, and recent archaeological discoveries.
**Times:** *Open Mar-9 Nov, daily 10-5.30. Winter season exterior only

**Fee:** *£3.60 (ch £1.80, concessions £2.70, Family £9.00)
**Facilities:** 🅿 🅿 🛋 ♿ (ramp outside, disabled parking, lift, toilets), shop, 🚌 (pre-booking preferred)

## CARLISLE
### Tullie House Museum & Art Gallery
Castle Street CA3 8TP
☎ 01228 534781 📄 01228 810249
**Email:** enquiries@tulliehouse.co.uk
**Web:** www.tulliehouse.co.uk
**Dir:** *M6 junct 42, 43 or 44 follow signs to city centre. Car park in Devonshire Walk*
Dramatic audio-visual displays, striking recreations of long vanished scenes and imaginative hands-on displays. There is something for everyone, no matter what age - the stunning underground Millennium Gallery or Border River pathway linking to Carlisle Castle.
**Times:** *Open: Nov-Mar, Mon-Sat 10-4, Sun 12-4; Apr-Jun & Sep-Oct, Mon-Sat 10-5, Sun 12-5; Jul-Aug, Mon-Sat 10-5, Sun 11-5. Closed 25-26 Dec & 1 Jan.

**Fee:** *Ground floor (including Art Gallery & Old Tullie House) - Free. Upper floors & Millennium Gallery - £5.20 (ch £2.60 concessions £3.60) Family ticket (2ad+3ch) £14.50
**Facilities:** 🅿 (5mins walk - disabled parking on site by request) 🍽 (Licensed) 🍴 ♿ (chair lift, ramped access, lifts to all floors, toilets), shop 🚫 (ex guide dogs) 🚌

## COCKERMOUTH
### Lakeland Sheep & Wool Centre
Egremont Road CA13 0QX
☎ 01900 822673 📄 01900 820129
**Email:** sheepshow@btconnect.com
**Web:** www.sheep-woolcentre.co.uk
**Dir:** *M6 junct 40, W on A66 to rdbt at Cockermouth on A66/A586 junct*
Come face to face with 19 different breeds of live sheep. There is also a stage show with 'One Man and his Dog' demonstration and our Jersey cow. Shows are four times daily, March-end Oct (Sun-Thu only) and are all held indoors.
**Times:** Open all year, daily 9.30-5.30 (Closed 25 Dec & 5-19 Jan).
**Fee:** £4.50 (ch £3.50) for sheep shows

**Facilities:** 🅿 🍽 (hot meals served 12-2 & 6-9) 🛋 ♿ (hearing loop system, toilets), shop, 🚫 (ex assist dogs) 🚌

**CUMBRIA**

**CONISTON**

### Steam Yacht Gondola

☎ 015394 41288 📠 015394 41962

**Email:** gondola@nationaltrust.org.uk

**Web:** www.nationaltrust.org.uk/gondola

**Dir:** *A593 to Coniston, follow signs near garage 'to boats' & S Y Gondola. Coniston Pier is at end of Lake Road.*

Originally launched in 1859, the graceful Gondola worked on Coniston Water until 1936. Now rebuilt, she came back into service in 1980, and visitors can once again enjoy her silent progress and old-fashioned comfort.

**Times:** *Open Apr-Oct to scheduled daily timetable. Trips commence from 11 at Coniston Pier. Piers at Coniston & Brantwood.

**Fee:** *Round trip £5.90 (ch £2.90). Family ticket (2 ad + 2 ch) £14.50

**Facilities:** 🅿 (charged) 🅿 (5 min walk) 🎫 £1.50, shop, ⊗ (ex outside salloons) 🚌 (pre-booking essential) 🐾

---

**DALTON-IN-FURNESS**

### South Lakes Wild Animal Park

Crossgates LA15 8JR

☎ 01229 466086 📠 01229 461310

**Email:** office@wildanimalpark.co.uk

**Web:** www.wildanimalpark.co.uk

**Dir:** *M6 junct 36, A590 to Dalton-in-Furness, follow tourist signs*

The north's leading zoo park is a unique safari on foot with many animals wandering free. Visitors can walk with kangaroos and emus in the bush, and watch parrots fly free in the trees. Hand feed (supervised at 2pm) families of nine different species of lemur, wonder at the amazing skills of gibbons, macaques and spider monkeys, and see the lions and tigers climb high into trees to catch their food. See both Amur and Sumatran tigers, and spectacled bears. An African plain is approximated by keeping four rhino, six giraffes and a family of baboons in the same field. Also see cheetah, red panda, and over 100 other species. There is a new Indonesian village-themed shopping area, and a new restaurant that overlooks the savannah.

**Times:** Open all year, daily 10-5 (last admission 4.15); Nov-Feb 10-4.30 (last admission 3.45). (Closed 25 Dec).

**Fee:** £10.50 (ch, pen, wheelchair users & registered blind £7). Reduced prices Nov-Mar.

**Facilities:** 🅿 🍴 🎫 ♿ (wheelchair users may need help, toilets), shop, ⊗ 🚌 (7 days advance notice preferable)

---

**EGREMONT**

### Florence Mine Heritage Centre

Florence Mine CA22 2NR

☎ 01946 825830 📠 01946 825830

**Email:** info@florencemine.co.uk

**Web:** www.florencemine.co.uk

**Dir:** *on A595 Egremont by-pass. Turn off at Wilton/Haile, follow signs*

Based in the last deep working, iron ore mine in Western Europe, the Florence Mine Heirtage Centre offers a mining museum, geology and mineral room, a reconstructed drift (or tunnel) and a research facility. Underground tours are also available all year, including weekdays, by prior arrangement. Please phone the mine for details. Suitable footwear and old clothes are advised for underground tours.

**Times:** *Open Apr-Oct, daily, 10-4. Nov-Mar, Mon-Fri 9.30-3.30

**Fee:** *Centre: £2 (ch £1); Mine Tour: £6.50 (ch £4.50)

**Facilities:** 🅿 🍴 🎫 ♿ (hands-on display, toilets), shop, ⊗ (ex guide dogs) 🚌 ♻

**CUMBRIA**

## HARDKNOTT CASTLE ROMAN FORT
**Hardknott Castle Roman Fort**
☎ 019467 26064 ▤ 013467 26115
**Email:** wasdale@nationaltrust.org.uk
**Web:** www.nationaltrust.org.uk
**Dir:** *9m NE of Ravenglass, at W end of Hardknott Pass*
One of the most dramatic Roman sites in Britain, with stunning views of the Lakeland falls. The fort was built between AD120 and AD138 and controlled the road from Ravenglass to Ambleside. The remains include the headquarters building and Commandant's house, with a bath house and parade ground outside the fort. It is on land owned by the National Trust as part of its Wasdale, Eskdales and Duddon property.

**Times:** Open any reasonable time. Access may be hazardous in winter.
**Fee:** *Free
**Facilities:** ⓟ Ⓧ (ex dogs on leads) ♨ ♿

## HAWKSHEAD
**The Beatrix Potter Gallery**
Main Street LA22 0NS
☎ 015394 36355 ▤ 015394 36187
**Email:** beatrixpottergallery@nationaltrust.org.uk
**Web:** www.nationaltrust.org.uk
**Dir:** *situated on main street in village centre*
An annually changing exhibition of Beatrix Potter's original illustrations from her children's storybooks, housed in the former office of her husband, solicitor William Heelis. The gallery also has a display on the life of the author as well as offering many activities for children.
**Times:** *Open Apr- 29 Oct & Good Fri, Sat-Wed 10.30-4.30 (last admission 4). Also open Thu in Jul/Aug. Admission is by timed ticket including NT members.

**Fee:** £3.80 (ch £1.90) Family ticket £9.50 (2ad+3ch)
**Facilities:** ⓟ (300mtrs) ▤ ♿ (Braille guide), shop, Ⓧ (ex guide dogs) 🚌 ♨

## HOLKER
**Holker Hall & Gardens**
Cark in Cartmel Grange-over-Sands LA11 7PL
☎ 015395 58328 ▤ 015395 58378
**Email:** publicopening@holker.co.uk
**Web:** www.holker-hall.co.uk
**Dir:** *from M6 junct 36, follow A590, signposted*
Dating from the 16th century, the new wing of the Hall was rebuilt in 1871, after a fire. It has a notable woodcarving and many fine pieces of furniture which mix happily with current family photographs. There are magnificent gardens, both formal and woodland and the Lakeland Motor Museum, exhibitions, deer park and adventure playground are further attractions.
**Times:** *Open 26 Mar-29 Oct, Sun-Fri 10.30-5.30. Hall Open 11-4.

**Fee:** *Gardens & Grounds £5.70 (ch 6-15 £3) Family ticket £15.50. All 3 attractions £10.50 (ch £6) Family ticket £29.
**Facilities:** ⓟ ⑩ (Licensed) ⊓ ▤ ♿ (ramps, wheelchairs & scooters available for hire, toilets), shop, 🚌 (booking preferred)

**CUMBRIA**

## KENDAL
### Museum of Lakeland Life
Abbot Hall LA9 5AL
☎ 01539 722464 📄 01539 722494
**Email:** info@lakelandmuseum.org.uk
**Web:** www.lakelandmuseum.org.uk
**Dir:** *M6 junct 36, follow signs to Kendal. Located at south end of Kendal beside Abbot Hall Art Gallery*
The life and history of the Lake District is captured by the displays in this museum, housed in Abbot Hall's stable block. The working and social life of the area are well illustrated by a variety of exhibits including period rooms, a Victorian Cumbrian street scene and a farming display. Two of the rooms are devoted to the memory the author Arthur Ransome. Craft demonstrations take place during the Easter and summer holidays

**Times:** *Open 12 Jan-9 Dec, Mon-Sat 10.30-5. (Closing at 4 Jan-Mar & Nov-Dec)
**Fee:** *£3.76 (ch & students £2.75). Family ticket £11. Combined ticket with Abbot Hall & Lakeland Life (same day), £5
**Facilities:** 🅿 Ⓟ (50mtrs) ☕ (Coffee Shop) 🚻 📋 ♿ (listening posts, large print labels, toilets), shop, guided tours ⊗ (ex service dogs) 🚌 (min 10 people)

## KESWICK
### Cars of the Stars Motor Museum
Standish Street CA12 5LS
☎ 017687 73757 📄 017687 72090
**Email:** cotsmm@aol.com
**Web:** www.carsofthestars.com
**Dir:** *M6 junct 40, A66 to Keswick, continue to town centre, close to Bell Close car park*
This unusual museum features celebrity TV and film vehicles. Some notable exhibits to look out for are Chitty Chitty Bang Bang, James Bond's DB5 Aston Martin, Harry Potter's Ford Anglia, Del Boy's Robin Reliant, the A-Team van and Batmobiles. Each vehicle is displayed in its individual film set.
**Times:** Open Feb half term. Daily Etr-Nov (wknds Dec) 10-5

**Fee:** *£4 (ch 3-14yrs £3)
**Facilities:** Ⓟ (100yds) ♿ shop, guided tours 🚌 (large parties split into 2 groups) ♨

## KESWICK
### Cumberland Pencil Museum
Southey Works Greta Bridge CA12 5NG
☎ 017687 73626 📄 017687 74679
**Email:** museum@acco-uk.co.uk
**Web:** www.pencils.co.uk
**Dir:** *M6 N onto A66 at Penrith. Left at 2nd Keswick exit, left at T-Junct, left over Greta Bridge*
Investigating the history and technology of an object most of us take utterly for granted, this interesting museum includes a replica of the Borrowdale mine where graphite was first discovered, the world's longest pencil, childrens activity area, and various artistic techniques that use pencils.
**Times:** Open daily 9.30-4 (hours may be extended during peak season). (Closed 25-26 Dec & 1 Jan)

**Fee:** £3 (ch & pen £1.50, students £2). Family ticket (3ad + 3ch) £7.50, group 10+ £2, ch & pen £1
**Facilities:** 🅿 Ⓟ (100mtrs) 🚻 ♿ (toilets), shop, 🚌 (pre-booking preferred)

## KESWICK
### Mirehouse
CA12 4QE

☎ 017687 72287

**Email:** info@mirehouse.com

**Web:** www.mirehouse.com

**Dir:** *3m N of Keswick on A591*

Visitors return to Mirehouse for many reasons: close links to Tennyson and Wordsworth, the setting of mountain and lake, the varied gardens, changing displays on the Poetry Walk, free children's nature notes, four woodland playgrounds, live classical piano music in the house and the generous Cumbrian cooking in the tearoom.

**Times:** Open Apr-Oct. Grounds: daily 10.30-5.30 House: Wed, Sun, (also Fri in Aug) 2-last entry 4.30. Parties by arrangement.

**Fee:** *House & grounds £4.60 (ch £2.30). Grounds only £2.20 (ch £1.10). Family ticket £13.80 (2 ad & up to 4 ch)

**Facilities:** 🅿 ⌂ ♿ (toilets) ⊗ (ex on leads & guide dogs) 🚌 (must pre-book) 🄑

## LAKESIDE
### Aquarium of the Lakes
Newby Bridge LA12 8AS

☎ 015395 30153 🖨 015395 30152

**Email:** aquariumofthelakes@reallive.co.uk

**Web:** www.aquariumofthelakes.co.uk

**Dir:** *M6, junct 36, take A590 to Newby Bridge. Turn right over bridge, follow Hawkshead Rd to Lakeside. Well signed*

Explore the secret world of the Lakes at Britain's unique freshwater aquarium. See menacing pike, eels, perch, charr and many more in over thirty naturally themed displays. Kids can get close to small mammals including harvest mice and brown rats. See diving ducks and carp in the incredible underwater tunnel, then find out more about British sharks and rays at the Morecombe Bay display. Regular lectures and events. See the aquarium website for details.

**Times:** Open all year, daily from 9. Closed 25 Dec.

**Fee:** *£7 (ch £4.50, pen £6). Family ticket (2ad+2ch £21, 2ad+3ch £25, 2ad+4ch £29).

**Facilities:** 🅿 (charged) ⌂ ♿ (lift to first floor, wheelchair, toilets), shop, guided tours ⊗ (ex guide dogs) 🚌 (pre-booking essential)

## NEAR SAWREY
### Hill Top
LA22 0LF

☎ 015394 36269 🖨 015394 36811

**Email:** hilltop@nationaltrust.org.uk

**Web:** www.nationaltrust.org.uk

**Dir:** *2m S of Hawkshead. Behind The Tower Bank Arms*

This small 17th-century house is where Beatrix Potter wrote many of her famous children's stories. It remains as she left it, and in each room can be found something that appears in one of her books. Note that there is a timed entry system to avoid overcrowding. Access to the garden and shop is also possible.

**Times:** Open 31 Mar-28 Oct Sat-Wed & Good Fri, 10.30-4.30 (Last admission 4) Also open Thu Jun-Aug

**Fee:** £5.40 (ch £2.70) Family ticket £13.50 (2ad+3ch)

**Facilities:** 🅿 (200mtrs - no parking for coaches) ♿ (Braille guide, handling items, access by arrangement), shop ⊗ (ex guide dogs) 🚌 Advance booking essential 🌺

## PENRITH
### Rheged - Enter into the Spirit of Cumbria
Redhills CA11 0DQ
☎ 01768 868000
🖹 01768 868002
**Email:** enquiries@rheged.com
**Web:** www.rheged.com
**Dir:** *M6 junct 40, on A66 near Penrith*
A cinema screen as big as six double decker buses
shows giant family movies daily. Rheged is also home
to the National Mountaineering Exhibition, twelve shops,
restaurants and a children's play area. There are year-
round daytime and evening events, including food and
drink festivals, films, lectures, children's fun days and
live music. Call for details.
**Times:** Open daily 10-5.30. (Closed 25 Dec)

**Fee:** Each attraction £5.95 (ch £4 & pen £4.95). Family
ticket £17
**Facilities:** 🅿 💬 (Open 10-4.30) ♿ (Wheelchairs and
motorised scooters, toilets), shop 🚫 (ex guide dogs)🚌

## PENRITH
### Wetheriggs Country Pottery
Clifton Dykes CA10 2DH
☎ 01768 892733
🖹 01768 892733 ext 231
**Email:** info@wetheriggs-pottery.co.uk
**Web:** www.wetheriggs-pottery.co.uk
**Dir:** *approx 2m off A6, S from Penrith, signed*
The only steam-powered pottery in Britain, with 7.5
acres of things to do. Wetheriggs includes the Pots of
Fun Studio, newt pond and play areas for kids as well
as places where you can throw or paint a pot and also
watch Designer-Makers at work. There's a chance to
purchase original paintings, prints, cards and sculpture,
a pottery museum and guided tours are available
throughout the year.

**Times:** *Open daily, Etr-Oct 10-5.30; Nov-Etr 10-4.30
**Fee:** *Free
**Facilities:** 🅿 🍴 (Licensed) ♿ (toilets), shop
🚫 (ex guide dogs) 🚌 (pre-booking essential)

## RAVENGLASS
### Ravenglass & Eskdale Railway
CA18 1SW
☎ 01229 717171
🖹 01229 717011
**Email:** steam@ravenglass-railway.co.uk
**Web:** www.ravenglass-railway.co.uk
**Dir:** *close to A595, Barrow to Carlisle road*
From the Lake Disrict National Park's only coastal
village of Ravenglass, small steam engines haul trains
through 7 miles of outstanding, unspoilt beauty to the
foot of England's highest mountains in Eskdale. Enjoy
the freedom of open or cosy covered carriages. Children
learn about steam with 'La'al Ratty', the Water-vole
Stationmaster. Thomas the Tank Engine days in May and
October.

**Times:** Open: trains operate daily mid Mar-early Nov.
Most winter wknds, plus daily in Feb Half term.
**Fee:** *Return fare £9 (ch 5-15 £4.50). Family tickets
available
**Facilities:** 🅿 (charged) 🅿 (200yds) 💬 (at the stations)
🍴 ⛱ ♿ (special coaches - prior notice advisable,
toilets), shop 🚌

## WHITEHAVEN
### The Beacon
West Strand CA28 7LY
☎ 01946 592302
🖨 01946 598150
**Email:** thebeacon@copelandbc.gov.uk
**Web:** www.thebeacon-whitehaven.co.uk
**Dir:** *A595, after Parton right onto New Rd. Follow one way system & town museum tourist signs to The Beacon on harbourside*

Home to the town's museum collection, The Beacon traces the social, industrial and maritime heritage of the area using local characters, audio-visual displays and museum pieces. Enjoy panoramic views of the town and coast from the Met Office Weather Gallery. Regular art exhibitions in Habour Gallery.

**Times:** *Open Tue-Sun, Etr-Oct 10-5.30, Nov-Mar 10-4.30.Open school & BH Mons. Closed 25 Dec.
**Fee:** *£4.50 (ch £2.90, pen £3.60) Family £13.50. Art gallery free.
**Facilities:** ℗ (charged) ℗ (100-400mtrs) ♿ (chair/stair lift, Braille signs, toilets), shop, guided tours ⊗ (except assistance dogs) 🚌

## WHITEHAVEN
### The Rum Story
27 Lowther Street CA28 7DN
☎ 01946 592933
🖨 01946 590595
**Email:** dutymanagers@rumstory.co.uk
**Web:** www.rumstory.co.uk
**Dir:** *A595, follow town centre signs*

Set in the original shop, courtyards, cellars and bonded warehouses of the Jefferson family, - the oldest rum trading family in the UK - this fascinating story takes the visitor back in time to the days of the rum trade, its links with the slave trade, sugar plantations, the Royal Navy, barrel-making and more. Set pieces include a tropical rainforest, an African village, a slave ship, and a cooper's workshop.

**Times:** Open daily, Apr-Sep 10-4.30, Oct-Mar 10-4. Closed 25 Dec & 1 Jan.
**Fee:** £4.95 (ch £2.95, concessions £3.95) Family £14.95. Groups 15+ £3
**Facilities:** ℗ (50 to 200 metres) ♿ (wheelchairs, wide doors, lifts, toilets), shop guided tours 🚌 1 coach at a time

## WINDERMERE
### Lake District Visitor Centre at Brockhole
LA23 1LJ
☎ 015394 46601
🖨 015394 45555
**Email:** infodesk@lake-district.gov.uk
**Web:** www.lake-district.gov.uk
**Dir:** *on A591, between Windermere and Ambleside, follow brown tourist signs*

Set in 32 acres of landscaped gardens and grounds, on the shore of Lake Windermere, this house became England's first National Park Visitor Centre in 1969. It offers exhibitions, audio-visual programmes, lake cruises, an adventure playground and an extensive events programme. Contact the Centre for a copy of their free Out and About guide.

**Times:** Open Apr-Oct daily, 10-5. Grounds & gardens open all year.
**Fee:** Free admission but pay & display parking.
**Facilities:** ℗ (charged) ♟ (Licensed) ⌇ ♿ (manual & electric wheelchairs, lifts, induction loops, toilets), shop 🚌

**CUMBRIA**

**CO DURHAM**

## BARNARD CASTLE
### The Bowes Museum
DL12 8NP

☎ 01833 690606 📠 01833 637163

**Email:** info@thebowesmuseum.org.uk

**Web:** www.thebowesmuseum.org.uk

**Dir:** *located in Barnard Castle, just off A66*

John and Joséphine Bowes founded the Bowes Museum over 100 years ago. The magnificent building houses a collection of treasures from fine and decorative art to major temporary exhibitions of international quality and interest. The icon of the collection is The Silver Swan, a unique life-size, musical automaton which plays every day. There are also works by El Greco, Goya and Canaletto. A continuous, rolling programme of major exhibitions is also in place.

**Times:** Open all year daily 11-5. Closed 25-26 Dec & 1 Jan.

**Fee:** £7 (ch under 16 free, concessions £6)

**Facilities:** 🅿 🅟 (10 mins walk) 🍴 📶 ♿ (lift, ramped entrance, reserved parking, audio guide/loop, toilets), shop guided tours audio commentaries ⊗ (ex guide dogs & in park) 🚌

## BEAMISH
### Beamish, The North of England Open Air Museum
☎ 0191 370 4000 📠 0191 370 4001

**Email:** museum@beamish.org.uk

**Web:** www.beamish.org.uk

**Dir:** *off A693 & A6076. Signed from A1M junct 63.*

Set in 200 acres of countryside, award winning Beamish vividly recreates life in the early 1800s and 1900s. Costumed staff welcome visitors to a 1913 town street, colliery village, farm and railway station; a re-creation of how people lived and worked. Ride on early electric tramcars, take a ride on a replica of an 1825 steam railway and visit Pockerley Manor.

**Times:** *Open Apr-29 Oct daily, 10-5; Oct-Mar 10-4, closed Mon & Fri & 11 Dec-1 Jan. (Last admission 3)

**Fee:** *Summer £16 (ch £10, pen £12.50). Winter £6 (ch & pen £6). Winter visit is centered on town & tramway only, other areas are closed.

**Facilities:** 🅿 ☕ (light refreshments) 🍴 📶 ♿ (not ideal for wheelchairs, assistance recommended, toilets), shop ⊗ (ex in grounds & assist dogs) 🚌 (must pre-book)

## BOWES
### The Otter Trust's North Pennines Reserve
Vale House Farm DL12 9RH

☎ 01833 628339 📠 01986 892461

**Web:** www.ottertrust.org.uk/Pennines_Home.html

**Dir:** *S side of A66 Scotch Corner to Penrith Rd, 2m W of Bowes*

Set in 230 acres of upland farmland, the Otter Trust reserve isn't just about otters, although there is an ongoing release programme that aims to protect the otter from extinction. Visitors can also see red and fallow deer, mouflon sheep, and a wide range of birds including curlew, oystercatchers, snipe, and black grouse. The visitor centre contains exhibits on some of the animals as well as local history, and overlooks the charming River Greta.

**Times:** *Open Apr-Oct, daily 10.30-6

**Fee:** *£5 (ch £3)

**Facilities:** 🅿 🍴 📶 ♿ (toilets), shop, ⊗ (ex guide dogs) 🚌 🅩

## COWSHILL
### Killhope The North of England Lead Mining Museum
Weardale DL13 1AR

☎ 01388 537505 📄 01388 537617

Email: killhope@durham.gov.uk

Web: www.durham.gov.uk/killhope

**Dir:** *beside A689 midway between Stanhope & Alston*

Equipped with hard hats and lamps, you can explore the working conditions of lead miners. The lead mine and 19th-century crushing mill have been restored to look as they would have done in the 1870s, and the 34ft water wheel has been restored to working order. There is also a visitor centre and mineral exhibition, a woodland walk, children's play area and a red squirrel and bird hide.

**Times:** Open Apr-Oct, daily 10.30-5 (BHs & summer school hols open until 5.30)

**Fee:** *Mine & Site: £6 (ch £3, concessions £5.50). Family £17. Site: £4.50 (ch £1.70, concessions £4). Family £11

**Facilities:** 🅿 🍴 📱 ♿ (2 electric scooters, sympathetic hearing scheme, toilets), shop, guided tours 🚌 (must pre-book)

## DARLINGTON
### Darlington Railway Centre & Museum
North Road Station DL3 6ST

☎ 01325 460532 📄 01325 287746

Email: museum@darlington.gov.uk

Web: www.drcm.org.uk

**Dir:** *0.75m N, off A167*

Housed in the carefully restored North Road Station, this museum's prize exhibit is *Locomotion*, which pulled the first passenger train on the Stockton to Darlington railway and was built by Robert Stephenson & Co in 1825. Several other steam locomotives are also shown, together with models and other exhibits relating to the Stockton and Darlington and the North Eastern Railway companies. Recently arrived at the museum for a two year period is an A2 Pacific No60532 'Blue Peter'.

**Times:** *Open daily 10-5. Closed 25-26 Dec & 1 Jan.

**Fee:** *£2.50 (ch £1.50, pen £1.50).

**Facilities:** 🅿 🅿 (50mtrs) 🍴 📱 ♿ (toilets), shop, guided tours 🚫 (ex guide dogs) 🚌

## DURHAM
### Durham Cathedral
DH1 3EH

☎ 0191 386 4266 📄 0191 386 4267

Email: enquiries@durhamcathedral.co.uk

Web: www.durhamcathedral.co.uk

**Dir:** *A690 into city, follow signs to car parks*

Founded in 1093 as a shrine to St Cuthbert, the cathedral is a remarkable example of Norman architecture, set in an impressive position high above the River Wear. A full programme of concerts throughout the year. St Cuthbert's Day Procession (phone for details).

**Times:** *Open all year, daily 9.30-6.15; 12 Jun-8 Sep 9.30-8. (Sun 12.30-5). Cathedral is closed to visitors during evening recitals & concerts.

**Fee:** *£4 donation requested

**Facilities:** 🅿 (in city centre) 📱 ♿ (large print guide, touch/hearing centre, stairclimber, toilets), shop, guided tours 🚫 (ex assist dogs) 🚌 (pre-booking) ♿

**CO DURHAM**

## DURHAM
### Oriental Museum
University of Durham Elvet Hill DH1 3TH
☎ 0191 334 5694 📄 0191 334 5694
**Email:** oriental.museum@durham.ac.uk
**Web:** www.dur.ac.uk/oriental.museum
**Dir:** *signed from A167 & A177*
The Marvels of China gallery introduces the visitor to contemporary China, its history and decorative arts. Other displays cover the Islamic World, Buddhism, Chinese archaeology, the story of writing, a Javanese Gamelan Orchestra and an Egyptian Gallery containing everything from mummies to magic amulets.
**Times:** *Open Mon-Fri 10-5, wknds 12-5. Closed Xmas-New Year.
**Fee:** *£1.50 (concessions 75p). Family ticket £3.50.

**Facilities:** 🅿 🅟 (200yds) ♿ (lifts to all floors, toilets), shop ⊗ 🚌 (pre-booking preferable)

## HARTLEPOOL
### Hartlepool's Maritime Experience
Maritime Avenue TS24 0XZ
☎ 01429 860077 📄 01429 867332
**Email:** info@hartlepoolsmaritimeexperience.com
**Web:** www.hartlepoolsmaritimeexperience.com
**Dir:** *from A19 take A179 and follow signs for marina then historic quay*
Britain's maritime heritage is brought to life, with the sights, sounds and smells of an 1800s quayside. Learn about the birth of the Royal Navy, and visit the Quayside shops, the admiral's house and the oldest warship afloat *HMS Trincomalee*. Other features include children's maritime adventure centre, regular demonstrations of sword fighting, and canon firing. There's a full programme of events, for further details see website.

**Times:** *Open all year daily 10-5. Closed 25-26 Dec & 1 Jan.
**Fee:** *£6.25 (ch £3.75, concessions £4.75). Family ticket (2ad+3ch) £16.50. Museum is free
**Facilities:** 🅿 🍴 (Licensed) 🚻 ♿ (all areas ramped or lift access, auto doors, toilets),shop, guided tours audio commentaries ⊗ (ex assist dogs) 🚌

## HARTLEPOOL
### HMS Trincomalee
Jackson Dock TS24 0SQ
☎ 01429 223193 📄 01429 864385
**Email:** office@hms-trincomalee.co.uk
**Web:** www.hms-trincomalee.co.uk
**Dir:** *From A19 take A689 or A179, follow signs for Hartlepool Historic Quay*
Originally built in 1817, the *HMS Trincomalee* is the oldest ship afloat in the UK and the last of the commissioned frigates of the Nelson era. Now fully restored in an award-winning maritime heritage project, visitors are invited to come aboard for a unique experience of navy life two centuries ago.
**Times:** *Open all year, Summer: 10-5, Winter: 10.30-4. Closed Xmas & New Year.

**Fee:** *£4.25 (ch, students, disabled, pen & unemployed £3.25. Family ticket (2ad+3ch) £11.75. Group tickets available.
**Facilities:** 🅿 🅟 (50yds) ♿ (3 out of the 4 decks are accessible by lift), shop, ⊗ (ex guide dogs) 🚌 (pre-booking)

## LANGLEY PARK
### Diggerland
DH7 9TT

☎ 08700 344437 🖷 09012 010300

**Email:** mail@diggerland.com

**Web:** www.diggerland.com

**Dir:** *A1(M) junct 62. Head W following signs to Consett. After 6m left at rdbt, signed Langley Park, then right into Riverside Industrial Estate*

An adventure park with a difference, where kids of all ages can experience the thrills of driving real earth moving equipment. Choose from various types of diggers and dumpers ranging from 1 ton to 8.5 tons. Supervised by an instructor complete the Dumper Truck Challenge or dig for buried treasure. New rides include JCB Robots, the Supertrack, Landrover Safari and Spin Dizzy. Even under 5s can join in the fun, with Mum or Dad's help of course.

**Times:** *Open mid Feb-Nov, 10-5, wknds BHs & school hols only

**Fee:** *£2.50 (pen £1.25, under 2's free). Additional charge to drive/ride machinery.

**Facilities:** 🅿 🛱 ♿ (toilets), shop ⊗ (ex guide dogs) 🚌

## SHILDON
### Locomotion: The National Railway Museum at Shildon
DL4 1PQ

☎ 01388 777999 🖷 01388 777999

**Email:** gill@hamer-loco.fsnet.co.uk

**Web:** www.locomotion.uk.com

**Dir:** *A1M junct 68, take A68 & A6072 to Shildon, attraction is 0.25m SE of town centre*

Timothy Hackwood (1786-1850) was an important figure in the development of steam travel. He constructed *Puffing Billy* for William Hedley, ran Stephenson's Newcastle Works, and also became the first superintendent of the Stockton & Darlington Railway. The museum and house detail Hackwood's life and the steam transport revolution, as well as displaying working models and locomotives from various periods. Steam train rides are available throughout the year, on event days. The Collections building contains 60 vehicles from the National Collection.

**Times:** * Telephone for details

**Fee:** *Free

**Facilities:** 🅿 🅟 (500yds) 🛱 🍽 ♿ (bus available to transport guests, please contact, toilets), shop, guided tours ⊗ (ex guide dogs) 🚌

## STAINDROP
### Raby Castle
Darlington DL2 3AH

☎ 01833 660202 🖷 01833 660169

**Email:** admin@rabycastle.com

**Web:** www.rabycastle.com

**Dir:** *on A688, Barnard Castle to Bishop Auckland road, 1m N of Staindrop*

This dramatic 14th-century castle, built by the Nevills has been home to Lord Barnard's family since 1626. It has an impressive gateway, nine towers, a vast hall and an octagonal Victorian drawing room that has re-emerged as one of the most striking interiors from the 19th century. Rooms contain fine furniture, impressive artworks and elaborate architecture. In the grounds are a deer park, large walled gardens, coach and carriage collections, a woodland adventure playground, a picnic area and gift shop.

**Times:** Open May, Jun & Sep, Wed & Sun only. Jul & Aug, Sun-Fri. Castle 1-5. Park & Gardens open daily (ex Sat) 11-5, open BH wk ends.

**Fee:** Castle, Park & Gardens £9 (ch £4 & pen £8). Family ticket £25 (2ad+3ch). Park & Gardens £4 (ch £2.50 & pen £3.50). Family ticket £12.50 (2ad+3ch). Party 12+

**Facilities:** 🅿 🅟 🛱 ♿ (most of ground floor accessible, DVD interpretation, toilets), shop, guided tours ⊗ (ex guide dogs & on lead) 🚌 (pre-book min 12 people)

TANFIELD
**Tanfield Railway**
Old Marley Hill Gateshead NE16 5ET
☎ 0191 388 7545 📄 0191 387 4784
**Email:** tanfield@ingsoc.demon.co.uk
**Web:** www.tanfield_railway.co.uk
**Dir:** *on A6076 1m S of Sunniside*
A 3-mile working steam railway and the oldest existing railway in the world. The Causey Arch, the first large railway bridge of its era, is the centrepiece of a deep wooded valley, with picturesque walks. You can ride in carriages that first saw use in Victorian times, and visit Marley Hill shed, the home of 35 engines; inside the shed you can see the stationary steam engine at work driving some of the vintage machine tools. The blacksmith is also often at work forging new parts for the restoration work. Special events are held throughout the year, please telephone for details.
**Times:** *Open all year, Summer daily 10-5; Winter daily 10-4. Trains: Sun & Summer BHs wknds; also Thu & Sat mid Jul-Aug. Santa's Specials Sat & Sun in Dec (booking essential). Mince pie specials Boxing Day.
**Fee:** *Admission free. Train travel £4.50 (under 5 free, ch & pen £2.50). Family discount tickets avalible £11.50.
**Facilities:** 🅿 Ⓟ 🍴 ♿ (all trains carry ramps for wheelchair access, toilets), shop 🚌 ♨

---

ALTRINCHAM
**Dunham Massey**
WA14 4SJ
☎ 0161 941 1025 📄 0161 929 7508
**Email:** dunhammassey@nationaltrust.org.uk
**Web:** www.nationaltrust.org.uk
**Dir:** *3m SW of Altrincham off A56, off M6 junct 19 or off M56 junct 7, then follow brown signs*
A fine 18th-century house, garden and park, home of the Earls of Stamford until 1976. The house contains fine furniture and silverware, and some thirty rooms, including the library, billiard room, fully-equipped kitchen, butler's pantry and laundry. The garden is on an ancient site with waterside plantings, mixed borders and fine lawns. There is also a 300-acre deer park. Telephone for details of special events.
**Times:** Open: Park, restaurant & shop open all year. House open 17 Mar-28 Oct, 12-5 (11 Sun & BH Mon). Garden, 11-5.30. Last entry 30mins before closing time.
**Fee:** House & Garden £7.50 (ch £3.75). House only £5 (ch £2.50). Group rate (pre-booked only) House & Garden £6. Family ticket £18.75. Reduced rate when arriving on public transport.
**Facilities:** 🅿 (charged) 🍴 (Licensed) 🍴 📖 ♿ (wheelchairs, lift, Braille & large print guide, parking, toilets) shop guided tours 🚫 (ex on lead in park) 🚌 (must pre-book) 🌿

---

ASHTON-UNDER-LYNE
**Portland Basin Museum**
Portland Place OL7 0QA
☎ 0161 343 2878 📄 0161 343 2869
**Email:** portland.basin@tameside.gov.uk
**Web:** www.tameside.gov.uk
**Dir:** *M60 junct 23 into Ashton town centre. Museum is near Cross Hill Street & car park*
Exploring the social and industrial history of Tameside, this museum is part of the recently rebuilt Ashton Canal Warehouse, built in 1834. Visitors can walk around a 1920s street, dress up in old hats and gloves, steer a virtual canal boat, and see the original canal powered waterwheel that once drove the warehouse machinery. It also features changing exhibitions and event programme - so there's always something new to see!
**Times:** *Open all year, Tue-Sun 10-5. (Closed Mon, ex BHs)
**Fee:** *Free
**Facilities:** 🅿 Ⓟ (100yds) 🍴 🍴 📖 ♿ (wheelchair, lift, loop system, toilets), shop 🚫 (ex guide dogs) 🚌

## BRAMHALL
### Bramall Hall & Park
Stockport SK7 3NX
☎ 0845 833 0974 🖺 0161 486 6959
**Email:** bramall.hall@stockport.gov.uk
**Web:** www.bramallhall.org.uk
**Dir:** *from A6 right at Blossoms public house through Davenport village then right - signed*
This large timber-framed hall dates from the 14th century, and is one of the finest black-and-white houses in the North West. It has rare 16th-century wall paintings and period furniture, and was the home of the Davenport family for 500 years. Much of the house is open to the public and available for hire for functions and events. Open air concerts and plays are a feature in summer.

**Times:** *Open all year, Apr-Sep Sun-Thu 1-5, Fri & Sat 1-4, BH 11-5; Oct-1 Jan Tue-Sun 1-4, BH 11-4; 2 Jan-Good Fri Sat & Sun 12-4. Closed 25-26 Dec.
**Fee:** *£3.95 (concessions £3). Family ticket £11.
**Facilities:** 🅿 (charged) ☕ (Open Summer 11-5, Winter 11-4) 🛗 🗄 ♿ (access for wheelchair users, toilets), shop, guided tours 🚫 (ex guide dogs) 🚌 (must be booked in advance)

## MANCHESTER
### Imperial War Museum North
The Quays Trafford Wharf Road Trafford Park M17 1TZ
☎ 0161 836 4000 🖺 0161 836 4012
**Email:** info@iwmnorth.org.uk
**Web:** www.iwm.org.uk
**Dir:** *M60 junct 9, join Parkway A5081 towards Trafford Park. At 1st island take 3rd exit onto Village Way. At next island take 2nd exit onto Warren Bruce Rd. Right at T-junct onto Trafford Wharf Rd. Alternatively, leave M602 junct 2 and follow signs*
This war museum is built to resemble three shards of a shattered globe, representing conflict on land, sea, and in the air. Inside are thousands of exhibits, performances, and recreations that explore the way that 20th and 21st century conflict has shaped our lives.

**Times:** Open daily Mar-Oct 10-6, Nov-Feb 10-5. Closed 24-26 Dec.
**Fee:** *Free Free
**Facilities:** 🅿 (charged) 🅟 (15 min walk - £4 all day) 🛗 🗄 ♿ (lifts, parking, wheelchairs, Braille sign in lift, toilets), shop, guided tours 🚫 (ex guide dogs) 🚌 (Pre-booked only) 🅿

## MANCHESTER
### Manchester Art Gallery
Mosley St M2 3JL
☎ 0161 235 8888 🖺 0161 235 8899
**Web:** www.manchestergalleries.org
**Dir:** *from M60 follow signs to city centre, gallery close to Town Hall and Central Library*
Manchester Art Gallery houses the city's magnificent art collection in stunning Victorian and contemporary surroundings. Highlights of the collection include outstanding Pre-Raphaelite works, crafts and design, and early 20th-century British art. The Clore Interactive Gallery has lively exhibits and multimedia facilities. There are also a wide range of events, from talks and tours to hands-on activities for children and adults. Contact for details of events and changing exhibitions.

**Times:** Open Tue-Sun, 10-5 (closed Mon except BH). Closed Good Fri, 24-26 & 31 Dec & 1 Jan.
**Fee:** *Free
**Facilities:** 🅟 (NCP-5 mins walk) 🍽 (Licensed) 🗄 ♿ (wheelchairs, induction loops, audio guides, toilets), shop guided tours audio commentaries (charged) 🚫 (ex assist dogs) 🚌 Pre-booking essential 🅿

**GREATER MANCHESTER**

## MANCHESTER
### Manchester Museum

The University Oxford Road M13 9PL

☎ 0161 275 2634 & 2643 ▤ 0161 275 2676

**Email:** anna.j.davey@man.ac.uk

**Web:** www.museum.man.ac.uk

**Dir:** *S of city centre on B5117*

The Manchester Museum has leading research facilities and collections in archaeology, botany, Egyptology, ethnology, mineralogy, numismatics, and zoology, among others. There are large galleries devoted to most of these departments, but the Egyptology collection is particularly impressive, and includes mummies excavated by Sir William Flinders Petrie.

**Times:** *Open all year, Mon-Sat 10-5, Sun & BHs 11-4.

**Fee:** *Free

**Facilities:** ❷ (charged) ⓟ ⴲ ⴵ (lift access, hearing loop, accessible parking, toilets), shop ⊗ (ex guide dogs) 🚌 (pre-booking required)

## MANCHESTER
### Manchester United Museum & Tour Centre

Sir Matt Busby Way Old Trafford M16 0RA

☎ 0870 442 1994 ▤ 0161 868 8861

**Email:** tours@manutd.co.uk

**Web:** www.manutd.com

**Dir:** *2m from city centre, off A56*

Opened in 1986, this is the first purpose-built British football museum. It covers the history of Manchester United in words, pictures, sound and vision, from its inception in 1878 to the present day. Fans can watch their favourite goals and walk down the tunnel to the pitchside (but are not allowed on the pitch).

**Times:** *Open daily 9.30-5 (open until 30mins before kick off on match days). Closed some days over Xmas & New Year.

**Fee:** *Stadium tour & Museum: £9 (ch & pen £6) Family ticket £25. Museum only: £5.50 (ch & pen £3.75) Family ticket £15.50.

**Facilities:** ❷ ⑩ (Licensed) ▤ ⴵ (wheelchair, audio visual scripts, toilets), shop, guided tours ⊗ (ex guide dogs) 🚌

## MANCHESTER
### Museum of Transport

Boyle Street Cheetham M8 8UW

☎ 0161 205 2122 ▤ 0161 205 1110

**Email:** e-mail@gmts.co.uk

**Web:** www.gmts.co.uk

**Dir:** *museum adjacent to Queens Rd bus depot. 1.25m N of city centre on Boyle St*

This museum is a must-see for fans of public transport! Among the many interesting exhibits are more than 80 beautifully restored buses and coaches from the region - the biggest collection in the UK. Displays of old photographs, tickets and other memorabilia complement the vehicles, some of which date back to 1890. Please telephone for details of special events, most of which, unsurprisingly, relate to transport in some way.

**Times:** Open all year Mar-Oct, 10-5; Nov-Feb, 10-4; Wed, Sat, Sun & BH ex Xmas

**Fee:** £4 (ch under 5 free, ch 5-15 & concessions £2, registered disabled, unemployed free). Family ticket £10 (2ad+3ch).

**Facilities:** ❷ ⑩ ⲷ (wknds & BHs) ⴵ (toilets), shop, guided tours ⊗ (ex assist dogs) 🚌 (Booking preferred)

## MANCHESTER
### The Museum of Science and Industry in Manchester

Liverpool Road Castlefield M3 4FP

☎ 0161 832 2244 & 832 1830 📄 0161 833 1471

**Email:** marketing@msim.org.uk

**Web:** www.msim.org.uk

**Dir:** *follow brown tourist signs from city centre*

This museum is on the site of the world's oldest passenger railway station. Colourful galleries packed full of fascinating facts and amazing artefacts bring the past to life. Walk away from your own shadow in Xperiment! The mind bending science centre, see wheels of industry turning in the Power Hall, and the planes that made flying history in the Air and Space Hall. A programme of changing exhibitions.

**Times:** *Open all year, daily 10-5. Last admission 4.30. Closed 24-26 Dec & 1 Jan. (Extended hrs for some special events)

**Fee:** *Free All permanent collections. Charges apply for special exhibitions.

**Facilities:** 🅿 (charged) 🅿 (10 mins walk) 🍴 (Licensed) 🚻 ♿ (lifts, wheelchair loan service, toilets), shop, guided tours 🚫 (ex guide dogs) 🚌 (no coach parking)

---

## MANCHESTER
### The Whitworth Art Gallery

The University of Manchester Oxford Road M15 6ER

☎ 0161 275 7450 📄 0161 275 7451

**Email:** whitworth@manchester.ac.uk

**Web:** www.manchester.ac.uk/whitworth

**Dir:** *follow brown tourist signs, on Oxford Rd B5117 to S of city centre. Gallery in Whitworth Park, opposite Manchester Royal Infirmary*

The gallery houses an impressive range of modern and historic drawings, prints, paintings and sculpture, as well as the largest collection of textiles and wallpapers outside London and an internationally famous collection of British watercolours. The gallery hosts an innovative programme of touring exhibitions. A selection of tour lectures, workshops and concerts complement the programme.

**Times:** *Open Mon-Sat 10-5, Sun 2-5. Closed Good Fri & Xmas-New Year.

**Fee:** *Free Free

**Facilities:** 🅿 🅿 (on road - car park full at peak times) 🚻 ♿ (wheelchair available, induction loop, Braille lift buttons, toilets), shop 🚫 (ex guide dogs) 🚌 (with prior notice) 🖾

---

## MANCHESTER
### Urbis

Cathedral Gardens M4 3BG

☎ 0161 605 8200 📄 0161 605 8201

**Email:** info@urbis.org.uk

**Web:** www.urbis.org.uk

**Dir:** *opposite to Victoria Railway Station*

Urbis explores the dynamic culture of the modern city. The top three floors of interactive exhibits explore cities around the world from Tokyo to Paris, revealing how different cities work, how they change and how they affect others. The exhibition programme covers photography, design, architecture, music and art.

**Times:** *Open daily, Sun-Wed, 10-6; Thu-Sat, 10-8.

**Fee:** Admission free (level one temporary exhibitions charge applies)

**Facilities:** 🅿 (200yds) ♿ (toilets), shop guided tours 🚫 (ex guide dogs) 🚌 (Advance booking required)

**GREATER MANCHESTER**

## SALFORD
**Salford Museum & Art Gallery**
Peel Park Crescent M5 4WU
☎ 0161 736 2649 📄 0161 745 9490
**Email:** salford.museum@salford.gov.uk
**Web:** www.salfordmuseum.org
**Dir:** *from N leave M60 junct 13, A666. From S follow signs from end of M602. Museum on A6*
The museum features a reconstruction of a 19th-20th century northern street with original shop fronts. Upstairs in the galleries there are temporary exhibitions and a gallery displaying paintings, sculptures and ceramics. Recent additions include the lifetimes gallery, featuring audio, IT zones, temporary exhibitions, a spectacular Pilkington's display and lots of hands-on activities and dressing up areas.

**Times:** *Open all year Mon-Fri 10-4.45, Sat & Sun 1-5. Closed Good Fri, Etr Sat, 25 & 26 Dec, 1 Jan.
**Fee:** *Free
**Facilities:** 🅿 Ⓟ (0.25m) 🍴 (Mon-Fri 10-3.30 Sun 1-4.30) 📖 ♿ (Braille & large print labels & visitor packs, hearing loop, toilets), shop, guided tours, audio commentaries 🚫 (ex guide dogs) 🚌 (must pre-book)

## SALFORD
**The Lowry**
Pier Eight Salford Quays M50 3AZ
☎ 0870 787 5774 📄 0161 876 2001
**Email:** info@thelowry.com
**Web:** www.thelowry.com
**Dir:** *M60 junct 12 for M602. Salford Quays is 0.25m from junct 3 of M602, follow brown Lowry signs*
The Lowry is an award-winning building housing galleries, shops, cafés and a restaurant, plus two theatres showing everything from West End plays and musicals, comedians, ballet and live bands. With regular family activity too, you can make a whole day of your visit.
**Times:** *Open daily from 10. Galleries, Sun-Fri from 11, Sat from 10. Closed 25 Dec.

**Fee:** *Free Lowry building & galleries free
**Facilities:** 🅿 (charged) Ⓟ (150 mtrs) ♿ (Sennheiser System, toilets) shop 🚫 (ex guide dogs) 🚌 (pre-booking advised

## STOCKPORT
**Hat Works Museum**
Wellington Mill Wellington Road South SK3 0EU
☎ 0845 833 0975 📄 0161 480 8735
**Email:** bookings.hatworks@stockport.gov.uk
**Web:** www.hatworks.org.uk
**Dir:** *M60 junct 1, follow signs for town centre. Museum opposite bus station*
Hat Works is the UK's only museum of the hatting industry, hats and headwear, offering an insight into a once flourishing industry. See how hats are made with a unique working collection of Victorian millinery machinery and take a tour with expert guides who will give visitors an insight into the Hatter's World. Browse an extensive collection of hats before relaxing in the Level 2 café. Contact for details of events throughout the year.

**Times:** *Open daily Mon-Fri 10-5, Sat, Sun & BHs 1-5. (Telephone for Xmas opening times)
**Fee:** *Free (Guided tours £2 per person)
**Facilities:** Ⓟ (5min walk - limited pay & display parking) 📖 ♿ (hearing loops, toilets), shop guided tours 🚫 (ex guide dogs) 🚌 Pre-booking essential

## UPPERMILL
**Saddleworth Museum & Art Gallery**
High Street nr Oldham OL3 6HS
☎ 01457 874093 ▤ 01457 870336
**Email:** curator@saddleworthmuseum.co.uk
**Web:** www.saddleworthmuseum.co.uk
**Dir:** *M62 E junct 22 or M62 W junct 21. On A670*
Based in an old mill building next to the Huddersfield canal, the museum explores the history of the Saddleworth area. Wool weaving is the traditional industry, displayed in the 18th-century Weaver's Cottage and the Victoria Mill Gallery. The textile machinery is run regularly by arrangement and there are regular exhibitions.
**Times:** Open all year: Apr-Oct, Mon-Sat 10-4.30; Sun 12-4; Nov-Mar, Mon-Sun 1-4; closed 24-25 Dec & 31 Dec & 1 Jan

**Fee:** *Museum - £2 (concessions £1) Family ticket £4. Art gallery - free
**Facilities:** ⓟ ⓟ (500-700yds) ▤ ♿ (stairlift, ramps, Braille & large print guides, wheelchair, toilets), shop ⊗ (ex guide dogs) 🚌 (pre-booked) ♨

## WIGAN
**Wigan Pier**
Wallgate WN3 4EU
☎ 01942 323666 ▤ 01942 701927
**Email:** wiganpier@wlct.org
**Web:** www.wiganpier.net
**Dir:** *follow brown tourist signs from M6 junct 25-27/ M61 junct 6-8*
Wigan Pier is a journey never to be forgotten. Part museum, part theatre, Wigan Pier is a mixture of entertainment and education. Step back in time at 'The Way We Were' heritage centre, visit the world's largest original Trencherfield Mill steam engine and view the auido-visial show or enjoy trips along the Leeds-Liverpool canal, walks in the grounds and events from a regular programme of activities

**Times:** *Open all year, Mon-Thu 10-5; Sun 11-5. Closed every Fri & Sat, 25-26 Dec & 1 Jan.
**Fee:** *£5.25 (concessions £4.25)
**Facilities:** ⓟ ⌷ ▤ ♿ (Braille guide, audio tape, large text leaflet, minicom, toilets), shop ⊗ (ex guide dogs) 🚌 (please telephone for details)

## BALLAUGH
**Curraghs Wild Life Park**
IM7 5EA
☎ 01624 897323 ▤ 01624 897327
**Email:** curraghswlp@gov.im
**Web:** www.gov.im/wildlife
**Dir:** *on main road halfway between Kirk Michael & Ramsey*
This park has been developed adjacent to the reserve area of the Ballaugh Curraghs and a large variety of animals and birds can be seen. A walk-through enclosure lets visitors explore the world of wildlife, including local habitats along the Curraghs nature trail. The miniature railway runs on Sundays.
**Times:** *Open all year Etr-Oct, daily 10-6. (Last admission 5). Oct-Etr, Sat & Sun 10-4.

**Fee:** *£5 (ch £2.50, under 5's free, pen £3). Party.
**Facilities:** ⓟ ⌷ ♿ (loan of wheelchair & electric wheelchair, toilets), shop, guided tours ⊗ (ex guide dogs by arrangement) 🚌

## CASTLETOWN
**Castle Rushen**
The Quay IM9 1LD
☎ 01624 648000 🖹 01624 648001
**Email:** enquiries@mnh.gov.im
**Web:** www.storyofmann.com
**Dir:** *centre of Castletown*
One of Europe's best preserved medieval castles, Castle Rushen is a limestone fortress rising out of the heart of the old capital of the island, Castletown. Once the fortress of the Kings and Lords of Mann, Castle Rushen is bought alive with rich decorations, and the sounds and smells of a bygone era.
**Times:** Open daily, Etr-Oct, 10-5.
**Fee:** £4.80 (ch £2.40) Family £12. Group from £3.80 each.

**Facilities:** Ⓟ (100yds - disc zone parking) 🔳 ♿ shop, ⊗ (ex guide dogs) 🚌 (pre-booking required)

## CASTLETOWN
**Nautical Museum**
☎ 01624 648000 🖹 01624 648001
**Email:** enquiries@mnh.gov.im
**Web:** www.storyofmann.com
**Dir:** *From Castletown centre, cross footbridge over harbour. Museum on right*
Set at the mouth of Castletown harbour The Nautical Museum is home to an 18th-century armed yacht, *The Peggy*, built in 1791 by Manxman George Quayle (and named after his mother). A replica sailmaker's loft, ship model and photographs bring alive Manx maritime life and trade in the days of sail.
**Times:** Open daily, Etr-Oct, 10-5.
**Fee:** £3.30 (ch £1.70). Family £8.30. Groups from £2.60

**Facilities:** Ⓟ (50yds) 🔳 ♿ shop, guided tours ⊗ (ex guide dogs) 🚌 (pre-booking advised)

## CASTLETOWN
**Old Grammar School**
IM9 1LE
☎ 01624 648000 🖹 01624 648001
**Email:** enquiries@mnh.gov.im
**Web:** www.storyofmann.com
**Dir:** *centre of Castletown, opposite the castle*
Built around 1200AD, the former capital's first church, St Mary's, has had a significant role in Manx education. It was a school from 1570 to 1930, saved from demolition in 1950 and evokes many memories of Victorian school life.
**Times:** Open daily, Etr-late Oct, 10-5.
**Fee:** Free

**Facilities:** Ⓟ Ⓟ (30yds - disc zone parking) 🪑 🔳 shop ⊗ (ex guide dogs) 🚌 (pre-booking advised) ♿

## CREGNEASH
**Cregneash Village Folk Museum**
☎ 01624 648000 📄 01624 648001
**Email:** enquiries@mnh.gov.im
**Web:** www.storyofmann.com
**Dir:** *2m from Port Erin/Port St Mary, signed*
The Cregneash story begins in Cummal Beg - the village information centre where you can experience what life was really like in a Manx crofting village during the early 19th century. As you stroll around this attractive village, set in beautiful countryside, call into Harry Kelly's cottage, a Turner's shed, a Weaver's house, and the Smithy. See how traditional crafts and trades are kept alive, still practised today by the village inhabitants. The Manx Four-horned Loghtan Sheep can be seen grazing along with other animals from the village farm.

**Times:** Open Etr-Oct, daily, 10-5.
**Fee:** £3.30 (ch £1.70) Family £8.30.
Group rates from £2.60
**Facilities:** 🅿 🍴 📷 ♿ (toilets), shop 🚫 (ex guide dogs) 🚌 (pre-booking required)

## DOUGLAS
**Manx Museum**
IM1 3LY
☎ 01624 648000 📄 01624 648001
**Email:** enquiries@mnh.gov.im
**Web:** www.storyofmann.com
**Dir:** *signed in Douglas*
The Island's Treasure House provides an exciting introduction to the Story of Mann where a specially produced film portrayal of Manx history complements the award winning displays. Galleries depict natural history, archaeology and the social development of the Island from 10,000 years ago to the present day. There are also examples of famous Manx artists in the National Art Gallery together with the Island's National archive and reference library

**Times:** Open daily all year, Mon-Sat, 10-5. Closed 25-26 Dec & 1 Jan.
**Fee:** Free
**Facilities:** 🅿 🅿 (30yds - parking discs required) 🍴 (Licensed) 🍴 📷 ♿ (lift, toilets), shop, audio commentaries 🚫 (ex guide dogs) 🚌 (pre-booking advised

## DOUGLAS
**Snaefell Mountain Railway**
Banks Circus IM1 5PT
☎ 01624 663366 📄 01624 663637
**Email:** info@busandrail.dtl.gov.im
**Web:** www.iombusandrail.info
**Dir:** *Manx Electric Railway from Douglas and change at Laxey*
Snaefell is the Isle of Man's highest mountain. Laid in 1895, it is Britain's oldest working mountain railway and runs up the four miles from the town of Laxey to the summit. At the top there is a café and several communication masts. On a clear day, England, Ireland, Scotland and Wales are all visible from the top of Snaefell.

**Times:** Open 30 Apr-Sep.
**Fee:** *Laxey-Summit: Return £7.40, Single, £4.40 (ch half fare).
**Facilities:** 🅿 shop 🚌

**ISLE OF MAN**

**ISLE OF MAN**

## LAXEY
### Great Laxey Wheel & Mines Trail
☎ 01624 648000 🖷 01624 648001
**Email:** enquiries@mnh.gov.im
**Web:** www.storyofmann.com
**Dir:** *signed in Laxey village*
Built in 1854, the Great Laxey Wheel, 22 metres in diameter, is the largest working water wheel in the world. It was designed to pump water from the lead and zinc mines and is an acknowledged masterpiece of engineering from the Victorian era. The wheel was christened by Lady Isabella, the wife of the Lieutenant Governor of the Isle of Man.
**Times:** Open Etr-Oct, daily, 10-5.
**Fee:** £3.30 (ch £1.70) Family £8.30. Group rates from £2.60

**Facilities:** 🅿 Ⓟ (100yds) ⼏ 🗊 ♿ shop, guided tours, ⊗ (ex guide dogs) 🚌 (pre-booking advised)

## PEEL
### House of Manannan
Mill Road IM5 1TA
☎ 01624 648000 🖷 01624 648001
**Email:** enquiries@mnh.gov.im
**Web:** www.storyofmann.com
**Dir:** *signed in Peel*
This £6 million centre is an unforgettable experience. Reconstructions, interactive displays, audio visual presentations and original material explore the Celtic, Viking and maritime traditions of the Isle of Man. A visit will leave you in awe of the diversity of Manx heritage and eager to learn more.
**Times:** Open daily, 10-5. Closed 25-26 Dec & 1 Jan.
**Fee:** £5.50 (ch £2.80) Family £13.80. Group rates from £4.40.

**Facilities:** 🅿 Ⓟ (50mtrs) 🗊 ♿ (toilets), shop, audio commentaries ⊗ (ex guide dogs) 🚌 (pre-booking advised)

## PEEL
### Peel Castle
IM5 1TB
☎ 01624 648000 🖷 01624 648001
**Email:** enquiries@mnh.gov.im
**Web:** www.storyofmann.com
**Dir:** *on St Patrick's Isle, facing Peel Bay, signed*
One of the Island's principle historic centres, this great natural fortress with its imposing curtain wall set majestically at the mouth of Peel Harbour is steeped in Viking heritage. The sandstone walls of Peel Castle enclose an 11th-century church and Round Tower, the 13th-century St German's Cathedral and the later apartments of the Lords of Mann. The site is owned by Manx National Heritage.
**Times:** Open Etr-Oct, daily, 10-5.

**Fee:** £3.30 (ch £1.70). Family £8.30. Group rates from £2.60.
**Facilities:** Ⓟ (100yds) 🗊 guided tours, audio commentaries ⊗ (ex guide dogs) 🚌 (pre-booking advised) ⊕

## RAMSEY
**The Grove**
IM8 3UA
☎ 01624 648000 🖷 01624 648001
**Email:** enquiries@mnh.gov.im
**Web:** www.storyofmann.com
**Dir:** *on W side of Andreas Rd. Signed in Ramsey*
This Victorian time capsule was a country house built
as a summer retreat for a Liverpool shipping merchant.
Rooms are filled with period furnishings together with
a costume exhibition. In the adjacent farmyard are
buildings containing displays on farming and 19th-
century vehicles. Around the grounds you may see
Loghtan sheep, ducks and perhaps a Manx cat. The site
is owned and run by Manx National Heritage.
**Times:** *Open Etr-late Oct, daily, 10-5.

**Fee:** *£3.30 (ch £1.70). Family £8.30. Group rates
from £2.60.
**Facilities:** ℗ ⭐ 🗐 ♿ shop, guided tours ⊗ (ex guide
dogs) 🚌 (pre-booking advised)

## BLACKPOOL
**Blackpool Zoo & Dinosaur Safari**
East Park Drive FY3 8PP
☎ 01253 830830 🖷 01253 830800
**Email:** info@blackpoolzoo.org.uk
**Web:** www.blackpoolzoo.org.uk
**Dir:** *M55 junct 4, follow brown tourist signs*
This modern zoo, built in 1972, houses over 1500
animals within its 32 acres of landscaped gardens.
There is a miniature railway, lots of close encounters
and animals in action, a children's play area, animal
feeding times and keeper talks throughout the day.
The Dinosaur Safari takes you on a walking trail with
32 lifesize dinosaurs in Jurassic gardens. Special events
include plays, music and a special dinosaur light show
complete with sound effects.

**Times:** *Open all year daily, summer 10-6; winter
10-dusk. Jul-Aug, Wed 10-9. Closed 25 Dec.
**Fee:** *£10 (ch £7, pen £8.50, disabled & carers £5,
concessions for groups). Family (2ad+2ch) £30,
(2ad+3 ch) £36.
**Facilities:** ℗ ℗ (50yds) ⭐ (Licensed) ⊓ 🗐
♿ (wheelchair loan, talking & signing tours, toilets),
shop, guided tours ⊗ 🚌 (prior booking preferred)

## CHARNOCK RICHARD
**Camelot Theme Park**
Chorley PR7 5LP
☎ 01257 452100 🖷 01257 452395
**Email:** kingarthur@camelotthemepark.co.uk
**Web:** www.camelotthemepark.co.uk
**Dir:** *from M6 junct 27/28, or M61 junct 8 follow brown
tourist signs*
Join Merlin, King Arthur and the Knights of the Round
Table at the magical kingdom of Camelot. Explore magic
lands filled with thrilling rides, spectacular shows, and
many more attractions. From white-knuckle thrills on The
Whirlwind spinning rollercoaster, to wet-knuckle thrills on
Pendragon's Plunge, there's something for everyone.
**Times:** Open 31 Mar-28 Oct.
**Fee:** *£16.50 (ch under 1 mtr, free). Family ticket £56

**Facilities:** ℗ ⊓ 🗐 ♿ (disabled car parking, toilets),
shop ⊗ (ex assist dogs) 🚌

**LANCASHIRE**

## CLITHEROE
**Clitheroe Castle Museum**
Castle House Castle Gate Castle Street BB7 1BA
☎ 01200 424635
**Email:** museum@ribblevalley.gov.uk
**Web:** www.ribblevalley.gov.uk/castlemuseum
**Dir:** *follow Clitheroe signs from A59 Preston-Skipton by-pass. Museum located in castle grounds near town centre*
The museum has a good collection of carboniferous fossils, and items of local interest. Displays include local history and the industrial archaeology of the Ribble Valley, while special features include the restored Hacking ferry boat believed to be the inspiration for Buckleberry Ferry featured in JRR Tolkien's *Fellowship of the Ring*, printer's and clogger's shops and Edwardian kitchen. The area is renowned for its early 17th-century witches, and the museum has a small display on witchcraft.
**Times:** *Open late Feb-Etr, Mon-Sat 11.15-4.30, Sun 1-4.30; Etr-Oct, daily inc BHs; Nov, Dec & Feb, wknds & school half terms. Closed Jan
**Fee:** *£2 (ch 50p, pen £1). Family ticket £4.50
**Facilities:** ℗ (500yds - disabled only parking at establishment) ⏛ ♿ shop, audio commentaries ⊘ (ex guide dogs) 🚌 ♨

## LEIGHTON HALL
**Leighton Hall**
Carnforth LA5 9ST
☎ 01524 734474 📠 01524 720357
**Email:** info@leightonhall.co.uk
**Web:** www.leightonhall.co.uk
**Dir:** *M6 junct 35 onto A6 & follow signs*
Early Gillow furniture is displayed among other treasures in the fine interior of this neo-Gothic mansion. Outside, a large collection of birds of prey can be seen, and flying displays are given each afternoon. There are also fine gardens, a maze and a woodland walk. A programme of events takes place throughout the year.
**Times:** Open May-Sep, Tue-Fri & BH Sun/Mon; Aug, Tue-Fri, Sun & BH Mon 12.30-5. Groups all year by arrangement
**Fee:** *£5.50 (ch 5-12 £4, concessions £5). Family ticket £17.
**Facilities:** ℗ ☕ (tearoom) ⏛ 🍴 ♿ shop, garden centre, guided tours ⊘ (ex guide dogs & in park) 🚌 ♨

## MARTIN MERE
**WWT Martin Mere**
Burscough,Ormskirk L40 0TA
☎ 01704 895181 📠 01704 892343
**Email:** info@martinmere.co.uk
**Web:** www.martinmere.co.uk
**Dir:** *signed from M61, M58 & M6, 6m from Ormskirk, off A59*
One of Britain's most important wetland sites, where you can get really close to a variety of ducks, geese and swans from all over the world as well as two flocks of flamingos. Thousands of wildfowl, including pink-footed geese, Bewick's and Whooper swans, winter here. Other features include a children's adventure playground, exhibition gallery, craft area and an educational centre. The Annual North West Bird Fair takes place during November and wild swans by floodlight from 1st November to 31st January.
**Times:** *Open all year, daily 9.30-5.30 (5 in winter). Closed 25 Dec.
**Fee:** *£6 (ch £3.80, concessions £4.80). Family ticket £15.55.
**Facilities:** ℗ ⏛ ♿ (wheelchair loan, Braille trail, heated hide, audio tours, toilets), shop ⊘ (ex guide dogs) 🚌 (pre-booking required)

PRESTON
## Harris Museum & Art Gallery
Market Square PR1 2PP
☎ 01772 258248 🖨 01772 886764
**Email:** harris.museum@preston.gov.uk
**Web:** www.harrismuseum.org.uk
**Dir:** *M6 junct 31, follow signs for city centre, park at bus station car park*
An impressive Grade I listed Greek Revival building containing extensive collections of fine and decorative art including a gallery of Clothes and Fashion. The Story of Preston covers the city's history and the lively exhibition programmes of contemporary art and social history are accompanied by events throughout the year.
**Times:** *Open all year, Mon & Wed-Sat 10-5, Tues 11-5, Sun 11-4.

**Fee:** *Free
**Facilities:** Ⓟ (5 mins walk - blue badge disabled parking only) 🚻 ♿ (wheelchair available, chair lift to mezzanine galleries, toilets), shop ⊗ (ex guide & assist dogs) 🚌 (contact prior to visit)

---

PRESTON
## The National Football Museum
Sir Tom Finney Way Deepdale PR1 6RY
☎ 01772 908442 🖨 01772 908444
**Email:** enquiries@nationalfootballmuseum.com
**Web:** www.nationalfootballmuseum.com
**Dir:** *2m from M6 juncts 31, 31A or 32. Follow brown tourist signs*
What location could be more fitting for a National Football Museum than Deepdale Stadium, the home of Preston North End, first winners of the professional football league in 1888-9? This fascinating trip through football past and present includes the FIFA Museum Collection, a fine display of memorabilia and artefacts; interactive displays that allow visitors to commentate on matches, and take virtual trips to every League ground in the country. Theres also an art gallery dedicated to the Beautiful Game.
**Times:** *Open all year Tue-Sat 10-5, Sun 11-5. Closed Mon ex BHs and school hols. Contact for opening times on match days.
**Fee:** Free
**Facilities:** Ⓟ Ⓟ (50mtrs) 🚻 ♿ (lifts, multi-sensory exhibitions, toilets), shop ⊗ (ex guide dogs) 🚌

---

RUFFORD
## Rufford Old Hall
Nr Ormskirk L40 1SG
☎ 01704 821254 🖨 01704 823823
**Email:** ruffordoldhall@nationaltrust.org.uk
**Web:** www.nationaltrust.org.uk
**Dir:** *M6 junct 27 & follow signs to Rufford. Hall on E side of A59*
There is a story that William Shakespeare performed here for the owner Sir Thomas Hesketh in the magnificent Great Hall. Built in 1530, Rufford Old Hall remained in the Hesketh family for over 400 years. The Carolean Wing, altered in 1821, features fine collections of 16th and 17th century oak furniture, arms, armour and tapestries. The grounds are laid out in a late Victorian style.

**Times:** *Open mid Mar-Oct, Sat-Wed. Hall 1-5 (last admission 4.30). Garden, restaurant & shop 11-5. Nov-Dec, Garden, restaurant & shop, Wed-Sun, 12-4.
**Fee:** *House and garden: £4.90 (ch £2.50). Family ticket £12. Groups £3.10 each (ch £1.30). Garden only £2.80 (ch £1.30). No groups Sun and BH Mon.
**Facilities:** Ⓟ 🍴 (Licensed) ⪥ 🚻 50p ♿ (Braille guide, wheelchairs, large print guide, toilets), shop, guided tours ⊗ (ex assist dogs) 🚌 (prior arrangement) 🌿 ♲

### SILVERDALE
**RSPB Leighton Moss Nature Reserve**
Myers Farm Carnforth LA5 0SW
☎ 01524 701601 📄 01524 702092
**Email:** leighton.moss@rspb.org.uk
**Web:** www.rspb.org.uk
**Dir:** *M6 junct 35, west on A501M for 0.5m. Turn right and head N on A6. Follow brown tourist signs*
The largest remaining reedbed in north-west England, this reserve covers 321 acres, and is home to a large concentration of bitterns, together with bearded tits, reed, sedge and grasshopper warblers, pochards, tufted ducks and marsh harriers. Black terns and ospreys regularly pass through in spring and greenshanks and various sandpipers in the autumn. Wintering wildfowl include large flocks of mallards, teals, wigeons, and shovelers.

**Times:** Reserve: Open daily 9-dusk . Visitor Centre daily 9.30-5. Feb-Oct 9.30-4.30 Nov-Jan. Closed 25 Dec.
**Fee:** £4.50 (ch £1, concessions £3) Family £9. RSPB members Free
**Facilities:** 🅿 ⛱ ♿ (stairlift available to tea room, toilets), shop, guided tours ⊗ (ex guide dogs) 🚌 (advance booking)

### BIRKENHEAD
**Historic Warships**
East Float Dock Road CH41 1DJ
☎ 0151 650 1573 📄 0151 650 1473
**Email:** manager@historicwarships.org
**Web:** www.historicwarships.org
**Dir:** *end of M53 all docks turn off follow tourist signs. From Liverpool Wallasey tunnel 1st exit after toll & follow brown heritage signs*
*HMS Onyx* served in the Falklands and is the only submarine afloat in the UK that visitors can explore. *HMS Plymouth*, an anti-submarine frigate also served in the Falklands. The U534 is the only WWII German U-Boat to be raised from the sea bed. Pre-booking required, only adults and children over 12 years (2 per adult) admitted to U-Boat.

**Times:** *Open all year, Sep-Mar daily 10-4, Apr-Aug daily 10-5. Closed 24-26 Dec, only open wknds for first 6 wks of year.
**Fee:** *£6.50 (ch £4.50, pen £5.50). Family ticket £19. Combined ships £15.50, U-Boat £9.
**Facilities:** 🅿 ⛱ ♿ (limited access to *HMS Plymouth*, multimedia tour of U534, toilets), shop, guided tours ⊗ (ex guide dogs) 🚌

### LIVERPOOL
**The Beatles Story**
Britannia Pavilion Albert Dock L3 4AD
☎ 0151 709 1963 📄 0151 708 0039
**Email:** info@beatlesstory.com
**Web:** www.beatlesstory.com
**Dir:** *follow signs to Albert Dock. Located outside Britannia Pavilion, next to Premier Travel Inn*
Relive the story of the four lads from Liverpool who took the world by storm and changed the face of popular music for ever. Features include a replica of the Cavern, George Harrison's first guitar, and exhibitions on John Lennon's post-Beatles career, the Quarrymen and the Yellow Submarine. The audio guide is narrated by John Lennon's sister, Julia, and other contributions come from the likes of George Martin, Pete Best and Gerry Marsden.

**Times:** Open all year 10-6 (last admission 5). Closed 25-26 Dec.
**Fee:** £8.99 (ch 5-16yrs £4.99 & concessions £5.99). Family ticket (2ad+3ch) £25.
**Facilities:** 🅿 (charged) Ⓟ (5 min walk) 🍴 ♿ (hearing loop, large print guide), shop, guided tours, audio commentaries ⊗ (ex guide dogs) 🚌 (pre-book only)

## LIVERPOOL
### The Grand National Experience

Aintree Racecourse Ormskirk Road L9 5AS

☎ 0151 522 2921 📄 0151 522 2920

**Email:** aintree@rht.net

**Web:** www.aintree.co.uk

**Dir:** *Aintree Racecourse on A59 Liverpool to Preston road, clearly signed*

A fascinating look at the Grand National, one of the World's greatest steeplechases. Visitors can sit in the jockeys' weighing-in chair, walk around the dressing rooms, watch video presentations, and view a gallery of paintings and photography depicting the race. There's also a chance for visitors to place bets in the Race of Champions.

**Times:** * Please telephone for details.

**Fee:** *Please telephone for details.

**Facilities:** 🅿 ⛱ ♿ (toilets), guided tours 🚫 (ex guide dogs) 🚌

## LIVERPOOL
### HM Customs & Excise National Museum

Merseyside Maritime Museum Albert Dock L3 4AQ

☎ 0151 478 4499 📄 0151 478 4590

**Web:** www.nmgm.org.uk

**Dir:** *Albert Dock - follow brown signs*

Enter the exciting world of smuggle busting where everyday items reveal their hidden secrets. Find a fake, rummage for hidden goods and spot a suspect traveller. Look into the illustrious past of HM Customs & Excise, it's the longest battle in history and it's still going on today! The museum is currently partially closed for refurbishment and is scheduled to reopen again fully in Spring 2008.

**Times:** *Open daily 10-5. Closed 23-26 Dec & 1 Jan.

**Fee:** *Free

**Facilities:** 🅿 🅿 (100yds) 🍴 (Licensed) ♿ (restricted wheelchair access, no access to basement, toilets), shop, 🚫 (ex guide dogs) 🚌 (prebooked)

## LIVERPOOL
### Liverpool Football Club Museum and Stadium Tour

Anfield Road L4 0TH

☎ 0151 260 6677 📄 0151 264 0149

**Email:** stephen.done@liverpoolfc.tv

**Web:** www.liverpoolfc.tv

Touch the famous 'This is Anfield' sign as you walk down the tunnel to the sound of the crowd at the LFC museum and tour centre. Celebrate all things Liverpool, past and present. Bright displays and videos chart the history of England's most successful football club and more recent glories are recalled. All five European cups are on display as well as the 2006 FA Cup.

**Times:** Open all year: Museum daily 10-5 last admission 4. Closed 25-26 Dec. Match days 9 until last admission - 1hr before kick off. Museum & Tour - tours are run subject to daily demand. Advance booking is essential to avoid disappointment.

**Fee:** Museum only, £5 (ch under 6 & pen £3). Family £13. Museum & Tour £10 (ch under 16 & pen £6). Family £25.

**Facilities:** 🅿 🅿 (0.5 km - match days-avoid trying to park) 🍴 (Licensed) ♿ (lifts, ramps to all areas for wheelchairs, toilets), shop, guided tours 🚫 (ex guide dogs) 🚌 (advance booking)

**MERSEYSIDE**

**MERSEYSIDE**

## LIVERPOOL
### Merseyside Maritime Museum
Albert Dock L3 4AQ
☎ 0151 478 4499 📄 0151 478 4590
**Web:** www.liverpoolmuseums.org.uk
**Dir:** *entry into Dock from The Strand*
Set in the heart of Liverpool's magnificent waterfront, the Merseyside Maritime Museum offers a unique insight into the history of the great port of Liverpool, its ships and its people. Visitors can follow the story of a 19th-century family as they emigrate to Australia and from August 2007 visit the International Slavery Museum to learn about the historic context of the slave trade and its enduring impact on the world.
**Times:** *Open daily 10-5. Closed 23-26 Dec & 1 Jan.
**Fee:** *Free

**Facilities:** 🅿 🍴 (Licensed) ♿ (lifts, wheelchairs, ramps, ex pilot boat & basement, toilets), shop, ⊗ (ex guide dogs) 🚌

## LIVERPOOL
### National Wildflower Centre
Court Hey Park Roby Road L16 3NA
☎ 0151 738 1913 📄 0151 737 1820
**Email:** info@nwc.org.uk
**Web:** www.nwc.org.uk
**Dir:** *M62 junct 5, take A5080 to rdbt. Exit into Roby Rd, entrance 0.5m on left*
The National Wildflower Centre promotes the creation of wildflower habitats around the country and provides educational materials, wildflower seeds and interactive facilities. The Centre has demonstration areas, children's activities, a working nursery, compost display and rooftop walk. Special Events: Green Fayre June 2007, special events through the summer, Knowsley Flower Show August 2007, Winter celebration December 2007.

**Times:** *Open Mar-Aug, daily 10-5.
**Fee:** *£3 (ch 5-16, pen, students & unemployed £1.50). Family ticket (2ad+2ch) £7.50. Season tickets & group discount tickets available.
**Facilities:** 🅿 🍴 📋 ♿ (electric buggy & wheelchair available, toilets), shop, garden centre guided tours ⊗ (ex guide dogs & in park) 🚌 (pre-booking required)

## LIVERPOOL
### Tate Liverpool
Albert Dock L3 4BB
☎ 0151 702 7400 & 7402 📄 0151 702 7401
**Email:** visiting.liverpool@tate.org.uk
**Web:** www.tate.org.uk/liverpool/
**Dir:** *within walking distance of Liverpool Lime Street train station*
Tate Liverpool is one of the largest galleries of modern and contemporary art outside London and is housed in a converted warehouse in the historic Albert Dock. The gallery is home to the National Collection of Modern Art in the North, and has four floors displaying work selected from the Tate Collection, as well as special exhibitions which bring together artwork loaned from around the world. Upcoming shows include Liverpool and the Avant-garde (until September 2007); Peter Blake (until September 2007), and Contemporary Chinese Art (until June 2007).
**Times:** Open Tue-Sun, BH Mon & all Mons in Jun-Aug, 10-5.50. Closed 24-26 Dec, 1 Jan & Good Fri
**Fee:** Admission free. £5 (concessions £4) for special exhibitions, phone for details.
**Facilities:** 🅿 (5 min walk - Pay & Display) 🍴 (licensed) ♿ (wheelchairs available, leaflets in Braille, hearing loop, toilets) shop, guided tours, audio commentaries ⊗ (ex assist dogs) 🚌

## LIVERPOOL
### World Museum Liverpool
William Brown Street L3 8EN

☎ 0151 478 4393

**Email:** themuseum@liverpoolmuseums.org.uk

**Web:** www.liverpoolmuseums.org.uk/wml/

**Dir:** *in city centre next to St George's Hall and Lime St, follow brown signs*

One of Britain's most interesting museums, the Liverpool Museum has diverse collections ranging from the Amazonian rain forests to the mysteries of outer space. Special attractions include the award-winning hands-on Natural History Centre and the Planetarium.

**Times:** *Open Mon-Sat 10-5, Sun noon-5. Closed 23-26 Dec & 1 Jan.

**Fee:** *Free

**Facilities:** Ⓟ ♿ (toilets), shop ⊗ (ex guide dogs) 🚌 (book in advance) ✉

---

## PRESCOT
### Knowsley Safari Park
L34 4AN

☎ 0151 430 9009 📄 0151 426 3677

**Email:** safari.park@knowsley.com

**Web:** www.knowsley.com

**Dir:** *M57 junct 2. Follow 'safari park' signs*

A five-mile drive through the reserves enables visitors to see lions, tigers, elephants, rhinos, monkeys and many other animals in spacious, natural surroundings. Also a children's amusement park, reptile house, pets' corner plus sealion shows. Other attractions include an amusement park and a miniature railway.

**Times:** Open all year, Mar-Oct, daily 10-4. Winter Nov-Feb, 11-3.

**Fee:** *£10 (ch & pen £7).

**Facilities:** Ⓟ ⊓ ♿ (toilets), shop, audio commentaries ⊗ (kennels provided) 🚌

---

## SOUTHPORT
### Pleasureland
Marine Drive PR8 1RX

☎ 0870 220 0204 📄 01704 537936

**Email:** mail@pleasurelandltd.freeserve.co.uk

**Web:** www.pleasureland.uk.com

**Dir:** *signed from town centre*

First openend in 1912, Pleasureland is now home to over 100 modern rides and attractions, including the TRAUMAtizer suspended rollercoaster, the Lucozade Space Shot, the Cyclone rollercoaster, Ghost Train and Lost Dinosaurs of the Sahara.

**Times:** Open Mar-Nov. opening times vary please call for information.

**Fee:** *£18 all day (juniors £12). Entry for 4 (adults and/or children) £60.

**Facilities:** Ⓟ (charged) Ⓟ (adjacent) ⊓ 📋 ♿ (access on some rides, toilets), shop ⊗ (ex guide dogs) 🚌

**MERSEYSIDE**

MERSEYSIDE / NORTHUMBERLAND

## ST HELENS
### World of Glass
Chalon Way East WA10 1BX
☎ 08700 114466 📄 01744 616966
**Email:** info@worldofglass.com
**Web:** www.worldofglass.com
**Dir:** *5mins from M62 junct 7*
Ideal for all the family, this fascinating attraction is in the heart of St Helens, a town shaped by glass-making. Features include the world's first continuous glass-making furnace, and two museum galleries that show glass in the ancient world and Victorian life in St Helens. There is also a Mirror Maze where Wizard Filigrano works, a café and a gift shop.
**Times:** *Open Tue-Sun & BH, 10-5. Closed 25-26 Dec & 1 Jan.

**Fee:** £5.30 (ch £3.80, pen £3.80) Family & group discounts.
**Facilities:** 🅿 Ⓟ (500yds) ☕ (10-4.30) 🍴 📓 £1.50 ♿ (Induction loop, toilets), shop, guided tours 🚫 (ex guide dogs) 🚌

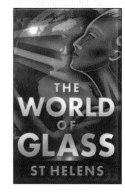

## ALNWICK
### Alnwick Castle
NE66 1NQ
☎ 01665 510777 📄 01665 510876
**Email:** enquiries@alnwickcastle.com
**Web:** www.alnwickcastle.com
**Dir:** *off A1 on outskirts of town, signed*
Set in a stunning landscape, Alnwick Castle overlooks the historic market town of Alnwick. Although it was originally built for the Percy family, who have lived here since 1309, - the current Duke and Duchess of Northumberland being the current tenants - the castle is best known as one of the locations that served as Hogwarts School in the Harry Potter movies. The castle is full of art and treasures and there are plenty of activities for all the family.

**Times:** *Open 5 Apr-29 Oct, daily 10-6 (last admission 4.30).
**Fee:** *£8.50 (ch £3.50, concessions £7.50). Family ticket £22.00. Party 14+.
**Facilities:** 🅿 Ⓟ (200mtrs) 🍽 (Licensed) 🍴 📓 ♿ (Castle lift for those able to walk a little, toilets), shop, guided tours 🚫 (ex assist dogs) 🚌

## ALNWICK
### The Alnwick Garden
Denwick Lane NE66 1YU
☎ 01665 511350 📄 01665 511351
**Email:** info@alnwickgarden.com
**Web:** www.alnwickgarden.com
**Dir:** *in centre of Alnwick*
A vision of the Duchess of Northumberland and the leading garden visitor attraction in North East England. The 12-acre garden is the creation of Belgian designers and British architect Sir Michael Hopkins designed the Pavilion and Visitor Centre. This unique project in a deprived rural area has transformed a derelict and forgotten plot into a stimulating landscape. Now in its second phase of development, the garden includes one of the largest wooden tree houses in the world, a Poison Garden, Labyrinth and Serpent Garden. An all weather attraction for all ages, accessible to all.
**Times:** Open all year Apr, May & Oct, daily 10-6; Jun-Sep daily, 10-7; Nov- Mar daily 10-4 (last admission 45 mins before closing)
**Fee:** *£8 (ch £2.50 in educational group otherwise free, concessions £7.50). Groups £6.25
**Facilities:** 🅿 🍴 📓 ♿ (ramps, w/chairs & scooters for hire, toilets), shop, garden centre, guided tours 🚫 (ex assist dogs) 🚌

## BAMBURGH
### Bamburgh Castle
NE69 7DF

☎ 01668 214515 & 214208 📠 01668 214060

**Email:** bamburghcastle@aol.com

**Web:** www.bamburghcastle.com

**Dir:** *A1 Belford by-pass, E on B1342 to Bamburgh*

Rising dramatically from a rocky outcrop, Bamburgh Castle is a huge, square Norman castle. Last restored in the 19th century, it has an impressive hall and an armoury with a large collection of armour from the Tower of London. The castle has wonderful views of the Farne Islands. Guide services are available.

**Times:** *Open 11 Mar-Oct, daily 11-5 (last admission 4.30).

**Fee:** *£6 (ch £2.50 & pen £5).

**Facilities:** 🅿 (charged) 🅿 (300yds - road side restrictions in village) 📷 50p ♿ (toilets), shop, guided tours ⊗ (ex guide dogs) 🚌 ♿

---

## BARDON MILL
### Vindolanda (Chesterholm)
Vindolanda Trust Hexham NE47 7JN

☎ 01434 344277 📠 01434 344060

**Email:** info@vindolanda.com

**Web:** www.vindolanda.com

**Dir:** *signed from A69 or B6318*

Vindolanda was a Roman fort and frontier town. It was started well before Hadrian's Wall, and became a base for 500 soldiers. The civilian settlement lay just west of the fort and has been excavated. The museum in the country house of Chesterholm nearby has displays and reconstructions. There are also formal gardens and an open-air museum with Roman Temple, shop and house.

**Times:** *Open Feb-Mar, daily 10-5. Apr-Sep 10-6, Oct & Nov 10-5.

**Fee:** *£4.50 (ch £2.90, student & pen £3.80, free admission for disabled). Saver ticket for joint admission to sister site - The Roman Army Museum £6.50 (ch £4.30, pen £5.50) Party. Family ticket £13, joint site family ticket £20.

**Facilities:** 🅿 ☕ (hot and cold light lunches) 🪑 📷 ♿ (please contact for further info, toilets), shop, guided tours, audio commentaries ⊗ (ex guide dogs) 🚌

---

## BERWICK-UPON-TWEED
### Paxton House
TD15 1SZ

☎ 01289 386291 📠 01289 386660

**Email:** info@paxtonhouse.com

**Web:** www.paxtonhouse.com

**Dir:** *3m from A1 Berwick-upon-Tweed bypass on B6461 Kelso road*

Built in 1758 for the Laird of Wedderburn, the house is a fine example of neo-Palladian architecture. Much of the house is furnished by Chippendale and there is a large picture gallery. The house is set in 80 acres beside the River Tweed, and the grounds include an adventure playground.

**Times:** Open daily from Apr-Oct, House & gallery 11-5 (last tour of house 4.15). Grounds 10-sunset.

**Fee:** House & Grounds: £6 (ch £3) Family ticket £16. Grounds only: £3 (ch £1.50) Family ticket £8.

**Facilities:** 🅿 🍴 (Licensed) 🪑 📷 ♿ (lifts to main areas of house, parking close to reception, toilets), shop, guided tours ⊗ (ex in grounds & assist dogs) 🚌

**NORTHUMBERLAND**

## CHILLINGHAM
### Chillingham Wild Cattle Park
Alnwick NE66 5NP
☎ 01668 215250
**Web:** www.chillingham-wildcattle.org.uk
**Dir:** *off B6348, follow brown tourist signs off A1 and A697*
The park at Chillingham boasts an extraordinary survival: a herd of wild white cattle descended from animals trapped in the park when the wall was built in the 13th century; they are the sole surviving pure-bred examples of their breed in the world. Binoculars are recommended for a close view. Visitors are accompanied into the park by the Warden.
**Times:** *Open Apr-Oct, daily 10-12 & 2-5, Sun 2-5. (Closed Tue).

**Fee:** *£4.50 (ch £1.50 & pen £3). Family ticket £10 (2ad + 2ch)
**Facilities:** 🅿 🍴 📇 £1 shop, guided tours 🚫 🚌 (max 50 people) ♿

## CORBRIDGE
### Corbridge Roman Site and Museum
NE45 5NT
☎ 01434 632349
**Web:** www.english-heritage.org.uk
**Dir:** *0.5m NW of Corbridge on minor road - signed*
Originally a fort, which evolved into a prosperous town during the Roman era. An excellent starting point to explore Hadrian's Wall. The museum houses a fascinating collection of finds.
**Times:** Open all year, Apr-Sep, daily 10-5.30 (last admission 5); Oct, daily 10-4; Nov-Mar, Sat-Sun 10-4. Closed 24-26 Dec & 1 Jan.
**Fee:** £3.80 (ch £1.90, concessions £2.90). Prices and opening times are subject to change. Please check web site or call 0870 333 1181 for the most up to date prices and opening times when planning your visit.
**Facilities:** 🅿 ♿ (toilets) 🚌 ⚙ ♿

## HOLY ISLAND (LINDISFARNE)
### Lindisfarne Castle
Berwick-upon-Tweed TD15 2SH
☎ 01289 389244 📠 01289 389909
**Email:** lindisfarne@nationaltrust.org.uk
**Web:** www.nationaltrust.org.uk
**Dir:** *8m S Berwick from A1 on Holy Island via 3m tidal causeway*
This 16th-century fort was restored by Sir Edwin Lutyens in 1903. The austere outside walls belie the Edwardian comfort within, which includes antique Flemish and English furniture, porcelain and polished brass. A small walled garden designed by Gertrude Jekyll is set on the southward facing slope, some 500 metres to the north of the castle. Spectatular views from the ramparts to the Farne Islands, Bamburgh Castle and beyond.

**Times:** *Open mid Mar-Oct, daily (closed Mon ex BHs). As Lindisfarne is a tidal island, the Castle opening times will vary. Garden open all year (10-dusk).
**Fee:** *Castle & garden £5.20 (ch £2.60) Family ticket £13. Garden only £1 (ch free)
**Facilities:** 🅿 (1m in village) 📇 ♿ (Braille guide), shop, guided tours 🚫 🚌 (pre-booking) 🌿

## HOUSESTEADS
**Housesteads Roman Fort**

Haydon Bridge NE47 6NN

☎ 01434 344363

**Web:** www.english-heritage.org.uk

**Dir:** *2.5m NE of Bardon Mill on B6318*

The jewel in the crown of Hadrian's Wall and the most complete Roman fort in Britain. These superb remains offer a glimpse of one of the world's greatest empires.

**Times:** Open all year, Apr-Sep, daily 10-6; Oct-Mar, daily 10-4. Closed 24-26 Dec & 1 Jan.

**Fee:** £3.80 (ch £1.90, concessions £2.90) Family £9.50. Prices and opening times are subject to change. Please check web site or call 0870 333 1181 for the most up to date prices and opening times when planning your visit.

**Facilities:** Ⓟ (0.25m from fort - charge payable) ⋈ ⅋ (disabled parking), shop 🚌 ♿

## ROTHBURY
**Cragside**

NE65 7PX

☎ 01669 620333 & 620150 🖷 01669 620066

**Email:** cragside@nationaltrust.org.uk

**Web:** www.nationaltrust.org.uk

**Dir:** *15m NW of Morpeth on A697, left onto B6341, entrance 1m N of Rothbury*

The aptly named Cragside was the home of Victorian inventor and landscape genius, Lord Armstrong, and sits on a rocky crag high above the Debden Burn. Crammed with ingenious gadgets it was the first house in the world to be lit by water-powered electricity. It the 1880s it also had hot and cold running water, central heating, fire alarms, telephones, and a passenger lift. The house has recently be re-wired, and re-opens in April 2007. In the estate there are forty miles of footpaths to explore, including a stroll through some of the best Victorian gardens in the country.

**Times:** *Open, Estate & Gardens: Apr-Oct, Tue-Sun & BH Mons 10.30-7; Nov-mid Dec Wed-Sun 11-4 (or dusk if earlier); (Last admission 1hr before closing).

**Fee:** *Estate & Gardens £6.50 (ch £3) Family £16. Winter opening £3 (ch £1.50) Family £7.50.

**Facilities:** Ⓟ ⋔ (Licensed) ⋈ ⅋ (ltd access, Braille guide, wheelchair path, lift, toilets), shop 🚌 (pre-booking) 🐾 ♿

## WARKWORTH
**Warkworth Castle & Hermitage**

Morpeth NE66 OUJ

☎ 01665 711423

**Web:** www.english-heritage.org.uk

The magnificent eight-towered keep of Warkworth Castle stands on a hill high above the River Coquet, dominating all around it. A complex stronghold, it was home to the Percy family, which at times wielded more power in the North than the King himself.

**Times:** Open all year. Castle; Apr-Sep, daily 10-5; Oct, daily 10-4; Nov-Mar, Sat-Mon 10-4. Hermitage; Apr-Sep, Wed, Sun & Bank Hols 11-5. Closed 24-26 Dec & 1 Jan.

**Fee:** Castle; £3.40 (ch £1.70, concessions £2.60) Family £8.50. Hermitage; £2.40 (ch £1.20, concessions £1.80). Prices and opening times are subject to change. Please check web site or call 0870 333 1181 for the most up to date prices and opening times when planning your visit.

**Facilities:** Ⓟ ⅋ (limited access), shop 🚌 ♯ ♿

**NORTHUMBERLAND**

**TYNE & WEAR**

## GATESHEAD
### The Baltic Centre for Contemporary Art
South Shore Road Gateshead Quays NE8 3BA
☎ 0191 478 1810 & 440 4944 📠 0191 478 1922
**Email:** info@balticmill.com
**Web:** www.balticmill.com
**Dir:** *follow signs for Quayside, Millennium Bridge.*
*15 mins' walk from Gateshead Metro & Newcastle*
*Central Station*
Once a 1950s grain warehouse, part of the old Baltic
Flour Mills, the Baltic Centre for Contemporary Art is an
international centre presenting a dynamic and ambitious
programme of complementary exhibitions and events. It
consists of five art spaces, cinema, auditorium, library
and archive, eating and drinking areas and a shop. Check
website for current events information.

**Times:** * Please see website for details
**Fee:** Free
**Facilities:** Ⓟ (charged) Ⓟ (0.25 mile) 🪑 ♿
(wheelchairs/scooters, Braille/large-print guides, toilets),
shop, guided tours 🚫 (ex guide & hearing dogs) 🚌 ♻️

## JARROW
### Bede's World
Church Bank NE32 3DY
☎ 0191 489 2106 📠 0191 428 2361
**Email:** visitor.info@bedesworld.co.uk
**Web:** www.bedesworld.co.uk
**Dir:** *off A185 near S end of Tyne tunnel*
The Venerable Bede lived over 1300 years ago and was
one of early Britain's greatest scholars, author of the
*Historia Ecclesiastica Gentis Anglorum* - the definitive
history of the early medieval period. As well as exhibits
detailing Bede's monastic life and work, the museum
re-creates an Anglo-Saxon farm and incorporates the
ruins of the medieval monastery of St Paul's. There
is also a herb garden based on Anglo Saxon and
medieval plants

**Times:** *Open all year, Apr-Oct, Mon-Sat 10-5.30, Sun
noon-5.30; Nov-Mar, Mon-Sat 10-4.30 & Sun 12-4.30;
Xmas-New YearOpening times vary.
**Fee:** *£4.50 (ch & concessions £3). Family ticket £10.
Concession Family ticket £7. Party rates 15+.
**Facilities:** Ⓟ Ⓟ (adjacent) 🍽️ (Licensed) 🪑 🗄️
♿ (wheelchair & elec. wheelchair on request, disabled
parking, toilets), shop 🚫 (ex guide dogs) 🚌

## NEWCASTLE UPON TYNE
### Centre for Life
Times Square NE1 4EP
☎ 0191 243 8210 📠 0191 243 8201
**Email:** info@life.org.uk
**Web:** www.life.org.uk
**Dir:** *A1M, A69, A184, A1058 & A167, follow signs to*
*Centre for Life or Central Station*
The Life Science Centre is an interactive, action-packed
day out that takes the visitor to the beginning of life and
back again. From single-celled organisms to dinosaurs,
from 4 billion years ago to today, this is a fascinating
attraction that deals with perhaps the most fundamental
subject of all: Life Itself.
**Times:** *Open all year Mon-Sat 10-6, Sun 11-6. Closed
25 Dec & 1 Jan. (Last entry subject to seasonal demand).

**Fee:** £6.95 (ch £4.50, concessions £5.50). Family
ticket £19.95.
**Facilities:** Ⓟ (charged) Ⓟ (200mtrs) 🪑
♿ (ramps, wheelchairs, induction loops, toilets), shop
🚫 (ex guide dogs) 🚌 (pre booking preferable)

## NEWCASTLE UPON TYNE
### Museum of Antiquities
The University NE1 7RU

☎ 0191 222 7849 ▤ 0191 222 8561
**Email:** m.o.antiquities@ncl.ac.uk
**Web:** www.ncl.ac.uk/antiquities
**Dir:** *Situated on main campus of Newcastle University between The Haymarket & Queen Victoria Rd*
Artefacts from north east England from prehistoric times to AD 1600 are on display here. The principal museum for Hadrian's Wall, this collection includes models of the wall, life-size Roman soldiers and a newly refurbished reconstruction of the Temple of Mithras.
**Times:** Open all year, daily (ex Sun), 10-5. Closed Good Fri, 24-26 Dec & 1 Jan.
**Fee:** Free

**Facilities:** ℗ (400yds) ⚲ ▤ ♿ (large print guide) shop guided tours ⊗ (ex guide dogs) 🚌

## SOUTH SHIELDS
### Arbeia Roman Fort & Museum
Baring Street NE33 2BB

☎ 0191 456 1369 ▤ 0191 427 6862
**Web:** www.twmuseums.org.uk
**Dir:** *5 mins' walk from town centre*
In South Shields town are the extensive remains of Arbeia, a Roman fort in use from the 2nd to 4th century. It was the supply base for the Roman army's campaign against Scotland. On site there are full size reconstructions of a fort gateway, a barrack block and part of the commanding officer's house. Archaeological evacuations are in progress throughout the summer.
**Times:** Open all year, Apr-Oct, Mon-Sat 10-5.30, Sun 1-5; Nov-Mar, Mon-Sat 10-3.30. Closed 25-26 Dec & 1 Jan

**Fee:** Fort & Museum free of charge ex for 'Timequest' Archaeological Interpretation Gallery £1.50 (ch & concessions 80p).
**Facilities:** ℗ (on road outside) ⚲ ▤ ♿ (pre-visit info pack and portable induction loop, toilets), shop, guided tours 🚌 (pre-booking preferred)

## SUNDERLAND
### National Glass Centre
Liberty Way SR6 0GL

☎ 0191 515 5555 ▤ 0191 515 5556
**Email:** info@nationalglasscentre.com
**Web:** www.nationalglasscentre.com
**Dir:** *A19 onto A1231, signposted from all major roads*
Housed in a striking modern building, the National Glass Centre celebrates the unique material and explains its history. Visitors can see the changing exhibitions of glass art, featuring pieces by leading artists. There is also the opportunity to witness the glass-making process and learn how it impacts on our lives. The brave can even walk on the glass roof 30 feet above the riverside.
**Times:** Open daily 10-5 (last admission to glass tour 4). Closed 25 Dec & 1 Jan.

**Fee:** *£3 (concessions £1.50). Family ticket £6.
**Facilities:** ℗ ♿ (lifts, ramps, parking facilites, toilets), shop, guided tours ⊗ (ex guide dogs) 🚌

**TYNE & WEAR**

## SUNDERLAND
**Sunderland Museum & Winter Gardens**
Burdon Rd SR1 1PP
☎ 0191 553 2323 🖹 0191 553 7828
**Email:** sunderland@twmuseums.org.uk
**Web:** www.twmuseums.org.uk/sunderland
**Dir:** *in city centre on Burdon Rd, short walk from Sunderland metro and mainline stations*
An award-winning attraction with wide-ranging displays and many hands-on exhibits that cover the archaeology and geology of Sunderland, the coal mines and shipyards of the area and the spectacular glass and pottery made on Wearside. Other galleries show the changes in the lifestyles of Sunderland women over the past century, works by LS Lowry and wildlife from all corners of the globe. The Winter Gardens are a horticultural wonderland where exotic plants from around the world can be seen growing to their full natural height in a spectacular glass and steel rotunda.
**Times:** Open all year, Mon-Sat 10-5, Sun 2-5.
**Fee:** Free
**Facilities:** ℗ (150 yds) ⭐ (Licensed) 🗐 ♿ (lifts to all floors, induction loops, toilets), shop, audio commentaries (charged) ⊗ (ex guide dogs) 🚌 (pre-booking prefered)

## TYNEMOUTH
**Blue Reef Aquarium**
Grand Parade NE30 4JF
☎ 0191 258 1031 🖹 0191 257 2116
**Email:** tynemouth@bluereefaquarium.co.uk
**Web:** www.bluereefaquarium.co.uk
**Dir:** *follow A19, taking A1058 coast road, signed Tynemouth. Situated on seafront*
From its position overlooking one of the North East's prettiest beaches, Blue Reef is home to a dazzling variety of creatures including seahorses, puffer fish, octopi, crabs, and even the deadly piranha. Visitors can walk through an underwater tunnel in a 250,000 litre tropical ocean tank. This offers close encounters with all manner of undersea wonders like sharks and stingrays.
**Times:** Open all year, daily from 10. Closed 25 Dec
**Fee:** £5.99 (ch 3-16 £3.99, concessions £4.99). Family ticket (2ad+2ch) £17.50, (2ad+3ch) £21.50.
**Facilities:** ℗ (charged) ℗ (pay and display) ⋒ 🗐 ♿ (wheelchair available, toilets), shop ⊗ (ex guide dogs) 🚌

## WALLSEND
**Segedunum Roman Fort, Baths & Museum**
Buddle Street NE28 6HR
☎ 0191 236 9347 🖹 0191 295 5858
**Email:** segedunum@twmuseums.org.uk
**Web:** www.twmuseums.org.uk
**Dir:** *A187 from Tyne Tunnel, signposted*
Hadrian's Wall was built by the Roman Emperor, Hadrian in 122AD, Segedunum was built as part of the Wall, serving as a garrison for 600 soldiers until the collapse of Roman rule around 410AD. This major historical venture shows what life would have been like then, using artefacts, audio-visuals, reconstructed buildings and a 34m high viewing tower. Plenty of special events including puppet shows, workshops, and Saturnalia. Contact for details.
**Times:** Open all year, Apr-Oct 10-5.30, Nov-Mar, 10-3.
**Fee:** *£3.95 (ch, pen & concessions £2.25). (ch 16 and under free)
**Facilities:** ℗ ℗ (50mtrs) ⋒ 🗐 ♿ (lifts, toilets), shop, guided tours audio commentaries (charged) ⊗ (ex guide dogs) 🚌

## WASHINGTON
### WWT Washington
District 15 NE38 8LE
☎ 0191 416 5454 📠 0191 416 5801
**Email:** washington@wwt.org.uk
**Web:** www.wwt.org.uk
**Dir:** *signposted off A195, A1231 & A182*
In a parkland setting, on the north bank of the River Wear, WWT Washington is the home of a wonderful collection of exotic wildfowl from all over the world. There is also a heronry where visitors can watch a colony of wild Grey Herons on CCTV. The 100-acre site includes an area for wintering wildfowl which can be observed from hides, and a flock of Chilean Flamingos. Other features include a discovery centre, waterfowl nursery, picture windows and a viewing gallery.

**Times:** *Open all year, daily 9.30-5 (summer) or 9.30-4 (winter). Closed 25 Dec.
**Fee:** *£5.95 (ch £3.75, concessions £4.75). Family £15.50
**Facilities:** 🅿 🍽 (Licensed) 🪑 ♿ (lowered windows in certain hides, wheelchairs to hire free, toilets), shop ⊗ (ex guide/hearing dogs) 🚌 (pre-booking required)

## WHITBURN
### Souter Lighthouse
Coast Road SR6 7NH
☎ 0191 529 3161 & 01670 773966 📠 0191 529 0902
**Email:** souter@nationaltrust.org.uk
**Web:** www.nationaltrust.org.uk
**Dir:** *on A183 coast road, 2m S of South Shields, 3m N of Sunderland*
When it opened in 1871, Souter was the most advanced lighthouse in the world, and warned shipping off the notorious rocks in the river approaches of the Tyne and Wear. Painted red and white and standing at 150ft high, it is a dramatic building and hands-on displays and volunteers help bring it to life. Visitors can explore the whole building with its engine room and lighthouse keeper's cottage. You can take part in hands-on activities concerning shipwrecks and the workings of the lighthouse, and see coastal creatures in the Rockpool Fishtank. Climb to the top of the lighthouse, or walk along the Leas, a 2.5 mile stretch of spectacular coastline.
**Times:** *Open Apr-29 Oct daily ex Fri (open Good Fri) 11-5 (last entry 30mins before closing).
**Fee:** *£4 (ch £2.50) Family ticket £10.50.
**Facilities:** 🅿 🅿 (200m) 🍽 🪑 ♿ (Braille guide, induction loops, tactile exhibits, toilets), shop ⊗ (ex guide dogs) 🚌 (pre-booking) 🦋

## BEMPTON
### RSPB Nature Reserve
Bridlington YO15 1JD
☎ 01262 851179 📠 01262 851533
**Dir:** *take cliff road from B1229, Bempton Village and follow brown tourist signs*
Part of the spectacular chalk cliffs that stretch from Flamborough Head to Speeton. This is one of the best sites in England to see thousands of nesting seabirds including gannets and puffins at close quarters. Viewpoints overlook the cliffs, which are best visited from April to July. Over 2 miles of chalk cliffs rising to 400ft with numerous cracks and ledges. Enormous numbers of seabirds nest on these cliffs including guillemots, razorbills, kittiwakes, fulmars, herring gulls and several pairs of shag. This is the only gannetry in England and is growing annually. Many migrants pass off-shore including terns, skuas and shearwaters. Wheatears, ring ouzels and merlins frequent the clifftop on migration. Grey seal and porpoise are sometimes seen offshore.
**Times:** * Visitor centreOpen daily, Mar-Oct 10-5. Nov -Dec 9.30-4.
**Fee:** *£3.50 per car, £6 per minibus, £10 per coach.
**Facilities:** 🅿 (charged) 🍴 (Snack bar) 🪑 ♿ (large print guide, toilets), shop 🚌 (pre-book only)

EAST RIDING OF YORKSHIRE

## BRIDLINGTON
### Sewerby Hall & Gardens
CHURCH LANE SEWERBY YO15 1EA
☎ 01262 673769 🖹 01262 673090
**Email:** sewerby.hall@eastring.gov.uk
**Web:** www.sewerby-hall.co.uk
**Dir:** *2m NE of Bridlington on B1255 towards Flamborough*
Sewerby Hall and Gardens, set in 50 acres of parkland overlooking Bridlington Bay, dates back to 1715. The Georgian House, with its 19th-century Orangery, contains art galleries, archaeological displays and an Amy Johnson Room with a collection of her trophies and mementoes. The grounds include magnificent walled Old English and Rose gardens and host many events throughout the year. Activities for all the family include a Children's Zoo and play areas, golf, putting, bowls, plus woodland and clifftop walks. Phone for details of special events.
**Times:** * Estate open all year, dawn-dusk. Hall open Etr-end Oct. Please contact for further details.
**Fee:** *£3.10 (ch 5-15 £1.50, pen £2.80). Family ticket £9.00. Group 10+
**Facilities:** 🅿 Ⓟ (600yds - No overnight parking) 🗲 ♿ (toilets), shop 🚌

## BURTON AGNES
### Burton Agnes Manor House
**Web:** www.english-heritage.org.uk
**Dir:** *in Burton Agnes, 5m SW of Bridlington on A166. 34 miles north-east of York.*
This 12th century stone fortified house founded by Roger de Stuteville is a rare and well-preserved example of a Norman dwelling. Some interesting Norman architectural features can still be seen, but the building was encased in brick during the 17th and 18th centuries. The house is located in the grounds of the Elizabethan Burton Agnes Hall but please note that the gardens are privately owned and not managed by English Heritage.
**Times:** Open Apr-Oct, daily 11-5.
**Fee:** Free
**Facilities:** ⌗ ⊗

## GOOLE
### The Waterways Museum
Dutch River Side DN14 5TB
☎ 01405 768730 🖹 01405 769868
**Email:** waterwaysmuseum@btinternet.com
**Web:** www.waterwaysmuseumandadventurecentre.co.uk
**Dir:** *M62 junct 36, enter Goole, turn right at next 3 sets of lights onto Dutch River Side. 0.75m and follow brown signs*
Discover the story of the Aire & Calder Navigation and the growth of the 'company town' of Goole and its busy port. Find out how to sail and, in the interactive gallery, see how wooden boats were built. Enjoy the unique 'Tom Pudding' story, brought to life through the vessels on the canal and the boat hoist in South Dock. Rediscover the Humber keels and sloops, and Goole's shipbuilding history through the objects, photos and memories of Goole people.
**Times:** *Open Mon-Fri 9-4.30 (Apr-Sep, Sun 12-5)
**Fee:** *£2.50 (concessions £1.50) Boat Trip £3.
**Facilities:** 🅿 Ⓟ 🗲 🗐 ♿ (disabled access on boats, nature trail, wheelchair, toilets), shop, guided tours audio commentaries ⊗ (ex guide dogs) 🚌 ⊠

## KINGSTON UPON HULL
### 'Streetlife' - Hull Museum of Transport
High Street HU1 1PS
☎ 01482 613902 📠 01482 613710
**Email:** museums@hullcc.gov.uk
**Web:** www.hullcc.gov.uk/museums
**Dir:** *A63 from M62, follow signs for Old Town*
This purpose built museum uses a 'hands-on' approach to trace 200 years of transport history. With a vehicle collection of national importance, state-of-the-art animatronic displays and authentic scenarios, you can see Hull's Old Town brought vividly to life. The mail coach ride uses the very latest in computer technology to recreate a Victorian journey by four-in-hand.
**Times:** *Open all year, Mon-Sat 10-5, Sun 1.30-4.30. Closed 24-25 Dec & Good Fri

**Fee:** *Free
**Facilities:** ℗ (500mtrs) ⊞ ♿ (toilets), shop ⊗ (ex guide dogs) 🚌 (pre-booked only) ♨

## KINGSTON UPON HULL
### The Deep
HU1 4DP
☎ 01482 381000 📠 01482 381010
**Email:** info@thedeep.co.uk
**Web:** www.thedeep.co.uk
**Dir:** *follow signs from city centre*
The Deep tells the story of the world's oceans using live animals and hands-on activities, with over 3000 fish and more than 40 sharks. Now featuring The Twilight Zone, an exhibition all about the weird and alien creatures from the deep sea like giant Pacific octopus, wolf eels and giant Japanese spider crabs.
**Times:** *Open all year, daily 10-6. Closed 24-25 Dec
**Fee:** *£8 (ch under 16 £6, pen £6). Family ticket (2ad+2ch) £25, (2ad+3ch) £30

**Facilities:** ℗ (charged) ℗ (0.25m) ⊞ 🎧 ♿ (signing for the deaf if booked in advance, tactile guides, toilets), shop, guided tours, audio commentaries (charged) ⊗ (ex guide dogs) 🚌 (must book in advance for group prices)

## ALDBOROUGH
### Aldborough Roman Site
Boroughbridge YO5 9ES
☎ 01423 322768
**Web:** www.english-heritage.org.uk
**Dir:** *0.75m SE of Boroughbridge, on minor road off B6265 within 1m of junct of A1 & A6055*
Aldborough was among one of the northernmost settlements in the Roman Empire. Today, the remains can still be glimpsed amidst the trees. Visitors can view two spectacular mosaic pavements still in their original positions and there is a chance to try your hand with a mosaic-making kit as well as handling a collection of real and replica objects from the period.
**Times:** *Open 19 Mar-Jul, Thu-Mon, 10-5; Aug, daily, 10-5; Sep, Thu-Mon, 10-5.

**Fee:** *£2.60 (ch £1.30, concessions £2.00). Opening times and prices are subject to change, for further details please phone 0870 333 1181
**Facilities:** ⊞ shop 🚌 ⚙ ♨

## AYSGARTH
**National Park Centre**

Leyburn DL8 3TH

☎ 01969 662910 📄 01969 662919

**Email:** aysgarth@ytbtic.co.uk

**Web:** www.yorkshiredales.org.uk

**Dir:** *off A684, Leyburn to Hawes road at Falls junct, Palmer Flatt Hotel & continue down hill over river, centre 500yds on left*

A visitor centre for the Yorkshire Dales National Park, with maps, guides, walks and local information. Interactive displays explain the history and natural history of the area. Plan the day ahead with a light lunch in the coffee shop. There are various guided walks throughout the year.

**Times:** *Open Apr-Oct, daily 10-5; Winter open Fri-Sun, 10-4.

**Fee:** *Free Parking: £2, over 2hrs £3

**Facilities:** 🅿 (charged) Ⓟ (0.25m) 🚻 ♿ (viewing platform at Falls, toilets), shop 🚫 (ex guide dogs) 🚌 by previous arrangement

## BEDALE
**Bedale Museum**

DL8 1AA

☎ 01677 423797

**Dir:** *on A684, 1.5m W of A1 at Leeming Bar. Opposite church, at N end of town*

Situated in a building dating back to the 17th century, the Bedale is a fascinating museum. The central attraction is the Bedale fire engine, which dates back to 1742. Other artefacts include documents, toys, craft tools and household utensils, which all help to give an absorbing frame of reference for the lifestyle of the period.

**Times:** Open all year Tue & Fri 10-12.30 & 2-4, Wed 2-4, Thu-Sat 10-12

**Fee:** Free Donation box available.

**Facilities:** 🅿 Ⓟ (20yds - 2hr disc, free long stay 400m) 📖 Booklets from 20p to £3.50 ♿ (toilets), shop 🚫 (ex guide dogs) 🚌 (prior booking preferred) 🖂

## BENINGBROUGH
**Beningbrough Hall & Gardens**

York YO6 1DD

☎ 01904 470666 📄 01904 470002

**Email:** beningbrough@nationaltrust.org.uk

**Web:** www.nationaltrust.org.uk

**Dir:** *off A19, 8m NW of York*

Beningbrough was built around 1716. It houses 100 portraits from the National Portrait Gallery in London. Ornately carved wood panelling is a feature of several of the rooms. There is also a fully equipped Victorian Laundry and walled garden.

**Times:** *Open early Mar-end Oct daily (ex Thu & Fri) Open Good Fri, Jul-Aug daily (ex Thu) 12-5. Grounds 11-5.30. Galleries & Grounds winter wkds Nov-Feb, Sat & Sun 11-3.

**Fee:** *Summer: £7 (ch £3.50) Winter : £4.50 (ch £2.50)

**Facilities:** 🅿 🍴 (Licensed) 🚻 📖 Guidebook available ♿ (access to Victorian laundry, shop & restaurant, toilets),  shop, guided tours audio commentaries 🚫 🚌 (pre booking req) 🐾 🖂

## BRIMHAM

### Brimham Rocks

Summerbridge Harrogate HG3 4DW

☎ 01423 780688 🖹 01423 781020

**Email:** brimhamrocks@nationaltrust.org.uk

**Web:** www.nationaltrust.org.uk

**Dir:** *10m NW of Harrogate, off B6265*

The Brimham Rocks stand on National Trust open moorland at a height of 987ft, enjoying spectacular views over the surrounding countryside. The area is filled with strange and fascinating rock formations and is rich in wildlife. Brimham House is now an information point and shop.

**Times:** *Open 8-dusk, (facilities may close in bad weather): shop with exhibition room, kiosk mid Mar-end May & Oct, Sat & Sun 11-5, end May-end Sep daily

11-5, early Nov-mid Dec, Sun 11-5. Also open daily; local school hols, BHs, 26 Dec & 1 Jan (weather permitting)

**Fee:** Cars (up to 4hrs £3, over 4hrs £4). Minibuses £7. Coaches £12. Motorcycles free. Nat Trust members free. Cars up to 4 hours £3.50. Cars over 4 hours £4.50.

**Facilities:** 🅿 (charged) ⛾ (refreshment kiosk) ⊐ 🚻 (adapted path steep in places, Braille/large print guide, toilets), shop 🚌 Need booking, not accepted when busy. 🐾

## DANBY

### The Moors Centre

Lodge Lane Whitby YO21 2NB

☎ 01439 772737 🖹 01287 660308

**Email:** moorscentre@ytbtic.co.uk

**Web:** www.moors.uk.net

**Dir:** *turn S off A171, follow Moors Centre Danby signs . Left at crossroads in Danby and then 2m, Centre at bend on right*

The ideal place to start exploring the North York Moors National Park. There is an exhibition about the area as well as events, video, a shop and local walks. The Moorsbus service also operates from this site - phone for details.

**Times:** Open all year, Apr-Oct, daily 10-5. Nov-Feb wknds only 11-4, Mar daily 11-4. Closed 25-26 Dec

**Fee:** *Free

**Facilities:** 🅿 (charged) ⛾ (contry tearoom) 🚻 📦 Walks Booklet £1.90 🚻 (woodland & garden trails, motorised & manual wheelchairs, toilets), shop ⊗ (ex guide dogs & in grounds) 🚌 (Max 60 people)

## ELVINGTON

### Yorkshire Air Museum & Allied Air Forces Memorial

Halifax Way York YO41 4AU

☎ 01904 608595 🖹 01904 608246

**Email:** museum@yorkshireairmuseum.co.uk

**Web:** www.yorkshireairmuseum.co.uk

**Dir:** *from York take A1079 then immediate right onto B1228, museum is signposted on right*

This museum and memorial is based around the largest authentic former WWII Bomber Command Station open to the public. It includes a restored tower, an air gunners museum, archives, an Airborne Forces display and Squadron memorial rooms. Among the exhibits are replicas of the pioneering Cayley Glider and Wright Flyer, and modern jets like the Harrier GR3 and Tornado GR1.

**Times:** Open daily, 10-5 (summer), 10-3.30 (winter). Closed 25 & 26 Dec.

**Fee:** *£5 (ch £3 & pen £4).

**Facilities:** 🅿 🍽 (Licensed) 🚻 📦 Guidebook £1, Educational resource apply on enquiry 🚻 (Access to all except top control tower, toilets), shop, guided tours, audio commentaries 🚌 (booked in advance)

**NORTH YORKSHIRE**

## FAIRBURN
### RSPB Nature Reserve
Fairburn Ings The Visitor Centre Newton Lane
Castleford WF10 2BH
☎ 01977 603796
**Email:** james.dean@rspb.org.uk
**Dir:** *W of A1, N of Ferrybridge. Signed from Allerton Bywater off A656. Signed Fairburn Village off A1*
One-third of the 700-acre RSPB reserve is open water, and over 270 species of birds have been recorded. A visitor centre provides information, and there is an elevated boardwalk, suitable for disabled visitors.
**Times:** * Access to the reserve via car park, open 9-dusk. Centre open 9.30-5 everyday. Car park open: 9-5. Closed 25-26 Dec.
**Fee:** *Free

**Facilities:** ❷ ⌐ 🗐 ♿ (raised boardwalk for wheelchair, toilets), shop ⊗ (ex guide dogs & in reserve) 🚌 (booked one month in advance) 🌀

## HARROGATE
### The Royal Pump Room Museum
Crown Place HG1 2RY
☎ 01423 556188 🖷 01423 556130
**Email:** museums@harrogate.gov.uk
**Web:** www.harrogate.gov.uk/museums
**Dir:** *A61 into town centre and follow brown heritage signs*
Housed in an early Victorian pump room over the town's sulphur wells, the museum tells the story of Harrogate's heyday as England's European spa. Visitors discover some of the amazing spa treatments; taste the sulphur water; and explore stories of Russian royalty, communal ox-roasts and early bicycles, among many others. From March 2007 there is an exploration of many aspects of Victorian life, which includes the work of local Victorian artist, William Powell Frith.
**Times:** Open all year, Mon-Sat 10-5, Sun 2-5, (Nov-Mar close at 4). Closed 24-26 Dec, 15-17 May, 1 & 8-19 Jan & 19-21 Feb for works.
**Fee:** *£2.80 (ch £1.50, concessions £1.70). Family rate £8 (2ad+2ch). Party. Combined seasonal tickets available for The Royal Pump Room Museum & Knaresborough Castle & Museum £10
**Facilities:** ℗ (100yds - restricted to 3hrs, need parking disc) 🗐 ♿ (toilets), shop, guided tours ⊗ (ex guide dogs) 🚌 (please book in advance)

## HELMSLEY
### Duncombe Park
York YO62 5EB
☎ 01439 778625 🖷 01439 771114
**Email:** liz@duncombepark.com
**Web:** www.duncombepark.com
**Dir:** *located in North York Moors National Park, off A170 Thirsk-Scarborough road, 1m from Helmsley market place*
Duncombe Park stands at the heart of a spectacular 30-acre early 18th-century landscape garden which is set in 300 acres of dramatic parkland around the River Rye. The house, originally built in 1713, was gutted by fire in 1879 and rebuilt in 1895. Its principal rooms are a fine example of the type of grand interior popular at the turn of the century. Home of the Duncombes for 300 years, for much of this century the house was a girls' school. In 1985 the present Lord and Lady Feversham made it a family home again and after major restoration, opened the house to the public in 1990. Part of the garden and parkland were designated a 250-acre National Nature Reserve in 1994. Special events include a Country Fair (May), an Antiques Fair (June), Steam Fair (July), Antiques Fair (November). Please telephone for details.
**Times:** Open: May-end Oct, Sun-Thu; Gardens, Parkland Centre tea room & shop & Parkland walks 11-5.30. House by guided tour only every hour from 12.30-3.30.
**Fee:** *House & Gardens £7.25 (ch 10-16, £3.25, concessions £5.50) Gardens & Parkland £4 (ch £2, concessions £3.50) Parkland only £2 (ch £1).
**Facilities:** ❷ ℗ (1m) 🍽 (Licensed) ⌐ ♿ (portable ramp, lift, wheelchair for loan, toilets), shop, guided tours ⊗ (guide dogs) 🚌 (group rates for 15+ pre booked)

## KIRBY MISPERTON
### Flamingo Land Theme Park & Zoo
The Rectory Malton YO17 6UX
☎ 01653 668287 📠 01653 668280
**Email:** info@flamingoland.co.uk
**Web:** www.flamingoland.co.uk
**Dir:** *turn off A64 onto A169, Pickering to Whitby road*
Set in 375 acres of North Yorkshire countryside with over 100 rides and attractions there's something for everyone at Flamingo Land. Enjoy the thrills and spills of 12 white knuckle rides or enjoy a stroll through the extensive zoo where you'll find tigers, giraffes, hippos and rhinos. The theme park also boasts 6 great family shows.
**Times:** Open daily, 30 Mar-28 Oct.
**Fee:** *£19 (ch 4-11 £16.50, ch under 3 free, pen £9.50). Family ticket (4 people) £70.

**Facilities:** 🅿 Ⓟ (50yds) 🍴 (various fast food and liciensed premises) 🍽 (Licensed) 🍴 📱 ♿ (parking, wheelchair hire, toilets), shop 🚌

## MALTON
### Castle Howard
YO60 7DA
☎ 01653 648333 📠 01653 648529
**Email:** house@castlehoward.co.uk
**Web:** www.castlehoward.co.uk
**Dir:** *15m NE of York, off A64, follow brown heritage signs*
Castle Howard is a magnificent 18th-century house with extensive collections and breathtaking grounds featuring temples, lakes and fountains. Attractions include historical character guides, outdoor tours, exhibitions, event programme plus lakeside adventure playground.
**Times:** *Open Mar-Oct. House open from 11 (last admission 4).Grounds & Stable courtyard open from 10.
**Fee:** *£9.50 (ch £6.50, pen £8.50). Grounds only £6.50 (ch £4.50, pen £6).

**Facilities:** 🅿 🍴 (Open 10am) 🍽 (Licensed) ♿ (wheelchair lift, free adapted transport to house, toilets), shop, garden centre, guided tours 🚫 (ex guide dogs) 🚌

## MALTON
### Eden Camp Modern History Theme Museum
Eden Camp YO17 6RT
☎ 01653 697777 📠 01653 698243
**Email:** admin@edencamp.co.uk
**Web:** www.edencamp.co.uk
**Dir:** *junct of A64 & A169, between York & Scarborough*
The story of the people's war unfolds in this museum devoted to civilian life in World War II. The displays, covering the blackout, rationing, the Blitz, the Home Guard and others, are housed in a former prisoner-of-war camp built in 1942 for German and Italian soldiers. Hut 13, covers the conflicts that Britain has been involved with from 1945 to present day. Huts 24-29 cover the military and political events of the war, whilst Hut 11 is dedicated to telling the story of World War I. The Museum also houses an extensive collection of military vehicles and equipment. Special Events: Escapers and Evaders April, All Services Commemorative Day and Parade 2nd Sun after August BH, Palestine Veterans Reunion Day 3rd Sat in Oct.
**Times:** Open 2nd Mon in Jan-23 Dec, 7 days a week, daily 10-5. (Last admission 4)
**Fee:** £4.50 (ch & pen £3.50) Party 10+.£3.50 - £1 discount on individual admission prices.
**Facilities:** 🅿 🍴 (self service hot food, snacks, bevarages) 🍴 ♿ (taped tours, Braille guides, toilets), shop, audio commentaries 🚌 (advise before arrival) 🐾

**NORTH YORKSHIRE**

## MIDDLESBROUGH
### Captain Cook Birthplace Museum
Stewart Park Marton TS7 8AT
☎ 01642 311211 ▤ 01642 515659
**Email:** captcookmuseum@middlesbrough.gov.uk
**Web:** www.middlesbrough.gov.uk
**Dir:** *3m S on A172*

Opened to mark the 250th anniversary of the birth of the voyager in 1728, this museum illustrates the early life of James Cook and his discoveries with permanent and temporary exhibitions. Located in spacious and rolling parkland, the site also offers outside attractions for the visitor. Recently refurbished, the museum has a special resource centre which has fresh approaches to presentation with computers, films, special effects, interactives and educational aids.

**Times:** *Open all year: Mar-Oct, Tue-Sun, 10-5.30. Nov-Feb 9-3.30. (Last entry 45 mins before closure). Closed Mon except BH, 24-28 Dec & 31 Dec-7 Jan.
**Fee:** *£2.40 (pen £1.20). Family ticket £6.
**Facilities:** ℗ ℗ (800yds) ⏍ ⏢ ♿ (lift to all floors, car parking, toilets), shop ⊗ (ex guide dogs) 🚌 (must pre-book)

## NEWBY HALL & GARDENS
### Newby Hall & Gardens
HG4 5AE
☎ 01423 322583 ▤ 01423 324452
**Email:** info@newbyhall.com
**Web:** www.newbyhall.com
**Dir:** *4m SE of Ripon & 2m W of A1M, off B6265, between Boroughbridge and Ripon*

A late 17th-century house with beautifully restored Robert Adam interiors containing an important collection of classical sculpture, Chippendale furniture and Gobelin tapestries. The gardens include a miniature railway, an adventure garden for children and a woodland walk.
**Times:** *Open Apr-Sep, Tue-Sun & BHs, also Mon in Jul & Aug; Gardens 11-5.30; House 12-5. (Last admission 5 Gardens, 4.30 House)

**Fee:** *House & Garden £8.20, (ch £5.70, pen £7.20). Gardens only £6.70 (ch £5, pen £5.70). Party rates and family tickets on application.
**Facilities:** ℗ ⏛ (licensed self service restaurant) ⏍ (Licensed) ⏢ ♿ (wheelchairs available, maps of wheelchair routes, toilets), shop, garden centre ⊗ (ex guide dogs) 🚌

## NORTH STAINLEY
### Lightwater Valley Theme Park
Ripon HG4 3HT
☎ 0870 458 0040 ▤ 0870 300 4440
**Email:** leisure@lightwatervalley.co.uk
**Web:** www.lightwatervalley.co.uk
**Dir:** *3m N of Ripon on A6108*

The family sized theme park with thrills of all sizes, from Europe's longest rollercoaster 'The Ultimate' and 'The Grizzly Bear', to family favourites such as the 'ladybird' rollercoaster and Grand Prix Go Karting along with spinning teacups, vintage cars and much more for younger children. New rides at the Lightwater Valley Theme Park include the Hornets Nest, Eagles Claw, and the Skyride. You just pay once and enjoy the fun all day long!

**Times:** Open 31 Mar-15 Apr, wknds only; 21 Apr-27 May inc BH Mon; daily from 2 Jun-2 Sep, wknds only, 8 Sep-21 Oct, daily 22 Oct-28 Oct. Gates open at 10, closes 4.30, depending on time of year.
**Fee:** *£15.95 over 1.2mtrs, £14.50 under 1.2mtrs, free under 1m; pen £7.95. Family ticket £58 (2ad+2ch) or (1ad+3ch under 16)
**Facilities:** ℗ ⏍ (Licensed) ⏢ ♿ (even pathways, toilets), shop, garden centre ⊗ (ex guide dogs) 🚌 (pre-booking preferred)

## PATELEY BRIDGE
### Stump Cross Caverns
Greenhow Harrogate HG3 5JL
☎ 01756 752780 📄 01756 752780
**Web:** www.stumpcrosscaverns.co.uk
**Dir:** *on B6265 between Pateley Bridge & Grassington*
Discovered by the brothers Mark and William Newbould in 1860, Stump Cross Caverns have been an attraction for visitors since 1863 when one shilling was charged for entrance. Among the few limestone show caves in Britain, these require no special clothing, experience or equipment, as walkways are gravel and concrete and floodlighting is provided. Stalagmites, stalagtites and calcite precipitation make this an eerie day out.
**Times:** Open daily, Mar-end of Nov, then wknds and school hols Dec, Jan, Feb 10-5.

**Fee:** *£5 (ch £3.95, ch under 4 free) free gift for ch in school hols
**Facilities:** 🅿 Ⓟ (300mtrs - parking for customers only) 🍴 £1 ♿ (ground floor and gardens accessible), shop guided tours 🚫 (ex guide dogs) 🚌 (max 3 at same time)

## PICKERING
### North Yorkshire Moors Railway
Pickering Station YO18 7AJ
☎ 01751 472508 📄 01751 476970
**Email:** admin@nymr.pickering.fsnet.co.uk
**Web:** www.northyorkshiremoorsrailway.com
**Dir:** *from A169 take road towards Kirkbymoorside, right at traffic lights, station 400yds on left*
Operating through the heart of the North York Moors National Park between Pickering and Grosmont, steam trains cover a distance of 18 miles. The locomotive sheds at Grosmont are open to the public. Events include Day Out with Thomas, Steam Gala, Santa Specials.
**Times:** *Open 29 Mar-Oct, daily; Dec, Santa specials and Xmas to New Year running. Further information available from Pickering Station.

**Fee:** *Return: £13 (ch £6.50, pen £11). Family ticket £28 (2ad+3ch), others on request. Party 20+.
**Facilities:** 🅿 (charged) Ⓟ (200m - £3 per day) 🍴 (at Pickering, Grosmont & Goathland) 🍴 (Licensed) 🏕 🍴 Simple child quiz sheets ♿ (ramp for trains, toilets), shop, guided tours (charged) 🚌 Maximum 150

## RICHMOND
### Richmond Castle
DL10 4QW
☎ 01748 822493
**Web:** www.english-heritage.org.uk
Overlooking the River Swale and market town of Richmond, the views from the keep are stunning. Built by William the Conqueror to subdue the rebellious North, the castle now houses an exciting interactive exhibition. The new Contemporary Heritage Garden offers a space for contemplation.
**Times:** Open all year, Apr-Sep, daily, 10-6; Oct-Mar, Thu-Mon, 10-4. Closed 24-26 Dec & 1 Jan.

**Fee:** £3.60 (ch £1.80, concessions £2.70) Family £9. Prices and opening times are subject to change. Please check web site or call 0870 333 1181 for the most up to date prices and opening times when planning your visit.
**Facilities:** Ⓟ (800 yds) 🏕 ♿ (toilets), shop 🚌 ♯ ♻

**NORTH YORKSHIRE**

RIPLEY

**Ripley Castle**

Harrogate HG3 3AY

☎ 01423 770152 🖹 01423 771745

**Email:** enquiries@ripleycastle.co.uk

**Web:** www.ripleycastle.co.uk

**Dir:** *off A61, Harrogate to Ripon road*

Ripley Castle has been home to the Ingilby family since 1320, and stands at the heart of an estate with deer park, lake and Victorian walled gardens. The Castle has a rich history and a fine collection of Royalist armour housed in the 1555 tower. There are also walled gardens, tropical hot houses, woodland walks, pleasure grounds and the National Hyacinth collection in spring.

**Times:** Open Oct-Nov & Mar-May, Tue, Thu, Sat & Sun 10.30-3, Jun-Sep daily 10.30-3, Dec-Feb wkends only, also BH and school hols. Groups all year by prior arrangement. Gardens open daily 9-5.30.

**Fee:** Castle & Gardens £6.50 (ch £4, pen £5.50). Gardens only £4 (ch £2.50, pen £3.50). Party £3.50.

**Facilities:** P (open daily 9.30-5) (Licensed) (mobility buggy for hire, audio loop, toilets), shop, garden centre (ex guide dogs) (by arrangement)

RIPON

**Fountains Abbey & Studley Royal**

HG4 3DY

☎ 01765 608888 🖹 01765 601002

**Email:** fountainsenquiries@nationaltrust.org.uk

**Web:** www.fountainsabbey.org.uk

**Dir:** *4m W of Ripon off B6265*

A world heritage site comprising the ruin of a 12th-century Cistercian Abbey and monastic watermill, an Elizabethan mansion and one of the best surviving examples of a Georgian water garden. Elegant ornamental lakes, canals, temples and cascades provide eye-catching vistas. The site also contains a Victorian St. Mary's Church and medieval deer park.

**Times:** *Open daily all year: Nov-Feb 10-4, Mar-Oct 10-5. Closed Fri Nov-Jan.

**Fee:** *£5.50 (ch £3). Family ticket £15

**Facilities:** P (Licensed) (pre-bk wheelchairs & batricars. Braille/large print guides, toilets), shop on lead at all times (booking essential)

SALTBURN-BY-THE-SEA

**Saltburn Smugglers Heritage Centre**

Old Saltburn, Next to Ship Inn TS12 1HF

☎ 01287 625252

**Web:** www.redcar-cleveland.gov.uk

**Dir:** *adjoining Ship Inn, on A174*

Follow the story of John Andrew King of Smugglers, who was at the heart of illicit local trade 200 years ago. Set in old fisherman's cottages, this centre skillfully blends costumed characters with authentic sounds and smells of the period. Saltburn itself also has many attractons including a recently renovated pier and a number of local celebrations throughout the year.

**Times:** Open Apr-Sep, daily 10-6: Winter Open by arrangement only telephone 01642 471069.

**Fee:** *£1.95 (ch £1.45). Family ticket £5.80. Party.

**Facilities:** P (200 mtrs - charged) schools only, shop (ex assisst dogs) pre-book

## SCARBOROUGH
**Scarborough Castle**

Castle Road YO11 1HY

☎ 01723 372451

**Web:** www.english-heritage.org.uk

**Dir:** *E of town centre*

This 12th-century fortress housed many important figures in history. Enjoy the spectacular coastal view and see the remains of the great keep still standing over three storeys high. Discover the castle's exciting history through the free audio tour.

**Times:** Open all year, Apr-Sep, daily 10-6; Oct, Thu-Mon, 10-5; Nov-Mar, Thu-Mon, 10-4. Closed 24-26 Dec & 1 Jan.

**Fee:** £3.50 (ch £1.80, concessions £2.60). Family £8.80. Prices and opening times are subject to change.

Please check web site or call 0870 333 1181 for the most up to date prices and opening times when planning your visit.

**Facilities:** ℗ (100yds) 🍴 ♿ (ex in keep) 🚌 ⊞ ▣

## SCARBOROUGH
**Sea Life & Marine Sanctuary**

Scalby Mills Road North Bay YO12 6RP

☎ 01723 376125 🖷 01723 376285

**Web:** www.sealife.co.uk

**Dir:** *follow brown tourist signs after entering Scarborough. Centre in North Bay Leisure Parks area of town*

Made up of three large white pyramids, this impressive marine sanctuary overlooks the white sandy beaches of the North Bay, Scarborough's Castle, and Peasholm Park. The sanctuary features Jurassic seas, jellyfish, Otter River, penguins, tropical sharks and sea turtles which can be seen in a colourful Caribbean style coral reef.

**Times:** *Open all year daily. Closed 25 Dec.

**Fee:** *Prices to be confirmed.

**Facilities:** ℗ (charged) ℗ (0.5m) 🍴 ♿ (lift to cafe, toilets), shop ⊗ (except guide dogs) 🚌

## SKINNINGROVE
**Cleveland Ironstone Mining Museum**

Deepdale Cleveland TS13 4AP

☎ 01287 642877 🖷 01287 642970

**Email:** visits@ironstonemuseum.co.uk

**Web:** www.ironstonemuseum.co.uk

**Dir:** *in Skinningrove Valley, just off A174 near coast between Saltburn and Whitby*

On the site of the old Loftus Mine, this museum offers visitors a glimpse into the underground world of Cleveland's ironstone mining past. Discover the special skills and customs of the miners who helped make Cleveland the most important ironstone mining district in Victorian and Edwardian England.

**Times:** Open Apr-Oct, Mon-Sat from 1 (last admission 4).Open main Summer school hols daily, also Sun pm.

**Fee:** £4 (ch £2). Family ticket (2ad+2ch) £10.

**Facilities:** ℗ ℗ (50yds + 500yds) 🍴 📓 Approx 60 books on mining heritage for sale. Costs vary. ♿ (2 wheelchairs on site. Induction loop, toilets), shop, guided tours ⊗ (ex guide dogs) 🚌 (pre-booking essential) ▣

## SKIPTON
**Skipton Castle**

BD23 1AW

☎ 01756 792442 🖺 01756 796100

**Email:** info@skiptoncastle.co.uk

**Web:** www.skiptoncastle.co.uk

**Dir:** *in town centre at head of High Street*

Skipton is one of the most complete and well-preserved medieval castles in England. Part of it dates from the 1650s when it was rebuilt after being partially damaged following the Civil War. However, the original castle was erected in Norman times and became the home of the Clifford family in 1310 and remained so until 1676. Illustrated tour sheets are available in a number of languages. Please see website for special events.

**Times:** *Open daily from 10, (Sun from noon). Last admission 6 (4pm Oct-Feb). Closed 25 Dec.

**Fee:** *£5.40 (inc illustrated tour sheet) (ch under 18 £2.90, under 5 free, concessions £4.80). Family ticket £15.90. Party 15+.

**Facilities:** ℗ (200m) ☐ (Light meals) ⇰ 🗐 Family Quiz 45p shop, garden centre guided tours ⊗ (ex on a lead) 🚌 (must book if meals req.)

## THIRSK
**Falconry Centre**

Sion Hill Hall Kirby Wiske YO7 4EU

☎ 01845 587522

**Email:** mail@falconrycentre.co.uk

**Web:** www.falconrycentre.co.uk

**Dir:** *follow brown tourist signs*

Set up to ensure that birds of prey would survive and to provide the public with a rare opportunity to see and enjoy these beautiful birds. Enjoy the excitement of falconry with over 70 birds and 30 species. The Falconry Centre also features flying displays, falconry courses (day and half days) and Hawk Walks as well as talks and presentations about promoting bird conservation across the UK and in the rest of the world.

**Times:** Open Mar-Oct, daily, 10.30-5.30.

**Fee:** *£5 (ch £3, under 3 free). Family ticket £14 (2ad+2ch)

**Facilities:** ℗ ⇰ 🗐 ♿ (toilets), shop ⊗ 🚌

## THIRSK
**Monk Park Farm Visitor Centre**

Bagby YO7 2AG

☎ 01845 597730 🖺 01845 597730

**Web:** www.monkpark.co.uk

**Dir:** *just off A170 Scarborough road or A19 from York*

Once a haven for the monks generations ago who made their living from the land, Monk Park is now a favourite for children. There is plenty for all ages to see and do, with indoor and outdoor viewing and feeding areas, a visitor centre, farm walks and a fitness trail. Animals range from rare sheep breeds and Shetland ponies to wallabies and llamas. The park has also been the venue for filming *Blue Peter* and *Vets in Practice*.

**Times:** Open Feb half term-Oct, daily, 11-5.30.

**Fee:** *£4 incl ch & concessions

**Facilities:** ℗ ⇰ ♿ (ramps, toilets), shop ⊗ (ex assist dogs) 🚌 ♨

## YORK
### DIG
St Saviourgate YO1 8NN
☎ 01904 654324 🖷 01904 627097
**Email:** enquiries@vikingjorvik.com
**Web:** www.digyork.co.uk
**Dir:** *follow A19 or A64 to city centre then pedestrian signs for attraction*
Dig is unusual way to discover York's Viking history. Visitors of all ages can get their hands dirty unearthing the secrets of the past with a trusty trowel, as well as learn about how archaeology is conducted in the field, and see what happens in a conservation lab.
**Times:** Open daily ex 24-25 Dec. Apr-Oct 10-6, Nov-Mar 10-5.

**Fee:** *£5.50. (ch, concessions £5) Family of 4 £16. Group rates available on request.
**Facilities:** ⓟ (50yds NCP) 🚻 ♿ (induction loop, sensory garden, hearing posts, toilets), shop ⊗ (ex guide dogs) 🚌 (pre-book tel:01904 543402)

## YORK
### Jorvik
Coppergate YO1 9WT
☎ 01904 543402 🖷 01904 627097
**Email:** enquiries@vikingjorvik.com
**Web:** www.vikingjorvik.com
**Dir:** *follow A19 or A64 to York. Jorvik in Coppergate shopping area city centre signed*
Explore York's Viking history on the very site where remains of the city of Jorvik were discovered. Encounter Viking residents, learn what life was like 1000 years ago.
**Times:** *Open all year, Apr-Oct daily 10-5; and Viking festival Nov-Mar daily 10-4. Closed 25 Dec opening times subject to change, please telephone for up to date details.
**Fee:** £7.75 (ch 5-15 £5.50, under 5 free, concessions £6.60) Family of 4 £21.95 & family of 5 £26.50. Telephone bookings on 01904 543403 (£1 booking fee per person at peak times).
**Facilities:** ⓟ (400 yds - limited to 3 hours) 🍴 (Apr-Oct) 🛗 ♿ (lift & time car designed to take wheelchair, hearing loop, toilets), shop, audio commentaries ⊗ (ex guide dogs) 🚌 (pre-booking preferred)

## YORK
### National Railway Museum
Leeman Road YO26 4XJ
☎ 01904 621261 🖷 01904 611112
**Email:** nrm@nmsi.ac.uk
**Web:** www.nrm.org.uk
**Dir:** *behind rail station. Signed from all major roads and city centre.*
The National Railway Museum is the world's largest railway museum. Housing *The Flying Scotsman*, three enormous galleries, interactive exhibits and daily events, the National Railway Museum mixes education with fun. Until Jan 2009, visitors to the NRM can take a ride on the London Eye-style Norwich Union Yorkshire Wheel. There is a charge for the wheel.

**Times:** Open all year, daily 10-6. Closed 24-26 Dec.
**Fee:** Free Admission may be charged for special events
**Facilities:** ⓟ (charged) ⓟ (100 mtrs - coach parking must be pre-booked) 🍴 (Holidays & special events only) 🍽 (Licensed) 🚻 ♿ (Please Touch evenings usually in June, toilets), shop, garden centre ⊗ (ex guide/hearing dogs) 🚌 Free parking if pre-booked.

## YORK
**The York Dungeon**

12 Clifford Street YO1 9RD

☎ 01904 632599 📄 01904 612602

**Email:** yorkdungeons@merlinentertainments.biz

**Web:** www.thedungeons.com

**Dir:** *A64/A19/A59 to city centre*

Deep in the heart of historic York lies the York Dungeon bringing more than 2,000 years of gruesomely authentic history vividly and literally back to life, so be warned, it always pays to keep your wits about you. The journey includes Dick Turpin, Witch Trials, Clifford's Tower, Pit of Despair, Guy Fawkes and Gorvik - the real Viking experience. The most recent addition is the Labyrinth of the Lost, which explores the Roman presence in York.

**Times:** *Open Apr-Sep 10.30-5 (last admission); Nov-Jan 11-4; Oct, Feb & Mar 10.30-4.30; Etr & Summer hols 10-5.30

**Fee:** *£10.95 (ch £7.95, concessions £8.95) Family ticket (2ad+2ch) £33.95

**Facilities:** Ⓟ (500yds) 🏛 Customer service/Marketing talks & packs ♿ (wheelchair ramps, stairlifts, award winning access, toilets), shop ⊗ (ex guide dogs) 🚌 (restricted in city, use coach parks)

## YORK
**Treasurer's House**

Minster Yard YO1 7JL

☎ 01904 624247 📄 01904 647372

**Email:** treasurershouse@nationaltrust.org.uk

**Web:** www.nationaltrust.org.uk

**Dir:** *in Minster Yard, on N side of Minster, in the centre of York*

Named after the Treasurer of York Minster and built over a Roman Road, the house is not all it seems. Nestled behind the Minster, the size, splendour and contents of the house are a constant surprise to everybody who visits - as are the famous ghost stories (a legion of Roman soldiers reputedly marches through the cellars). Children's trails, and access to the tea room is free.

**Times:** *Open mid Mar-end Oct, daily except Fri, 11-5.

**Fee:** *£4.80 (ch £2.40). Family ticket £12 (2+3). House and Ghost Cellar £6.80 (ch £3.60)

**Facilities:** Ⓟ (800 mtrs) 🍽 ♿ (Braille guide/tactile pictures/induction loop/scented path)⊗ (ex guide dogs) 🚌 (booking req.) 🦋 ♨

## YORK
**York Castle Museum**

The Eye of York YO1 1RY

☎ 01904 653611 📄 01904 671078

**Web:** www.york.gov.uk

**Dir:** *city centre, next to Clifford's Tower*

Fascinating exhibits that bring memories to life, imaginatively displayed through reconstructions of period rooms and two indoor streets, complete with cobbles, a Hansom cab and a park. The museum is housed in the city's former prison and is based on an extensive collection of 'bygones' acquired at the beginning of the twentieth century. It was one of the first folk museums to display a huge range of everyday objects in an authentic setting. The Victorian street includes a pawnbroker, a tallow candle factory and a haberdasher's shop. There is even a reconstruction of the original sweet shop of the York chocolate manufacturer, Joseph Terry. An extensive collection of many other items ranging from musical instruments to costumes and a gallery of domestic gadgets from Victorian times to the 1960s are further attractions to this remarkable museum. The museum also has one of Britain's finest collections of Militaria. The museum includes the cell where highwayman Dick Turpin was held. Please contact the museum for details of exhibitions and events.

**Times:** *Open all year, Apr-Oct Mon-Sat 9.30-5.30, Sun 10-5.30; Nov-Mar, Mon-Sat 9.30-4, Sun 10-4. Closed 25-26 Dec & 1 Jan.

**Fee:** *£4.50 (ch, pen, students & UB40 £3.15). Family ticket £13.50. Party 10+.

**Facilities:** ♿ (toilets) shop ⊗ 🚌

## YORK

**York Minster**

Deangate YO1 7HH

☎ 01904 557216 🖹 01904 557218

**Email:** visitors@yorkminster.org

**Web:** www.yorkminster.org

**Dir:** *easy access via A19, A1 or A64*

Enjoy the peaceful atmosphere of the largest Gothic
cathedral in Northern Europe, a place of worship and
a treasure house of stained glass. Take an audio tour of
the Undercroft to find out about the Minster's fascinating
history and climb the Tower for amazing views.

**Times:** *Open from 7 for services. Visitors Mon-Sat 9-5
(9.30 in winter), Sun noon-3.45. Phone for 2007 details.

**Fee:** *£5 (ch16 free, concessions £4). Small charge also
for the Undercroft and Tower.

**Facilities:** ⓟ (440yds) ♿ (tactile model, Braille
& large print guide, toilets), shop, guided tours, audio
commentaries ⊗ (ex assist dogs) 🚌 (advance booking)

## YORK

**Yorkshire Museum**

Museum Gardens YO1 7FR

☎ 01904 551800 🖹 01904 551802

**Email:** yorkshire.museum@york.gov.uk

**Web:** www.york.gov.uk

**Dir:** *park & ride service from 4 sites near
A64/A19/A1079 & A166, also 3 car parks within
short walk*

The Yorkshire Museum is set in 10 acres of botanical
gardens in the heart of the historic City of York, and
displays some of the finest Roman, Anglo-Saxon, Viking
and Medieval treasures ever discovered in Britain. The
Middleham jewel, a fine example of English Gothic
jewellery, is on display, and in the Roman Gallery, visitors
can see a marble head of Constantine the Great. The
Anglo-Saxon Gallery houses the delicate silver-gilt
Ormside bowl and the Gilling sword.

**Times:** *Open all year, daily 10-5.

**Fee:** *£3.95 (concessions £2.50) Family ticket £11.50.

**Facilities:** ⓟ (5 mins walk) 🚻 ♿ (ramps & lift, toilets),
shop ⊗ 🚌

## ROTHERHAM

**Magna Science Adventure Centre**

Sheffield Road Templeborough S60 1DX

☎ 01709 720002 🖹 01709 820092

**Email:** ebodley@magnatrust.co.uk

**Web:** www.visitmagna.co.uk

**Dir:** *M1 junct 33/34, follow Templeborough sign off rdbt,
then brown heritage signs*

Magna is the UK's first Science Adventure Centre,
an exciting exploration of Earth, Air, Fire and Water. A
chance for visitors to create their own adventure through
hands-on interactive challenges. Visit the four Adventure
Pavilions, two shows and Sci-Tec outdoor adventure
playground and have fun unearthing the mysteries of
our world.

**Times:** *Open all year, daily (ex some Mons), 10-5

**Fee:** *£9.95 (ch & concessions £7.95). Family ticket
(2ad+1ch) £25

**Facilities:** ⓟ ⓟ 🍽 (Open everyday 10-5pm) 🚻 ♿ (lifts,
portable seating, wheelchair hire, toilets) shop guided
tours ⊗ (ex guide dogs) 🚌 (min 12 must pre-book)

## SHEFFIELD
### Kelham Island Museum

Alma Street S3 8RY

☎ 0114 272 2106 📄 0114 275 7847

**Email:** postmaster@simt.co.uk

**Web:** www.simt.co.uk

**Dir:** *0.5m NW of city centre, take A61 N to West Bar, follow signs*

The story of Sheffield, its industry and life, with the most powerful working steam engine in Europe, reconstructed workshops, and craftspeople demonstrating traditional 'made in Sheffield' skills - this is a 'living' museum. During the year Kelham Island stages events, displays and temporary exhibitions culminating in the annual Christmas Victorian Market.

**Times:** *Open Mon-Thu 10-4, Sun 11-4.45. Closed Fri and Sat. CheckOpening days/times at Xmas & New Year before travelling.

**Fee:** £4 (concessions £3). Family ticket £8.

**Facilities:** 🅿 ☕ (open 11-3) 📷 ♿ (wheelchair on request, toilets), shop ⊗ 🚌 ♿

---

## SHEFFIELD
### Millennium Galleries

Arundel Gate S1 2PP

☎ 0114 278 2600 📄 0114 278 2604

**Email:** info@sheffieldgalleries.org.uk

**Web:** www.sheffieldgalleries.org.uk

With four different galleries under one roof, the Millennium Galleries has something for everyone. Enjoy new blockbuster exhibitions drawn from the collections of Britain's national galleries and museums, including the Victoria & Albert Museum and Tate Gallery. See the best of contemporary craft and design in a range of exhibitions by established and up-and-coming makers. Be dazzled by Sheffield's magnificent and internationally important collection of decorative and domestic metal-work and silverware. Discover the Ruskin Gallery with its wonderful array of treasures by Victorian artist and writer John Ruskin.

**Times:** *Open daily Mon-Sat 10-5, Sun 11-5.

**Fee:** *Free Special Exhibitions: £4 (ch 5-16 £2, concessions £3) family ticket £9.

**Facilities:** 🅿 ♿ (hearing loop, toilets), shop ⊗ (ex guide dogs) 🚌

---

## BRADFORD
### Bradford Industrial Museum and Horses at Work

Moorside Mills Moorside Road Eccleshill BD2 3HP

☎ 01274 435900 📄 01274 636362

**Web:** www.bradfordmuseums.org

**Dir:** *off A658*

Moorside Mills is an original spinning mill, now part of a museum that brings vividly to life the story of Bradford's woollen industry. There is the machinery that once converted raw wool into cloth, and the mill yard rings with the sound of iron on stone as shire horses pull trams, haul buses and give rides. Daily demonstrations and changing exhibitions.

**Times:** Open all year, Tue-Sat 10-5, Sun 12-5. Closed Mon ex BH, Good Fri, 25-26 Dec

**Fee:** Free

**Facilities:** 🅿 📷 ♿ (induction loop in lecture theatre, lift, toilets), shop ⊗ (ex guide dogs) 🚌 ♿

## BRADFORD
### National Museum of Photography, Film & Television
BD1 1NQ

☎ 0870 7010200 🖹 01274 723155

**Email:** talk.nmpft@nmsi.ac.uk

**Web:** www.nmpft.org.uk

**Dir:** *2m from end of M606, follow signs for city centre*

Experience the past, present and future of photography, film and television with amazing interactive displays and spectacular 3D IMAX cinema.

**Times:** *Open all year, Tue-Sun, BHs & main school hols 10-6. Closed Mon.

**Fee:** *Admission to permanent galleries free, IMAX Cinema £6.50 (concessions £4.30). Groups 20% discount.

**Facilities:** Ⓟ (adjacent) 🍽 (Licensed) 🚻 ♿ (tailored tours, Braille signs, induction loop, cinema seating, toilets), shop ⊗ (ex guide dogs) 🚌 no coach parking on site

## BRADFORD
### The Colour Museum
Perkin House 1 Providence Street BD1 2PW

☎ 01274 390955 🖹 01274 392888

**Email:** museum@sdc.org.uk

**Web:** www.colour-experience.org

**Dir:** *from city centre follow signs B6144 Haworth, then brown heritage signs*

Europe's only Museum of Colour comprises two galleries packed with visitor-operated exhibits demonstrating the effects of light and colour, including optical illusions, and the story of dyeing and textile printing. There is a programme of special exhibitions and events. Please telephone for details.

**Times:** *Open 2 Jan-18 Dec, Tue-Sat, 10-4.

**Fee:** *£2 (concessions £1.50). Family ticket £4

**Facilities:** Ⓟ (200 yds) ♿ (lifts, ramps at door, toilets), shop ⊗ (ex guide dogs) 🚌 (prior booking)

## HALIFAX
### Bankfield Museum
Boothtown Rd Akroyd Park HX3 6HG

☎ 01422 354823 & 352334 🖹 01422 349020

**Email:** bankfield-museum@calderdale.gov.uk

**Web:** www.calderdale.gov.uk

**Dir:** *on A647 Bradford via Queensbury road, 0.5m from Halifax town centre*

Built by Edward Akroyd in the 1860s, this Renaissance-style building is set in parkland on a hill overlooking the town. It has an outstanding collection of costumes and textiles from around the world, including a gallery featuring East European textiles. There is also a section on toys, and the museum of the Duke of Wellington's Regiment is housed here. There is a lively programme of events, workshops and activities. Please ring for details.

**Times:** *Open all year, Tue-Sat 10-5, Sun 1-4, BH Mon 10-5.

**Fee:** Free

**Facilities:** Ⓟ Ⓟ (50yds - restricted access for coaches) ♿ (audio guide & tactile objects, toilets), shop ⊗ (ex guide dogs) 🚌

**WEST YORKSHIRE**

### HALIFAX
**Eureka! The Museum for Children**
Discovery Road HX1 2NE
☎ 01422 330069 📄 01422 330275
**Email:** info@eureka.org.uk
**Web:** www.eureka.org.uk
**Dir:** *M62 junct 24 follow heritage signs to Halifax - A629*
With over 400 'must touch' exhibits, interactive activities
and challenges, visitors are invited to embark upon a
journey of discovery through four main gallery spaces:
Me and My Body, Living and Working Together, Our
Global Garden and SoundSpace, an interactive music
gallery inviting children to explore the science behind
sound, rhythm and technology.
**Times:** *Open all year, daily 10-5. Closed 24-26 Dec
**Fee:** £6.50 (ch under 3 £1.95, ch under 1 free) Family
Saver ticket admits 5 £29.50. Special group rates
available.
**Facilities:** 🅿 (charged) 🅿 (5 mins - pay & display
parking) 🍽 (fast food and healthy options) 🚻 ♿ (lift, staff
trained in basic sign language, large print, toilets), shop,
audio commentaries 🚫 (ex guide dogs) 🚌 (booking
essential)

### HALIFAX
**Halifax Visitor Centre and Art Gallery**
HX1 1RE
☎ 01422 368725
**Email:** halifax@ytbtic.co.uk
**Web:** www.calderdale.gov.uk
**Dir:** *follow brown tourist signs, close to railway station*
The merchants of Halifax built the elegant and unique
hall in 1770, and it has over 300 merchant's rooms
around a courtyard, now housing an art gallery and
visitor centre. There are around eight temporary
exhibitions each year including art, craft, design
and photography.
**Times:** *Open all year daily. Closed 25-26 Dec. Art
Gallery, Tue-Sun & BH Mon 10-5.
**Fee:** *Free

**Facilities:** 🅿 (50 yds) 🚻 ♿ (lifts, shopmobility on
site & audio guide available, toilets), shop 🚫 (ex
guide dogs) 🚌

### HAREWOOD
**Harewood House & Bird Garden**
Leeds LS17 9LG
☎ 0113 218 1010 📄 0113 218 1002
**Email:** business@harewood.org
**Web:** www.harewood.org
**Dir:** *junct A61/A659 Leeds to Harrogate road*
Designed in 1759 by John Carr, Harewood House is
home to the Queen's cousin, the Earl of Harewood. His
mother, HRH Princess Mary, Princess Royal lived at
Harewood for 35 years and much of her memorabilia is
still displayed. The House, renowned for its stunning
architecture and exquisite Adam interiors, contains a rich
collection of Chippendale furniture, fine porcelain and
outstanding art collections from Italian Renaissance
masterpieces and Turner watercolours to contemporary
works. The old kitchen contains the best collection of
noble household copperware in the country giving visitors
a glimpse into below stairs life. The grounds include a
restored parterre terrace, oriental rock garden, walled
garden, lakeside and woodland walks, a bird garden and
for youngsters, an adventure playground.
**Times:** *Open 4 Feb-30 Oct, (grounds until 17 Dec),
Grounds (inc Bird Gardens) daily from 10, House
from 11.
**Fee:** Mon-Fri £12.50. Sat-Sun, £14.50. (ch and student,
Mon-Fri, £7.20, Sat-Sun, £9, pen, Mon-Fri, £11, Sat-
Sun, £13.50) Family, Mon-Fri, £41.50, Sat-Sun, £49.
**Facilities:** 🅿 🍽 (Licensed) 🚻 ♿ (electric ramp, lift,
toilets), shop guided tours audio commentaries
🚫 (ex guide dogs or in gardens ) 🚌 (pre-booking
essential)

## HAWORTH
### Keighley & Worth Valley Railway & Museum
Keighley BD22 8NJ
☎ 01535 645214 & 677777 📄 01535 647317
**Email:** admin@kwvr.co.uk
**Web:** www.kwvr.co.uk
**Dir:** *1m from Keighley on A629 Halifax road, follow brown signs*

The line was built mainly to serve the valley's mills, and passes through the heart of Brontë country. Beginning at Keighley (shared with Network Rail), it climbs up to Haworth, and terminates at Oxenhope, which has a storage and restoration building. At Haworth there are locomotive workshops and at Ingrow West, an award-winning museum.

**Times:** *Open every wknd, please phone for other times.
**Fee:** *All day fares: Family Day Rover £25, Adult Day Rover £12 (ch 5-15 £6 under 5's free, pen concessionary). Single and day returns, group rates available, phone for details.
**Facilities:** ℗ (charged) Ⓟ (100yds - free at some stations) ☕ (Buffet at 2 stations) 🎋 ♿ (level access to all sites, ramps on trains and stations, toilets), shop 🚌

---

## KEIGHLEY
### Cliffe Castle Museum & Gallery
Spring Gardens Lane BD20 6LH
☎ 01535 618230 📄 01535 610536
**Web:** www.bradfordmuseums.org
**Dir:** *NW of town off A629*

Built as a millionaire's mansion, the house displays Victorian interiors, together with collections of local and natural history, ceramics, dolls, geological items and minerals. The grounds have a play area and an aviary. Temporary exhibitions occur throughout the year and learning activities and events for children take place in the *In*Sight room.
**Times:** Open all year, Tue-Sat 10-5, Sun 12-5.Open BH Mon. Closed Good Fri & 25-28 Dec.
**Fee:** Free

**Facilities:** ℗ 🎋 📱 ♿ (toilets), shop, garden centre ⊗ (ex guide dogs) 🚌 ♻

---

## LEEDS
### Abbey House Museum
Abbey Walk Abbey Road Kirkstall LS5 3EH
☎ 0113 230 5492 📄 0113 230 5499
**Email:** abbey.house@leeds.gov.uk
**Web:** www.leeds.gov.uk
**Dir:** *3m W of city centre on A65*

Displays at this museum include an interactive childhood gallery, a look at Kirkstall Abbey, and an exploration of life in Victorian Leeds. Three reconstructed streets allow the visitor to immerse themselves in the sights and sounds of the late 19th century, from the glamourous art furnishers shop to the life of the impoverished widow washerwoman.
**Times:** Open all year Tue-Fri 10-5, Sat noon-5, Sun 10-5. Closed Mon ex BH Mon (open 10-5)

**Fee:** £3.50 (ch £1.50 accompanied by an adult, concessions £2.50). Family ticket £5
**Facilities:** ℗ Ⓟ (disabled parking adjacent) 🎋 ♿ (Braille plaques on wall, tactile tours by request, toilets), shop ⊗ (ex guide dogs) 🚌 (Pre-booking required)

**WEST YORKSHIRE**

**WEST YORKSHIRE**

## LEEDS
### Leeds Industrial Museum at Armley Mills
Canal Road Armley LS12 2QF
☎ 0113 263 7861
**Web:** www.leeds.gov.uk
**Dir:** *2m W of city centre, off A65*
Once the world's largest woollen mill, Armley Mills evokes memories of the 18th-century woollen industry, showing the progress of wool from the sheep to knitted clothing. The museum has its own 1930s cinema illustrating the history of film projection, including the first moving pictures taken in Leeds. There are demonstrations of static engines and steam locomotives, a printing gallery and a journey through the world of textiles and fashion.
**Times:** Open all year, Tue-Sat 10-5, Sun 1-5. (Last entry 1 hr before closing). Closed Mon ex BHs.
**Fee:** £3 (ch £1, concessions £1.50).
**Facilities:** ❷ ⼌ 🖼 ♿ (chair-lifts between floors, toilets), shop ⊗ 🚌 (min 10 people)

## LEEDS
### Royal Armouries Museum
Armouries Drive LS10 1LT
☎ 0113 220 1999 & 0990 106 666 🖹 0113 220 1955
**Email:** enquiries@armouries.org.uk
**Web:** www.royalarmouries.org
**Dir:** *off A61 close to Leeds centre, follow brown heritage signs.*
The museum is an impressive contemporary home for the renowned national collection of arms and armour. The collection is divided between five galleries: War, Tournament, Self-Defence, Hunting and Oriental. The Hall of Steel features a 100ft-high mass of 3000 pieces of arms and armour. Visitors are encouraged to take part in and handle some of the collections. Live demonstrations and interpretations take place throughout the year.
**Times:** Open daily, from 10-5. Closed 24-25 Dec
**Fee:** Free
**Facilities:** ❷ (charged) ⊑ (coffee shop, hot and cold food) ⼌ ♿ (induction loops, wheelchairs, signers, low level counter, toilets), shop ⊗ (ex guide & hearing dogs) 🚌

## LEEDS
### Temple Newsam Estate
LS15 0AE
☎ 0113 264 7321 (House) & 5535 (Park)
🖹 0113 260 2285
**Web:** www.leeds.gov.uk
**Dir:** *4m from city centre on A63 or 2m from M1 junct*
This Tudor and Jacobean mansion boasts extensive collections of decorative arts in their original room settings, including an incomparable Chippendale collection. Set in 1500 acres of parkland (landscaped by 'Capability' Brown), there is a Rare Breeds Centre, and the gardens have a magnificent display of rhododendrons. Free audio guides tour you around the house and tell you more about the people who lived there. On special days, visitors can join in with the laundry maids washing at the dolly tub, watch the blacksmith hammer out shoes and see logs cut at the saw-mill.
**Times:** Open all year. House: Tue-Sat 10-5, Sun 1-5; Nov-28 Dec & Mar, Tue-Sat 10-4, Sun 12-5.Open Bank Hols. Home Farm: Tue-Sun, 10-4 (3 in winter); Gardens: 10-dusk. Estate: daily, dawn-dusk. Closed Jan-Feb re-opens 28 Feb.
**Fee:** House: £3.50, Farm: £3, Joint, £5.50. Ch; House: £2.50, Farm: £2, Joint: £3.50. Family; House: £9, Farm: £8, Joint: £14.
**Facilities:** ❷ (charged) ⼌ 🖼 ♿ (ramps for full access to parkland, electric wheelchairs, toilets), shop, guided tours, audio commentaries ⊗ (ex guide dogs) 🚌 (min 10 people)

## LEEDS
### Thackray Museum
Beckett St LS9 7LN

☎ 0113 244 4343 📠 0113 247 0219

**Email:** info@thackraymuseum.org

**Web:** www.thackraymuseum.org

**Dir:** *M1 junct 43, onto M621 junct 4. Follow signs for York & St James Hospital, then brown tourist signs*

Housed in a large Victorian building, next to the famous St James's Hospital, the Thackray Museum offers a unique hands-on experience. A cow from Gloucester, green mould and smelly toilets - all these things have helped transform our lives. Walk back in time and explore the sights, sounds and smells of Victorian slum life. Also the interactive Bodyworks Gallery offers the chance to explore the workings of the human body.

**Times:** Open all year, daily 10-5.(last admission 3) Closed 24-26 & 31 Dec & 1 Jan

**Fee:** *£5.50 (ch 4-16 £4, concessions £4.50). Family ticket (2ad+3ch) £18. Group rates available.

**Facilities:** 🅿 (charged) Ⓟ (0.5m) 🍴 (hot and cold food) 🍴 📱 60p ♿ (wheelchairs, induction loop, large texts, toilets), shop ⊗ (ex guide dogs) 🚌 (booking required)

## LEEDS
### Tropical World
Canal Gardens Roundhay Park LS8 2ER

☎ 0113 266 1850 📠 0113 237 0077

**Web:** www.leeds.gov.uk

**Dir:** *3m N of city centre off A58 at Oakwood*

The atmosphere of the tropics is recreated here as visitors walk on the beach among exotic trees. A waterfall cascades into a rock-pool and other pools contain terrapins and carp. There are reptiles, insects and more than 30 species of butterfly. Feel the dry heat of the desert and the darkness of the nocturnal zone, and watch out for the piranhas and other exotic fish in the depths of the aquarium.

**Times:** *Open Winter (GMT), daily 10-4 (last admission 3.30); Summer (BST), 10-6 (last admission 5.30)

**Fee:** *£3 (ch 8-15 £2, under 8's & Leeds card holders free)

**Facilities:** 🅿 Ⓟ (street outside) ♿ (toilets), shop ⊗ (ex guide dogs) 🚌 pre-book and term time only

## OAKWELL HALL
### Oakwell Hall
Nutter Lane Birstall WF17 9LG

☎ 01924 326240 📠 01924 326249

**Email:** oakwell.hall@kirklees.gov.uk

**Web:** www.oakwellhallcountrypark.co.uk

**Dir:** *6m SE of Bradford, off M62 junct 26/27, follow brown heritage signs, turn off A652 onto Nutter Lane*

A moated Elizabethan manor house, furnished as it might have looked in the 1690s. Extensive 110-acre country park with visitor information centre, period gardens, nature trails, arboretum and children's adventure playground.

**Times:** Open all year, daily Mon-Fri 11-5; Sat & Sun 12-5. Closed Good Fri & 24 Dec-1 Jan.

**Fee:** *Hall £1.50 (ch & wheelchair users 60p). Family ticket £3.30. Charges Mar-Oct. Free admission Nov-Feb. Vistor centre and park free all year.

**Facilities:** 🅿 Ⓟ (0.5m - charge made on major event days) 🍴 (Oak Tree Cafe) 🍴 ♿ (large print & Braille guide, induction loops, toilets), shop, guided tours ⊗ (ex guide dogs) 🚌 (booking essential)

## WAKEFIELD
### National Coal Mining Museum For England
Caphouse Colliery New Road Wakefield WF4 4RH
☎ 01924 848806 🖹 01924 844567
**Email:** info@ncm.org.uk
**Web:** www.ncm.org.uk
**Dir:** *on A642 between Huddersfield & Horbury*
A unique opportunity to go 140 metres underground down one of Britain's oldest working mines. Take a step back in time with one of the museum's experienced local miners who will guide parties around the under-ground workings, where models and machinery depict methods and conditions of mining from the early 1800s to present day. Other attractions include the Hope Pit, pit-head baths, Victorian steam winder, nature trail and adventure playground and meet the last ever working pit ponies. You are strongly advised to wear sensible footwear and warm clothing.
**Times:** Open all year, daily 10-5. Closed 24-26 Dec & 1 Jan.
**Fee:** Free
**Facilities:** ℗ ⊑ (licensed) 🍽 (licensed) ⋔ 📋 £1 ♿ (induction loop, audio tours, 2 w'chairs for underground, toilets), shop 🚫 (ex guide dogs) 🚌

## WAKEFIELD
### Wakefield Art Gallery
Wentworth Terrace WF1 3QW
☎ 01924 305796 🖹 01924 305770
**Email:** museumsandarts@wakefield.gov.uk
**Web:** www.wakefield.gov.uk/cultureandleisure
**Dir:** *N of city centre by Wakefield College and Clayton Hospital*
Wakefield was home to two of Britain's greatest modern sculptors - Barbara Hepworth and Henry Moore. The art gallery, which has an important collection of 20th-century paintings and sculptures, has a special room devoted to these two local artists. There are frequent temporary exhibitions of both modern and earlier works.
**Times:** Open all year, Tue-Sat 10.30-4.30, Sun 2-4.30.
**Fee:** Free
**Facilities:** ℗ (on street parking restricted to 2hrs) ⋔ 📋 ♿ shop 🚫 (ex guide dogs) 🚌 pre-book required 🐾

## WEST BRETTON
### Yorkshire Sculpture Park
Wakefield WF4 4LG
☎ 01924 832631 🖹 01924 832600
**Email:** info@ysp.co.uk
**Web:** www.ysp.co.uk
**Dir:** *M1 junct 38, follow brown heritage signs to A637. Left at rdbt, attraction signed*
Set in the beautiful grounds and gardens of a 500 acre, 18th-century country estate, this is one of the world's leading open-air galleries and presents a changing programme of international sculpture exhibitions. The landscape provides a variety of magnificent scenic vistas of the valley and lakes. The Visitor Centre provides all-weather facilities including a large restaurant, shop, coffee bar, audio-visual auditorium and meeting rooms.
**Times:** *Open all year 10-6 (summer) 10-5 (winter). Please phone for details of Xmas closures
**Fee:** *Free. Car parking £3, coaches £8
**Facilities:** ℗ (charged) 🍽 (licensed) ⋔ ♿ (free scooters, parking, trail accessible for wheelchairs, toilets), shop guided tours 🚫 (ex assist dogs) 🚌 (Pre-bookings only. 01924 830642) 🐾

# South & East England

A line of punts for hire on the willow tree lined River Cam, Cambridge

**BEDFORDSHIRE**

## BEDFORD

### Bedford Museum

Castle Lane MK40 3XD

☎ 01234 353323 🖺 01234 273401

**Email:** bmuseum@bedford.gov.uk

**Web:** www.bedfordmuseum.org

**Dir:** *close to town bridge and Embankment*

Embark on a fascinating journey through the human and natural history of north Bedfordshire, pausing briefly to glimpse at wonders from more distant lands. Go back in time and visit the delightful rural room sets and the Old School Museum, where Blackbeard's Sword, 'Old Billy' the record breaking longest-living horse, and numerous other treasures and curiosities can be found. Housed in the former Higgins and Sons Brewery, Bedford Museum is situated within the gardens of what was once Bedford Castle, beside the Great Ouse embankment. The courtyard and galleries provide an excellent setting for the varied collections.

**Times:** *Open all year, Tue-Sat 11-5, Sun 2-5. (Closed Mon ex BH Mon afternoon, Good Fri & Xmas).

**Fee:** *Free

**Facilities:** ℗ (50mtrs) 🏻 📱 ♿ (lift available on request, subject to staff availability, toilets), shop ⊗ (ex guide dogs) 🚌

## LEIGHTON BUZZARD

### Leighton Buzzard Railway

Pages Park Station Billington Road LU7 4TN

☎ 01525 373888 🖺 01525 377814

**Email:** info@buzzrail.co.uk

**Web:** www.buzzrail.co.uk

**Dir:** *0.75m SE on A4146 signposted in and around Leighton Buzzard, near rdbt junct with A505*

The Leighton Buzzard Railway offers a 70-minute journey into the vanished world of the English light railway, with its sharp curves, steep gradients, level crossings and unique roadside running. Built in 1919 to serve the local sand industry, the railway has carried a steam passenger service, operated by volunteers, since 1968.

**Times:** Open 11 Mar-28 Oct, Sun; 9 Apr, 7 & 28 May & 27 Aug, Mon; 31 Jul-21 Aug, Tue; 4 & 11 Apr, 30 May-22 Aug & 24 Oct, Wed; 2-23 Aug, Thu; 6 Apr, Fri; 7 Apr, 5 & 26 May, 4 Aug-15 Sep & 6 Oct, Sat.

**Fee:** Return ticket £6 (ch 2-15 £3, ch under 2 free, concessions £5). Party 10+.

**Facilities:** ⊕ ℗ 🏻 📱 ♿ (platform & train access for wheelchairs, toilets) shop guided tours 🚌 (advance booking essential)

## LUTON

### Stockwood Park Museum

Stockwood Country Park Farley Hill LU1 4BH

☎ 01582 738714 & 546739 🖺 01582 546763

**Email:** museum.gallery@luton.gov.uk

**Web:** www.luton.gov.uk/museums

**Dir:** *signposted from M1 junct 10 and from Hitchin, Dunstable, Bedford and from Luton town centre*

The Museum is set in period gardens which incorporate the Ian Hamilton Finlay Sculpture Gardens. The Mossman collection of horse-drawn vehicles traces the history of transport from Roman times to the 1940s. Craft demonstrations are held at weekends in the summer. Please telephone for details of special events.

**Times:** *Open all year; Mar-Oct, Tue-Sun 10-5; Nov-Mar, wknds 10-4. (closed Xmas & 1 Jan)

**Fee:** *Free

**Facilities:** ⊕ ℗ (200mtrs - coach parking by appointment) 🏻 📱 ♿ (stair lift, parking, induction loop, automatic door, toilets) shop audio commentaries ⊗ (ex guide & hearing dogs) 🚌 (advance bookings) ♿

## OLD WARDEN
### The Shuttleworth Collection
Old Warden Park SG18 9EA
☎ 01767 627927 📄 01767 627949
**Web:** www.shuttleworth.org
**Dir:** *2m W from rdbt on A1, Biggleswade by-pass*
Housed in eight hangars on a classic grass aerodrome, 40 working historic aeroplanes span the progress of aviation with exhibits ranging from a 1909 Bleriot to a 1941 Spitfire. A garage of roadworthy motor vehicles explores the eras of the 1898 Panhard Levassor to the Railton sports car of 1937. The 19th-century coach house displays horse-drawn vehicles from 1880 to 1914.
**Times:** Open Apr-Oct 10-5 (last admission 4), Nov-Mar 10-4 (last admission 3). Closed Xmas-New Year.
**Fee:** *£8 (concessions £7). Most flying displays £16.

**Facilities:** 🅿 🍴 (Licensed) ⛱ 🗐 £3 ♿ (wheelchairs, toilets) shop guided tours ⊗ (ex on leads/guide dogs) 🚍

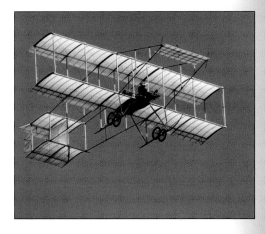

## SANDY
### RSPB Nature Reserve
The Lodge Shop SG19 2DL
☎ 01767 680541 📄 01767 683508
**Email:** claire.wallace@rspb.org.uk
**Web:** www.rspb.org.uk
**Dir:** *1m E, on B1042 Potton road*
The headquarters of the Royal Society for the Protection of Birds. The house and buildings are not open to the public, but there are waymarked paths and formal gardens, and two species of woodpecker, nuthatches and woodland birds may be seen, as may muntjac deer. Another feature is the specialist wildlife garden created in conjunction with the Henry Doubleday Association.
**Times:** *Open all year, Mon-Fri 9-5, Sat, Sun & BHs 10-5. Closed 25-26 Dec.

**Fee:** *£3 (ch under 16 £1, concessions £1.50). Family ticket (2ad+2ch) £6.
**Facilities:** 🅿 🅿 (300mtrs) ⛱ ♿ (partial access, toilets), shop ⊗ (ex in restricted areas) 🚍

## WHIPSNADE
### Whipsnade Wild Animal Park
Dunstable LU6 2LF
☎ 01582 872171 📄 01582 872649
**Email:** marketing@zsl.org
**Web:** www.whipsnade.co.uk
**Dir:** *signposted from M1 junct 9 & 12*
Located in beautiful Bedfordshire countryside, Whipsnade is home to more than 2,500 rare and exotic animals and is one of the largest conservation centres in Europe. Hop aboard the Jumbo Express, a fantastic steam train experience, and see elephants, rhino, yaks, camels and deer, along with wild horses, and learn about their lives in the wilds of Asia and Africa. Other highlights include the Lions of the Serengeti, the sealion pool, and Birds of the World. The Discover Centre is home to tamarins, turtles, big snakes and sea horses among others. Visitors can also enjoy the picnic areas, keeper talks and animal shows.
**Times:** Open all year, daily. (Closed 25 Dec). Closing times vary.
**Fee:** Seasonal pricing. Telephone or see website for up-to-date pricing.
**Facilities:** 🅿 (charged) ⛱ 🗐 £3.50 ♿ (1 carer free per registered disabled visitor, toilets), shop, guided tours ⊗ 🚍 (must use car park outside)

### WILDEN
**Bedford Butterfly Park**
Renhold Road MK44 2PX
☎ 01234 772770 📄 01234 772773
**Email:** enquiries@bedford-butterflies.co.uk
**Web:** www.bedford-butterflies.co.uk
**Dir:** *Signed from Gt Barford, E of Bedford*
Wildflower meadows, wildlife garden and bird hide are just a few of the countryside pleasures to be enjoyed at the park. A tropical house features exotic flowers, butterflies, waterfalls and ponds. Children's activities are a regular event at weekends and during the holidays.
**Times:** Open 4 Jan-4 Feb & 8 Nov-23 Dec, Thu-Sun 10-4. Daily 8 Feb-4 Nov, 10-5.
**Fee:** Jan-mid Feb & Nov-Dec £4.25 (ch under 16yrs £3.50, under 3yrs free, concessions £3.50). Mid Feb-Oct £4.75 (ch under 16yrs £3.90, under 3yrs free, concessions £4.25).
**Facilities:** 🅿 ☕ (light lunch & afternoon tea) 🪑 📷 ♿ (toilets), shop, guided tours ⊗ (ex guide dogs) 🚌 (pre book only)

### WOBURN
**Woburn Abbey**
MK17 9WA
☎ 01525 290333 📄 01525 290271
**Email:** admissions@woburnabbey.co.uk
**Web:** www.discoverwoburn.co.uk
**Dir:** *Just off M1 junct 12/13*
Set in a beautiful 3,000 acre deer park, Woburn Abbey has been the home of the Russell family for nearly 400 years, and is now occupied by the 15th Duke of Bedford. Built on a Cistercian Monastery founded in 1145, the Abbey was given to the 1st Earl in the will of Henry VIII. It houses one of the most important private art collections in the world, including paintings by Gainsborough, Reynolds, Van Dyck and Cuyp. Wooburn Abbey is where the concept of afternoon tea was introduced by Anna Maria, wife of the 7th Duke, back in the 19th century. There are extensive formal gardens and a fine antiques centre.
**Times:** * 8 Apr-1 Oct
**Fee:** *Deer Park & Abbey Grounds £2. House £10.50 (ch 5-15yrs £6, under 5's free, concessions £9.50)
**Facilities:** 🅿 🍽 (Licensed) 🪑 ♿ (wheelchairs accommodated by prior arrangement, toilets), shop, guided tours, audio commentaries ⊗ 🚌

### WOBURN
**Woburn Safari Park**
Woburn Park MK17 9QN
☎ 01525 290407 📄 01525 290489
**Email:** info@woburnsafari.co.uk
**Web:** www.discoverwoburn.co.uk
**Dir:** *Signposted from M1 junct 13*
Set in the 3,000 acres of parkland belonging to Woburn Abbey, Woburn Safari Park has an extensive collection of many species. Visitors can tour the reserves from the safety of their own car, and experience the thrill of being alongside white rhino, buffalo, giraffes and Siberian tigers. Walk-through areas are home to wallabies, squirrel monkeys, and lemurs, and feature a full programme of keeper talks and demonstrations. All attractions are included in the entry price.
**Times:** *11 Mar-29 Oct 10-5. 30 Oct-9 Mar wknds only 11-3. (Closed 23-24 Dec)
**Fee:** *Please phone for details
**Facilities:** 🅿 🍽 (Licensed) 🪑 📷 ♿ (toilets) shop guided tours audio commentaries (charged) ⊗ 🚌

## BRACKNELL
### The Look Out Discovery Centre
Nine Mile Ride RG12 7QW
☎ 01344 354400 🖷 01344 354422
**Email:** thelookout@bracknell-forest.gov.uk
**Web:** www.bracknell-forest.gov.uk/lookout
**Dir:** *3m S of town centre. From M3 junct 3, take A322 to Bracknell and from M4 junct 10, take A329(M) to Bracknell. Follow brown tourist signs*

A hands-on, interactive science and nature exhibition where budding scientists can spend many hours exploring and discovering over 70 fun-filled exhibits within five themed zones, linked to the National Curriculum. Zones include Light and Colour, Forces and Movement and the Body and Perception. A new exciting zone, Woodland and Water, has a vortex, stream, ant colony and many more interactive exhibits. Climb the 88 steps to the Look Out tower and look towards Bracknell and beyond or enjoy a nature walk in the surrounding 2,600 acres of Crown Estate woodland. Interactive shows for the public and schools running throughout the year. Please note the tower is closed when wet.

**Times:** Open all year (Closed 24-26 Dec, 8-12 Jan)
**Fee:** £5.20 (ch & concessions £3.45). Family (2 ad + 2 ch or 1 ad + 3 ch) £13.85.
**Facilities:** 🅿 Ⓟ (100mtrs - No cars to park in coach parking area) ☕ (Hot/cold food & drinks) ⛱ 🗇 £1.95 ♿ (lift to 1st floor, toilets), shop ⊗ (ex guide dogs) 🚌 (pre book)

## HAMPSTEAD NORREYS
### The Living Rainforest
RG18 0TN
☎ 01635 202444 🖷 01635 202440
**Email:** enquiries@livingrainforest.org
**Web:** www.livingrainforest.org
**Dir:** *follow brown tourist signs from M4/A34*

By providing education and supporting research into the relationship between humanity and the rainforests, this wonderful attraction hopes to promote a more sustainable future. Visitors to the Living Rainforest will see plants and wildlife that are under threat in their natural habitat, and be encouraged to take part in a large variety of activities, workshops and exhibitions.

**Times:** *Open all year daily 10-5.15. (Closed from 1pm 24 Dec & 25-26 Dec)
**Fee:** *£5.95 (concessions £5.35, ch 5-14 £3.95 & ch 3-4 £2.95)
**Facilities:** 🅿 ☕ (Serves baguettes, tea, coffee, cakes) ⛱ ♿ (toilets), shop ⊗ (ex guide dogs) 🚌

## LOWER BASILDON
### Beale Park
Lower Basildon Reading RG8 9NH
☎ 0870 777 7160 🖷 0870 777 7120
**Web:** www.bealepark.co.uk
**Dir:** *M4 junct 12, follow brown tourist signs to Pangbourne, A329 towards Oxford*

Beale Park is home to an extraordinary collection of birds and animals including peacocks, swans, owls and parrots. It also offers a steam railway, rare breeds of farm animals, a great pet corner, meerkats, wallabies, ring-tailed lemurs, a deer park, three splash pools, a huge adventure playground, acres of gardens, and sculptures in a traditional, family park beside the Thames. There are summer riverboat trips and excellent lake and river fishing.

**Times:** Open Mar-Oct.
**Fee:** £6.50 (ch £4.50, under 2 free, pen £5.50). Family (2 & 2 ch) £20
**Facilities:** 🅿 🍽 (Licensed) ⛱ ♿ (wheelchair available, parking, toilets), shop ⊗ (ex guide dogs) 🚌 (advance bookings preferred) 🈺

**BERKSHIRE**

**BERKSHIRE**

## READING
### Museum of English Rural Life
University of Reading Redlands Road RG1 5EX
☎ 0118 378 8660 📄 0118 378 5632
Email: merl@reading.ac.uk
Web: www.merl.org.uk
Dir: *close to the Royal Berkshire Hospital*
Recently moved to larger premises, this museum houses
a national collection of agricultural, domestic and crafts
exhibits, including wagons, tools and a wide range of
other equipment used in the English countryside over
the last 150 years. Special facilities are available for
school parties. The museum also contains extensive
documentary and photographic archives, which can be
studied by appointment. There is a regular programme
of events and activities, please see website for details.

Times: *Open all year, Tue-Fri, 10-4.30, Sat & Sun
2-4.30 (Closed BHs & Xmas-New Year).
Fee: *Free
Facilities: ℗ 📄 ᬥ (Chair lifts, hearing loop, toilets),
shop ⊗ (ex guide dogs) 🚌 ♿

## RISELEY
### Wellington Country Park
Reading RG7 1SP
☎ 0118 932 6444 📄 0118 932 6445
Email: info@wellington-country-park.co.uk
Web: www.wellington-country-park.co.uk
Dir: *signposted off A33, between Reading & Basingstoke*
All the ingredients of a family day out are provided in 350
acres of woodland walks, barbecues and picnic areas,
nature trails, adventure playground and fishing lake.
Attractions appealing to younger and older children
include; miniature railway, variety of children's play
areas, crazy golf and 'in season' rowing boat hire. The
park also has a highly recommended touring campsite.
Times: Open Mar-Oct, daily 10-5.30.
Fee: *£6 (ch £4, under 3's free, concessions £5)

Facilities: ℗ ☐ (Drinks & snacks) 🎋 ᬥ (fishing platform
& nature trail, toilets) shop 🚌 (advanced notice required)

## WINDSOR
### LEGOLAND Windsor
Winkfield Road SL4 4AY
Email: customer.services@legoland.co.uk
Web: www.legoland.co.uk
Dir: *on B3022 Windsor to Ascot road signposted
from M3 junct 3 & M4 junct 6*
With over 50 interactive rides, live shows, building
workshops, driving schools and attractions. Set in
150 acres of beautiful parkland, LEGOLAND Windsor
is a different sort of family theme park. An atmospheric
and unique experience for the whole family, a visit to
LEGOLAND Windsor is more than a day out, it's a lifetime
of memories.
Times: *Open daily 12 Mar-5 Nov
Fee: *£24 (ch £22)

Facilities: ℗ (charged) ℗ ☐ (various) 🎋
ᬥ (signing staff, wheelchair hire, parking, toilets), shop
⊗ (ex guide dogs) 🚌 (pre-booking 2wks)

## WINDSOR
**Windsor Castle**
SL4 1NJ
☎ 020 7766 7304 📠 020 7930 9625
**Email:** bookinginfo@royalcollection.org.uk
**Web:** www.royalcollection.org.uk
**Dir:** *M4 junct 6 & M3 junct 3*
Covering 13 acres, this is the official residence of HM The Queen, and the largest inhabited castle in the world. Begun as a wooden fort by William the Conqueror, almost every monarch since has contributed to the further development of the castle. A visit will take in the magnificent state apartments, St George's chapel, Queen Mary's dolls house, the drawings gallery, and between October and March, the semi-state rooms created by George IV.

**Times:** Open all year, daily except Good Fri, 19 Jun & 25-26 Dec. Nov-Feb, 9.45-4.15 (last admission 3), Mar-Oct 9.45-5.15 (last admission 4). As Windsor Castle is a royal residence the opening arrangements may be subject to change at short notice - 24hr info line 01753 831118
**Fee:** *£13.50 (ch under 17 £7.50, under 5's free, concessions £12) Family ticket £34.50 (2ad+3ch)
**Facilities:** ℗ (400yds) 🍴 ♿ (contact 020 7766 7324, toilets) shop guided tours audio commentaries 🚫 (ex guide dogs) 🚌 (no parking)

## AYLESBURY
**Tiggywinkles Visitor Centre & Hedgehog World Museum**
Aston Road HP17 8AF
☎ 01844 292511
**Email:** mail@sttiggywinkles.org.uk
**Web:** www.tiggywinkles.com
**Dir:** *Turn off A418 towards Haddenham then follow signs to 'Wildlife Hospital'*
Look through the glass into our bird and mammal nursery wards in the hospital. Find out all about the hospital, our patients and their treatment on our education boards dotted around the gardens. See some of the other hospital wards on our CCTV monitor. Wander round the world's first Hedgehog Memorabilia Museum or watch the foxes in their permanent enclosure. Try to catch a glimpse of one of our permanent badgers or see the deer in the recovery paddocks. The animals live as natural a life as possible, so don't be surprised if they do not come out to visit.
**Times:** *Open Etr-Sep, daily 10-4
**Fee:** *£4.20 (ch & concessions £3). Family ticket £12.20.
**Facilities:** ℗ 🍴 20p ♿ shop 🚫 📷

## BEACONSFIELD
**Bekonscot Model Village and Railway**
Warwick Road HP9 2PL
☎ 01494 672919 📠 01494 675284
**Email:** info@bekonscot.co.uk
**Web:** www.bekonscot.com
**Dir:** *M40 junct 2, 4m M25 junct 16, take A355 and follow signs to Model Village*
A miniature world, depicting rural England in the 1930s. A Gauge 1 model railway meanders through six little villages, each with their own tiny population and town/country landscapes. Rides on the sit-on miniature railway (with its recent extension) take place weekends and school holidays.
**Times:** Open mid Feb-Oct, 10-5.
**Fee:** Telephone for prices

**Facilities:** ℗ ℗ (10mtrs) 🍴 25p ♿ (wheelchair loan by prior booking, toilets), shop 🚫 (ex guide dogs) 🚌 (preferably pre-booked)

**BERKSHIRE / BUCKINGHAMSHIRE**

### BLETCHLEY
**Bletchley Park**

The Mansion Bletchley Park Milton Keynes MK3 6EB

☎ 01908 640404 📠 01908 274381

**Email:** info@bletchleypark.org.uk

**Web:** www.bletchleypark.org.uk

**Dir:** *Approach Bletchley from V7 Saxon St. At rdbt, southern end of Saxon St under railway bridge towards Buckingham & follow signs to Bletchley Park*

Known as 'Station X' during World War II, this was the home of the secret scientific team that worked to decipher German military messages sent using the Enigma code machine. Visitors can find out more about the Enigma machine; the 'bombes', computers used to crack the code; Alan Turing who worked on the project; as well as see a number of other displays including the use of pigeons during the war, wartime vehicles, and a Churchill collection.

**Times:** *Open daily 9.30-5.30 (Tours at 11 & 2). Wknds open 10.30-5. Closed 25 & 26 Dec.

**Fee:** *£10 (ch & conc £8) Family £25 under 8's free.

**Facilities:** 🅿 (charged) Ⓟ (500yds - off site parking free) ⚘ ♿ (toilets), shop 🚌

### CHALFONT ST GILES
**Chiltern Open Air Museum**

Newland Park Gorelands Lane HP8 4AB

☎ 01494 871117 📠 01494 872774

**Email:** coamuseum@netscape.net

**Web:** www.coam.org.uk

**Dir:** *M25 junct 17, M40 junct 2. Follow brown signs*

Saved from demolition and moved brick by brick to Newland Park, this collection of old buildings includes barns, granaries and even a tin chapel. Step back in time and get a feel of the 1940s in a fully furnished Prefab, or experience 50AD at the Iron Age House. Demonstrations at Chiltern including brick making, rug making, black smithing and storytelling. Regular living history re-enactments.

**Times:** *Open 31 Mar-Oct, daily 10-5.

**Fee:** *£6 (ch £3.50, concessions £5) Family ticket (2 adults & 2 ch) £16.50.

**Facilities:** 🅿 ⚘ ♿ (Braille guide books & taped guides available, wheelchairs, toilets), shop ⊗ (ex on lead) 🚌 (advanced booking required)

### GREAT MISSENDEN
**The Roald Dahl Museum & Story Centre**

81-83 High Street HP16 0AL

☎ 01494 892192 📠 01494 892191

**Email:** info@roalddahlmuseum.org

**Web:** www.roalddahlmuseum.org

**Dir:** *From London/Amersham turn left off A413 into Great Missenden link road*

Roald Dahl's life and displays from his unique archive in the village where he lived for over 70 years. Discover more of the world famous writer and some of his contemporaries. Unearth secrets about the people and places which inspired Dahl's tales, and in interactive galleries, discover how he wrote. Use the touch-screens to read his hand written notes and visit a replica of his writing hut. Check out top tips from today's leading authors - use your own Ideas Book just as Dahl did and you too could be a writer! Rolling programme of workshops and events.

**Times:** *Open all year, Tue-Fri & BH Mon 10-5. Closed 25-26 Dec

**Fee:** *£4.50 (ch 3-18 & concessions £3.50, under 3's free). Family ticket £15

**Facilities:** Ⓟ (3 mins walk) ⚘ ♿ (audio loops, tactile maps, toilets), shop ⊗ (ex assist dogs)

## MIDDLE CLAYDON
### Claydon House
Buckingham MK18 2EY

☎ 01296 730349 📠 01296 738511

**Email:** claydon@nationaltrust.org.uk

**Web:** www.nationaltrust.org.uk

**Dir:** *M40 junct 9 off A413 in Padbury, follow National Trust signs. Entrance by north drive only*

The rather sober exterior of this 18th-century house gives no clue to the extravagances that lie inside, in the form of fantastic rococo carvings. Ceilings, cornices, walls and overmantels are adorned with delicately carved fruits, birds, beasts and flowers by Luke Lightfoot. The Chinese room is particularly splendid. There is also a spectacular parquetry staircase.

**Times:** *House Open 25 Mar-29 Oct, Sat-Wed 1-5. Last admission 4.30. (Closed Good Fri).

**Fee:** *£5.50 (ch £2.70). Family ticket £13. Grounds £4.50. Private Gardens £2.50

**Facilities:** ℗ 🍴 (Licensed) 🪑 🏷 (50p-£3.50) ♿ (Braille guide, photograph albums, toilets) guided tours 🚫 (ex guide dogs or in park) 🚌 (max 2 coaches per day) 🌺 ♻

## QUAINTON
### Buckinghamshire Railway Centre
Quainton Road Station Aylesbury HP22 4BY

☎ 01296 655720 📠 01296 655720

**Email:** bucksrailcentre@btopenworld.com

**Web:** www.bucksrailcentre.org

**Dir:** *Signed off A41 (Aylesbury-Bicester road) at Waddesdon, 7m NW of Aylesbury*

Housed in a former Grade II listed building, the Centre features an interesting and varied collection of about 20 locomotives with 40 carriages and wagons from places as far afield as South Africa, Egypt and America. Items date from the 1800s up to the 1960s. Visitors can take a ride on full-size and miniature steam trains, and stroll around the 20-acre site to see locomotives and rolling stock. The Centre runs locomotive driving courses for visitors. Regular 'Days out with Thomas' events take place throughout the year.

**Times:** *Open with engines in steam Apr-Oct, Sun & BH Mon; School hol Wed; 10.30-5.30. Dec Sat & Sun Santa's Magical Steamings-advanced booking essential. Also open for static viewing Wed-Sat.

**Fee:** *Steaming Days; £6 (ch & pen £4). Family ticket £18. BH wknds £7 (ch & pen £5). Family ticket £20. Static viewing £3 (ch & pen £2).

**Facilities:** ℗ 🪑 ♿ (ramped bridge with wheelchair lift, toilets), shop 🚌

## WADDESDON
### Waddesdon Manor
Aylesbury HP18 0JH

☎ 01296 653211, 653226 & 653203

📠 01296 653212

**Email:** waddesdonmanor@nationaltrust.org.uk

**Web:** www.waddesdon.org.uk

**Dir:** *entrance off A41, 6m NW of Aylesbury*

Built in the 19th century by Baron Ferdinand de Rothschild, this French-style chateau was created as a showcase for his fine collection of French decorative arts. Its Victorian gardens are known for its parterre, seasonal displays, walks, views, fountains and statues. The aviary is stocked with species that were once part of Baron Ferdinand's collection and the wine cellar contains Rothschild wines dating back to 1868. Special

**Events:** Please telephone 01296 653226 for details of events running throughout the year.

**Times:** *Gardens: 29 Mar-23 Dec, Wed-Sun & BH Mons 10-5.Open 18-19 Dec. 7 Jan-26 Mar wknds only. House: 29 Mar-29 Oct, Wed-Sun & BH Mons 11-4. (East Wing for Xmas 15 Nov-23 Dec Wed-Sun & 18-19 Dec 12-4).

**Fee:** *House & Gardens £12 (ch £8.50), pre-Xmas £9 (ch £4.50). Gardens £5 (ch £2.50). Bachelors Wing £3 (Under 5's free).

**Facilities:** ℗ 🍴 (Licensed) ♿ (wheelchairs, Braille guide, parking, scented plants, toilets), shop, audio commentaries (charged) 🚫 (ex guide dogs) 🚌 (pre book) 🌺

## WEST WYCOMBE
### The Hell-Fire Caves
High Wycombe HP14 3AJ
☎ 01494 524411 (office) & 533739 (caves)
📄 01494 471617
**Email:** mary@west-wycombe-estate.co.uk
**Web:** www.hellfirecaves.co.uk
**Dir:** *on A40 in West Wycombe*
The entrance to West Wycombe caves is halfway up the hill that dominates the village. On the summit stands the parish church and the mausoleum of the Dashwood family. The caves are not natural but were dug on the orders of Sir Francis Dashwood between 1748 and 1752. Sir Francis, the Chancellor of the Exchequer, was also the founder of the Hell Fire Club, whose members were reputed to have held outrageous and blasphemous parties in the caves, which extend approximately half a mile underground. The entrance, from a large forecourt, is a brick tunnel that leads into the caves, where tableaux and curiosities are exhibited.
**Times:** Open all year, Apr-Oct, daily 11-6; Nov-Mar, Sat & Sun 1-5.
**Fee:** *£4 (ch, concessions £3). Family ticket £12 (max 3 ch)
**Facilities:** 🅿 🅿 (200mtrs) 🍵 (tearoom) 🚻 ♿ (toilets), shop 🚫 (ex guide dogs) 🚌 (advance booking)

## CAMBRIDGE
### Cambridge & County Folk Museum
2/3 Castle Street CB3 0AQ
☎ 01223 355159
**Email:** info@folkmuseum.org.uk
**Web:** www.folkmuseum.org.uk
**Dir:** *off A14 onto A3019, museum NW of town*
This timber-framed inn houses items covering the everyday life of the people of Cambridgeshire from the early times to the present day. There are also temporary exhibitions. Special exhibitions and children's activity days take place throughout the year. Please telephone for details.
**Times:** *Open all year, Apr-Sep, Mon-Sat 10.30-5, Sun 2-5. Oct-Mar, Tue-Sat 10.30-5, Sun 2-5. (Last admissions 30 mins before closing). Closed 1 Jan, Good Fri, 24-31 Dec
**Fee:** *£3 (ch 5-12 £1, concessions £2) one free ch with every full paying adult.
**Facilities:** 🅿 (300yds - pay and display on street parking) 🚻 ♿ (Braille touch tables, tape guides & large print guides, toilets), shop 🚫 (ex guide dogs) 🚌 (pre-booking essential) 🎫

## CAMBRIDGE
### Cambridge University Botanic Garden
Cory Lodge Bateman Street CB2 1JF
☎ 01223 336265 📄 01223 336278
**Email:** enquiries@botanic.cam.ac.uk
**Web:** www.botanic.cam.ac.uk
**Dir:** *1m S of city centre*
The Cambridge University Botanic Garden is a 40-acre oasis of beautifully landscaped gardens and glasshouses close to the heart of the historic city. Opened on its present site in 1846, the garden showcases a collection of some 8000 plant species. This Grade II heritage landscape features the Rock Garden, displaying alpine plants, the Winter and Autumn Gardens, tropical rainforest and seasonal displays in the Glasshouses, the historic Systematic Beds, the Scented Garden, Herbaceous Beds and the finest collection of trees in the east of England.
**Times:** *Open all year daily Apr-Sep 10-6; Feb-Mar, Oct 10-5, Nov-Jan 10-4. Glasshouses close 30mins before garden. Please call to check Christmas closure. Entry by Bateman St & Station Rd gates on wkdays & by Bateman St gate only at wknds & BH.
**Fee:** £3 (concessions £2.50).
**Facilities:** 🅿 (on street parking or park & ride) 🍵 (closes 30mins before garden) 🚻 🎟 £2 ♿ (guiding service, manual & motorised wheelchairs-prebooked, toilets), shop, guided tours 🚫 (ex guide dogs) 🚌 (pre book) 🎫

## CAMBRIDGE
### Scott Polar Research Institute Museum
Lensfield Road CB2 1ER
☎ 01223 336540 🖹 01223 336549
**Email:** enquiries@spri.cam.ac.uk
**Web:** www.spri.cam.ac.uk
**Dir:** *1km S of City Centre*

An international centre for polar studies, including a museum featuring displays of Arctic and Antarctic expeditions, with special emphasis on those of Captain Scott's attempts to reach the South Pole as well as the exploration of the Northwest Passage in the late 19th and early 20th centuries. Other exhibits include Eskimo work and other arts of the polar regions, as well as displays on current scientific exploration. Public lectures run from October to December and February to April.

**Times:** *Open all year, Tue-Sat 2.30-4. Closed some BHs wknds, public & university hols.
**Fee:** *Free
**Facilities:** ℗ (400mtrs) 🗐 ♿ shop ⊗ (ex guide dogs) 🚌 (pre-booking essential) ♨

## DUXFORD
### Imperial War Museum Duxford
Cambridge CB2 4QR
☎ 01223 835000 🖹 01223 837267
**Email:** duxford@iwm.org.uk
**Web:** www.iwm.org.uk
**Dir:** *off M11 junct 10, on A505*

Duxford is one of the world's most spectacular aviation heritage complexes with a collection of nearly 200 aircraft, the American Air Museum and a fine collection of military vehicles plus special exhibitions including The Battle of Britain, Normandy Experience and Monty. The Museum holds four Air Shows throughout the summer plus other special events such as the Military Vehicle Show and Flying Proms. The museum also has its very own history serving as an airbase in both World Wars.

**Times:** *Open all year, mid Mar-mid Oct daily 10-6; mid Oct-mid Mar daily 10-4. (Closed 24-26 Dec)
**Fee:** *£13 (pen £11 & concessions £8). (Ch under 16yrs free). Different rates apply for air shows.
**Facilities:** ℗ ⊡ (2 cafés) 🍴 (Licensed) ⊼ ♿ (w/chair available-phone in advance, ramps, toilets) shop guided tours ⊗ (ex guide dogs) 🚌

## ELY
### Ely Cathedral
CB7 4DL
☎ 01353 667735 🖹 01353 665658
**Email:** receptionist@cathedral.ely.anglican.org
**Web:** www.cathedral.ely.anglican.org
**Dir:** *A10 or A142, 15m from Cambridge*

The Octagon Tower of Ely Cathedral can be seen for miles as it rises above the surrounding flat fenland. A monastery was founded on the site by St Etheldreda in 673, but the present cathedral church dates from 1083 and is a magnificent example of Romanesque architecture.

**Times:** *Open daily, Summer 7-7, Winter 7.30-6 (5pm Sun).
**Fee:** £5.20 (ch free in family group). (concessions £4.50). Group reductions (15+)
**Facilities:** ℗ (walking distance) ⊼ ♿ (touch tour for blind/partially sighted, toilets) shop guided tours ⊗ (ex assist dogs) 🚌 (pre-book)

## HAMERTON
### Hamerton Zoo Park
Nr Sawtry PE28 5RE
☎ 01832 293362 🖹 01832 293677
**Email:** office@hamertonzoopark.com
**Web:** www.hamertonzoopark.com
**Dir:** *off A1 junct 15, signed Sawtry*
A wildlife breeding centre, dedicated to the practical conservation of endangered species including gibbons, marmosets, lemurs, wildcats, meerkats, sloths and many more. There is also a large and varied bird collection, with several species unique to Hamerton. Over 120 species in all. Other attractions include a children's play area, and new creature contact sessions.
**Times:** *Open Summer daily 10.30-6; Winter daily 10.30-4. Closed 25 Dec

**Fee:** *Prices on application
**Facilities:** 𝐏 🏕 ⅍ (toilets), shop ⊗ 🚌

## LINTON
### Linton Zoological Gardens
Hadstock Road CB1 6NT
☎ 01223 891308 🖹 01223 891308
**Web:** www.lintonzoo.co.uk
**Dir:** *M11 junct 9/10, on B1052 off A1307 between Cambridge & Haverhill, signposted*
Linton Zoo places emphasis on conservation and education where visitors can see a combination of beautiful gardens and a wealth of wildlife from all over the world. There are many rare and exotic creatures to see including tapirs, snow leopards, tigers, lions, zebra, tamarin monkeys, lemurs, owls, parrots, giant tortoises, snakes, tarantula spiders and many others. The zoo is set in 16-acres of gardens with plenty of picnic areas, children's play area and bouncy castle.

**Times:** *Open all year, daily 10.30-4, (last admission 3). Hours extended during summer. Closed 25-26 Dec.
**Fee:** *£7 (ch 2-13 £4.50, concessions £6.50)
**Facilities:** 𝐏 🏕 📋 ⅍ (toilets), shop ⊗ 🚌 (pre-book)

## PETERBOROUGH
### Flag Fen Bronze Age Centre
The Droveway Northey Road PE6 7QJ
☎ 01733 313414 🖹 01733 349957
**Email:** office@flagfen.freeserve.co.uk
**Web:** www.flagfen.com
**Dir:** *Join A1139, exit at Boongate junct. At rdbt 3rd exit, through lights and turn right. At t-junct turn right, Flag Fen is signed*
Although visitors enter this site through a 21st-century roundhouse, the rest of their day will be spent in the Bronze Age, some 3,000 years ago. Flag Fens Museum contains artefacts found over the last 20 years of excavating on site, and includes among them the oldest wheel in Britain. In the park there is a reconstructed Bronze Age settlement and Iron Age roundhouse, while in the Preservation Hall visitors can see the excavated Bronze Age processional way that spanned over one mile. The Hall also contains a 60-ft mural depicting the fens in ancient times.
**Times:** Open daily Oct-Mar 10-4 (last admission 3), Apr-Sep 10-5 (last admission 4). Closed 24 Dec-2 Jan
**Fee:** *£4.75 (pen £4.25, ch & students £3.50). Family £13.
**Facilities:** 𝐏 ☕ (Tea/coffee only during Winter) 🏕 📋 £2.50 ⅍ (toilets), shop, guided tours (charged) ⊗ (ex guide dogs) 🚌 (pre-book)

## PETERBOROUGH
### Railworld
Oundle Road PE2 9NR

☎ 01733 344240 & 319362 📄 01733 319362

**Email:** railworld@aol.com

**Web:** www.railworld.net

**Dir:** *from A1(M) Peterborough, turn onto A1139 then off at junct 5 to city centre. At 1st rdbt, follow Little Puffer tourist signs. Entrance for Railworld is off Oundle Rd at city end through car park*

An exhibition centre and museum dedicated to all things rail related, especially the environment. Attractions include model railways, hands on exhibits, a rail industry showcase, hover-trains, local rail history gallery and a car.

**Times:** Mar-Oct daily 11-4, Nov-Feb Mon-Fri 11-4

**Fee:** £5 (ch £2.50, concessions £4). Family £13 (up to 4 ch).

**Facilities:** 🅿 Ⓟ (200mtrs - Height barrier 7.5ft opened on request) ☕ (Mar-Oct wknds only) 🍴 📱 ♿ (reasonable access, toilets), shop, guided tours ⊗ (ex guide dogs & outside) 🚌 (Notice required for height barrier)

---

## THORNHAUGH
### Sacrewell Farm & Country Centre
Peterborough PE8 6HJ

☎ 01780 782254 📄 01780 781370

**Email:** info@sacrewell.fsnet.co.uk

**Web:** www.sacrewell.org.uk

**Dir:** *E of A1/A47 intersection. Brown tourist signs from both directions*

Treasures of farming and the country await discovery at this farm and 18th-century watermill spread across 35 acres. All aspects of agriculture and country life through the ages are here including listed buildings, a working watermill, a mill house and farm bygones. Farm animals, tractor rides, mini maze and pedal tractors are just a few of the activities to be experienced. There's also a choice of indoor or outdoor play areas for children.

**Times:** Open all year daily Mar-Sep, 9.30-5; Oct-Feb 10-4. (Closed 24 Dec-2 Jan).

**Fee:** *£5.25 (ch £3.75, concessions £4.25) Family ticket £15.

**Facilities:** 🅿 🍴 📱 £2.99 ♿ (upstairs in watermill not accessible, toilets), shop, guided tours 🚌 (pre book)

---

## WANSFORD
### Nene Valley Railway
Wansford Station Stibbington Peterborough PE8 6LR

☎ 01780 784444 📄 01780 784440

**Email:** nvrorg@aol.com

**Web:** www.nvr.org.uk

**Dir:** *A1 at Stibbington, W of Peterborough, 1m south of the A47 junct*

Originally opened as a working railway in 1845, closed in 1966, then re-opened in 1977 as a tourist railway, Nene Valley Railway has steam and diesel engines, carriages and wagons from Europe including the UK. All the sights and sounds of the golden age of steam come alive here. Travelling between Yarwell Junction, Wansford and Peterborough the 7.5 miles of track pass through the heart of the 500-acre Ferry Meadows Country Park. Nene Valley Railway is also the home of 'Thomas'- children's favourite engine.

**Times:** * Train services operate on Sun from Jan; wknds from Apr-Oct; Wed from May, plus other mid-week services in summer.

**Fee:** £10.50 (ch 3-15 £5.50, concessions £8). Family ticket £26.

**Facilities:** 🅿 Ⓟ (adjacent) ☕ (at Wansford Station) 🍴 ♿ (disabled access to trains, toilets) shop 🚌

## WATERBEACH
**The Farmland Museum and Denny Abbey**
Ely Road CB5 9PQ
☎ 01223 860988 🖹 01223 860988
**Email:** f.m.denny@tesco.net
**Web:** www.dennyfarmlandmuseum.org.uk
**Dir:** *on A10 between Cambridge and Ely*
Explore two areas of rural life at this fascinating museum.
The Abbey tells the story of those who have lived there,
including Benedictine monks, Franciscan nuns, and the
mysterious Knights Templar. The farm museum features
the craft workshops of a wheelwright, a basketmaker,
and a blacksmith. There is also a 1940s farmworker's
cottage and a village shop. Special events on Easter,
May and August Bank Holidays.
**Times:** Open daily Apr-Oct, noon-5

**Fee:** £3.90 (ch £1.70, concessions £3)
**Facilities:** 🅿 ☕ (Open wknds only) ⛱ ♿ (wheelchairs,
toilets), shop, guided tours 🚌 (pre-booking required)

## WOODHURST
**The Raptor Foundation**
The Heath St Ives Road PE28 3BT
☎ 01487 741140 🖹 01487 841140
**Email:** heleowl@aol.com
**Web:** www.raptorfoundation.org.uk
**Dir:** *B1040 to Somersham, follow brown signs*
Permanent home to over 250 birds of which there are
40 different varieties; the Foundation also provides
medical care for injured birds and returns rehabilitated
ones to the wild. This is a unique opportunity to meet and
learn about birds of prey. Depending on weather and time
of year flying demonstrations are held, usually three
times a day and audiences have the chance to
participate in displays. There are nearly 60 birds in the
flying team, so each display has a different set of birds.

Educational trail linking to new education room.
**Times:** *Open all year, daily 10-5. Closed 25-26 Dec
& 1 Jan.
**Fee:** *£4 (ch £2.50 ages 2-5 £1, concessions £3)
**Facilities:** 🅿 ⛱ ♿ (ramped areas, toilets), shop, guided
tours ⊗ 🚌

## BRENTWOOD
**Kelvedon Hatch Secret Nuclear Bunker**
CM14 5TL
☎ 01277 364883 🖹 01277 365260
**Email:** bunker@japer.demon.co.uk
**Web:** www.secretnuclearbunker.co.uk
**Dir:** *on A128 Brentwood to Chipping Ongar road at
Kelvedon Hotel*
Witness the three phases of the bunker's life. From its
role with the RAF where the overall tactical controller
would react to a nuclear attack from Britain's enemies,
through to its role as Regional Government HQ. When
there could have been up too 600 personnel, possibly
including the Prime Minister, organising the survival of
the civilian population in the aftermath of nuclear war.
See for yourself the equipment and rooms needed to

support the plotting of nuclear fall-out patterns.
**Times:** * Mar-Oct, wkdays 10-4 wknds 10-5; Nov-Feb,
Thu-Sun 10-4.
**Fee:** *£6 (ch £4). Family ticket (2ad+2ch) £15.
**Facilities:** 🅿 ☕ (snacks) ⛱ 🍴 ♿ (stairlift, ramps,
toilets), shop, audio commentaries ⊗ (ex guide dogs)
🚌 ♿

## CASTLE HEDINGHAM
### Colne Valley Railway & Museum

Castle Hedingham Station Halstead CO9 3DZ

☎ 01787 461174

**Web:** www.colnevalleyrailway.co.uk

**Dir:** *4m NW of Halstead on A1017*

Many former Colne Valley and Halstead railway buildings have been rebuilt here. Stock includes seven steam locomotives plus 80 other engines, carriages and wagons. Visitors can dine in style in restored Pullman carriages while travelling along the line. Please telephone for a free timetable and details of the many special events.

**Times:** *Open all year, daily 10-dusk. Steam days, rides from 12-4. Closed 23 Dec-1 Feb. Steam days every Sun and BH from Mothering Sun to end Oct, Wed of school

summer hols & special events. Railway Farm Park open May-Sep. Phone 01787 461174 for timetable information

**Fee:** *Steam days: £6 (ch £3, pen £5) Family ticket £18. Diesel days £5 (ch £2.50); Family ticket £15. NB: Prices are provisional

**Facilities:** ℗ ⌨ (when trains operate & on train service) ⊓◎⏐ (Licensed) ⊓ ♿ (ramps for wheelchairs to get onto carriages, toilets), shop ⊗ (ex guide dogs) 🚌 (pre-booking)

---

## COLCHESTER
### Colchester Castle Museum

Castle Park High St CO1 1TJ

☎ 01206 282939 📠 01206 282925

**Web:** www.colchestermuseums.org.uk

**Dir:** *at E end of High St*

The largest Norman castle keep in Europe - built over the remains of the magnificent Roman Temple of Claudius which was destroyed by Boudicca in AD60. Colchester was the first capital of Roman Britain, and the archaeological collections are among the finest in the country. Please telephone for details about the range of events held throughout the year.

**Times:** *Open all year, Mon-Sat 10-5, Sun 11-5. Closed Xmas/New Year

**Fee:** *£4.50 (ch & concessions £2.90, under 5's free)

**Facilities:** ℗ (town centre) ⊓ ♿ (all parts accessible except vaults/roof tour, toilets), shop ⊗ (ex guide dogs) 🚌 (book in advance)

---

## COLCHESTER
### Colchester Zoo

Stanway Maldon Road CO3 0SL

☎ 01206 331292 📠 01206 331392

**Email:** enquiries@colchester-zoo.co.uk

**Web:** www.colchester-zoo.co.uk

**Dir:** *turn off A12 onto A1124 and follow elephant signs*

One of England's finest zoos, Colchester Zoo has over 250 species of animal. Visitors can meet the elephants, handle a snake, and see parrots, seals, penguins and birds of prey all appearing in informative daily displays. Enclosures include Spirit of Africa with baby elephants Kito and Jambo, Playa Patagonia where sea lions swim above your head in a 24mtr underwater tunnel, Penguin Shores, the Wilds of Asia for orang-utans, Chimp World, and the Kingdom of the Wild, with giraffes, zebras and

rhinos. There is also an undercover soft play complex, road train, four adventure play areas, eating places and gift shops, all set in 60 acres of gardens.

**Times:** Open all year, daily from 9.30. Last admission 5.30 (1hr before dusk out of season). Closed 25 Dec.

**Fee:** *£13.50 (ch 3-14 £7.50).

**Facilities:** ℗ ⊓◎⏐ (Licensed) ⊓ ▤ ♿ (easy route developed, but zoo has hills, electric scooters, toilets), shop ⊗ (ex guide dogs) 🚌 (must book in advance for reduced rates)

**ESSEX**

**ESSEX**

## NEWPORT
### Mole Hall Wildlife Park
Widdington Saffron Walden CB11 3SS
☎ 01799 540400 & 541359 ▤ 01799 542408
**Email:** enquiries@molehall.co.uk
**Web:** www.molehall.co.uk
**Dir:** *M11 junct 8 between Stansted & Saffron Walden, off B1383*
The Park covers 20 acres and has been lovingly developed by the Johnstone family for over 40 years. The wide variety of animals range from South American Lama Guanaco to Red Squirrels, Leopard-like Serval Cat and the Formosan Sika Deer, which is extinct in the wild. Mole Hall is also home to two species of otter, being the first regular breeders in the UK of the North American Otter. Other residents include chimpanzees, capuchins, lemurs and much more. In the tropical butterfly pavilion, see butterflies on the wing and free flying small birds. Tarantulas, snakes, pools of aquatic life, small monkeys, tortoises and lovebirds. Small children will also be entertained by the straw castle, water maze, sand pit and play area.
**Times:** Open all year, daily 10-5.30 (or dusk). Closed 25 Dec. Butterfly House and Water Maze open mid Mar-Oct.
**Fee:** *£6.30 (ch £4.30 under 3's free, pen, student & disabled £3).
**Facilities:** ❷ ⊼ ♿ (Difficult access in wet weather for wheelchairs, toilets) shop garden centre ⊗ (ex guide dogs) 🚌

## SOUTHEND-ON-SEA
### Southend Museum, Planetarium & Discovery Centre
Victoria Avenue SS2 6ES
☎ 01702 434449 ▤ 01702 349806
**Email:** southendmuseum@hotmail.com
**Web:** www.southendmuseums.co.uk
**Dir:** *take A127 or A13 towards town centre. Museum is adjacent to Southend Victoria Railway Station*
A fine Edwardian building housing displays of archaeology, natural history and local history, telling the story of man in the south-east Essex area. Also the only planetarium in the South East. Ring for details of special events, or see website.
**Times:** *Open Central Museum: Tue-Sat 10-5 (Closed Sun -Mon & BH); Planetarium: Wed-Sat, shows at 11, 2 & 4.
**Fee:** Central Museum free. Planetarium £2.60 (ch & pen £1.90). Family tickets £8. Party rates on request.
**Facilities:** ❷ (charged) ❷ (50mtrs - disabled only behind museum) ♿ (planetarium not accessible, disabled access to centre), shop ⊗ (ex guide dogs) 🚌 (advance notice required) ⌨

## STANSTED
### House on the Hill, Toy Museum
CM24 8SP
☎ 01279 813567 ▤ 01279 816391
**Email:** office@mountfitchetcastle.com
**Web:** www.mountfitchetcastle.com
**Dir:** *off B1383 in the centre of Stansted Mountfitchet*
The House on the Hill is a large, privately-owned toy museum, housed on two floors covering 7,000 sq. ft. It houses a huge variety of toys, books and games from the late Victorian period up to the 1970s. There is a space display, Teddy Bears' picnic, Action Man, Sindy, Barbie, military displays and much more. Additional exhibitions of film, theatre, rock 'n' roll and television memorabilia are on show, plus end-of-the-pier slot machines.
**Times:** *Open all year daily, 10-5; (closed for a few days over the Xmas period & Mon in Jan & Feb)
**Fee:** *£4 (ch under 14 £3.30, pen £3.50). Party 15+.
**Facilities:** ❷ (charged) ❷ (100mtrs - pay & display) ⊼ shop ⊗ (ex guide dogs) 🚌 (pre-booking)

## STANSTED
### Mountfitchet Castle & Norman Village
Mountfitchet CM24 8SP
☎ 01279 813237 📄 01279 816391
**Email:** office@mountfitchetcastle.com
**Web:** www.mountfitchetcastle.com
**Dir:** *off B1383, in village centre. 5 min from M11 junct 8*
Norman motte and bailey castle and village reconstructed
as it was in Norman England of 1066, on its original
historic site. A vivid illustration of village life in Domesday
England, complete with houses, church, seige tower,
seige weapons, and many types of animals roaming
freely. There are animated wax figures in all the buildings
to give historical information to visitors.
**Times:** *Open daily, mid Mar-mid Nov, 10-5.
**Fee:** *£6.50 (ch under 2 free, ch 3-13 £5, pen £5.50).

**Facilities:** ℗ (charged) ℗ (100mtrs - pay & display
car park) 🍽 (hot snacks, cakes) 🍴 📄 20p ♿ (laser
commentaries, toilets), shop ⊗ (ex guide dogs)
🚌 (must pre-book)

## WALTHAM ABBEY
### Lee Valley Park Farms
Stubbins Hall Lane Crooked Mile EN9 2EG
☎ 01992 892781 & 702200 📄 01992 899561
**Email:** hayeshill@leevalleypark.org.uk
**Web:** www.leevalleypark.org.uk
**Dir:** *M25 junct 26, follow to Waltham Abbey. 2m from
Waltham Abbey on B914*
Set in the heart of Lee Valley Country Park, Hayes
Hill Farm offers young and old the chance to view
many types of farm animals. Meet a variety of rare
breeds in the traditional-style farmyard. In the pet centre,
see many creatures from meerkats to chipmunks.
During summer, there are tractor and trailor rides to
Holyfield Hall, a nearby 700-acre working dairy and
arable farm.

**Times:** *Open all year, Mon-Fri 10-4.30, wknds &
BHs 10-5.30.
**Fee:** *£4.10 (ch 3+ £3.10, concessions £3.60).
Family (2ad+3ch) £16.50
**Facilities:** ℗ ℗ (0.5m) 🍴 📄 ♿ (graded concrete
paths, signed routes, toilets), shop 🚌

## WALTHAM ABBEY
### Royal Gunpowder Mills
Beaulieu Drive EN9 1JY
☎ 01992 707370 📄 01992 707372
**Email:** info@royalgunpowdermills.com
**Web:** www.royalgunpowdermills.com
**Dir:** *M25 junct 26. Follow signs for A121 to Waltham
Abbey at rdbt, entrance in Beaulieu Drive*
Set in 175 acres of parkland, this amazing scientific
complex has 21 buildings of historical importance.
Before it closed in 1991 this was a site of major scientific
research and development, including work on Congreve's
Rocket in the early 19th century, up to more recent work
on ejector seats and fuel for rocket motors. Explosives
were made in many of the buildings on the site which
are connected by five miles of navigational canals.

**Times:** *Open 30 Apr-25 Sep, 11-5, last entry at
3.30. (Wknds and BHs only)
**Fee:** *£5.50 (ch £3, concessions £4.70, under 5's
free) Family £17
**Facilities:** ℗ 🍴 📄 ♿ (ramps, lift, tactile with audio
tour, toilets), shop ⊗ (ex guide dogs) 🚌 4 coaches
on one visit

**ESSEX**

GREATER LONDON

## BRENTFORD
### Kew Bridge Steam Museum
Green Dragon Lane TW8 0EN
☎ 020 8568 4757 📠 020 8569 9978
**Email:** info@kbsm.org
**Web:** www.kbsm.org
**Dir:** *Underground - Kew Gardens, District line then 391 bus. Museum 100yds from N side of Kew Bridge*
This Victorian pumping station has steam engines and six beam engines, five of which are working and one of which is the largest in the world. The Grand Junction 90 inch engine is over 40 feet high, and weighs around 250 tons. A diesel house and waterwheel can also be seen along with London's only steam narrow-gauge railway, which operates every Sunday (Mar-Nov). The Water for Life Gallery tells the hisstory of London's water supply.

**Times:** Open all year (ex Mon) daily 11-5. Engines in steam, wknds & BHs.
**Fee:** *Wkdays £4.25, wknds £5.75 (ch free, concessions available)
**Facilities:** 🅿 Ⓟ (100mtrs - single yellow lines in street) ⛾ (open wknds only) 🍴 🗐 ♿ (wheelchairs, large print guide, toilets) shop guided tours 🚌 (by prior arrangement only)

## CHESSINGTON
### Chessington World of Adventures
Leatherhead Road KT9 2NE
☎ 0870 444 7777 📠 01372 725050
**Web:** www.chessington.com
**Dir:** *M25 junct 9/10, on A243*
With over 90% of its rides suitable for under-12s, this is the ideal place for an action-packed family day out. Very small children are entertained in Animal Land, Land of the Dragons, and on the Toytown fun-rides. Among the multitude of fun-packed areas are Beanoland, the Mystic East, the Forbidden Kingdom, Mexicana, Transylvania, and the Market Square. Chessington has recently seen the introduction of the bubbletastic Bubbleworks water ride, where riders float in bubble tubs over chutes, fountains and foam. The Monkey and Bird Garden is a new animal attraction, as is Creature Features with skunks, porcupines and meerkats. Plenty of special events and shows including Halloween fun and TV characters.

**Times:** *Open 27 Mar-Oct (excluding some off peak days in Sep) either 10-5 or 10-6 (telephone for details). Zoo opens 9.30
**Fee:** *£29 (ch £19.50) 1 ch under 12 free with each full paying adult. Family ticket (2 ad & 2 ch) £58
**Facilities:** 🅿 🍴 (Licensed) 🍴 ♿ (some rides not accessible, disabled guide available, toilets), shop 🚫 (ex assist dogs) 🚌 (12+ advanced booking recommended)

## CHISLEHURST
### Chislehurst Caves
Old Hill BR7 5NB
☎ 020 8467 3264 📠 020 8295 0407
**Email:** enquiries@chislehurstcaves.co.uk
**Web:** www.chislehurstcaves.co.uk
**Dir:** *off A222 near Chislehurst railway stn. Turn into station approach, then right & right again into Caveside Close*
Miles of mystery and history beneath your feet. Grab a lantern and get ready for an amazing adventure! Visit the caves and your whole family can travel back in time as you explore the maze of passageways dug through the chalk deep beneath Chislehurst. Accompanied by an experienced guide on a 45-minute tour you'll see the tunnels made famous as a shelter during the Second World War, visit the cave's church, druid altar, the haunted pool and much more.

**Times:** Open all year, Wed-Sun, 10-4. Daily during local school hols (incl half terms). Closed Xmas.
**Fee:** £5 (ch & pen £3).
**Facilities:** 🅿 🍴 (Licensed) 🍴 🗐 £1.50 ♿ (toilets), shop guided tours 🚫 (ex guide dogs) 🚌 (pre-booking)

## HAM
### Ham House
Ham Street Richmond TW10 7RS
☎ 020 8439 8241 📄 020 8332 6903
**Email:** hamhouse@nationaltrust.org.uk
**Web:** www.nationaltrust.org.uk/hamhouse
**Dir:** *W of A307, between Kingston & Richmond*
Built in 1610, the Ham House was enlarged in the 1670s
when it was at the heart of Restoration court life and
intrigue. It was then occupied by the same family until
1948. The formal garden is significant for its survival in
an area known as the cradle of the English Landscape
Movement. There are also opportunities to see open-air
theatre and take a ghost tour. Contact for details.
**Times:** *Open Gardens: all year, Sat-Wed 11-6 or dusk
if earlier. Closed 25-26 Dec & 1 Jan. House: 25 Mar-29

Oct, Sat-Wed 1-5. (Last admission 4.30).
**Fee:** *House & Garden £8 (ch £4). Family ticket £19.
Garden only £4 (ch £2). Family ticket £9.
**Facilities:** 🅿 Ⓟ (400yds - disabled parking on site only)
🛏 📋 £1 ♿ (Braille guide, wheelchairs, induction loop,
lift, parking, toilets), shop, guided tours ⊗ (ex assist
dogs) 🚌 (pre booking required) 🌿

## HAMPTON COURT
### Hampton Court Palace
KT8 9AU
☎ 0870 752 7777 📄 020 8781 9669
**Email:** hamptoncourt@hrp.org.uk
**Web:** www.hrp.org.uk
**Dir:** *A3 to Hook underpass then A309. Train from
Waterloo - Hampton Court, 2mins walk from station*
With over 500 years of royal history Hampton Court
Palace has something to offer everyone, from the
magnificent State Apartments to the domestic reality
of the Tudor Kitchens. Costumed guides and audio tours
bring the palace to life and provide an insight into how
life in the palace would have been in the time of Henry
VIII and William III. There is also an exhibition that
explores community life after the departure of the

monarchy from the Palace, along with an audio
installation in the world famous maze. The newest
addition is a multi-sensory experience involving the
Tudor kitchens.
**Times:** Open all year from 10, closes 6 mid Mar-mid
Oct, 4.30 mid Oct-mid Mar. Closed 24-26 Dec.
**Fee:** £12.30 (ch £8, concessions £10). Family £36.40
**Facilities:** 🅿 (charged) Ⓟ (500 mtrs - no overnight in
Palace car park) 🍽 (Licensed) 🛏 ♿ (lifts, buggies for
gardens, wheelchairs, wardens to assist, toilets), shop,
guided tours, audio commentaries ⊗ (ex guide/hearing
dogs) 🚌

## KEW
### Kew Gardens (Royal Botanic Gardens)
Richmond TW9 3AB
☎ 020 8332 5655 📄 020 8332 5197
**Email:** info@kew.org
**Web:** www.kew.org
**Dir:** *Underground - Kew Gardens*
Kew Gardens is a paradise throughout the seasons.
Lose yourself in the magnificent glasshouses and
discover plants from the world's deserts, mountains
and oceans. Wide-open spaces, stunning vistas, listed
buildings (including the Pagoda and the Palm House)
and wildlife contribute to the Gardens unique
atmosphere. As well as being famous for its beautiful
gardens, Kew is world renowned for its contribution
to botanical and horticultural science.

**Times:** *Open all year, Gardens daily 9.30. Closing
times vary (seasonal, visit website or phone to verify).
Closed 24 & 25 Dec.
**Fee:** £9.50 (ch under 17 free, concessions £6.50).
**Facilities:** 🅿 (charged) Ⓟ (0.2m - nearby parking
is free after 10am) 🍽 (Licensed) ♿ (16 seat bus tour:
enquiries ring 020 8332 5643, toilets), shop, garden
centre, guided tours ⊗ (ex guide dogs) 🚌

**GREATER LONDON**

## TWICKENHAM
### Marble Hill House
Richmond Road TW1 2NL
☎ 020 8892 5115 🖨 020 8607 9976
**Web:** www.english-heritage.org.uk
A magnificent Thames-side Palladian villa built for
Henrietta Howard, mistress of King George II, set in
66 acres of riverside parklands.
**Times:** Open Apr-Oct, Sat 10-2, Sun & BHs 10-5. Tours
on Tue & Wed 12 & 3. Closed Nov-Mar but pre-booked
groups by arrangement. Closed 22 Dec-7 Feb.
**Fee:** £4 (ch £2, concessions £3). Family ticket £10.
Closed 22 Dec-7 Feb. Prices and opening times are
subject to change. Please check web site or call
0870 333 1181 for the most up to date prices and
opening times when planning your trip

**Facilities:** 🅿 †◎┤ (Licensed) 🪑 ♿ (toilets), shop
🚫 (ex on lead in certain areas) 🚐 ♯ 🆑

## TWICKENHAM
### Museum of Rugby & Twickenham Stadium Tours
Rugby Football Union Rugby Road TW1 1DZ
☎ 0870 405 2021 🖨 020 8892 2817
**Email:** museum@rfu.com
**Web:** www.rfu.com/microsites/museum/
**Dir:** *A316, follow signs to museum*
Combine a behind the scenes guided tour of the world's
most famous rugby stadium with a visit to The Museum
of Rugby. The tour includes breathtaking views from the
top of the North Stand, a visit to the England dressing
room and ends by walking through the players tunnel
to pitch side. The multi-media museum appeals to
enthusiasts of all ages and charts the history and
world-wide growth of rugby.

**Times:** *Open, Tue-Sat 10-
5 (last museum admission
4.30), Sun 11-5 (last
admission 4.30). Closed
post Twickenham match
days, Etr Sun, 24-26 Dec &
1 Jan. On match days
museum only available to
ticket holders.
**Fee:** *Museum & Tour £9
(concessions £6). Family
£30.
**Facilities:** 🅿 🗐 ♿ (toilets)
shop  guided tours
🚫 (ex guide dogs) 🚐

## TWICKENHAM
### Orleans House Gallery
Riverside TW1 3DJ
☎ 020 8831 6000 🖨 020 8744 0501
**Email:** m.denovellis@richmond.gov.uk
**Web:** www.richmond.gov.uk
**Dir:** *Richmond road A305, Orleans Rd is on right just
past Orleans Park School*
Stroll beside the Thames and through the woodland
gardens of Orleans House, where you will find stunning
18th-century interior design and an excellent public art
gallery. Visitors of all ages can try out their own artistic
talents in pre-booked workshops, and wide-ranging
temporary exhibitions and showcases of work by local
artists are held throughout the year - please telephone
for details.

**Times:** *Open Oct-Mar, Tue-Sat 1-4.30, Sun & BH
2-4.30; Apr-Sep Tue-Sat 1-5.30, Sun & BH 2-5.30.
**Fee:** *Free
**Facilities:** 🅿 🅿 (surrounding areas - coach space not
currently available) 🪑 ♿ (handling objects & large print
labels for some exhibitions, toilets), shop 🚫 (ex guide
dogs) 🚐 (booking prefered) 🆑

## FOREST
### German Occupation Museum
GY8 0BG

☎ 01481 238205

**Dir:** *Behind Forest Church near the airport*

The museum has the Channel Islands' largest collection of Occupation items, with tableaux of a kitchen, bunker rooms and a street during the Occupation. Audio-visual displays convey the stories of the islanders, whilst recreations of rooms and scenes are shown through realistic dioramas. There are also collections of German equipment. Liberation Day (9th May) is celebrated every year with special events and exhibitions.

**Times:** Open Apr-Oct 10-4.30, Nov-Mar 10-12.30 (Closed Mon).

**Fee:** £3.75 (ch £2). Free admission for disabled.

**Facilities:** ℗ ⊓ 🗐 ♿ (ramps & handrails), guided tours ⊗ (ex assist dogs) 🚌 ♨

## ROCQUAINE BAY
### Fort Grey and Shipwreck Museum
St Peter's GY7 9BY

☎ 01481 265036 📠 01481 263279

**Email:** admin@museums.gov.gg

**Web:** www.museum.guernsey.net

**Dir:** *on coast road at Rocquaine Bay*

The fort is a Martello tower, built in 1804, as part of the Channel Islands' extensive defences. It is nicknamed the 'cup and saucer' because of its appearance, and houses a museum devoted to ships wrecked on the treacherous Hanois reefs nearby. The museum contains many salvaged artefacts and related illustrations.

**Times:** Open Etr-Oct, 10-5

**Fee:** *Fort Grey, £2.50 (pen £1.25), 3 Venue Ticket £9 (pen £5)

**Facilities:** ℗ (opposite fort) ⊓ 🗐 shop guided tours ⊗ (ex guide dogs) 🚌 (pre-booking essential)

## ST ANDREW
### German Military Underground Hospital & Ammunition Store
La Vassalerie GY6 8XR

☎ 01481 239100

**Dir:** *St Andrews Parish, centre of island*

The largest structure created during the German Occupation of the Channel Islands, a concrete maze of about 75,000 sq. ft, which took slave workers three-and-a-half years to complete, at the cost of many lives. Most of the equipment has been removed, but the central heating plant, hospital beds and cooking facilities can still be seen.

**Times:** *Open Jul-Aug, daily 10-noon & 2-4.30; May-Jun & Sep, daily 10-noon & 2-4; Apr & Oct, daily 2-4; Mar & Nov, Sun & Thu 2-3.

**Fee:** *£3 (ch £1).

**Facilities:** ℗ ♿ shop 🚌 ♨

**GUERNSEY**

## ST PETER PORT
**Castle Cornet**
GY1 1AU
☎ 01481 721657 📠 01481 715177
**Email:** admin@museums.gov.gg
**Web:** www.museum.guernsey.net
**Dir:** *5 mins walk from St Peter Port bus terminus.*
The history of this magnificent castle spans eight
centuries and its buildings now house several museums,
the Refectory Café and a shop. Soldiers fire the noonday
gun in a daily ceremony. Look for the Maritime Museum
that charts Guernsey's nautical history, the 'Story of
Castle Cornet' with its mystery skeleton and the 201
squadron RAF Museum.
**Times:** Open Etr-end Oct, daily 10-5.
**Fee:** *£6 (pen £4). 3 venue ticket £9 (pen £5)

**Facilities:** Ⓟ (100 yds- time limit) 📖 shop guided tours
Ⓧ (ex guide dogs )🚌 (prior booking preferred)

## ALDERSHOT
**Airborne Forces Museum**
Browning Barracks Queens Avenue GU11 2BU
☎ 01252 349619 📠 01252 349203
**Dir:** *M3 take A325 to Aldershot then next left*
The museum traces the history of the Parachute
Regiment and British Airborne Forces since 1940.
Using weapons, equipment, dioramas and briefing
models it depicts the story of airborne actions such as
the early raids, D-Day, Arnhem, the Rhine Crossing,
and post-war campaigns such as Suez, the Falklands
and Kosovo.
**Times:** *Open all year, Mon-Fri 10-4.30 (last admission
3.45), Sat-Sun & BH 10-4. Closed Xmas.
**Fee:** *£3 (ch, pen & former members of the Regiment
£1, under 5's free)

**Facilities:** Ⓟ ♿ (wheelchair ramps), shop, guided tours
Ⓧ (ex guide dogs) 🚌 ⊗

## AMPFIELD
**The Sir Harold Hillier Gardens**
Jermyns Lane Romsey SO51 0QA
☎ 01794 368787 📠 01794 368027
**Email:** info@hilliergardens.org.uk
**Web:** www.hilliergardens.org.uk
**Dir:** *3m NE of Romsey, signed off A3090 & A3057*
Established in 1953, this 180-acre public garden
comprises the greatest collection of hardy trees and
shrubs in the world. A garden for all seasons with
stunning range of seasonal colour and interest and
featuring eleven national plant collections. Champion
trees, the Gurkha Memorial Garden and the largest
Winter Garden of its kind in Europe. Events take place
all year round and the gardens feature a purpose-built
Visitor and Education Pavilion. Contact for details.

**Times:** Open all year, daily, 10-6 (or dusk if earlier).
Closed 25-26 Dec.
**Fee:** £7.50 (ch under 16 free, concessions £6.50).
Group bookings £6
**Facilities:** Ⓟ 🍴 (Licensed) 🪑 📖 ♿ (all ability path,
toilets), shop, garden centre, guided tours Ⓧ (ex guide
dogs) 🚌 (prior booking preferred)

## ANDOVER
### Finkley Down Farm Park
SP11 6NF

☎ 01264 352195 🖷 01264 363172

**Email:** admin@finkleydownfarm.co.uk

**Web:** www.finkleydownfarm.co.uk

**Dir:** *signed from A303 & A343, 1.5m N of A303 & 2m E of Andover*

This fun family farm park is jam packed with things to do. You can join in with feeding time, groom a pony, cuddle a rabbit, or collect duck eggs. Lots of activities are scheduled throughout the day, or kids can just let off steam in the playground or on the trampolines. From chipmunks to chinchillas, pygmy goats to peacocks, and lambs to llamas, Finkley Down Farm has something for everyone.

**Times:** *Open mid Mar-Oct, daily 10-6. Last admission 5.

**Fee:** *£5.75 (ch £4.75, pen £5.25). Family ticket £20 (2ad+2ch).

**Facilities:** 🅿 Ⓟ 🛱 ♿ (toilets), shop ⊗ (ex guide dogs) 🚌

## ASHURST
### Longdown Activity Farm
Longdown Southampton SO40 7EH

☎ 023 8029 3326 🖷 023 8029 3376

**Email:** enquiries@longdownfarm.co.uk

**Web:** www.longdownfarm.co.uk

**Dir:** *off A35 between Lyndhurst & Southampton*

Fun for all the family at Longdown Activity Farm with a variety of hands-on activities every day, including small animal handling and bottle feeding calves and goat kids. There are indoor and outdoor play areas, with trampolines and ball pools. Tearoom, picnic area and excellent gift shop.

**Times:** Open Feb-Dec, daily 10-5.

**Fee:** *£6 (ch 3-14 & pen £5). Saver ticket £21 (2ad+2ch).

**Facilities:** 🅿 🛱 ♿ (concrete path for wheelchairs, toilets) shop guided tours ⊗ (kennels provided) 🚌 (pre-booking required)

## BASINGSTOKE
### Milestones - Hampshire's Living History Museum
Basingstoke Leisure Park Churchill Way West RG21 6YR

☎ 01256 477766 🖷 01256 477784

**Email:** jane.holmes@hants.gov.uk

**Web:** www.milestones-museum.com

**Dir:** *M3 junct 6, take ringway road West and follow brown signs for Leisure Park*

Milestones brings Hampshire's recent past to life through stunning period street scenes and exciting interactive areas, all under one roof. Nationally important collections of transport, technology and everyday life are presented in an entertaining way. Staff in period costumes, mannequins and sounds all bring the streets to life.

**Times:** Open Tue-Fri & BHs 10-5, Sat-Sun 11-5. Closed 25-26 Dec & 1 Jan.

**Fee:** *£7.25 (ch £4.25, under 5s free, concessions £6.50). Family ticket (2ad+2ch) £21.

**Facilities:** 🅿 Ⓟ (50mtrs) ⊡ (daily 10-4.30) 🛱 ♿ (induction loops, subtitles screens, scooters, wheelchairs, toilets) shop, audio commentaries ⊗ (ex guide dogs) 🚌 (must be pre-booked for discount)

**HAMPSHIRE**

## BEAULIEU
**Beaulieu : National Motor Museum**
Brockenhurst SO42 7ZN
☎ 01590 612345 📠 01590 612624
**Email:** info@beaulieu.co.uk
**Web:** www.beaulieu.co.uk
**Dir:** *M27 junct 2, A326, B3054, then follow tourist signs*
Set in the heart of William the Conqueror's New Forest, on the banks of the Beaulieu River, stands this 16th-century house. It has become most famous as the home of the National Motor Museum. The site also contains the picturesque abbey building ruins, which have an exhibition on life in the middle ages, and various family treasures and memorabilia. The Secret Army Exhibition tells the story of the secret agents trained at the Beaulieu 'Finishing School' during WWII.

**Times:** *Open all year - Palace House & Gardens, National Motor Museum, Beaulieu Abbey & Exhibition of Monastic Life, May-Sep 10-6; Oct-Apr 10-5. Closed 25 Dec.
**Fee:** *Please contact for current prices.
**Facilities:** 🅿 Ⓟ (1.5m) 🪑 🗑 ♿ (ramp access, lift to upper level, induction loop, toilets), shop, guided tours 🚌

## BREAMORE
**Breamore House & Countryside Museum**
Fordingbridge SP6 2DF
☎ 01725 512468 📠 01725 512858
**Email:** breamore@ukonline.co.uk
**Web:** www.breamorehouse.com
**Dir:** *turn off A338, between Salisbury & Fordingbridge and follow signs for 1m*
The handsome manor house was completed in around 1583 and has a fine collection of paintings, china and tapestries. The museum has good examples of steam engines, and uses reconstructed workshops and other displays to show how people lived and worked a century or so ago. There is also a children's playground.
**Times:** *Open Apr, Tue, Sun & Etr, May-Sep, Tue-Thu & Sat, Sun & BH; daily 2-5.30 (Countryside Museum 1pm).

**Fee:** *£7 (ch £5). Party £6 each.
**Facilities:** 🅿 Ⓟ (300yds - disabled only close to house) 🗑 ♿ (ramps, parking, recorded message & book about 1st floor, toilets), shop, guided tours (charged) ⊗ (ex guide dogs) 🚌 (pre-booking preferred) ♨

## BUCKLER'S HARD
**Buckler's Hard Village & Maritime Museum**
Beaulieu Brockenhurst SO42 7XB
☎ 01590 616203 📠 01590 612624
**Email:** info@bucklershard.co.uk
**Web:** www.bucklershard.co.uk
**Dir:** *M27 junct 2, A326, B3054 then follow tourist signs to Beaulieu & Buckler's Hard*
An enticing port of call, the historic and picturesque shipbuilding village of Buckler's Hard is where ships from Nelson's fleet were built. After setting a course for the Buckler's Hard Story and authentically reconstructed 18th-century Historic Cottages savour the sights and sounds of the countryside on a ramble along the Riverside Walk or enjoy a cruise on the Beaulieu River on 'Swiftsure' during the summer months.

**Times:** *Open all year, Etr-Sep 10.30-5, winter 11-4. Closed 25 Dec.
**Fee:** *Please contact for current prices.
**Facilities:** 🅿 🍽 (Licensed) 🪑 🗑 ♿ (toilets), shop, guided tours 🚌

## EXBURY
### Exbury Gardens & Railway
Exbury Estate Office Southampton SO45 1AZ
☎ 023 8089 1203 📄 023 8089 9940
**Email:** nigel.philpott@exbury.co.uk
**Web:** www.exbury.co.uk
**Dir:** *from M27 W junct 2, 3m from Beaulieu, off B3054*
A 200-acre landscaped woodland garden on the east bank of the Beaulieu River, with one of the finest collections of rhododendrons, azaleas, camellias and magnolias in the world - as well as many rare and beautiful shrubs and trees. A labyrinth of tracks and paths enable you to explore the beautiful gardens and walks. Year round interest is ensured in various parts of the gardens and a steam railway takes visitors on a 20-minute journey around the gardens.

**Times:** *Open Mar-5 Nov, daily 10-5.30; Santa Steam Specials in Dec
**Fee:** *£5-£7.50 (ch under 3 free, ch 3-15 £1-£1.50, pen £4.50-£6.50, £6 Mon-Fri). Railway £2.50-£3.
**Facilities:** 🅿 🅿 (100yds) 🍽 (Licensed) ⛱ ♿ (free wheelchair loans & access maps, buggy tours £3.50, toilets), shop, garden centre, guided tours 🚌

## FAREHAM
### Royal Armouries Fort Nelson
Portsdown Hill Road PO17 6AN
☎ 01329 233734 📄 01329 822092
**Email:** fnenquiries@armouries.org.uk
**Web:** www.royalarmouries.org
**Dir:** *from M27 junct 11, follow brown tourist signs for Royal Armouries.*
Home to the Royal Armouries' collection of over 350 big guns and cannon, this superbly restored Victorian fort overlooks Portsmouth Harbour. Built in the 1860s to deter a threatened French invasion, there are secret tunnels, underground chambers and grass ramparts to explore with daily guided tours. Events throughout the year include re-enactments and the Royal Armouries Military Tattoo. Contact Fort Nelson for details.

**Times:** Open Apr-Oct, daily 10-5 (Tue 11-5); Nov-Mar, daily 10.30-4 (Tue 11.30-4)
**Fee:** *Free (there may be a charge for special events/workshops)
**Facilities:** 🅿 ⛱ ♿ (access & audio guide, ramps, induction loop, wheelchair, toilets) shop guided tours audio commentaries ⊗ (ex guide & hearing dogs) 🚌 (pre-booking advised for catering)

## GOSPORT
### Explosion! Museum of Naval Firepower
Priddy's Hard PO12 4LE
☎ 023 9250 5600 📄 023 9250 5605
**Email:** info@explosion.org.uk
**Web:** www.explosion.org.uk
**Dir:** *M27 junct 11, A32 and follow signs*
Explosion! The Museum of Naval Firepower is set in the green Heritage Area of Priddy's Hard in Gosport on the shores of Portsmouth Harbour, telling the story of naval firepower from the days of gunpowder to modern missiles. Come face to face with the atom bomb, the Exocet missile and the Gatling Gun and take a trip into the fascinating story of the men and women who supplied the Royal Navy. Walk around the buildings that were a state secret for 200 years and discover the Grand Magazine, an amazing vault once packed full with gunpowder, now a stunning multimedia film show.
**Times:** Open all year, Apr-Oct & all school hols, daily 10-5.30; Nov-Mar, Thu, Sat & Sun 10-4.30. Closed 24-26 Dec.
**Fee:** £5 (ch £3.50, pen £4.50). Family ticket £15
**Facilities:** 🅿 ⛱ 🍽 ♿ (toilets), shop, guided tours ⊗ (ex guide dogs) 🚌 (pre-booking required)

**HAMPSHIRE**

## GOSPORT
### Royal Navy Submarine Museum

Haslar Jetty Road Portsmouth Harbour PO12 2AS

☎ 023 9252 9217 & 9251 0354 ▤ 023 9251 1349

**Email:** rnsubs@rnsubmus.co.uk

**Web:** www.rnsubmus.co.uk

**Dir:** *M27 junct 11, follow signs*

The great attraction of this museum is the chance to see inside a submarine, and there are guided tours of *HMS Alliance*, as well as displays exploring submarine development. Two periscopes from *HMS Conqueror* can be seen in the reconstruction of a nuclear submarine control room, giving panoramic views of Portsmouth Harbour. The Navy's first submarine is back on display in a new gallery and exhibition space.

**Times:** *Open all year, Apr-Oct 10-5.30; Nov-Mar 10-4.30. Closed 24 Dec-1 Jan. (Allow 3 hrs for visit. Last tour 1 hour before closing).

**Fee:** *£4 (ch & pen £2.75). Family ticket £11 (2ad+4ch). Party 12+. Discounted entry scheme Defence of the Realm, in association with Southern Military Museums.

**Facilities:** 🅿 Ⓟ (0.5m) ⌂ ⛭ (information in Braille, lift to upper gallery, toilets), shop ⊗ (ex guide dogs) 🚌

## HAVANT
### Staunton Country Park

Middle Park Way PO9 5HB

☎ 023 9245 3405 ▤ 023 9249 8156

**Email:** amanda.fallbrown@hants.gov.uk

**Web:** www.hants.gov.uk/staunton

**Dir:** *off B2149, between Havant & Horndean*

Set in the Regency pleasure grounds of Sir George Staunton, 19th-century traveller, Orientalist and patron of horticulture, Staunton boasts an ornamental farm, the largest ornamental glasshouses on the South Coast, 1,000 acres of parkland, with ancient woodland and intriguing follies and much, much more. Children can feed farm animals, or visit the play area while the grown-ups stroll through the walled gardens.

**Times:** Open 10-5 (4 winter).

**Fee:** *£5 (ch £3.60, pen £4.10).

**Facilities:** 🅿 Ⓟ (50yds) 🍴 ⌂ 📷 60-75p ⛭ (wheelchairs for visitors, most areas accessible, toilets), shop, guided tours ⊗ (ex in parkland) 🚌 (pre-booking essential)

## HIGHCLERE
### Highclere Castle & Gardens

Newbury RG20 9RN

☎ 01635 253210 ▤ 01635 255315

**Email:** theoffice@highclerecastle.co.uk

**Web:** www.highclerecastle.co.uk

**Dir:** *4.5m S of Newbury, off A34*

This splendid early Victorian mansion stands in beautiful parkland on the site of a previous house, which in turn was built on the site of an even earlier house owned by the Bishops of Winchester. It has sumptuous interiors and numerous Old Master pictures. Also shown are early finds by the 5th Earl of Carnarvon, one of the men who discovered Tutankhamun's tomb. During the First World War it was a hospital, and in the Second World War it was a home for evacuee children.

**Times:** *Open Jun-Aug, Mon-Fri; 2 BHs wknds in May, Aug BH Mon 11-4 (last entry 3). Telephone 01635 253210 before travelling as Highclere Castle reserves the right to close at other times.

**Fee:** *£7.50 (ch 4-15 £4, concessions £6). Family ticket (2ad + 2ch or 1ad + 3ch) £18 Grounds & gardens only free.

**Facilities:** 🅿 ☕ (self-service tearooms) Licensed ⌂ ⛭ (wheelchair available, toilets), shop ⊗ (ex guide dogs) 🚌

## LIPHOOK
### Hollycombe Steam Collection
Iron Hill Midhurst Road GU30 7LP
☎ 01428 724900 📠 01428 723682
**Email:** info@hollycombe.co.uk
**Web:** www.hollycombe.co.uk
**Dir:** *1m SE Liphook on Midhurst road, follow brown tourist signs*

A comprehensive collection of working steam-power, including a large Edwardian fairground, three railways, one with spectacular views of the South Downs, traction engine hauled rides, steam agricultural machinery, pets corner, sawmill and even a paddle steamer engine.
**Times:** *Open 2 Apr-8 Oct Sun & BHs, 30 Jul-28 Aug, daily 12-5
**Fee:** *£8.50 (ch 3-15 & pen £7).

**Facilities:** 🅿 🍴 ♿ (toilets), shop, guided tours 🚫 (ex assist dogs) 🚌

## LYNDHURST
### New Forest Museum & Visitor Centre
Main Car Park High Street SO43 7NY
☎ 023 8028 3444 📠 023 8028 4236
**Email:** office@newforestmuseum.org.uk
**Web:** www.newforestmuseum.org.uk
**Dir:** *leave M27 at Cadnam & follow A337 to Lyndhurst. Museum signed*

The story of the New Forest - history, traditions, character and wildlife, told through an audio-visual show and exhibition displays. With life-size models of Forest characters, and the famous New Forest embroidery. Events and exhibitions throughout the year, contact for details.
**Times:** Open all year daily, from 10. Closed 25 & 26 Dec.

**Fee:** £3 (concessions £2.50). Family ticket (2ad+4ch) £9 , under 8yrs free.
**Facilities:** 🅿 (charged) 🍴 ♿ (lift to 1st floor, toilets), shop 🚌

## MARWELL
### Marwell Zoological Park
Colden Common SO21 1JH
☎ 01962 777407 📠 01962 777511
**Email:** marwell@marwell.org.uk
**Web:** www.marwell.org.uk
**Dir:** *M3 junct 11 or M27 junct 5. Zoo located on B2177, follow brown tourist signs*

Marwell has over 200 species of rare and wonderful animals including tigers, snow leopards, rhino, meerkats, hippo and zebra. Highlights include The World of Lemurs, Encounter Village with unusual domesticated animals, Tropical World with its rainforest environment, Into Africa for giraffes and monkeys, Penguin World and Desert Carnivores. Recent additions include an exciting new snow leopard enclosure and a walkway that enables visitors to come face to face with the giraffes. Marwell is dedicated to saving endangered species and every visit helps conservation work. With road and rail trains, holiday activities, restaurant, gift shops and adventure play-grounds Marwell provides fun and interest for all ages.
**Times:** *Open all year, daily 10-6 (summer), 10-4 (winter). (Last admission 90 mins before closing). Closed 25 Dec.
**Fee:** *£13.50 (ch £10, pen £11.50). Family ticket (2ad+2ch) £45. Prices include a 10% donation
**Facilities:** 🅿 🍴 🍴 🍴 ♿ (wheelchairs & tours for visually impaired/disabled groups, toilets), shop, guided tours 🚫 🚌

**HAMPSHIRE**

## MIDDLE WALLOP
**Museum of Army Flying**
Stockbridge SO20 8DY
☎ 01264 784421 📄 01264 781694
**Email:** enquiries@flying-museum.org.uk
**Web:** www.flying-museum.org.uk
**Dir:** *on A343, between Andover & Salisbury*
One of the country's finest historical collections of military kites, gliders, aeroplanes and helicopters. Imaginative dioramas and displays trace the development of Army flying from before the First World War to more recent conflicts in Ireland, the Falklands and the Gulf. Sit at the controls of a real Scout helicopter and test your skills on the flight simulator, plus children's education centre and 1940s house.
**Times:** *Open all year, daily 10-4.30. Closed week prior to Xmas. Evening visits by special arrangement.
**Fee:** *£6 (ch £3.50, concessions £4) Family £18. Party 10+.
**Facilities:** 🅿 🍴 (Licensed) 🌂 📋 ♿ (lifts to upper levels, toilets), shop, guided tours ⊗ (ex assist dogs) 🚌 (restaurant prefers notice)

## MINSTEAD
**Furzey Gardens**
Lyndhurst SO43 7GL
☎ 023 8081 2464 & 2297 📄 023 8081 2297
**Email:** info@furzey-gardens.org
**Web:** www.furzey-gardens.org
**Dir:** *1m S of junct A31/M3 Cadnam off A31 or A337 near Lyndhurst*
A large thatched gallery is the venue for refreshments and displays of local arts and crafts, and the eight acres of peaceful glades which surround it include winter and summer heathers, rare flowering trees and shrubs and a mass of spring bulbs. There is a 16th-century cottage, lake, and the nursery, run by the Minstead Training Project for Young People with Learning Disabilities, sells a wide range of produce.
**Times:** Gardens open daily, 10-5 (or dusk if earlier). Gallery open: Mar-Oct, 10-5 & wknds unitl mid Dec. Closed Xmas.
**Fee:** *Mar-Oct: £4.50 (ch £1.50, pen £3.50) Family £10
**Facilities:** 🅿 🅿 (0.5m) 🌂 📋 ♿ (garden access for wheelchair visitors with assistance, toilets), shop, garden centre ⊗ (ex guide dogs) 🚌 (prior booking required)

## MOTTISFONT
**Mottisfont Abbey & Garden**
Romsey SO51 0LP
☎ 01794 340757 📄 01794 341492
**Email:** mottisfontabbey@nationaltrust.org.uk
**Web:** www.nationaltrust.org.uk/mottisfontabbey
**Dir:** *4.5m NW Romsey, 1m W of A3057*
Mottisfont Abbey is an 18th-century house adapted from a 12th-century priory. The north front shows its medieval church origins quite clearly, and the garden has splendid old trees and a walled garden planted with the national collection of old-fashioned roses. The estate includes Mottisfont village and surrounding farmland and woods.
**Times:** * Garden & House: 27 Feb-2 Jun, Sat-Wed 11-5; 3-30 Jun daily from 11-5 (garden to 8.30); 1 Jul-3 Sep, Sat-Thu 11-5; 4 Sep-29 Oct, Sat-Wed 11-5. Garden only 4 Feb-26 Mar 11-4, 30 Oct-17 Dec Sat-Sun 11-4. (Last admission to grounds 1hr before closing).
**Fee:** *£7 (ch £3.50) Family ticket £17.50
**Facilities:** 🅿 🍴 (last orders 4.45) 🍴 (Licensed) 🌂 📋 10p ♿ (Braille guide, wheelchair available, driven buggy, toilets), shop, garden centre ⊗ (ex assist dogs) 🚌 booking essential 🌸

## NEW ALRESFORD
### Watercress Line
The Railway Station SO24 9JG
☎ 01962 733810 🖪 01962 735448
**Email:** info@watercressline.co.uk
**Web:** www.watercressline.co.uk
**Dir:** *stations at Alton & Alresford signed off A31, follow brown tourist signs*
The Watercress Line runs through ten miles of scenic countryside between Alton and Alresford. All four stations are `dressed' in period style, and there's a locomotive yard and picnic area at Ropley. Special events inlcude the Thomas the Tank Engine and Santa Specials. 2007 is the 30th anniversary of the lines re-opening.
**Times:** *Open May-Sep, Tue-Thu & wknds; Jan-Apr & Oct, wknds only.

**Fee:** *Unlimited travel for the day, £10 (ch £5, pen £9). Family ticket £25. Charge for dogs.
**Facilities:** Ⓟ (charged) Ⓟ (200mtrs - parking at Alresford & Alton only) 🖵 (buffet at Alresford) 🍴 (Licensed) 🚻♿ (ramp access to trains, toilets), shop, guided tours 🚍 (prior booking preferred)

## NEW MILTON
### Sammy Miller Mototcycle Museum
Bashley Cross Road BH25 5SZ
☎ 01425 620777 🖪 01425 619696
**Email:** info@sammymiller.co.uk
**Web:** www.sammymiller.co.uk
**Dir:** *signed off A35, 15m W of Southampton, 10m E of Bournemouth, N of New Milton town centre*
The museum houses over 300 rare and classic bikes and with machines dating back to 1900, some are the only surviving examples of their type. The Racing collection features World Record breaking bikes and their history, including the first bike to lap a Grand Prix Course at over 100 miles per hour. Special events include marque days.
**Times:** Open daily 10-4.30. (Closed 2 Jan-mid-Feb)
**Fee:** £4.90 (ch £2.50).

**Facilities:** Ⓟ Ⓟ (100yds) 🍴 (Licensed) 🚻♿ (special rates for disabled people, toilets), shop, guided tours 🚫 (ex guide dogs) 🚍

## OWER
### Paultons Park
Romsey SO51 6AL
☎ 023 8081 4442 🖪 023 8081 3025
**Email:** info@paultons.co.uk
**Web:** www.paultonspark.co.uk
**Dir:** *exit M27 junct 2, near junct A31 & A36*
Paultons Park offers a great day out for all the family with over 50 different attractions. Many fun activities include new Cobra ride, drop rides, roller coaster, 6-lane astroglide, teacup ride, log flume, pirate ship swingboat, dragon roundabout, and wave-runner coaster. Attractions for younger children include Kid's Kingdom, Tiny Tots Town, Rabbit Ride, the Magic Forest where nursery rhymes come to life, Wonderful World of Wind in the Willows and the Ladybird ride. In beautiful parkland

setting with extensive 'Capability' Brown gardens landscaped with ponds and aviaries for exotic birds; lake and hedge maze. There is also the Romany Experience Museum with unique collection of gypsy wagons and the Village Life Museum. Something for everyone.
**Times:** *Open mid Mar-Oct, daily 10-6; Nov & Dec, wknds only until Xmas.
**Fee:** *£13.50 (ch under 14). Children under 1m tall enter for free. Range of Family Supersavers.
**Facilities:** Ⓟ 🍴 (Licensed) 🚻♿ (pre-booked wheelchair hire, some rides unsuitable, toilets), shop 🚫 (ex guide dogs) 🚍

**HAMPSHIRE**

## PORTCHESTER
**Portchester Castle**
Castle Street PO16 9QW
☎ 023 9237 8291
**Web:** www.english-heritage.org.uk
**Dir:** *off A27*
Discover 2,000 years of history from the Roman beginnings of Portchester Castle to the years of medieval splendour. Stand where Henry V rallied his troops before setting out to defeat the French at the Battle of Agincourt in 1415.
**Times:** Open all year, Apr-Sep, daily 10-6; Oct-Mar, daily 10-4. Closed 24-26 Dec & 1 Jan.
**Fee:** £3.90 (ch £2, concessions £2.90). Prices and opening times are subject to change. Please check web site or call 0870 333 1181 for the most up to date prices and opening times when planning your visit.
**Facilities:** 𝐏 & shop ⊗ (ex on lead in certain areas) 🚐 ⚏ ♨

## PORTSMOUTH
**Blue Reef Aquarium**
Clarence Esplanade Portsmouth PO5 3PB
☎ 023 9287 5222 🖷 023 9229 4443
**Email:** portsmouth@bluereefaquarium.co.uk
**Web:** www.bluereefaquarium.co.uk
**Dir:** *on approach to city follow brown tourist signs to seafront or Aquarium. Located on Southsea seafront between D-Day Museum and The Hoverport*
Spectacular underwater walkthrough tunnels offer amazing sights of exotic coral reefs - home to sharks and shimmering shoals of brightly-coloured fish. Mediterranean and tropical waters are recreated in giant ocean tanks, home to a stunning array of undersea life including seahorses, puffer fish, coral and piranhas. Visit the website for current special events.
**Times:** *Open daily from 10. Closing times vary with season, please telephone for details.
**Fee:** £7.50 (pen £6.50, ch 3-16 £4.99)
**Facilities:** 𝐏 (under 50mtrs) 🍴 🖷 & (all on 1 level, toilets), shop, guided tours ⊗ (ex assist dogs) 🚐

## PORTSMOUTH
**City Museum & Records Office**
Museum Rd PO1 2LJ
☎ 023 9282 7261 🖷 023 9287 5276
**Email:** mvs@portsmouthcc.gov.uk
**Web:** www.portsmouthcitymuseums.co.uk/
**Dir:** *M27/M275 into Portsmouth, follow museum symbol signs*
Dedicated to local history, fine and decorative art, 'The Story of Portsmouth' presents room settings showing life here from the 17th century to the 1950s. The 'Portsmouth at Play' exhibition features leisure pursuits from the Victorian period to the 1970s. The museum has a fine and decorative art gallery, plus regular temporary exhibitions. The Record Office contains the official records of the City of Portsmouth from the 14th century.
**Times:** *Open all year, Apr-Oct daily 10-5.30; Nov-Mar daily 10-5. Closed 24-26 Dec and Record Office closed on public holidays.
**Fee:** *Free
**Facilities:** 𝐏 𝐏 (200mtrs) 🍴 & (induction loops, lift & wheelchairs, parking, toilets), shop ⊗ (ex guide & assist dogs) 🚐 (pre-booking) ♨

## PORTSMOUTH
### D-Day Museum & Overlord Embroidery
Clarence Esplanade PO5 3NT
☎ 023 9282 7261 ▤ 023 9287 5276
**Email:** mvs@portsmouthcc.gov.uk
**Web:** www.ddaymuseum.co.uk
**Dir:** *M27/M275 into Portsmouth, follow D-Day Museum & seafront signs*
Portsmouth's D-Day Museum tells the dramatic story of the Allied landings in Normandy in 1944. Centrepiece is the magnificent 'Overlord Embroidery' made of 34 individual panels and 83 metres in length. Experience the world's largest ever seaborne invasion, and step back in time to scenes of wartime Britain. Military equipment, vehicles, landing craft and personal memories complete this special story.

**Times:** *Open all year, Apr-Sep daily 10-5.30. Oct-Mar, 10-5. Closed 24-26 Dec
**Fee:** £6 (ch £3.60, pen £4.50). Family ticket £15.60
**Facilities:** ℗ (charged) ℗ (200-400yds) ☕ (May-Sep) ⊞ ♿ (induction loops, sound aids, w/chairs available, toilets), shop, audio commentaries (charged) ⊗ (ex guide & helper dogs) 🚌 (pre-booking)

## PORTSMOUTH
### Portsmouth Historic Dockyard
HM Naval Base PO1 3LJ
☎ 023 9283 9766 ▤ 023 9283 8228
**Email:** enquiries@historicdockyard.co.uk
**Web:** www.historicdockyard.co.uk
**Dir:** *M27/M275 & follow brown historic waterfront and dockyard signs*
Portsmouth Historic Dockyard is home to the world's greatest historic ships: *Mary Rose* - King Henry VIII's favourite ship, *HMS Victory* - Lord Nelson's flagship at the Battle of Trafalgar and *HMS Warrior* - the first iron-hulled warship. In addition, the Royal Naval Museum has the most significant, permanent collections relating to Nelson and the Battle of Trafalgar, and Action Stations gives an interactive insight into the modern day Royal Navy.

**Times:** *Open Apr-Oct, daily 10-6; Nov-Mar, daily 10-5.30. Last entry, 30 minutes before closing
**Fee:** *All inclusive ticket: £16 (ch & pen £13, under 5's free). Family £46
**Facilities:** ℗ (charged) ℗ (200yds) ⊞ ♿ (wheelchairs, facilities for visually & hearing impaired, toilets), shop, guided tours, audio commentaries ⊗ (ex assist dogs) 🚌 (advisable to book)

## PORTSMOUTH
### Southsea Castle
Clarence Esplanade PO5 3PA
☎ 023 9282 7261 ▤ 023 9287 5276
**Email:** mvs@portsmouthcc.gov.uk
**Web:** www.southseacastle.co.uk
**Dir:** *accessible from M27, A27, A3M, A2030, follow castle signposts*
Part of Henry VIII's national coastal defences, this fort was built in 1544 and has since been used as a prison. In the 'Time Tunnel' experience, the ghost of the castle's first master gunner guides you through the dramatic scenes from the castle's eventful history. Audio-visual presentation, underground passages, Tudor military history displays, artillery, and panoramic views of the Solent and Isle of Wight.

**Times:** *Open all year, Apr-Sep, daily 10-5.30; Oct-Mar, daily 10-5.
**Fee:** £3 (ch & students £1.80, ch accompanied under 13 free, pen £2.25). Family ticket £7.80.
**Facilities:** ℗ ℗ (300-400yds) ⊞ ♿ (wheelchair available), shop ⊗ (ex guide & assist dogs) 🚌 (pre-booking)

**HAMPSHIRE**

HAMPSHIRE

### PORTSMOUTH
**Spitbank Fort**
Town Quay House 99 Gosport Road PO16 0PY
☎ 01329 242077 📠 02392 504207
**Email:** info@spitbankfort.co.uk
**Web:** www.spitbankfort.co.uk
**Dir:** *Ferries depart from HM Naval Base Portsmouth, Portsmouth Hard, Gosport Ferry Pontoon, by the side of Portsmouth Harbour Railway Stn and Gunwarf Quays shopping centre*
Built in the 1860s as part of the coastal defences against the French, this massive granite and iron fortress stands a mile out to sea, with magnificent views across the Solent. The interior is a maze of passages connecting over 50 rooms on two levels and it is now a unique entertainment venue for all ages and tastes.

**Times:** Open all year
**Fee:** *Boat ride takes approx 20 mins. Pub nights: (Wed/Thu) £17.50 (ch £10). Parties: (Fri/Sat) £25 (adult only). Sun Lunch: £17.50 (ch £10)
**Facilities:** Ⓟ ⌨ (licensed) 🍽 (Licensed) ♿ (many steps), guided tours ⊗ (ex guide dogs) 🚌

---

### RINGWOOD
**Moors Valley Country Park**
Horton Road Ashley Heath BH24 2ET
☎ 01425 470721 📠 01425 471656
**Email:** moorsvalley@eastdorsetdc.gov.uk
**Web:** www.moors-valley.co.uk
**Dir:** *1.5m from Ashley Heath rdbt on A31 near Three Legged Cross*
Fifteen hundred acres of forest, woodland, heathland, lakes, river and meadows provide a home for a wide variety of plants and animals, and there's a Visitor Centre, Adventure Playground, picnic area, Moors Valley Railway, Tree Top Trail and the 'Go Ape'- high ropes course (book on 0870 444 5562). Cycle hire is also available.
**Times:** Open all year, 8-dusk (8pm at latest). Visitor centre open 9.30-4.30 (later in summer). Closed 25 Dec.

**Fee:** No admission charge but parking up to £7 per day.
**Facilities:** Ⓟ (charged) 🍴 ♿ (scooter & wheelchairs, toilets), shop 🚌 (pre-booked)

---

### ROCKBOURNE
**Rockbourne Roman Villa**
Fordingbridge SP6 3PG
☎ 01725 518541
**Web:** www.hants.gov.uk/museum/rockbourne
**Dir:** *from Salisbury exit A338 at Fordingbridge, take B3078 westwards through Sandleheath & follow signs. Or turn off A354 Salisbury to Blandford road, W of Coombe Bissett*
Discovered in 1942, the site features the remains of a 40-room Roman villa and is the largest in the area. Displays include mosaics and a very rare hypocaust system. The museum displays the many artefacts found on the site during excavations. Roman re-enactments are performed - please ring for details.
**Times:** *Open Apr-Sep, daily 10.30-6. (Last adm 5.30)

**Fee:** *£2.25 (concessions £1.25).
**Facilities:** Ⓟ 🍴 📓 20p ♿ (ramps in & out of museum, toilets), shop ⊗ (ex guide/hearing dogs) 🚌 (must be pre-booked) 📧

## SELBORNE
### Gilbert White's House & The Oates Museum
High Street Alton GU34 3JH
☎ 01420 511275 📄 01420 511040
**Email:** info@gilbertwhitehouse.org.uk
**Web:** www.gilbertwhitehouse.org.uk
**Dir:** *on village High Street*
Charming 18th-century house, home of famous naturalist, the Rev. Gilbert White, author of *The Natural History and Antiquities of Selborne*. Over 20 acres of garden and parkland, shop and tea parlour serving some 18th-century fare. There is also an exhibition on Captain Lawrence Oates and his ill-fated expedition to the South Pole in 1911-12. Special events include an unusual plants fair and concert evening in June, Gilbert White day in July and mulled wine day in December.

**Times:** *Open Tue-Sun & BH, Jan-24 Dec, 11-5. Last admissions 4.30
**Fee:** *£6 (ch free, concessions £5).
**Facilities:** Ⓟ (100mtrs) 🍽 (Licensed) ♿ (toilets), shop, garden centre, guided tours ⊗ (ex guide dogs) 🚌 (pre-booking)

## SHERBORNE ST JOHN
### The Vyne
Basingstoke RG24 9HL
☎ 01256 883858 📄 01256 881720
**Email:** thevyne@nationaltrust.org.uk
**Web:** www.nationaltrust.org.uk
**Dir:** *4m N of Basingstoke, off A340, signed from A33, A339 & A340*
Built in the early 16th-century for Lord Sandys, Henry VIII's Lord Chamberlain, the house acquired a classical portico in the mid-17th century and has a fascinating Tudor chapel with renaissance glass, a palladian staircase and a wealth of old panelling and fine furniture. The attractive grounds feature herbaceous borders and a wild garden, with lawns, lakes and woodland walks.
**Times:** *Open House & Gardens 20 Mar-Oct daily (ex Thu & Fri) 1-5, wknds 11-5. Gardens open wknds in Feb & Mar, 11-5 & 11-5 Mon-Wed). **Fee:** *House & Grounds £7.50 (ch £3.75). Family £18.75, Group £6.30. Grounds & Gardens only £4.50 (ch £2.25) **Facilities:** Ⓟ 🖵 (open 11-5, lunch 12-2) 🍽 (Licensed) 🪑 📱 ♿ (Braille guides, hearing loop, touch tours, toilets) shop guided tours ⊗ (ex assist dogs) 🚌 (must pre-book) 🌸

## SOUTHAMPTON
### Southampton City Art Gallery
Civic Centre Commercial Rd SO14 7LP
☎ 023 8083 2277 📄 023 8083 2153
**Email:** art.gallery@southampton.gov.uk
**Web:** www.southampton.gov.uk/art
**Dir:** *situated on the Watts Park side of the Civic Centre, a short walk from the station, on Commercial Rd*
The largest gallery in the south of England, with the finest collection of contemporary art in the country outside London. Varied displays of landscapes, portrait paintings or recent British art are always available, as well as a special display, selected by members of the public.
**Times:** Open all year, Tue-Sat 10-5, Sun 1-4. Closed 25-27 & 31 Dec.
**Fee:** *Free

**Facilities:** Ⓟ (50yds - nearby street parking is 1hr only) 🍽 📱 ♿ (free BSL signed tours by arrangement, 'touch tour', toilets) shop guided tours ⊗ (ex guide dogs) 🚌 (over 50 people, call ahead of visit) ♿

## SOUTHAMPTON
### Southampton Maritime Museum
The Wool House Town Quay SO14 2AR
☎ 023 8022 3941 & 8063 5904 📠 023 8033 9601
**Email:** museums@southampton.gov.uk
**Web:** www.southampton.gov.uk/leisure
**Dir:** *on the waterfront, near to the Town Quay*
The Wool House was built in the 14th century as
a warehouse for wool, and now houses a maritime
museum, with models and displays telling the history
of the Victorian and modern port of Southampton. There
are exhibitions of the *Titanic*, *The Queen Mary* and an
interactive area for children.
**Times:** Open Tue-Fri 10-4; Sat 10-1 & 2-4; Sun 1-4
**Fee:** *Free
**Facilities:** ℗ (400yds - metered parking adjacent)

📷 ♿ (hearing loop on Titanic presentation), shop, audio
commentaries ⊗ (ex guide dogs) 🚌 (pre-booking) ♨

## WEYHILL
### The Hawk Conservancy Trust
Andover SP11 8DY
☎ 01264 773850 📠 01264 773772
**Email:** info@hawk-conservancy.org
**Web:** www.hawk-conservancy.org
**Dir:** *3m W of Andover, signed from A303*
This is the largest centre in the south for birds of prey
from all over the world including eagles, hawks, falcons,
owls, vultures and kites. Exciting birds of prey
demonstrations are held daily at noon, 2pm, and
3.30pm, including the 'Valley of the Eagles' at 2pm.
Different birds are flown at these times and visitors may
be able to hold a bird and adults can fly a Harris hawk.
**Times:** Open Feb half term-Oct half term, daily from
10.30-5.30 (last admission 4).

**Fee:** *£8.75 (ch £5, concessions £8). Family ticket
£27.50
**Facilities:** ℗ 🍴 🪑 📷 ♿ (wheelchair area in grounds,
viewing areas in hides, ramps, toilets), shop, guided tours
⊗ 🚌 (pre-book for party rates)

## WHITCHURCH
### Whitchurch Silk Mill
28 Winchester Street RG28 7AL
☎ 01256 892065 📠 01256 893882
**Email:** silkmill@btinternet.com
**Web:** www.whitchurchsilkmill.org.uk
**Dir:** *halfway between Winchester & Newbury signposted
clearly on the A34. Located in centre of the town*
The mill is idyllically located on the River Test. Whitchurch
Silk Mill is the oldest surviving textile mill in Southern
England. Fine silks and ribbons are still woven for
interiors and fashion. See the 19th-century waterwheel
pounding and learn about winding, warping and weaving.
There is a programme of exhibitions, workshops and
children's activities.
**Times:** *Open Tue-Sun & BH Mon 10.30-5 (last

admission 4.15). Closed 24 Dec-1 Jan.
**Fee:** *£3.50 (ch £1.75, pen & students £3). Family
ticket (2 adults & 3 ch) £8.75.
**Facilities:** ℗ ℗ ⌨ (self-service) 🪑 ♿ (disabled parking
adjacent site, toilets), shop, guided tours (charged),
audio commentaries ⊗ (ex guide dogs) 🚌 (advance
booking essential)

## WINCHESTER
### Hospital of St Cross
St Cross SO23 9SD

☎ 01962 851375 ▤ 01962 878221

**Email:** administrator@stcrosshospital.co.uk

**Web:** www.stcrosshospital.co.uk

**Dir:** *on B3335, 0.5m from M3 junct 11*

A beautiful group of Grade I listed medieval and Tudor buildings, in a tranquil setting by the water meadows, St. Cross is home to 25 elderly brothers. In keeping with tradition, they wear gowns and trencher hats and act as visitor guides. The hospital is world-famous for its ancient and unique tradition of the Wayfarers Dole - a beaker of beer and a morsel of bread is given by the porter to all visitors who request it. Visitors can admire the medieval and Tudor architecture, explore the medieval hall, the Georgian kitchen and the Tudor cloister as well as the walled garden with many plants of American origin.

**Times:** Open all year, Apr-Oct, 9.30-5; Nov-Mar 10.30-3.30. (Closed Good Fri, 25 Dec, Sun mornings (summer) and Sun (winter)

**Fee:** £2.50 (ch 50p, pen £2).

**Facilities:** ❷ ℗ (50yds) ⍭ ▤ ♿ (toilets), shop, guided tours ⊗ (ex guide dogs) 🚌 1 at a time

---

## WINCHESTER
### INTECH - Family Science Centre
Telegraph Way Morn Hill SO21 1HX

☎ 01962 863791 ▤ 01962 868524

**Email:** htct@intech-uk.com

**Web:** www.intech-uk.com

**Dir:** *M3 junct 10 S or junct 9 N onto A31 then B3404 Alresford road*

This purpose-built, 3500 square metre family attraction houses 100 interactive exhibits, which demonstrate the science and technology of the world around us in an engaging way. The philosophy is most definitely 'hands-on', and the motto of the centre is 'Doing is Believing'. Exhibits deal with things like viscosity, tornados, and Newton's Cradle among others. Activities and science shows take place during school holidays.

**Times:** Open all year, daily 10-4. Closed Xmas.

**Fee:** *£6.50 (ch £4, pen £5) Family ticket (2ad + 2ch) £18.90

**Facilities:** ❷ ⍭ ▤ ♿ (toilets), shop ⊗ (ex guide dogs) 🚌 Pre-booked visits only

---

## WINCHESTER
### The Great Hall
Castle Avenue SO23 8PJ

☎ 01962 846476 ▤ 01962 841326

**Email:** the.great.hall@hants.gov.uk

**Web:** www.hants.gov.uk/discover/places/great-hall.html

**Dir:** *situated at top of High St. Park & Ride recommended*

The only surviving part of Winchester Castle, once home to the Domesday Book, this 13th-century hall was the centre of court and government life. Built between 1222-1235 during the reign of Henry III, it is one of the largest and finest five bay halls in England to have survived to the present day. The Round Table based on the Arthurian Legend and built between 1230-1280 hangs in the hall. Queen Eleanor's Garden is a re-creation of a late 13th century ornamental garden.

**Times:** Open all year, Mar-Oct daily 10-5; Nov-Feb, daily 10-5, wknds 10-4. Closed 25-26 Dec.

**Fee:** *Free

**Facilities:** ℗ (200yds) ▤ ♿ (toilets), shop, guided tours ⊗ (ex guide/hearing dogs) 🚌 (no parking for coaches)

HAMPSHIRE

### WINCHESTER
**Winchester Cathedral**
1 The Close SO23 9LS
☎ 01962 857200 & 866854 📄 01962 857201
**Email:** cathedral.office@winchester-cathedral.org.uk
**Web:** www.winchester-cathedral.org.uk
**Dir:** *in city centre - follow city heritage signs*
The longest medieval church in Europe, founded in 1079 on a site where Christian worship had already been offered for over 400 years. Among its treasures are the 12th-century illuminated Winchester Bible, the font, medieval wall paintings and Triforium Gallery Museum. Items of interest include Jane Austen's tomb and the statue of the Winchester diver, William Walker, who in 1905 saved the cathedral by underpinning its foundations, working up to six hours a day over a period of six years, often in 20 feet of water. Visitors can also descend into the crypt to see a sculpture by Anthony Gormley, best known as creator of The Angel of The North, or ascend to the tower and bell chamber.
**Times:** *Open all year, daily 8.30-5.30. (Subject to services and special events).
**Fee:** *Admission free, voluntary donations: £4 (concessions £3).
**Facilities:** ℗ (500mtrs) 📋 ♿ (chair lift to east end of Cathedral, touch & hearing model, toilets) shop guided tours ⊗ (ex guide dogs) 🚌 (advance booking essential)

### HATFIELD
**Hatfield House**
AL9 5NQ
☎ 01707 287010 📄 01707 287033
**Email:** visitors@hatfield-house.co.uk
**Web:** www.hatfield-house.co.uk
**Dir:** *2m from junct 4 A1(M) on A1000, 7m from M25 junct 23. House is opposite Hatfield railway station*
The house, built by Robert Cecil in 1611, is the home of the 7th Marquess of Salisbury and is full of exquisite tapestries, furniture and famous paintings. It includes the national collection of model soldiers and children's play area. Events take place throughout the year - see website for details.
**Times:** Open Etr Sat-Sep. House: Wed-Sun & BHs 12-4; Park & West Garden: daily 11-5.30. East Garden, Thu.
**Fee:** House, park & West Garden: £9 (ch £4.50, pen £8.50). Park only £2.50 (ch £1.50, pen £2.50), Park & West Garden £5 (ch £4, pen £5). Park & Gardens on Thu: £7.50 (ch £7, pen £6). House tour £5.
**Facilities:** ℗ 🍴 (Licensed) 🎪 📋 ♿ (lift to 1st floor, wheelchairs, toilets), shop, guided tours ⊗ (ex in park) 🚌 (prior booking required)

### KNEBWORTH
**Knebworth House, Gardens & Country Park**
SG3 6PY
☎ 01438 812661 📄 01438 811908
**Email:** info@knebworthhouse.com
**Web:** www.knebworthhouse.com
**Dir:** *direct access from A1(M) junct 7 Stevenage South*
Home of the Lytton family since 1490, the original Tudor Manor was transformed in 1843 by the spectacular high Gothic decoration of Victorian novelist Sir Edward Bulwer Lytton. The grounds include a Gertrude Jekyll herb garden, a maze, recently restored walled garden, a dinosaur trail in the wilderness garden, a miniature railway, and a deer park.
**Times:** Open daily 31 Mar-15 Apr, 26 May-3 Jun, 30 Jun-5 Sep; wknds & BHs 24-25 March, 21 Apr-20 May, 9-24 Jun, 8-30 Sep. Park, playground & gardens 11-5.30; House 12-5 (last admission 4.15)
**Fee:** House & grounds £9 (ch & pen £8.50) Family ticket £31. Grounds £7, family ticket £24.
**Facilities:** ℗ 🎪 📋 ♿ (transport to door, wheelchair available, toilets), shop, garden centre guided tours audio commentaries ⊗ (ex guide dogs & in park) 🚌

## LONDON COLNEY
### de Havilland Aircraft Heritage Centre
Salisbury Hall AL2 1EX
☎ 01727 826400 & 822051(info) 🖹 01727 826400
**Email:** w4050.dhamt@fsmail.net
**Web:** www.dehavillandmuseum.co.uk
**Dir:** *M25 junct 22. Follow signs for 'Mosquito Aircraft Museum' onto B556*
The oldest aircraft museum in Britain, opened in 1959 to preserve and display the de Havilland Mosquito prototype on the site of its conception. A working museum with displays of 20 de Havilland aircraft and sections together with a comprehensive collection of de Havilland engines and memorabilia. Selective cockpits are open to enter. Education storyboard 'maze style' now open.

**Times:** Open first Sun Mar-last Sun Oct, Sun & BHs 10.30-5.30, Tue, Thu & Sat 2-5.30.
**Fee:** *£5 (ch under 5 free, ch 5-16 £3, pen £4) Family ticket £13 (2ad+2ch)
**Facilities:** 🅿 Ⓟ (adjacent - space restrictions at major events) 🍴 🗎 £3.50 ♿ (w/chairs available, toilets), shop, guided tours 🚫 (ex assist dogs) 🚌 (1 months notice)

## ST ALBANS
### Museum of St Albans
9A Hatfield Road AL1 3RR
☎ 01727 819340 🖹 01727 837472
**Email:** history@stalbans.gov.uk
**Web:** www.stalbansmuseums.org.uk
**Dir:** *city centre on A1057 Hatfield road*
Exhibits include the Salaman collection of craft tools, and reconstructed workshops. The history of St Albans is traced from the departure of the Romans up to the present day. There is a special exhibition gallery with a surprising variety of exhibitions and a wildlife garden with picnic area.
**Times:** *Open all year, daily 10-5, Sun 2-5. Closed 25-26 Dec.
**Fee:** *Free

**Facilities:** 🅿 Ⓟ (0.5m) 🍴 🗎 ♿ (toilets). shop 🚫 (ex guide dogs) 🚌 (no coach parking on site, pre-book)

## ST ALBANS
### Verulamium Museum
St Michaels AL3 4SW
☎ 01727 751810 🖹 01727 859919
**Email:** museum@stalbans.gov.uk
**Web:** www.stalbansmuseums.org.uk
**Dir:** *follow signs for St Albans, museum signed*
Verulamium was one of the largest and most important Roman towns in Britain - by the lst century AD it was declared a 'municipium', giving its inhabitants the rights of Roman citizenship, the only British city granted this honour. A mosaic and underfloor heating system can be seen, and the museum has wall paintings, jewellery, pottery and other domestic items. On the second week-end of every month legionaries occupy the galleries and describe the tactics and equipment of the Roman Army.

**Times:** *Open all year wkdys 10-5.30, Sun 2-5.30. Closed 25-26 Dec.
**Fee:** *£3.30 (ch, concessions £2). Family ticket £8. Subject to change.
**Facilities:** 🅿 (charged) 🍴 🗎 ♿ (ramp access to main entrance, toilets), shop 🚫 (ex guide dogs) 🚌 (max 60, must pre-book)

**HERTFORDSHIRE**

## TRING
**The Walter Rothschild Zoological Museum**
Akeman Street HP23 6AP
☎ 020 7942 6171 📄 020 7942 6150
**Email:** tring-enquiries@nhm.ac.uk
**Web:** www.nhm.ac.uk/museum/tring
**Dir:** *signed from A41*
An unusual museum, founded in the 1890s by Lionel
Walter, 2nd Baron Rothschild, scientist, eccentric and
natural history enthusiast, it became part of the Natural
History Museum in 1937 and houses more than 4000
specimens from whales to fleas, and humming birds
to tigers.
**Times:** Open all year, Mon-Sat 10-5, Sun 2-5. Closed
24-26 Dec.
**Fee:** *Free

**Facilities:** ❷ Ⓟ (on street) 🎪 📄 20p ♿ (ramps, virtual
tour, disabled parking space, toilets), shop ⊗ (ex guide
dogs) 🚌 (no parking at site, must park in town)

## ST BRELADE
**Jersey Lavender Farm**
Rue du Pont Marquet JE3 8DS
☎ 01534 742933 📄 01534 745613
**Email:** admin@jerseylavender.co.uk
**Web:** www.jerseylavender.co.uk
**Dir:** *on B25 from St Aubin's Bay to Redhouses*
Jersey Lavender grows nine acres of lavender, distils
out the essential oil and creates a range of fine toiletry
products. Visitors are able to see the whole process
from cultivating, through to harvesting, distillation and
the production of the final product. There is a national
collection of lavenders, extensive gardens, herb beds
and walks among the lavender fields. There are also
other herbs that are grown and distilled, namely
eucalyptus, rosemary and tea tree.

**Times:** *Open 10 May-18 Sep, Tue-Sun 10-5.
**Fee:** *£3.25 (ch under 14 free pen £3).
**Facilities:** ❷ ☕ (Tea room, ligth lunches, cakes)
♿ (free wheelchair loan, toilets), shop, garden centre
🚌 (prior appointment only)

## ST CLEMENT
**Samares Manor**
JE2 6QW
☎ 01534 870551 📄 01534 768949
**Email:** enquiries@samaresmanor.com
**Web:** www.samaresmanor.com
**Dir:** *2m E of St Helier on St Clements Inner Rd*
The manor stands in 14 acres of beautiful gardens.
The Japanese Garden occupies an artificial hill, and
has a series of waterfalls cascading over Cumberland
limestone. There are farm animals, a craft centre, a
children's play area, tours of the manor house, a
children's nature trail and the Jersey Rural Life and
Carriage Museum. The Jersey Royal Rifle and Carriage
Museum is situated in the manor's early Victorian
courtyard.

**Times:** *Open 8 Apr-14 Oct.
**Fee:** *£5.60 (ch under 16 £1.95, pen £5.20).
**Facilities:** ❷ 🍴 (Licensed) 📄 ♿ (toilets), shop, garden
centre guided tours ⊗ (ex guide dogs) 🚌 (by prior
arrangement)

## ST HELIER
### Maritime Museum & Occupation Tapestry Gallery

New North Quay JE2 3ND

☎ 01534 811043 🖺 01534 874099

**Email:** marketing@jerseyheritagetrust

**Web:** www.jerseyheritagetrust.org

**Dir:** *alongside Marina, opposite Liberation Square*

This converted 19th-century warehouse houses the tapestry consisting of 12 two-metre panels that tells the story of the occupation of Jersey during the Second World War. Each of the 12 parishes took responsibility for stitching a panel, making it the largest community arts project ever undertaken on the island. The Maritime Museum celebrates the relationship of islanders and the sea, including an award-winning hands-on experience.

**Times:** *Open all year, daily 10-5. Winter closing at 4.

**Fee:** *£6 (ch under 6 free, concessions £5.20). Discount and family tickets

**Facilities:** ℗ (paycards in public car parks) ♿ (Braille books, audio guide etc, toilets), shop, audio commentaries ⊗ (ex guide dogs) 🚌 (prebooking)

## ST LAWRENCE
### JERSEY WAR TUNNELS

Les Charrieres Malorey JE3 1FU

☎ 01534 860808 🖺 01534 860886

**Email:** info@jerseywartunnels.com

**Web:** www.jerseywartunnels.com

**Dir:** *bus route 8A from St Helier*

On 1 July 1940 the Channel Islands were occupied by German forces, and this vast complex dug deep into a hillside is the most evocative reminder of that Occupation. A video presentation, along with a large collection of memorabilia, illustrates the lives of the islanders at war and a further exhibition records their impressions during 1945, the year of liberation.

**Times:** *Open 14 Feb-19 Dec, daily 9.30-5.30 (last admission 4).

**Fee:** *£8 (ch £4, students & serving armed forces £6 & pen £7).

**Facilities:** ❷ ℗ (50yds) 🍴 (Hot & cold food) 🍽 (Licensed) ♿ (ramp to restaurant & lift in Visitor Centre to restaurant, toilets) shop ⊗ (ex guide dogs) 🚌

## ST OUEN
### The Channel Islands Military Museum

Five Mile Road

☎ 01534 723136

**Email:** damienhorn@jerseymail.co.uk

**Dir:** *N end of 5 Mile Rd, at rear of Jersey Woollen Mill & across rd from Jersey Pearl*

The museum is housed in a German coastal defence bunker, which formed part of Hitler's Atlantic Wall. It has been restored, as far as possible, to give the visitor an idea of how it looked. The visitor can also see German uniforms, motorcycles, weapons, documents, photographs and other items from the 1940-45 occupation of the island.

**Times:** *Open wk before Etr-Oct

**Fee:** *£4 (ch £2) Groups by arrangement.

**Facilities:** ❷ ℗ (100mtrs) ♿ (all parts accessible ex 1 small room, toilets) shop ⊗ (ex guide dogs) 🚌 (pre-booking required) ♨

JERSEY

ST PETER

**The Living Legend**

Rue de Petit Aleval JE3 7ET

☎ 01534 485496 🖷 01534 485855

**Email:** info@jerseyslivinglegend.co.je

**Web:** www.jerseyslivinglegend.co.je

**Dir:** *from St Helier, along main esplanade & right to Bel Royal. Left and follow road to attraction, signed from German Underground Hospital*

Pass through the granite archways into the landscaped gardens and the world of the Jersey Experience where Jersey's exciting past is recreated in a three dimensional spectacle featuring Stephen Tompkinson, Tony Robinson and other well-known names. Learn of the heroes and villains, the folklore and the story of the island's links with the UK and its struggles with Europe. Other attractions include an adventure playground, street entertainment, the Jersey Craft and Shopping Village, a range of shops and the Jersey Kitchen Restaurant. Two 18-hole adventure golf courses are suitable for all ages. Jersey Karting is a formula one style experience. A unique track featuring adult and cadet karts.

**Times:** *Open daily, Mar-Nov 9.30-5, Sat-Sun 10-5

**Fee:** *£7.10 (ch 7-13 £4.85, pen £6.80, student £5.50, disabled £5.60).

**Facilities:** Ⓟ 🍴 (Licensed) ♿ (wheelchair available, toilets), shop 🚫 (ex guide dogs) 🚌

---

TRINITY

**Durrell Wildlife Conservation Trust**

Les Augres Manor La Profunde Rue JE3 5BP

☎ 01534 860000 🖷 01534 860001

**Email:** info@durrell.org

**Web:** www.durrell.org

Gerald Durrell's unique sanctuary and breeding centre for many of the world's rarest animals. Visitors can see these remarkable creatures, some so rare that they can only be found here, in modern, spacious enclosures in the gardens of the 16th-century manor house. Major attractions are the magical Aye-Ayes from Madagascar and the world-famous family of Lowland gorillas. There is a comprehensive programme of keeper talks, animal displays, activities and exhibitions throughout the year. Contact for further details.

**Times:** *Open all year, daily 9.30-6 (summer); 9.30-5 (winter). Closed 25 Dec.

**Fee:** *£11.50 (ch 4-16 £7.40, pen £8.50).

**Facilities:** Ⓟ 🍴 ⛩ ♿ (toilets), shop 🚫 🚌

---

BEKESBOURNE

**Howletts Wild Animal Park**

Canterbury CT4 5EL

☎ 0870 750 4647 🖷 01303 264944

**Email:** info@totallywild.net

**Web:** www.totallywild.net

**Dir:** *off A2, 3m S of Canterbury, follow brown tourist signs*

Set in 90 acres of parkland, Howletts is home to some of the world's most rare and endangered animals. Howletts boasts the UK's largest group of African elephants, Indian and Siberian tigers, many small cats and rare monkeys and the world's largest group of Western Lowland gorillas. Glass fronted tiger enclosures, children's adventure playground and the new Jurassic Mine with ice and gem cave are not to be missed. Visit the new Natureworks Arts and Craft Studio for painting, pottery, arts and crafts and the new open-topped Javan Langur enclosure where the endangered monkeys can be seen in a natural environment.

**Times:** *Open all year, daily 10-6 during summer (last admission 4.30), 10-dusk during winter (last admission 3). Closed 25 Dec.

**Fee:** £13.95 (ch 4-14 £10.95, pen £8.95). Family ticket (2 ad & 2 ch) £42, (2 ad & 3 ch) £49.

**Facilities:** Ⓟ 🍴 (Licensed) ⛩ ♿ (wheelchairs for hire, book in advance, toilets), shop, garden centre 🚫 🚌 (pre-booking preferred)

## BELTRING
### Hop Farm & Country Park
Paddock Wood Tonbridge TN12 6PY
☎ 01622 872068 📄 01622 872630
**Email:** enquiry@thehopfarm.co.uk
**Web:** www.thehopfarm.co.uk
**Dir:** *on A228 at Paddock Wood*
The Hop Farm is a popular South East family visitor attraction and event location. Set among a large collection of Victorian Oast houses, attractions include museums and exhibitions, indoor and outdoor play areas, animal farm and shire horses, and restaurant and gift shop. Special events throughout the year include craft shows, motor shows and food and drink festivals.
**Times:** *Open from 10. Closed 24-26 Dec, 23 May & 20 June

**Fee:** *£7.50 (ch 4-15 £6.50). Family ticket (2ad+2ch) £27.
**Facilities:** 🅿 🍽 (Licensed) 🪑 ♿ (toilets) shop 🚌 (pre-booking essential)

## BIRCHINGTON
### Powell-Cotton Museum, Quex House & Gardens
Quex Park CT7 0BH
☎ 01843 842168 📄 01843 846661
**Email:** powell-cotton.museum@virgin.net
**Web:** www.powell-cottonmuseum.co.uk
**Dir:** *W of Margate on A28. In Birchington right into Park Lane before rdbt in town centre. Entrance 600yds on left*
Major Powell-Cotton spent much of his life on the study of African animals and many different cultures. This museum, founded in 1895, is his legacy, consisting of animal dioramas, photographs, extensive notes, and artefacts from around the world. Also on display in Quex House, the family home, are collections of Eastern and Asian furniture, Kashmir walnut wall carvings, Chinese silk embroidery, and English period furniture. All set within 15 acres of mature gardens, including a Victorian walled garden. Various events throughout the summer.
**Times:** *Open Apr-Oct, Tue-Thu, Sun & BH 11-5, Quex House 2-4.30; Mar, Sun 11-4, Quex House closed Nov-Feb.
**Fee:** *Summer £5 (ch & pen £4, under 5's free), Family ticket (2ad+3ch) £14. Winter £4 (ch & pen £3), Family ticket (2ad+3ch) £10. Garden only £1.50 (ch & pen £1).
**Facilities:** 🅿 🅟 (10min walk) 🍴 (Café/Restaurant) 🍽 (Licensed) 🪑 📖 ♿ (two wheelchairs available, toilets), shop, guided tours 🚫 (ex assistance dogs) 🚌

## CANTERBURY
### Canterbury Roman Museum
Butchery Lane Longmarket CT1 2JR
☎ 01227 785575 📄 01227 455047
**Email:** museums@canterbury.gov.uk
**Web:** www.canterbury-museum.co.uk
**Dir:** *in centre close to cathedral and city centre car parks*
Step below today's Canterbury to discover an exciting part of the Roman town including the real remains of a house featuring fine mosaics. Experience everyday life in the reconstructed market place and see exquisite silver and glass. Try your skills on the touch screen computer, and in the hands-on area with actual archaeological finds. Use the computer animation of Roman Canterbury to join the search for the lost temple and see what can discover.

**Times:** *Open all year, Mon-Sat 10-5 & Sun (Jun-Oct) 1.30-5. (Last admission 4). Closed Good Fri & Xmas period.
**Fee:** £3 (ch 5-18, disabled, pen & students £1.85). Family ticket £7.60
**Facilities:** 🅟 (walking distance) ♿ (lift, toilets) shop 🚫 (ex guide dogs) 🚌 (pre-booking essential)

**KENT**

**KENT**

## CANTERBURY
### Canterbury West Gate Towers
St. Peter's Street CT1 2RA
☎ 01227 789576 📠 01227 455047
**Email:** museums@canterbury.gov.uk
**Web:** www.canterbury-museum.co.uk
**Dir:** *at end of main street beside river. Entrance under main arch*

The last of the city's fortified gatehouses sits astride the London road with the river as a moat. Rebuilt in around 1380 by Archbishop Sudbury, it was used as a prison for many years. The battlements give a splendid panoramic view of the city and are a good vantage point for photographs. Arms and armour can be seen in the guardroom, and the towers have cells. Brass rubbings can be made and children can try on replica armour.

**Times:** *Open all year (ex Good Fri & Xmas period), Mon-Sat; 11-12.30 & 1.30-3.30. Last admission 15 mins before closure.
**Fee:** £1.20 (ch & concessions 70p). Family ticket £2.80.
**Facilities:** Ⓟ (100yds) shop ⊗ (ex guide dogs) 🚌 (maximum of 25 at one time) ♨

## CANTERBURY
### Druidstone Park
Honey Hill Blean CT2 9JR
☎ 01227 765168 📠 01227 768860
**Web:** www.druidstone.net
**Dir:** *3m NW on A290 from Canterbury*

Take a break from urban stress at Druidstone Park where you can explore the idyllic garden setting with enchanted woodland walks where dwells the sleeping dragon and other magical creatures. See the mystical Oak Circle with the old man of the oaks, or perhaps discover the fabulous display of bluebells and budleja in the summer. There's also a children's farmyard, adventure play areas, under-cover picnic areas, a gift shop and cafeteria.
**Times:** *Open Etr-Nov, daily, 10-5.30.
**Fee:** *£5.10 (ch £3.80 & pen £4.30). Family ticket £15

**Facilities:** Ⓟ �🏛 ♿ (toilets) shop ⊗ (except guide dogs) 🚌

## CANTERBURY
### Museum of Canterbury
Stour Street CT1 2RA
☎ 01227 475202 📠 01227 455047
**Email:** museums@canterbury.gov.uk
**Web:** www.canterbury-museum.co.uk
**Dir:** *in the Medieval Poor Priests' Hospital, just off St Margaret's St or High St*

Discover the story of Canterbury in new interactive displays and see the city's treasures including the famous Canterbury Cross. Try the fun activities in the Medieval Discovery Gallery, find out about the mysteries surrounding Christopher Marlowe's life and death and spot friend or foe planes in the WW2 Blitz gallery. Meet favourite children's TV character Bagpuss and friends and enjoy the Rupert Bear Museum.

**Times:** *Open all year, Mon-Sat 10.30-5 & Sun (Jun-Sep) 1.30-5 (last admission 4). (Closed Good Fri & Xmas period).
**Fee:** £3.30 (concessions £2.20). Family ticket £8.70 (2 ad & 3 ch)
**Facilities:** Ⓟ (walking) ♿ (toilets), shop ⊗ (ex guide dogs) 🚌 (pre-booked preferred) ♨

## CANTERBURY
### The Canterbury Tales
St. Margaret's Street CT1 2TG
☎ 01227 479227 📠 01227 765584
**Email:** info@canterburytales.org.uk
**Web:** www.canterburytales.org.uk
**Dir:** *In heart of city centre, located in St Margaret's St*
Step back in time to experience the sights sounds and smells of the Middle Ages in this reconstruction of 14th century England. Travel from the Tabard Inn in London, to St. Thomas Becket's Shrine in Canterbury with Chaucer's colourful pilgrims. Their tales of chivalry, romance and intrigue are brought vividly to life for you to enjoy along your journey.
**Times:** Open Mar-Jun 10-5, Jul-Aug 9.30-5, Sep-Oct 10-5 & Nov-Feb 10-4.30. Closed 25 & 26 Dec, 1 Jan

**Fee:** *£7.25 (ch £5.25, concessions £6.25) Family ticket (2 ad & 2 ch) £22.50
**Facilities:** Ⓟ (200mtrs) ♿ (notice required for wheelchairs, hearing loop facility, toilets), shop, audio commentaries ⊗ (ex guide dogs) 🚌 (must pre-book)

## CHATHAM
### Fort Amherst Heritage Park & Caverns
Dock Road ME4 4UB
☎ 01634 847747 📠 01634 830612
**Email:** info@fortamherst.com
**Web:** www.fortamherst.com
**Dir:** *adjacent to A231 dock road, 0.5m from Chatham Dockyard*
A fine Georgian fortress set in over 15 acres of attractive parkland. A fascinating collection of caves, tunnels, gun-batteries and barracks gives visitors an insight into the life of the Napoleonic soldier. Please telephone for details of special events, including historic re-enactments.
**Times:** *Open Mar-Sep Sat-Sun and every day during school hols. 10.30-4

**Fee:** *£6 (concessions £4) Family ticket £16.
**Facilities:** Ⓟ Ⓟ (across road) 🏕 ♿ (road access up to fort, toilets) shop ⊗ (ex guide dogs) 🚌 (pre-booking recommended)

## CHATHAM
### The Historic Dockyard Chatham
ME4 4TZ
☎ 01634 823807 📠 01634 823801
**Email:** info@chdt.org.uk
**Web:** www.thedockyard.co.uk
**Dir:** *M20 & M2 junct 3, follow signs for Chatham on A229. Then A230 and A231, following brown tourist signs. Brown anchor signs lead to visitors' entrance*
The Historic Dockyard celebrates over 400 years of naval history in one 80-acre site. Exhibits include Battle Ships with WWII destroyer *HMS Cavalier* and the spy sub Ocelot. Lifeboat with a display of 15 full size boats, archive film and artefacts; and Wooden Walls which looks at the life of a carpenter's apprentice in the 18th century. The naval architecture is spectacular.

**Times:** *Open mid Feb-early Nov, daily 10-6. Last entry 4.
**Fee:** *£10 (ch 5-15 £6.50, concessions £7.50). Family ticket (2ad+2ch) £26.50, additional child £3.25
**Facilities:** Ⓟ Ⓟ 🍽 (Licensed) 🏕 ♿ (wheelchair available, virtual tours, toilets), shop, guided tours 🚌

KENT

**KENT**

## DOVER
### Crabble Corn Mill
Lower Road River CT17 0UY
☎ 01304 823292 ▤ 01304 823292
**Email:** miller@ccmt.org.uk
**Web:** www.ccmt.org.uk
**Dir:** *A2 to Whitfield rdbt then 2nd turning down Whitfield Hill, left. At traffic lights right into River Crabble, under railway bridge and 1st right. Mill 500mtrs on left*
Visit this beautifully restored working Kentish water mill dating from 1812. Regular demonstrations of waterwheel working and making stoneground wholemeal flour from Kentish organic wheat. There's flour for sale, as well as home-baked produce in café. An exhibition space regularly displays work of local artists and craftspeople.

**Times:** *Open all year, Mar-Sep, daily 11-5; Winter, Sun only (except by appointment).Open all year for groups by arrangement. Closed Xmas & Jan.
**Fee:** *Self guided tours: £2.50 (ch 5-15 yrs £1.50, pen & students £2). Family ticket £6. Guide tours: £3 (ch 5-15 yrs £2.20, pen & students £2.50). Family ticket £6.50.
**Facilities:** ❷ Ⓟ (50mtrs) ⌂ ♿ shop ⊗ (ex guide dogs) 🚌 (must pre-book) ♨

## DOVER
### Dover Castle & Secret Wartime Tunnels
CT16 1HU
☎ 01304 211067 ▤ 01304 214739
**Web:** www.english-heritage.org.uk
Various exhibitions demonstrate how Dover Castle has served as a vital strategic centre for the Iron Age onwards. In May 1940 the tunnels under the castle became the nerve centre for 'Operation Dynamo' - the evacuation of Dunkirk. These wartime secrets are now revealed for all to see.
**Times:** Open Apr-Jul, 10-6, daily; Aug, 9.30-6, daily. Sep, 10-6, daily. Oct, 10-5, daily. Nov-Jan, 10-4, Thu-Mon. Feb-Mar, 10-4 daily. Closed 24-26 Dec & 1 Jan. Note: Keep closes at 5pm on Sat if hospitality event booked

**Fee:** £9.50 (ch £4.80, concessions £7.10). Family £23.80. Prices and opening times are subject to change. Please check web site or call 0870 333 1181 for the most up-to-date prices and opening times when planning your visit.
**Facilities:** ❷ Ⓟ (400 yds) ⍾ ♿ shop ⊗ (ex on lead in certain areas) 🚌 ⊞ ♨

## EYNSFORD
### Eagle Heights
Lullingstone Lane Dartford DA4 0JB
☎ 01322 866466 ▤ 01322 861024
**Email:** office@eagleheights.co.uk
**Web:** www.eagleheights.co.uk
**Dir:** *M25 junct 3/A20 towards West Kingsdown. Right after 2 rdbts onto A225. Follow brown signs*
Eagle Heights is an impressive display of birds of prey from all over the world featuring between 150 and 200 birds at any one time. Many are flown out across the Darenth Valley twice daily. Meet the owls, pygmy goat and rabbits in the paddock.
**Times:** *Open Mar-Nov daily 10.30-5. Nov, Jan-Feb wknd only 11-4. Dec closed.
**Fee:** *£6.95 (ch £4.95 4-14yrs, concessions £5.95)

**Facilities:** ❷ Ⓟ ⛾ (tearooms, light lunches and snacks) ⌂ ♿ (toilets), shop ⊗ 🚌

## FAVERSHAM
### Fleur de Lis Heritage Centre
10-13 Preston Street ME13 8NS
☎ 01795 534542
**Email:** ticfaversham@btconnect.com
**Web:** www.faversham.org/society
**Dir:** *3 minutes drive from M2 junct 6*
Recently expanded and updated, and housed in
16th-century premises, the Centre features colourful
displays and room settings that vividly evoke the 2000-
year history of Faversham. Special features include
the 'Gunpowder Experience' and a working old-style
village telephone exchange, one of only two remaining
in Britain. In July, during the Faversham Open House
Scheme, over 20 historic properties in the town are
opened to the public.

**Times:** *Open all year, Mon-Sat, 10-4; Sun 10-1.
**Fee:** £2 (ch & pen £1)
**Facilities:** Ⓟ (200yds) 🍴 ♿ (DVD show of parts that
are inaccessible, toilets), shop 🚌

## GROOMBRIDGE PLACE
### Groombridge Place Gardens & Enchanted Forest
Tunbridge Wells TN3 9QG
☎ 01892 861444 🖷 01892 863996
**Email:** office@groombridge.co.uk
**Web:** www.groombridge.co.uk
**Dir:** *M25 junct 5, follow A21 S, exit at A26 signed
Tunbridge Wells, then take A264 - follow signs to
Groombridge village and Groombridge Place Gardens*
This award-winning attraction, set in 200 acres, features
a series of magnificent walled gardens set against the
backdrop of a romantic 17th-century moated manor.
Explore the white rose garden, the 'Drunken Topiary', the
'Secret Garden' and the 'Enchanted Forest', where the
imagination is stimulated by the 'Dark Walk' and 'Groms'

Village'. There are also bird of prey flying displays, canal
boat cruises, and a full programme of special events.
**Times:** Open Apr-Nov, daily 10-5.30
**Fee:** *£8.70 (ch 3-12 & pen £7.20). Family ticket
(2ad+2ch) £29.50. Groups 20+ available on request.
**Facilities:** Ⓟ 🍴 🍴 ♿ (toilets), shop, guided tours
🚫 (ex guide/hearing dogs) 🚌 (must pre-book)

## HAWKINGE
### Kent Battle of Britain Museum
Aerodrome Road CT18 7AG
☎ 01303 893140
**Email:** kentbattleofbritainmuseum@btinternet.com
**Web:** www.kbobm.org
**Dir:** *off A260, 1m along Aerodrome road*
Once a Battle of Britain station, today it houses the
largest collection of relics and related memorabilia of
British and German aircraft involved in the fighting. Also
shown, full-size replicas of the Hurricane, Spitfire and
Me109 used in Battle of Britain films. A new memorial
was dedicated to commemorate the 60th anniversary of
the Battle of Britain. Artefacts on show, recovered from
over 600 battle of Britain aircraft, all form a lasting
memorial to all those involved in the conflict.

**Times:** *Open Etr-Sep, daily 10-5; Oct, daily 11-4.
(Last admission 1 hour before closing).
**Fee:** *£3.50 (ch £2, pen £3). Group 20+.
**Facilities:** Ⓟ Ⓟ (adjacent to car park) 🍴 ♿ shop
🚫 (ex guide dogs) 🚌 (advanced notice preferred) 🅳

**KENT**

### HEVER
#### Hever Castle & Gardens
Edenbridge TN8 7NG
☎ 01732 865224 🖨 01732 866796
**Email:** mail@hevercastle.co.uk
**Web:** www.hevercastle.co.uk
**Dir:** *M25 junct 5 or 6, 3m SE of Edenbridge, off B2026*
This enchanting, double-moated, 13th-century castle was the childhood home of Anne Boleyn. Restored by the American millionaire William Waldorf Astor, it shows superb Edwardian craftsmanship. Astor also transformed the grounds, creating topiary, a yew maze, 35-acre lake and Italian gardens filled with antique sculptures. There is also a 100-metre herbaceous border, 'splashing' water maze' on the Sixteen Acre Island, as well as a woodland walk known as Sunday Walk.

**Times:** *Open Mar-Nov, daily. Castle 12-6, Gardens 11-6. (Last admission 5). (Closes 4pm Mar & Nov).
**Fee:** *Castle & Gardens £9.80 (ch 5-14 £5.30, pen £8.20). Family ticket £24.90. Gardens only £7.80 (ch 5-14 £5, pen £6.70). Family ticket £20.60
**Facilities:** ❷ ❑ (Licensed) ❙ ❺ (wheelchairs available, toilets), shop, garden centre 🚌 (pre book, min 15)

### HYTHE
#### Romney Hythe & Dymchurch Railway
TN28 8PL
☎ 01797 362353 & 363256 🖨 01797 363591
**Email:** info@rhdr.org.uk
**Web:** www.rhdr.org.uk
**Dir:** *M20 junct 11, off A259 signed New Romney*
The world's smallest public railway has its headquarters here. The concept of two enthusiasts coincided with Southern Railway's plans for expansion, and so the thirteen-and-a-half mile stretch of 15 inch gauge railway came into being, running from Hythe through New Romney and Dymchurch to Dungeness Lighthouse.
**Times:** *Open daily Etr-Sep, also wknds in Mar & Oct. For times apply to: The Manager, RH & DR, New Romney, Kent.

**Fee:** *Charged according to journey.
**Facilities:** ❷ (charged) ❑ (New Romney & Dungeness Stations) ❙ ❺ (stairlift to Toy & Model Museum, toilets), shop 🚌 (pre-booking preferred)

### IGHTHAM
#### Ightham Mote
Ivy Hatch Sevenoaks TN15 0NT
☎ 01732 810378 & 811145 (info line)
🖨 01732 811029
**Email:** igthammote@nationaltrust.org.uk
**Web:** www.nationaltrust.org.uk
**Dir:** *2.5m S off A227, 6m E of Sevenoaks*
This moated manor house, nestling in a sunken valley, dates from 1330. The main features of the house span many centuries and include the Great Hall, old chapel and crypt, Tudor chapel with painted ceiling, drawing room with Jacobean fireplace, frieze and 18th-century handpainted Chinese wallpaper and the billiards room. There is an extensive garden as well as interesting walks in the surrounding woodland. Following completion of all conservation work visitors can enjoy the most extensive visitor route to date, including the bedroom of Charles Henry Robinson who bequeathed Ightham Mote to the National Trust.
**Times:** *Open 12 Mar-29 Oct, daily ex Tue & Sat, 10-5.30. Open Good Fri. (Last admission 5).
**Fee:** *£8.50 (ch £4). Family ticket £21.
**Facilities:** ❷ ❑ (Licensed) ❙ ❐ ❺ (wheelchairs, special parking ask at office, virtual tour, toilets), shop, garden centre guided tours ⊗ (ex hearing & guide dogs) 🚌 (booking essential) ❦

## LAMBERHURST
### Scotney Castle Garden & Estate
TN3 8JN

☎ 01892 893898 📄 01892 890110

**Email:** scotneycastle@nationaltrust.org.uk

**Web:** www.nationaltrust.org.uk

**Dir:** *1m S, of Lamberhurst on A21*

The beautiful gardens at Scotney were planned in the 19th century around the remains of the old, moated Scotney Castle. There is something to see at every time of year, with spring flowers followed by rhododendrons, azaleas and a mass of roses, and then superb autumn colours. Estate walks all year through 770 acres of woodlands and meadows, estate explorer map available.

**Times:** *Open Garden: Apr-end Oct. Old Castle: May-mid Sep, Wed-Sun & 4 Nov-17 Dec wknds only 11-6 or sunset if earlier. BH Mon 11-6. Closed Good Fri. (Last admission 1hr before closing).

**Fee:** *£5.20 (ch £2.60) Family £13

**Facilities:** 🅿 🛏 ♿ (wheelchair hire, Braille/large print guidebook, audio tape, toilets) shop garden centre guided tours ⊗ (ex guide & hearing dogs) 🚌 (booking essential) 🦌

---

## LYDD
### RSPB Nature Reserve
Boulderwall Farm Dungeness Road TN29 9PN

☎ 01797 320588 📄 01797 321962

**Email:** dungeness@rspb.org.uk

**Web:** www.rspb.org.uk

**Dir:** *off Lydd to Dungeness road, 1m SE of Lydd, follow tourist signs*

This Royal Society for the Protection of Birds coastal reserve comprises 2,106 acres of shingle beach and flooded pits. An excellent place to watch breeding terns, gulls and other water birds. Wheatears, great crested and little grebes also nest here, and outside the breeding season there are large flocks of teals, shovelers, and goldeneyes, goosanders, smews and both Slavonian and red-necked grebes.

**Times:** *Open: Visitor Centre all year, daily 10-5 (10-4 Nov-Feb). Reserve open all year, daily 9am-9pm (or sunset if earlier). Closed 25-26 Dec.

**Fee:** *£3 (ch £1, concessions £2).

**Facilities:** 🅿 🛏 📖 ♿ (access by car to some hides, toilets), shop, guided tours ⊗ (ex guide dogs) 🚌 (pre-booking required)

---

## LYMPNE
### Port Lympne Wild Animal Park, Mansion & Garden
Hythe CT21 4PD

☎ 0870 750 4647 📄 01303 264944

**Email:** info@totallywild.net

**Web:** www.totallywild.net

**Dir:** *M20 junct 11, follow brown tourist signs*

A 400-acre wild animal park that houses hundreds of rare animals: Indian elephants, rhinos, wolves, bison, snow leopards, Siberian and Indian tigers, gorillas and monkeys. New features include a glass-fronted lion enclosure and an open-topped woodland home for the Colobus monkeys. The mansion designed by Sir Herbert Baker is surrounded by 15 acres of spectacular gardens. Inside, notable features include the restored Rex Whistler Tent Room, a Moroccan patio, and the hexagonal library where the Treaty of Paris was signed after the First World War. Visit the Spencer Roberts mural room and the Martin Jordan animal mural room.

**Times:** *Open all year, daily 10-6 (closes at dusk in summer). (Last admission 4.30 summer, 3 winter. Closed 25 Dec.

**Fee:** *£13.95 (ch 4-14 & pen £10.95). Family ticket £42 (2ad+2ch) £49 (2ad+3ch).

**Facilities:** 🅿 🍴 (Licensed) 🛏 📖 £1.50 ♿ (very limited access for disabled, special route available, toilets), shop, garden centre ⊗ 🚌 (pre-booking preferred)

**KENT**

**KENT**

## MAIDSTONE
### Leeds Castle
ME17 1PL

☎ 01622 765400 📄 01622 735616
**Email:** enquiries@leeds-castle.co.uk
**Web:** www.leeds-castle.com
**Dir:** *7m E of Maidstone at junct 8 of M20/A20,*
*clearly signed*

Set on two islands in the centre of a lake, Leeds Castle has been called the 'loveliest castle in the world', and was home to six medieval Queens of England, as well as being Henry VIII's Royal Palace. Among the treasures inside are many paintings, tapestries and furnishings. Attractions in the grounds include formal gardens, exotic aviary, dog collar museum, vineyard, woodland walks, toddlers' play area, yew maze with secret underground grotto and daily falconry displays. Plenty of special events, contact for details.
**Times:** *Open daily, Apr-Sep 10-7 (Castle 10.30-7) Last admission 5. Oct-Mar 10-5 (Castle 10.30-5) Last admission 3. Last entry to the castle is 30min after the last admission time.
**Fee:** *Fully incl ticket £13.50 (ch £8, concessions £11).
**Facilities:** ℗ ⵏⵔⵉ (Licensed) ⵏ 🪑 ⵃ (Braille information, induction loops & wheelchair, lift, toilets), shop, guided tours, audio commentaries (charged) ⊗ (ex assist dogs) 🚌

## MAIDSTONE
### Maidstone Museum & Bentlif Art Gallery
St Faith's Street ME14 1LH

☎ 01622 602838
**Email:** museum@maidstone.gov.uk
**Web:** www.museum.maidstone.gov.uk
**Dir:** *close to County Hall & Maidstone E train stn,*
*opp Fremlin's Walk*

Set in an Elizabethan manor house which has been much extended over the years, this museum houses an outstanding collection of fine and applied arts, including watercolours, furniture, ceramics, and a collection of Japanese art and artefacts. The museum of the Queen's Own Royal West Kent Regiment is also housed here. Please apply or call for details of temporary exhibitions, workshops etc.
**Times:** Open all year, Mon-Sat 10-5.15, Sun & BH Mon 11-4. Closed 25-26 Dec & 1 Jan
**Fee:** *Free
**Facilities:** ℗ (150 mtrs) 🖵 (Mon-Sat 10-4, Sun & BH 11-3) 🪑 ⵃ (Lifts) shop ⊗ (ex guide dogs) 🚌

## MAIDSTONE
### Museum of Kent Life
Lock Lane Sandling ME14 3AU

☎ 01622 763936 📄 01622 662024
**Email:** enquiries@museum-kentlife.co.uk
**Web:** www.museum-kentlife.co.uk
**Dir:** *from M20 junct 6 onto A229 Maidstone road, follow*
*signs for Aylesford*

Kent's award-winning open air museum is home to an outstanding collection of historic buildings which house exhibitions on life in Kent over the last 100 years. An early 20th-century village hall and reconstruction of cottages from the 17th & 20th-centuries are more recent buildings to be viewed.
**Times:** *Open Feb-Nov, daily 10-5, in winter open every wknd 10-3.
**Fee:** *£6.50 (ch 4-15 £4.50, under 4's free, pen £5). Family ticket £20.
**Facilities:** ℗ ℗ (20yds) ⵏⵔⵉ ⵏ ⵃ (wheelchairs available, ramps, transport available, toilets), shop 🚌

## PENSHURST
### Penshurst Place & Gardens
Tonbridge TN11 8DG
☎ 01892 870307 📄 01892 870866
**Email:** enquiries@penshurstplace.com
**Web:** www.penshurstplace.com
**Dir:** *M25 junct 5 take A21 Hastings road then exit at Hildenborough & follow signs*
Built between 1340 and 1345, the original house is perfectly preserved. Enlarged by successive owners between the 15th and 17th centuries, the great variety of architectural styles showcases the extensive collections of furniture, tapestries and paintings. The Baron's Hall is the oldest and finest in the country, and the house is set in magnificent formal gardens. There also a toy museum and woodland trail.

**Times:** *Open: wknds from early Mar, daily Mar-late Oct. GroundsOpen 10.30-6. House open noon-4.
**Fee:** *House & Grounds £7.50 (ch 5-16 £5, concs £7). Family £21. Grounds only £6 (ch 5-16 £5, concs £5.50) Family £18. Party 20+. Garden season ticket £35.
**Facilities:** 🅿 Ⓟ (220yds) 🍴 (Licensed) 🎍 ♿ (Braille & large print, toilets), shop 🚫 🚌 (pre-booking required)

## RAMSGATE
### Ramsgate Maritime Museum
Clock House Pier Yard Royal Harbour CT11 8LS
☎ 01843 570622
**Email:** museum@ekmt.fsnet.co.uk
**Web:** www.ekmt.fsnet.co.uk
**Dir:** *follow Harbour signs*
The Maritime Museum Ramsgate is housed in the early 19th-century Clock House, and contains four galleries depicting various aspects of the maritime heritage of the East Kent area. A temporary gallery/conservation room features a 17th-century naval gun. The 'Dunkirk Little Ship' motor yacht *Sundower* may also be visited by prior arrangement.
**Times:** *Open Etr-Sep, Tue-Sun 10-5. Oct-Etr Thu-Sun 11-4.30.

**Fee:** *Combined ticket for museum £1.50. (ch & pen 75p). Family £4.
**Facilities:** 🅿 (charged) Ⓟ (100-500yds) 📋 ♿ (restricted) shop 🚫 (ex assist dogs) 🚌 📷

## ROLVENDEN
### C M Booth Collection of Historic Vehicles
Falstaff Antiques 63 High St TN17 4LP
☎ 01580 241234
**Email:** info@morganmuseum.co.uk
**Web:** www.morganmuseum.co.uk
**Dir:** *on A28, 3m from Tenterden*
Not just vehicles, but various other items of interest connected with transport. There is a unique collection of three-wheel Morgan cars, dating from 1913, and the only known Humber tri-car of 1904, as well as a 1929 Morris van, a 1936 Bampton caravan, motorcycles and bicycles. There is also a toy and model car display.
**Times:** Open all year, Mon-Sat 10-5.30. Closed 25-26 Dec.
**Fee:** £2 (ch £1)

**Facilities:** Ⓟ (roadside) shop 🚌 (max 20, must pre-book)

**KENT**

**KENT**

## ROYAL TUNBRIDGE WELLS
### Tunbridge Wells Museum and Art Gallery
Civic Centre Mount Pleasant TN1 1JN
☎ 01892 554171 & 526121 ▤ 01892 554131
**Email:** museum@tunbridgewells.gov.uk
**Web:** www.tunbridgewellsmuseum.org
**Dir:** *adjacent to Town Hall, off A264*
This combined museum and art gallery tells the story of the borough of Tunbridge Wells. There are collections of costume, art, dolls and toys along with natural and local history from dinosaur bones to the original Pantiles for which Tunbridge Wells was famous. There is also a large collection of Tunbridge ware, the intricate wooden souvenirs made for visitors to the Wells. The art gallery features a changing programme of contemporary and historic art, touring exhibitions, and local art and craft.

**Times:** Open all year, daily 9.30-5. Sun 10-4. Closed BHs & Etr Sat.
**Fee:** *Free
**Facilities:** ℗ (200 yds) ▤ ♿ (parking adjacent to building) shop ⊗ (ex guide dogs) 🚌 (pre-booking) ♨

## STROOD
### Diggerland
Medway Valley Leisure Park Roman Way ME2 2NU
☎ 08700 344437 ▤ 09012 010300
**Email:** mail@diggerland.com
**Web:** www.diggerland.com
**Dir:** *M2 junct 2, follow A228 towards Rochester. At rdbt turn right. Diggerland on right*
An adventure park with a huge difference. Experience the thrills of driving real earth moving equipment and drive a digger yourself. Choose from various types of diggers and dumpers ranging from 1 ton to 8.5 tons. Complete the Dumper Truck Challenge or dig for buried treasure (supervised by an instructor). New rides include JCB Robots, the Supertrack, Landrover Safari, Spin Dizzy and the Diggerland Tractors.

**Times:** *Open all year, 10-5, wknds, BHs & school hols only
**Fee:** *£2.50 for all over 2yrs (pen £1.25) Additional charges to ride/drive real machinery
**Facilities:** ℗ ℗ (200yds) 🍴 ♿ (toilets) shop ⊗ (ex guide dogs) 🚌

## SWINGFIELD MINNIS
### The Butterfly Centre
MacFarlanes Garden Centre Folkestone CT15 7HX
☎ 01303 844244 ▤ 01303 844244
**Email:** macfarlanes@gardensandtress.fsnet.co.uk
**Dir:** *on A260 by junction with Elham-Lydden road*
Within the complex of a retail garden centre a tropical greenhouse garden is home to scores of colourful free-flying butterflies from all over the world. These exotic insects flutter delicately amongst tropical plants such as bougainvillea, oleander and banana. The temperate section houses British butterflies, with many favourite species, and if you look carefully you will spot some rare species too.
**Times:** *Open Apr-1 Oct, daily 10-5. Closed Etr Sun.
**Fee:** *£3 (ch £2 & concessions £2.50). Family ticket (2ad+2ch) £8.50.
**Facilities:** ℗ 🍴 🍴 ▤ ♿ (toilets) shop, garden centre, guided tours ⊗ (ex guide dogs) 🚌 (only three coaches at one time)

## LONDON E2
### V & A Museum of Childhood

Cambridge Heath Road E2 9PA
☎ 020 8980 2415 🖷 020 8983 5225
**Email:** moc@vam.ac.uk
**Web:** www.museumofchildhood.org.uk
**Dir:** *Underground – Bethnal Green*

The V&A Museum of Childhood celebrates its 150th birthday in 2007. It has recently re-opened following a £4.7 million transformation. There is a stunning new entrance, fully updated galleries and displays, a brand new gallery and expanded public spaces. The galleries include Creativity, Moving Toys, World in the East End, Design in Focus, and Children in Trouble. There is also a full programme of activities. Exhibitions include a birthday celebration of Dick Bruna's Miffy the rabbit, Picasso's natural history, and *Lost in Space*.

**Times:** Open all year, daily 10-5.50, closed 25-26 Dec, 1 Jan.
**Fee:** Free
**Facilities:** ℗ (metered parking) 🚻 🗐 ♿ (disabled parking by arrangement, toilets) shop, guided tours ⊗ 🚌 (prior booking) ♨

## LONDON E14
### Museum in Docklands

West India Quay E14 4AL
☎ 0870 444 3855 & 3856 🖷 0870 444 3858
**Email:** info@museumindocklands.org.uk
**Web:** www.museumindocklands.org.uk
**Dir:** *Signposted from West India Quay DLR*

Housed in a converted 18th-century warehouse the museum explores the 2,000 year history of London's river, port and people. Four floors of interactive displays and a unique collection journeys through the history of the Thames, from the first Roman settlements to the Docklands of the 21st century. A changing programme of activities for all ages includes character re-enactments, talks by history experts, films and guided walks through Docklands. The soft play gallery, Mudlarks, is a great place for under elevens – discover archaeological finds on the foreshore, or reconstruct a model Canary Wharf.

**Times:** *Open all year, daily 10-6 (last admission 5.30)
**Fee:** *£5 (ch16 free, concessions £3)
**Facilities:** ℗ (opp rear museum – disabled parking on quayside) 🚻 ♿ (w/chairs, power scooters & various aids) shop, audio commentaries (charged) ⊗ (ex guide dogs)

## LONDON EC2
### Bank of England Museum

Bartholomew Lane EC2R 8AH
☎ 020 7601 5545 🖷 020 7601 5808
**Email:** museum@bankofengland.co.uk
**Web:** www.bankofengland.co.uk/museum
**Dir:** *museum housed in Bank of London, entrance in Bartholomew Lane. Bank underground, exit 2*

The museum tells the story of the Bank of England from its foundation in 1694 to its role in today's economy. Interactive programmes with graphics and video help explain its many and varied roles. Popular exhibits include a unique collection of banknotes and a genuine gold bar, which may be handled.

**Times:** *Open all year, Mon-Fri 10-5. Closed wknds & BHs. Open on day of Lord Mayor's Show.
**Fee:** *Free
**Facilities:** ℗ (10 mins walk) 🗐 ♿ (special need presentation, advance notice helpful, toilets) shop, audio commentaries (charged) ⊗ (ex assist dogs) 🚌 (no parking) ♨

LONDON EC2

**Museum of London**

150 London Wall EC2Y 5HN

☎ 0870 444 3851 🖹 0870 444 3853

**Email:** info@museumoflondon.org.uk

**Web:** www.museumoflondon.org.uk

**Dir:** *Underground - St Paul's, Barbican. N of St Paul's Cathedral at the end of St Martins le Grand and S of the Barbican. S of Aldersgate St*

The Museum of London has a permanent collection that is dedicated to the story of London and its people, and a varied exhibition programme with major temporary exhibitions and topical displays each year. There are also smaller exhibitions in the foyer gallery and a programme of lectures and events that explore London's history.

**Times**: *Open all year, Mon-Sat 10-5.50, Sun 12-5.50. Last admission 5.30.

**Fee:** *Free

**Facilities:** 🅟 Ⓟ (NCP opp museum – disabled/single decker coaches only) ⛩ ♿ (w/chairs & power scooters, lifts & induction loops, toilets) shop, audio commentaries (charged) 🚫 (ex guide dogs) 🚌 (free parking for coaches if pre-booked)

LONDON EC3

**Tower of London**

Tower Hill EC3N 4AB

☎ 0870 756 6060

**Web:** www.hrp.org.uk

**Dir:** *Underground – Tower Hill*

Perhaps the most famous castle in the world, the Tower of London has played a central part in British history. The White Tower, built by William the Conqueror as a show of strength to the people of London, remains one of the most outstanding examples of Norman military architecture in Europe. For hundreds of years the Tower was used, among other things, as the State Prison and Place of Execution. Two of Henry VIII wives and Lady Jane Grey all lost their heads here. The Yeoman Warders, or 'Beefeaters' play an important role in the protection of the Tower – home of the Crown Jewels – and are informative and entertaining. Look out for the ravens, whose continued residence is said to ensure that the Kingdom does not fall. The Crowns and Diamonds exhibition features a number of crowns never displayed to the public before. The first recorded visitor to the Royal Armouries, was as long ago as 1489. The displays include arms and armour dating from the Norman ages.

**Times:** *Open all year, Mar-Oct, Mon-Sat 9-6, Sun 10-6 (last admission 5); Nov-Feb, Tue-Sat 9-5, Sun 10-5 (last admission 4). Closed 24-26 Dec & 1 Jan.

**Fee:** *£12 (ch £7.80 under 5's free, concessions £9). Family ticket (2ad+3ch) £36.

**Facilities:** Ⓟ (100yds – NCP Lower Thames St) 🍽 (Licensed) ♿ (access guide booking – 020 7488 5694, toilets) shop 🚫 (ex guide dogs) 🚌 (no parking coaches)

LONDON EC4

**St Paul's Cathedral**

St Pauls Courtyard EC4M 8AD

☎ 020 7246 8348 🖹 020 7248 3104

**Email:** chapterhouse@stpaulscathedral.org.uk

**Web:** www.stpauls.co.uk

Completed in 1710, Sir Christopher Wren's architectural masterpiece is the cathedral church of the Bishop of London, and arose, like so much of this area of London, from the ashes of the Great Fire of London in 1666. Among the historic figures buried here are Nelson and the Duke of Wellington, while Holman Hunt's masterpiece, *Light of the World* hangs in the nave. St Paul's also hosted the weddings of Charles and Diana, and the funeral of Sir Winston Churchill. Impressive views of London can be seen from the Golden Gallery.

**Times:** *Open Cathedral, Crypt, Ambulatory, Mon-Sat 8.30. Galleries 9.30. (Last admission 4). Cathedral may close for special services.

**Fee:** £9 (ch £3.50, concessions £8) Family £21.50 (2ad+2ch).

**Facilities:** Ⓟ (400mtrs – meter parking in area) ♿ (toilets) shop, guided tours, audio commentaries (charged) 🚫 (ex guide dogs) 🚌

LONDON

## LONDON N7
### Freightliners City Farm
Sheringham Road Islington N7 8PF
☎ 020 7609 0467 📄 020 7609 9934
**Email:** robert@freightlinersfarm.org.uk
**Web:** www.freightlinersfarm.org.uk
**Dir:** *off Liverpool Rd*

A city farm bringing rural life into an urban setting. A variety of animals can be seen at the farm, including cows, pigs, goats, sheep and poultry. Some interesting building projects are taking place at the farm, including a strawbale building, solar dome, an outside bread oven and a continental beehive. A Saturday market offers organic produce, arts and crafts and much more.
**Times:** *Open Winter: 10-4. Summer: 10-4.45
**Fee:** *Free

**Facilities:** Ⓟ (charged) Ⓟ (20mtrs – pay & display) 🪑 ♿ (toilets) shop, garden centre, guided tours ⊗ (ex guide dogs) 🚌 ♨

## LONDON NW1
### London Zoo
Regents Park NW1 4RY
☎ 020 7449 6235 📄 020 7586 6177
**Email:** marketing@zsl.org
**Web:** www.londonzoo.co.uk
**Dir:** *Underground - Camden Town or Regents Park*

London Zoo is home to over 12,000 animals, insects, reptiles and fish. First opened in 1828, the Zoo can claim the world's first aquarium, insect and reptile house. Theres lots to do, plenty to see and so much to learn. Get closer to your favourite animals, learn about them at the keeper talks and watch them show off their skills at special events. By visiting London Zoo, visitors help protect endangered species, conserve natural habitats and bring learning to life for all ages.

**Times:** Open all year, daily from 10, (closing time dependant on time of year). Closed 25 Dec.
**Fee:** *£14.50 (ch 3-15 £11.50, concessions £12.70).
**Facilities:** Ⓟ (charged) Ⓟ (5mins walk) £9 charge 🍴 (Licensed) 🪑 ♿ (wheelchairs & booster scooter available, toilets) shop, guided tours ⊗ 🚌

## LONDON NW1
### Madame Tussaud's and Stardome
Marylebone Road NW1 5LR
☎ 0870 400 3000
**Email:** csc@madame-tussauds.com
**Web:** www.madame-tussauds.com
**Dir:** *Underground - Baker Street*

Madame Tussaud's world-famous waxwork collection was founded in Paris in 1770. It moved to England in 1802 and found a permanent home in London's Marylebone Road in 1884. The 21st century has brought new innovations and new levels of interactivity. Listen to Kylie Minogue whisper in your ear, become an A-list celeb in the 'Blush' nightclub, and take your chances in a high security prison populated by dangerous serial killers. Madame Tussaud's has recently been combined with the equally memorable London Planetarium, where visitors can interact with characters from Disney's *Treasure Planet*.

**Times:** *Open all year 9.30-5.30 (9-6 wknds/summer)
**Fee:** *£17.99 (ch under 16 £13.99. (Includes entry into Stardome & The Wonderful World of Stars).
**Facilities:** Ⓟ (200mtrs) 🍴 (Licensed) ♿ (all parts accessible except Spirit of London ride, toilets) shop, ⊗ (ex guide dogs) 🚌

**LONDON**

**LONDON NW1**

## The Jewish Museum

Raymond Burton House 129-131 Albert Street
Camden Town NW1 7NB
☎ 020 7284 1997 🖷 020 7267 9008
**Email:** marketing@jewishmuseum.org.uk
**Web:** www.jewishmuseum.org.uk
**Dir:** *Underground - Camden Town, 3 mins walk from station*

Attractive galleries illustrating Jewish history and religious life in Britain and beyond. One of the world's finest collections of Jewish ceremonial art. There are constantly-changing temporary exhibitions, events and workshops. 2006/7 sees an exhibition on Polish educator, Janusz Korczak, who went to the Nazi death camps with children from his orphanage. In May 2007 there will be an exhibition on Jewish boxers. This year is also the 75th anniversary of the Jewish Museum. The site will be closing for re-development in autumn 2007, please call for further details.

**Times:** Open Mon-Thu, 10-4, Sun 10-5. Closed Jewish Festivals.
**Fee:** £3.50 (ch, students, disabled & UB40 £1.50, pen £2.50) Family ticket £8.
**Facilities:** ℗ (outside museum – pay & display parking) 🖺 Free or £1 ♿ (induction loop in lecture room linked to audio-visual unit, toilets) shop ⊗ (ex guide dogs) 🚌 (must pre-book)

**LONDON NW3**

## Kenwood House

Hampstead Lane NW3 7JR
☎ 020 8348 1286 🖷 020 7973 3891
**Web:** www.english-heritage.org.uk
**Dir:** *Underground – Hampstead*

Set in splendid parkland beside Hampstead Heath, this outstanding neo-classical house was owned by Edward Guinness, the brewing magnate who bequeathed the estate and part of his art collection to the nation. Kenwood House is now in the care of English Heritage. Works by Rembrandt, Vermeer, Turner, Gainsborough and Reynolds are displayed within the sumptuous public rooms and represent one of the most important collections of paintings ever given to the nation. The grounds are steep in places but easily accessible and form a perfect amphitheatre for open-air concerts during the summer. Scenes from *Notting Hill* and *Mansfield Park* were filmed here.

**Times:** Open all year, Apr-Oct, daily 11-5; Nov-Mar, daily 11-4. Closed 24-26 Dec & 1 Jan.
**Fee:** Free
**Facilities:** ℗ ﹖◍﹗ (Licensed) ⊼ ♿ (toilets) shop 🚌 ⚏ ⊕

**LONDON NW8**

## Lord's Tour & M.C.C. Museum

Lord's Ground NW8 8QN
☎ 020 7616 8595 & 8596 🖷 020 7266 3825
**Email:** tours@mcc.org.uk
**Web:** www.lords.org
**Dir:** *Underground - St John's Wood*

Established in 1787, Lord's is the home of the MCC and cricket. Guided tours take you behind the scenes, and highlights include the Long Room and the MCC Museum, where the Ashes and a large collection of paintings and memorabilia are displayed. The Museum is open on match days for spectators.

**Times:** Open all year, Oct-Mar tours at 12 & 2. Apr-Sep 10, 12 & 2 (restrictions on some match days). Telephone for details & bookings.

**Fee:** *Guided tour £8 (ch £5, concessions £6). Family ticket (2ad+2ch) £22. Party 25+. Museum only £3 (concessions £1) plus ground admission (match days only).
**Facilities:** ℗ ℗ (surrounding roads – no parking on match days, no coaches) ﹖◍﹗ (Licensed) ⊼ ♿ (by arrangement, toilets) shop, guided tours ⊗ (ex guide dogs) 🚌 (prior booking)

## LONDON NW9
### Royal Air Force Museum
Grahame Park Way Hendon NW9 5LL
☎ 020 8205 2266 📠 020 8358 4981
**Email:** groups@rafmuseum.org
**Web:** www.rafmuseum.org
**Dir:** *within easy reach of the A5, A41, M1 and North Circular A406 roads. Tube on Northern Line to Colindale. Rail to Mill Hill Broadway station. Bus route 303 passes the door*

Take off to the Royal Air Force Museum and soar through the history of aviation from the earliest balloon flights to the latest Eurofighter. Gaze at a world-class collection of over 100 aircraft, aviation/wartime memorabilia and artefacts together with a sound and light show that takes you back in time to the Battle of Britain. The Aeronauts Interactive Centre offers hands-on entertainment and education for all ages and includes cockpit controls, co-ordination tests, engine lifting, air speed, drop zone and pilot testing.

**Times:** Open daily 10-6. (Last admission 5.30). Closed 24-26 Dec & 1 Jan.
**Fee:** Free
**Facilities:** 🅿 Ⓟ (0.5m – only available while museum is open) 🍴 (Licensed) 🪑 ♿ (lifts, ramps & wheelchairs available, toilets) shop, guided tours 🚫 (ex guide dogs) 🚌 (pre-booking preferred)

## LONDON SE1
### British Airways London Eye
Riverside Building County Hall Westminster Bridge Road SE1 7PB
☎ 0870 500 0600 📠 0870 990 8882
**Email:** customer.services@ba-londoneye.com
**Web:** www.ba-londoneye.com
**Dir:** *Underground – Waterloo/Westminster*

British Airways London Eye is one of the most inspiring and visually dramatic additions to the London skyline. At 135m/443ft high, it is the world's tallest observation wheel, allowing you to see one of the world's most exciting cities from a completely new perspective. The London Eye takes you on a gradual, 30 minute, 360 degree rotation, revealing parts of the city, which are simply not visible from the ground. For Londoners and visitors alike, it is the best way to see London and its many celebrated landmarks. The London Eye provides the perfect location for private parties and entertaining and offers a wide variety of in-flight hospitality packages, like champagne and canapés, which are available to enjoy within the privacy of a private capsule.

**Times:** *Open daily, Oct-May, 10-8; Jun-Sep, 10-9. Closed 25 Dec & annual maintenance.
**Fee:** *£13 (ch under 5 free, ch £6.50, disabled visitors £10). Fast track entry £25.
**Facilities:** Ⓟ (500yds) 📱 ♿ (Braille guidebooks, w/chair hire, T-loop, carer ticket, toilets) shop, audio commentaries (charged) 🚫 (ex guide & hearing dogs) 🚌 (drop off and pick up areas)

## LONDON SE1
### Design Museum
Shad Thames SE1 2YD
☎ 0870 909 9009 📠 0870 909 1909
**Email:** info@designmuseum.org
**Web:** www.designmuseum.org
**Dir:** *Turn off Tooley St onto Shad Thames. Underground London Bridge or Tower Hill*

The Design Museum is the first museum in the world to be dedicated to 20th and 21st century design. Since opening in 1989, it has become one of London's most inspiring attractions and has won international acclaim for its ground-breaking exhibition and education programmes. As one of the leading museums of design, fashion and architecture, the Design Museum has a changing programme of exhibitions, combining compelling insights into design history with innovative contemporary design.

**Times:** Open all year, daily 10-5.45 (last entry 5.15). Late opening on Fri during summer months only, 9 (last entry 8.30). Closed 25 Dec.
**Fee:** £7 (ch under 12 free, concessions £4)
**Facilities:** Ⓟ (3 mins – Gainsford St car park is chargeable) 📱 ♿ (ramped entrance, wheelchair & lift, toilets) shop 🚫 (ex guide dogs) 🚌 (pre-booking required)

**LONDON**

## LONDON SE1
### Florence Nightingale Museum

St Thomas' Hospital Gassiot House
2 Lambeth Palace Road SE1 7EW
☎ 020 7620 0374 ▤ 020 7928 1760
**Email:** info@florence-nightingale.co.uk
**Web:** www.florence-nightingale.co.uk
**Dir:** *Underground - Westminster, Waterloo. On the site of St Thomas' Hospital*

Florence Nightingale needs no introduction, but this museum shows clearly that she was more than 'The Lady with the Lamp'. Beautifully designed, the museum creates a personal setting in which a large collection of Florence's personal items including childhood souvenirs, her dress, furniture from her houses and the honours awarded to her in later years are displayed. There is a small military history collection of souvenirs from the Crimean War, including military medals and a military nursing uniform.

**Times:** *Open Mon-Fri 10-5; wknds & BHs 10-4.30. (Last admission 1hr before closing). Closed Good Fri, Etr Sat & Sun & 22 Dec-2 Jan.

**Fee:** £5.80 (ch & concessions £4.80). Family ticket (2ad+ up to 5ch) £16. Discounted rates for pre-booked groups of 15+.

**Facilities:** Ⓟ (charged) ▤ ﬞ (toilets) shop, guided tours Ⓧ (ex guide dogs) 🚌 (must pre-book)

## LONDON SE1
### Golden Hinde Educational Trust

6A Horseshoe Wharf Clink Street SE1 9FE
☎ 020 7403 0123 ▤ 020 7407 5908
**Email:** info@goldenhinde.co.uk
**Web:** www.goldenhinde.co.uk
**Dir:** *On the Thames path between Southwark Cathedral and the new Globe Theatre*

A full size replica of Sir Francis Drake's famous 16th-century galleon. Just like the original, this *Golden Hinde* has circumnavigated the globe. You can explore the five decks, and replica furnishings add to the atmosphere. Special events include Living History re-enactments. There are holiday workshops for children and the ship is also available for private hire.

**Times:** *Open all year, 10-6. Visitors are advised to check opening times as they may vary due to closures for functions.

**Fee:** *£5.50 (ch & concessions £5). Family (2ad+3ch) £18

**Facilities:** Ⓟ (on street parking) ▤ £1.50 shop, guided tours Ⓧ (ex guide dogs) 🚌

## LONDON SE1
### HMS Belfast

Morgans Lane Tooley Street SE1 2JH
☎ 020 7940 6300 ▤ 020 7403 0719
**Email:** hmsbelfast@iwm.org.uk
**Web:** www.iwm.org.uk/hmsbelfast
**Dir:** *Underground - London Bridge/Tower Hill/Monument. Rail: London Bridge*

Europe's last surviving big gun armoured warship from the Second World War, *HMS Belfast* was launched in 1938 and served in the North Atlantic and Arctic with the Home Fleet. She led the Allied naval bombardment of German positions on D-Day, and was saved for the nation in 1971. A tour of the ship will take you from the Captain's Bridge through nine decks to the massive Boiler and Engine Rooms. You can visit the cramped Mess decks, Officers' Cabins, Galley, Sick Bay, Dentist and Laundry.

**Times:** *Open all year, daily. Mar-Oct 10-6 (last admission 5.15); Nov-Feb 10-5 (last admission 4.15). Closed 24-26 Dec.

**Fee:** *£8.50 (ch under 16 free, concessions £5.25). Party £6.50 per person.

**Facilities:** ⽊ ▤ ﬞ (wheelchair lift for access on board, toilets) shop, audio commentaries Ⓧ (ex guide dogs) 🚌 (pre booking required)

## LONDON SE1
### Imperial War Museum

Lambeth Rd SE1 6HZ

☎ 020 7416 5320 & 5321 📄 020 7416 5374

**Email:** mail@iwm.org.uk

**Web:** www.iwm.org.uk

**Dir:** *Underground – Lambeth North, Elephant & Castle or Waterloo*

Founded in 1917, this museum illustrates and records all aspects of the two World Wars and other military operations involving Britain and the Commonwealth since 1914. There are always special exhibitions and the programme of special and family events include film shows and lectures. The museum also has a wealth of military reference material, although some reference departments are open to the public by appointment only.

**Times:** Open all year, daily 10-6. Closed 24-26 Dec.

**Fee:** Free admission (charges apply for some temporary exhibitions)

**Facilities:** Ⓟ (on street, 100mtrs – metered Mon-Fri) 🍽 🍴 📋 ♿ (parking & w/chair hire book in advance, study room, T-Loop, toilets) shop, audio commentaries (charged) ⊗ (ex guide dogs) 🚌 (book in advance)

## LONDON SE1
### London Aquarium

County Hall Riverside Building Westminster Bridge Rd SE1 7PB

☎ 020 7967 8000 📄 020 7967 8029

**Email:** info@londonaquarium.co.uk

**Web:** www.londonaquarium.co.uk

**Dir:** *Underground-Waterloo & Westminster. On south bank next to Westminster Bridge, nr Big Ben & London Eye*

The London Aquarium is one of Europe's largest displays of global aquatic life with over 350 species in over 50 displays, ranging from the mystical seahorse to the deadly stonefish. The huge Pacific display is home to a variety of jacks, stingrays and seven sharks. Come and witness the spectacular Atlantic feed where our team of divers hand-feed rays and native British sharks. The rainforest feed incorporates a frenzied piranha attack with the amazing marksmanship of the archerfish. There is also a range of education tours and literature to enhance any visit.

**Times:** *Open all year, daily 10-6. (Last admission 1hr before closing). Closed 25 Dec. Late opening over summer months see website for details.

**Fee:** *Peak – £9.75 (ch 3-14 £6.25, ch under 3 free, concessions & registered disabled £7.50) Family ticket (2ad+2ch) £29. Off peak – £8.75 (ch 3-14 £5.25, ch under 3 free, concessions & registered disabled £6.50). Family ticket (2ad+2ch) £25.

**Facilities:** Ⓟ (300mtrs) 📋 ♿ (wheelchairs available, toilets) shop, guided tours, audio commentaries (charged) ⊗ (ex guide & hearing dogs) 🚌

## LONDON SE1
### Shakespeare's Globe Exhibition and Theatre Tour

21 New Globe Walk Bankside SE1 9DT

☎ 020 7902 1500 📄 020 7902 1515

**Email:** info@shakespearesglobe.com

**Web:** www.shakespeares-globe.org

**Dir:** *Underground London Bridge, walk along Bankside. Mansion House, walk across Southwark Bridge. St Pauls, walk across Millennium Bridge*

Guides help to bring England's theatrical heritage to life at the 'unparalleled and astonishing' recreation of this famous theatre built 'in the round'. Discover what an Elizabethan audience would have been like, find out about the rivalry between the Bankside theatres, the bear baiting and the stews, hear about the penny stinkards and find out what a bodger is.

**Times:** *Open all year, May-Sep, daily 9-12 (12-5 Rose Theatre tour); Oct-Apr 10-5.

**Fee:** *Oct-Apr £8 (ch £5.50, pen & students £6.50). May-Sep £8.50 (ch £6, pen & students £7) Group rates available.

**Facilities:** Ⓟ (0.5m – very limited on-street parking) ♿ (parking spaces, 'touch tours' available by appointment, toilets) shop ⊗ (ex guide & hearing dogs) 🚌 (advance booking recommended)

**LONDON**

## LONDON SE1
**Tate Modern**
Bankside SE1 9TG
☎ 020 7887 8008 (info) & 8888 ▤ 020 7401 5052
**Email:** information@tate.org.uk
**Web:** www.tate.org.uk
**Dir:** *Underground - Southwark, Blackfriars*
This is the UK's largest museum of modern art and is housed in the impressive Bankside power station. Entrance to the permanent collection, which includes works from artists like Picasso, Warhol and Dali, is free. Tate Modern also holds world-acclaimed temporary exhibitions as well as education programmes, events and activities.
**Times:** Open all year, Sun-Thu 10-6 (last admission 5.15), Fri & Sat 10am-10pm (last admission 9.15).

Closed 24-26 Dec.
**Fee:** Free. A charge is made for special exhibitions.
**Facilities:** ℗ (reserved for mobility impaired) ▤ ♿ (parking & wheelchairs available call 020 7887 8888, toilets) shop, guided tours, audio commentaries (charged) Ⓧ (ex guide dogs) 🚌 (pre-booking required)

## LONDON SE1
**The London Dungeon**
28-34 Tooley Street SE1 2SZ
☎ 020 7403 7221 ▤ 020 7378 1529
**Email:** london.dungeon@merlinentertainments.biz
**Web:** www.thedungeons.com
**Dir:** *Next to London Bridge Station*
Blood and guts, torture and terror, are all part of the re-enactments of some of the most gruesome events in British history. Brave the Great Fire of London, sail down the Thames towards Traitor's Gate, or visit Executioners corner. You can also meet some especially Wicked Women. Step back to the 1660s to dodge the rats inhabiting 'The Great Plague', then dodge the flames at The Great Fire before examining the facts concerning The Ripper known as Jack.

**Times:** Open all year, daily, Apr-Sep 10-5.30; Oct-Mar 10.30-5. Late night opening in the Summer. Telephone for exact times.
**Fee:** £16.95 (ch £11.95, concessions £13.95).
**Facilities:** ℗ (NCP 200yds) ▤ £3.95 ♿ (cards for deaf visitors, toilets) shop, guided tours Ⓧ (ex guide dogs) 🚌 (pre-booking required)

## LONDON SE1
**The Tower Bridge Exhibition**
Tower Bridge Road SE1 2UP
☎ 020 7940 3985 ▤ 020 7357 7935
**Email:** enquiries@towerbridge.org.uk
**Web:** www.towerbridge.co.uk
**Dir:** *Underground - Tower Hill or London Bridge*
One of the capital's most famous landmarks, its glass-covered walkways stand 142ft above the Thames, affording panoramic views of the river. Much of the original machinery for working the bridge can be seen in the engine rooms. The Tower Bridge Exhibition uses state-of-the-art effects to present the story of the bridge in a dramatic and exciting fashion.
**Times:** *Open all year, Apr-Sep 10-6.30 (last ticket 5.30); Oct-Mar 9.30-6 (last ticket 5)

**Fee:** *£5.50 (ch £3, concessions £4.25) Family tickets from £14.
**Facilities:** ℗ (100yds) ▤ ♿ (toilets) shop Ⓧ (ex guide dogs) 🚌

## LONDON SE1
### Winston Churchill's Britain at War Experience
64/66 Tooley Street SE1 2TF
☎ 020 7403 3171 📄 020 7403 5104
**Email:** info@britainatwar.org.uk
**Web:** www.britainatwar.co.uk
**Dir:** *mid way down Tooley St, between London Bridge & Tower Bridge. 2min walk from London Bridge Stn*
A realistic adventure back to the home front to experience life in war-torn Britain during World War II. Take the lift to the underground, where many spent sleepless nights. Explore evacuation, weddings, rationing, air-raids, gas masks, the blackout and walk through the London blitz.
**Times:** Open all year, Apr-Sep 10-6; Oct-Mar 10-5 (last entry 1hr before closing). Closed 24-26 Dec.
**Fee:** *£9.50 (ch 5-16 £4.85, concessions £5.75). Family ticket (2ad+2ch) £25.
**Facilities:** Ⓟ (400mtrs) 🍴 £7.50 ♿ (toilets) shop ⊗ (ex guide dogs) 🚌 (pre-booking)

## LONDON SE10
### Cutty Sark Clipper Ship
King William Walk Greenwich SE10 9HT
☎ 020 8858 2698 📄 020 8858 6976
**Email:** enquiries@cuttysark.org.uk
**Web:** www.cuttysark.org.uk
**Dir:** *situated in dry dock beside Greenwich Pier*
The fastest tea clipper ever, built in 1869, she once sailed 363 miles in a single day. Preserved in dry dock since 1957, her graceful lines dominate the riverside at Greenwich. The world's only surviving tea clipper with an amazing history is the highpoint of the age of sail. *Cutty Sark* contains the largest collection of merchant figureheads in the world and fascinating and historic crew quarters.
**Times:** *Open daily 10-4.30. Currently undergoing restoration. It is planned to keep the ship open as much as possible during the conservation programme, to allow members of the public to experience the science of ship preservation and maintain its heritage.
**Fee:** *£4.50 (ch £3.25, concessions £3.75). Family ticket £12.
**Facilities:** Ⓟ (50mtrs) 🍴 £3.95 ♿ shop, guided tours ⊗ (ex guide dogs) 🚌

## LONDON SE10
### National Maritime Museum
Romney Rd SE10 9NF
☎ 020 8312 6565 📄 020 8312 6632
**Email:** bookings@nmm.ac.uk
**Web:** www.nmm.ac.uk
**Dir:** *central Greenwich*
Britain's seafaring history displayed in an impressive modern museum. Themes include exploration and discovery, Nelson, trade and empire, passenger shipping and luxury liners, maritime London, costume, art and the sea, and the future of the sea. There are interactive displays for children.
**Times:** *Open all year, daily 10-5 (10-6 Jul-Aug). Closed 24-26 Dec.
**Fee:** *Free, except special exhibtions.
**Facilities:** Ⓟ (50 yds - parking in Greenwich limited) 🍷 (licensed) 🍽 (licensed) 🪑 🍴 ♿ (wheelchairs, advisory service for hearing/sight impaired, toilets) shop, guided tours, audio commentaries ⊗ (assist dogs) 🚌

**LONDON**

## LONDON SE10

### Royal Observatory Greenwich

Greenwich Park Greenwich SE10 9NF

☎ 020 8312 6565 📠 020 8312 6632

**Email:** bookings@nmm.ac.uk

**Web:** www.nmm.ac.uk

**Dir:** *off A2, Greenwich Park, enter from Blackheath Gate only*

Charles II founded the Royal Observatory in 1675 'for perfecting navigation and astronomy'. It stands at zero meridian longitude and is the original home of Greenwich Mean Time. It houses an extensive collection of historic timekeeping, astronomical and navigational instruments. New astronomy galleries and the Peter Harrison Planetarium will open in June 2007.

**Times:** Open all year, daily 10-5 (10-6 Jul-Aug). Partial closures 31 Dec, 1 Jan and Marathon day.

**Fee:** Free Royal Observatory free

**Facilities:** ℗ (charged) 🚻 📶 ♿ (assistance on request, toilets) shop, guided tours ⊗ 🚌

## LONDON SE18

### Firepower

Royal Arsenal Woolwich SE18 6ST

☎ 020 8855 7755 📠 020 8855 7100

**Email:** info@firepower.org.uk

**Web:** www.firepower.org.uk

**Dir:** *A205, right at Woolwich ferry onto A206, attraction signed*

Firepower is the Royal Artillery Museum in the historic Royal Arsenal. It spans 2000 years of artillery and shows the development from Roman catapult to guided missile to self-propelled gun. Put science into action with touchscreen displays and be awed by the big guns.

**Times:** *Open Wed-Sun & BHs 11-5.30. Phone for winter opening times.

**Fee:** *£6.50 (ch 4.50, concessions £5.50) Family tickets & group discounts (10+) available.

**Facilities:** ℗ (charged) ℗ (0.5m) 🚻 ♿ (wheelchairs available, toilets) shop ⊗ (ex guide dogs) 🚌 (pre-booking required)

## LONDON SW1

### Buckingham Palace

Buckingham Palace Rd SW1 1AA

☎ 020 7766 7300 📠 020 7930 9625

**Email:** bookinginfo@royalcollection.org.uk

**Web:** www.royalcollection.org.uk

**Dir:** *Underground - Victoria, Green Park, St James' Park*

Buckingham Palace has been the official London residence of Britain's sovereigns since 1837. Today it serves as both the home and office of Her Majesty the Queen. Nineteen State Rooms, which open for eight weeks a year, form the heart of the working palace and more than 50,000 people visit each year as the guests at State, ceremonial and official occasions and garden parties. After visiting the State Rooms, visitors can enjoy a walk along the south side of the garden, which offers superb views of the west front of the Palace and the 19th-century lake.

**Times:** Open Aug-Sep 9.45-6 (last admission 3.45). Entry by timed-ticket.

**Fee:** *£14 (ch under 17 £8, ch under 5 free, concessions £12.50) Family ticket (2ad+3ch) £36.

**Facilities:** ℗ (200yds – very limited, driving not recommended) 📶 ♿ (ex gardens, pre-booking essential - 020 7766 7324, toilets) shop, audio commentaries ⊗ (ex guide dogs) 🚌 (no coach parking)

## LONDON SW1
### Churchill Museum & Cabinet War Rooms

Clive Steps King Charles Street SW1A 2AQ

☎ 020 7930 6961 🖩 020 7839 5897

**Email:** cwr@iwm.org.uk

**Web:** www.iwm.org.uk

**Dir:** *Underground - Westminster exit 6 or St James Park*

Learn more about the man who inspired Britain's finest hour at the interactive and innovative Churchill Museum, the world's first major museum dedicated to the life of the 'Greatest Briton'. Step back in time and discover the secret underground headquarters that were the nerve centre of Britain's war effort. Located in the heart of Westminster, visitors can view this complex of historic rooms left as they were in 1945, while at the same time taking in the new Churchill Museum.

**Times:** *Open all year, daily 9.30-6. (last admission 5). Closed 24-26 Dec.

**Fee:** *£10 (ch under 16 free, concessions £8). Party 10+ £8 (concessions £7)

**Facilities:** ℗ (2 mins walk – meter parking) 🗐 ♿ (education service, object handling session, induction loop, toilets) shop, audio commentaries ⊗ (ex guide dogs) 🚌 (max 45 people in one group)

## LONDON SW1
### Houses of Parliament

Westminster SW1A 0AA

☎ 020 7219 4272 🖩 020 7219 5839

**Web:** www.parliament.uk

**Dir:** *Underground – Westminster*

The Houses of Parliament occupy the site that was once the Palace of Westminster, a royal palace for nearly 1,000 years. In 1834 a devastating fire destroyed most of the building leaving Westminster Hall (c.1097), where Charles I and Guy Fawkes were put on trial, the Jewel Tower and St Stephen's crypt. The new building was designed by Pugin and reflects the medieval origins of the Palace. Visitors will see the Queen's Robing Room, the Royal Gallery, the Chambers of both the House of Lords and House of Commons, the voting lobbies, as well as other areas normally hidden from public view.

**Times:** *Open 24 Jul-4 Sep, Mon, Tue, Fri & Sat, 9.15-4.30, Wed & Thu, 1.15-4.30; 18 Sep-2 Oct, Mon, Fri & Sat, 9.15-4.30, Tue, Wed & Thu 1.15-4.30. Times are for 1st and last tours of the day.

**Fee:** *£7 (ch 5-16 £5, concessions £5) Family ticket £22. Foreign language tours £7.50-£9. Group rates on application.

**Facilities:** ℗ (50mtrs – limited parking, metered) ♿ (touch & sound model for visually impaired, toilets) shop ⊗ (ex guide dogs)

## LONDON SW1
### Tate Britain

Millbank SW1P 4RG

☎ 020 7887 8888 & rec info 8008

**Email:** information@tate.org.uk

**Web:** www.tate.org.uk

**Dir:** *Underground - Pimlico*

Tate Britain is the national gallery of British art from 1500 to the present day, from Tudors to the Turner Prize. Tate holds the greatest collection of British art in the world, including works by Blake, Constable, Epstein, Gainsborough, Gilbert and George, Hatoum, Hirst, Hockney, Hodgkin, Hogarth, Moore, Rossetti, Sickert, Spencer, Stubbs and Turner. The gallery is the world centre for the understanding and enjoyment of British art. Tate Britain also has regular special exhibitions that reflect the history of British art, and numerous public events. See website for details.

**Times:** Open daily 10-5.50. Closed 24-26 Dec.

**Fee:** *Free. Donations welcomed. Prices vary for special exhibitions.

**Facilities:** ℗ (100mtrs – metered parking) ⬚ (Self-service) 🍽 (Licensed) 🚻 🗐 ♿ (wheelchairs on request, parking by prior arrangement, toilets) shop, guided tours, audio commentaries (charged) ⊗ (ex guide & hearing dogs) 🚌 (contact in advance)

**LONDON**

## LONDON SW1
### Westminster Abbey

Broad Sanctuary SW1P 3PA

☎ 020 7222 5152 & 7654 4900 📠 020 7233 2072

**Email:** press@westminster-abbey.org

**Web:** www.westminster-abbey.org

**Dir:** *Underground – Westminster, St James's Park.
Parliament Square and opposite the Houses of Parliament*

Westminster Abbey was originally a Benedictine monastery, re-founded by Edward the Confessor, it became his burial place shortly after it was completed. The abbey has been the setting for most coronations since William the Conqueror in 1066. The present building, begun by Henry III in 1245, is one of the most visited churches in the world.

**Times:** *Open Abbey: Mon-Fri 9.30-3.45, Sat 9-1.45. Wed late night til 7. (Last admission 1hr before closing). No tourism on Sun, visitors welcome at services. The Abbey may close at short notice for special services.

**Fee:** *£8 (ch & concessions £6). Family ticket (2ad+2ch) £18.

**Facilities:** ♿ (induction loop) shop, guided tours, audio commentaries, (charged) ⊗ (ex guide dogs) 🚌

## LONDON SW1
### Westminster Cathedral

Victoria Street SW1P 1QW

☎ 020 7798 9055 📠 020 7798 9090

**Email:** barrypalmer@rcdow.org.uk

**Web:** www.westminstercathedral.org.uk

**Dir:** *300 yds from Victoria Station*

Westminster Cathedral is a fascinating example of Victorian architecture. Designed in the Early Christian Byzantine style by John Francis Bentley, its strongly oriental appearance makes it very distinctive. The foundation stone was laid in 1895 but the interior decorations are not fully completed. The Campanile Bell Tower is 273ft high and has a four-sided viewing gallery with magnificent views over London. The lift is open daily 9am-5pm Mar-Nov but shut Mon-Wed from Dec-Feb.

**Times:** *Open all year, daily 7am-7pm.

**Fee:** Free

**Facilities:** Ⓟ (0.25m – 2hr metered parking) ☕ (open 10-4) 🍴 20p-£4.95 ♿ (all parts accessible except side chapels, loop system) shop, guided tours ⊗ (ex guide dogs) 🚌 ♿

## LONDON SW7
### Natural History Museum

Cromwell Road SW7 5BD

☎ 020 7942 5000 📠 020 7942 5075

**Email:** feedback@nhm.ac.uk

**Web:** www.nhm.ac.uk

**Dir:** *Underground - South Kensington*

This vast and elaborate Romanesque-style building, with its terracotta facing showing relief mouldings of animals, birds and fishes, covers an area of four acres. Holding over 70 million specimens from all over the globe, from dinosaurs to diamonds and earthquakes to ants, the museum provides a journey into Earth's past, present and future. Discover more about the work of the museum through a daily programme of talks from museum scientists or go behind the scenes of the Darwin Centre, the museum's scientific research centre.

**Times:** *Open daily 10-5.50 (last admission 5.30). Closed 24-26 Dec.

**Fee:** *Free. Charge made for some special exhibitions.

**Facilities:** Ⓟ (180yds – limited parking, use public transport) 🍴 (Licensed) 🪑 🍴 Varies ♿ (top floor/one gallery not accessible, wheelchair hire, toilets) shop, guided tours ⊗ (ex guide dogs) 🚌

## LONDON SW7
### Science Museum

Exhibition Road South Kensington SW7 2DD

☎ 0870 870 4868 🖹 020 7942 4421

**Email:** sciencemuseum@nmsi.ac.uk

**Web:** www.sciencemuseum.org.uk

**Dir:** *Underground - South Kensington, signed from tube stn*

See iconic objects from the history of science, from Stephenson's *Rocket* to the *Apollo 10* command module; be amazed by a 3D IMAX movie; take a ride in a simulator; visit an exhibition; and encounter the past, present and future of technology in seven floors of free galleries, including the famous hands-on section where children can have fun investigating science with the Museum's dedicated Explainers. The Museum is free, but charges apply to the IMAX cinema, special exhibitions and simulators.

**Times:** Open all year, daily 10-6. Closed 24-26 Dec.

**Fee:** Admission free. Charges apply for IMAX 3D cinema, simulators & some special exhibitions.

**Facilities:** ℗ (metered 0.5m away) ☕ (open 10-5.30) 🍴 (Licensed) ⛱ 🛗 ♿ (personal 2hr tour of museum, hearing loop, toilets) shop, guided tours (charged) 🚫 (ex guide dogs) 🚌 (no coach parking)

## LONDON SW7
### Victoria and Albert Museum

Cromwell Road South Kensington SW7 2RL

☎ 020 7942 2000

**Email:** vanda@vam.ac.uk

**Web:** www.vam.ac.uk

**Dir:** *Underground - South Kensington, Museum situated on A4, Buses C1, 14, 74, 414 stop outside the Cromwell Road entrance*

The world's finest museum of art and design, with collections spanning 3000 years, and comprising sculpture, furniture, fashion and textiles, paintings, silver, glass, ceramics, jewellery, books, prints, and photographs from Britain and all over the world. Highlights include the national collection of paintings by John Constable, the Dress Court showing fashion from 1500 to the present day, a superb Asian collection, the Jewellery Gallery including the Russian Crown Jewels, and the 20th Century Gallery, devoted to contemporary art and design. The stunning British Galleries 1500-1900 tell the story of British design from the Tudor age to the Victorian era.

**Times:** *Open all year, Mon-Sun 10-5.45. Wed & last Fri of month open late, 10am-10pm. Closed 24-26 Dec.

**Fee:** *Free admission but some exhibitions may carry an extra charge.

**Facilities:** ℗ (500yds – limited, charged parking) 🍴 (Licensed) ⛱ ♿ (Facilities available. Call for details 020 7942 2211, toilets) shop 🚫 (ex guide dogs) 🚌 (must pre-book)

## LONDON SW13
### London Wetland Centre

Queen Elizabeth Walk SW13 9WT

☎ 020 8409 4400 🖹 020 8409 4401

**Email:** info@wetlandcentre.org.uk

**Web:** www.wwt.org.uk

**Dir:** *underground - Hammersmith.*

An inspiring wetland landscape in Barnes SW13, that stretches over 105 acres alongside the River Thames. Not far from the heart of London, a total of 30 wild wetland habitats have been created, from reservoir lagoon to ponds, lakes and reedbeds, and all are home to a wide variety of wildlife, particularly waterbirds.

**Times:** Winter 9.30-4, Summer 9.30-5.

**Fee:** *£7.25 (ch £4.50 & concessions £6). Family ticket £18.50. Groups 10+. Car park £2 charge on Sun & BHs per vehicle.

**Facilities:** ℗ (charged) ⛱ ♿ (ramps, lifts, toilets) shop 🚫 (ex guide dogs) 🚌 (must book in advance) ♻

**LONDON**

LONDON

## LONDON W1
### Pollock's Toy Museum
1 Scala Street W1T 2HL
☎ 020 7636 3452
**Email:** pollocks@btconnect.com
**Web:** www.pollockstoymuseum.com
**Dir:** *Underground – Goodge St*
Teddy bears, wax and china dolls, dolls' houses, board games, toy theatres, tin toys, mechanical and optical toys, folk toys and nursery furniture, are among the attractions to be seen in this appealing museum. Items from all over the world and from all periods are displayed in two small, interconnecting houses with winding staircases and charming little rooms.
**Times:** *Open all year, Mon-Sat 10-5. Closed BH, Sun & Xmas.

**Fee:** *£3 (ch 3-18 £1.50)
**Facilities:** Ⓟ (100yds – Central London restrictions) ♿ shop 🚌

## LONDON W12
### BBC Television Centre Tours
BBC Television Centre Wood Lane W12 7RJ
☎ 0870 603 0304 📄 020 8576 7466
**Email:** bbctours@bbc.co.uk
**Web:** www.bbc.co.uk/tours
**Dir:** *Underground – Central Line/White City*
Take a look behind the scenes at the world's most famous TV centre. As the BBC TV Centre is a working building, no guarantees can be made as to what visitors will see, although dressing rooms, the News Centre, the Weather Centre, and various studios are all possible. The uncertain nature of the visit means that no two are the same, and that only pre-booked guided tours are available. For children 7 years and over there are tours to find out what goes on behind the scenes of CBBC's television programmes.
**Times:** *Open Mon-Sat. Tours at 10, 10.20, 10.40, 1.15, 1.30, 1.45, 3.30, 3.45 & 4. Closed Xmas & BHs. All tours must be pre-booked.
**Fee:** *£8.95 (concessions £7.95, student £6.50). Family ticket £25
**Facilities:** Ⓟ (10min walk) ♿ (pre-arranged disabled parking, wheelchair & sign language available, toilets) shop, guided tours 🚫 (ex assist dogs) 🚌

## LONDON WC1
### British Museum
Great Russell Street WC1B 3DG
☎ 020 7323 8000 📄 020 7323 8616
**Email:** information@thebritishmuseum.ac.uk
**Web:** www.thebritishmuseum.ac.uk
**Dir:** *Underground – Russell Sq, Tottenham Court Rd, Holborn*
Of the world and for the world, the British Museum brings together astounding examples of universal heritage, for free. Enter through the largest covered square in Europe. Pick up your audio guide, children's pack or What's On programme. Then discover the world through objects like the Aztec mosaics, the Rosetta Stone, El Anatsui's African textiles or the colossal Ramesses II. And if you want a more relaxed viewing, a fantastic evening meal or some world cinema, come late – every Thursday and Friday.
**Times:** *Open all year, Gallery: Sat-Wed 10-5.30 & Thu-Fri 10-8.30. Great Court: Sun-Wed 9-6, Thu-Sat 9am-11pm. Closed Good Fri, 24-26 Dec & 1 Jan.
**Fee:** *Free admission except for special exhibitions
**Facilities:** Ⓟ (5 mins walk) 🍽 (Licensed) 🍴 📗 ♿ (parking by arrangement, toilets) shop, guided tours, audio commentaries (charged) 🚫 (ex guide/companion dogs) 🚌 (educational groups must book by phone)

## LONDON WC1
### Petrie Museum of Egyptian Archaeology
Malet Place Univerity College London WC1E 6BT
☎ 020 7679 2884 ▤ 020 7679 2886
**Email:** petrie.museum@ucl.ac.uk
**Web:** www.petrie.ucl.ac.uk
**Dir:** *on 1st floor of the D M S Watson building, in Malet Place, off Torrington Place*
One of the largest and most inspiring collections of Egyptian archaeology anywhere in the world. The displays illustrate life in the Nile Valley from prehistory, through the era of the Pharoahs to Roman and Islamic times. Especially noted for its collection of the personal items that illustrate life and death in Ancient Egypt, including the world's earliest surviving dress (c 2800BC).
**Times:** *Open all year, Tue-Fri 1-5, Sat 10-1. Closed for 1 wk at Xmas/Etr.
**Fee:** *Free
**Facilities:** ▤ ♿ (wheelchair lift, toilets) shop, guided tours ⊗ (ex guide dogs) 🚌 (max 50 people) ♨

## LONDON WC1
### The Cartoon Museum
35 Little Russell Street WC1A 2HH
☎ 020 7580 8155 ▤ 020 7631 0793
**Email:** info@cartoonmuseum.org
**Web:** www.cartoonmuseum.org
**Dir:** *left off New Oxford St into Museum St, then left into Little Russell St*
The main galleries display over 200 original cartoons, comics, cartoon strips and caricatures by many of the greatest and funniest of British cartoonists past and present. There is also a programme of temporary exhibitions which change regularly.
**Times:** Open all year Tue-Sat 10.30-5.30, Sun 12-5.30.
**Fee:** £3 (ch under 18 free, concessions £2)
**Facilities:** ℗ (charged) ℗ ▤ ♿ (hearing loop, large print labels, toilets) shop, guided tours ⊗ (ex assist dogs) 🚌 (maximum 50)

## LONDON WC2
### Hunterian Museum
The Royal College of Surgeons 35-43 Lincoln's Inn Fields WC2A 3PE
☎ 020 7869 6560 ▤ 020 7869 6564
**Email:** museums@rcseng.ac.uk
**Web:** www.rcseng.ac.uk
**Dir:** *Underground - Holborn*
The Hunterian Museum at the Royal College of Surgeons houses over 3,000 anatomical and pathological preparations collected by the surgeon John Hunter (1728-1793). New interpretive displays explore Hunter's life and work, the history of the Hunterian Museum and the College, and the development of surgery from the 18th century to the present. The MacRae Gallery provides a dedicated space for learning based on the museum's reserve collections. The museum also stages a changing programme of temporary exhibitions, lectures and other public events on themes related to the history and current practice of surgery.
**Times:** Open all year Tues-Sat 10-5. Closed 21 Dec-3 Jan, Good Fri & Etr Sat.
**Fee:** Free
**Facilities:** ℗ (15mtrs – pay & display 8.30-6.30pm) ▤ ♿ (Descriptive tours by arrangement, toilets) shop, guided tours ⊗ (ex guide dogs) 🚌 (must pre-book) ♨

LONDON

## LONDON WC2
### National Gallery
Trafalgar Square WC2N 5DN
☎ 020 7747 2885 🖷 020 7747 2423
**Email:** information@ng-london.org.uk
**Web:** www.nationalgallery.org.uk
**Dir:** *Underground - Charing Cross, Leicester Square, Embankment & Piccadilly Circus. Rail: Charing Cross. Located on N side of Trafalgar Sq*
All the great periods of Western European painting, from 1260-1900, are represented here. The Gallery's particular treasures include Velázquez's *Toilet of Venus*, Leonardo da Vinci's Cartoon (*The Virgin and Child with Saints Anne and John the Baptist*), Rembrandt's *Belshazzar's Feast*, Van Gogh's *Sunflowers*, and Titian's *Bacchus and Ariadne*. The British paintings include Gainsborough's *Mr and Mrs Andrews* and Constable's *Haywain*. Free guided tours everyday.
**Times:** Open all year, daily 10-6, (Wed until 9). Special major charging exhibitions open normal gallery times. Closed 24-26 Dec & 1 Jan.
**Fee:** Free. Admission charged for some major exhibitions.
**Facilities:** ℗ (100yds) 🍽 (Licensed) 📶 ♿ (wheelchair, induction loop, lift, deaf/blind visitor tours, toilets) shop, guided tours, audio commentaries (charged) 🚫 (ex guide & hearing dogs) 🚌 (must register on arrival at information desk)

## LONDON WC2
### National Portrait Gallery
St Martin's Place WC2H 0HE
☎ 020 7306 0055 🖷 020 7306 0056
**Web:** www.npg.org.uk
**Dir:** *Underground - Charing Cross, Leicester Square. Buses to Trafalgar Square*
The National Portrait Gallery is home to the largest collection of portraiture in the world featuring famous British men and woman who have created history from the Middle Ages until the present day. Over 1,000 portraits are on display across three floors from Henry VIII and Florence Nightingale to The Beatles and HM The Queen. And, if you want to rest those weary feet, visit the fabulous Portrait Restaurant on the top floor with roof-top views across London. Special events take place throughout the year, see website for details.
**Times:** *Open all year, Mon-Wed & Sat-Sun 10-6, Thu-Fri 10-9. Closed Good Fri, 24-26 Dec & 1 Jan. (Gallery closure commences 10mins prior to stated time).
**Fee:** *Free (ex special exhibitions)
**Facilities:** ℗ (200yds) 🍽 (Licensed) 📶 ♿ (stair climber, touch tours, audio guide, print captions, toilets) shop, audio commentaries (charged) 🚫 (ex guide dogs) 🚌 (10+ must pre-book)

## BANHAM
### Banham Zoo
The Grove Norwich NR16 2HE
☎ 01953 887771 & 887773 🖷 01953 887445
**Email:** info@banhamzoo.co.uk
**Web:** www.banhamzoo.co.uk
**Dir:** *on B1113, signed off A11 and A140. Follow brown tourist signs*
Set in 35 acres of magnificent parkland, see hundreds of animals ranging from big cats to birds of prey and siamangs to shire horses. Tiger Territory is a purpose-built enclosure for Siberian tigers, including a rock pool and woodland setting. See also Lemur Island and Tamarin and Marmoset Islands. The Heritage Farm Stables & Falconry displays Norfolk's rural heritage with majestic shire horses and birds of prey. Other attractions include Children's Farmyard Barn and Adventure Play Area.
**Times:** *Open all year, daily from 10. (Last admission 1 hour before closing). Closed 25 & 26 Dec.
**Fee:** *Please phone Zoo for details
**Facilities:** ℗ ℗ (50mtrs) 🚻 (seasonal opening) 🍽 (Licensed) 🪑 ♿ (3 wheelchairs for hire, parking, toilets) shop, audio commentaries 🚫 🚌

## BRESSINGHAM
### Bressingham Steam Museum & Gardens
Diss IP22 2AB

☎ 01379 686900 & 687386 🖺 01379 686907

**Email:** info@bressingham.co.uk

**Web:** www.bressingham.co.uk

**Dir:** *on A1066 2.5m W of Diss, between Thetford & Diss*
Alan Bloom is an internationally recognised nurseryman
and a steam enthusiast, and has combined his interests
to great effect at Bressingham. There are three miniature
steam-hauled trains, including a 15in gauge running
through the wooded Waveney Valley. The Dell Garden has
5,000 species of perennials and alpines. There is a
steam roundabout and the Norfolk fire museum is
housed here. Various events are held, including Dad's
Army Day, Friends of Thomas the Tank Engine.

**Times:** Open: Apr-Sep, daily 10.30-5.30 (Mar & Oct
10.30-4.30). (Last admission 1 hour before closing time)
**Fee:** £7-£12 (ch 3-16 £5-£8, pen £7-£10). Family £22-
£35. Season tickets available.
**Facilities:** 🅿 🍽 (Licensed) 🚻 🎫 ♿ (wheelchairs can be
taken onto Nursery & Waveney lines, toilets) shop, garden
centre, guided tours ⊗ (ex guide dogs) 🚌 (pre-book)

## FAKENHAM
### Pensthorpe Nature Reserve & Gardens
Pensthorpe NR21 0LN

☎ 01328 851465 🖺 01328 855905

**Email:** info@pensthorpe.com

**Web:** www.pensthorpe.co.uk

**Dir:** *1m from Fakenham on the A1067 to Norwich*
Covering 500 acres of beautiful Wensum Valley
countryside, with five lakes which are home to one of the
largest collections of waterfowl and waders in Europe.
Spacious walk-through enclosures and a network of
hardsurfaced pathways ensures close contact with birds
at the water's edge. Gardens by acclaimed designers Piet
Dudolf and Julie Toll.
**Times:** *Open Jan-Mar, daily 10-4. Apr-Dec, 10-5
**Fee:** *£7 (ch £3.50, pen £5.50)

**Facilities:** 🅿 🚻 🎫 50p ♿ (network of hard surfaced
pathways ensures access, toilets) shop, guided tours
⊗ (ex guide dogs) 🚌

## FILBY
### Thrigby Hall Wildlife Gardens
NR29 3DR

☎ 01493 369477 🖺 01493 368256

**Web:** www.thrigbyhall.co.uk

**Dir:** *on unclass road off A1064, between Acle &
Caister-on-Sea*
The 250-year-old park of Thrigby Hall is now the home of
animals and birds from Asia, and the lake has
ornamental wildfowl. There are tropical bird houses, a
unique blue willow pattern garden and tree walk and a
summer house as old as the park. The enormous jungled
swamp hall has special features such as underwater
viewing of large crocodiles.
**Times:** *Open all year, daily from 10.
**Fee:** *£7.90 (ch 4-14 £5.90, pen £6.90).

**Facilities:** 🅿 🅿 (200yds) 🚻 🎫 £1 ♿ (wheelchairs
available, ramps, parking, toilets) shop, guided tours
⊗ (ex guide dogs) 🚌 (pre-book)

## GREAT BIRCHAM
**Bircham Windmill**
King's Lynn PE31 6SJ
☎ 01485 578393
**Email:** birchamwindmill@btinternet.com
**Web:** www.birchamwindmill.co.uk
**Dir:** *0.5m W off unclassified Snettisham road.*
This windmill is one of the last remaining in Norfolk and one of only a few open to the public. The sails turn when there is sufficient wind. The adjacent tea room serves home-made cakes, light lunches and cream teas. There is also a bakery shop and cycle hire. In addition there is a programme of events throughout the year, including crafts fairs and events on a number of weekends.
**Times:** Open Etr-Sep, 10-5.
**Fee:** *£3.25 (ch £2, pen £3)

**Facilities:** Ⓟ 🚽 75p ♿ (toilets) shop 🚌 (prior arrangement only)

## GREAT YARMOUTH
**Merrivale Model Village**
Marine Parade NR30 3JG
☎ 01493 842097
**Web:** www.merrivalemodelvillage.co.uk
**Dir:** *Marine parade seafront, next to Wellington Pier*
Set in more than an acre of attractive landscaped gardens, this comprehensive miniature village is built on a scale of 1:12, and features naturalistic streams, a lake and waterfalls. Among the models are a working fairground, a stone quarry, houses, shops, and a garden railway. There are even illuminations at dusk! The Penny Arcade is a display of the old penny slot machines and provides a nostalgic opportunity to play with these old seaside amusements.
**Times:** Open daily Etr-end Oct

**Fee:** Please telephone for details, or visit website
**Facilities:** Ⓟ (opposite) 🪑 ♿ (toilets) shop 🚌

## GRESSENHALL
**Gressenhall Farm and Workhouse**
Dereham NR20 4DR
☎ 01362 860563 📠 01362 860385
**Email:** gressenhall.museum@norfolk.gov.uk
**Web:** www.museums.norfolk.gov.uk
**Dir:** *on B1146 3m NW of Dereham, follow brown signs*
This fascinating journey through the history of rural Norfolk includes an historic workhouse, a traditional farm, extensive collections, and a new adventure playground. The farm has lambs and piglets as well as horses working the fields. Visitors can explore the grounds, gardens and country trails, then take a break in the café.
**Times:** *Open 12-19 Feb, 11-4. 26 Mar-29 Oct, 10-5.
**Fee:** *£7 (ch £4.65, under 4's free, concessions £5.95)
**Facilities:** Ⓟ 🪑 🚽 ♿ (sound guide, wheelchair loan, toilets) shop, guided tours, audio commentaries 🚫 (ex assist dogs) 🚌

## GRIMES GRAVES
**Grimes Graves**
Lynford Thetford IP26 5DE
☎ 01842 810656
**Web:** www.english-heritage.org.uk
**Dir:** *7m NW of Thetford off A134*
Not graves at all, these unique and remarkable Neolithic flint mines are the earliest major industrial site in Europe. Between 2,200 and 2,500BC early miners sunk shafts up to 30 feet deep to locate seams of flint which were used for axes and tools. Impressively, evidence from archaeological digs suggest that these early miners used deer antlers as a digging tool.
**Times:** Open 3-31 Mar; Thu-Mon, 10-5; Apr-Sep, daily 10-6; Oct, Thu-Mon 10-5.
**Fee:** £2.70 (ch £1.40, concessions £2) Family £6.80.

Prices and opening times are subject to change. Please check web site or call 0870 333 1181 for the most up to date prices and opening times when planning your visit.
**Facilities:** ❷ ♿ (exhibition area, grounds only, access track rough) shop 🚌 ♯ ♿

## HEACHAM
**Norfolk Lavender**
Caley Mill King's Lynn PE31 7JE
☎ 01485 570384 📄 01485 571176
**Email:** admin@norfolk-lavender.co.uk
**Web:** www.norfolk-lavender.co.uk
**Dir:** *follow signs on A149 & A148. Car park entrance on B1454, 100yds E of junct with A149*
This is the largest lavender-growing and distilling operation in Britain. Different coloured lavenders are grown in strips and harvested in July and August. There are also herb gardens and a fragrant Plant Centre, as well as guided tours of the distillery and gardens.
**Times:** Open all year, daily, Apr-Oct 9.30-5; Nov-Mar 9.30-4. (Closed 25-26 Dec & 1 Jan).
**Fee:** *Admission to grounds free. Guided tours £3 (May-

Sep). Trip to Lavender Field £5, mid Jul-mid Aug.
**Facilities:** ❷ 🍴 (Licensed) ♿ (2 wheelchairs for loan, toilets) shop, garden centre, guided tours 🚌

## HOLKHAM
**Holkham Hall & Bygones Museum**
Wells-Next-The-Sea NR23 1AB
☎ 01328 710227 📄 01328 711707
**Email:** enquiries@holkham.co.uk
**Web:** www.holkham.co.uk
**Dir:** *off A149, 2m W of Wells-next-the-Sea, coaches should use B1105 at New Holkham, signed Holkham Coaches*
This classic Palladian mansion was built between 1734 and 1764 by Thomas Coke, 1st Earl of Leicester, and is home to his descendants. It has a magnificent alabaster entrance hall and the sumptuous state rooms house Roman statuary, fine furniture and paintings by Rubens, Van Dyck, Gainsborough and others. The Bygones Museum, housed in the stable block, has over 5,000

items of domestic and agricultural display – from gramophones to fire engines. The adjacent (and free) History of Farming exhibition illustrates how a great agricultural estate such as Holkham works and has evolved.
**Times:** Open 25 May-Sep, Sun-Thu 12-5; also Sat-Mon & all BHs, 12-5
**Fee:** Hall £7 (ch £3.50). Bygones £5 (ch £2.50). Combined ticket Hall & Bygones: £10 (ch £5). Family ticket £25.
**Facilities:** ❷ ℗ (in Holkham Village) 🍴 📖 ♿ (wheelchair ramps, stairclimbing equipment, toilets) shop, guided tours, audio commentaries (charged) ⊗ (ex guide dogs) 🚌 (prior booking advised)

**NORFOLK**

## HORSEY
**Horsey Windpump**
NR29 4EF
☎ 01493 393904
**Web:** www.nationaltrust.co.uk
**Dir:** *15m N of Great Yarmouth, on the B1159 4m NE of Martham*
Set in a remote part of the Norfolk Broads, the windpump mill was built 200 years ago to drain the area, and then rebuilt in 1912 by Dan England, a noted Norfolk millwright. It has been restored since being struck by lightning in 1943, and overlooks Horsey Mere and marshes, noted for the wild birds and insects as a site of International Importance for Nature Conservation.
**Times:** *Open Mar; Sat-Sun 10-4.30, Apr-Oct; Wed-Sun 10-4.30, BH Mon 10.30-4.

**Fee:** *£2 (ch £1). NT members free entry & parking. Mooring fees payable to the Horsey Estate (inc NT members).
**Facilities:** ♿ (charged) ♿ (parking, ramps to ground floor, toilets) shop 🚌 (limited to 10 in windpump for large groups) 🌿

## HORSHAM ST FAITH
**City of Norwich Aviation Museum**
Old Norwich Road Norwich NR10 3JF
☎ 01603 893080 📄 01603 893080
**Email:** norwichairmuseum@hotmail.com
**Web:** www.cnam.co.uk
**Dir:** *follow brown tourist signs from A140 Norwich to Cromer road*
A massive Avro Vulcan bomber, veteran of the Falklands War, dominates the collection of military and civilian aircraft at this museum. There are several displays relating to the aeronautical history of Norfolk, including some on the role played by Norfolk-based RAF and USAAF planes during World War II, and a section dedicated to the operations of RAF Bomber Command's 100 group.

**Times:** *Open all year, Apr-Oct Tue-Sat, 10-5. Sun & BH Mons 12-5 (Mons during school hols). Nov-Mar, Wed & Sat 10-4. Sun 12-4.
**Fee:** £3.25 (ch & concessions £1.50, pen £2.75) Family ticket £9.
**Facilities:** ♿ 🪑 ♿ (assistance available) shop ⊗ (ex guide dogs) 🚌 (guided tours for groups by arrangment)

## HOUGHTON
**Houghton Hall**
Kings Lynn PE31 6UE
☎ 01485 528569 📄 01485 528167
**Email:** administrator@houghtonhall.com
**Web:** www.houghtonhall.com
**Dir:** *1.25m off A148. 13m E of King's Lynn & 10m W of Fakenham on A148*
Houghton Hall, built in the 1720s by Sir Robert Walpole, Britain's first Prime Minister, is one of the grandest surviving Palladian Houses in England. The spectacular 5-acre walled garden, has been divided into areas for fruit and vegetables, spacious herbaceous borders, and formal rose gardens with over 150 varieties. A collection of Model Soldiers contains over 20,000 figures laid out in various battle formations. There are musical events in the

summer, and the Houghton horse trials in August.
**Times:** * House open 1.30-5 (last entry 4.30). Grounds and Soldier Museum open 11-5.30.
**Fee:** *£7 (ch £3). Fam £16. Grounds only £4.50 (ch £2).
**Facilities:** ♿ Ⓟ 🍴 (Licensed) 🪑 📋 ♿ (lift, motorised buggies, toilets) shop, guided tours ⊗ (ex guide dogs) 🚌 pre-book

## HUNSTANTON
### Hunstanton Sea Life Sanctuary
Southern Promenade PE36 5BH
☎ 01485 533576 ▤ 01485 533531
**Web:** www.sealsanctuary.co.uk
**Dir:** *A149 King's Lynn to Hunstanton, then follow brown Sea Life signs.*
With over 30 fascinating displays of marine life, this marvellous aquarium offers close encounters with starfish, sharks, octopus, eels and many other underwater wonders. There are feeding demonstrations, talks and special presentations. The latest addition is Claws: this involves six displays featuring strange clawed creatures from around the world.
**Times:** Open all year, daily from 10. (Closed 25 Dec)
**Fee:** *£9.95 (ch £7.25 & concessions £7.95)

**Facilities:** ℗ (charged) ℗ ⊟ ♿ (toilets) shop ⊗ (ex guide dogs) 🚌 (pre-booking required)

## LENWADE
### Dinosaur Adventure Park
Weston Park NR9 5JW
☎ 01603 876310 ▤ 01603 876315
**Email:** info@dinosaurpark.co.uk
**Web:** www.dinosaurpark.co.uk
**Dir:** *From A47 or A1067 follow brown signs to Park*
Set in 100 acres of wooded parkland, the Dinosaur Adventure Park has lots of entertainment for all the family. Visitors can help the Ranger track T-Rex on the Dinosaur Trail and meet giants from the past including the new addition, spinosaurus. They can also make friends with animals from hedgehogs to wallabies, or bugs and snakes in the secret animal garden. There is a new adventure play area including a Climb-o-saurus, Raptor Racers, Jurassic Putt Crazy Golf, and the Lost

World Amazing Adventure.
**Times:** *Open daily until 10 Sep & Oct half term; 11 Sep-22 Oct, Fri-Sun.
**Fee:** *£7.95 (ch & pen £6.95, under 3's free)
**Facilities:** ℗ ⊟ ▤ ♿ (Swing, toilets) shop, guided tours, audio commentaries (charged) ⊗ (ex guide dogs) 🚌 (book in advance)

## NORWICH
### Norwich Castle Museum & Art Gallery
Castle Meadow NR1 3JU
☎ 01603 493625 ▤ 01603 493623
**Email:** museums@norfolk.gov.uk
**Web:** www.museums.norfolk.gov.uk
**Dir:** *in city centre*
The Castle keep was built in the 12th century, and the museum houses displays of art, archaeology, natural history, Lowestoft porcelain, Norwich silver, a large collection of paintings (with special emphasis on the Norwich School of Painters) and British ceramic teapots. There are also guided tours of the dungeons and battlements. A programme of exhibitions, children's events, gallery and evening talks take place throughout the year. Please ring for details.

**Times:** Open all year, Mon-Fri 10-4.30, Sat 10-5, Sun 1-5; School hols, Mon-Sat 10-5.30, Sun 1-5.
**Fee:** *All zones £5.95 (ch 4-16 £4.45, concessions £4.95). Castle & History Zone £3.95 (ch £2.95, concessions £3.35). Art & Exhibitions Zone £3.45 (ch £2.60, concessions £2.95)
**Facilities:** ℗ (200mtrs) ⊟ ▤ ♿ (lift to first floor, disabled parking, virtual tour, toilets) shop, guided tours ⊗ (ex guide dogs) 🚌

**NORFOLK**

**NORFOLK**

## NORWICH
### The Bridewell
Bridewell Alley NR2 1AQ
☎ 01603 629127 📠 01603 765651
**Email:** museums@norfolk.gov.uk
**Web:** www.museums.norfolk.gov.uk
**Dir:** *in city centre, Lanes area, 5 min from Norwich Market Place*
Built in the late 14th century, this flint-faced merchant's house was used as a prison from 1583 to 1828. It now houses displays illustrating the trades and industries of Norwich during the past 200 years, including a large collection of locally made boots and shoes. There are also a reconstructed 1930s pharmacy, pawnbroker's shop and a blacksmith's smithy. Fans of Norwich City FC will enjoy the exhibition on the team's history.

**Times:** *Open Apr-28 Oct, Tue-Fri 10-4.30; Sat 10-5. School hols, Mon-Sat 10-5.
**Fee:** £3 (ch £1.60, concessions £2.50) Family ticket £6.90.
**Facilities:** Ⓟ (5 min walk) 🍴 shop ⊗ (ex guide dogs) 🚌

## OXBOROUGH
### Oxburgh Hall
Kings Lynn PE33 9PS
☎ 01366 328258 📠 01366 328066
**Email:** oxburghhall@nationaltrust.org.uk
**Web:** www.nationaltrust.org.uk
**Dir:** *Signed from A134 at Stoke ferry & Swaffham*
The outstanding feature of this 15th-century moated building is the 80ft-high Tudor gatehouse which has remained unaltered throughout the centuries. Henry VII lodged in the King's Room in 1487. A parterre garden of French design stands outside the moat. Rare needlework by Mary, Queen of Scots and Bess of Hardwick is on display. A particular attraction is a genuine 16th-century priest's hole, which is accessible to members of the public.

**Times:** *Open House: 25 Mar-29 Oct, daily (ex Thu & Fri) 1-5, BH Mon 11-5, (last admission 4.30). Garden: 1-19 Mar, wknds, 11-4; 25 Mar-29 Oct daily (ex Thu & Fri) 11-5.30 (4.30 Oct); Aug daily 11-5.30.
**Fee:** *House & Gardens £6.50 (ch £3.25), Family ticket £17. Gardens only £3.25 (ch £1.65). Party 15+ £5.50.
**Facilities:** Ⓟ 🍴 (Licensed) 🪑 🍴 Free-£3.50 � (DVD tour of first floor, wheelchairs available, touch tour, toilets) shop, guided tours ⊗ (ex guide dogs) 🚌 (pre-booking required) 🌿

## REEDHAM
### Pettitts Animal Adventure Park
Nr Great Yarmouth NR13 3UA
☎ 01493 700094 & 701403 📠 01493 700933
**Email:** pettittsreedham@aol.com
**Web:** www.pettittsadventurepark.co.uk
**Dir:** *off A47 at Acle then follow brown signs*
These three parks in one are aimed at younger children. There are over 50 attractions and rides to be enjoyed including a railway and roller coaster; the adventure play area has a golf course, ball pond and tearoom; and entertainment is provided by clowns, puppets and live musicians. Among the animals that can be seen are miniature horses, donkeys and Pigmy goats, wallabies, birds of prey, parrots, goats, alpacas and reindeer.
**Times:** *Open daily 19 Mar-30 Oct, 10-5/5.30.

**Fee:** *£7.95, (ch £7.95, under 3's free, concessions £5.85)
**Facilities:** Ⓟ Ⓟ (100yds) 🪑 � (ramps to all areas, toilets) shop ⊗ (ex assist dogs) 🚌

## SANDRINGHAM
### Sandringham House, Gardens & Museum
PE35 6EN

☎ 01553 612908 ▤ 01485 541571

**Email:** visits@sandringhamestate.co.uk

**Web:** www.sandringhamestate.co.uk

**Dir:** *off A148*

The private country retreat of Her Majesty The Queen, this neo-Jacobean house was built in 1870 for King Edward VII. The main rooms used by the Royal Family, when in residence, are open to the public. Sixty acres of glorious grounds surround the House and offer beauty and colour throughout the season. Sandringham Museum contains fascinating displays of Royal memorabilia. A new exhibition, Behind the Lines, features caricatures and cartoons from the Duke of Edinburghs private collection.

**Times:** *Open Etr Sat-mid Jul & early Aug-Oct. HouseOpen 11-4.45, Museum 11-5 & Grounds 10.30-5.

**Fee:** *House, Museum & Grounds: £8 (ch £5, pen £6.50). Family ticket £21.

**Facilities:** ℗ ☺ (Licensed) ⚲ ▤ £2.95 ♿ (wheelchair loan, free transport in grounds, Braille guide, toilets) shop, garden centre ⊗ (ex guide dogs) 🚌

## SHERINGHAM
### North Norfolk Railway (The Poppy Line)
Sheringham Station NR26 8RA

☎ 01263 820800 ▤ 01263 820801

**Email:** enquiries@nnrailway.co.uk

**Web:** www.nnr.co.uk

**Dir:** *from A148 take A1082. Next to large car park by rdbt in town centre*

A full size heritage railway running between Sheringham and Holt, with an intermediate station at Weybourne. The route runs for 5.5m along the coast, through the heathland and features genuine Victorian stations. A replica railway goods shed houses the new William Marriott Railway Museum at Holt.

**Times:** *Open mid Feb-Oct and wknds in Dec; daily steam trains mid Mar-end Oct, Santa specials. Please telephone or see website for details

**Fee:** *£9 (ch £5.50, pen £8). Family ticket £27, cycles & dogs £1.

**Facilities:** ℗ (charged) ℗ (adjacent – limited free spaces at Weybourne Stn) ⚲ ▤ £3 ♿ (ramps to trains, carriage converted for wheelchair access, toilets) shop, guided tours 🚌 (advance booking required)

## SOUTH WALSHAM
### Fairhaven Woodland & Water Garden
School Road Norwich NR13 6DZ

☎ 01603 270449 ▤ 01603 270449

**Web:** www.fairhavengarden.co.uk

**Dir:** *follow brown heritage signs from A47 onto B1140 to South Walsham. Through village towards Gt Yarmouth. Left into School Rd, 100yds past South Walsham Hall*

These delightful woodland and water gardens offer a combination of cultivated and wild flowers. In spring there are masses of primroses and bluebells, with azaleas and rhododendrons in several areas. Candelabra primulas and some unusual plants grow near the waterways, and in summer the wild flowers provide food for butterflies, bees and dragonflies. Summer flowers include Day Lilies, Ligularia, Hostas, Hydrangeas and flowering shrubs.

**Times:** Open daily 10-5, May-Aug extended opening Wed & Thu 10-9. Closed 25 Dec.

**Fee:** *£4.50 (ch £2, under 5 free, pen & concessions £4). Single membership tickets £15. Family membership ticket £35. Dog membership £2.50.

**Facilities:** ℗ ℗ (20 yards) ⚲ ▤ ♿ (ramp, grab rail, toilets) shop, garden centre, guided tours 🚌

NORFOLK

### THURSFORD GREEN
**Thursford Collection**

Thursford Fakenham NR21 0AS

☎ 01328 878477 📠 01328 878415

**Email:** admin@thursfordcollection.co.uk

**Web:** www.thursford.com

**Dir:** *1m off A148. Halfway between Fakenham and Holt*

This exciting collection specialises in music organs, with a Wurlitzer cinema organ, fairground organs, barrel organs and street organs among its treasures. There are live musical shows every day. The collection also includes showmen's engines, ploughing engines and farm machinery. There is a children's play area and a breathtaking 'Venetian gondola' switchback ride.

**Times:** Open Good Fri-last Sun in Sep, daily, 12-5. Closed Sat.

**Fee:** *£5.75 (ch under 4 free, ch 4-14 £3.25, students £5 pen £5.45). Party 15+ £5 each.

**Facilities:** 🅿 🍽 (Licensed) 🪑 ♿ (toilets) shop, guided tours 🚫 (ex guide dogs) 🚌

### TITCHWELL
**RSPB Nature Reserve**

King's Lynn PE31 8BB

☎ 01485 210779 📠 01485 210779

**Email:** titchwell@rspb.org.uk

**Dir:** *6m E of Hunstanton on A149, signed entrance*

On the Norfolk coast, Titchwell Marsh is the RSPB's most visited reserve. Hundreds and thousands of migrating birds pass through in spring and autumn and many stay during the winter, providing an opportunity to see many species of ducks, waders, seabirds and geese and also the RSPB emblem bird, the Avocet.

**Times:** Open at all times. Visitor Centre daily 9.30-5 (4 Nov-Mar).

**Fee:** Free (car parking charge of £4 for non RSPB members).

**Facilities:** 🅿 (charged) ☕ (open 9.30-4.30) 🪑 📷 ♿ (ramps to hides, wheelchair bays in hides, toilets) shop, guided tours 🚌 (advance booking essential)

### WELLS-NEXT-THE-SEA
**Wells & Walsingham Light Railway**

NR23 1QB

☎ 01328 711630

**Dir:** *A149 Cromer road*

Originally a mile long beach railway the line covers the four miles between Wells and Walsingham, and is the longest ten and a quarter inch gauge track in the world. The main station at Wells has a restored signal box which provides refreshments and souvenirs. This is also the home of the unique Garratt Steam Locomotive *'Norfolk Hero'* an engine specially built for this line. The railway has 5 bridges and passes through some very pretty countryside, particularly noted for its wild flowers and butterflies.

**Times:** *Open daily Good Fri-end Oct.

**Fee:** £7 return (ch £5.50 return).

**Facilities:** 🅿 ♿ shop 🚌 (pre-booking required) 🚫

## WELNEY
### WWT Welney
Hundred Foot Bank Wisbech PE14 9TN
☎ 01353 860711 ▤ 01353 860711
**Email:** welney@wwt.org.uk
**Web:** www.wwt.org.uk
**Dir:** *off A1101, N of Ely*
This important wetland site on the beautiful Ouse Washes is famed for the breathtaking spectacle of wild ducks, geese and swans which spend the winter here. Impressive observation facilities, including hides, towers and an observatory, offer outstanding views of the huge numbers of wildfowl which include Bewicks and Whooper swans, wigeon, teal and shoveler. Floodlit evening swan feeds take place between November and February. There are two hides for wheelchair users.

**Times:** *Open all year, daily 10-5. Closed 25 Dec.
**Fee:** *£4.50 (ch £2.70, pen £3.70). Family ticket £12
**Facilities:** ❷ ⩤ ♿ (toilets) shop ⊗ (ex guide/hearing dogs) ▭ (Pre-booking required)

## WEST RUNTON
### Norfolk Shire Horse Centre
West Runton Stables Cromer NR27 9QH
☎ 01263 837339 ▤ 01263 837132
**Email:** bakewell@norfolkshirehorse.fsnet.co.uk
**Web:** www.norfolk-shirehorse-centre.co.uk
**Dir:** *off A149 in village of West Ranton half-way between Cromer & Sheringham, follow brown signs*
The Shire Horse Centre has a collection of draught horses and some breeds of mountain and moorland ponies. There are also exhibits of horse-drawn machinery, waggons and carts, and harnessing and working demonstrations are given twice every day. Other attractions include a children's farm, a photographic display of draught horses past and present, talks and a video show. There is a riding school on the premises as well. Please telephone for details of special events.
**Times:** Open Apr-25 Oct daily (last admission 3.45); Apr & May after Etr Closed Fri & Sat; Jun-Aug closed Sat; Sep-Oct closed Fri & Sat
**Fee:** £4.50 (ch £5.50, pen £6.50).
**Facilities:** ❷ ⩤ ♿ (video room, concrete yards all ramped, toilets) shop ▭

## WEYBOURNE
### The Muckleburgh Collection
Weybourne Military Camp Holt NR25 7EG
☎ 01263 588210 & 588608 ▤ 01263 588425
**Email:** info@muckleburgh.co.uk
**Web:** www.muckleburgh.co.uk
**Dir:** *on A149, coast road, 3m W of Sheringham*
The largest privately-owned military collection of its kind in the country, which incorporates the Museum of the Suffolk and Norfolk Yeomanry. Exhibits include restored and working tanks, armoured cars, trucks and artillery of WWII, and equipment and weapons from the Falklands and the Gulf War. Live tank demonstrations are run daily (except Sat) during school holidays.
**Times:** Open 11-18 Feb, 28 Feb-28 Mar (Sat only), Apr-28 Oct, daily ex Sat after 16 Oct.Open 10-5
**Fee:** £6 (ch £3.50 & pen £5). Family ticket £14.50.
**Facilities:** ❷ ⑩ ⩤ ♿ (ramped access, wheelchairs available, toilets) shop ⊗ (ex guide, kennels provided) ▭

**NORFOLK**

## BANBURY
**Banbury Museum**
Spiceball Park Road OX16 2PQ
☎ 01295 259855 📄 01295 269469
**Email:** banburymuseum@cherwell-dc.gov.uk
**Web:** www.cherwell-dc.gov.uk/banburymuseum
**Dir:** *M40 junct 11 straight across at first rdbt into Hennef
Way, left at next rdbt into Concord Ave, right at next rdbt
& left at next rdbt, Castle Quay Shopping Centre &
Museum on right*
Come and visit Banbury's stunning new museum
situated in an attractive canal-side location in the centre
of Banbury. Exciting modern displays tell of Banbury's
origins and historic past. The Civil War; the plush
manufacturing industry; the Victorian market town;
costume from the 17th century to the present day;

Tooley's Boatyard and the Oxford Canal, are just some of
the subjects illustrated in the museum.
**Times:** *Open all year, Mon-Sat, 10-5, Sun 10.30-4.30.
**Fee:** Free
**Facilities:** Ⓟ (500yds) 🍽️ (Licensed) 📵 ♿ (toilets) shop,
guided tours ⊗ (ex guide dogs) 🚌 (must pre-book)

## BURFORD
**Cotswold Wildlife Park**
Oxford OX18 4JW
☎ 01993 823006 📄 01993 823807
**Web:** www.cotswoldwildlifepark.co.uk
**Dir:** *on A361 2m S of A40 at Burford*
This 160-acre landscaped zoological park, surrounds a
listed Gothic-style manor house. There is a varied
collection of animals from all over the world, many of
which are endangered species such as Asiatic lions,
leopards, white rhinos and red pandas. There's an
adventure playground, a children's farmyard, and train
rides during the summer. The park has also become one
of the Cotswold's leading attractions for garden
enthusiasts, with its exotic summer displays and varied
plantings offering interest all year.

**Times:** Open all year, daily from 10, (last admission 4.30
Mar-Sep, 3.30 Oct-Feb). Closed 25 Dec.
**Fee:** £9.50 (ch 3-16 & pen £7).
**Facilities:** Ⓟ 🍽️ (Licensed) ⛱️ ♿ (parking, free hire of
wheelchairs, toilets) shop 🚌

## DIDCOT
**Didcot Railway Centre**
OX11 7NJ
☎ 01235 817200 📄 01235 510621
**Email:** didrlyc@globalnet.co.uk
**Web:** www.didcotrailwaycentre.org.uk
**Dir:** *on A4130 at Didcot Parkway Station*
Based around the original GWR engine shed, the Centre
is home to the biggest collection anywhere of Great
Western Railway steam locomotives, carriages and
wagons. A typical GWR station has been re-created and a
section of Brunel's original broad gauge track relaid, with
reconstruction of the *'Fire Fly'* locomotive of 1840.
**Times:** Open all year, Sat & Sun. Daily 31 Mar-16 Apr,
26 May-3 Jun, 23 Jun-2 Sep. Steamdays, Easter 6-9
Apr, 28 Apr-2 Sep (Sat & Sun), Wed 11 Jul-29 Aug. Day

out with Thomas 9-11 Mar, 5-7 Oct. Thomas Santa
Special 7-24 Dec, Fri-Sun.
**Fee:** £4-£9.50 depending on event (ch £3-£8, pen
£3.50-£8).
**Facilities:** Ⓟ (100yds) 🍽️ ⛱️ 📵 ♿ (advance notice
recommended, awkward steps at entrance, toilets) shop,
guided tours 🚌

## HENLEY-ON-THAMES
### River & Rowing Museum
Mill Meadows RG9 1BF
☎ 01491 415600 📄 01491 415601
**Email:** museum@rrm.co.uk
**Web:** www.rrm.co.uk
**Dir:** *off A4130, signed to Mill Meadows*
This award-winning River and Rowing Museum is the only museum dedicated to rowing and the 'Quest for Speed'; from the Greek Trireme to modern Olympic rowing boats. See the boats that won gold in Sydney and the Royal Regatta at Henley, and the River Thames from source to sea with its rich history and varied wildlife. There is a permanent *Wind in the Willows* exhibition recreating the drawings of E. H. Shepard using models, lighting and sound to bring the classic book to life.

**Times:** Open: May-Aug 10-5.30. Sep-Apr 10-5. Closed 24-25 & 31 Dec & 1 Jan.
**Fee:** £7 (concs £6). Fam ticket from £20. Party 10+.
**Facilities:** ❷ ⓟ (museum entrance) 🍴 (lunches and tea) 📄 ♿ (lift access, ramps at entrance, toilets) shop, audio commentaries 🚫 (ex guide dogs) 🚍 Discount for pre booked parties of 10

## MAPLEDURHAM
### Mapledurham House
Reading RG4 7TR
☎ 0118 972 3350 📄 0118 972 4016
**Email:** mtrust1997@aol.com
**Web:** www.mapledurham.co.uk
**Dir:** *off A4074, follow brown heritage signs from Reading*
The small community at Mapledurham includes the house, a watermill and a church. The fine Elizabethan mansion, surrounded by quiet parkland that runs down to the River Thames, was built by the Blount family in the 16th century. The estate has literary connections with the poet Alexander Pope, with Galsworthy's *Forsyte Saga* and Kenneth Graham's *Wind in the Willows*, it was also a location for the film *The Eagle has Landed.*
**Times:** *Open Etr-Sep, Sat, Sun & BHs 2-5.30 Picnic area 2-5.30. (Last admission 5). Group visits midweek by arrangement.
**Fee:** *Combined house, watermill & grounds £6.50 (ch £3). House & grounds £4 (ch £2). Watermill & grounds £3 (ch £1.50).
**Facilities:** ❷ 🍴 (Tea room) 🚻 ♿ shop guided tours 🚫 (ex in grounds) 🚍 (Tue-Thu pm & wknds only)

## MAPLEDURHAM
### Mapledurham Watermill
Reading RG4 7TR
☎ 0118 972 3350 📄 0118 972 4016
**Email:** mtrust1997@aol.com
**Web:** www.mapledurham.co.uk
**Dir:** *off A4074, follow brown heritage signs from Reading*
Close to Mapledurham House stands the last working corn and grist mill on the Thames, still using traditional wooden machinery and producing flour for local bakers and shops. The watermill's products can be purchased in the shop. When Mapledurham House is open the mill can be reached by river launch.
**Times:** *Open Etr-Sep, Sat, Sun & BHs 2-5.30. Picnic area 2-5.30. (Last admission 5). Groups midweek by arrangement.
**Fee:** *Watermill & grounds £3 (ch £1.50)
**Facilities:** ❷ 🍴 (Tea room) 🚻 ♿ shop, guided tours 🚍 (min 40 people)

**OXFORDSHIRE**

## OXFORD
### Ashmolean Museum of Art & Archaeology
Beaumont Street OX1 2PH
☎ 01865 278000 📠 01865 278018
**Web:** www.ashmol.ox.ac.uk
**Dir:** *city centre, opposite The Randolph Hotel*
The oldest museum in the country, opened in 1683, the Ashmolean contains Oxford University's priceless collections. Many important historical art pieces and artefacts are on display, including work from Ancient Greece through to the twentieth century.
**Times:** Open all year, Tue-Sat 10-5, Sun 12-5 BH Mons 10-5. Closed Etr & during St.Giles Fair in early Sep, Xmas & 1 Jan.
**Fee:** Free. Guided tours by arrangement.
**Facilities:** ℗ (100-200mtrs – pay & display)
🍴 (Licensed) 📖 ♿ (entry ramp from Beaumont St. Tel. before visit, toilets) shop, guided tours ⊗ 🚌 (big parties split 15 max, booking req)

## OXFORD
### Harcourt Arboretum
Nuneham Courtenay OX44 9PX
☎ 01865 343501 📠 01865 341828
**Email:** piers.newth@obg.ox.ac.uk
**Web:** www.botanic-garden.ox.ac.uk
**Dir:** *400yds S of Nuneham Courtenay on A4074*
Six miles south of Oxford and part of of the plant collection of the Oxford Botanic Garden, Harcourt Arboretum covers 75 acres of mixed woodland with fine specimen trees, meadow, pond and rhododendron walks. The Arboretum runs a diverse programme of events throughout the year, from bird spotting to plant sales and craft weekends to theatrical productions.
**Times:** Open Apr-Nov, daily 10-5, Dec-Mar, Mon-Fri 10-4.30. Closed 22 Dec-4 Jan.
**Fee:** £2 pay & display for car park or £5 for 1yr season ticket.
**Facilities:** ℗ (charged) 📖 £2 ♿ (toilets) guided tours ⊗ (ex guide dogs) 🚌 (no parking for coaches) ♿

## OXFORD
### Museum of the History of Science
Old Ashmolean Building Broad Street OX1 3AZ
☎ 01865 277280 📠 01865 277288
**Email:** museum@mhs.ox.ac.uk
**Web:** www.mhs.ox.ac.uk
**Dir:** *next to Sheldonian Theatre in city centre, on Broad St*
The first purpose built museum in Britain, it was orginally the Ashmolean museum and built in 1683. It is now home to the world's finest collection of early scientific instruments used in astronomy, navigation, surveying, physics and chemistry.
**Times:** *Open Tue-Sat 12-4, Sun 2-5. Closed Xmas and Etr Hols.
**Fee:** Free
**Facilities:** ℗ (300mtrs – limited street parking, meters)
📖 Various ♿ (lift, toilets) shop, guided tours, audio commentaries (charged) ⊗ (ex guide dogs) 🚌 (Max 15 people, pre-book only) ♿

## OXFORD
### Oxford University Museum of Natural History

Parks Road OX1 3PW

☎ 01865 272950 🖺 01865 272970

**Email:** info@oum.ox.ac.uk

**Web:** www.oum.ox.ac.uk

**Dir:** *opposite Keble College*

Built between 1855 and 1860, this museum of the natural sciences was intended to satisfy a growing interest in biology, botany, archaeology, zoology, entomology and so on. The museum reflects Oxford University's position as a 19th-century centre of learning, with displays of early dinosaur discoveries, Darwinian evolution and Elias Ashmole's collection of preserved animals. Although visitors to the Pitt-Rivers Museum must pass through the University Museum, the two should not be confused.

**Times:** Open daily 12-5. Times vary at Xmas & Etr.

**Fee:** Free

**Facilities:** Ⓟ (200mtrs – meter parking) 🛋 📋 🕁 (lift access to gallery, toilets) shop ⊗ 🚌 ♿

## OXFORD
### Pitt Rivers Museum

South Parks Road OX1 3PP

☎ 01865 270927 🖺 01865 270943

**Email:** prm@prm.ox.ac.uk

**Web:** www.prm.ox.ac.uk

**Dir:** *10 min walk from city centre, visitors' entrance on Parks Rd through the Oxford Univiersity Museum of Natural History*

The museum is one of the city's most popular attractions. It is part of the University of Oxford and was founded in 1884. The collections held at the museum are internationally acclaimed, and contain many objects from different cultures of the world and from various periods of history. Displayed in context, they are all grouped by type, or purpose.

**Times:** Open all year. Mon-Sun 12-4.30. Closed Xmas & Etr, Open BHs.

**Fee:** Free

**Facilities:** 📋 🕁 (audio guide, wheelchair trail, toilets) shop, audio commentaries (charged) ⊗ (ex guide dogs) 🚌 ♿

## OXFORD
### University of Oxford Botanic Garden

Rose Lane OX1 4AZ

☎ 01865 286690 🖺 01865 286693

**Email:** postmaster@obg.ox.ac.uk

**Web:** www.botanic-garden.ox.ac.uk

**Dir:** *E end of High St on banks of River Cherwell*

Founded in 1621, this botanic garden is the oldest in the country. There is a collection of over 7,000 species of plants from all over the world. Consisting of 3 sections: the Glasshouses contain plants that need protection from the British weather. The area outside the Walled Garden contains a water garden and rock garden as well as the spring border and autumn border. Within the Walled Garden plants are grouped by country of origin, botanic family or economic use.

**Times:** Open all year daily: 9-4.30 Jan-Feb & Nov-Dec (last admission 4.15). Mar-Apr, Sep-Oct 9-5 (last admission 4.15) May-Aug 9-6.

**Fee:** £2.70 (ch free, disabled with 1 carer free, concessions £2).

**Facilities:** Ⓟ (0.5m – park and ride system) 📋 £3 🕁 (toilets) shop, guided tours (charged) ⊗ (ex guide dogs) 🚌 (pre-booked)

OXFORDSHIRE

### OXFORD
**Unlocked - Oxford Castle**
44-46 Oxford Castle OX1 1AY
☎ 01865 260666 🖷 01865 260660
**Email:** info@oxfordcastleunlocked.co.uk
**Web:** www.oxfordcastleunlocked.co.uk
**Dir:** *in city centre off New Rd*
For the first time in 1,000 years, the secrets of Oxford Castle will be 'unlocked' revealing episodes of violence, executions, great escapes, betrayal and even romance. Walk through these ancient buildings and experience the stories that connect the real people to these extraordinary events.
**Times:** Open daily 10-5.30 (last tour 4.30). Closed 25 Dec.
**Fee:** *£6.95 (ch £5.25, concessions £5.95)

**Facilities:** Ⓟ ♿ (lift & ramp, toilets) shop, guided tours, audio commentaries Ⓧ (ex assist dogs) 🚌

### WITNEY
**Cogges Manor Farm Museum**
Church Lane Cogges OX28 3LA
☎ 01993 772602 🖷 01993 703056
**Web:** www.cogges.org
**Dir:** *0.5m SE off A4022*
Dedicated to Oxfordshire rural life in the 19th century, the museum includes the Manor, dairy and walled garden. The audio tour brings this Victorian farm to life with characters from Cogges past. The first floor of the manor contains period rooms where maids may be found going about their work. The farm museum has traditional breeds of farm animals and milking and butter making are just part of the living history features. Special events take place through the season.
**Times:** Open Apr-Oct, Tue-Fri 10.30-5.30, Sat, Sun & BH Mon, 12-5.30. Early closing Oct. Closed Good Fri.
**Fee:** *£5.40 (ch £2.30, concessions £3.85). Family ticket £13.90 (2ad+2ch).
**Facilities:** Ⓞ Ⓟ (300yds) 🍴 📷 ♿ (wheelchair available, audio tour, toilets) shop, audio commentaries 🚌 (pre-booking)

### WOODSTOCK
**Blenheim Palace**
OX20 1PX
☎ 08700 602080 🖷 01993 810570
**Email:** admin@blenheimpalace.com
**Web:** www.blenheimpalace.com
**Dir:** *M40 junct 9, follow signs to Blenheim, on A44 8m N of Oxford*
Home of the 11th Duke of Marlborough and birthplace of Sir Winston Churchill, Blenheim Palace is an English Baroque masterpiece. Fine furniture, sculpture, paintings and tapestries are set in magnificent gilded staterooms that overlook sweeping lawns, formal gardens and the 2,100-acre park, which is open to visitors.
**Times:** Palace & Gardens mid Feb-mid Dec (ex Mon & Tue in Nov & Dec) daily 10.30-5.30 (last admission 4.45). Park daily all year 9-4.45. Closed 25 Dec.
**Fee:** Palace, Park & Gardens £12-£14 (ch £6.50-£8.50, concessions £9.50-£11.50). Park & Gardens £7-£9 (ch £2.50-£4.50, concessions £5-£7)
**Facilities:** Ⓞ Ⓟ (in Woodstock) 🍴 (Licensed) 🍴 ♿ (lift, ramps, disabled parking, buggies, wheelchairs, toilets) shop, guided tours Ⓧ assist dogs 🚌

## WOODSTOCK
### The Oxfordshire Museum
Fletcher's House Park Street OX20 1SN

☎ 01993 811456 🖺 01993 813239

**Email:** oxon.museum@oxfordshire.go.uk

**Web:** www.oxfordshire.gov.uk/the_oxfordshire_museum

**Dir:** *A44 Evesham-Oxford, follow signs for Blenheim Palace. Museum opposite church*

Situated in the heart of the historic town of Woodstock, the award-winning re-development of Fletcher's House provides a home for the new county museum. Set in attractive gardens, the museum celebrates Oxfordshire in all its diversity and features collections of local history, art, archaeology, landscape and wildlife as well as a gallery exploring the country's innovative industries from nuclear power to nanotechnology. Interactive exhibits offer new learning experiences for visitors of all ages. The museum's purpose built Garden Gallery houses a variety of touring exhibitions of regional and national interest.

**Times:** Open all year, Tue-Sat 10-5, Sun 2-5. Closed Good Fri, 25-26 Dec & 1 Jan. Galleries closed on Mon, but open BH Mons, 2-5.

**Fee:** Free

**Facilities:** ℗ (outside entrance – free parking) ⌾ (Licensed) ⍝ 📋 ♿ (chair lifts to all galleries, toilets) guided tours ⊗ (ex guide dogs) 🚌 (pre-booked only) ♻

## BUNGAY
### The Otter Trust
Earsham NR35 2AF

☎ 01986 893470 🖺 01986 892461

**Dir:** *off A143, 1m W of Bungay*

The Otter Trust was the largest otter conservation organisation in Britain. Founded over 30 years ago it has carried out a programme of otter breeding in order to re-introduce otters to the wild. This has been successful and now that otters numbers have considerably improved the trust no longer breeds otters at Earsham. The grounds cover 23 acres with three lakes and walks along the banks of the River Waveney which are still open to the public. Hand-reared fallow deer are very tame and walk freely in the grounds.

**Times:** Open Apr (or Good Fri if earlier)- Sep, daily 10.30-6. Last entry 5

**Fee:** £6 (ch over 3 £3). Disabled person in wheelchair free.

**Facilities:** ❶ ⍝ 📋 ♿ (toilets) shop ⊗ (ex guide dogs) 🚌

## EASTON
### Easton Farm Park
Woodbridge IP13 0EQ

☎ 01728 746475 🖺 01728 747861

**Email:** info@eastonfarmpark.co.uk

**Web:** www.eastonfarmpark.co.uk

**Dir:** *signed from A12 at Wickam Market, and from A1120*

Award-winning Farm Park is situated on the banks of the River Deben. There are lots of breeds of farm animals, including Suffolk Punch horses, ponies, pigs, lambs, calves, goats, rabbits, guinea pigs & poultry. Chicks hatching and egg collecting daily. Free hug-a-bunny & pony rides every day.

**Times:** Open Mar-end Sep, daily 10.30-6. AlsoOpen Feb & Oct half term hols and wknds in Dec.

**Fee:** £6.25 (ch under 1 free, ch 1-16 £4.75 pen £5.75). Family £20.

**Facilities:** ❶ ⍝ 📋 ♿ (special parking and wheelchairs, toilets) shop 🚌

OXFORDSHIRE / SUFFOLK

**SUFFOLK**

## FLIXTON
### Norfolk & Suffolk Aviation Museum
Buckeroo Way The Street Bungay NR35 1NZ
☎ 01986 896644
**Email:** nsam.flixton@virgin.net
**Web:** www.aviationmuseum.net
**Dir:** *off A143, take B1062, 2m W of Bungay*
Situated in the Waveney Valley, the museum has over 50 historic aircraft. There is also a Bloodhound surface-to-air missile, the 446th Bomb Group Museum, RAF Bomber Command Museum, the Royal Observer Corps Museum, RAF Air-Sea Rescue and Coastal Command and a souvenir shop. Among the displays are Decoy Sites and Wartime Deception, Fallen Eagles - Wartime Luftwaffe Crashes and an ex-Ipswich airport hangar made by Norwich company Boulton and Paul Ltd.

**Times:** Open Apr-Oct, Sun-Thu 10-5 (last admission 4); Nov-Mar, Tue, Wed & Sun 10-4 (last admission 3). Closed late Dec-early Jan.
**Fee:** Free
**Facilities:** 🅿 Ⓟ (100yds) ⊼ 🗐 only for school visits 🌢 (helper advised, ramps/paths to all buildings, toilets) shop 🚌 Advance booking preferred 🖾

## HORRINGER
### Ickworth House, Park & Gardens
Bury St Edmunds IP29 5QE
☎ 01284 735270 🗎 01284 735175
**Email:** ickworth@ntrust.org.uk
**Web:** www.nationaltrust.org.uk/ickworth
**Dir:** *2.5m SW of Bury St Edmunds in Horringer on A143*
The eccentric Earl of Bristol created this equally eccentric house, begun in 1795, to display his collection of European art. The Georgian Silver Collection is considered the finest in private hands. 'Capability' Brown designed the parkland, and also featured are a vineyard, waymarked walks and an adventure playground. 2007 sees the 50th anniversary of the opening of Ickworth by the National Trust. Birthday celebrations will take place throughout the year.

**Times:** Open: House 19 Mar-4 Nov, Mon, Tue, Fri, wknds and BHs, 1-5 (4.30 in Oct and Nov) Garden: 19 Mar-4 Nov, Mon, Tue, Fri, wknds and BHs, 10-5. Oct-17 Mar, Mon, Tue, Fri, wknds and BHs, 11-4. Park: daily 8-8.
**Fee:** *House, Garden & Park £6.70 (National Trust members & ch under 5 free, ch £3) Garden & park £3.10 (ch 90p). Discount for pre-booked parties.
**Facilities:** 🅿 🍽 (Licensed) ⊼ 🗐 £1 or £5 deposit on returnable back pack 🌢 (Braille guide, batricars, hearing loop, large print guides, toilets) shop, guided tours 🚫 (ex guide dogs and on lead) 🚌 (Pre-book) 🦋

## LEISTON
### Long Shop Museum
Main Street IP16 4ES
☎ 01728 832189 🗎 01728 832189
**Email:** longshop@care4free.net
**Web:** www.longshop.care4free.net
**Dir:** *Turn off A12, follow B1119 from Saxmundham to Leiston. Museum is in the middle of town*
Discover the Magic of Steam through a visit to the world famous traction engine manufacturers. Trace the history of the factory and Richard Garrett engineering. See the traction engines and road rollers in the very place that they were built. Soak up the atmosphere of the Long Shop, built in 1852 as one of the first production line engineering halls in the world. An award-winning museum with five exhibition halls full of items from the glorious age of steam and covering 200 years of local, social and industrial history.
**Times:** Open Apr-Oct, Mon-Sat 10-5, Sun 11-5.
**Fee:** £4 (ch under 5 free, ch £2, concessions £3.50) Family £10.
**Facilities:** 🅿 Ⓟ (adjacent – 1 hour) ⊼ 🗐 🌢 (wheelchair available, toilets) shop, guided tours 🚫 (ex guide dogs) 🚌 🖾

## LONG MELFORD
### Kentwell Hall
Sudbury CO10 9BA

☎ 01787 310207 🖷 01787 379318

**Email:** info@kentwell.co.uk

**Web:** www.kentwell.co.uk

**Dir:** *signposted off A134, between Bury St Edmunds & Sudbury*

Kentwell Hall is a moated red brick Tudor manor with gardens, woodland walks and a rare breeds farm. Restoration started in 1971 and still continues today. The house and grounds are open to the public at certain times of the year, and recreations of Tudor and 1940s life take place at weekends. Ring for details.

**Times:** Open: Gardens & Farm: Mar, Sun, 11-4. House, Gardens and Farm: Apr-Jun, Sun-Wed and daily in Jul, Aug and Sep 12-5.Open: BH and school hols.

**Fee:** *House, Garden & Farm £7.15 (ch £4.60, pen £6.15). Garden & Farm only £5 (ch £3.30, pen £4.30).

**Facilities:** ❷ 🛱 🍴 ♿ (wheelchair ramps & 3 wheelchairs for loan, toilets) shop guided tours 🚫 (ex guide dogs) 🚌 (must pre-book)

## LOWESTOFT
### East Anglia Transport Museum
Chapel Rd Carlton Colville NR33 8BL

☎ 01502 518459 🖷 01502 584658

**Email:** enquiries@eatm.org.uk

**Web:** www.eatm.org.uk

**Dir:** *3m SW of Lowestoft, follow brown signs from A12, A146 & B1384*

A particular attraction of this museum is the reconstructed 1930s street scene which is used as a setting for working vehicles: visitors can ride by tram, trolley bus and narrow gauge railway. Other motor, steam and electrical vehicles are exhibited. There is also a woodland picnic area served by trams.

**Times:** Open: Apr-Sep, Sun and BH 11-5. From Jun, Thu and Sat, 2-4.

**Fee:** £5 (ch 5-15 £3.50) pen £4. Price includes rides. Party rates available.

**Facilities:** ❷ 🛱 ♿ (toilets) shop guided tours 🚌

## LOWESTOFT
### New Pleasurewood Hills
Leisure Way Corton NR32 5DZ

☎ 01502 586000 (admin) & 508200 (info)

🖷 01502 567393

**Email:** info@pleasurewoodhills.co.uk

**Web:** www.pleasurewoodhills.co.uk

**Dir:** *off A12 at Lowestoft*

There are over 40 rides, shows and attractions at New Pleasurewood Hills, set in 50 acres of beautiful parkland. Old favourites such as the Tidal Wave Watercoaster and the Fairytale Fantasy Ride combine with more recent attractions such as Formula K Raceway Go-Karts, the new 100ft Drop Tower, the Crazy Coaster and the Double Decker Carousel.

**Times:** *Open Apr-Oct & Xmas. Telephone for details.

**Fee:** *£13 over 1.25mtr, £11 under 1.25mtr, under 1mtr free, family ticket (2 ad & 2 ch) £46. Telephone for details.

**Facilities:** ❷ 🍴 (Licensed) 🛱 ♿ (all shows accessible, most ride operators able to assist, toilets) shop 🚫 (ex guide dogs) 🚌 (pre-booking prefered)

**SUFFOLK**

SUFFOLK

## NEWMARKET
**National Horseracing Museum and Tours**
99 High Street CB8 8JH
☎ 01638 667333 ▤ 01638 665600
**Web:** www.nhrm.co.uk
**Dir:** *located in centre of High St*
This friendly award-winning museum tells the story of the
people and horses involved in racing in Britain. Have a go
on the horse simulator in the hands-on gallery and chat
to retired jockeys and trainers about their experiences.
Special mini bus tours visit the gallops, a stable and yard
and horses' swimming pool.
**Times:** Open Etr-end Oct, Tue-Sun (also BH Mons &
Mons in Jul & Aug) 11-5. 10 opening on race days.
**Fee:** *£4.50 (ch £1.50, concessions £3.50). Family ticket
£10 (2ad+2ch).

**Facilities:** Ⓟ (300yds - coach drop off in front of
museum) � (Licensed) ⏃ ▤ ♿ (ramps & lift, toilets)
shop, guided tours Ⓧ (ex guide dogs) 🚌 (pre-booking
preferred)

## STOWMARKET
**Museum of East Anglian Life**
IP14 1DL
☎ 01449 612229 ▤ 01449 672307
**Email:** enquiries@eastanglianlife.org.uk
**Web:** www.eastanglianlife.org.uk
**Dir:** *located in centre of Stowmarket, signed from A14 &
B1115*
This 70-acre, all-weather museum is set in an attractive
river-valley site with 3km of woodland and riverside
nature trails. There are reconstructed buildings, including
a working water mill, a smithy and also a wind pump,
and the Boby Building houses craft workshops. There are
displays on Victorian domestic life, gypsies, farming and
industry. These include working steam traction engines,
the only surviving pair of Burrell ploughing engines of

1879, and a working Suffolk Punch horse. William Bone
Building, illustrating the history of Ransomes of Ipswich.
**Times:** Open late March-end Oct.
**Fee:** £6.50 (ch 4-16 £3.50, concessions £5.50). Family
ticket (2ad+2/3ch) £17.50. 1ad family £11. Party 10+.
**Facilities:** Ⓟ (adjacent) ⎐ (museum bistro) ⏃
♿ (w/chairs & 2 buggies available, special vehicle
acilities, toilets) shop, guided tours Ⓧ (ex on a lead)
🚌 (need to pre-book)

## SUFFOLK WILDLIFE PARK
**Africa Alive!**
Kessingland NR33 7TF
☎ 01502 740291 ▤ 01502 741104
**Email:** info@africa-alive.co.uk
**Web:** www.africa-alive.co.uk
**Dir:** *just S of Lowestoft off A12*
Set in 80 acres of dramatic coastal parkland, visitors can
explore the sights and sounds of Africa at Africa Alive!
There are giraffes, rhinos, cheetah, hyenas and many
more, including a bird's-eye view of the new lion
enclosure. There are lots of daily feeding talks and animal
encounter sessions, a magnificent bird of prey display,
and the free Safari Roadtrain that makes the journey
around the park with live commentary and fascinating
animal facts – a great favourite with children.

**Times:** Open all year, daily from 10. Closed 25-26 Dec.
**Fee:** *Please call park reception for full admission prices
**Facilities:** Ⓟ 101 ⏃ ♿ (wheelchairs available for hire,
toilets) shop, audio commentaries Ⓧ 🚌

## WEST STOW
**West Stow Anglo Saxon Village**
West Stow Country Park Icklingham Road
Bury St Edmunds IP28 6HG
☎ 01284 728718 ▤ 01284 728277
**Email:** weststow@stedsbc.gov.uk
**Web:** www.stedmundsbury.gov.uk/weststow.htm
**Dir:** *off A1101, 7m NW of Bury St Edmunds. Follow
brown heritage signs*
The village is a reconstruction of a pagan Anglo-Saxon
settlement dated 420-650 AD. Seven buildings have
been reconstructed on the site of the excavated
settlement. There is a visitors' centre and a children's
play area. A new Anglo-Saxon Centre houses the original
objects found on the site. The village is located in the
West Stow Country Park. The park is 125 acres with
river, lake, woodland and heath and has many trails
and paths.
**Times:** *Open all year, daily 10-5. Last entry 4 (3.30 in
Winter) Except Xmas period.
**Fee:** *£5 (ch £4). Family ticket £15. (Prices subject to
change for special events)
**Facilities:** 🅿 ⓟ (500 yds) ⛟ 🍴 free with entry
♿ (ramps, toilets) shop, guided tours 🚫 (ex guide dogs)
🚌 (booking preferred, one group only)

## WESTLETON
**RSPB Minsmere Nature Reserve**
SAXMUNDHAM IP17 3BY
☎ 01728 648281 ▤ 01728 648770
**Email:** minsmere@rspb.org.uk
**Web:** www.rspb.org.uk/reserves/minsmere
**Dir:** *signed from A12 at Yoxford & Blythburgh and from
Westleton Village*
Set on the beautiful Suffolk coast, Minsmere offers an
enjoyable day out for all. Nature trails take you through a
variety of habitats to the excellent birdwatching hides.
Spring is a time for birdsong, including nightingales and
booming bitterns. In summer, you can watch breeding
avocets and marsh harriers. Autumn is excellent for
migrants, and in winter, hundreds of wildfowl visit the
reserve. Look out for otters and red deer. The visitor
centre has a well-stocked shop and licensed tearoom,
and you can find out more about the reserve.
There is a programme of events throughout the year,
including several for children and families. Self-guided
activity booklets for families.
**Times:** Open daily (ex 25-26 Dec) 9-9 (or dusk if earlier).
Visitor centre: 9-5 (9-4 Nov-Jan).
**Fee:** £5 (ch £1.50, concessions £3). Family ticket £10.
RSPB members free
**Facilities:** 🅿 ⓟ (0.75m – no overnight parking) ⛟ 🍴
♿ (batricar available for loan, booking advised, toilets)
shop guided tours 🚫 (ex guide dogs) 🚌 (advance
booking)

## CHERTSEY
**Thorpe Park**
Staines Road KT16 8PN
☎ 0870 444 4466 ▤ 01932 566367
**Web:** www.thorpepark.com
**Dir:** *M25 junct 11 or 13 and follow signs via A320 to
Thorpe Park*
Conveniently situated close to both the M25 and the M3,
fun-loving families and thrill-seekers come alive at
Thorpe Park, home to some of the most exciting
rollercoaster experiences in Europe. There are over 25
rides, including *Stealth*, Europe's fastest and tallest
launch rollercoaster. Another unique ride is *Colossus*, the
world's first 10-loop roller.
**Times:** *Open: 15 Mar-5 Nov (ex 2-5, 9-12 Oct).Opening
times vary throughout, check in advance.
**Fee:** *From £28.50 (ch under 1m free, ch 4-11 from
£20).
**Facilities:** 🅿 🍴 (Licensed) ⛟ ♿ (some rides not
accessible, wheelchair hire available, toilets) shop
🚫 (ex assist dogs) 🚌 (pre-booking preferred)

## FARNHAM
### Birdworld & Underwaterworld
Holt Pound GU10 4LD
☎ 01420 22140 🖨 01420 23715
**Email:** bookings@birdworld.co.uk
**Web:** www.birdworld.co.uk
**Dir:** *3m S of Farnham on A325*

Birdworld is the largest bird collection in the country and includes toucans, pelicans, flamingoes, ostriches and many others. Underwater World is a tropical aquarium with brilliant lighting that shows off collections of marine and freshwater fish, as well as the swampy depths of the alligator exhibit. Visitors can also visit some beautiful gardens, the Jenny Wren farm and the Heron Theatre.
**Times:** Open daily, 10-6 (summer), 10-4.30 (winter).
**Fee:** *£9.95 (ch 3-14 £8.25, pen £8.25). Family ticket

(2ad+2ch) £32.95
**Facilities:** 𝐏 ℗ �🅞 🍴 ㅠ 📱 20p-£2 ♿ (wheelchairs available, toilets) shop, garden centre ⊗ (ex guide dogs) 🚌 (book in advance)

## GODSTONE
### Godstone Farm
RH9 8LX
☎ 01883 742546 🖨 01883 740380
**Email:** havefun@godstonefarm.co.uk
**Web:** www.godstonefarm.co.uk
**Dir:** *M25 junct 6, S of village, signed*

An ideal day out for children, Godstone Farm has lots of friendly animals, big sand pits and play areas. There are chicks, rabbits and piglets born all year round as well as lambs in the spring and goats in the summer. Visitors are encouraged to handle the small animals and there are shetland ponies and llamas to be stroked. For rainy days there is an Indoor Play Barn, at an extra cost of 80p.
**Times:** *Open Mar-Oct, 10-6 (last admission 5); Nov-Feb 10-5 (last admission 4). Closed 25 & 26 Dec.

**Fee:** *Contact for admission prices.
**Facilities:** 𝐏 ㅠ 📱 20p ♿ (toilets) shop ⊗ (ex guide dogs) 🚌

## GUILDFORD
### Dapdune Wharf
Wharf Road GU1 4RR
☎ 01483 561389 🖨 01483 531667
**Email:** riverwey@nationaltrust.org.uk
**Web:** www.nationaltrust.org.uk/riverwey
**Dir:** *off Woodbridge Rd to rear of Surrey County Cricket Ground*

The visitor centre at Dapdune Wharf is the centrepiece of one of the National Trust's most unusual properties, the River Way Navigations. A series of interactive exhibits and displays allow you to discover the fascinating story of Surrey's secret waterway, one of the first British rivers to be made navigable. See where huge Wey barges were built and climb aboard *Reliance*, one of the last surviving barges. Children's trails and special events run throughout the season.
**Times:** *Open Apr-Oct, Thu-Mon 11-5. River trips Thu-Mon 11-5 (conditions permitting)
**Fee:** *£3.50 (ch £2). Family ticket £10. National Trust Members free.
**Facilities:** 𝐏 ℗ (0.25m) ☕ (small tearoom) ㅠ ♿ (Braille guide, toilets) shop, guided tours ⊗ (ex on leads) 🚌 (prior booking required) 🌿 📷

## HASCOMBE
### Winkworth Arboretum
Hascombe Road Godalming GU8 4AD
☎ 01483 208477 🖹 01483 208252
Email: winkwortharboretum@nationaltrust.org.uk
Web: www.nationaltrust.org.uk/winkwortharboretum
Dir: *2m SE of Godalming, E side of B2130, follow brown tourist signs from Godalming*
This lovely woodland covers a hillside of nearly 100 acres, with fine views over the North Downs. The best times to visit are April and May for the azaleas, bluebells and other flowers, and October for the autumn colours. A delightful Victorian boathouse is open Apr-Oct with fine views over Rowes Flashe lake. There are many rare trees and shrubs in group plantings for spring and autumn colour effect.

**Times:** Open all year, daily during daylight hours. (Could close when weather is bad)
**Fee:** *£4.50 (ch £2). Family ticket £10, additional family member £1.75.
**Facilities:** ℗ ☕ (small tearoom) 🍴 Donations accepted 🚻 (suggested route, free entry for helpers, toilets) shop, guided tours ⊗ (ex on lead) 🚌 (by appointment) 🌿

## OUTWOOD
### Outwood Windmill
Outwood Common Redhill RH1 5PW
☎ 01342 843458 & 843644 🖹 01342 843458
Email: info@outwoodwindmill.co.uk
Web: www.outwoodwindmill.co.uk
Dir: *M25 junct 6, take A25 through Godstone towards Redhill, after 1m turn S off A25 at Bletchingly, between The Prince Albert & The White Hart. Mill 3m on left*
This award-winning example of a post-mill dates from 1665 and is the oldest working windmill in England and one of the best preserved in existence. Standing 400ft above sea level, it is surrounded by common land and National Trust property. Ducks and geese wander freely in the grounds.

**Times:** Open: Every Sun from Etr-Sep and BH. Mon and Wed for booked parties.
**Fee:** £3 (ch £2).
**Facilities:** ℗ (10yds) 🍴 £1.25 🚻 (toilets) shop, guided tours, audio commentaries 🚌 (pre-booking required) ⊘

## PAINSHILL PARK
### Painshill Park
Portsmouth Road KT11 1JE
☎ 01932 868113 🖹 01932 868001
Email: info@painshill.co.uk
Web: www.painshill.co.uk
Dir: *W of Cobham on A245*
Within its 160 acres created by Charles Hamilton as a series of subtle and surprising vistas, 'The Hamilton Landscapes' include authentic 18th-century plantings, a working vineyard, Gothic Temple, Chinese Bridge, Crystal Grotto, Turkish Tent and the restored Hermitage and Gothic Tower.

**Times:** Open: Apr-Oct, 10.30-6. Nov-Mar, 10.30-4. Closed 25-26 Dec.
**Fee:** £6.60 (ch 5-16 £3.85, concessions £5.80).
Pre-booked adult groups 10+ £5.80 Please telephone 01932 868113 for prices. For more details check website.
**Facilities:** ℗ 🍴 £2.50 🚻 (wheelchairs & buggies available – pre-booked, toilets) shop, guided tours, audio commentaries ⊗ (ex on lead) 🚌 (must pre-book)

### REIGATE
**Reigate Priory Museum**
Bell Street RH2 7RL
☎ 01737 222550
**Web:** www.reigatepriorymuseum.org.uk
**Dir:** *in Priory Park close to town centre, use Bell St car park on A217*
The Priory Museum is housed in Reigate Priory which was originally founded before 1200, this Grade I listed building was converted to a mansion in Tudor times. Notable features include the magnificent Holbein fireplace, 17th-early 18th-century oak staircase and murals. The small museum has changing exhibitions on a wide range of subjects, designed to appeal to both adults and children. The collection includes domestic bygones, local history and costume.

**Times:** *Open Etr-early Dec, Wed & Sat, 2-4.30 in term time.
**Fee:** *Donations welcome.
**Facilities:** ℗ (50yds) 🍴 for school parties ♿ (hands on facilities) shop, guided tours ⊗ (ex assist dogs) 🚌 (must pre-book) ⊜

### TILFORD
**Rural Life Centre**
Reeds Road Farnham GU10 2DL
☎ 01252 795571 📠 01252 795571
**Email:** rural.life@lineone.net
**Web:** www.rural-life.org.uk
**Dir:** *off A287, 3m S of Farnham, signed*
The museum covers village life from 1750 to 1960. It is set in over ten acres of garden and woodland and incorporates purpose-built and reconstructed buildings, including a chapel. Displays show village crafts and trades, such as wheelwrighting, thatching, ploughing and gardening. The historic village playground provides entertainment for children and there is an arboretum featuring over 100 trees from around the world.
**Times:** Open mid Mar-end Oct, Wed-Sun & BH 10-5;

Winter Wed & Sun only 11-4
**Fee:** £5.50 (ch £3.50 & pen £4.50). Family ticket £16 (2ad+2ch)
**Facilities:** ℗ 🍴 (Licensed) 🍴 🍴 £1.25 ♿ (3 wheelchairs for use, toilets) shop, guided tours 🚌 (pre-booked)

### WEYBRIDGE
**Brooklands Museum**
Brooklands Road KT13 0QN
☎ 01932 857381 📠 01932 855465
**Email:** info@brooklandsmuseum.com
**Web:** www.brooklandsmuseum.com
**Dir:** *M25 junct 10/11, museum off B374*
Brooklands racing circuit was the birthplace of British motorsport and aviation. From 1907 to 1987 it was a world-renowned centre of engineering excellence. The Museum features old banked track and the 1-in-4 Test Hill. Many of the original buildings have been restored including the Clubhouse, the Shell and BP Petrol Pagodas, and the Malcolm Campbell Sheds in the Motoring Village. Many motorcycles, cars and aircraft are on display. Ring for details of special events.

**Times:** Open Mon-Sun & BHs 10-5 (4 in winter).
**Fee:** *£7 (ch under 5 free, ch 6-16 £5, concessions £6). Family ticket (2ad+3ch) £20.
**Facilities:** ℗ 🍴 ♿ (toilets) shop ⊗ (ex guide dogs) 🚌

SURREY

## ALFRISTON
### Drusillas Park
Polegate BN26 5QS
☎ 01323 874100 🖨 01323 874101
**Email:** info@drusillas.co.uk
**Web:** www.drusillas.co.uk
**Dir:** *off A27 near Alfriston 12m from Brighton & 7m from Eastbourne*
Situated amidst the stunning scenery of the Cuckmere Valley at Alfriston, Drusillas is widely recognised as the best small zoo in England. There are over 100 animal species in naturalistic environments, including meerkats, bats, penguins, monkeys, reptiles and creepy crawlies. The large adventure play area is paradise for anyone who needs to let off steam and the many attractions provide endless entertainment.

**Times:** Open all year, daily 10-6 (winter 10-5). Closed 24-26 Dec.
**Fee:** *Family super saver tickets: Family of 3 £31.50, family of 4 £42, family of 5 £52.50
**Facilities:** 🅿 ☕ (good quality fast food) 🍴 (Licensed) 🚻 📷 ♿ (rear train carriage & sensory trails, toilets) shop, audio commentaries 🚫 (ex guide dogs) 🚌

## BATTLE
### 1066 Battle of Hastings Abbey & Battlefield
TN33 0AD
☎ 01424 773792 🖨 01424 775059
**Web:** www.english-heritage.org.uk
**Dir:** *A21 onto A2100*
Explore the site of the Battle of Hastings, where on 14th October 1066, one of the most famous events in English history took place. In a single day's battle, William of Normandy defeated Harold of England, became known as William the Conqueror and changed the course of English history. There is a free interactive wand tour of the battlefield and atmospheric abbey ruins.
**Times:** *Open all year, Apr-Sep, daily 10-6; Oct-Mar, daily 10-4. Closed 24-26 Dec & 1 Jan.
**Fee:** *£5.30 (ch £2.70, concessions £4). Family £13.30.

Opening times and prices are subject to change, for further details please phone 0870 333 1181
**Facilities:** 🅿 (charged) ♿ shop 🚌 ♯ ♨

## BATTLE
### Yesterday's World
89-90 High Street Hastings TN33 0AQ
☎ 01424 775378 & 774269 🖨 01424 775174
**Email:** info@yesterdaysworld.co.uk
**Web:** www.yesterdaysworld.co.uk
**Dir:** *M25 junct 5, A21 onto A2100 towards Battle, opposite Battle Abbey Gatehouse*
A fun day out for all the family, as the past is brought to life. Walk down the cobbled streets of yesteryear and meet the colourful characters in over 30 shop and room settings including a 1930s grocer's and a Victorian kitchen. The exhibition contains many rarities from the 1850s onwards, including some of Queen Victoria's personal effects and letters written by the present queen. The museum is housed in beautiful gardens with children's play village, miniature golf and summer tea rooms. Special Events: Please visit website for details of events running throughout the year.
**Times:** *Open all year, Winter, daily 9.30-5.30; Summer, daily 9.30-6. Closed 25-26 Dec and 1 Jan.
**Fee:** *£5.95 (ch £3.95, pen £4.95). Family ticket £16.99. Discount for groups of 15+.
**Facilities:** 🅿 (100yds – £2.50 per day) ☕ (Opened October 2006) 🚻 📷 Free-£5 ♿ (limited access for wheelchairs, toilets) shop, audio commentaries 🚌 pre-book only

## BODIAM
**Bodiam Castle**
TN32 5UA
☎ 01580 830436 🖷 01580 830398
**Email:** bodiamcastle@nationaltrust.org.uk
**Web:** www.nationaltrust.org.uk/places/bodiamcastle
**Dir:** *2m E of A21 Hurst Green*
With its tall round drum towers at each corner, Bodiam is
something of a fairytale castle. It was built in 1386 by Sir
Edward Dalnygrigge, for comfort and defence. The walls
measure some 6ft 6in thick, and the great gatehouse
was defended by gun loops and three portcullises.
**Times:** Open 10 Feb-Oct, daily 10.30-6 (dusk if earlier);
Nov-Feb, Sat & Sun 10.30-4 (dusk if earlier). (Last
admission 1 hour before closing).
**Fee:** *£4.20 (ch £2.10). Family ticket £10.50. Group
15+ £3.60, (ch £1.80). Car £2, Coach £5.
**Facilities:** 🅿 (charged) 📖 Guidebooks and childrens
packs available. ♿ (Braille/large print guides, parking on
request, toilets) shop 🐕 (ex guide dogs) 🚍 (booking
recommended as limited number) 🐾

## BRIGHTON
**Brighton Museum & Art Gallery**
Royal Pavilion Gardens BN1 1EE
☎ 01273 290900 🖷 01273 292841
**Email:** museums@brighton-hove.gov.uk
**Web:** www.brighton.virtualmuseum.info
**Dir:** *A23/M23 from London. In city centre near seafront.
New entrance in Royal Pavilion Gardens*
A £10 million redevelopment has transformed Brighton
museum into a state-of-the-art visitor attraction. Dynamic
and innovative new galleries, including fashion, 20th-
century design and world art, featuring exciting
interactive displays appealing to all ages. The museum
also benefits from a spacious new entrance located in
the Royal Pavilion gardens and provides full disabled
access.
**Times:** Open Tue-Sat 10-5, Sun 2-5. (Closed Mon ex
BHs).
**Fee:** Free
**Facilities:** 🅿 (5 mins walk – Church St NCP & on street)
📖 ♿ (lift, tactile exhibits, induction loops, ramps, toilets)
shop 🐕 (ex guide dogs) 🚍 Call in advance ⌨

## BRIGHTON
**Royal Pavilion**
BN1 1EE
☎ 01273 290900 🖷 01273 292871
**Email:** visitor.services@brighton-hove.gov.uk
**Web:** www.royalpavilion.org.uk
**Dir:** *M23/A23 from London. In city centre near seafront.
15 min walk from rail station*
Acclaimed as one of the most exotically beautiful
buildings in the British Isles, the Royal Pavilion was the
magnificent seaside residence of George IV. This
breathtaking Regency palace is decorated in Chinese
style, with a romanticised Indian exterior, and surrounded
by restored Regency gardens.
**Times:** Open all year, Apr-Sep, daily 9.30-5.45 (last
admission 5); Oct-Mar, daily 10-5.15 (last admission
4.30). Closed 25&26 Dec.
**Fee:** *£7.50 (ch £5, concessions £5.75) Family ticket
(1ad+upto 2ch) £11.50 (2ad+upto 2ch) £19. Groups
20+ £6.20 each.
**Facilities:** 🅿 (5 mins walk - NCP & on Church St) 📖
♿ (wheelchairs, audio guides, toilets) shop, guided tours,
audio commentaries 🐕 (ex guide dogs) 🚍 (contact in
advance)

## BRIGHTON
### Sea Life Centre
Marine Parade BN2 1TB

☎ 01273 604234 ▤ 01273 681840

**Email:** slcbrighton@merlinentertainments.biz

**Web:** www.sealife.co.uk

**Dir:** *next to Brighton Pier between Marine Parade & Madeira Drive*

Experience spectacular marine displays, set in the world's oldest functioning aquarium. Take a look at over 100 species in their natural habitat, including seahorses, sharks and rays. Over forty exhibits include Adventures at 20,000 Leagues complete with NASA-designed walk-through observation tunnel. Features also include a Captain Pugwash quiz trail, a soft play area, a café and a giftshop.

**Times:** *Open all year, daily 10-5. (Last admission 4).Open later on wknds in summer & school hols. Closed 25 Dec.

**Fee:** *£9.95 (ch £7.50, concessions £8.50).

**Facilities:** ℗ (200yds – pay & display) ▤ Guide book £3.75 ♿ (Access in majority of Centre, toilets) shop ⊗ (ex guide dogs) 🚌

## EAST DEAN
### Seven Sisters Sheep Centre
Gilberts Drive BN20 0AA

☎ 01323 423302 ▤ 01323 423302

**Email:** sevensisters.sheepcentre@talk21.com

**Web:** www.sheepcentre.co.uk

**Dir:** *3m W of Eastbourne on A259. Turn left in village of East Dean to Birling Gap and sea, 0.5m on left*

The Sheep Centre has possibly the largest collection of sheep in the world, where over 40 different breeds can be visited at this family run farm. See lambs being born, sheep sheared and milked, cheese making and spinning. Take in the agricultural heritage and history of sheep on the South Downs.

**Times:** Open 3 Mar-7 May & 30 Jun-2 Sep, 2-5 (11-5 wknds/E Sussex school holidays)

**Fee:** £4 (ch £3 & concessions £3.50)

**Facilities:** ❶ (charged) ℗ ⊼ ♿ shop, guided tours ⊗ (ex guide dogs) 🚌 (pre-book) ♿

## EASTBOURNE
### How We Lived Then Museum of Shops & Social History
20 Cornfield Terrace BN21 4NS

☎ 01323 737143

**Email:** howwelivedthen@btconnect.com

**Web:** www.how-we-lived-then.co.uk

**Dir:** *just off seafront, between town centre & theatres, signed*

Over the last 50 years, Jan and Graham Upton have collected over 100,000 items which are now displayed on four floors of authentic old shops and room-settings, transporting visitors back to their grandparents' era. Other displays, such as seaside souvenirs, wartime rationing and Royal mementoes, help to capture 100 years of social history.

**Times:** Open all year, daily, 10-5.30 (last entry 5). Winter times subject to change, telephone establishment.

**Fee:** *£4 (ch 5-15 £3, under 5's free, pen £3.50). Party 10+.

**Facilities:** ℗ (outside) ▤ Free-£1 ♿ (no charge) shop 🚌 (must pre-book) ♿

**EAST SUSSEX**

### HALLAND
**Bentley Wildfowl & Motor Museum**
Lewes BN8 5AF
☎ 01825 840573 📠 01825 841322
**Email:** barrysutherland@pavilion.co.uk
**Web:** www.bentley.org.uk
**Dir:** *7m NE of Lewes, signposted off A22, A26 & B2192*
Hundreds of swans, geese and ducks from all over the
world can be seen on lakes and ponds along with
flamingoes and peacocks. There is a fine array of
Veteran, Edwardian and Vintage vehicles, and the house
has splendid antiques and wildfowl paintings. The
gardens specialise in old fashioned roses. Other
attractions include woodland walks, a nature trail,
education centre, adventure playground and a miniature
train.

**Times:** *Open 17 Mar-Oct, daily 10.30-4.30. House
Open from noon, Apr-Nov, Feb & part of Mar, wknds only.
Estate closed Dec & Jan. House closed all winter.
**Fee:** *Summer £5.50 (ch 4-15 £3.80, pen & students
£4.50). Family ticket (2 ad & 4 ch) £17.50. Winter
£4.20. Special rates for disabled.
**Facilities:** 🅿 🚻 ♿ (wheelchairs available, toilets) shop
⊗ (ex guide dogs) 🚌

---

### HASTINGS & ST LEONARDS
**1066 Story in Hastings Castle**
Castle Hill Road West Hill TN34 3RG
☎ 01424 781111 & 781112 (info line)
📠 01424 781186
**Email:** bookings@discoverhastings.co.uk
**Web:** www.hastings.gov.uk
**Dir:** *close to A259 seafront, 2m from B2093*
The ruins of the Norman castle stand on the cliffs, close
to the site of William the Conqueror's first motte-and-
bailey castle in England. It was excavated in 1825 and
1968, and old dungeons were discovered in 1894. An
unusual approach to the castle can be made via the West
Hill Cliff Railway.
**Times:** *Open daily, Oct-26 Mar 11-3.30, 27 Mar-Sep
10-5. Closed 24-26 Dec.

**Fee:** *£3.40 (ch £2.25, pen & students £2.75, disabled
free). Family ticket £10 (fee entitles visitor to third off
Caves & Underwater World)
**Facilities:** 🅿 (seafront – time restrictions, pay & display)
🚻 ♿ (concrete slope, some uneven ground) shop
⊗ (ex guide dogs) 🚌 must pre-book ♿

---

### HASTINGS & ST LEONARDS
**Smugglers Adventure**
St Clements Caves West Hill TN34 3HY
☎ 01424 422964 📠 01424 721483
**Email:** smugglers@discoverhastings.co.uk
**Web:** www.discoverhastings.co.uk
**Dir:** *follow brown signs on A259, coast road, through
Hastings. Use seafront car park, then take West Cliff
railway or follow signed footpath*
A Smuggler's Adventure is a themed experience housed
in a labyrinth of caverns and passages deep below the
West Hill. Visitors first tour a comprehensive exhibition
and museum, followed by a video theatre, before
embarking on the Adventure Walk – a trip through
several acres of caves with life-size tableaux, push-
button automated models and dramatic scenic effects

depicting life in the days of 18th-century smuggling.
**Times:** *Open all year daily, Etr-Sep 10-5.30; Oct-Etr
11-4.30. Closed 24-26 Dec.
**Fee:** *£5.95 (ch £3.95, concessions £4.95). Family ticket
£16.50.
**Facilities:** 🅿 (500yds – parking meters on some streets)
shop ⊗ (ex guide dogs) 🚌

## HERSTMONCEUX
### The Observatory Science Centre
Hailsham BN27 1RN
☎ 01323 832731 📠 01323 832741
**Email:** info@the-observatory.org
**Web:** www.the-observatory.org
**Dir:** *0.75m N of Wartling village*
From the 1950s to the 1980s this was part of the Royal Greenwich Observatory, and was used by astronomers to observe and chart movements in the night sky. Visitors can learn about not only astronomy, but also other areas of science in a series of interactive and engaging displays. There are also exhibitions, a discovery park, and a collection of unusual giant exhibits.
**Times:** *Open daily from 28 Jan-3 Dec.Open wkends of Jan 7/8, 14/15, 21/22 and Dec 9/10.

**Fee:** *£6.50 (ch 4-15 £4.75). Family ticket (2ad+3ch or 1ad+4ch) £19.50, Family of 5 £22.30.
**Facilities:** 🅿 🚻 📱 ♿ (ramps & disabled entrance, lift to 1st floor, toilets) shop, guided tours ⊗ (ex guide dogs) 🚌

## LEWES
### Lewes Castle & Barbican House Museum
169 High Street BN7 1YE
☎ 01273 486290 📠 01273 486990
**Email:** castle@sussexpast.co.uk
**Web:** www.sussexpast.co.uk
**Dir:** *N of High St off A27/A26/A275*
High above the medieval streets stands Lewes Castle, begun soon after the Norman Conquest by William de Warenne as his stronghold in Sussex and added to over the next 300 years, culminating in the magnificent Barbican. Thomas Read Kemp and his family owned and updated the ruins during Georgian times. Barbican House is next to the castle, and now houses a museum covering the area from pre-history to the late medieval period. Visitors can climb to the top of the castle, from where they are rewarded by stunning views. A 'sound and light' show in the museum below tells the story of the town of Lewes through the ages.
**Times:** *Open daily, Tue-Sat 10-5.30, Sun, Mon & BHs 11-5.30. (Last admission 30 mins before closing). Closed Xmas & Mon in Jan.
**Fee:** *£4.50 (ch (5-15) £2.25, concessions £4). Family ticket (2ad+2ch) £11.70, (1ad+4ch) £9.20. Disabled/Carer £2.25 each.
**Facilities:** 🅿 (on street parking) shop, guided tours ⊗ (ex guide dogs) 🚌 (discount for pre-booked groups only)

## NEWHAVEN
### Paradise Park & Gardens
Avis Road BN9 0DH
☎ 01273 512123 📠 01273 616005
**Email:** promotions@paradisepark.co.uk
**Web:** www.paradisepark.co.uk
**Dir:** *signed off A26 & A259*
A perfect day out for plant lovers whatever the season. Discover the unusual garden designs with waterfalls, fountains and lakes, including the Caribbean garden and the tranquil Oriental garden. The Conservatory Gardens complex contains a large variety of the world's flora divided into several zones. There's also a Sussex history trail and Planet Earth with moving dinosaurs and interactive displays, plus rides and amusements for children.

**Times:** *Open all year, daily 9-6. Closed 25-26 Dec.
**Fee:** *£7.99 (ch £5.99). Family ticket £19.99 (2ad+2ch).
**Facilities:** 🅿 🍽 (9-5.30 (Apr-Oct), 9-5 (Nov-Mar) 🍴 🚻 📱 ♿ (all areas level or ramped, toilets) shop, garden centre, guided tours ⊗ (ex guide dogs) 🚌

SHEFFIELD PARK STATION

**Bluebell Railway**

Sheffield Park Station Uckfield TN22 3QL

☎ 01825 720800 & 722370 🖷 01825 720804

**Email:** info@bluebell-railway.co.uk

**Web:** www.bluebell-railway.co.uk

**Dir:** *4.5m E of Haywards Heath, off A275, 10m S of East Grinstead A22-A275*

A volunteer-run heritage steam railway with nine miles of track running through pretty Sussex countryside. Please note that there is no parking at Kingscote Station. If you wish to board the train here, catch the bus (service 473) which connects Kingscote and East Grinstead.

**Times:** *Open all year, Sat & Sun, daily May-Sep & during school holidays. Santa Specials run Dec. For timetable and information regarding trains contact above.

**Fee:** *3rd class return fare £9.50 (ch £4.70). Family ticket £27. Admission to Sheffield Park Station only £1.60 (ch 80p). Other tickets available on request. Maybe subject to change, please telephone for details.

**Facilities:** Ⓟ Ⓟ (0.5m) 🍴 (Licensed) 🪑 ♿ (special carriage for wheelchairs & carers with lift, toilets) shop, guided tours 🚌 (book in advance, groups of 20+)

---

AMBERLEY

**Amberley Working Museum**

Arundel BN18 9LT

☎ 01798 831370 🖷 01798 831831

**Email:** office@amberleymuseum.co.uk

**Web:** www.amberleymuseum.co.uk

**Dir:** *on B2139, between Arundel and Storrington, adjacent to Amberley railway station*

36-acre open-air museum dedicated to the industrial heritage of the south east of England. Traditional craftspeople on site (including a blacksmith and potter), working narrow-gauge railway and vintage bus collection, Connected Earth telecommunications display, Seeboard Electricity Hall, stationary engines, print workshop, woodturners, wheelwrights, nature trails, restaurant, shop and much more.

**Times:** *Open 12 Mar-2 Nov, Wed-Sun & BH Mon 10-5.30 (last admission 4.30). Also open daily during school hols.

**Fee:** *£7.20 (ch 5-16 £4, pen & students £6.20). Family ticket (2ad+3ch) £20.

**Facilities:** Ⓟ 🪑 ♿ (wheelchairs available for loan & large print guides, toilets) shop 🚌

---

ARUNDEL

**Arundel Castle**

BN18 9AB

☎ 01903 882173 🖷 01903 884581

**Email:** info@arundelcastle.org

**Web:** www.arundelcastle.org

**Dir:** *on A27 between Chichester & Worthing*

Set high on a hill in West Sussex, this magnificent castle and stately home, seat of the Dukes of Norfolk for nearly 1000 years, commands stunning views across the River Arun and out to sea. Climb to the keep and battlements; marvel at a fine collection of 16th-century furniture; portraits by Van Dyke, Gainsborough, Canaletto and others; tapestries and the personal possessions of Mary, Queen of Scots; wander in the grounds and renovated Victorian flower and vegetable gardens.

**Times:** Open Apr-Oct, Sun-Fri 11-5, CastleOpen 12-5. (Last admission 4). Closed Sat.

**Fee:** *£12 (ch 5-16 £7.50, pen £9.50). Family ticket £32. Party 20+.

**Facilities:** Ⓟ (charged) Ⓟ (70yds – large vehicles must park off site) ☕ (Light lunches, snacks.) ♿ (chair lift, toilets) shop, guided tours 🚫🐕 (ex assist dogs) 🚌 (pre-booking advised)

## ARUNDEL
### WWT Arundel
Mill Road BN18 9PB
☎ 01903 883355 🖷 01903 884834
**Email:** arundel@wwt.org.uk
**Web:** www.wwt.org.uk
**Dir:** *signed from A27 & A29*
More than a thousand ducks, geese and swans from all over the world can be found here, many of which are so friendly, they will eat from your hand. The wild reserve attracts a variety of birds and includes a reedbed habitat considered so vital to the wetland wildlife it shelters that it has been designated a Site of Special Scientific Interest. Visitors can walk right through this reedbed on a specially designed boardwalk. There is a packed programme of events and activities throughout the year.

**Times:** *Open all year, daily; summer 9.30-5; winter 9.30-4.30. (Last admission summer 5; winter 4). Closed 25 Dec.
**Fee:** *£6.75 (ch £3.25, pen £5.25). Family ticket £17.
**Facilities:** 🅿 Ⓟ 🍽 (Licensed) 🛉 ♿ (level paths, free wheelchair loan, toilets) shop ⊗ (ex guide & hearing dogs) 🚍 (pre-booking required)

## BIGNOR
### Bignor Roman Villa & Museum
Pulborough RH20 1PH
☎ 01798 869259 🖷 01798 869259
**Email:** bignorromanvilla@care4free.net
**Web:** www.pyrrha.demon.co.uk
**Dir:** *6m S of Pulborough & 6m N of Arundel on A29, signed. 8m S of Petworth on A285, signed*
Rediscovered in 1811, this Roman house was built on a grand scale. It is one of the largest known, and has spectacular mosaics. The heating system can also be seen, and various finds from excavations are on show. The longest mosaic in Britain (82ft) is on display here in its original position.
**Times:** Open Mar-Apr, Tue-Sun & BH 10-5; May daily 10-5; Jun-Sep daily 10-6, Oct daily 10-5

**Fee:** *£4.35 (ch 5-15 £1.85, pen £3.10). Party 10+ 20% discount. Guided tours by arrangement.
**Facilities:** 🅿 ☕ (light refreshments available) 🛉 📖 10p ♿ (most areas accessible) shop, guided tours ⊗ (ex guide dogs) 🚍 (pre-booking preferred)

## CHICHESTER
### Mechanical Music & Doll Collection
Church Rd Portfield PO19 4HN
☎ 01243 372646 🖷 01243 370299
**Dir:** *1m E of Chichester, signed off A27*
Housed in a Victorian former church, this collection is a unique opportunity to see and hear barrel organs, polyphons, musical boxes, fair organs etc – all fully restored and playing. The organs are played as part of the tour of 100 years of mechanical music – a magical musical tour to fascinate and entertain all ages. The doll collection contains fine examples of Victorian and Edwardian china and wax dolls, and felt and velvet dolls of the 1920s.
**Times:** *Open Jun-Sep, Wed 1-4; Group bookings anytime in the year by prior arrangement.

**Fee:** *£2.50 (ch £1.25).
**Facilities:** 🅿 ♿ shop, guided tours ⊗ (ex guide dogs) 🚍 (prior booking essential) ♲

## FISHBOURNE
**Fishbourne Roman Palace**
Salthill Road Chichester PO19 3QR
☎ 01243 785859 📄 01243 539266
**Email:** adminfish@sussexpast.co.uk
**Web:** www.sussexpast.co.uk
**Dir:** *off A27 onto A259 into Fishbourne. Turn right into Salthill Rd & right into Roman Way*
This is the largest known Roman residence in Britain. It was occupied from the 1st to the 3rd centuries AD, and has many beautiful mosaic floors. 25 of these can still be seen in varying states of completeness, including others rescued from elsewhere in the area. Outside, part of the garden has been replanted to its original 1st-century plan. The museum displays a collection of finds from the excavations and tells the story of the site's discovery. A computer-generated, audio-visual presentation helps bring the site back to life, as it would have been many centuries ago.
**Times:** Open all year, daily Feb-15 Dec. Feb, Nov-Dec 10-4; Mar-Jul & Sep-Oct 10-5; Aug 10-6. Winter wknds 10-4.
**Fee:** *£6.50 (ch 5-15 £3.40, concessions £5.50, registered disabled £4.90). Family ticket £16.60 (2ad+2ch).
**Facilities:** 🅿 🍴 📱 ♿ (self guiding tapes & tactile objects for the blind, toilets) shop, guided tours 🚫 (ex guide dogs) 🚌

## GOODWOOD
**Goodwood House**
Chichester PO18 0PX
☎ 01243 755048 📄 01243 755005
**Email:** curator@goodwood.co.uk
**Web:** www.goodwood.co.uk
**Dir:** *3m NE of Chichester*
The Sussex Downs and 12,000 acres of working country estate provide a glorious backdrop to this magnificent Regency house, which has been the home of the Dukes of Richmond for over 300 years. The gilded, richly-decorated State Apartments include the luxurious Yellow Drawing Room and the unique Egyptian Dining Room. The art collection includes paintings by George Stubbs and Canaletto.
**Times:** Open end Mar-Sep, Sun & Mon, 1-5; Aug, Sun-Thu. Closed for occasional events.
**Fee:** £8 (ch under 12 free, ch & student £4, pen £7). Groups 20+ £7 each.
**Facilities:** 🅿 ♿ (ramp at front of house, disabled parking area, toilets) shop, guided tours 🚫 (ex guide dogs) 🚌 (advance booking)

## LITTLEHAMPTON
**Look & Sea! Visitor Centre**
63-65 Surrey Street BN17 5AW
☎ 01903 718984 📄 01903 718036
**Email:** info@lookandsea.co.uk
**Web:** www.lookandsea.co.uk
**Dir:** *on harbour front 10 mins walk from Littlehampton Station*
An interactive museum exploring the history and geography of Littlehampton and the surrounding area. Inside the modern waterfront building you can meet the 500,000-year-old Boxgrove Man, become a ship's captain in an interactive computer game, and enjoy spectacular panoramic views of the Sussex coast from the circular glass tower.
**Times:** *Open all year, daily 9-5
**Fee:** *£2.95 (ch £2.50, concessions £2.50).
**Facilities:** 🅿 (20 mtrs) 🅿 (Ground floor) ♿ (toilets) shop 🚫 (ex guide dogs) 🚌 (pre book in advance)

## LOWER BEEDING
### Leonardslee Lakes & Gardens

Horsham RH13 6PP

☎ 01403 891212 🖹 01403 891305

**Email:** gardens@leonardslee.com

**Web:** www.leonardslee.com

**Dir:** *4m SW from Handcross, at junct of B2110 & A281*

This Grade I listed garden is set in a peaceful valley with walks around seven beautiful lakes. It is a paradise in spring, with banks of rhododendrons and azaleas along paths lined with bluebells. Wallabies live in parts of the valley, deer in the parks and wildfowl on the lakes. Enjoy the Rock Garden, the fascinating Bonsai, the new 'Behind the Doll's House' exhibition and the collection of Victorian Motorcars (1889-1900).

**Times:** *Open Apr-Oct, daily 9.30-6

**Fee:** *Apr & Jun-Oct £6, May (Mon-Fri) £8, (wknds & BH) £9 (ch £4 anytime).

**Facilities:** 🅿 🍴 (Licensed) shop garden centre ⊗ 🚌 (pre booking preferred)

---

## PETWORTH
### Petworth House & Park

GU28 0AE

☎ 01798 342207 & 343929 🖹 01798 342963

**Email:** petworth@nationaltrust.org.uk

**Web:** www.nationaltrust.org.uk/petworth

**Dir:** *in town centre, A272/283*

Petworth House is an impressive 17th-century mansion set in a 700 acre Deer Park, landscaped by 'Capability' Brown, and immortalised in Turner's paintings. There is a fine art collection including work by Van Dyck, Titian, and Turner, as well as sculpture, ceramics and fine furniture. The fascinating Servants' Quarters show the domestic side of life of this great estate.

**Times:** *Open Apr-Oct 11-5 last entry 4.30 (closed Thu-Fri)

**Fee:** *£8 (ch £4). Family ticket £20. Party 15+ £7 each. NT members free. Pleasure Ground £3 (ch £1.50).

**Facilities:** 🅿 🅿 (600mtrs) Pentworth Car park £2 NT members free ☕ (licensed) 🍴 (Licensed) 🗐 50p ♿ (wheelchairs available, Braille guide, virtual tour, toilets) shop, audio commentaries (charged) ⊗ (ex guide/hearing dogs) 🚌 (must pre-book) 🌿

---

## PULBOROUGH
### Parham House & Gardens

Parham Park Storrington RH20 4HS

☎ 01903 744888 & 742021 🖹 01903 746557

**Email:** enquiries@parhaminsussex.co.uk

**Web:** www.parhaminsussex.co.uk

**Dir:** *midway between A29 & A24, off A283*

Surrounded by a deer park, fine gardens and 18th-century pleasure grounds in a beautiful downland setting, this Elizabethan family home contains an important collection of paintings, furniture, carpets and rare needlework. There are four acres of walled garden with huge herbaceous borders, greenhouse, orchard and herb garden. A brick and turf maze has been created in the grounds – designed with children in mind, it is called 'Veronica's Maze'.

**Times:** *Open Etr Sun-Sep, Wed, Thu, Sun & BH Mons (also open Tue & Fri in Aug). Gardens open 12-6; House 2-6 (last entry 5).

**Fee:** *House & Gardens £6.50 (ch 5-15 £2.50, pen & disabled visitors £5.50). Family ticket £15.50. Gardens only £5 (ch £1). Party rates available.

**Facilities:** 🅿 ☕ (12-2, 2.30-5.30) 🪑 🗐 ♿ (wheelchairs, ramps, recorded tour tape, parking, toilets) shop, garden centre, audio commentaries (charged) ⊗ (ex guide dogs & in grounds) 🚌 (pre-booking for group rates)

WEST SUSSEX

## PULBOROUGH
### RSPB Pulborough Brooks Nature Reserve
Uppertons Barn Visitor Centre Wiggonholt RH20 2EL
☎ 01798 875851
**Email:** pulborough.brooks@rspb.org.uk
**Web:** www.rspb.org.uk
**Dir:** *signed on A283, 2m SE of Pulborough*
Set in the scenic Arun Valley and easily reached via the visitor centre at Wiggonholt, this is an excellent reserve for year-round family visits. A nature trail winds through hedgerow-lined lanes to viewing hides overlooking water-meadows. Breeding summer birds include nightingales and warblers, ducks and wading birds, and nightjars and hobbies on nearby heathland. Unusual wading birds and hedgerow birds regularly pass through on spring and autumn migration.

**Times:** *Open daily, Reserve: 9-9, (or sunset if earlier). Visitor centre: 10-5. Reserve closed 25 Dec, Visitor Centre closed 25-26 Dec.
**Fee:** *£3.50 (ch £1, concessions £2.50). Family ticket £7.
**Facilities:** ❷ Ⓟ (200mtrs) ☕ (closes 4.45pm) 🎪 ♿ (free hire electric buggy and wheelchair, toilets) shop ⊗ (ex guide dogs) 🚌 (advance booking essential)

## SINGLETON
### Weald & Downland Open Air Museum
Chichester PO18 0EU
☎ 01243 811348 🖷 01243 811475
**Email:** office@wealddown.co.uk
**Web:** www.wealddown.co.uk
**Dir:** *6m N of Chichester on A286*
A showcase of English architectural heritage, where historic buildings have been rescued from destruction and rebuilt in a parkland setting. Vividly demonstrating the evolution of building techniques and use of local materials, these fascinating buildings bring to life the homes, farms and rural industries of the south east of the past 500 years.
**Times:** Open all year, Mar-Oct, daily 10.30-6. Call or see website for winter opening.

**Fee:** *£7.95 (ch £4.25, pen £6.95). Family ticket (2ad+3ch) £21.95.
**Facilities:** ❷ ☕ (Light lunches, refreshments) 🎪 ♿ (separate entrance and ramps available for some buildings, toilets) shop, guided tours ⊗ (ex on lead) 🚌 pre-book only

## TANGMERE
### Tangmere Military Aviation Museum
Chichester PO20 2ES
☎ 01243 775223 🖷 01243 789490
**Email:** info@tangmere-museum.org.uk
**Web:** www.tangmere-museum.org.uk
**Dir:** *off A27, 3m E of Chichester towards Arundel*
Based at an airfield that played an important role during the World Wars, this museum spans 80 years of military aviation. There are photographs, documents, aircraft and aircraft parts on display along with a Hurricane replica, Spitfire replica and cockpit simulator. A hangar houses a Supermarine Swift and the record-breaking aircraft *Meteor* and *Hunter*. Aircraft outside include; Lockheed T33, English Electric Lightning, De Havilland Sea Vixen, McDonnell Douglas Phantom F4, Gloster Meteor and a

Westland Whirlwind helicopter.
**Times:** *Open Mar-Oct, daily 10-5.30; Feb & Nov, daily 10-4.30.
**Fee:** *£5 (ch £1.50 & pen £4) Family £11.50 (2ad+2ch).
**Facilities:** ❷ ☕ (hot meals provided seats about 30) 🎪 ♿ (wheelchairs available, toilets) shop ⊗ (ex guide dogs) 🚌 ♿

## WISBOROUGH GREEN
**Fishers Farm Park**
Newpound Lane RH14 0EG
☎ 01403 700063 📄 01403 700823
Email: info@fishersfarmpark.co.uk
Web: www.fishersfarmpark.co.uk
Dir: *follow brown & white tourist boards on all roads approaching Wisborough Green*

This all-weather, all-year farm and adventure park, provides a mixture of farmyard and dynamic adventure play. Amongst the attractions there are barns, paddocks and stables with animals that can be petted and stroked; pony, horse and donkey rides, animal demonstrations and rides on a combine harvester and a tractor-trailer. The adventure play features a giant paddling pool, bumper boats, slides, mini-mazes and a 1950s Merry-Go-Round.

**Times:** Open all year, daily, 10-5. Closed 26-26 Dec.
**Fee:** *From £7.75 (ch 2 yrs from £4, ch 3-16 yrs from £7.25, concessions from £6.25)
**Facilities:** 🅿 🅿 (100mtrs) ☕ (open 10.30-4.15) 🛆 📖 ♿ (toilets) shop ⊗ 🚌 (not on wkdays during summer hols)

## ALUM BAY
**The Needles Old Battery**
West High Down Totland Bay PO30 0JH
☎ 01983 754772 📄 01983 756978
Email: isleofwight@nationaltrust.org.uk
Web: www.nationaltrust.org.uk/isleofwight
Dir: *at Needles Headland, W of Freshwater Bay and Alum Bay, B3322*

The threat of a French invasion prompted the construction in 1862 of this spectacularly sited fort, which now contains exhibitions on the Battery's involvement in both World Wars, as well as the Headland's intriguing past as part of the secret rocket testing programme. Two of the original gun barrels are displayed in the parade ground and a 60-yard tunnel leads to a searchlight emplacement perched above the Needles Rocks giving magnificent views of the Dorset coastline beyond.

**Times:** *Open 26 Mar-29 Oct Sat-Thu 10.30-5. Jul-Aug daily.
**Fee:** *£3.90 (ch £1.95). Family ticket £8.90. May be subject to change.
**Facilities:** 🅿 (0.5m) 🛆 📖 £1 ♿ (ramp & audio tours, hearing loops, toilets) shop, guided tours (charged) 🚌 Pre-book only ✂

## ALUM BAY
**The Needles Park**
PO39 0JD
☎ 0870 458 0022 📄 01983 755260
Email: info@theneedles.co.uk
Web: www.theneedles.co.uk
Dir: *signed on B3322*

Overlooking the Needles on the western edge of the island, the park has attractions for all the family: included in the wide range of facilities is the spectacular chair lift to the beach to view the famous coloured sand cliffs, Needles Rocks and lighthouse. Other popular attractions are Alum Bay Glass and the Isle of Wight Sweet Manufactory. Kids will enjoy the Junior Driver roadway, and the Jurassic golf course.

**Times:** *Open Apr-30 Oct, daily 10-5. Hours extended in high season & on special event days
**Fee:** *No admission charged for entrance to Park. All day car park charge £3. Pay-as-you-go attractions or Supersaver Attraction discount ticket.
**Facilities:** 🅿 (charged) 🍴 (Licensed) 🛆 ♿ (designated parking, toilets) shop 🚌

## ARRETON
### Robin Hill Country Park
Downend Newport PO30 2NU
☎ 01983 527352 🖹 01983 527347
**Email:** dj@robin-hill.com
**Web:** www.robin-hill.com
**Dir:** *0.5m from Arreton next to Hare & Hounds pub*
Set in 88 acres of beautiful woodland and countryside,
Robin Hill has a wide variety of activities and attractions
including; Tree Top Trail, Mazes, Snake Slides, Troll Island,
Squirrel Tower, Toboggan Run and Falconry Centre. A
5-year garden project is underway and the new
Woodland Centre offers nature displays and wildlife
cameras.
**Times:** *Open 27 Mar-29 Oct, daily 10-5
(last admission 4).

**Fee:** *£7.50, pen £5.50, disabled £4.
Saver ticket for 4 £27.
**Facilities:** 🅿 🚻 ♿ (most areas are accessible, ramps
access, toilets) shop 🚫 (ex on lead) 🚌

## BEMBRIDGE
### Bembridge Windmill
PO35 5SQ
☎ 01983 873945 🖹 01983 873 945
**Email:** isleofwight@nationaltrust.org.uk
**Web:** www.nationaltrust.org.uk/Isleofwight
**Dir:** *0.5m S of Bembridge on B3395*
Built around 1700, this is the only surviving windmill on
the island and has much of its original machinery intact.
It was last used in 1913, and the stone-built tower with
its wooden cap and machinery has been restored so that
visitors can explore its four floors. The mill also provides
breathtaking views across glorious, unspoilt countryside.
**Times:** *Open 27 Mar-29 Oct, Sun-Fri, 10-4.30. Jul, Aug
& Sep daily. May be subject to change.
**Fee:** *£2.10 (ch £1.05) Family £6

**Facilities:** 🅿 (200yds) ☕ (kiosk selling refreshments) 🚻
🖹 Donation ♿ (hearing loop, pictorial guide, audio guide,
Braille guide) shop, guided tours, audio commentaries
🚫 (ex guide dogs) 🚌 (pre-book) 🦋

## BLACKGANG
### Blackgang Chine Fantasy Park
Ventnor PO38 2HN
☎ 01983 730330 🖹 01983 731267
**Email:** info@blackgangchine.com
**Web:** www.blackgangchine.com
**Dir:** *follow signs from Ventnor for Whitnell & Niton. From
Niton follow signs for Blackgang*
Opened as scenic gardens in 1843 covering some 40
acres, the park has imaginative play areas, water
gardens, maze and coastal gardens. Set on the steep
wooded slopes of the chine are the themed areas
Smugglerland, Nurseryland, Dinosaurland, Fantasyland
and Frontierland. St Catherine's Quay has a maritime
exhibition showing the history of local and maritime
affairs.

**Times:** *Open mid Mar-end Oct daily, 10-5; late Jul-early
Sep open until 10.
**Fee:** *Combined ticket (as from 15 May) to chine,
sawmill & quay £8.50. Saver ticket (4 people) £31.
**Facilities:** 🅿 (charged) ☕ (130 seat, self service) 🚻 🖹
History book £2, School Pack ♿ (toilets) shop, guided
tours 🚌

## BRADING
### Brading The Experience
46 High Street PO36 0DQ

☎ 01983 407286 🖥 01983 402112

**Email:** info@bradingtheexperience.co.uk

**Web:** www.bradingtheexperience.co.uk

**Dir:** *on A3055, in Brading High St*

Brading The Experience is more than just a waxworks! Comprising Great British Legends Gallery, 16th-century Rectory Mansion filled with famous and infamous characters from the past, Chamber of Horrors, award-winning Courtyards, Animal World, World of Wheels and The Pier.

**Times:** Open all year, Summer 10-5.30, Winter 10.30-5 (last admission 1.5hrs before closing)

**Fee:** £6.75 (ch 5-15, £4.75, under 5 free, pen £5.50).

OAP £5.75 Family £21 (2ad+2ch), Family £25 (2ad+3ch). Party 20+.

**Facilities:** 🅿 🅟 (100yds - coaches must use nearby car park) ☕ (indoor & conservatory seating) 🗐 School pack F.O.C/Individuals 25p ♿ (disabled route planner, toilets) shop 🚌 booking recommended

## BRADING
### Lilliput Antique Doll & Toy Museum
High Street PO36 0DJ

☎ 01983 407231

**Email:** lilliput.museum@btconnect.com

**Web:** www.lilliputmuseum.com

**Dir:** *A3055 Ryde/Sandown road, in Brading High Street*

This private museum contains one of the finest collections of antique dolls and toys in Britain. There are over 2000 exhibits, ranging in age from 2000BC to 1945 with examples of almost every seriously collectable doll, many with royal connections. Also dolls' houses, teddy bears and rare and unusual toys.

**Times:** *Open all year, daily, 10-5.

**Fee:** *£1.95 (ch & pen £1.15, ch under 5 free). Party on request.

**Facilities:** 🅟 (200 yds) 🗐 For school groups upon request only. ♿ (ramps provided on request) shop, guided tours 🚌

## CARISBROOKE
### Carisbrooke Castle
Newport PO30 1XY

☎ 01983 522107 🖥 01983 528632

**Web:** www.english-heritage.org.uk

**Dir:** *1.25m SW of Newport, off B3401*

A royal fortress and prison to King Charles I for the final year of his life, Carisbrooke Castle is set on a sweeping ridge at the heart of the Isle of Wight. The displays include personal memorabilia and relics from the imprisonment of Charles I, the history of the castle and a wide range of exhibits illustrating the social history of the island. Don't miss the donkeys that can be seen working a 16th-century wheel to draw water from the well.

**Times:** Open all year, Apr-Sep, daily 10-5; Oct-Mar, daily 10-4. Closed 24-26 Dec & 1 Jan.

**Fee:** £5.50 (ch £2.80, concessions £4.10). Family £13.80. Prices and opening times are subject to change. Please check web site or call 0870 333 1181 for the most up to date prices and opening times when planning your visit.

**Facilities:** 🅿 ☕ (open Apr-Oct) ♿ shop 🚌 ⊞ ⊘

**ISLE OF WIGHT**

## OSBORNE HOUSE
**Osborne House**
East Cowes PO32 6JY
☎ 01983 200022 🖹 01983 281380
**Web:** www.english-heritage.org.uk
**Dir:** *1m SE of East Cowes*
The beloved seaside retreat of Queen Victoria offers a glimpse into the private life of Britain's longest reigning monarch. The royal apartments are full of treasured mementos; and Queen Victoria's role as Empress of India is celebrated in the decoration of the Durbar Room. Visit the gardens and the charming Swiss Cottage.
**Times:** House open: Apr-Sep, daily, 10-5; Oct, daily, 10-4; Nov-Mar, 10-4, Wed-Sun (guided tours only, must pre-book, last tour 2.30. House & grounds close 4. During Xmas tour season 11 Nov-7 Jan, last tour time is 3). Closed 24-26 Dec & 1 Jan. On 22-23, 28-29 J
**Fee:** House & Gardens: £9.50 (ch £4.80, concessions £7.10). Family £23.80. Garden only: £5.50 (ch £2.80, concessions £4.10). Family £13.80. Prices and opening times are subject to change. Please check web or call 0870 333 1181
**Facilities:** 🅿 ⛶ (open Apr-Oct) ⛱ ♿ shop
⊗ 🚌 ⊞ ⌨

## PORCHFIELD
**Colemans Animal Farm**
Colemans Lane PO30 4LX
☎ 01983 522831 🖹 01983 537534
**Email:** info@colemansfarm.net
**Web:** www.colemansfarm.com
**Dir:** *A3054 Newport to Yarmouth road, follow brown tourist signs*
Ideal for young children, this extensive petting farm has donkeys, goats, rabbits, guinea pigs, pigs, Highland cattle, Shetland ponies, chickens, ducks and geese. There is also a fun barn with slides and swings, an adventure playground, a Tractor Fun Park, and an Old Barn Café for adults who need to relax. Visitors can cuddle, stroke and feed the animals at special times throughout the day. Other special events run all day.
**Times:** Open mid Mar-end Oct, Tue-Sun, 10-4.30 (last admission recommended 3.30). (Closed Mon, ex during school and BHs).Open for pre-booked events out of season.
**Fee:** £5.95 (ch £4.95, concessions £4.50), family ticket £18.
**Facilities:** 🅿 ⛶ (16th-century barn café) ⛱ ♿ (toilets) shop 🚌

## SANDOWN
**Dinosaur Isle**
Culver Parade PO36 8QA
☎ 01983 404344 🖹 01983 407502
**Email:** dinosaur@iow.gov.uk
**Web:** www.dinosaurisle.com
Britain's first purpose-built dinosaur attraction where, in a building reminiscent of a Pterosaur flying across the Cretaceous skies, you can walk back through fossilised time. In recreated landscape meet life sized models of the island's famous five – Neovenator, Eotyrannus, Iguandon, Hypsilophodon and Polacanthus. Look out for the flying Pterodactyls and skeletons as they are found, watch volunteers preparing the latest finds or try the many hands-on activities.
**Times:** Open all year daily, Apr-Sep 10-6; Oct 10-5; Nov-Mar 10-4. Closed 24-26 Dec & 1 Jan, please phone to confirm opening Jan-10 Feb. Last admission 1hr before closing.
**Fee:** *£4.75 (ch 3-15 £2.75, concessions £3.50) Family £13 (2+2)
**Facilities:** 🅿 (charged) ⛱ 📱 ♿ (toilets) shop, guided tours ⊗ (assist dogs) 🚌

## SHANKLIN
### Shanklin Chine
12 Pomona Rd PO37 6PF
☎ 01983 866432 📄 01983 866145
**Email:** jillshanklinchine1@msn.com
**Web:** www.shanklinchine.co.uk
**Dir:** *turn off A3055 at lights, left into Hope Rd & continue onto Esplanade for entrance*
Part of Britain's national heritage, this scenic gorge at Shanklin is a magical world of unique beauty and a haven for rare plants and wildlife. A path winds through the ravine with overhanging trees, ferns and other flora covering the steep sides. 'The Island-Then and Now' is an exhibition detailing the history of the Isle of Wight, including its military importance in WWII.
**Times:** * 31 Mar-25 May, 10-5. 26 May-10 Sep, 10-10.
11 Sep-29 Oct, 10-5.
**Fee:** *£3.75 (ch under 14 £2, concessions £2.75). Family ticket £9.50 (2ad+2ch), £11.50 (2ad +3ch). Group rates available.
**Facilities:** 🅿 (charged) Ⓟ (450yds) ☕ (Tea Room) ♿ (access via lower entry only, toilets) shop 🚌 (groups of 30 at a time) ♻

## VENTNOR
### Ventnor Botanic Garden
Undercliff Drive PO38 1UL
☎ 01983 855397 📄 01983 856756
**Email:** alison.ellsbury@iow.gov.uk
**Web:** www.botanic.co.uk
**Dir:** *on A3055 coastal road, 1.5m W of Ventnor*
Due to the unique microclimate of the 'Undercliff', plants that can only survive in a Mediterranean climate thrive on the Isle of Wight. Built on the site of a Victorian hospital for TB sufferers, the garden was founded in 1970 by Sir Harold Hillier, and opened in 1972 by the late Earl Mountbatten. The garden has plants from Australasia, Africa, America, the Mediterranean, and the Far East, and is a great day out for anyone interested in exotic flora.
**Times:** Gardens: Open all year; Visitor Centre & Green
House: Mar-Oct, daily 10-5 & Nov-Feb, wknds only 10-4
**Fee:** Free admission to Gardens & Visitor Centre; Green House £1
**Facilities:** 🅿 (charged) ☕ (Closes 30 minutes before visitor centre) 🍴 🏛 Garden Trail £1 ♿ (lifts in visitor centre, wheelchairs, 2 lifts, toilets) shop, garden centre, guided tours ⊗ (guide dogs) 🚌

**ISLE OF WIGHT**

**The Needles**

# West Country

Durdle Door

## BRISTOL
**At-Bristol**

Anchor Road Harbourside BS1 5DB

☎ 0845 345 1235 📄 0117 915 7200

**Email:** information@at-bristol.org.uk

**Web:** www.at-bristol.org.uk

**Dir:** *from city centre, A4 to Anchor Rd. Located on left opposite Cathedral*

For the interactive adventure of a lifetime head for At-Bristol's three attractions on the city's habourside. A clever fusion of sci-fi architecture and historic buildings are home to 'Wildwalk', a breathtaking journey through the plant and animal kingdoms; Explore, the UK's most exciting hands-on science centre; and enjoy the big screen in the IMAX theatre, the largest cinema screen in the West of England.

**Times:** *Open all year, term-time wkdays 10-5, wknds & school hols 10-6. (Closed 25 Dec).

**Fee:** Ticket for 3 attractions £20 (ch £15, concessions £15). Family ticket £62.

**Facilities:** ℗ (charged) ℗ (0.5m - 2 metre height restriction on vehicles) 🚻 📶 ♿ (induction loop & mini com 0117 914 3475, toilets) shop ⊗ (ex guide dogs) 🚌

## BRISTOL
**Bristol Zoo Gardens**

Clifton BS8 3HA

☎ 0117 974 7399 📄 0117 973 6814

**Email:** information@bristolzoo.org.uk

**Web:** www.bristolzoo.org.uk

**Dir:** *M5 junct 17, take A4018 then follow brown elephant signs. Also signed from city centre*

From the smallest and rarest tortoise in the world to the largest ape, there are 300 exotic and endangered species to explore. The Zoo is dedicated to conservation and involved in international breeding programmes. In Zona Brazil, visitors can experience first hand, the stunning and diverse species found in the threatened coastal rainforests of Brazil. A winding wooden walkway will lead you past stunning birds, dainty agouti, grazing tapirs, and the world's largest living rodent - the capybara. Award-winning Seal & Penguin Coasts enable visitors to come face-to-face with penguins and seals in their natural element - beneath the waves - through transparent underwater walkways. Other favourites include Bug World, Twilight World, Meet the Lemurs, and the Reptile House.

**Times:** Open all year, daily (ex 25 Dec). 9-5.30 (British summer time), 9-4.30 (standard hrs)

**Fee:** £11 (ch £7, concessions £9.70). Family ticket (2ad+2 ch) £33.

**Facilities:** ℗ (charged) 🍴 (Licensed) 🚻 ♿ (wheelchairs/electric scooters for use in zoo grounds, toilets) shop, guided tours ⊗ (kennels for guide dogs) 🚌

## BRISTOL
**Bristol's Blaise Castle House Museum**

Henbury Road Henbury BS10 7QS

☎ 0117 903 9818

**Email:** general_museum@bristol-city.gov.uk

**Web:** www.bristol-city.gov.uk/museums

**Dir:** *4m NW of city, off B4057*

Built in the 18th century for a John Harford, a Quaker banker, this mansion is now Bristol's Museum of Social History with a collection of over 30,000 objects. The museum contains exhibits of everyday life from centuries past including a Bristol at Home display with everything from cooking utensils to early vacuum cleaners. John Harford was also responsible for nearby Blaise Hamlet, a picturesque estate village, designed by John Nash and built to house the estate servants and tenants.

**Times:** Open all year, Sat-Wed 10-5. (Closed 25-26 Dec).

**Fee:** *Free

**Facilities:** ℗ ℗ (200yds) 🚻 ♿ shop guided tours ⊗ (ex guide dogs) 🚌 (pre booking) ✉

## BRISTOL
### Bristol's City Museum & Art Gallery

Queen's Road Clifton BS8 1RL
☎ 0117 922 3571 📠 0117 922 2047
**Email:** general_museum@bristol-city.gov.uk
**Web:** www.bristol-city.gov.uk/museums
**Dir:** *follow signs to city centre, then follow tourist board signs to City Museum & Art Gallery*

Housed in a magnificant building in the centre of Bristol, there are regional and international collections that represent ancient history, dinosaurs, natural sciences and archaeology and in the art gallery there are seven galleries devoted to fine and applied arts. Displays include Bristol ceramics, silver, Chinese and Japanese ceramics. A full programme of special exhibitions take place throughout the year. Ring for details.

**Times:** Open all year, daily 10-5. (Closed 25-26 Dec).
**Fee:** *Free
**Facilities:** Ⓟ (400yds) 🍴 ♿ (lift, toilets) shop guided tours ⊗ (ex guide dogs) 🚌 (pre-booking) ♻

## BRISTOL
### British Empire & Commonwealth Museum

Station Approach Temple Meads BS1 6QH
☎ 0117 925 4980 📠 0117 925 4983
**Email:** admin@empiremuseum.co.uk
**Web:** www.empiremuseum.co.uk
**Dir:** *in city centre, near Temple Meads station*

Exploring the dramatic 500-year history of the rise and fall of the British Empire and the emergence of the modern Commonwealth, this internationally acclaimed museum uses video stations, interactive exhibits, and computer games, as well as more traditional techniques. Visitors have the opportunity to dress in period costume, learn Morse code or sample exotic spices. The museum is divided into three sections: Britain's first empire 1500-1790, the British Empire at its height 1790-1914, and Independence and Beyond, and is housed in a restored railway terminus built by Brunel. A visit to the museum includes entry to the hands-on exhibition Pow Wow.

**Times:** *Open all year, daily 10-5. (Closed 25-26 Dec)
**Fee:** *£6.95 (ch 5-15yrs £3.95, concessions £5.95). Family of 4 £16.
**Facilities:** Ⓟ (charged) Ⓟ (500yds) 🥤 (hot/cold drinks and snacks) 🍴 ♿ (all but one conference room accessible, lifts, toilets) shop, guided tours ⊗ (ex guide dogs) 🚌

## BRISTOL
### Brunel's SS Great Britain

Great Western Dock Gas Ferry Road BS1 6TY
☎ 0117 926 0680 📠 0117 925 5788
**Email:** admin@ssgreatbritain.org
**Web:** www.ssgreatbritain.org
**Dir:** *off Cumberland Rd*

Built and launched in Bristol in 1843, Isambard Kingdom Brunel's maritime masterpiece was the first ocean-going, propeller-driven, iron ship. After a life as a passenger liner, troop transport, cargo carrier and floating warehouse, she was abandoned in the Falkland Islands in 1937. In 1970 she was towed back to Bristol, restored to her former glory, and is now conserved in the Great Western Dock where she was built.

**Times:** *Open all year daily 10-5.30, 4.30 in winter. (Closed 18, 24-25 Dec).
**Fee:** *£8.95 (ch £4.95, under 3yrs free, concessions £6.95). Family ticket (2ad+3ch) £24.95. Annual ticket. Last ticket sale 1hr before closing.
**Facilities:** Ⓟ (charged) Ⓟ (200yds) 🥤 (Dockyard Café Bar, Winter 10-4.30) 🍴 (call for details) ♿ (toilets) shop, guided tours, audio commentaries ⊗ (ex guide dogs) 🚌

## BRISTOL
### HorseWorld
Staunton Manor Farm Staunton Lane Whitchurch
BS14 0QJ
☎ 01275 540173 📠 01275 540119
**Email:** visitor.centre@horseworld.org.uk
**Web:** www.horseworld.org.uk
**Dir:** *A37 Bristol to Wells road, follow brown signs from Maes Knoll traffic lights*
One of the largest horse rescue centres in Britain, set in Mendip-stone farm buildings on the edge of Bristol. Meet the friendly horses, ponies and donkeys. There is much to see and do including a miniature farm, 'touch and groom' areas, pony rides, daily animal care presentations, nature trail, educational displays, a video theatre and an adventure playground. There is also a tearoom.

**Times:** *Open all year daily 10-5 (Winter; closed Mon)
**Fee:** *£5.50 (ch £4.25, concessions £5)
**Facilities:** 🅿 🚻 ♿ (toilets) shop 🚌

## BRISTOL
### Maritime Heritage Centre
Gas Ferry Road BS1 6UN
☎ 0117 926 0680 📠 0117 925 5788
**Email:** commerical@ss-great-britain.com
**Web:** www.ss-great-britain.com
**Dir:** *M5 junct 18, follow brown signs 'Anchor'*
Exploring 200 years of Bristol shipbuilding, with special reference to Charles Hill & Son, and their predecessor, James Hillhouse, the Maritime Heritage centre is located on the quayside by the Great Western Dock. It forms part of the *SS Great Britain* and John Cabot's *Matthew* experience.
**Times:** *Open all year, daily 10-5.30, 4.30 in winter. (Closed 24 & 25 Dec).
**Fee:** *Admission is for the museum, the SS Great Britain & the Matthew £6.25 (ch £3.75, pen £5.25). Family ticket (2 adults & 2 ch) £16.50. Party 20+.
**Facilities:** 🅿 (charged) Ⓟ (200/300 yds - max 4hr) ♿ (toilets) shop ⊗ (ex guide dogs) 🚌 (pre-booked)

## BODMIN
### Pencarrow
Washaway PL30 3AG
☎ 01208 841369 📠 01208 841722
**Email:** pencarrow@aol.com
**Web:** www.pencarrow.co.uk
**Dir:** *4m NW of Bodmin, signposted off A389 & B3266*
Still a family home, this Georgian house has a superb collection of pictures, furniture and porcelain. The 50 acres of formal and woodland gardens include a Victorian rockery, a lake, 700 different rhododendrons and an acclaimed conifer collection. There is also a craft centre, a children's play area and a programme of special events throughout the year. Ring for details.
**Times:** House: Apr-25 Oct, Sun-Thu 11-5 (last house tour 4). Gardens: Daily Mar-Oct 9.30-5.30.

**Fee:** House & Garden £8. Gardens only £4 (ch £1). Family ticket £22. Party 20-30 £7 each, Party 31+ £6 each.
**Facilities:** 🅿 ⛻ (Licensed café) 🚻 🍽 £2.50 ♿ (1 wheelchair, disabled parking at house, toilets) shop, garden centre, guided tours, audio commentaries ⊗ (ex in grounds) 🚌 (prior bookings)

## CAMELFORD
### British Cycling Museum
The Old Station PL32 9TZ
☎ 01840 212811 📠 01840 212811
**Web:** www.chycor.co.uk/britishcyclingmuseum
**Dir:** *1m N of Camelford on B3266 at junct with B3314*
Located within easy reach of Camelford, the nation's
foremost museum of cycling history covers bicycles from
1818 to the present day, with over 400 cycles on display.
The museum also holds more than 1,000 cycling
medals, fobs and badges; an extensive library of bicycle
related publications; displays of gas, candle, battery and
oil lighting; and a fascinating collection of advertising
posters and enamel signs. There is also an old cycle
repair shop.
**Times:** Open all year, Sun-Thu 10-5.

**Fee:** *£3.25 (ch 5-17 £1.90).
**Facilities:** 🅿 ⛱ ♿ shop, guided tours
⊗ (ex guide dogs) 🚐 ☏

## DOBWALLS
### Dobwalls Family Adventure Park
Liskeard PL14 6HB
☎ 01579 320325 & 321129 📠 01579 321345
**Email:** dobwallsadventurepark@hotmail.com
**Web:** www.dobwallsadventurepark.co.uk
**Dir:** *turn off A38 in centre of Dobwalls and follow the
brown signs for approx 0.5m*
Plenty to do here, with stretches of miniature American
railroads to ride – there are steam and diesel locos,
visitors can take the Rio Grande ride through the forests
or the Union Pacific route over the prairies. There is also
Adventureland – action-packed areas filled with both
indoor and outdoor adventure play equipment.
**Times:** *Open Etr to Oct, daily 10.30-5 (10-5.30 high
season). Closed some days in Apr, May & Oct

**Fee:** *£8.95 (ch under 2 free, pen & disabled £5.50).
Family tickets available from £17.50-£52.95.
Groups 20+ £5.50 each.
**Facilities:** 🅿 ⛱ ♿ (manual wheelchairs subject to
availability, toilets) shop 🚐

## FALMOUTH
### National Maritime Museum Cornwall
Discovery Quay TR11 3QY
☎ 01326 313388 📠 01326 317878
**Email:** enquiries@nmmc.co.uk
**Web:** www.nmmc.co.uk
**Dir:** *follow signs from A39 for park/float ride and
museum*
Just one of the reasons to visit this important museum, is
to enjoy the breathtaking views from its 29-metre tower,
one of only three natural underwater viewing locations in
the world. There are hands-on interactives, audio-visual
immersive experiences, talks, special exhibitions and the
opportunity to get out onto the water and discover marine
life around the coastline. Use the Park & Float and sail to
the museum in a classic ferry.

**Times:** *Open daily 10-5. Closed 25 & 26 Dec
**Fee:** £7 (ch & concessions £4.80). Family ticket (2ad &
3ch) £18.50.
**Facilities:** 🅿 (charged) 🅿 (400 metres) 🍴 (locally
sourced food) ⛱ 🍴 ♿ (wheelchairs provided on arrival,
toilets) shop, guided tours ⊗ (ex guide dogs)
🚐 (prior booking)

## GOONHAVERN
### World in Miniature
Bodmin Road TR4 9QE

☎ 0870 458 4433 🖹 01872 572829

**Email:** info@worldinminiature.co.uk

**Web:** www.worldinminiature.co.uk

**Dir:** *turn off A30 at Boxheater junct onto B3285*

There are six major attractions for the price of one at this theme park. Visitors can stroll amongst famous landmarks such as the Taj Mahal and the Statue of Liberty, all in miniature scale and set in spectacular gardens. Then there is Tombstone, a wild-west town complete with saloon, bank, shops, livery stable and jail. The Adventure Dome is the original super cinema 180, direct from the USA, which shows two exciting films. Don't miss Jurassic Adventure World, Super X Simulator and the children's fairground rides. The 12-acre gardens are beautifully landscaped with over 70,000 plants and shrubs.

**Times:** *Open Etr-Oct, daily from 10.

**Fee:** *£6 (ch 4-14 & pen £4.50). Family ticket (2 ad & 2 ch) £19.

**Facilities:** 𝐏 🅰 ♿ (toilets) shop, garden centre 🚌

## GWEEK
### National Seal Sanctuary
Helston TR12 6UG

☎ 01326 221361 & 221874 🖹 01326 221210

**Email:** slcgweek@merlin-entertainments.com

**Web:** www.sealsanctuary.co.uk

**Dir:** *pass RNAS Culdrose & take A3293 & then B3291 to Gweek, the sanctuary is signed from village*

Britain's largest seal rescue facility – offering a unique opportunity to learn more about these beautiful creatures. The sanctuary has a hospital and nursery as well as convalescence and resident pools. Every year it rescues, rehabilitates and releases around 30 sick or abandoned seal pups. Newest residents are Chaff and Mika, South African Cape fur seals.

**Times:** *Open all year, daily from 10. Closed 25 Dec.

**Fee:** *Please call for admission prices.

**Facilities:** 𝐏 ⬚ (BBQ in Summer) 🅰 ♿ (toilets) shop, 🚌 (pre-booking advised)

## HELSTON
### Goonhilly Satellite Earth Station Experience
Goonhilly Downs TR12 6LQ

☎ 0800 679593 🖹 01326 221438

**Email:** goonhilly.visitorscentre@bt.com

**Web:** www.goonhilly.bt.com

**Dir:** *7m from Helston on B3293, Helston to St Keverne road*

Making a dramatic impression on the Lizard Peninsula landscape, this is the largest earth station in the world, with over 60 dishes. Opened in 1962 with only one dish, Goonhilly now handles millions of e-mails, phone calls, and TV broadcasts. In the fully interactive visitors' centre, explore the world of communications, experience tomorrow's technology today, and see your own animated 3D virtual head.

**Times:** Mid Feb-Mar, 11-4, closed Mon, Apr-May, 10-5 daily, Jun-Sep, 10-6 daily, Oct, 10-5 daily, Nov-Dec, 11-4, closed Mon. Closed 5 Jan-9 Feb.

**Fee:** *£6.50 (ch5-16 £4.50, under 4's free; conc £5)

**Facilities:** 𝐏 🅰 📱 £4.95 ♿ (induction loop, wheelchair height terminals, toilets) shop, guided tours, audio commentaries 🚫 (ex guide dogs) 🚌

## HELSTON
### The Flambards Experience
Culdrose Manor TR13 0QA
☎ 01326 573404 📠 01326 573344
**Email:** info@flambards.co.uk
**Web:** www.flambards.co.uk
**Dir:** *0.5m SE of Helston on A3083, Lizard road*
Three award-winning, all-weather attractions can be visited on one site here. Flambards Victorian Village, a recreation of streets, shops and houses from 1830-1910 and Britain in the Blitz, a life-size wartime street with shops, a pub and a living room with Morrison shelter. The Science Centre is a playground that brings physics alive for the whole family. In addition there are exciting rides and play areas for young visitors. The Wildlife Experience features lizards, snakes, large spiders and birds of prey.

**Times:** *Open winter 11-4. Summer 10-5. Times vary.
**Fee:** *£12.50 (ch 5-14 £9.55 over 55's £6.95). Family of 3 £31.50, of 4 £41, of 5 £50, of 6 £58.50.
**Facilities:** 🅿 🍴 ♿ (95% accessible, free loan of wheelchairs, route guides, toilets) shop, garden centre, audio commentaries (charged) 🚫 (ex guide dogs) 🚌 (15+ party to be pre-booked)

## LANHYDROCK
### Lanhydrock
Bodmin PL30 5AD
☎ 01208 265950 📠 01208 265959
**Email:** lanhydrock@nationaltrust.org.uk
**Web:** www.nationaltrust.org.uk
**Dir:** *2.5m SE of Bodmin, signed from A30, A38 & B3268*
Part-Jacobean, part-Victorian building that gives a vivid picture of life in Victorian times. The 'below stairs' sections have a huge kitchen, larders, dairy, bakehouse, cellars, and servants' quarters. The long gallery has a moulded ceiling showing Old Testament scenes, and overlooks the formal gardens with their superb clipped yews and bronze urns. The higher garden, famed for its magnolias and rhododendrons, climbs the hillside behind the house.

**Times:** Open mid Mar-Oct: House daily (ex Mon), 11-5.30 (11-5 in Oct), open BH Mon. Gardens daily from mid Feb, (last admission half hour before closing). Winter: Gardens, Nov-Feb during daylight hours.
**Fee:** House & Grounds £9.40 (ch £4.70). Grounds £5.30 (ch £2.65). Family ticket £23.50 one adult £14.10. Pre-booked group £8 each (ch £4 each)
**Facilities:** 🅿 🅿 (600yds) 🍴 (Licensed) 🍴 ♿ (lift, self drive buggy pre-book, wheelchairs, toilets) shop garden centre 🚫 (ex on lead in park) 🚌 (must pre-book) 🌿

## LAUNCESTON
### Launceston Steam Railway
St Thomas Road PL15 8DA
☎ 01566 775665
**Dir:** *turn off A30 Launceston, well signed*
Built as a subsidiary of the Great Western Railway the Launceston Steam Railway links the historic town of Launceston with the hamlet of New Mills. Tickets are valid for unlimited travel on the day of issue and you can break your journey at various points along the track. Launceston Station houses railway workshops, a transport museum, gift shop and book shop. Alongside the railway are the remains of Launceston Priory, destroyed after Henry VIII's Dissolution of the Monastries, the remains were rediscoverd when the railway was built in 1886.

**Times:** Open Whitsun to mid Sep, daily ex Sat.
**Fee:** *£6.75 (ch £4.40, concessions £5). Family ticket £20 (2 ad & up to 4 ch). Dogs 50p.
**Facilities:** 🅿 🅿 (100yds) car park closes 5.30pm, ☕ (snacks, cakes, sandwiches) 🍴 ♿ shop 🚌 ♿

## LAUNCESTON
### The Tamar Otter Sanctuary
North Petherwin PL15 8GW
☎ 01566 785646 📄 01986 892461
**Web:** www.ottertrust.org.uk/Tamar_Home.html
**Dir:** *5m NW off B3254 Bude road*
The Tamar Otter Sanctuary has a breeding programme
for the British otter and has to date bred and released
over 100 otters into the wild. Visitors to the sanctuary
can see otters in large natural enclosures, as well as
fallow and muntjac deer, waterfowl, and wallabies. There
is a rehabilitation centre for orphaned otters and a
dormouse conservation project. The Sanctuary also has
nature trails, a visitor centre, picnic areas, refreshments
and a shop.

**Times:** *Open Apr-Oct, daily 10.30-6
**Fee:** *£6 (ch £3.50)
**Facilities:** 🅿 🌧 ♿ shop ⊗ (ex guide dogs) 🚌 ♻

## LOOE
### The Monkey Sanctuary Trust
St Martins PL13 1NZ
☎ 01503 262532 📄 01503 262532
**Email:** info@monkeysanctuary.org
**Web:** www.monkeysanctuary.org
**Dir:** *signposted on B3253 at No Man's Land between
East Looe & Hessenford*
Visitors can see a colony of Amazonian woolly monkeys
in extensive indoor and outdoor territory. There are also
conservation gardens, children's play area, activity room,
a display room and vegetarian café. In addition a bat
cave is on site where visitors can watch a colony of rare
'horseshoe' bats.
**Times:** Open Sun-Thu from the Sun before Etr-end Sep.
Also open Autumn Half Term.

**Fee:** *£6 (under 5's free, ch £3.50 & concession £4.50).
Family ticket (2ad+2ch) £16.
**Facilities:** 🅿 ☕ (vegetarian, snacks, lunches) 🌧 📄
♿ (toilets) shop ⊗ 🚌 (coach width limited to 7ft 6in)

## MARAZION
### St Michael's Mount
Penzance TR17 0HT
☎ 01736 719476 & 710507 📄 01736 719930
**Email:** godolphin@manor-office.co.uk
**Web:** www.nationaltrust.org.uk
**Dir:** *access is by Causeway on foot at low tide. 0.5m S of
A394 at Marazion*
There is plenty of parking at Marazion and the tiny island
is a short stroll over the causeway at low tide, or a ferry
boat ride at high tide in the summer. St Michael's Mount
rises dramatically from the sea, a medieval castle to
which a magnificent east wing was added in the 1870s.
It is home to Lord St Leven, whose ancestor John St
Aubyn acquired it in the 17th century. There is much to
see and do including the house and St Michael's Church.

**Times:** Open Apr-Oct, Mon-Fri 10.30-5.30. Last
admission 4.45 on the island; Nov-Mar, telephone for
details.
**Fee:** £6.40 (ch £3.20) Family ticket £16. Party 20+
£5.60 each.
**Facilities:** 🅿 (on mainland) 🍴 (Licensed) 🌧
♿ (Braille guide, sandchair available) shop, guided tours
⊗ (ex guide dogs) 🚌 (advance booking) 🌿

## MAWNAN SMITH
### Glendurgan
TR11 5JZ

☎ 01872 862090 📠 01872 865808

**Email:** glendurgan@nationaltrust.org.uk

**Web:** www.nationaltrust.org.uk

**Dir:** *4m SW of Falmouth. 0.5m SW of Mawnan Smith on road to Helford Passage*

This delightful garden, set in a valley above the River Helford, was started by Alfred Fox in 1820. The informal landscape contains trees and shrubs from all over the world, including the Japanese loquat and tree ferns from New Zealand. There is a laurel maze, and a Giant's Stride which is popular with children. The house is not open.

**Times:** Open mid Feb-Oct, Tue-Sat & BH Mon. Last admission 4.30 (Closed Good Fri).

**Fee:** £5.20 (ch £2.60). Family ticket £13, family 1 ad £7.80

**Facilities:** ❷ Ⓟ (600yds)gates locked 5.30pm ☕ (self service tea house) ♿ (Braille guide, limited access to gardens/ground floor, toilets) shop, garden centre ⊗ (ex guide dogs) 🚌 (advance booking) 💐

---

## NEWQUAY
### Blue Reef Aquarium
Towan Promenade TR7 1DU

☎ 01637 878134 📠 01637 872578

**Email:** newquay@bluereefaquarium.co.uk

**Web:** www.bluereefaquarium.co.uk

**Dir:** *from A30 follow signs to Newquay, follow Blue Reef Aquarium signs to car park in town centre*

Take the ultimate undersea safari at the Blue Reef Aquarium. Discover Cornish marine life from native sharks and rays to the incredibly intelligent and playful octopus. From here journey through warmer waters to watch the magical seahorses, unusual shape shifting, jet-propelled cuttlefish and the vibrant, swaying tentacles of living sponges and anemones. Continue your safari through the underwater tunnel below a tropical sea. Where you will encounter the activities of a coral reef alive with shoals of brightly coloured fish and the graceful, black tip reef sharks which glide silently overhead. Daily talks and regular feeding demonstrations bring the experience to life.

**Times:** Open all year, daily 10-5. (Closed 25 Dec).Open until 6 during summer holidays.

**Fee:** *£6.99 (ch £4.99, concessions £5.99).

**Facilities:** Ⓟ (5mins walk – prior contact for disabled parking) ☕ (hot and cold food and drink) 🪑 ♿ (lifts, wheelchair, ramps, toilets) shop ⊗ (ex guide & service dogs) 🚌

---

## NEWQUAY
### Dairy Land Farm World
Summercourt TR8 5AA

☎ 01872 510246 📠 01872 510349

**Email:** info@dairylandfarmworld.co.uk

**Web:** www.dairylandfarmworld.com

**Dir:** *Signed from A30 at exit for Mitchell/Summercourt*

Visitors can watch while the cows are milked to music on a spectacular merry-go-round milking machine. The life of a Victorian farmer and his neighbours is explored in the Heritage Centre, and a Farm Nature Trail features informative displays along pleasant walks. Children will have fun getting to know the farm animals in the Farm Park. They will also enjoy the playground, assault course and indoor play areas.

**Times:** *Open daily, late Mar-Oct 10-5. (Bull pen additional winter openings Thu-Sun & school hols, please telephone for more information)

**Fee:** *£7.25 (ch £6.25, under 3s free, pen £5.25). Family Supersaver £25 (2 ad & up to 3 ch). Telephone about parties & groups.

**Facilities:** ❷ ☕ (light lunches and snacks) 🪑 ♿ (wheelchairs for loan; disabled viewing gallery for the milking machine, toilets) shop ⊗ 🚌 (advance booking)

**CORNWALL**

**CORNWALL**

## NEWQUAY
### Newquay Zoo
Trenance Gardens TR7 2LZ
☎ 01637 873342 🗎 01637 851318
**Email:** info@newquayzoo.org.uk
**Web:** www.newquayzoo.org.uk
**Dir:** *off A3075 and follow signs to Zoo*
There's always something new at Newquay Zoo. Explore the rainforest exhibit in the tropical house where you'll discover a world of exotic animals. Water cascades down the ancient temple walls to pools filled with tropical fish. Spot the iguanas, sloths and flying foxbats, and explore the mini-beasts room complete with Arrow Poison Frog enclosure. Among the sub-tropical lakeside gardens live hundreds of animals from around the world ranging from small monkeys to shy red pandas. Look out for meerkats on sentry duty, penguins splashing in their pool, or glimpse the endangered lemurs and fossa. The zoo gardens feature a Tarzan trail, children's play area, dragon maze, as well as picnic areas, snack bar and gift shop.
**Times:** *Open Apr-Sep, daily 9.30-6; Oct-Mar 10-dusk. (Closed 25 Dec)
**Fee:** Check website for admission charges.
**Facilities:** 🅿 (charged) Ⓟ (100yds – pay & display. Refunded on zoo entry) 🍽 (Licensed) 🏕 ♿ (80% access, wheelchairs, guided tours, sensory sculpture, toilets) shop ⊗ (ex guide dogs) 🚌 (booking preferred)

## PENDEEN
### Geevor Tin Mine
Penzance TR19 7EW
☎ 01736 788662 🗎 01736 786059
**Email:** bookings@geevor.com
**Web:** www.geevor.com
**Dir:** *Beside the B3306 Lands End to St Ives road. From Penzance take A3071 towards St Just, then the B3318 towards Pendeen. From St Ives follow B3306 to Pendeen*
A preserved tin mine and museum provide an insight into the methods and equipment used in the industry that was once so important in the area. The Geevor Tin Mine only actually stopped operation in 1990. Guided tours let visitors see the tin treatment plant, and a video illustrates the techniques employed. The underground tour is well worth the trip.
**Times:** Open daily except Sat 9-5, closes at 4pm Nov-Mar. Closed 21-26, 31 Dec & 1 Jan.
**Fee:** *£7.50 (ch & students £4.30, pen £7) Family £21
**Facilities:** 🅿 Ⓟ 🍽 🏕 📖 ♿ (lift, ramps, toilets) shop, guided tours ⊗ 🚌

## PENTEWAN
### The Lost Gardens of Heligan
St Austell PL26 6EN
☎ 01726 845100 🗎 01726 845101
**Email:** info@heligan.com
**Web:** www.heligan.com
**Dir:** *signposted from A390 & B3273*
Heligan, seat of the Tremayne family for more than 400 years, is one of the most mysterious estates in England. At the end of the 19th-century its thousand acres were at their zenith, but only a few years after the Great War, bramble and ivy were already drawing a green veil over this sleeping beauty. Today the garden offers 200 acres for exploration, which include productive gardens, pleasure grounds, sustainably-managed farmland, wetlands, and ancient woodlands. Please telephone for details of spring-time and harvest-time events and for summer evening theatre.
**Times:** *Open daily 10-6 (last admission 4.30pm): winter 10-dusk. Closed 24-25 Dec.
**Fee:** *£7.50. Please telephone to confirm concessions prices.
**Facilities:** 🅿 Ⓟ (2m) 🍴 (Licensed) 🍽 (Licensed) 🏕 ♿ (free loan of wheelchairs and trained access advisors, toilets) shop, garden centre 🚌 (booking essential)

## POOL

**Cornish Mines & Engines**

Redruth TR15 3NP

☎ 01209 315027 & 210900 🖷 01209 315027

**Email:** jane.affleck@nationaltrust.org.uk

**Dir:** *2m W of Redruth on A3047, signposted from A30, Pool exit*

Impressive relics of the tin mining industry, these great beam engines were used for pumping water from 2000ft down and for lifting men and ore from the workings below ground. The mine at East Pool has been converted into the Cornwall Industrial Heritage Centre which includes audio visual theatre giving background to all aspects of Cornwall's industrial heritage.

**Times:** *Open Apr-Oct, Sun-Fri 11-5.

**Fee:** *£5 (ch £2.50, under 5's free, 2 adult family £12.50, 1 adult family £7.50) Groups 15+ £4.30 each.

**Facilities:** 🅿 ℗ (100mtrs) ♿ ⛪ (lift to all levels, toilets) shop, guided tours ⊗ (ex guide dogs) 🚌 (pre-booked) ❧

## ST AUSTELL

**Charlestown Shipwreck & Heritage Centre**

Quay Road Charlestown PL25 3NJ

☎ 01726 69897 🖷 01726 69897

**Email:** admin@shipwreckcharlestown.com

**Web:** www.shipwreckcharlestown.com

**Dir:** *signed off A390 from St. Austell close to Eden Project*

Charlestown is a small and unspoilt village with a unique sea-lock, china-clay port, purpose built in the 18th century. The Shipwreck and Heritage Centre was originally a dry house for china clay built on underground tunnels. Now it houses the largest display of shipwreck artefacts in the UK, along with local heritage, diving exhibits, and a Titanic display. A recent addition is a Nelson display to commemorate the Battle of Trafalgar.

**Times:** Open Mar-Oct, daily 10-5 (later in high season). (Last admission 1 hour before closing)

**Fee:** £5.95 (ch under 10 free if accompanied by paying adult, ch under 16 £2.50, concessions £3.95) group prices on request.

**Facilities:** 🅿 (charged) ℗ (150yds) ⛩ (Licensed) 🍴 ⛪ (ramps in place, toilets) shop, guided tours ⊗ not in restaurant 🚌 pre-booking preferred

## ST AUSTELL

**Eden Project**

Bodelva PL24 2SG

☎ 01726 811911 🖷 01726 811912

**Email:** information@edenproject.com

**Web:** www.edenproject.com

**Dir:** *overlooking St Austell Bay signposted from A390/A30/A391*

An unforgettable experience in a breathtaking location, the Eden Project is a gateway into the fascinating world of plants and human society. Space age technology meets the lost world in the biggest greenhouse ever built. Located in a 50-metre deep crater the size of 30 football pitches are two gigantic geodesic conservatories: the Humid Tropics Biome and the Warm Temperate Biome. This is a startling and unique day out.

**Times:** *Open daily Mar-Oct 10-6 (last admission 4.30), Nov-Mar 10-4.30 (last admission 3).

**Fee:** *£13.80 (ch 5-15 £5, student £7 concessions £10). Family ticket £34. Annual membership available.

**Facilities:** 🅿 ♿ ⛪ (wheelchairs, car shuttle to visitor centre/biomes, toilets) shop, garden centre, guided tours ⊗ (ex guide dogs) 🚌 (must be pre-booked 01726 811903)

**CORNWALL**

## TREDINNICK
### Cornwall's Crealy Great Adventure Park
Trelow Farm Wadebridge PL27 7RA
☎ 01841 541215
**Email:** shirespark@tiscali.co.uk
**Dir:** *signposted off A39*
The Crealy Great Adventure Park is a fun-packed day out for all the family. The excitement includes 'The Haunted Castle', full of demons, skeletons and ghosts; the 'Dragon Kingdom', an indoor adventure zone with slides, climbs, ropes, balls and towers. Take a walk through the Enchanted Forest to Greengate Meadow and meet fully animated moles, Mr Badger and their woodland friends. New attractions include Thunder Falls, a double log flume ride, the Raging River Watercoaster and a Viking Warrior Pirate Ship. There are acres of outdoor adventure play

with aerial bridges and steep slides as well as train rides around the lakes and the majestic Shire Horses including new born foals with farmyard friends.
**Times:** *Open Good Friend Oct, daily 10-5.
**Fee:** *£8 (ch £7, pen £5)
**Facilities:** ℗ ⑩ (Licensed) 🍴 ♿ (most areas are ramped, toilets) shop 🚐 ⊘

## WENDRON
### Poldark Mine and Heritage Complex
Helston TR13 0ER
☎ 01326 573173 🖨 01326 563166
**Email:** info@poldark-mine.com
**Web:** www.poldark-mine.com
**Dir:** *3m from Helston on B3297 Redruth road, follow brown signs*
The centre of this attraction is the 18th-century tin mine where visitors can join a guided tour of workings which retain much of their original character. The site's Museum explains the history of tin production in Cornwall from 1800BC through to the 19th century and the fascinating story of the Cornish overseas. In addition to the Museum, the audio-visual presentation gives more insight into Cornwall's mining heritage.

**Times:** *Open Etr-1st wk Nov, 10-5.30 (last tour 4).
**Fee:** *Guided Underground Tour: £5.95 (ch 5-15 £3.95) Family (2aduls+2ch) £16.45.
**Facilities:** ℗ 🍴 ♿ (newly refurbished museum allowing disabled access) shop 🚐 (prior booking preferred)

## ZENNOR
### Wayside Folk Museum
St Ives TR26 3DA
☎ 01736 796945
**Dir:** *4m W of St Ives, on B3306*
Until the 19th century Zennor remained in considerable isolation. There were no roads and everything came by packhorse. Consequently life didn't change very much. With such a wealth of ancient implements and local customs Colonel 'Freddie' Hurst founded the folk museum in 1937. It covers every aspect of life in Zennor and the surrounding district from 3,000BC to the 1930s. Over 5,000 items are displayed in 16 display areas and cover the activities of wheelwrights, blacksmiths, local agriculture, fishing and mining. There are items from local wrecks and archaeological artefacts as well as

many items of domestic life. A photographic exhibition entitled People of the Past tells the story of the village. The museum also contains a watermill to which visitors have access.
**Times:** *Open Etr-end Oct, daily 10.30-5.30.
**Fee:** *£3 (ch £1.85). Party rates 10+.
**Facilities:** ℗ (50yds) 🍴 🍽 ♿ (not suitable for wheelchair users) shop 🚐 (book for discount)

## BEER
### Pecorama Pleasure Gardens
Underleys EX12 3NA
☎ 01297 21542 📄 01297 20229
**Email:** pecorama@btconnect.com
**Web:** www.peco-uk.com
**Dir:** *from A3052 take B3174, Beer road, signed*
Overlooking Beer, a miniature steam and diesel
passenger line offers visitors a stunning view of Lyme
Bay as it runs through the Pleasure Gardens. Attractions
include an aviary, crazy golf, a children's activity area,
Peco Millennium Garden and an exhibition of railway
modelling in various small gauges. Please telephone for
details of events running throughout the year.
**Times:** Open Etr-Oct , Mon-Fri 10-5.30, Sat 10-1.Open
Sun Etr & 27 May-early Sep.

**Fee:** *£5.75 (ch 4-14 £3.80, pen £5.25, over 80 &
under 4 free)
**Facilities:** 🅿 Ⓟ (0.5m) ⛻ (Restaurant car from Pullman
train.) 🍽 (Licensed) 🚻 ♿ (access with helper,
wheelchair. Garden steep in places, toilets) shop guided
tours Ⓧ (ex guide dogs) 🚌 (advanced booking
preferred)

## BICTON
### Bicton Park Botanical Gardens
East Budleigh Exeter EX9 7BJ
☎ 01395 568465 📄 01395 568374
**Email:** info@bictongardens.co.uk
**Web:** www.bictongardens.co.uk
**Dir:** *2m N of Budleigh Salterton on B3178, leave M5 at
junct 30 & follow brown tourist signs*
Unique Grade I-listed 18th-century historic gardens with
palm house, orangery, plant collections, extensive
countryside museum, indoor and outdoor activity play
areas, pinetum, arboretum, nature trail, woodland railway
garden centre and restaurant. All this set in 63 acres of
beautiful parkland that has been cherished for 300 years.
**Times:** Open Winter 10-5, Summer 10-6. Closed 25 &
26 Dec.

**Fee:** *£5.95 (ch & concessions £4.95). Family ticket (2
ad, 2 ch) £19.95.
**Facilities:** 🅿 🍽 (Licensed) 🚻 ♿ (adapted carriage on
woodland railway, wheelchairs, toilets) shop, garden
centre 🚌

## BLACKMOOR GATE
### Exmoor Zoological Park
South Stowford Bratton Fleming EX31 4SG
☎ 01598 763352 📄 01598 763352
**Email:** exmoorzoo@fsbdial.co.uk
**Web:** www.exmoorzoo.co.uk
**Dir:** *off A361 onto A399, follow brown tourist signs*
Exmoor Zoo is both personal and friendly. Open since
1982 it is an ideal family venue, catering particularly for
the younger generation. The zoo participates in international breeding programmes, and specialises in smaller
animals, many endangered, such as the golden headed
lion tamarins. Over 14 species of this type of primate are
exhibited. Contact pens are provided throughout and
children are encouraged to participate. Twice daily guided
tours at feeding times along with handling sessions.

**Times:** *Open daily, Apr-Oct 10-6; Nov-Mar 10-4.
**Fee:** *£7.50 (ch £5.50, concessions £6.50).
**Facilities:** 🅿 🚻 📋 ♿ (toilets) shop, guided tours
Ⓧ (ex guide dogs) 🚌 (booking advisable)

**DEVON**

**DEVON**

## BUCKFASTLEIGH
**Buckfast Butterfly Farm &**
**Dartmoor Otter Sanctuary**
TQ11 0DZ
☎ 01364 642916
**Email:** contact@ottersandbutterflies.co.uk
**Web:** www.ottersandbutterflies.co.uk
**Dir:** off A38, at Dart Bridge junct, follow tourist signs
Visitors can wander around this specially designed, undercover tropical garden, where free-flying butterflies and moths from around the world can be experienced as they flutter around the trees and shrubs. The otter sanctuary has large enclosures with underwater viewing areas. There are three types of otters that can be seen – the native British otter along with Asian and North American otters.

**Times:** Open Good Fri-end Oct, daily 10-5.30 or dusk (if earlier).
**Fee:** *£5.95 (ch £4.50, pen £5.50). Family ticket £16.95.
**Facilities:** ❷ ⓟ (100yds) ☐ (Light refreshments and lunches) ⊼ 📋 ♿ (wheelchair ramps) shop, guided tours ⊗ (ex guide dogs) 🚌

## CHITTLEHAMPTON
**Cobbaton Combat Collection**
Cobbaton Umberleigh EX37 9RZ
☎ 01769 540740 📄 01769 540141
**Email:** info@cobbatoncombat.co.uk
**Web:** www.cobbatoncombat.co.uk
**Dir:** signed from A361 & A377
World War II British and Canadian military vehicles, war documents and military equipment can be seen in this private collection. There are over 50 vehicles including tanks, one a Gulf War Centurian, and a recently added Warsaw Pact section. There is also a section on 'Mum's War' and the Home Front. The Home Front section is now in a new purpose-built building.
**Times:** *Open Apr-Oct, daily (ex Sat) 10-5; Jul-Aug daily. Winter most wkdays, phone for details.

**Fee:** *£5.25 (ch £3.75, pen £4.75).
**Facilities:** ❷ ☐ (summer only) ⊼ ♿ (most areas accessible, toilets) shop ⊗ (ex guide dogs, outside) 🚌

## CHUDLEIGH
**Canonteign Falls**
Exeter EX6 7NT
☎ 01647 252434 📄 01647 52617
**Email:** info@canonteignfalls.com
**Web:** www.canonteignfalls.com
**Dir:** off A38 at Chudleigh/Teign Valley junct onto B3193 and follow tourist signs for 3m
A magical combination of waterfalls, woodlands and lakes. Set in the beautiful Teign Valley Canonteign Falls is the highest waterfall in England, falling almost vertically for 220 feet. The whole area can be explored via laid walks and trails; there is a junior commando course, a fern centre, picnic areas, a restaurant and a shop.
**Times:** *Open all year, summer 10-6, winter 10-dusk. Last admission 1 hour before closing

**Fee:** *£5.75 (ch £3.50, pen £4.75). Family ticket £16.50.
**Facilities:** ❷ ☐ (hot and cold snacks, summer bbq) 🍽 (Licensed) ⊼ 📋 ♿ (grounds partly accessible, toilets) shop, guided tours 🚌

## CHURSTON FERRERS
**Greenway Garden**

Brixham TQ5 0ES

☎ 01803 842382 📄 01803 661900

**Email:** greenway@nationaltrust.org.uk

**Web:** www.nationaltrust.org.uk/devoncornwall

**Dir:** *off A3022 into Galmpton. Follow Manor Vale Rd into village then follow brown signs for Greenway Garden*

Greenway is a beautiful woodland garden set on the banks of the River Dart which time seems to have passed by. A garden held on the edge of wilderness, renowned for rare half-hardy trees and shrubs, underplanted by native wild flowers, Devon's best kept secret. The surrounding estate has many walks which give stunning views over the estuary. Travel by river to enjoy this peaceful haven. Greenway is not easily accessible, having some steep and slippery paths and all visitors are asked to wear walking shoes and to follow routes and directions according to their suitability on the day.

**Times:** *Open Mar-7 Oct, Wed-Sat, 10.30-5.

**Fee:** *£5 (ch £2.50) Groups £4.25. Green visitors (not by car) £4.25 (ch £2).

**Facilities:** 🅿 🍴 📱 ♿ (part access to garden, Braille guide, large print, T Loop, toilets) shop, guided tours ⊗ (ex guide dogs & in parkland) 🚌 (up to 25 people) 🦋

## CLOVELLY
**The Milky Way Adventure Park**

Bideford EX39 5RY

☎ 01237 431255 📄 01237 431735

**Email:** info@themilkyway.co.uk

**Web:** www.themilkyway.co.uk

**Dir:** *on A39, 2m from Clovelly*

One of the West Country's leading sites for the biggest rides and the best shows. Attractions include Clone Zone - Europe's first interactive adventure ride featuring a suspended roller coaster; Time Warp - indoor adventure play area; daily displays from the North Devon Bird of Prey Centre; archery centre; golf driving nets; railway; pets corner and more. 'Droid Destroyer Dodgems' invites pilots to save the Earth from the Vega Asteroid. Look out for the Thatched Café or the Galactic Café.

**Times:** Open Apr-Oct, daily 10.30-6.

**Fee:** *£8 (ch under 1m £6, pen £6, under 3's free).

**Facilities:** 🅿 🍴 ♿ (ramps, toilets) shop 🚌 (pre-booking preferred)

## CLYST ST MARY
**Crealy Adventure Park**

Sidmouth Road Exeter EX5 1DR

☎ 01395 233200 📄 01395 233211

**Email:** fun@crealy.co.uk

**Web:** www.crealy.co.uk

**Dir:** *M5 junct 30 onto A3052 Exeter to Sidmouth road*

Crealy Adventure Park offers an unforgettable day for all the family with Tidal Wave log flume, El Pastil Loco Coaster, Queen Bess Pirate Ship, Techno Race Karts, Bumper Boats, Victorian Carousel, Funosaurus show and all weather play area. Visit the Animal Realm to ride, feed, milk, groom or cuddle the animals. Relax on the Prairie Train through the world's 1st Sunflower Maze.

**Times:** *Open all year, Jan-mid July & 6 Sep-Dec, daily 10-5. Closed winter term time Mon-Tue; mid Jul-5 Sep, daily 10-6.

**Fee:** *£8.95-£9.95 (ch under 92cm free, pen £6.20-£7.20). Party 4+ £8.65-£9.65. Lower rates during winter months

**Facilities:** 🅿 🅿 (20mtrs) 🍽 (Licensed) 🍴♿ (carers admitted free, rollercoaster has disabled facility, toilets) shop 🚌 (prior notice preferred)

**DEVON**

## COMBE MARTIN
### Combe Martin Wildlife & Dinosaur Park
Ilfracombe EX34 0NG
☎ 01271 882486 📄 01271 883869
**Email:** info@dinosaur-park.com
**Web:** www.dinosaur-park.com
**Dir:** *M5 junct 27 then A361 towards Barnstaple, turn right onto A399*
The land that time forgot. A subtropical paradise with hundreds of birds and animals and realistic animatronic dinosaurs! There are sealion shows, falconry displays, animal handling sessions and the UK's only Wolf Education and Research Centre. Animals include meerkats, snow leopards, timber wolves, monkeys and apes. There are additional attractions, a spectacular light-show and the most unique train ride in the UK.

**Times:** *Open 18 Mar-29 Oct, daily 10-5.30 (last admission 3).
**Fee:** *£12 (ch 3-15 £7, ch under 3 free, pen £8). Family (2ad+2ch) £34.
**Facilities:** 🅿 Ⓟ (no caravans or large vehicles) 🍴 (fast food, drinks and snacks) 🪑 📦 ♿ (toilets) shop ⊗ 🚌 (pre-booking preferred)

## CULLOMPTON
### Diggerland
Verbeer Manor EX15 2PE
☎ 08700 344437 📄 0901 2010 300
**Email:** mail@diggerland
**Web:** www.diggerland.com
**Dir:** *M5 junct 27. E on A38 & at rdbt turn right onto A3181. Diggerland is 3m on left*
An adventure park with a difference, where kids of all ages can experience the thrills of driving real earth moving equipment. Choose from various types of diggers and dumpers ranging from 1 ton to 8.5 tons. Supervised by an instructor complete the Dumper Truck Challenge or dig for buried treasure. New rides include JCB Robots, the Supertrack, Landrover Safari and Spin Dizzy. Even under 5's can join in, with mum or dad's help. Please

telephone for details of events during school and Bank Holidays.
**Times:** *Open mid Feb-Nov, BHs & school hols.
**Fee:** *£2.50 (pen £1.25, under 2's free). Additional charge to drive/ride machinery.
**Facilities:** 🅿 🪑 ♿ shop ⊗ (ex guide dogs) 🚌

## DARTMOUTH
### Woodlands Leisure Park
Blackawton TQ9 7DQ
☎ 01803 712598 📄 01803 712680
**Email:** fun@woodlandspark.com
**Web:** www.woodlandspark.com
**Dir:** *W, off A3122*
A family day out of variety and fun with 60 acres of unique indoor and outdoor attractions, with 13 family rides. The park features; 3 Watercoasters, 500mtr Toboggan Run, Boats and 15 Playzones. Entertain the family for hours in the incredible indoor playcentres with action challenges and interactive play including rides, a train, Trauma Tower with 50ft sheer drop and Master Blaster. Superb Falconry Centre with flying displays, animals and birds galore.

**Times:** Open daily 10 Mar-4 Nov, 5 Nov-Mar wknds and school holidays only.
**Fee:** £9.25 (under 92cms Free). Family ticket £35.20 (2ad+2ch).
**Facilities:** 🅿 🪑 (wknds only in winter, and school hols) 🪑 📦 ♿ (ramps, toilets) shop ⊗ (ex guide dogs) 🚌 (over 10 persons)

## DREWSTEIGNTON
### Castle Drogo
EX6 6PB

☎ 01647 433306 📄 01647 433186

**Email:** castledrogo@nationaltrust.org.uk

**Web:** www.nationaltrust.org.uk

**Dir:** *5m S of A30 Exeter-Okehampton. Coaches turn off A382 at Sandy Park*

India tea baron Julius Drewe's dream house. This granite castle, built between 1910 and 1930, is one of the most remarkable works of Sir Edward Lutyens, and combines the grandeur of a medieval castle with the comfort of the 20th century. A great country house with terraced formal garden, woodland spring garden, huge circular croquet lawn and colourful herbaceous borders. Standing at more than 900ft overlooking the wooded gorge of the River Teign with stunning views of Dartmoor, and delightful walks.

**Times:** Castle open 17 Mar-4 Nov, daily (ex Tue) 11-5. Garden, tearooms & shop open 17 Mar-4 Nov daily.

**Fee:** *House & garden £6.80 (ch £3.30). Family £16.50. Garden only £4.50 (ch £2.50)

**Facilities:** 🅿 🚻 ♿ (Braille & large print guide, touch list, toilets) shop, garden centre, guided tours ⊗ (ex guide/hearing dogs) 🚌 (40 people per group) ❧

## EXMOUTH
### The World of Country Life
Sandy Bay EX8 5BU

☎ 01395 274533 📄 01392 227131

**Dir:** *M5 junct 30, take A376 to Exmouth. Follow signs to Sandy Bay*

All-weather family attraction including owl displays and a safari train that rides through a forty-acre deer park. Kids will enjoy the friendly farm animals, pets' centre and the animal nursery. The perfect place for wet weather, two acres of buildings contain a Victorian street and superb displays of working models from a bygone age, including agricultural machinery, steam and vintage vehicles. All in all there are thousands of exhibits to be enjoyed. In addition there is an adventure playground with an indoor Pirate Ship Adventure.

**Times:** *Open Etr-Oct, daily 10-5.

**Fee:** *£8 (ch 3-17 & pen £7). Family ticket (2 ad & 2 ch) £28.

**Facilities:** 🅿 🚻 ♿ (all parts accessible ex 'safari train', toilets) shop ⊗ (ex guide dogs) 🚌

## ILFRACOMBE
### Watermouth Castle & Family Theme Park
EX34 9SL

☎ 01271 863879 📄 01271 865864

**Web:** www.watermouthcastle.com

**Dir:** *3m NE off A399, midway between Ilfracombe & Combe Martin*

A popular family attraction with lots to see and do including mechanical music demonstrations, a musical water show, dungeon labyrinths, Victorian displays, bygone pier machines, animated fairy tale scenes, a tube slide, mini golf, a children's carousel, swingboats, aeroplane ride, water fountains, river ride, gardens and even a maze.

**Times:** *Open Apr-end Oct, closed Sat. (Also closed some Mon & Fri off season). Ring for further details.

**Fee:** *£10 (ch 3-13 £8.50 & pen £7)

**Facilities:** 🅿 🍴 (Self service) 🚻 🎁 ♿ (special wheelchair route, toilets) shop ⊗ (ex guide dogs) 🚌 (must pre-book)

## KINGSBRIDGE
### Cookworthy Museum of Rural Life
The Old Grammar School 108 Fore Street TQ7 1AW
☎ 01548 853235
**Email:** wcookworthy@talk21.com
**Web:** www.devonmuseums.net
**Dir:** *A38 onto A384, then A381 to Kingsbridge, museum at top of town*
The 17th-century schoolrooms of this former grammar school are now the setting for another kind of education. Reconstructed room-sets of a Victorian kitchen, an Edwardian pharmacy, a costume room and extensive collection of local historical items are gathered to illustrate South Devon life. A walled garden and farm gallery are also features of this museum, founded to commemorate William Cookworthy, 'father' of the English china clay industry. The Local Heritage Resource Centre with public access databases, microfilm of local newspapers since 1855 and Devon record service point are available to visitors. Please ring for details of special events. All in a Day's Work explores and celebrates the long tradition of skilled craftsmen and women.
**Times:** Open all year, 26 Mar-Sep, Mon-Sat 10.30-5; Oct 10.30-4. Nov-Mar groups by arrangement. Local Heritage Resource Centre open all year, Mon-Thu 10-12 & Wed also 2-4, other times by appointment.
**Fee:** £2 (ch £1, concessions £1.50). Family ticket £5 (2ad+4ch).
**Facilities:** ℗ (100mtrs - max 3hrs) ⃫ ▤ ♿ (Braille labels on selected exhibits, viewing gallery, toilets) shop, guided tours ⊘ (ex guide dogs) 🚌 (max 50 people) ♺

## LYDFORD
### Lydford Gorge
EX20 4BH
☎ 01822 820320 & 820441 ▤ 01822 822000
**Email:** lydfordgorge@nationaltrust.org.uk
**Web:** www.nationaltrust.org.uk
**Dir:** *off A386, between Okehampton & Tavistock*
The spectacular gorge has been formed by the River Lyd, which has cut into the rock and caused swirling boulders to scoop out potholes in the stream bed. This has created some dramatic features, notably the Devil's Cauldron close to Lydford Bridge. At the end of the gorge is the 90ft-high White Lady Waterfall.
**Times:** *Open Mar-Sep, daily 10-5; Oct, daily 10-4. (Winter opening Nov-Mar, please ring for details).
**Fee:** *£5 (ch 5-16 £2.50, under 5 free). Family ticket (2ad & 3ch) £12.50.
**Facilities:** ℗ ℗ (400yds – limited coach parking, book in advance) ⊒ (tearoom) ⃫ ▤ £1 ♿ (easy access path, audio tapes, braille guide, toilets) shop, garden centre, guided tours 🚌 (book in advance for parking) ♼

## MORWELLHAM
### Morwellham Quay
Tavistock PL19 8JL
☎ 01822 832766 & 833808 ▤ 01822 833808
**Email:** enquiries@morwellham-quay.co.uk
**Web:** www.morwellham-quay.co.uk
**Dir:** *4m W of Tavistock, off A390. Midway between Gunnislake & Tavistock. Signed*
A unique, open-air museum based around the ancient port and copper mine workings in the heart of the Tamar Valley. Journey back into another time as costumed interpreters help you re-live the daily life of a 19th-century mining village and shipping quay. A tramway takes you deep into the workings of the George and Charlotte mine. Special events include music festivals, classic car shows, and a Victorian food festival.
**Times:** *Open all year (ex Xmas wk) 10-6 (4.30 Nov-Etr). Last admission 3.30 (2.30 Nov-Etr).
**Fee:** *£8.90 (ch 5-16 £6, pen & students £7.80). Family ticket (2ad + 2ch) £26
**Facilities:** ℗ ⊒ (Jul-Aug) ⦿ (Licensed) ⃫ ▤ ♿ (difficult areas in Victorian village, toilets) shop, guided tours, 🚌 (advance booking preferred)

## NEWTON ABBOT
### Hedgehog Hospital at Prickly Ball Farm
Denbury Rd East Ogwell TQ12 6BZ
☎ 01626 362319 & 330685 📄 01626 330685
**Email:** enquiries@pricklyballfarm.co.uk
**Web:** www.pricklyballfarm.co.uk
**Dir:** *1.5m from Newton Abbot on A381 towards Totnes, follow brown heritage signs*
See, touch and learn about this wild animal. In mid-season see baby hogs bottle feeding. Find out how the prickly patients are returned to the wild. There are talks throughout the day, with a big screen presentation, telling all about hedgehogs and how to encourage them into your garden. There are also pony and cart rides, goat walking, pony grooming, lamb feeding (in season), and a petting zoo.

**Times:** *Open Etr-end Oct, 10-5. (Recommended last admission 3.30)
**Fee:** *£5.75 (ch 4-14 £4.75, ch under 3 free, concessions £5). Family ticket £18.95.
**Facilities:** 🅿 🍴 ♿ (large print menu, use of wheelchair, Braille menu, toilets) shop, guided tours ⊗ (ex guide dogs) 🚌

## PAIGNTON
### Paignton & Dartmouth Steam Railway
Queens Park Station Torbay Road TQ4 6AF
☎ 01803 555872 📄 01803 664313
**Email:** mail@pdsr.eclipse.co.uk
**Web:** www.paignton-steamrailway.co.uk
**Dir:** *from Paignton follow brown tourist signs*
Steam trains run for seven miles from Paignton to Kingswear on the former Great Western line, stopping at Goodrington Sands, Churston, and Kingswear, connecting with the ferry crossing to Dartmouth. Combined river excursions available. Ring for details of special events.
**Times:** *Open Jun-Sep, daily 9-5.30 & selected days Oct & Apr-May.
**Fee:** *Paignton to Kingswear £7.40 (ch £5.10, pen £6.80). Family £23. Paignton to Dartmouth (including ferry) £9 (ch £6, pen £8.50). Family £28.
**Facilities:** 🅿 (5mins walk) 🍽 (buffet at Kingswear & Paignton Station) ♿ (wheelchair ramp for boarding train, toilets) shop 🚌

## PAIGNTON
### Paignton Zoo Environmental Park
Totnes Road TQ4 7EU
☎ 01803 697500 📄 01803 523457
**Email:** info@paigntonzoo.org.uk
**Web:** www.paigntonzoo.org.uk
**Dir:** *1m from Paignton town centre on A3022 Totnes road. Follow brown signs*
Paignton is one of Britain's biggest zoos, set in a beautiful and secluded woodland valley. A tour will take you through some of the world's threatened habitats - Forest, Savannah, Wetland and Desert, with hundreds of species, many of them endangered and part of conservation breeding programmes. There are regular keeper talks, a children's play area, and special events throughout the year.

**Times:** Open all year, daily 10-6 (5 in winter). Last admission 5 (4 in winter). Closed 25 Dec.
**Fee:** £11.35 (ch 3-15 £7.60, conc £9.35). Family ticket (2ad & 2ch) £34.10. (including Living Coasts £49.15).
**Facilities:** 🅿 🅿 (100yds) 🍽 (Licensed) 🍴♿ (some steep hills, wheelchair loan-booking essential, toilets) shop guided tours ⊗ (ex guide dogs) 🚌

**DEVON**

## PLYMOUTH
### The Elizabethan House
32 New Street The Barbican PL1 7FW
☎ 01752 304774 📄 01752 304775
**Email:** enquiry@plymouthmuseum.gov.uk
**Web:** www.plymouthmuseum.gov.uk
**Dir:** *A38/A374 follow signs to city centre, house located just behind Southside Street*
On Plymouth's historic Barbican, find an ancient doorway and go back in time to Drake's Plymouth. Home of an Elizabethan merchant or sea captain, the house is an opportunity to see how an Elizabethan mariner might have lived. A rare Tudor time-capsule with furniture and fabrics dating back to the 1600s.
**Times:** *Open Apr-Sep, Tue-Sat & BH Mon, 10-5 (last entry 4.30)

**Fee:** *£1.30 (ch 80p). Family tickets & other concessions available
**Facilities:** ℗ (200yds) ♿ shop garden centre ⊛

## POWDERHAM
### Powderham Castle
Exeter EX6 8JQ
☎ 01626 890243 📄 01626 890729
**Email:** castle@powderham.co.uk
**Web:** www.powderham.co.uk
**Dir:** *signed off A379 Exeter/Dawlish road*
Built between 1390 and 1420, this ancestral home of the Earls of Devon was damaged in the Civil War. The house was restored and altered in later times and is set in beautiful rose gardens with views over the deer park to the Exe Estuary. Much of the house is open to the public and in the grounds there is a Secret Garden, Falconry displays, Archery and a Fort. From antique fairs to concerts there is a varied programme of special events – please telephone for details.

**Times:** *Open Etr-end Oct, 10-5.30 (last admission 5). Closed Sat.
**Fee:** *£7.45 (ch £4.15, pen £4.25). Family ticket £19.90 concessions £5.65
**Facilities:** 🅿 ℗ (200yds) ☕ (light lunches) 🍴 (Licensed) ⊞ ♿ (ramps, toilets) shop, garden centre 🚌

## SALCOMBE
### Overbeck's
Sharpitor TQ8 8LW
☎ 01548 842893 📄 01548 845020
**Email:** overbecks@nationaltrust.org.uk
**Web:** www.nationaltrust.org.uk
**Dir:** *1.5m SW of Salcombe, signed from Malborough & Salcombe, narrow approach road*
The garden is on the most southerly tip of Devon, and the mild temperatures allow many exotic plants to flourish. The Edwardian house displays toys, dolls and a natural history collection, and there is a secret room for children where they can search for 'Fred' the friendly ghost.
**Times:** *Open Apr-Jul, Sun-Fri 11-5.30; Aug, daily 11-5.30; Sep, Sun-Fri 11-5.30; Oct, Sun-Thu 11-5. Gardens open all year, 10-6 (or sunset if earlier).

**Fee:** Gardens & house £5.80 (ch £2.90). Family ticket £14.50.
**Facilities:** 🅿 ℗ (600yds – approach steep/narrow: no coaches) ☕ (light lunches) ⊞ ♿ (ramp from garden, Braille guide, hearing loop) shop, guided tours (charged) 🚫 (ex assist dogs) 🚌 (by arrangement only) 🌿

## SOUTH MOLTON
### Quince Honey Farm
EX36 3AZ

☎ 01769 572401 📄 01769 574704
**Email:** info@quincehoney.co.uk
**Web:** www.quincehoney.com
**Dir:** *3.5m W of A361, on N edge of South Molton*

Follow the story of honey and beeswax from flower to table. This exhibition allows you to see the world of honey bees close up and in complete safety. The interactive displays open the hives at the press of a button, revealing the honeybees' secret life in all its complexity. After viewing the bees at work, the fruits of their labour are available in the café or shop.
**Times:** *Open daily, Apr-Sep 9-6; Oct 9-5; Shop only Nov-Etr 9-5, closed Sun. Closed 25 Dec-4 Jan.

**Fee:** *£3.95 (ch 5-16 £2.75, pen £3.25)
**Facilities:** 🅿 ⬚ (self service) 🍴 📷 ♿ (toilets) shop ⊗ (ex guide dogs) 🚌

## TORQUAY
### Babbacombe Model Village
Hampton Avenue Babbacombe TQ1 3LA

☎ 01803 328669 & 315315 📄 01803 315173
**Email:** ss@babbacombemodelvillage.co.uk
**Web:** www.babbacombemodelvillage.co.uk
**Dir:** *follow brown tourist signs from outskirts of town*

Set in four acres of beautifully maintained, miniature landscaped garden, the village contains over 400 models and 1200ft of model railway. City Lights, an evening illuminations feature, depicts Piccadilly Circus in miniature. At the end of your visit, enjoy a new facility that offers breathtaking views over the model village. Vintage model railway layout; the Aquaviva, an evening water, light and sound spectacular and the new 'Silvers Model Circus'.

**Times:** * May-Sep, 10-9.30 (10-5 Sat), winter 10-3.30 (ex 18 Nov-Dec, 10-7).
**Fee:** *£6.90 (ch £4.50, pen £5.90). Family ticket £20.
**Facilities:** 🅿 (charged) Ⓟ (street parking )🍴 ⊙ 🍴 📷 ♿ (push button audio information, toilets) shop, garden centre 🚌

## TORQUAY
### 'Bygones'
Fore Street St Marychurch TQ1 4PR

☎ 01803 326108 📄 01803 326108
**Web:** www.bygones.co.uk
**Dir:** *follow tourist signs into Torquay and St Marychurch*

Step back in time in this life-size Victorian exhibition street of over 20 shops including a forge, pub and period display rooms, housed in a former cinema. Exhibits include a large model railway layout, illuminated fantasyland, railway memorabilia and military exhibits including a walk-through World War I trench. At Christmas the street is turned into a winter wonderland. A new set piece features Babbacombe's John Lee ('the man they couldn't hang') in his cell. There is something here for all the family.

**Times:** *Open all year, Summer 10-6, (Wed & Thur 10-9.30, Jul-Aug); Spring & Autumn 10-6; Winter 10-4, wknds & school hols 10-5. (Last entry 1hr before closing).
**Fee:** *£5.50 (ch 4-14 £3.50, pen £4.95). Family ticket (2ad & 2ch) £16. Prices may change, contact in advance.
**Facilities:** Ⓟ (50yds) 📷 £1.50 ♿ (ramp) shop ⊗ (ex guide dogs) 🚌 (by arrangement) ⊛

## TORQUAY
### Kents Cavern
Cavern House 91 Ilsham Road Wellswood TQ1 2JF
☎ 01803 215136 📄 01803 211034
**Email:** caves@kents-cavern.co.uk
**Web:** www.kents-cavern.co.uk
**Dir:** *1.25m NE off B3199, follow brown tourist signs. 1m from Torquay Harbour*
Probably the most important Palaeolithic site in Britain and recognised as one of the most significant archaeological areas. This is not only a world of spectacular natural beauty, but also a priceless record of past times, where a multitude of secrets of mankind, animals and nature have become trapped and preserved over the last 500,000 years. 170 years after the first excavations and with over 80,000 remains already unearthed, modern research is still discovering new clues to our past. Please visit website for details of special events.
**Times:** *Open all year daily from 10, last tour 3.30 Nov-Feb, 4 Mar-Jun & Sep-Oct, 4.30 Jul-Aug. For up to date info visit website.
**Fee:** *Daytime: £6.50 (ch 4-15 £5) Family £21. Ghost evening tour: £5.50. For up to date info visit website.
**Facilities:** 🅿 ⓟ (on road outside) 🚼 (limited Nov-Mar) 🍽 (Licensed) 🪑 ♿ (toilets) shop ⊗ (ex guide dogs) 🚌

## TORQUAY
### Living Coasts
Beacon Quay TQ1 2BG
☎ 01803 202470 📄 01803 202471
**Email:** info@livingcoasts.org.uk
**Web:** www.livingcoasts.org.uk
**Dir:** *once in Torquay follow A379 and brown tourist signs to Torquay harbour*
Living Coasts is an unusual and ambitious attraction that allows visitors to take a trip around the coastlines of the world without leaving Torquay. Specially designed environments are home to fur seals, puffins, penguins, ducks, rats, and waders among others. All the animals can be seen above and below the water, while the huge meshed aviary allows the birds to fly free over your head. Visitors can obtain special joint tickets which will allow them to visit nearby Paignton Zoo.
**Times:** Open daily from 10. Closed 25 Dec.
**Fee:** £6.75 (ch over 3 £4.70, concessions £5.25). Family ticket (2ad+2ch) £20.50
**Facilities:** ⓟ 🚼 (hot and cold food) 🍴 ♿ (pre-booked wheelchair hire, toilets) shop ⊗ (ex assist dogs) 🚌 (prefer bookings in advance)

## UFFCULME
### Coldharbour Mill Working Wool Museum
Coldharbour Mill Cullompton EX15 3EE
☎ 01884 840960 📄 01884 840858
**Email:** info@coldharbourmill.org.uk
**Web:** www.coldharbourmill.org.uk
**Dir:** *2m from M5 junct 27, off B3181. Follow signs to Willand, then brown signs to museum*
The picturesque Coldharbour Mill is set in idyllic Devon countryside. It has been producing textiles since 1799 and is now a working museum, still making knitting wools and fabrics on period machinery. The Fox Gallery exhibits a variety of temporary exhibitions including textiles, photography, mixed media and craft. With machine demonstrations, a water wheel and steam engines, Coldharbour Mill is a great day out.
**Times:** * Mar-Sep 10.30-5, Oct-Feb 11-4
Fee: *£6.25 (ch 5-16 £2.95, pen £5.75). Family ticket £17.
**Facilities:** 🅿 🚼 (waterside cafe) 🍽 (Licensed) 🪑 ♿ (helpful guides & lift, indoor restaurant not accessible, toilets) shop, guided tours ⊗ (ex guide dogs or in grounds) 🚌 (by appointment; evenings available)

## ABBOTSBURY

**Abbotsbury Swannery**

New Barn Road DT3 4JG

☎ 01305 871858 📄 01305 871092

**Email:** info@abbotsbury-tourism.co.uk

**Web:** www.abbotsbury-tourism.co.uk

**Dir:** *turn off A35 at Winterborne Abbas near Dorchester. Abbotsbury on B3157 coastal road, between Weymouth and Bridport*

Abbotsbury is the breeding ground of the only managed colony of mute swans. The swans can be seen safely at close quarters, and the site is also home or stopping point for many wild birds. The highlight of the year is the cygnet season, end of May to the end of June, when there may be over 100 nests on site. Visitors can often take pictures of cygnets emerging from eggs at close quarters. There is an audio-visual show, as well as mass feeding at noon and 4pm daily, and an ugly duckling trail. Childrens play area available.

**Times:** *Open 18 Mar-29 Oct, daily 10-6 (last admission 5).

**Fee:** *£7.50 (ch £4.50 & pen £7).

**Facilities:** 🅿 🍴 (Licensed) 🎪 📋 £5 ♿ (free wheelchair loan, herb garden for blind, toilets) shop, guided tours 🚫 🚌

## BLANDFORD FORUM

**Royal Signals Museum**

Blandford Camp DT11 8RH

☎ 01258 482248 📄 01258 482084

**Email:** info@royalsignalsmuseum.com

**Web:** www.royalsignalsmuseum.com

**Dir:** *signed off the B3082 Blandford/Wimborne road & A354 Salisbury road. Follow brown signs for the museum.*

The Royal Signals Museum depicts the history of military communications, science and technology from the Crimea to current day. As well as displays on all major conflicts involving British forces, there are the stories of the ATS, the Long Range Desert Group, Air Support, Airborne, Para and SAS Signals. D-Day and Dorset explores the Royal Signals involvement in Operation Overlord. Trails and interactive exhibits for children.

**Times:** *Open Mar-Oct Mon-Fri 10-5, Sat-Sun 10-4. Closed 10 days over Xmas & New Year

**Fee:** *£6 (ch £4, pen £5). Family £17.50

**Facilities:** 🅿 🅿 (100m) 🎪 📋 ♿ (ramps & lifts, toilets) shop, guided tours 🚫 (ex guide dogs) 🚌 Notice preferable

## BOURNEMOUTH

**Oceanarium**

Pier Approach West Beach BH2 5AA

☎ 01202 311993 📄 01202 311990

**Email:** oceanarium@reallive.co.uk

**Web:** www.oceanarium.co.uk

**Dir:** *from A338 Wessex Way, follow Oceanarium signs*

Explore the secrets of the ocean in an adventure that will take you to some of the world's most amazing waters. The Oceanarium Bournemouth brings you face to face with a vast array of creatures from piranhas and clownfish to tiny freshwater turtles. Take a walk through the amazing underwater tunnel to get even closer to sharks, sea turtles, stingrays and eels.

**Times:** *Open all year, daily from 10. Late night opening during school summer hols. Closed 25 Dec.

**Fee:** *Telephone for admission charges.

**Facilities:** 🅿 (100mtrs) ♿ (toilets) shop guided tours 🚫 (ex guide dogs) 🚌 (Must pre-book on 01202 311993 ext.25)

## BOVINGTON CAMP
**The Tank Museum**
BH20 6JG
☎ 01929 405096 📠 01929 405360
**Email:** info@tankmuseum.org
**Web:** www.tankmuseum.org
**Dir:** *off A352 or A35, follow brown tank signs from Bere Regis & Wool*
The Tank Museum houses the world's finest international collection of Armoured Fighting Vehicles with over 300 vehicles from 26 countries. Tanks in Action displays are held every Thursday at noon during July and September, every Tuesday from end July to August Bank Holiday, and every Sunday in August. Armoured vehicle rides are available throughout the summer, and various special events take place – please telephone for details.

**Times:** *Open all year, daily 10-5.
Closed 21-27 Dec 2006.
**Fee:** *£10 (ch £7, pen £9). Family saver £28 (2ad+2ch); £26 (1ad+3ch). Group rates available.
**Facilities:** 🅿 Ⓟ (100mtrs) ☕ (main season only) 🍽 (Licensed) ⏏ 📷 ♿ (wheelchairs available & audio tours, toilets) shop, guided tours, audio commentaries ⊗ (ex in grounds) 🚌

## BROWNSEA ISLAND
**Brownsea Island**
Poole Harbour BH13 7EE
☎ 01202 707744 📠 01202 701635
**Email:** brownseaisland@nationaltrust.org.uk
**Web:** www.nationaltrust.org.uk
**Dir:** *located in Poole Harbour*
This is a 250-acre nature reserve partly managed by the Dorset Trust for Nature Conservation. The island is most famous as the site of the first scout camp, held by Lord Baden-Powell in 1907. Scouts and Guides are still the only people allowed to stay here overnight. One of the few places in Britain where red squirrels can be seen, it is also a haven for seabirds.
**Times:** *Open daily 25 Mar -21 Jul, 10-5; 22 Jul -3 Sep, 10-6; 4-30 Sep 10-5; 1-29 Oct, 10-4

**Fee:** *£4.40 (ch £2.20). Family ticket £11. Group £3.80 (ch £1.90)
**Facilities:** 🍽 ⏏ 📷 ♿ (Braille/Audio guide, 2 selfdrive vehicles- booking advised, toilets) shop ⊗ 🚌 (by written arrangement) 🌿 ♻

## DORCHESTER
**Dinosaur Museum**
Icen Way DT1 1EW
☎ 01305 269880 📠 01305 268885
**Email:** info@thedinosaurmuseum.com
**Web:** www.thedinosaurmuseum.com
**Dir:** *off A35 into Dorchester, museum in town centre just off High East St*
Britain's award-winning museum devoted to dinosaurs has an appealing mixture of fossils, skeletons, life-size reconstructions and interactive displays such as the 'feelies'. There are audio-visual presentations and computer displays providing an all-round family attraction with new displays each year. It is part of the Jurassic Coast experience.
**Times:** *Open all year, daily 9.30-5.30 (10-4.30 Nov-

Mar). Closed 24-26 Dec.
**Fee:** *£6.50 (ch £4.75, concessions £5.50, under 4's free). Family ticket £19.95
**Facilities:** Ⓟ (50yds) 📷 ♿ (many low level displays) shop, guided tours 🚌 (pre-booking essential)

## DORCHESTER
### Dorset Teddy Bear Museum
Eastgate High East St & Salisbury St DT1 1JU
☎ 01305 266040 🖷 01305 268885
Email: info@teddybearmuseum.co.uk
Web: www.teddybearmuseum.co.uk
Dir: off A35, museum in town centre near Dinosaur
Museum

There are three different ways to indulge in teddy bears
here. Enter the enchanting world of the teddy bear in the
wonderful family museum with every type of teddy from
the very earliest, over 100 years ago, to today's TV
favourites. The teddy bear house, home of Mr Edward
Bear and his extended family, has life-sized teddy bears
comfortably at home. The nearby teddy bear shop is jam-
packed with teddies and soft toys.

**Times:** *Open daily, 10-5.30, (4.30 in winter). Closed
24-26 Dec.
**Fee:** £5.50 (ch £3.75, under 4's free, pen & concessions
£4.50). Family £17
**Facilities:** Ⓟ (150mtrs) 🍴 shop Ⓧ (ex guide dogs)
🚌 (pre-booking essential)

## DORCHESTER
### Tutankhamun Exhibition
High West St DT1 1UW
☎ 01305 269571 🖷 01305 268885
Email: info@tutankhamun-exhibition.co.uk
Web: www.tutankhamun-exhibition.co.uk
Dir: off A35 into Dorchester town centre

The exhibition recreates the excitement of one of the
world's greatest discoveries of ancient treasure. A
reconstruction of the tomb and recreations of its
treasures are displayed. The superbly preserved
mummified body of the boy king can be seen,
wonderfully recreated in every detail. Facsimiles of some
of the most famous treasures, including the golden
funerary mask and the harpooner can be seen in the
final gallery.

**Times:** *Open all year daily, Apr-Oct, 9.30-5.30; Nov-Mar
wkdays 9.30-5, wknds 10-4.30. Closed 24-26 Dec.
**Fee:** £6.50 (ch £4.75, concessions £5.50, under 5's
free). Family ticket £19.95
**Facilities:** Ⓟ (200yds) 🍴 ♿ shop, guided tours
(charged) Ⓧ (ex guide dogs) 🚌 (pre-booking essential)

## ORGANFORD
### Farmer Palmer's Farm Park
Poole BH16 6EU
☎ 01202 622022 🖷 01202 622182
Email: info@farmerpalmers.co.uk
Web: www.farmerpalmer.co.uk
Dir: From Poole, just off A35 straight over rdbt past
Bakers Arms, signed on left, 2nd turning, 0.5m after rdbt

Family owned and run Farmer Palmers has been
specially designed for families with children 8 years and
under. Many activities include meeting and learning about
the animals, climbing the straw mountain, going for a
tractor trailer ride and exercising in the soft play area.
Lots of undercover activities, so this is a fun and busy
day for the family, whatever the weather.
**Times:** *Open 11-19 Feb, daily 10-4; 20 Feb-24 Mar &
30 Oct-17 Dec Fri & wknds 10-4, 25 Mar-29 Oct, daily
10-5.30.
**Fee:** *£4.95 (ch 4.75, under 2yrs free, concessions
£4.50). Family (2 ad, 2ch) £18.50. Disabled & carer
£4.50 each.
**Facilities:** Ⓟ Ⓟ (adjacent) 🍴 ♿ (ramps & wide
doorways, toilets) shop Ⓧ (ex guide dogs) 🚌 (pre book)

DORSET

**DORSET**

## POOLE
**Waterfront Museum**
4 High St BH15 1BW
☎ 01202 262600 📄 01202 262622
**Email:** museums@poole.gov.uk
**Web:** www.boroughofpoole.com/museums
**Dir:** *off Poole Quay*
The Waterfront Museum tells the story of Poole's history with displays and hands-on activities, including the Studland Bay wreck and trade with Newfoundland. The museum is undergoing a major refurbishment, and is due to re-open in mid-2007. Please contact the Poole Museums Service for further information. Scalplen's Court and the Tudor Garden remain open. The local history centre with research facilities on local and family history will also remain open during the refurbishment.

**Times:** Local History Centre only: Tue-Sat 10-3 (closed on Tue following a BH).
**Fee:** *Free Free
**Facilities:** Ⓟ (250mtrs) 📓 ♿ (Scaplen's Court not accessible, toilets) shop ⊗ (ex guide dogs) 🚌

## SWANAGE
**Swanage Railway**
Station House BH19 1HB
☎ 01929 425800 📄 01929 426680
**Email:** general@swanrail.freeserve.co.uk
**Web:** www.swanagerailway.co.uk
**Dir:** *signed from A351*
The railway from Swanage to Wareham was closed in 1972, and in 1976 the Swanage Railway took possession and have gradually restored the line, which now runs for 6 miles, passing the ruins of Corfe Castle. On train meals are offered on the Wessex Belle, the Travelling Tavern and the Dorsetman. Ring for details of special events.
**Times:** Open every wknd ex Jan, daily Apr-Oct.
**Fee:** *Swanage-Corfe/Norden £7.50 return (ch & concessions £5.50 return). Family ticket £21. Day Rover

£8.50 (ch & concessions £6.50)
**Facilities:** Ⓟ Ⓟ (Park & Ride Norden) ☕ (station buffet at Swanage & Norden) 🍽 (Licensed) 🪑 ♿ (disabled persons coach) shop 🚌 (prior booking)

## WEST LULWORTH
**Lulworth Castle & Park**
BH20 5QS
☎ 0845 450 1054 📄 01929 400563
**Email:** estate.office@lulworth.com
**Web:** www.lulworth.com
**Dir:** *from Wareham, W on A352 for 1m, left onto B3070 to E Lulworth, follow tourist signs*
Glimpse life below stairs in the restored kitchen, and enjoy glorious views from the top of the tower of this historic castle set in beautiful parkland. The 18th-century chapel is the first Catholic chapel built in England after the Reformation. Children will enjoy the animal farm, play area, indoor activity room and pitch and putt.
**Times:** *Open 25 Mar-Sep, Sun-Fri 10.30-6; 2 Oct-Dec, Sun-Fri 10.30-4; 2-7 Jan, Sun-Fri 10.30-4; 23-24 Mar,

Sun-Fri 10.30-4. Closed 24-25 Dec & 7-21 Jan.
**Fee:** *£7.00 (ch £4.00, concessions £5.00) non-jousting season. £8.50 (ch £4.50, concessions £7.00) jousting season. Family £21.00 (2 ad + 3 ch), £15 (1 ad + 3 ch).
**Facilities:** Ⓟ ☕ (open 10.30-5 summer, 10.30-4 winter) 🪑 ♿ (limited in castle due to Grade I listing, toilets) shop 🚌

## WEYMOUTH
### Deep Sea Adventure & Sharky's Play Warehouse

9 Custom House Quay Old Harbour North DT4 8BG
☎ 0871 222 5760 📄 0871 222 5760
**Email:** enquiries@deepsea-adventure.co.uk
**Web:** www.deepsea-adventure.co.uk
**Dir:** *A35 to Weymouth, then Old Harbour North. Attraction between pavillion & town bridge. Follow brown tourist signs.*

A fascinating attraction telling the story of underwater exploration and marine exploits. Discover the history of Weymouth's Old Harbour, compelling tales of shipwreck survival, explore the Black Hole and search for Ollie the Oyster. Also a unique display telling the gripping tale of the Titanic disaster. Sharky's Play Area is four floors of fun-packed adventure. Separate toddler area for the under fives. 'Paint your own Pottery' studio can also be found on site. Laser shoot out evenings now available.
**Times:** *Open all year, daily from 9.30. Closed 25-26 Dec & 1 Jan.
**Fee:** *Sharky's Play Zone: Adults free (ch £3.50). Deep Sea Adventure: £3.95 (ch 5-15 £2.95, concessions £3.50).
**Facilities:** Ⓟ (100yds) 🍽 (Licensed) 📔 ♿ (lift & sign language for deaf, toilets) shop, guided tours, audio commentaries 🚫 (ex guide dogs) 🚌

## WEYMOUTH
### RSPB Nature Reserve Radipole Lake

The Swannery Car Park DT4 7TZ
☎ 01305 778313 📄 01305 778313
**Web:** www.rspb.org.uk
**Dir:** *close to seafront & railway station*

Covering 222 acres and including a large reedbed, flood meadows and open water, the Reserve offers firm paths, hide and a visitor centre. Several types of warblers, mute swans, gadwalls, teals and great crested grebes may be seen, and the visitor centre has viewing windows overlooking the lake. Families are well provided with special walks and trails and the free loan of Wildlife Explorer backpacks. Phone for details of special events.
**Times:** *Open daily 9-5
**Fee:** Small fee for North Hide only if not RSPB members
**Facilities:** Ⓟ (charged) Ⓟ (Council car park) ⛱
♿ (toilets) shop 🚌 (advance booking)

## WEYMOUTH
### Sea Life Park & Marine Sanctuary

Lodmoor Country Park DT4 7SX
☎ 01305 788255 📄 01305 760165
**Email:** slcweymouth@merlinentertainments.biz
**Web:** www.sealifeeurope.com
**Dir:** *on A353*

A unique mix of indoor and outdoor attractions set in 7 acres. The park offers a day of fun, bringing you face to face with penguins, otters, seals and much more. A recent addition is the unique Turtle Sanctuary for green-back turtles from the Cayman Islands. The current inhabitants were bred in captivity and the accompanying displays are intended to raise awareness of these endearing animals.
**Times:** *Open all year, daily from 10. (Closed 25 Dec).
**Fee:** *£10.50 (ch £7.50, concessions £7.95)
**Facilities:** Ⓟ (charged) 🍽 ⛱ ♿ (toilets) shop 🚫 (ex guide dogs) 🚌

**DORSET**

## WIMBORNE
### Kingston Lacy House, Garden & Park
BH21 4EA
☎ 01202 883402 (Mon-Fri) & 880413 (infoline)
🖹 01202 882402
**Email:** kingstonlacy@nationaltrust.org.uk
**Web:** www.nationaltrust.org.uk
**Dir:** *1.5m W of Wimborne, B3082*
Kingston Lacy House was the home of the Bankes family for over 300 years. The original house is 17th century, but in the 1830s was given a stone façade. The Italian marble staircase, Venetian ceiling, treasures from Spain and an Egyptian obelisk were also added. There are outstanding pictures by Titian, Rubens, Velasquez, Reynolds and Van Dyck. No photography is allowed in the house.

**Times:** *Open: House 18 Mar-29 Oct, 11-5, Wed-Sun. Garden & Park 10.30-6, daily 3 Nov-17 Dec, 10.30-4, Fri-Sun 3 Feb-20 Mar, 10.30-4, Sat-Sun.
**Fee:** *House, Garden & Park £9 (ch £4.50) Family £22. Park & Gardens only £4.50 (ch £2.30) Family £11.
**Facilities:** ℗ ⛾ (open 10.30-5.30) 🍽 (Licensed) ⛌ ♿ (wheelchairs, large print & Braille guides, parking, toilets) shop, guided tours ⊗ (ex on leads in park & wood) 🚌 (must book in advance) ✿ 📷

## WIMBORNE
### Priest's House Museum and Garden
23-27 High Street BH21 1HR
☎ 01202 882533 🖹 01202 882533
**Email:** priestshouse@eastdorset.gov.uk
**Dir:** *located on High Street, opposite The Minster*
An award-winning local history museum, set in an historic house. The 17th-century hall, Georgian parlour and working Victorian kitchen reveal the history of the building and its inhabitants. The museum houses exhibitions on East Dorset from prehistoric to modern times. There are regular special exhibitions and a walled garden to explore.
**Times:** *Open Apr-Oct, Mon-Sat, 10-4.30.
**Fee:** *£3 (ch £1, concesssions £2). Family & season ticket £7.50

**Facilities:** ℗ (200yds) ⛌ 📷 ♿ (hands on archaeology gallery) shop guided tours ⊗ (ex guide dogs) 🚌 (advance booking required) 📷

## WIMBORNE
### Stapehill Abbey, Crafts & Garden
Wimborne Road West BH21 2EB
☎ 01202 861686 🖹 01202 894589
**Dir:** *2.5m E off A31 at Canford Bottom rdbt*
This early 19th-century abbey, home for nearly 200 years to Cistercian nuns, is now a busy working crafts centre with many attractions under cover. There are award-winning landscaped gardens, parkland and picnic spots, and the Power to the Land exhibition. There is also a childrens play area, a coffee shop and a gift shop. Telephone for details of special events.
**Times:** *Open Etr-Sep, daily 10-5; Oct-Etr, Wed-Sun 10-4. Closed 22 Dec-Feb.
**Fee:** *£7.50 (ch 4-16 £4.50, students & pen £7). Family ticket (2ad+2ch) £19.50.

**Facilities:** ℗ ⛌ ♿ (toilets) shop garden centre ⊗ (ex guide dogs) 🚌

## WOOL
### Monkey World

Longthorns BH20 6HH

☎ 01929 462537 & 0800 456600 📠 01929 405414

**Email:** apes@monkeyworld.org

**Web:** www.monkeyworld.org

**Dir:** *1m N of Wool on Bere Regis road*

Set up in order to rescue monkeys and apes from abuse and illegal smuggling and now celebrating its 20th anniversary, Monkey World houses over 160 primates in 65 acres of Dorset woodland. There are 58 chimps, the largest group outside Africa, as well as gibbons, woolly monkeys, orang-utans, lemurs, marmosets and macaques. There are keeper talks every half hour, and a Great Ape Play Area for the kids. To help the work of the centre there is an adoption scheme which includes free admission to the park for one year.

**Times:** Open daily 10-5 (Jul-Aug 10-6). (Last admission 1 hour before closing)

**Fee:** *£9 (ch & concessions £6.50). Family ticket (1ad+2ch) £20, (2ad+2ch) £27. Group 15+ £8 (£5.50).

**Facilities:** 🅿 🍴 ♿ (toilets) shop guided tours ⊗ (ex guide dogs) 🚌 (pre-booking advised)

---

## BERKELEY
### Berkeley Castle

GL13 9BQ

☎ 01453 810332 📠 01453 512995

**Email:** info@berkeley.castle.com

**Web:** www.berkeley-castle.com

**Dir:** *just off A38 midway between Bristol & Gloucester. From M5 take junct 14 or 13*

Berkeley Castle is the amazing fortress home of the Berkeley family, who have lived in the building since the Keep was completed in 1153. The castle is still intact, from dungeon to elegant drawing rooms, and reflects nearly a thousand years of English history: a king's murder, the American Colonies and London's Berkeley Square to mention just a few. Rose-clad terraces surround this most romantic castle.

**Times:** *Open Apr-2 Oct, Tue-Sat & BH Mon 11-4, Sun 2-5; Oct, Sun only 2-5.

**Fee:** *Castle & Gardens & Butterfly House: £7.50 (ch 5-15 £4.50, pen £6). Family ticket (2ad+2ch) £21.

**Facilities:** 🅿 🍴 ♿ (Special tours can be arranged) shop, garden centre, guided tours ⊗ (ex guide dogs) 🚌 (pre-booking essential)

---

## BOURTON-ON-THE-WATER
### Birdland

Rissington Road Cheltenham GL54 2BN

☎ 01451 820480 📠 01451 822398

**Email:** simonb@birdland.co.uk

**Web:** www.birdland.co.uk

**Dir:** *on A429*

Birdland is a natural setting of woodland, river and gardens which is inhabited by over 500 birds. Flamingos, pelicans, penguins, cranes, storks, cassowarys and waterfowl can be seen on various aspects of the water habitat. Over 50 aviaries accommodate parrots, falcons, pheasants, hornbills, touracos, pigeons, ibis and many more. Tropical, Toucan and Desert Houses are home to the more delicate species.

**Times:** Open all year, Apr-Oct, daily 10-6; Nov-Mar, daily 10-4. (Last admission 1hr before closing). Closed 25 Dec.

**Fee:** £5.20 (pen £4.20). Family ticket (2ad+2ch) £15.

**Facilities:** 🅿 (adjacent) 🍴 ♿ (toilets) shop, audio commentaries 🚌

GLOUCESTERSHIRE

### BOURTON-ON-THE-WATER
**Model Village**
Old New Inn Cheltenham GL54 2AF
☎ 01451 820467 🖹 01451 810236
**Email:** reception@theoldnewinn.co.uk
**Web:** www.theoldnewinn.co.uk
In the garden of the Old New Inn is a model version of
the village. Built of Cotswold stone to a scale of one-
ninth, it is a perfect replica of the village in the 1930s
when it was constructed. The work of an earlier inn
owner and a team of local craftsmen it includes a metre
wide miniature River Windrush, a working model waterwheel, churches and shops, with tiny trees, shrubs and
alpine plants.
**Times:** Open all year 10-5.45 (summer), 10-dusk
(winter). Closed 25 Dec.

**Fee:** £3 (ch £2.50, pen £2.75).
**Facilities:** Ⓟ (500yds) ♚ (Licensed) shop ⊗ (ex guide
dogs) 🚌 (coaches to park on central coach park)

### CHEDWORTH
**Chedworth Roman Villa**
Yanworth GL54 3LJ
☎ 01242 890256 🖹 01242 890909
**Email:** chedworth@nationaltrust.org.uk
**Web:** www.nationaltrust.org.uk
**Dir:** *3m NW of Fossebridge on A429*
The remains of a Romano-British villa, excavated in
1864-66 and known as 'Britains oldest county house'.
Set in a beautiful wooded combe, there are fine 4th-
century mosaics, two bath houses, and a temple with a
spring. The museum houses the smaller finds and there
is also a 9-minute video programme. Telephone for
further details of special events.
**Times:** *Open 1-25 Mar, daily 11-4; 26 Mar-28 Oct,
daily 10-5; 26 Oct-12 Nov, daily 11-4.

(Closed Mons ex BH Mon).
**Fee:** *£5.50 (ch £3). Family ticket £14.
**Facilities:** Ⓟ ⊼ ♿ (audio tour, induction loop, Braille
guide, toilets) shop guided tours ⊗ 🚌 (pre-booked) 🦋

### CIRENCESTER
**Corinium Museum**
Park Street GL7 2BX
☎ 01285 655611
**Email:** museums@cotswold.gov.uk
**Web:** www.cotswold.gov.uk
**Dir:** *in town centre*
Discover the treasures of the Cotswolds at the new
Corinium Museum. Two years and over £5 million in the
making, it has been transformed into a must-see
attraction. Featuring archaeological and historical
material from Cirencester and the Cotswolds, from
prehistoric times to the 19th century. The museum is
known for its Roman mosaic sculpture and other material
from one of Britain's largest Roman towns. New on
display are Anglo-Saxon treasures from Lechlade

bringing to life this little known period. The museum also
houses Medieval, Tudor, Civil War and 18th-19th century
displays.
**Times:** *Open Mon-Sat 10-5, Sun 2-5. Closed 25-26
Dec & 1 Jan.
**Fee:** £3.90 (ch & students £2.00, pen £2.90). Family
ticket £9.
**Facilities:** Ⓟ (2mins walk) ♚ 📋 ♿ (Large print &
Braille guides, toilets) shop, guided tours ⊗ assisst dogs
🚌 (booking advised)

## CLEARWELL
### Clearwell Caves Ancient Iron Mines
Coleford Royal Forest of Dean GL16 8JR

☎ 01594 832535 🖷 01594 833362

**Email:** jw@clearwellcaves.com

**Web:** www.clearwellcaves.com

**Dir:** *1.5m S of Coleford town centre, off B4228 follow brown tourist signs*

These impressive natural caves have also been mined since the earliest times for paint pigment and iron ore. Today visitors explore nine large caverns with displays of local mining and geology. Colour room where ochre pigments are still produced and blacksmith shop. Deep level excursions available for more adventurous visitors, must be pre booked. Christmas fantasy event when the caverns are transformed into a world of light and sound.

**Times:** Open Mar-Oct daily 10-5; Jan-Feb Sat-Sun 10-5; Christmas Fantasy 1-24 Dec, daily 10-5.

**Fee:** £5 (ch £3, concessions £4.50) Family ticket £14.

**Facilities:** 🅿 Ⓟ (150mtrs) 🍽 (Light lunches) 🚻 ♿ (hands-on exhibits, Braille guide book, contact in advance, toilets) shop, guided tours 🚫 (ex guide & hearing dogs) 🚌 (pre-booked if guide required)

## CRANHAM
### Prinknash Abbey and Visitors Centre
GL4 8EX

☎ 01452 812066 🖷 01452 813322

**Email:** prinknashshop@waitrose.com

**Web:** www.prinknashabbey.org.uk

**Dir:** *on A46 between Cheltenham & Stroud*

Set in a large park, the old priory building is a 12th to 16th-century house, used by Benedictine monks and guests of Gloucester Abbey until 1539. It became an abbey for Benedictine monks from Caldey Island in 1928. Home to the reconstruction of the Great Orpheus Pavement. It is the largest mosaic in Britain, as mentioned in the *Guinness Book of Records*. Also visit the bird and deer park.

**Times:** Open all year. Abbey Church: April-end Oct 9- 5.30, Nov-end Mar 10-4.30. Closed Good Fri, 25-26 Dec.

**Fee:** *Admission free to grounds. Orpheus Pavement £3.25 (ch 1.75). Family ticket £7.

**Facilities:** 🅿 🍽 (snacks) 🚻 🖼 ♿ (Radar approved, toilets) shop 🚌

## CRANHAM
### Prinknash Bird & Deer Park
GL4 8EU

☎ 01452 812727 🖷 01452 812727

**Web:** www.prinknash-bird-and-deerpark.com

**Dir:** *A46 Stroud. Follow brown tourist signs*

Nine acres of parkland and lakes make a beautiful home for black swans, geese and other water birds. There are also exotic birds such as white and Indian blue peacocks and crown cranes, as well as tame fallow deer and pygmy goats. The Golden Wood is stocked with ornamental pheasants, and leads to the reputedly haunted monks' fishpond, which contains trout. An 80-year-old, free-standing, 16ft tall Wendy House in the style of a Tudor house has recently been erected near the picnic area.

**Times:** *Open all year, daily 10-5 (4 in winter). Closed 26 Dec & Good Fri.

**Fee:** *£5 (ch £3.50, pen £4.50). Party 10+ £4 (ch £3, pen £4).

**Facilities:** 🅿 Ⓟ (100mtrs - 450 car spaces, 10 coach spaces) 🚻 🖼 ♿ (toilets) shop 🚫 🚌 🎫

GLOUCESTERSHIRE

## DYRHAM
### Dyrham Park
SN14 8ER

☎ 0117 937 2501 🖹 0117 937 1353
**Email:** dyrhampark@nationaltrust.org.uk
**Web:** www.nationaltrust.org.uk
**Dir:** *8m N of Bath, 2m from M4 junct 18*

Dyrham Park is a splendid Baroque Country house, with interiors that have hardly altered since the late 17th century. It has contemporary Dutch-style furnishings, Dutch pictures and blue-and-white Delft ware. Around the house is an ancient park with fallow deer, where Dyrham derives its name. In the beautiful gardens, famous for the tulip festival in April, is a medieval church.

**Times:** *House 24 Mar-29 Oct, 12-4.45, Fri-Tue. Garden 24 Mar-29 Oct, 11-5, Fri-Tue. Park all year, 11-5, all week. Shop 24 Mar-29 Oct, 11-5, Fri-Tue. Tea room, 24 Mar-29 Oct, 11-5, Fri-Tue.

**Fee:** *House £9 (ch £4.50). Family £22.50 Ground only £3.50 (ch £1.80). Family £8). Park only £2.30 (ch £1.10). Family £5.20

**Facilities:** 🅿 🍴 (Licensed) 🆓 ♿ (Braille/audio guides, stairclimber, free bus from car park, toilets) shop guided tours ⊗ (ex in dog walk area) 🚌 (by appointment) 🐾 ♨

---

## GLOUCESTER
### Gloucester City Museum & Art Gallery
Brunswick Road GL1 1HP

☎ 01452 396131 🖹 01452 410898
**Email:** city.museum@gloucester.gov.uk
**Web:** www.gloucester.gov.uk
**Dir:** *centre of Gloucester*

The museum and art gallery provides something for everyone. Of particular note is an impressive range of Roman artefacts including the Rufus Sita tombstone; the amazing Iron Age Birdlip Mirror; one of the earliest backgammon sets in the world; dinosaur fossils; and paintings by famous artists such as Turner and Gainsborough. There is an exciting range of temporary exhibitions from contemporary art and textiles to dinosaurs and local history; children's holiday activities and regular special events.

**Times:** Open all year, Tue-Sat 10-5.
**Fee:** *Free Admission free to everyone
**Facilities:** 🅿 (500yds) 📖 ♿ (lift to 1st floor galleries, induction loops, toilets) shop ⊗ (ex guide dogs) 🚌 (advance booking)

---

## GLOUCESTER
### Gloucester Folk Museum
99-103 Westgate Street GL1 2PG

☎ 01452 396868 & 396869 🖹 01452 330495
**Email:** folk.museum@gloucester.gov.uk
**Web:** www.gloucester.gov.uk
**Dir:** *from W - A40 & A48; from N - A38 & M5, from E - A40 & B4073; from S - A4173 & A38*

Three floors of splendid timber-framed buildings dating from the 16th and 17th centuries along with newer buildings housing the Dairy, Ironmonger's shop and Wheelwright and Carpenter workshops. Displays explore local history, domestic life, crafts, trades and industries from 1500 to the present day. A wide range of exhibitions, hands-on activities, events, demonstrations and role play sessions are held throughout the year. There is an attractive cottage garden and courtyard for events, often with live animals, and outside games.

**Times:** Open all year, Tue-Sat, 10-5
**Fee:** *Free
**Facilities:** 🅿 (500yds) 🆓 ♿ (virtual tour in Protal gallery, induction loops) shop ⊗ (ex guide dogs) 🚌 (book in advance)

## GLOUCESTER
### Nature in Art

Wallsworth Hall Tewkesbury Road Twigworth GL2 9PA

☎ 01452 731422 & 0845 450 0233 🖹 01452 730937

**Email:** enquiries@nature-in-art.org.uk

**Web:** www.nature-in-art.org.uk

**Dir:** *0.5m off main A38 between Gloucester and Tewkesbury, 2m N of Gloucester. Follow tourist signs*

Nature is the theme at this museum and art gallery, set in a Georgian Mansion, with exhibits including sculpture, tapestries and ceramics. There is an 'artist in residence' programme Feb-Nov, and events include monthly talks, film showings and a full programme of exhibitions and art courses. Work from over 60 countries spanning 1,500 years is included in the collection. From Picasso to Japanese prints – there is something for everyone.

**Times:** Open all year, Tue-Sun & BHs 10-5. Closed 24-26 Dec.

**Fee:** *£4.50 (ch, concessions £4.00, ch under 8 free). Family ticket £13. Party 15+.

**Facilities:** 🅿 ⛾ (home made snacks and meals) 🍴 (Licensed) 🪑 ♿ (lift & ramps at entrance, toilets) shop, guided tours 🚫 (ex guide dogs) 🚌 (must pre-book) ♻

## GLOUCESTER
### The National Waterways Museum

Llanthony Warehouse The Docks GL1 2EH

☎ 01452 318200 🖹 01452 318202

**Email:** bookingsnwm@thewaterwaystrust.org

**Web:** www.nwm.org.uk

**Dir:** *From M5, A40 and within the city follow brown signs for historic docks*

Based in Gloucester Docks, this museum takes up three floors of a seven-storey Victorian warehouse, and documents the 200-year history of Britain's water-based transport. The emphasis is on hands-on experience, including working models and engines, interactive displays, actual craft, computer interactions and the national collection of inland waterways. Boat trips are also available between Easter and October.

**Times:** *Open all year, daily 10-5. (Last admission 4). Closed 25 Dec.

**Fee:** £5.95 (under 5's free, concessions £4.95). Family ticket £17.50

**Facilities:** 🅿 (charged) 🅿 (2 mins walk - no overnight parking) ⛾ (lunches, snacks, coffee shop) 🍴 🪑 🗐 ♿ (wheelchair, lifts, limited access to floating exhibits, toilets) shop 🚫 (ex guide dogs) 🚌 (Parties 10+ pre-booking helpful)

## GUITING POWER
### Cotswold Farm Park

Cheltenham GL54 5UG

☎ 01451 850307 🖹 01451 850423

**Email:** info@cotswoldfarmpark.co.uk

**Web:** www.cotswoldfarmpark.co.uk

**Dir:** *signed off B4077 from M5 junct 9*

At the Cotswold Farm Park there are nearly 50 breeding herds and flocks of the rarest British breeds of sheep, cattle, pigs, goats, horses, and poultry. Lots of activities for children including rabbits and guinea pigs to cuddle, lambs and calves to bottle feed, tractor and trailer rides, battery powered tractors and safe rustic-themed play areas indoors and outdoors. Lambing occurs in early May, followed by shearing and then milking demonstrations later in the season.

**Times:** Open mid Mar-mid Sep, daily (then open wknds only until end Oct & Autumn half term 10.30-5).

**Fee:** *£5.50 (ch £4.50 pen £5). Family ticket £18.

**Facilities:** 🅿 🪑 🗐 £6 teachers pack ♿ (ramps, toilets) shop, audio commentaries 🚫 (ex guide dogs) 🚌 (prior booking required)

# 1001 Great Family Days Out

## LYDNEY
### Dean Forest Railway
Norchard Railway Centre New Mills Forest Rd GL15 4ET
☎ 01594 843423 (info) & 845840
**Email:** commercial@deanforestrailway.co.uk
**Web:** www.deanforestrailway.co.uk
**Dir:** *At Lydney, turn off the Gloucester to Chepstow A48 road and follow brown tourist signs to Norchard Railway Centre, on B4234 Lydney-Parkend road*
Travel on a heritage steam railway through the beautiful and historic Forest of Dean. A relaxing round trip of over 8 miles to the recently opened Parkend Station. There's free car parking at Norchard Station (near Lydney) with a well-stocked gift shop, museum and café. Regular family events include Thomas the Tank Engine and Santa Specials.

**Times:** *Open Apr-Oct, Sun; Jun-Sep, Wed, Sat, Sun; also Tue & Thu in Aug and BH's; Dec wknds (Santa Specials) & New Year.
**Fee:** *£8 (under 5's free, ch £5, pen £7). Family ticket (2ad+2ch) £24. Different charges may apply to events.
**Facilities:** ♿ ☕ (only on steam & diesel days) ⛽ ⛱ ♿ (specially adapted coach for wheelchairs, phone for details, toilets) shop, guided tours
🚌 (prior arrangements for large parties)

## MORETON-IN-MARSH
### Cotswold Falconry Centre
Batsford Park GL56 9QB
☎ 01386 701043
**Email:** geoffdalton@yahoo.co.uk
**Web:** www.cotswold-falconry.co.uk
**Dir:** *1m W of Moreton-in-Marsh on A44*
Conveniently located by the Batsford Park Arboretum, the Cotswold Falconry gives daily demonstrations in the art of falconry. The emphasis here is on breeding and conservation, and eagles, hawks, owls and falcons can be viewed in their aviaries as well as when they are used for flying displays.
**Times:** Open mid Feb-mid Nov, 10.30-5.30. (Last admission 5).
**Fee:** *£6 (ch 4-15 £2.50, concessions £5). Joint ticket with Batsford Arboretum £10 (ch 4-15 £4, concessions £9.50).
**Facilities:** ♿ ☕ (tea room in garden centre) ⛱ ♿ (no steps, wide doorways, toilets) shop, garden centre, guided tours ⊗ (ex on leads in arboretum) 🚌 (pre-book)

## NEWENT
### National Birds of Prey Centre
GL18 1JJ
☎ 0870 9901992 📠 01531 821389
**Email:** katherine@nbpc.co.uk
**Web:** www.nbpc.co.uk
**Dir:** *follow A40, right onto B4219 towards Newent. Follow brown tourist signs from Newent town*
Trained birds can be seen at close quarters in the Hawk Walk and the Owl Courtyard and there are also breeding aviaries, a gift shop, bookshop, picnic areas, coffee shop and children's play area. Birds are flown three times daily in summer and winter, giving an exciting and educational display. There are over 80 aviaries on view with 40 species.
**Times:** *Open Feb-Oct, daily 10.30-5.30.
**Fee:** *£6.75 (ch £4, pen £5.75). Family ticket £18.50 (2ad+2ch).
**Facilities:** ♿ ⛱ ♿ (special tours available, pre-booking required, toilets) shop ⊗ 🚌

## NEWENT
### The Shambles Victorian Village
Church Street GL18 1PP

☎ 01531 822144

**Web:** www.shamblesnewent.co.uk

**Dir:** *close to town centre near church*

Cobbled streets, alleyways, cottages and houses set in over an acre with display shops and trades, even a tin chapel and cottage garden all helping to recreate the feel and atmosphere of a small Victorian town. There are over 80 shops to peer into and with a focus on the 1890's each building is furnished as if occupied but the inhabitant has just popped out for a moment. A fascinating experience for young and old alike.

**Times:** *Open mid Mar-end Oct, Tue-Sun & BHs 10-5 (or dusk); Nov-Dec wknds only.

**Fee:** *£4.35 (ch £2.75, pen £3.75).

**Facilities:** ℗ (100yds) ☐ (seasonal) ⊼ ♿ (toilets) shop, 🚌 (advanced bookings prefered)

## NORTHLEACH
### Keith Harding's World of Mechanical Music
The Oak House High Street GL54 3ET

☎ 01451 860181 🖺 01451 861133

**Email:** keith@mechanicalmusic.co.uk

**Web:** www.mechanicalmusic.co.uk

**Dir:** *at crossroads of A40 & A429*

A fascinating collection of antique clocks, musical boxes, automata and mechanical musical instruments, restored and maintained in the world-famous workshops and displayed in a period setting. Much of the collection is played by the guides during regular tours. There is also an exhibition of coin operated instruments which visitors can play.

**Times:** Open all year, daily 10-6.  Last tour 5. Closed 25-26 Dec.

**Fee:** *£6 (ch £3, concessions £5). Discounts for families & groups.

**Facilities:** ℗ ℗ (50yds) ♿ (Safety rails, non-slip floor, toilets) shop guided tours ⊗ (ex guide dogs) 🚌 (more than 30, split into 2 groups)

## SLIMBRIDGE
### WWT Slimbridge
GL2 7BT

☎ 0870 33 44 000 🖺 01453 890827

**Email:** slimbridge@wwt.org.uk

**Web:** www.wwt.org.uk

**Dir:** *off A38, signed from M5 junct 13 & 14*

Slimbridge is home to the world's largest collection of exotic wildfowl – and the only place in Europe where all six types of flamingo can be seen. Up to 8,000 wild birds winter on the 800-acre reserve of flat fields, marsh and mudflats on the River Severn. Facilities include a tropical house, discovery centre, shop and restaurant.

**Times:** *Open all year, daily from 9.30-5 (winter 4). Closed 25 Dec.

**Fee:** *£6.75 (ch £4, pen £5.50). Family ticket £18.50.

**Facilities:** ℗ ⧖ (Licensed) ⊼ ♿ (wheelchair loan, tapes for blind, hearing pads & loops, toilets) shop ⊗ (ex guide & hearing dogs) 🚌 (pre-booking required)

**GLOUCESTERSHIRE**

## SNOWSHILL
**Snowshill Manor**
Broadway WR12 7JU
☎ 01386 852410 ▤ 01386 842822
**Email:** snowshillmanor@nationaltrust.org.uk
**Web:** www.nationaltrust.org.uk
**Dir:** *3m SW of Broadway, off A44*
Arts and crafts garden designed by its owner Charles Paget Wade in collaboration with M.H. Baillie Scott. It was designed as a series of outdoor rooms to compliment the traditional Cotswold manor house filled with his unique collection of craftsmanship including clocks, toys, bicycles, musical instruments and Japanese armour. This was the first National Trust garden to be managed following organic principles. It is a lively mix of cottage flowers, bright colours and delightful scents with stunning views across Cotswold countryside.
**Times:** * House: 25 Mar-29 Oct, 12-5, Wed-Sun; Garden: 25 Mar-29 May, 11-5.30, Thu-Sun, 4 May-30 Oct, 11-5.30, Wed-Sun; Shop: As garden, also 4 Nov-10 Dec, 12-4, Sat & Sun; Restaurant: As shop
**Fee:** *House & Garden: £7.30, (ch £3.65). Family £18.50, groups £6.20. Garden, Restaurant & Shop: £4, (ch £2). Family £10
**Facilities:** ❷ ⫪❂⫪ (Licensed) ♿ (Braille guides, audio tapes, 2 manual wheelchairs, toilets) shop ⊗ (ex guide dogs) 🚌 (prior arrangement by letter) ✤

## SOUDLEY
**Dean Heritage Centre**
Camp Mill GL14 2UB
☎ 01594 822170 ▤ 01594 823711
**Email:** deanmuse@btconnect.com
**Web:** www.deanheritagemuseum.com
**Dir:** *on B4227, in Forest of Dean*
The Centre tells the story of this unique area, and its people, from pre-historic times to present day. Displays include a reconstructed cottage, a working beam engine from Lightmore Colliery, charcoal burners' camp and art gallery. There are also nature trails with animals. There is an adventure playground that includes a maze and swing bridge. Library and research facilities are available by appointment. Annual events include the Sheep Fair in April and a Herb Day in July.
**Times:** *Open all year, daily, Winter 10-4, Summer 10-5.30. Closed 24-26 Dec & 1 Jan.
**Fee:** *£4.50 (ch £2.50, under 5's free, pen & concessions £3.50). Family ticket £13.
**Facilities:** ❷ (charged) ℗ (100yds) 🍴 ♿ (lift, ramps, help from establishment staff, toilets) shop, guided tours ⊗ (ex guide dogs) 🚌

## WESTONBIRT
**Westonbirt - The National Arboretum**
Tetbury GL8 8QS
☎ 01666 880220 ▤ 01666 880559
**Web:** www.westonbirtarboretum.com
**Dir:** *3m S Tetbury on A433*
Begun in 1829, this arboretum contains one of the finest and most important collections of trees and shrubs in the world. There are 18,000 specimens, planted from 1829 to the present day, covering 600 acres of landscaped Cotswold countryside. Magnificent displays of Rhododendrons, Azaleas, Magnolias and wild flowers, and ablaze with colour in the autumn from the national collection of Japanese Maples.
**Times:** *Open all year, daily 10-8 or sunset. Visitor centre & shop all year. Closed Xmas & New Year.
**Fee:** *Mar-Nov £6.50 Family ticket £13. Nov-Mar £5 (pen £4) Family ticket £11.
**Facilities:** ❷ ⫪❂⫪ (Licensed) 🍴 ♿ (electric & manual wheelchair for loan, telephone to book, toilets) shop, garden centre, guided tours 🚌 (pre-booking requested)

## WINCHCOMBE
### Sudeley Castle, Gardens & Exhibitions
Cheltenham GL54 5JD
☎ 01242 602308 📠 01242 602959
**Email:** enquiries@sudeley.org.uk
**Web:** www.sudeleycastle.co.uk
**Dir:** *B4632 to Winchcombe, Castle is signed from town*
Sudeley Castle was home to Katherine Parr, who is buried in the Chapel. Henry VIII, Anne Boleyn, Lady Jane Grey and Elizabeth I all stayed or visited here; and it was the headquarters of Prince Rupert during the Civil War. The Queen's Garden is famous for its rose collection. There are exhibitions, a full and varied special events programme and plant centre.
**Times:** Please phone for current opening times.
**Fee:** Please phone for current admission rates.

**Facilities:** ❷ Ⓟ (1.5m - Limited parking nearby) 🍴 (Licensed) 🎋 📷 ♿ (limited access to gardens only, parking, toilets) shop, garden centre, guided tours ⊗ 🚌 (pre-booking requested)

## BATH
### American Museum
Claverton Manor BA2 7BD
☎ 01225 460503 📠 01225 469160
**Email:** info@americanmuseum.org
**Web:** www.americanmuseum.org
**Dir:** *2.5m SE*
Claverton Manor is just two miles south east of Bath, in a beautiful setting above the River Avon. The house was built in 1820 by Sir Jeffrey Wyatville, and is now a museum of American decorative arts. The gardens are well worth seeing, and include an American arboretum and a replica of George Washington's garden at Mount Vernon. The Folk Art Gallery and the New Gallery are among the many exhibits in the grounds along with seasonal exhibitions.

**Times:** *Open mid Mar-Oct, Tue-Sun 2-5. Gardens 12-6.Open Mon in Aug & BHs.
**Fee:** *£6.50 (ch £3.50, con £6).
**Facilities:** ❷ 🎋 📷 £2 ♿ (toilets) shop, guided tours 🚌 (must pre-book)

## BATH
### Bath Aqua Theatre of Glass
105-107 Walcot Street BA1 5BW
☎ 01225 428146
**Email:** sales@bathaquaglass.com
**Web:** www.bathaquaglass.com
In the heart of the city's artisan quarter – right in the city centre, this is an ideal place to learn about the history of glass and watch the ancient craft of glass blowing and stained glass making in action. There are children's activities and a Glass Museum which features examples of Old Bristol Blue glass. Also on site are antique stained glass windows from Bath Abbey Chambers, now renovated and restored.
**Times:** *Open all year, daily, 9.30-5. Closed Sun, Oct-Etr.
**Fee:** *£3.50 (ch & concessions £2). Family of 4 £8.

**Facilities:** 📷 ♿ (toilets) shop, guided tours, audio commentaries (charged) ⊗ 🚌

**SOMERSET**

## BATH
### Bath Postal Museum
27 Northgate Street BA1 1AJ
☎ 01225 460333
**Email:** info@bathpostalmuseum.org
**Web:** www.bathpostalmuseum.org
**Dir:** *On entering city fork left at mini rdbt. After all traffic lights into Walcot St. Podium car park facing*
Discover how 18th-century Bath influenced and developed the Postal System, including the story of the Penny Post. The first letter sent with a stamp was sent from Bath. Visitors can explore the history of written communication from Egyptian clay tablets, thousands of years ago, to the first Airmail flight from Bath to London in 1912. See the Victorian Post Office and watch continuous video films including the in-house production entitled 'History of Writing'. Visit the children's activity room and shop.
**Times:** Open all year, Mon-Sat 11-4.30. (Last admission Mar-Oct 4.30, Oct-Mar 4). Closed Sun, 25-26 Dec & 1 Jan.
**Fee:** £2.90 (ch under 5 free, ch £1.50, students £1.90 & pen £2.40). Family and Party 10+ tickets available.
**Facilities:** ℗ (50yds - no on-street parking) 🗐 ♿ (films and computer games for hearing impaired) shop, guided tours ⊗ (ex guide dogs) 🚌 (pre-booking required)

## BATH
### Museum of Bath at Work
Julian Road BA1 2RH
☎ 01225 318348 🖷 01225 318348
**Email:** mobaw@hotmail.com
**Web:** www.bath-at-work.org.uk
**Dir:** *from city centre, off Lansdown Rd into Julian Rd. Museum next to church on right*
Two thousand years of Bath's commercial and industrial development are explored with exhibits on 'The Story of Bath Stone', a Bath cabinet makers workshop, a 1914 Horstmann car and a reconstruction of J B Bowlers' engineering and mineral water business. New for 2007 is the exhibition: How We Work Now: Bath at Work Today.
**Times:** *Open all year, Etr-1 Nov, daily 10.30-5; Nov-Etr, wknds 10.30-5. Closed 25-26 Dec.
**Fee:** *£4 (concessions £3). Family ticket £10.
**Facilities:** ℗ (0.25m) ⊟ 🗐 £2.50 ♿ (audio guides, ramps) shop, guided tours, audio commentaries (charged) ⊗ (ex guide dogs) 🚌 (pre-book) 🈂

## BATH
### Museum of Costume
Bennett Street BA1 2QH
☎ 01225 477173 🖷 01225 477743
**Email:** costume_bookings@bathnes.gov.uk
**Web:** www.museumofcostume.co.uk
**Dir:** *Museum near city centre. Parking in Charlotte Street car park.*
The Museum of Costume is one of the finest collections of fashionable dress in the world, covering the period from the late 16th-century to the present day. It is housed in Bath's famous 18th-century Assembly Rooms designed by John Wood the Younger in 1771. Entrance to the Assembly Rooms is free.
**Times:** Open all year, daily Jan-Feb 11-4; Mar-Oct 11-5; Nov-Dec 11-4. Closed 25 & 26 Dec.
**Fee:** *£6.50 (ch £4.50). Family ticket £18. Combined ticket with Roman Baths, £13 (ch £7.60).
**Facilities:** ℗ (5 mins walk - park & ride recommended) ⊡ (open 11-4) 🗐 ♿ (audio guides available, toilets) shop, guided tours, audio commentaries ⊗ (ex guide dogs) 🚌 (20+ party, book in advance)

## BATH
### Roman Baths & Pump Room
Abbey Church Yard BA1 1LZ
☎ 01225 477785 ▤ 01225 477743
**Email:** romanbaths_bookings@bathnes.gov.uk
**Web:** www.romanbaths.co.uk
**Dir:** *M4 junct 18, A46 into city centre*
Built 2,000 years ago next to Britain's only hot spring the baths served pilgrims and the sick visiting the adjacent Temple of Sulis Minerva. Above the Temple Courtyard, the regency Pump Room was a popular meeting place in the 18th century. The hot springs remain and no visit is complete without a taste of the famous hot spa water.
**Times:** Open all year, Mar-Jun & Sep-Oct, daily 9-5; Jul & Aug daily 9am-9pm; Jan-Feb & Nov-Dec, daily 9.30-4-30. Closed 25-26 Dec. (Last exit 1hr after closing).

**Fee:** *£10 (£11 Jul-Aug) (ch £6). Family ticket £28. Combined ticket with Museum of Costume £13 (ch £7.60). Disabled visitors free admission to ground floor.
**Facilities:** ⓟ (5 mins walk - park & ride recommended) ⊙ (Licensed) ▤ ♿ (sign language & audio tours, toilets) shop, guided tours, audio commentaries ⊗ (ex guide dogs) 🚌 (party 20+ booking in advance essential)

## BATH
### Sally Lunn's Refreshment House & Museum
4 North Parade Passage BA1 1NX
☎ 01225 461634 ▤ 01225 447090
**Email:** enquiries@sallylunns.co.uk
**Web:** www.sallylunns.co.uk
**Dir:** *centre of Bath, follow signs, next to Bath Abbey*
This Tudor building is Bath's oldest house and was a popular 17th-century meeting place. The traditional 'Sally Lunn' is similar to a brioche, and is popularly believed to carry the name of its first maker who came to Bath in 1680. The bun is still served in the restaurant, and the original oven, Georgian cooking range and a collection of baking utensils are displayed in the museum.
**Times:** *Open all year, Museum - Mon-Fri 10-6, Sat 10-5, Sun 11-5. Closed 25-26 Dec & 1 Jan.

**Fee:** *30p (concessions free).
**Facilities:** ⓟ (2-3 min walk – cards required for street parking) ⊙ (Licensed) ▤ ♿ (Braille menu available) shop, guided tours, audio commentaries ⊗ (ex guide dogs) 🚌 (must be booked in advance)

## BATH
### The Building of Bath Museum
Countess of Huntingdons Chapel The Vineyards
The Paragon BA1 5NA
☎ 01225 333895 ▤ 01225 445473
**Email:** enquiries@bathmuseum.co.uk
**Web:** www.bath-preservation-trust.org.uk
**Dir:** *Take A4, 2nd exit at mini rdbt. Along road on right*
This new museum relates the fascinating story of how Georgian Bath was created. 17th-century Bath was a medieval market town but in the space of 100 years it was transformed into one of the most beautiful and glamorous cities in Europe. The exhibition depicts elegant society life in Beau Nash's spa resort and explains how the houses were constructed. After a visit, the street scene outside seems like an extension of the exhibition.

Ring for details of special events such as concerts and lectures.
**Times:** Open 15 Feb-30 Nov, Tue-Sun & BHs 10.30-5.
**Fee:** £4 (ch £2, concessions £3, children under 6 free). Family ticket £10. Party 10+
**Facilities:** ⓟ (500mtrs) ▤ ♿ shop, guided tours ⊗ (ex guide dogs) 🚌

**SOMERSET**

## CRICKET ST THOMAS
### The Wildlife Park at Cricket St Thomas
Chard TA20 4DB
☎ 01460 30111 📠 01460 30817
**Email:** wildlifepark.cst@bourne-leisure.co.uk
**Web:** www.wild.org.uk
**Dir:** *3m E of Chard on A30, follow brown heritage signs.*
The Wildlife Park offers you the chance to see more than 60 species of animals at close quarters. Visitors can learn about what is being done to save endangered species, take a walk through the Lemur Wood, ride on the Safari Train or visit the Children's Farm. During peak season, park mascot Larry the Lemur stars in his very own show.
**Times:** Open all year, daily 10-6 last admission 4, (10-4.30, last admission 3 in winter). Closed 25 Dec.

**Fee:** £8.25 (ch 3-14 £6.25, under 3's free, pen £7.25). Family ticket £26 (2ad+3ch).
**Facilities:** ❷ ⭐ (Licensed) ⛱ 🗐 £2.95 ♿ (some steep slopes, toilets) shop, guided tours, audio commentaries ⊗ (ex guide dogs) 🚌

## SPARKFORD
### Haynes International Motor Museum
Yeovil BA22 7LH
☎ 01963 440804 📠 01963 441004
**Email:** info@haynesmotormuseum.co.uk
**Web:** www.haynesmotormuseum.co.uk
**Dir:** *from A303 follow A359 towards Castle Cary, museum clearly signed*
Spectacular collection of historic cars, motorcycles and motoring memorabilia. Vehicles range from a 1903 Oldsmobile to sports cars of the 50s and 60s and modern day classics. Also at the Museum is a 70 seat video cinema, the Hall of Motorsports, a millennium hall featuring modern classics and super-cars, and a picnic area and children's adventure playground. The museum also has its own test circuit.

**Times:** *Open all year, Mar-Oct, daily 9.30-5.30; Nov-Feb, 10-4.30. Closed 24-26 Dec & 1 Jan.
**Fee:** *£6.95 (ch £3.75, concessions £5.50). Family £8.95 (1ad+1ch), £21 (2ad+3ch).
**Facilities:** ❷ ⭐ (Licensed) ⛱ 🗐 ♿ (ramps & loan wheelchairs available, toilets) shop ⊗ (ex guide dogs & in grounds) 🚌

## WASHFORD
### Tropiquaria Animal and Adventure Park
Watchet TA23 0QB
☎ 01984 640688 📠 01984 641105
**Email:** office@tropiquaria.co.uk
**Web:** www.tropiquaria.co.uk
**Dir:** *on A39, between Williton and Minehead*
Housed in a 1930s BBC transmitting station, the main hall has been converted into an indoor jungle with a 15-foot waterfall, tropical plants and free-flying birds. (Snakes, lizards, iguanas, spiders, toads and terrapins are caged!). Downstairs is the submarine crypt with local and tropical marine life. Other features include landscaped gardens, the Shadowstring Puppet Theatre, and 'Wireless in the West' museum. Also two new full size pirate adventure ships are moored on the front lawn accessible to pirates of all ages! The park has an indoor playcastle for adventure and fun whatever the weather.
**Times:** Open Apr-Sep, daily 10-6 (last entry 4.30); Oct daily 11-5 (last entry 4); Nov-Mar wknds 11-4 (last entry 3).
**Fee:** *£6.95 (ch & pen £5.95).
**Facilities:** ❷ ⛱ ♿ (ramp to pirate galleon & indoor castle, toilets) shop ⊗ (ex guide dogs) 🚌 (pre-booking required)

SOMERSET

## WESTON-SUPER-MARE
### North Somerset Museum
Burlington Street BS23 1PR

☎ 01934 621028 ▤ 01934 612526

**Email:** museum.service@n-somerset.gov.uk

**Web:** www.n-somerset.gov.uk/museum

**Dir:** *in centre of Weston-super-Mare*

This museum, housed in the former workshops of the Edwardian Gaslight Company, has displays on the seaside holiday, an old chemist's shop, a dairy and Victorian pavement mosaics. Adjoining the museum is Clara's Cottage, a Westonian home of the 1900s with period kitchen, parlour, bedroom and back yard. One of the rooms has an additional display of Peggy Nisbet dolls. Other displays include wildlife gallery, Mendip minerals, mining and local archaeology and costume.

**Times:** *Open all year: Mon-Sat 10-4.30. Closed 25-27 Dec & 1 Jan.

**Fee:** *£3.90 (ch free when accompanied by an adult, pen £2.85)

**Facilities:** Ⓟ (800yds - 1 disabled parking space outside museum) ♿ (Hearing loop at reception, toilets) shop, ⊗ (ex guide dogs) 🚌

---

## WESTON-SUPER-MARE
### The Helicopter Museum
The Heliport Locking Moor Road BS24 8PP

☎ 01934 635227 ▤ 01934 645230

**Email:** office@helimuseum.fsnet.co.uk

**Web:** www.helicoptermuseum.co.uk

**Dir:** *outskirts of town on A371, near M5 junct 21*

The world's largest rotary-wing collection and the only helicopter museum in Britain. More than 70 helicopters and autogyros are on display - including examples from France, Germany, Poland, Russia and the United States, from 1935 to the present day - with displays of models, engines and other components explaining the history and development of the rotocraft. Special events include 'Open Cockpit Days', when visitors can learn more about how a helicopter works.

**Times:** Open all year, Nov-Mar, Wed-Sun 10-4.30; Apr-Oct 10-5.30.Open daily during Etr & Summer school hols 10-5.30. Closed 24-26 Dec & 1 Jan.

**Fee:** *£5.30 (ch under 5 free, ch 5-16 £3.30, pen £4.30). Family ticket (2ad+2ch) £14.50, (2ad+3ch) £16.50. Party 12+.

**Facilities:** Ⓟ 🅿 🖼 £1 ♿ (large print and Braille information sheet, toilets) shop, guided tours, 🚌 (advance notice required)

---

## WOOKEY HOLE
### Wookey Hole Caves & Papermill
Wells BA5 1BB

☎ 01749 672243 ▤ 01749 677749

**Email:** witch@wookey.co.uk

**Web:** www.wookey.co.uk

**Dir:** *M5 junct 22 follow signs via A38 & A371, from Bristol & Bath A39 to Wells then 2m to Wookey Hole*

Britain's most spectacular caves and legendary home of the infamous Witch of Wookey. The 19th-century paper mill houses a variety of fascinating attractions including a Cave Museum, Victorian Penny Arcade, Magical Mirror Maze, Haunted Corridor of Crazy Mirrors, and the Wizard's Castle play area. Visitors can also see paper being made in Britain's only surviving handmade paper mill. Puppet theatre shows, magic lessons, an enchanted fairy garden and Dinosaur Valley round off this family day out in Wookey Gorge.

**Times:** *Open all year, Nov-Mar, daily 10-4; Apr-Oct, daily 10-5. Closed 25 Dec.

**Fee:** *£10.90 (ch 4-14 & concessions £8.50, under 4's free).

**Facilities:** Ⓟ 🍴 (Licensed) 🅿 🖼 £1.50 ♿ (papermill only accessible, toilets) shop, guided tours ⊗ (ex guide dogs) 🚌

### YEOVILTON
**Fleet Air Arm Museum**
Royal Naval Air Station Ilchester BA22 8HT
☎ 01935 840565 ▤ 01935 842630
**Email:** info@fleetairarm.com
**Web:** www.fleetairarm.com
**Dir:** *on B3151, just off junct of A303 and A37*
The Fleet Air Arm Museum has the largest collection of naval aircraft anywhere in Europe. Situated alongside Europe's largest naval air station, where visitors may see Sea Harriers and helicopters. Inside the museum you can board Concorde; be transported by a simulated helicopter flight to the replica flight deck of the aircraft carrier *HMS Ark Royal* and experience the thrills of a working flight deck. The site includes an adventure playground, a licensed restaurant, and a shop.

**Times:** *Open all year, daily Apr-Oct 10-5.30; Nov-Mar, Wed-Sun 10-4.30. Closed 24-26 Dec.
**Fee:** *£10 (ch under 5 free, ch 5-16 £7, concessions £8). Family ticket (2ad+3ch) £30.
**Facilities:** ❷ ℗ ᛏ⊙ᛏ (Licensed) 🛏 ▤ ♿ (wheelchairs available, toilets) shop guided tours ⊗ (ex guide dogs) 🚌 (pre-book)

### AVEBURY
**Alexander Keiller Museum**
High Street Nr Marlborough SN8 1RF
☎ 01672 539250 ▤ 01672 538038
**Email:** avebury@nationaltrust.org.uk
**Web:** www.nationaltrust.org.uk
**Dir:** *6m W of Marlborough. 1m N of Bath Rd A4 on A4361 and B4003*
The Avebury Stone Circle is one of the most important megalithic monuments in Europe, and was built before Stonehenge. The museum, including an exhibition in the 17th-century threshing barn, presents the full archaeo-logical story of the stones using finds from the site, along with interactive and audio-visual displays.
**Times:** *Open Apr-Oct, daily 10-6; Nov-Mar 10-4. Closed 24-26 Dec

**Fee:** *£4.20 (ch £2.10) Family £10.50 (2ad+3ch) Family £7.50 (1ad+3ch). Groups £3.60 (ch 1.80).
**Facilities:** ❷ (charged) ℗ (In village) ⎙ (organic vegetarian lunches) ᛏ⊙ᛏ (Licensed) 🛏 ♿ (Braille guide, large print guide, drop off point, toilets) shop ⊗ (ex guide dogs) 🚌 ♨

### CALNE
**Bowood House & Gardens**
Wiltshire SN11 0LZ
☎ 01249 812102 ▤ 01249 821757
**Email:** houseandgardens@bowood.org
**Web:** www.bowood.org
**Dir:** *off A4 Chippenham to Calne road, in Derry Hill village*
Built in 1624, the house was finished by the first Earl of Shelburne, who employed celebrated architects, notably Robert Adam, to complete the work. Adam's library is particularly admired, and also in the house is the laboratory where Dr Joseph Priestley discovered the existence of oxygen in 1774. The house overlooks terraced gardens towards the 40-acre lake and some beautiful parkland. The gardens were laid out by 'Capability' Brown in the 1760s, and are carpeted with daffodils, narcissi and bluebells in spring. There is also an adventure playground and new soft play area.
**Times:** *Open mid Apr-Oct, daily 11-6, including BH. Rhododendron Gardens (separate entrance off A342) open 6 weeks during mid Apr-early Jun, 11-6.
**Fee:** *House & Gardens £7.50 (ch 2-4 £3.80; 5-15 £5; pen £6.50). Family ticket (2ad+2ch) £22.50. Rhododendrons only £4.80 (pen £4.30). £1 discount if house visited on same day.
**Facilities:** ❷ ⎙ (hot and cold food) 🛏 ♿ (parking by arrangement, DVD tour of upstairs, toilets) shop, guided tours ⊗ (ex assist dogs) 🚌

## LACOCK

**Lacock Abbey, Fox Talbot Museum & Village**
Chippenham SN15 2LG
☎ 01249 730227 (abbey) & 730459 📄 01249 730501
**Web:** www.nationaltrust.org.uk
**Dir:** *3m S of Chippenham, E of A350, car park signed*
This magnificent country house was converted from a medieval abbey in late Victorian times. There are extensive servants' quarters, gardens and a wooded estate. The surrounding village is well preserved and presents an impressive example of domestic Wiltshire architecture. The Fox Talbot Museum displays the history of photography and the work of William Henry Fox Talbot known as the 'father of photography'.
**Times:** * Museum, Cloisters & Grounds, Mar-Oct, daily 11-5.30. Closed Good Fri. Abbey, 27 Mar-Oct daily, ex

Tue, 1-5.30. Closed Good Fri.
**Fee:** *Museum, Abbey, Grounds & Cloisters £7.80 (ch £3.90) Family ticket £20 (2ad+2ch). Garden, Cloisters & Museum £4.80 (ch £2.40) Family ticket £12.20 (2ad+2ch). Abbey, Cloisters & Grounds £6.30 (ch £3.20) Family ticket £16.10 (2ad+2ch). Museum (winter) £3.40
**Facilities:** 🅿 (charged) 🍴 ♿ (manual wheelchairs, Braille/large print & audio guides, toilets) shop, 🚫 🚌 🐾 ♿

## LONGLEAT

**Longleat**
The Estate Office Warminster BA12 7NW
☎ 01985 844400 📄 01985 844885
**Email:** enquiries@longleat.co.uk
**Web:** www.longleat.co.uk
**Dir:** *turn off A36 Bath-Salisbury road onto A362 (Warminster-Frome road)*
Nestling within magnificent 'Capability' Brown landscaped parkland in the heart of Wiltshire, Longleat House is widely regarded as one of the most beautiful stately homes open to the public. It has many treasures including paintings by Tintoretto and Wooton and exquisite Flemish tapestries. Longleat is also renowned for its safari park, the first of its kind in the UK, with hundreds of animals in natural woodland and parkland

settings. Other attractions for a fun family day out include the 'Longleat Hedge Maze', the 'Adventure Castle', 'Longleat Railway', 'Pets' Corner' and the 'Safari Boats'.
**Times:** * Daily Apr-5 Nov. Telephone for opening times
**Fee:** *Longleat passport: £19 (ch 3-14 yrs & pen £15)
**Facilities:** 🅿 🍴 (Licensed) 🍴 🍽 ♿ (informative leaflet available or see website, toilets) shop, guided tours 🚌

## MARLBOROUGH

**Crofton Beam Engines**
Crofton Pumping Station Crofton SN8 3DW
☎ 01672 870300
**Email:** enquiries@croftonbeamengines.org
**Web:** www.croftonbeamengines.org
**Dir:** *signed from A4/A338/A346 & B3087 at Burbage*
The oldest working beam engine in the world still in its original building and still doing its original job, the Boulton and Watt 1812, can be found in this rural spot. Its companion is a Harvey's of Hayle of 1845. Both are steam driven, from a hand-stoked, coal-fired boiler, and pump water into the summit level of the Kennet and Avon Canal with a lift of 40ft.
**Times:** Open daily 6 Apr-Sep, 10.30-5 (last entry 4.30). 'In Steam' Etr, BH wknds & last wknd of Jun, Jul & Sep.

**Fee:** *In Steam wknd: £5 (ch £1, under 5 free & pen £4). Family ticket £10. Non-In Steam days £3 (ch £1, pen £2.50) Family £7
**Facilities:** 🅿 (charged) 🍴 ♿ (phone warden in advance, sighted guides provided) shop 🚌 (must pre-book)

## SALISBURY
### Salisbury Cathedral
33 The Close SP1 2EJ

☎ 01722 555120 ▤ 01722 555116

**Email:** visitors@salcath.co.uk

**Web:** www.salisburycathedral.org.uk

**Dir:** *S of city centre & Market Sq*

Built in one phase between 1220 and 1258, the Cathedral is probably Britain's finest piece of medieval architecture. The 123 metres high spire is the tallest in England. The Chapter House displays a magnificent frieze depicting scenes from Genesis and Exodus and the finest surviving Magna Carta. The surrounding Cathedral Close contains two museums, two small stately homes and acres of lawn.

**Times:** Open all year, daily 7.15am-6.15pm; Jun-Aug, Mon-Sat 7.15am-7.15pm.

**Fee:** Suggested voluntary donations: £4 (ch 5-17 £2, concessions £3.50). Family £8.50.

**Facilities:** Ⓟ (100yds) ⪥ ▤ ♿ (loop system, interpretative model for blind, wheelchairs, toilets) shop, guided tours 🚌

## SALISBURY
### The Medieval Hall
Cathedral Close SP1 2EY

☎ 01722 412472 & 324731 ▤ 01722 339983

**Email:** medieval.hall@ntworld.com

**Web:** www.medieval-hall.co.uk

**Dir:** *look for signs within Salisbury Cathedral Close*

Visit the historic 13th-century Medieval Hall and watch the fascinating 40-minute sound and picture guide to the city and region. A witty and informative soundtrack, (available in six different languages) specially composed music and some startling effects accompany hundreds of images to provide an insight into Salisbury's extraordinary past, the colourful city of today, and many of the attractions in the area. Enjoy refreshments 'while you watch'. Contact the Hall for full details of special events.

**Times:** *Open Apr-Sep, 11-5. Also open throughout year for pre-booked groups. Occasionally closed for special events.

**Fee:** *£2.25 (ch under 18 £1.75, ch under 6 free). Family tickets available

**Facilities:** Ⓟ (charged) Ⓟ (150m) ☕ (Tea, coffee & biscuits) ♿ (ramp access) shop 🚌 (no coaches permitted to enter Close) ⊗

## STONEHENGE
### Stonehenge
SP4 7DE

☎ 01980 624715

**Web:** www.english-heritage.org.uk

**Dir:** *2m W of Amesbury on junct A303 and A344/A360*

Britain's greatest prehistoric monument and a World Heritage Site. What visitors see today are the substantial remains of the last in a series of monuments erected between c3,000 and 1,600BC. The dramatic stone circle is surrounded by more than 300 burial sites and other pre-historic remains.

**Times:** Open all year, mid Mar-May, daily 9.30-6; Jun-Aug, daily 9-7; Sep-mid Oct, daily 9.30-6; mid Oct-mid Mar, daily 9.30-4. Closed 24-26 Dec & 1 Jan.
Note: Usual facilities may not apply around Summer

Solstice 20-22 June, please check

**Fee:** £5.90 (ch £3, concessions £4.40). Family ticket £14.80. Prices and opening times are subject to change. Please check web site or call 0870 333 1181 for the most up-to-date prices and opening times when planning your visit.

**Facilities:** Ⓟ ♿ shop ⊗ (ex guide & hearing dogs) 🚌 ⌗ ⊗

## STOURHEAD

**Stourhead**

Stourhead Estate Office Warminster BA12 6QD

☎ 01747 841152 ▤ 01747 842005

**Email:** stourhead@nationaltrust.org.uk

**Web:** www.nationaltrust.org.uk

**Dir:** *At Stourton off B3092, 3m NW Mere A303, follow brown tourist signs*

An outstanding example of the English landscape style, this splendid garden was designed by Henry Hoare II and laid out between 1741 and 1780. Classical temples, including the Pantheon and Temple of Apollo, are set around the central lake at the end of a series of vistas, which change as the visitor moves around the paths and through the mature woodland with its extensive collection of exotic trees.

**Times:** * Garden open all year 9-7 (or dusk if earlier). House open 18 Mar-Oct ,11.30-4.30 (closed Wed & Thu); King Alfred tower open 18 Mar-Oct, daily 11.30-4.30.

**Fee:** *Garden & House £10.40 (ch £5.20) Family ticket £24.70, groups £9.90, Garden or House £6.20, ch £3.40, King Alfred Tower £2.30, ch £1.20.

**Facilities:** ℗ ⊩◉⊩ (Licensed) ⊓ ♿ (wheelchairs, electric buggy, telephone in advance, toilets) shop, garden centre, guided tours ⊗ (ex in gardens Nov-Feb only) 🚌 🌿

## SWINDON

**STEAM - Museum of The Great Western Railway**

Kemble Drive SN2 2TA

☎ 01793 466646 ▤ 01793 466615

**Email:** steampostbox@swindon.gov.uk

**Web:** www.swindon.gov.uk/steam

**Dir:** *from M4 junct 16 & A420 follow brown signs to 'Outlet Centre' & Museum*

This fascinating day out tells the story of the men and women who built, operated and travelled on the Great Western Railway. Hands-on displays, world-famous locomotives, archive film footage and the testimonies of ex-railway workers bring the story to life. A reconstructed station platform, posters and holiday memorabilia recreate the glamour and excitement of the golden age of steam. Located next door to the McArthurGlen Designer Outlet Great Western, STEAM offers a great day out for all. Good value group packages, special events and exhibitions and shop.

**Times:** Open daily 10-5. Closed 25-26 Dec & 1 Jan

**Fee:** £5.95 (ch £3.80, pen £3.90) Family ticket £14.70 (2ad+2ch)

**Facilities:** ℗ (100yds - disabled parking 20yds) ♿ (wheelchair or scooter can be pre-booked, toilets) shop, ⊗ (ex guide dogs) 🚌 (book in advance)

## TEFFONT MAGNA

**Farmer Giles Farmstead**

Salisbury SP3 5QY

☎ 01722 716338 ▤ 01722 716993

**Email:** tdeane6995@aol.com

**Web:** www.farmergiles.co.uk

**Dir:** *11m W of Stonehenge, off A303 to Teffont. Follow brown signs*

A forty-acre working farm on the Wiltshire Downs where visitors can feed the farm animals, groom a donkey and milk a cow. There are inside and outside play areas, pets corner, a lake and waterfall, nature walks, exhibitions and tractor rides. As well as a restaurant and gift shop there are attractive picnic areas.

**Times:** *Open 18 Mar-5 Nov, daily 10-6, wknds in winters, 10-dusk. Party bookings all year.

**Fee:** *£3.95 (ch £2.85, under 2's free & pen £3.50) Family ticket £13.

**Facilities:** ℗ ℗ (adjacent) ⊩◉⊩ (Licensed) ⊓ ♿ (complete access for disabled/wheelchairs available for use, toilets) shop, 🚌 (telephone prior to visit)

**WILTSHIRE**

## TISBURY
### Old Wardour Castle
SP3 6RR

☎ 01747 870487

**Web:** www.english-heritage.org.uk

**Dir:** *2m SW*

This 14th-century castle stands in a romantic lakeside setting. Landscaped grounds and elaborate rockwork grotto surround the unusual hexagonal ruins. Scenes from the Kevin Costner film, *Robin Hood - Prince of Thieves*, were filmed here.

**Times:** Open all year,  Apr-Jun & Sep, daily 10-5; Jul-Aug, daily 10-6; Oct, daily 10-4; Nov-Mar, Sat-Sun 10-4. Closed 24-26 Dec & 1 Jan.

**Fee:** £3.20 (ch £1.60, concessions £2.40). Prices and opening times are subject to change. Please check web site or call 0870 333 1181 for the most up-to-date prices and opening times when planning your visit.

**Facilities:** ℗ ♿ 🚌 ⌗ ♿

## WESTBURY
### Brokerswood Country Park
Brokerswood BA13 4EH

☎ 01373 822238 & 823880 📄 01373 858474

**Email:** woodland.park@virgin.net

**Web:** www.brokerswood.co.uk

**Dir:** *off A36 at Bell Inn, Standerwick. Follow brown signs from A350*

Brokerswood Country Park's nature walk leads through 80 acres of woodlands, with a lake and wildfowl. Facilities include a woodland visitor centre (covering wildlife and forestry), two children's adventure playgrounds (Etr-Oct school holidays & wknds only), guided walks and the woodland railway, over a third of a mile long.

**Times:** *Open all year; Park open daily 10-5. Closed 24-26 Dec & 1 Jan. Ring for museum opening hours.

**Fee:** *£3.50 (ch 3-16yrs £2.50, pen £3)

**Facilities:** ℗ ⛱ ♿ (ramp access to cafe, toilets) shop, 🚌 (pre-booked only)

## WILTON [NEAR SALISBURY]
### Wilton House
Salisbury SP2 0BJ

☎ 01722 746720 & 746729 (24 hr line)

📄 01722 744447

**Email:** tourism@wiltonhouse.com

**Web:** www.wiltonhouse.com

**Dir:** *3m W of Salisbury, on A30, 10m from Stonehenge & A303*

This fabulous Palladian mansion amazes visitors with its treasures, including magnificent art, fine furniture and interiors by Inigo Jones. The traditional and modern gardens, some designed by the 17th Earl, are fabulous throughout the season and continue to delight visitors, whilst the adventure playground is a firm favourite with children.

**Times:** *Open 2 Apr-Oct, daily, 10.30-5.30. (Last admission 4.30). House closed Mon, ex BHs.

**Fee:** *£9.75 (ch 5-15 £5.50, students & pen £8). Family ticket £24.

**Facilities:** ℗ ⊑ (10.30-5) ⛱ ♿ (induction loop, toilets) shop garden centre guided tours ⊗ (ex assist dogs) 🚌 (pre-booking required – min 15 people)

Scotland

## ABERDEEN
### Satrosphere Science Centre
179 Constitution Street AB24 5TU

☎ 01224 640340 📄 01224 622211

**Email:** info@satrosphere.net

**Web:** www.satrosphere.net

**Dir:** *located very close to Beach Esplanade. Follow signs to fun beach, then attraction*

Satrosphere, the Discovery Place, is different from many museums or exhibition centres. It is an Interactive Centre where everything is 'hands-on'. Visitors can learn through discovery and exploration, from more than 50 exhibits which will challenge and amaze. There are also special weekend events that combine fun-packed experiments, live shows and demonstrations that bring science alive. Things are always changing, so every visit is different.

**Times:** Open daily, 10-5. Closed 25-26 Dec and 1-2 Jan.

**Fee:** *£5.75 (under 3's free, ch & concessions £4.50).

**Facilities:** 🅿 Ⓟ (500yds) ♿ (toilets) shop ⊗ (ex guide dogs) 🚌

## ALFORD
### Alford Valley Railway
AB33 8AD

☎ 019755 62326 & 62811 📄 019755 63182

**Dir:** *A944 Alford Village*

It's not just railway enthusiasts that will delight in taking this narrow-gauge passenger railway between Alford and Haughton Park Station. It's a scenic one-mile trip with views of Bennachie travelling through the golf course and a tree-lined avenue. There's also a large play area available for children and walkways that lead down to the River Don. Diesel traction also features.

**Times:** *Open Apr, May & Sep wknds 1-5, Jun-Aug daily from 1 (30 min service). Party bookings also available at other times.

**Fee:** £2.50 (ch £1) return fare.

**Facilities:** 🅿 Ⓟ (100yds) 🍴 ♿ (ramps at station platforms, toilets), shop, guided tours audio commentaries 🚌 ♿

## BALMORAL
### Balmoral Castle Grounds & Exhibition
AB35 5TB

☎ 013397 42534 📄 013397 42034

**Email:** info@balmoralcastle.com

**Web:** www.balmoralcastle.com

**Dir:** *on A93 between Ballater & Braemar*

Queen Victoria and Prince Albert first rented Balmoral Castle in 1848, and Prince Albert bought the property four years later. He commissioned William Smith to build a new castle, which was completed by 1856 and is still the Royal Family's Highland residence. Country walks and pony trekking can be enjoyed, and an exhibition of paintings and other works of art can be seen in the castle ballroom, together with a Travel and Carriage exhibition and a wildlife exhibition.

**Times:** *Open Apr-Jul, daily 10-5.

**Fee:** *£5 (ch under 16 £1, pen £4)

**Facilities:** Ⓟ (100yds) 🍴 ♿ (wheelchairs & battricars available, reserved parking, toilets), shop ⊗ (ex guide dogs/in grounds) 🚌

## CRATHES
**Crathes Castle & Garden**
Banchory AB31 5QJ
☎ 01330 844525 🖷 01330 844797
Email: crathes@nts.org.uk
Web: www.nts.org.uk
Dir: *On A93, 3m E of Banchory*
This impressive 16th-century castle with magnificent
interiors has royal associations dating from 1323. There
is a large walled garden and a notable collection of
unusual plants, including yew hedges dating from 1702.
The grounds contain six nature trails, one suitable for
disabled visitors, and an adventure playground.
Times: *Open: Castle & Visitor Centre: Apr-Sep, daily
10-5.30, Oct daily 10-4.30. To help enjoy your visit & for
safety reasons, admission to the castle is by timed ticket
(limited numbers: entry may be delayed). Garden &
grounds all year, daily 9-sunset. Times
Fee: *£9 (concessions £6.50) Admission free to NTS
members. For other details please phone 0131 243
9387 or check website.
Facilities: 🅿 🍴 (Licensed) 🚻 ♿ (tape for visually
impaired, toilets), shop ⊗ (ex guide dogs)
🚌 (pre-booking required) ♨ ♿

## KEMNAY
**Castle Fraser**
Inverurie AB51 7LD
☎ 01330 833463
Email: castlefraser@nts.org.uk
Web: www.nts.org.uk
Dir: *off A944, 4m N of Dunecht*
The massive Z-plan castle was built between 1575 and
1636 and is one of the grandest of the Castles of Mar.
The interior was remodelled in 1838 and some
decoration of that period survives. A formal garden inside
the old walled garden, estate trails, a children's play area
and a programme of concerts are among the attractions.
Times: *Open Apr-Jun & Sep, Fri-Tue 12-5.30, Jul-Aug,
daily 11-5.30. Times may change for 2007 please
telephone or check website
Fee: *£7 (concessions £5.25) Groups adult £5.60,
child £1, please book groups in advance. Admission
free to NTS members. For other details please phone
0131 243 9387
Facilities: 🅿 ☕ (tea room) 🚻 ♿ shop, garden centre,
(ex guide dogs, certain areas) 🚌 (pre-booking required)
♨ ♿

## MACDUFF
**Macduff Marine Aquarium**
11 High Shore AB44 1SL
☎ 01261 833369 🖷 01261 831052
Email: macduff.aquarium@aberdeenshire.gov.uk
Web: www.macduff-aquarium.org.uk
Dir: *off A947 and A98 to Macduff, aquarium signed*
Exciting displays feature local sealife. The central exhibit,
unique in Britain, holds a living kelp reef. Divers feed the
fish in this tank. Other displays include an estuary exhibit,
splash tank, rock pools, deep reef tank and ray pool.
Young visitors especially enjoy the touch pools. There are
talks, video presentations and feeding shows throughout
the week.
Times: *Open 10-5 daily (last admission 4.15). Closed
25-26 Dec & 31 Dec-2 Jan
Fee: *£5 (ch £2.50, concessions £3). Family ticket
(2ad+2ch) £13.75. Groups 10+
Facilities: 🅿 🅿 (adjacent) 🚻 📋 ♿ (audio tour
for visually impaired, toilets) shop, guided tours
⊗ (ex guide dogs) 🚌

**ABERDEENSHIRE**

## MARYCULTER
### Storybook Glen
AB12 5FT

☎ 01224 732941 📄 01224 732941

**Web:** www.storybookglenaberdeen.co.uk

**Dir:** *5m W of Aberdeen on B9077. Signposted between Peterculter and Milltimber.*

In this child's fantasy land, favourite nursery rhyme and fairytale characters are brought to life in a magical world of make believe and fun. Grown-ups can enjoy the nostalgia too and there's the 20 acres of Deeside country to explore with its flowers, plants, trees and waterfalls. There's also Dingle Dell Gift and Garden Centre to peruse.

**Times:** *Open Mar-Oct, daily 10-6; Nov-Feb, daily 10-4.

**Fee:** *£4.85 (ch £3.50, pen £3.60).

**Facilities:** 🅿 ☕ (self service) 🍽 (Licensed) ♿ (toilets) shop, garden centre ⊗ (ex guide dogs) 🚌

## MINTLAW
### Aberdeenshire Farming Museum
Aden Country Park AB42 5FQ

☎ 01771 622807 📄 01771 623558

**Email:** heritage@aberdeenshire.gov.uk

**Web:** www.aberdeenshire.gov.uk/heritage

**Dir:** *1m W of Mintlaw on A950*

Housed in 19th-century farm buildings, once part of the estate which now makes up the Aden Country Park. Two centuries of farming history and innovation are illustrated, and the story of the estate is also told. The reconstructed farm of Hareshowe shows how a family in the north-east farmed during the 1950s . Access by guided tour only.

**Times:** *Open May-Sep, daily 11-4.30; Apr & Oct, wknds only noon-4.30. (Last admission 30 mins before closing). ParkOpen all year, Apr-Sep 7-10, winter 7-7.

**Fee:** Free

**Facilities:** 🅿 (charged) Ⓟ (200yds) 🍴 ♿ (sensory garden, toilets), guided tours ⊗ (ex guide dogs) 🚌 (pre-booking essential) ♿

## OYNE
### Archaeolink
Berryhill Insch AB52 6QP

☎ 01464 851500 📄 01464 851544

**Email:** info@archaeolink.co.uk

**Web:** www.archaeolink.co.uk

**Dir:** *1m off A96 on B9002*

A stunning audio-visual show, a Myths and Legends Gallery and a whole range of interpretation techniques help visitors to explore what it was like to live 6,000 years ago. In addition there are landscaped walkways, and outdoor activity areas including an Iron Age farm, Roman marching camp and Stone Age settlement in the 40-acre park. Enjoy daily hands-on activities for all ages, guided tours with costumed guides or relax in the coffee shop. Special weekend events held regularly.

**Times:** *Open all year daily, Apr-Oct 10-5, Nov-Mar 11-4.

**Fee:** *£4.75 (ch 3-16 £3.25, concessions £4.25) Family from £11.25

**Facilities:** 🅿 Ⓟ (100yds) 🍴 ♿ (induction loop in theatre, wheelchair, toilets) shop guided tours ⊗ (ex guide dogs) 🚌 (book in advance)

## PITMEDDEN
### Pitmedden Garden
Ellon AB41 7PD
☎ 01651 842352 🖷 01651 843188
**Email:** aclipson@nts.scot.demon.co.uk
**Web:** www.nts.org.uk
**Dir:** *1m W of Pitmedden on A920*
The fine 17th-century walled garden, with sundials, pavilions and fountains dotted among the parterres, has been authentically restored, and there is a Museum of Farming Life and a woodland walk.
**Times:** *Open May-Sep, daily 10-5.30. Grounds: all year, daily. Times may change for 2007 please telephone or check website
**Fee:** *£5 (concessions £3.75) Family ticket £13.50. Groups adult £4 (ch/school £1). Please book groups in advance. Admission free to NTS members. For other details please phone 0131 243 9387 or check website.
**Facilities:** 🅿 ☕ (tea room) 🎌 ♿ (2 wheelchairs available, toilets), shop 🚌 ☃ 🈯

## TURRIFF
### Fyvie Castle
Fyvie AB53 8JS
☎ 01651 891266 🖷 01651 891107
**Email:** aclipson@nts.scot.demon.co.uk
**Web:** www.nts.org.uk
**Dir:** *8m SE of Turriff on A947*
This superb castle, founded in the 13th century, has five towers, each built in a different century, and is one of the grandest examples of Scottish Baronial. It contains the finest wheel stair in Scotland, and a 17th-century morning room, lavishly furnished in Edwardian style. The collection of portraits is exceptional, and there are also displays of arms and armour and tapestries.
**Times:** *Open Apr-Jun & Sep, Fri-Tue 12-5; Jul-Aug, daily 11-5. Grounds all year, daily, 9.30-sunset. Times may change for 2007 please telephone or check website
**Fee:** *£7 (concessions £5.25) Family ticket £19. Groups adult £5.60 (ch/school £1). Please book groups in advance. Admission free to NTS members. For other details please phone 0131 243 9387
**Facilities:** 🅿 🎌 ♿ (small lift, Braille sheets, toilets), shop 🚫 (ex guide dogs) 🚌 (pre-booking required) ☃ 🈯

## BRECHIN
### Pictavia Visitor Centre
Brechin Castle Centre Haughmuir DD9 6RL
☎ 01356 626241 🖷 01307 473764
**Email:** ecdev@angus.gov.uk
**Web:** www.pictavia.org.uk
**Dir:** *off A90 at Brechin*
Find about more about the ancient pagan nation of the Picts, who lived in Scotland nearly 2000 years ago. Visitors can learn about Pictish culture, art and religion through film, interactive displays and music. There are also nature and farm trails, a pets' corner, and an adventure playground.
**Times:** *Open daily, Etr-mid Oct, Mon-Sat 9.30-5.30, Sun 10.30-5.30; mid Oct-Etr, Mon-Sat 9.30-5, Sun 10-5. Closed 25-26 Dec & 1-2 Jan
**Fee:** *£3.25 (ch & concessions £2.25)
**Facilities:** 🅿 🎌 ♿ (toilets) shop, garden centre, guided tours 🚫 (ex assist dogs) 🚌

**ABERDEENSHIRE / ANGUS**

### GLAMIS
**Angus Folk Museum**
Kirkwynd Cottages Forfar DD8 1RT
☎ 01307 840288 📄 01307 840233
**Web:** www.nts.org.uk
**Dir:** *off A94, in Glamis*
A row of stone-roofed, late 18th-century cottages now
houses the splendid Angus Folk Collection of domestic
equipment and cottage furniture. Across the wynd,
an Angus stone steading houses 'The Life on the
Land' exhibition.
**Times:** *Open Apr-Jun & Sep, Fri-Tue 12-5; Jul & Aug
12-5. Times may change for 2007 please telephone
or check website
**Fee:** *£5 (concessions £3.75) Groups adult £4 (ch/school
group £1), groups please book in advance. Family ticket
£13.50. Admission free to NTS members. For other
details please phone 0131 243 9387 or check web
**Facilities:** 🅿 ♿ (toilets) 🚫 (ex guide dogs)
🚌 (pre-booking required) 🏕 ♻

### GLAMIS
**Glamis Castle**
BY FORFAR DD8 1RJ
☎ 01307 840393 📄 01307 840733
**Email:** enquires@glamis-castle.co.uk
**Web:** www.glamis-castle.co.uk
**Dir:** *5m W of Forfar on A94*
Glamis Castle is the family home of the Earls of
Strathmore and Kinghorne and has been a royal
residence since 1372. It is the childhood home of the
late Queen Mother, the birthplace of her daughter the late
Princess Margaret and the setting for Shakespeare's play
*Macbeth.* Though the Castle is open to visitors it remains
the home of the Strathmore family. Each year there are
Highland games, a transport extravaganza, the Scottish
Prom, and a countryside festival. Contact for exact dates.
**Times:** Open Mar-Oct, 10-6. Nov-Dec as advertised.
(Last admission 4.30).
**Fee:** *Castle & grounds £7.30 (ch £4.10, pen & students
£6.10). Family ticket £21. Grounds only £3.50 (ch, pen
& students £2.50). Group 20+
**Facilities:** 🅿 🅿 (1m) 🍴 (Licensed) 🪑 🗑 ♿ (castle
tour not suitable due to stairs, toilets), shop, guided tours
🚫 (ex in grounds, guide dogs) 🚌

### KIRRIEMUIR
**J M Barrie's Birthplace**
9 Brechin Road DD8 4BX
☎ 01575 572646
**Email:** aclipson@nts.scot.demon.co.uk
**Web:** ww.nts.org.uk
**Dir:** *on A90/A926, 6m NW of Forfar*
The creator of *Peter Pan,* Sir James Barrie, was born
in Kirriemuir in 1860. The upper floors of No 9 Brechin
Road are furnished as they may have been when Barrie
lived there, and the adjacent house, No 11, houses an
exhibition. The wash-house outside was his first 'theatre'
and gave him the idea for Wendy's house in Peter Pan.
**Times:** *Open Apr-Jun & Sep, Fri-Tue 12-5; Jul-Aug,
daily 12-5. Times may change for 2007 please telephone
or check website
**Fee:** *£5 (concessions £3.75) Groups adult £4 (ch/schoo
£1), please book groups in advance. Family ticket
£13.50. Admission free to NTS members. For other
details please phone 0131 243 9387 or check web site
**Facilities:** 🅿 (100yds) ♿ (stairlift, audio programmes),
shop 🚫 (ex guide dogs) 🚌 (pre-booking required) 🏕 ♻

## MONTROSE
### House of Dun

DD10 9LQ

☎ 01674 810264 🖷 01674 810722

**Email:** houseofdun@nts.org.uk

**Web:** www.nts.org.uk

**Dir:** *on A935, 3m W of Montrose*

This Georgian house, overlooking the Montrose Basin, was built for Lord Dun in 1730 and is noted for the exuberant plasterwork of the interior. Family portraits, fine furniture and porcelain are on display, and royal mementos connected with a daughter of King William IV and the actress Mrs Jordan, who lived here in the 19th century. There is a walled garden and woodland walks.

**Times:** *Open House: Apr-Jun, & Sep, Fri-Tue 12-5, Jul-Aug, daily 12-5. Garden & grounds all year daily 9.30-sunset. Times may change for 2007 please telephone or check website

**Fee:** *£7 (concessions £5.25) Family ticket £19. Groups adult £5.60 (ch/school £1). Please book groups in advance. Admission free to NTS members. For other details please phone 0131 243 9387 or check web site

**Facilities:** ❷ �🍽🏠 ♿ (Braille sheets, house wheelchair & stair lift, toilets), shop ⊗ (ex guide dogs) 🚌 (pre-booking required) 🍴 ♨

## ARROCHAR
### Argyll Forest Park

Forestry Commission Ardgartan Visitor Centre G83 7AR

☎ 01301 702597 🖷 01301 702597

**Email:** robin.kennedy@forestry.gsl.gov.uk

**Dir:** *on A83 at foot of The Rest and Be Thankful*

This park was the very first to be made accessible to the public back in 1935. Extending over a large area of hill ground and forest, Argyll Forest Park is noted for its rugged beauty. Numerous forest walks and picnic sites allow exploration; the Arboretum walks and the route between Younger Botanic Gardens and Puck's Glen are particularly lovely. The Forestry Commission hosts many events in the park including talks, tours, education and conservation events. See the website or call for further details.

**Times:** Open all year.

**Fee:** Free

**Facilities:** ❷ 🏠 shop 🚌

## AUCHINDRAIN
### Auchindrain Museum

Nr Inveraray PA32 8XN

☎ 01499 500235 🖷 01499 500235

**Email:** manager@auchindrain-museum.org.uk

**Web:** www.auchindrain-museum.org.uk

**Dir:** *6m SW of Inveraray on A83*

Auchindrain is an unusual attraction that brings an original township (or farming village) back to life. On entering the Museum visitors step back in time to witness how the local community lived, worked on the land and played. The original township buildings are furnished with objects from the period and give a fascinating glimpse into the lives of the people who once lived and worked at Auchindrain.

**Times:** Open Apr-Oct, daily 10-5.

**Fee:** *£4.50 (ch £2.20, pen £3.50). Family ticket £12.

**Facilities:** ❷ 🏠 📱 shop 🚌 ♨

**ANGUS / ARGYLL & BUTE**

## BARCALDINE
### Scottish Sea Life Sanctuary
Oban PA37 1SE
☎ 01631 720386 📄 01631 720529
**Email:** obansealife@merlinentertainments.biz
**Web:** www.sealsanctuary.co.uk
**Dir:** *10m N of Oban on A828 towards Fort William*
Set in one of Scotland's most picturesque locations, the Scottish Sea Life Sanctuary provides dramatic views of native undersea life including stingrays, seals, octopus and catfish. There are daily talks and feeding demonstrations and during the summer young seals can be viewed prior to their release back into the wild. Recent additions include Otter Creek - a large naturally landscaped enclosure with deep diving pool with underwater viewing and cascading streams through other pools and 'Into the Deep', a themed interactive area displaying living creatures from the deep. There is a restaurant, gift shop, children's play park and a nature trail.
**Times:** *Open all year, mid Feb-Nov, daily 10-5. Dec & Jan; Sat-Sun & school hols only
**Fee:** *£7.95 (ch £5.50, pen £6.50). Group 15+.
**Facilities:** 🅿 ☕ (Lochsite restaurant) 🍴 🎪 📷 ♿ (assistance available for wheelchairs, toilets), shop ⊗ (ex guide dogs) 🚌

## BENMORE
### Benmore Botanic Garden
Dunoon PA23 8QU
☎ 01369 706261 📄 01369 706369
**Email:** benmore@rbge.org.uk
**Web:** www.rbge.org.uk
**Dir:** *7m N of Dunoon on A815*
From the formal gardens, through the hillside woodlands, follow the paths to a stunning viewpoint with a spectacular outlook across the garden and the Holy Loch to the Firth of Clyde and beyond. Amongst many highlights are the stately conifers, the magnificent avenue of giant redwoods, and an extensive magnolia and rhododendron collection.
**Times:** *Open Mar & Oct daily 10-5, Apr-Sep daily 10-6
**Fee:** *£3.50 (ch £1, concs £3). Family £8. Party rates.
**Facilities:** 🅿 🍴 (Licensed) 📷 ♿ (toilets), shop, garden centre, guided tours, audio commentaries (charged) ⊗ (ex guide dogs) 🚌

## CRAIGNURE
### Mull & West Highland Narrow Gauge Railway
Craignure (old pier) Station Isle of Mull PA65 6AY
☎ 01680 812494 (in season) or 01680 812567
📄 01680 300595
**Email:** mullrail@dee-emm.co.uk
**Web:** mullrail.co.uk
**Dir:** *0.25m from Craignure Ferry Terminal, just off road to Iona, by Police station*
The first passenger railway on a Scottish island, opened in 1983. Both steam and diesel trains operate on the ten-and-a-quarter inch gauge line, which runs from Craignure to Torosay Castle. The 1.25 mile line offers dramatic woodland and mountain views taking in Ben Nevis, Glencoe and the Isle of Lismore.
**Times:** Open Etr-end Oct, 11-5
**Fee:** *Return £4 (ch £3); Single £3 (ch £2). Family ticket return £12, single £8, Dogs free.
**Facilities:** 🅿 📷 £2 ♿ (provision to carry person seated in wheelchair on trains) shop 🚌

## INVERARAY
**Inveraray Castle**

PA32 8XE

☎ 01499 302203 🗎 01499 302421

**Email:** enquiries@inveraray-castle.com

**Web:** www.inveraray-castle.com

**Dir:** *on A83 Glasgow to Campbeltown road*

The Castle is currently home to the Duke of Argyll, Head of the Clan Campbell, whose family have lived in Inveraray since the 15th century. Designed by Roger Morris and decorated by Robert Mylne, the fairytale exterior belies the grandeur of the gracious interior. The Armoury Hall contains some 1300 pieces including Brown Bess muskets, Lochaber axes, 18th-century Scottish broadswords, and swords from the Battle of Culloden. Other rooms contain fine French tapestries, Scottish, English and French furniture, and a wealth of other works of art. There is also a unique collection of china, silver and family artefacts.

**Times:** *Open 1st Sat in Apr-last Sun in Oct. Mon-Sat 10-5.45, Sun 1-5.45.

**Fee:** £6.30 (ch under 16 £4.10, concessions £5.20) Family ticket £17. School parties. Groups 20+. 20% discount. School parties £2.10 per child.

**Facilities:** 🅿 🅟 (0.5 miles) ☕ (Tearoom-light snacks, teas, coffees) 🇦 🗐 ♿ (toilets) shop, guided tours ⊗ (ex guide dogs and in grounds) 🚌 Larger parties to pre-book

## INVERARAY
**Inveraray Jail**

Church Square PA32 8TX

☎ 01499 302381 🗎 01499 302195

**Email:** Info@Inverarayjail.co.uk

**Web:** www.inverarayjail.co.uk

**Dir:** *on A82/A83 Campbeltown road*

Enter Inveraray Jail and step back in time. See furnished cells and experience prison sounds and smells. Ask the 'prisoner' how to pick oakum. Turn the heavy handle of an original crank machine, take 40 winks in a hammock or listen to Matron's tales of day-to-day prison life. Visit the magnificent 1820 courtroom and hear trials in progress. Imaginative exhibitions including 'Torture, Death and Damnation' and 'In Prison Today'. Also a fully preserved Black Maria, built in 1891.

**Times:** Open all year, Nov-Mar, daily 10-5 (last admisssion 4); Apr-Oct, daily 9.30-6 (last admission 5). Closed 25-26 Dec & 1-2 Jan.

**Fee:** *£6.25 (ch £3.15, pen £4.15). Family ticket £17.20.

**Facilities:** 🅟 (100 yds) 🗐 £2 ♿ (wheelchair ramp at rear, induction loop in courtroom, toilets) shop, guided tours ⊗ (ex on leads) 🚌 (pre-booked preferred)

## LOCHAWE
**Cruachan Power Station**

Visitor Centre Dalmally PA33 1AN

☎ 01866 822618 🗎 01866 822509

**Email:** visit.cruachan@scottishpower.com

**Web:** www.visitcruachan.co.uk

**Dir:** *A85 18m E of Oban*

A vast cavern hidden 1km inside Ben Cruachan, which contains a 400,000-kilowatt hydro-electric power station, driven by water drawn from a high-level reservoir further up the mountain. A guided tour takes you inside the mountain and reveals the generators and the processes by which electricity is created in their underground cavern. Call for further details.

**Times:** Open Etr-Nov, daily 9.30-5 (last tour 4.15). (Winter hours available on request).

**Fee:** *£5 (ch 6-16 £2, concessions £4.50)

**Facilities:** 🅿 🇦 ♿ (toilets) shop ⊗ (ex guide dogs) 🚌

## DUNDEE
### Camperdown Country Park
Coupar Angus Road DD2 4TF
☎ 01382 431818 📄 01382 431810
**Email:** camperdown@dundeecity.gov.uk
**Web:** www.camperdownpark.com
**Dir:** *A90 to Dundee then onto A923 Coupar-Angus road, left at 1st rdbt to attraction*
Camperdown is Dundee's largest park, covers an area of over 400 acres and is home to some 190 species of tree. There is a good range of facilities, including an 18-hole golf course, a putting green, boating pond, children's play area, footpaths and woodland trails, and Camperdown Wildlife Centre. There is also a year-round calendar of special events. Contact the Country Park for further details.

**Times:** Open Park: all year. Wildlife Centre: Mar-Sep, daily 10-4.30 (last admission 3.45), Oct-Mar 10-3.30 (last admission 2.45).
**Fee:** Park - free admission. Wildlife Centre charged.
**Facilities:** 🅿 ⛱ ♿ (ramps, toilets), shop, guided tours ⊗ (ex guide dogs and on leads) 🚌 😊

## DUNDEE
### Discovery Point & RRS Discovery
Discovery Quay DD1 4XA
☎ 01382 201245 📄 01382 225891
**Email:** info@dundeeheritage.sol.co.uk
**Web:** www.rrsdiscovery.com
**Dir:** *follow brown heritage signs for Historic Ships*
Discovery Point is the home of *RRS Discovery*, Captain Scott's famous Antarctic ship. Spectacular lighting, graphics and special effects re-create key moments in the Discovery story. The restored bridge gives a captain's view over the ship and the River Tay. Learn what happened to the ship after the expedition, during the First World War and the Russian Revolution, and find out about her involvement in the first survey of whales' migratory patterns.

**Times:** Open Apr-Oct, Mon-Sat 10-6. Sun 11-6; Nov-Mar, Mon-Sat 10-5. Sun 11-5.
**Fee:** *£6.45 (ch £3.85, pen & concessions £4.90). Group £5.15 (ch £3.50, pen & concessions £4)
**Facilities:** 🅿 (charged) Ⓟ (20 yds) 🍽 (Licensed) 📋 ♿ (in-house wheelchairs & lifts, parking, ramps, toilets), shop, guided tours ⊗ (ex guide & hearing dogs) 🚌

## DUNDEE
### HM Frigate Unicorn
Victory Dock DD1 3BP
☎ 01382 200900 & 200893 📄 01382 200923
**Email:** frigateunicorn@hotmail.com
**Web:** www.frigateunicorn.org
**Dir:** *from W follow A85 from A90 at Invergowrie. From E follow A92. Near N end of Tay Road Bridge. Follow signs for City Quay.*
The Unicorn is the oldest British-built warship afloat, and Scotland's only example of a wooden warship. Today she houses a museum of life in the Royal Navy during the days of sail, with guns, models and displays.
**Times:** Open all year Apr-Oct, daily 10-5; Nov-Mar, Wed-Fri 12-4, Sat & Sun 10-4. Closed Mon-Tue & 2 weeks at Xmas & New Year.

**Fee:** £4 (concessions £3). Family ticket £9-£11. Groups 10+ £2.50 each.
**Facilities:** 🅿 Ⓟ (10min walk - limit 3hrs and is free) 📋 £2.50 ♿ (audio visual presentations, introductory video), shop, guided tours ⊗ (ex guide dogs on deck area) 🚌 (pre-booking advised)

## DUNDEE
### Mills Observatory

Balgay Park Glamis Road DD2 2UB

☎ 01382 435967 📠 01382 435962

**Email:** mills.observatory@dundeecity.gov.uk

**Web:** www.dundeecity.gov.uk/mills

**Dir:** *1m W of city centre, in Balgay Park, on Balgay Hill. Vehicle entrance at Glamis Rd gate to Balgay Park*

The observatory was built in 1935, and has a Victorian 10in Cooke refracting telescope among its instruments. The gallery has displays on astronomy and space exploration; visitors can view a safe projection of the sun on bright days. There is a small planetarium for booked groups only. The observatory is open at night during the winter months with children's activities during the summer holidays.

**Times:** Open all year, Apr-Sep, Tue-Fri 11-5, Sat & Sun 12.30-4; Oct-Mar, Mon-Fri 4-10, Sat & Sun 12.30-4. Closed 25-26 Dec & 1-3 Jan.

**Fee:** Free except for planetarium shows extra, £1 (ch 50p) Groups £10.

**Facilities:** 🅿 Ⓟ (0.25m) 🍴 📷 ♿ (portable telescopes available, images on screen, toilets), shop, guided tours 🚫 (ex guide dogs) 🚌 (pre-booking preferred)

## DUNDEE
### Verdant Works

West Henderson's Wynd DD2 5BT

☎ 01382 225282 📠 01382 221612

**Email:** info@dundeeheritage.sol.co.uk

**Web:** www.verdantworks.com

**Dir:** *follow brown tourist signs*

Dating from 1830, this old Jute Mill covers 50,000 sq ft and has been restored as a living museum of Dundee and Tayside's textile history and award-winning European Industrial Museum. Phase I explains what jute is and how Dundee became the centre of its production. Working machinery illustrates the production process and Phase II deals with the uses of jute and Dundee's social history.

**Times:** *Open Apr-Oct; Mon-Sat 10-5, Sun 11-5. Nov-Mar; Mon-Sat 10-4, Sun 11-4. Venue closes 1hr after last entry. Please check for winter opening times. Closed 25-26 Dec & 1-2 Jan

**Fee:** *£5.95 (ch £3.85, pen & concessions £4.45). Family ticket (2ad+2ch) £17.

**Facilities:** 🅿 (charged) Ⓟ (50yds) ♿ (wheelchairs, induction loops, toilets), shop 🚫 (ex guide & hearing dogs) 🚌 (prior notice required)

## EDINBURGH
### Camera Obscura & World of Illusions

Castlehill Royal Mile EH1 2ND

☎ 0131 226 3709 📠 0131 225 4239

**Email:** info@camera-obscura.co.uk

**Web:** www.camera-obscura.co.uk

**Dir:** *next to Edinburgh Castle*

A unique view of Edinburgh in this world of illusions. As the lights go down, a brilliant moving image of the surrounding city appears. The scene changes as a guide operates the camera's system of revolving lenses and mirrors.

**Times:** *Open all year, daily, Apr-Oct 9.30-6; Nov-Mar 10-5. Closed 25 Dec. Open later Jul-Aug, phone for details.

**Fee:** *£5.75 (ch £3.70, students & pen £4.60)

**Facilities:** Ⓟ (300mtrs) shop 🚫 (ex guide dogs) 🚌 (max 70 people)

EDINBURGH
**Dynamic Earth**
Holyrood Rd EH8 8AS
☎ 0131 550 7800 🖹 0131 550 7801
Email: enquiries@dynamicearth.co.uk
Web: www.dynamicearth.co.uk
Dir: *on edge of Holyrood Park, opposite Palace of Holyrood House*
Take a walk through Scotland's geological history. Travel back in time to follow the creation of Planet Earth. Be shaken by a volcano, feel the chill of polar ice and get caught in a tropical rainstorm. A new addition is the Journey to the Centre of the Earth. Please visit website for details of events running throughout the year.
Times: Open Apr-Oct daily & Nov-Mar Wed-Sun 10-5, (last entry 3.50); Jul-Aug daily, 10-6, (last entry 4.50).
Fee: £8.95 (ch £5.45).
Facilities: ℗ (charged) ℗ (500yds - multi storey) ☕ (Hot and cold meals and snacks) ⌿ ♿ (audio guides, large print gallery guides, toilets), shop, audio commentaries (charged) ⊗ (ex guide dogs) 🚌 (pre-booked)

EDINBURGH
**Edinburgh Castle**
EH1 2NG
☎ 0131 225 9846
Web: www.historic-scotland.gov.uk
This historic stronghold stands on the precipitous crag of Castle Rock. One of the oldest parts is the 11th-century chapel of the saintly Queen Margaret, but most of the present castle evolved later, during its stormy history of sieges and wars, and was altered again in Victorian times. The Scottish crown and other royal regalia are displayed in the Crown Room.
Times: *Open all year, Apr-Sep daily 9.30-6; Oct-Mar 9.30-5. Closed 25-26 Dec.
Fee: *£10.30 (ch £4.50, concessions £8.50). Please phone or check website for further details.
Facilities: ℗ (charged) 🍴 (Licensed) ♿ (free transport to top of Castle Hill lift, toilets), shop ⊗ 🚌 ⧉ ⧉

EDINBURGH
**Edinburgh Zoo**
Murrayfield EH12 6TS
☎ 0131 334 9171 🖹 0131 314 0382
Email: marketing@rzss.org.uk
Web: www.edinburghzoo.org.uk
Dir: *3m W of city centre on A8 towards Glasgow*
Scotland's largest wildlife attraction, set in 80 acres of leafy hillside parkland, just ten minutes from the city centre. With over 1,000 animals ranging from the tiny poison arrow frog to massive white rhinos, including many threatened species. See the world's largest penguin pool with underwater viewing, and the Darwin Maze, based on the theme of evolution.
Times: *Open all year, Apr-Sep, daily 9-6; Oct & Mar, daily 9-5; Nov-Feb, daily 9-4.30.
Fee: *£8.50 (ch 3-14 & disabled £5.50, student £6.50, pen £6).
Facilities: ℗ (charged) ℗ (by main entrance - time restrictions apply) 🍴 (Licensed) ⌿ ♿ (wheelchair loan free, 1 helper free - phone in advance, toilets), shop ⊗ (ex guide dogs) 🚌

## EDINBURGH
### Georgian House

7 Charlotte Square EH2 4DR

☎ 0131 226 3318 📄 0131 226 3318

**Email:** thegeorgianhouse@nts.org.uk

**Web:** www.nts.org.uk

**Dir:** *2 mins walk W end of Princes Street*

The house is part of Robert Adam's splendid north side of Charlotte Square, the epitome of Edinburgh New Town architecture. The lower floors of No 7 have been restored in the style of the early 1800s, when the house was new. There also videos of life in the New Town, and this house in particular.

**Times:** *Open Apr-Oct, daily 10-5; Mar & Nov-24 Dec daily 11-3. Times may change for 2007 please telephone or check website

**Fee:** *£5 (concessions £3.75) Family ticket £13.50. Groups adult £4 (ch/school £1). Please book groups in advance. Admission free for NTS members. For other details please phone 0131 243 9387 or check web site.

**Facilities:** Ⓟ (100yds, disabled directly outside) ♿ (induction loop, Braille guide), shop Ⓝ (ex guide dogs) 🚌 (pre-booking required) 🎌 ♻

## EDINBURGH
### Mary King's Close

2 Warriston's Close High Street EH1 1PG

☎ 08702 430160 📄 0131 225 0671

**Email:** info@realmarykingsclose.com

**Web:** www.realmarykingsclose.com

**Dir:** *off High St, opposite St. Giles Cathedral*

Step back in time to walk through a warren of hidden streets, deep beneath The Royal Mile. Meet some of the real characters who used to inhabit these closes and hear tales of extraordinary apparitions as you are guided through dramatic episodes from Edinburgh's hidden past.

**Times:** Apr-Oct, 10-9 (last tour), Sun-Sat. Nov-Mar, 10-4 (last tour), Sun-Fri, 10-9 (last tour) Sat. Closed 25 Dec.

**Fee:** *£8 (ch £6, concessions £7).

**Facilities:** Ⓟ ♿ (hearing loop, toilets) shop, guided tours, audio commentaries Ⓝ (ex guide dogs) 🚌 (pre-booked only)

## EDINBURGH
### Museum of Scotland

Chambers Street EH1 1JF

☎ 0131 247 4422 📄 0131 220 4819

**Email:** info@nms.ac.uk

**Web:** www.nms.ac.uk

**Dir:** *situated in Chambers St in Old Town. A few mins walk from Princes St and The Royal Mile*

The museum is a striking landmark in Edinburgh's historic Old Town. It houses more than 10,000 of the nation's most precious artefacts, as well as everyday objects which throw light on life in Scotland through the ages. Admission to the Royal Museum which is adjacent to the Museum of Scotland is also free. Contact for details of special events.

**Times:** *Open all year, Mon-Sun 10-5. Closed 25 Dec.

Please telephone for times on 26 Dec and 1 Jan.

**Fee:** Free. A charge for special exhibitions

**Facilities:** Ⓟ (off street – metered parking) ♿ (toilets) shop, guided tours, audio commentaries Ⓝ (ex assist dogs) 🚌

EDINBURGH
**National Gallery of Scotland**
The Mound EH2 2EL
☎ 0131 624 6200 📄 0131 343 3250
**Email:** enquiries@nationalgalleries.org
**Web:** www.nationalgalleries.org
**Dir:** *off Princes Street*
Occupying a handsome neo-classical building designed
by William Playfair, the gallery is home to Scotland's
greatest collection of European paintings and sculpture
from the Renaissance to Post-Impressionism. It contains
notable collections of works by Old Masters,
Impressionists and Scottish artists.
**Times:** *Open all year, daily 10-5, Thu until 7. 1 Jan
noon-5. Closed 25-26 Dec.
**Fee:** *Free. Charges for some major exhibitions.

**Facilities:** Ⓟ (150yds - pay and display) 🍴 (Licensed)
♿ (ramps & lift, room A1 not accessible, toilets), shop,
guided tours ⊗ (ex guide dogs) 🚌 (prior booking
prefered)

EDINBURGH
**National War Museum of Scotland**
Edinburgh Castle EH1 2NG
☎ 0131 247 4413 📄 0131 225 3848
**Email:** info@nms.ac.uk
**Web:** www.nms.ac.uk
**Dir:** *at Edinburgh Castle, a few minutes walk up
the Royal Mile to Castlehill*
Explore the Scottish experience of war and military
service over the last 400 years. A chance to experience
the poignant stories of the Scots who went to war,
through their letters and personal treasures.
**Times:** *Open all year, daily, Apr-Oct, 9.45-5.45;
Nov-Mar, daily, 9.45-4.45 Closed 25-26 Dec.
**Fee:** *£10.30 (ch £4.50, ch under 5 free, concessions
£8.50) NMS members £8.30.

**Facilities:** Ⓟ ♿ (courtesy vehicle runs from the Castle
ticket kiosk, toilets) shop ⊗ (ex assist dogs) 🚌 ♿

EDINBURGH
**Palace of Holyroodhouse**
EH8 8DX
☎ 0131 556 5100 📄 020 7930 9625
**Email:** bookinginfo@royalcollection.org.uk
**Web:** www.royalcollection.org.uk
**Dir:** *at east end of Royal Mile*
The Palace grew from the guest house of the Abbey
of the Holyrood, said to have been founded by David I
after a miraculous apparition. Mary, Queen of Scots had
her court here from 1561 to 1567, and 'Bonnie' Prince
Charlie held levees at the Palace during his occupation
of Edinburgh. Today the Royal Apartments are used
by HM The Queen for state ceremonies and official
entertaining, and are finely decorated with works of
art from the Royal Collection.

**Times:** Open daily, Apr-Oct 9.30-6 (last admission 5);
Nov-Mar 9.30-4.30 (last admission 3.30). Closed Good
Fri, 25-26 Dec and when The Queen is in residence.
**Fee:** £8.80 (ch under 17 £4.80, concessions £7.80).
Family ticket (2ad+3ch) £22.50.
**Facilities:** Ⓟ (charged) Ⓟ (200yds) ♿ (first floor by lift,
wheelchair available, toilets), shop, audio commentaries
⊗ (ex guide dogs) 🚌

## EDINBURGH
**Royal Botanic Garden Edinburgh**

Inverleith Row EH3 5LR

☎ 0131 552 7171 🖷 0131 248 2901

**Email:** info@rbge.org.uk

**Web:** www.rbge.org.uk

**Dir:** *1m N of city centre, off A902*

Established in 1670, on an area the size of a tennis court, the Garden is now over 70 acres of beautifully landscaped grounds. Spectacular features include the Rock Garden and the Chinese Hillside. The amazing glasshouses feature Britain's tallest palm house and the magnificent woodland gardens and arboretum.

**Times:** *Open all year, daily; Apr-Sep, 10-7; Mar & Oct, 10-6; Nov-Feb, 10-4. Closed 25 Dec & 1 Jan. (Facilities close 30 mins before Garden)

**Fee:** Free

**Facilities:** Ⓟ (free on street - restricted at certain times) ⓘ (Licensed) 🗐 70p-£2.50 ᵷ (wheelchairs available at east/west gates, toilets), shop, garden centre, guided tours  audio commentaries (charged) ⊗ (ex guide dogs) 🚌

## EDINBURGH
**Scottish National Gallery of Modern Art**

Belford Rd EH4 3DR

☎ 0131 624 6200 🖷 0131 343 3250

**Email:** enquiries@nationalgalleries.org

**Web:** www.nationalgalleries.org

**Dir:** *in West End, 20min walk from Haymarket station*

An outstanding collection of 20th-century painting, sculpture and graphic art. Includes major works by Matisse, Picasso, Bacon, Moore and Lichtenstein and an exceptional group of Scottish paintings. Set in leafy grounds with a sculpture garden.

**Times:** *Open all year, daily 10-5. New Year's Day noon-5. Closed 25-26 Dec.

**Fee:** *Free. Admission charged to some major exhibitions.

**Facilities:** ❷ ᵷ (ramps & lift, toilets), shop, guided tours ⊗ (ex guide dogs) 🚌

## EDINBURGH
**The Edinburgh Dungeon**

31 Market Street EH1 1QB

☎ 0131 240 1000 & 240 1002 🖷 0131 240 1002

**Email:** edinburghdungeon@merlinentertainments.biz

**Web:** www.thedungeons.com

**Dir:** *close to Waverly Train Station*

From the same team at The London Dungeon, there comes a Scottish feast of fun with history's horrible bits. A mixture of live actors, rides, shows and special effects take the brave visitor back into a dark past that includes such delights as the Judgement of Sinners, the Plague, Burke & Hare: Bodysnatchers, and Clan Wars, which attempts to recreate the horror of the Glencoe Massacre of 1692. A new attraction is Inferno, which explores the Great Fire of Edinburgh in 1828.

**Times:** *Open all year ex Xmas. Please telephone for times.

**Fee:** *£11.95 (ch 5-14 £7.95, concessions £9.95). Family £37.75

**Facilities:** Ⓟ (100mtrs - metered bays limited to 1-2hrs) 🗐 £4.50 ᵷ (toilets), shop, guided tours ⊗ (ex guide dogs) 🚌 no parking

**CITY OF EDINBURGH**

## EDINBURGH
**The Royal Yacht Britannia**
Ocean Terminal Leith EH6 6JJ
☎ 0131 555 5566 📄 0131 555 8835
**Email:** enquiries@tryb.co.uk
**Web:** www.royalyachtbritannia.co.uk
**Dir:** *follow signs to North Edinburgh & Leith. Situated within Ocean Terminal*
Visit the Royal Yacht Britannia, now in Edinburgh's historic port of Leith. Start in the Visitor Centre where you can discover the ship's history. Then step aboard for a self-led audio tour which takes you around five decks. Highlights include the State Apartments, Admiral's Cabin, Engine Room, Laundry, and the Royal Marine's Barracks.
**Times:** Open Jan-Mar & Oct-Dec: 10-3.30 (last admission). Apr-Sep 9.30-4.30 (last admission). Closed 25 Dec & 1 Jan.
**Fee:** *£9 (ch 5-17 £5, concessions £7). Family ticket (2ad+3ch) £25.
**Facilities:** 🅿 ℗ (adjacent - parking charges Mon-Fri) ♿ (lift to ship, all areas ramped, written scripts, toilets) shop, audio commentaries ⊗ (ex guide dogs) 🚌 (pre-booking required)

## SOUTH QUEENSFERRY
**Hopetoun House**
EH30 9SL
☎ 0131 331 2451 📄 0131 319 1885
**Email:** marketing@hopetounhouse.com
**Web:** www.hopetounhouse.com
**Dir:** *2m W of Forth Road Bridge, off A904*
Hopetoun House at South Queensferry is just a short drive from Edinburgh and has all the ingredients for a great family day out. Whether it is a leisurely stroll, afternoon tea or a touch of nostalgia you crave, Hopetoun will fit the bill. Built some 300 years ago, it is a delight to wander the corridors and historical rooms of one of the most splendid examples of the work of Scottish architects, Sir William Bruce and William Adam. It shows some of the finest examples in Scotland of carving, wainscoting and ceiling painting. With 100 acres of parkland including a deer park, the gardens are a colourful carpet of seasonal flowers. After a gentle walk, indulge yourself with a traditional tea and a browse through our shop.
**Times:** *Open daily Etr-Sep, 11-5.30.
**Fee:** *£8 (ch £4.25). Grounds £3.70 (ch £2.20).
**Facilities:** 🅿 ℗ (disable parking at entrance of house) 🪑 🍴 ♿ (ramps, toilets), shop, guided tours ⊗ (ex on leads) 🚌

## GLASGOW
**Burrell Collection**
2060 Pollokshaws Rd G43 1AT
☎ 0141 287 2550 📄 0141 287 2597
**Email:** museums@cls.glasgow.gov.uk
**Web:** www.glasgowmuseums.com
**Dir:** *3.5m S of city centre*
Set in Pollok Country Park, this award-winning building makes the priceless works of art on display seem almost part of the woodland setting. Shipping magnate Sir William Burrell's main interests were medieval Europe, Oriental art and European paintings. Colourful paintings and stained glass show the details of medieval life. Furniture, paintings, sculpture, armour and weapons help to complete the picture. Rugs, ceramics and metalwork represent the art of Islam. There is also a strong collection of Chinese and other Oriental ceramics. Paintings on display include works by Bellini, Rembrandt and the French Impressionists.
**Times:** *Open all year, Mon-Thu & Sat 10-5, Fri & Sun 11-5. Closed 24-25 & 31 (pm) Dec & 1-2 Jan
**Fee:** *Free
**Facilities:** 🅿 (charged) 🍴 (Licensed) ♿ (wheelchairs available, tape guides, lifts, toilets) shop ⊗ 🚌 ♿

## GLASGOW
### Clydebuilt - Scottish Maritime Museum at Braehead

Braehead Shopping Centre King Inch Road G51 4BN

☎ 0141 886 1013 🖷 0141 886 1015

**Email:** clydebuilt@tinyworld.co.uk

**Web:** www.scottishmaritimemuseum.org

**Dir:** *M8 junct 25A, 26, follow signs for Braehead Shopping Centre, then Green car park*

On the banks of the River Clyde, home of the Scottish shipbuilding industry, visitors can discover how Glasgow's famous ships were built, from the design stages through to the launch. There are also displays on the textile and cotton industries, iron and steel, and tobacco. Hands-on activities allow you to operate a ship's engine, become a ship's riveter, and steer a virtual ship up the Clyde.

**Times:** *Open Mon-Sat 10-5.30; Sun 11-5.

**Fee:** *£4.25 (ch £2.50, concessions £3). Family ticket £10

**Facilities:** 🅿 🅿 (500yds) 🍴 📷 20p ♿ (lift/ramps/wheelchairs from shopping centre, toilets), shop, guided tours 🚫 (ex guide dogs) 🚌 ♻

## GLASGOW
### Glasgow Science Centre

50 Pacific Quay G51 1EA

☎ 0 0871 540 1000 🖷 0871 540 1006

**Email:** admin@glasgowsciencecentre.org

**Web:** www.glasgowsciencecentre.org

**Dir:** *M8 junct 24 or M77 junct 21, follow brown signs, across Clyde from SECC*

The centre is home to many entertaining and exciting attractions and contains hundreds of interactive exhibits. Highlights include the Scottish Power Planetarium, Scotland's only IMAX cinema and the 127 meter tall Glasgow Tower, a remarkable free-standing structure that gives breathtaking views of the city (check availability before visiting). GSC presents the world of science and technology in new and exciting ways.

**Times:** Open 2 Jan-26 Mar, 10-6. 27 Mar daily 10-6

**Fee:** Science Mall* or Imax: £6.95 (ch & concessions £4.95). Science Mall & Imax: £9.95 (ch & concessions £7.95). 10% off for groups 4+. * Scottish Power Planeterium extra £2.

**Facilities:** 🅿 (charged) 🅿 (SECC) 🍴 📷 ♿ (induction loops, toilets) shop 🚫 (ex guide/hearing dogs) 🚌

## GLASGOW
### Museum of Transport

1 Bunhouse Road G3 8DP

☎ 0141 287 2720 🖷 0141 287 2692

**Email:** museums@cls.glasgow.gov.uk

**Web:** www.glasgowmuseums.com

**Dir:** *1.5m W of city centre*

Visit the Museum of Transport and the first impression is of gleaming metalwork and bright paint. All around you there are cars, caravans, carriages and carts, fire engines, buses, steam locomotives, prams and trams. The museum uses its collections of vehicles and models to tell the story of transport by land and sea, with a unique Glasgow flavour. Visitors can even go window shopping along the recreated Kelvin Street of 1938. Upstairs 250 ship models tell the story of the great days of Clyde shipbuilding. The Museum of Transport has something for everyone.

**Times:** *Open all year, Mon-Thu & Sat 10-5, Fri & Sun 11-5.

**Fee:** *Free

**Facilities:** 🅿 (charged) 🅿 (100yds) ♿ (assistance available, toilets), shop 🚫 (ex guide dogs) 🚌 ♻

GLASGOW
### People's Palace & Winter Gardens
Glasgow Green G40 1AT
☎ 0141 271 2951 📄 0141 271 2960
**Email:** museums@cls.glasgow.gov.uk
**Web:** www.glasgowmuseums.com
**Dir:** *1m SE of city centre*
Glasgow grew from a medieval town located by the Cathedral to the Second City of the British Empire. Trade with the Americas, and later industry, made the city rich. But not everyone shared in Glasgow's wealth. The People's Palace on historic Glasgow Green shows how ordinary Glaswegians worked, lived and played. Visitors can discover how a family lived in a typical one-room Glasgow 'single end' tenement flat, see Billy Connolly's amazing banana boots, learn to speak Glesga, take a trip 'doon the watter' and visit the Winter Gardens.
**Times:** *Open all year, Mon-Thu & Sat 10-5, Fri & Sun 11-5. Closed 24-25 & 31 Dec [pm] & 1-2 Jan
**Fee:** *Free
**Facilities:** Ⓟ (50yds) ♿ (lifts, toilets) shop garden centre
🚫 🚌 ♻

GLASGOW
### Tenement House
145 Buccleuch Street Garnethill G3 6QN
☎ 0141 333 0183
**Email:** tenementhouse@nts.org.uk
**Web:** www.nts.org.uk
**Dir:** *N of Charing Cross*
This shows an unsung but once-typical side of Glasgow life: it is a first-floor flat, built in 1892, with a parlour, bedroom, kitchen and bathroom, furnished with the original recess beds, kitchen range, sink, and coal bunker, among other articles. The home of Agnes Toward from 1911 to 1965, the flat was bought by an actress who preserved it as a 'time capsule'. The contents vividly portray the life of one section of Glasgow society.
**Times:** *Open Mar-Oct, daily 2-5. Wkday morning visits available for pre-booked educational & other groups. Times may change for 2007 please telephone or check website
**Fee:** *£3.50 (concessions £2.60) Family ticket £9.50. Groups adult £2.80 (ch/school £1). Admission free to NTS members. For other details please phone 0131 243 9387
**Facilities:** Ⓟ (100yds - restricted, recommend parking in town) ♿ (Braille guide) 🚫 (ex guide dogs)
🚌 (pre-booking required, wkday am only) ☃ ♻

GLASGOW
### The Lighthouse
11 Mitchell Lane G1 3NU
☎ 0141 221 6362 📄 0141 221 6395
**Email:** enquiries@thelighthouse.co.uk
**Web:** www.thelighthouse.co.uk
**Dir:** *in city centre*
Scotland's National Centre for Architecture, Design and the City. Extending over six floors and one of the biggest centres of its kind in Europe. Home to the award-winning Mackintosh Centre, devoted to the art, architecture and design of Charles Rennie Mackintosh. There are also temporary exhibition spaces with a thought provoking programme. A place of discovery and learning, another feature of The Lighthouse is the uninterrupted view over Glasgow's cityscape. Climb the helical staircase in the Mackintosh Tower or use the lift to the Level 6 Viewing Platform and spot some significant buildings that make up Glasgow's architectural tapestry.
**Times:** Open all year, Mon & Wed-Sat, 10.30-5, Tue 11-5, Sun noon-5.
**Fee:** *£3 (ch £1, concessions £1.50)
**Facilities:** Ⓟ (50mtrs) 🍴 ♿ (induction loop, toilets), shop, guided tours 🚫 (ex assist dogs) 🚌 (no coach parking near building)

## GLASGOW
### The Scottish Football Museum
Hampden Park G42 9BA
☎ 0141 616 6139 🖷 0141 616 6101
**Email:** info@scottishfootballmuseum.org.uk
**Web:** www.scottishfootballmuseum.org.uk
**Dir:** *3m S of city centre, follow brown tourist signs*
Using 2,500 pieces of footballing memorabilia, the
Scottish Football Museum covers such themes as
football's origins, fan culture, other games influenced by
football, and even some social history. The exhibits
include the world's oldest football, trophy and ticket, and
a reconstructed 1903 changing room and press box.
**Times:** Open Mon-Sat 10-5, Sun 11-5. Closed match
days, special events and Xmas/New Year, please
telephone in advance for confirmation

**Fee:** Museum £5.50 (ch under 16 & concessions £2.75)
Stadium £6 (ch under 16 & concessions £3). Combined
Ticket £8.50 (ch under 16 & concessions £4.25)
Children under 5 free.
**Facilities:** 🅿 Ⓟ (1-2 min walk) 🗐 ♿ (ramps throughout,
toilets) shop, guided tours ⊗ (ex guide dogs) 🚌 (book-
ing required)

## GLASGOW
### The Tall Ship at Glasgow Harbour
100 Stobcross Road G3 8QQ
☎ 0141 222 2513 🖷 0141 222 2536
**Email:** info@thetallship.com
**Web:** www.thetallship.com
**Dir:** *from M8 junct 19 onto A814 follow signs for
attraction*
Visit The Tall Ship at Glasgow Harbour and step back in
time to the days of sail. Experience Glasgow's maritime
history at first hand and explore the UK's only remaining
Clydebuilt sailing ship, the Glenlee. Exhibitions on board
and in the visitor centre on the quayside tell the story of
the ship and the Glasgow Harbour area. If you have ever
wondered what it would have been like to be a sailor on
a tall ship, this is your chance to find out! Children can

have fun by joining in the hunt for Jock, the ship's cat.
An unmissable experience, The Tall Ship offers guided
tours, changing exhibitions, children's activities, a nautical
gift shop and café.
**Times:** *Open daily Mar-Oct 10-5, Nov-Feb 10-4.
**Fee:** *£4.95 (1 ch free with paying adult/concession,
additional ch £2.50, concessions £3.75).
**Facilities:** 🅿 Ⓟ (50yds) 🎋 🗐 ♿ (toilets), shop, guided
tours 🚌 (pre-booking required)

## ALVA
### Mill Trail Visitor Centre
Glentana Mill West Stirling St FK12 5EN
☎ 01259 769696 🖷 01259 763100
**Dir:** *on A91 approx 8m E of Stirling*
In the heart of Scotland's woollen mill country, the Centre
recounts the history of Scotland's woollen and tweed
traditions, and features machines from spinning wheels
to large motorised looms of the type in use today. Hear
12 year-old Mary describe her working day as a mill girl
150 years ago, and then contrast her story with our
modern working woollen mill. Factory bargains and local
crafts, tourist information centre, café.
**Times:** *Open all year, Jan-Jun 10-5; Jul-Aug 9-5; Sep-
Dec 10-5.
**Fee:** *Free

**Facilities:** 🅿 🎋 ♿ (toilets) shop ⊗ (ex guide dogs)
🚌 (prebooked)

**DUMFRIES & GALLOWAY**

## CAERLAVEROCK
### WWT Caerlaverock
Eastpark Farm DG1 4RS
☎ 01387 770200 ▤ 01387 770539
**Email:** caerlaverock@wwt.org.uk
**Web:** www.wwt.org.uk
**Dir:** *9m SE of Dumfries, signed from A75*
This internationally important wetland is the winter habitat of the entire Svalbard population of Barnacle Geese which spends the winter on the Solway Firth. Observation facilities include 20 hides, 3 towers and a heated observatory. A wide variety of other wildlife can be seen, notably the rare Natterjack Toad and a family of Barn Owls which can be observed via a CCTV system.
**Times:** *Open daily 10-5. Closed 25 Dec.
**Fee:** *£4.40 (ch £2.70 & concessions £3.60). Family ticket £11.50
**Facilities:** ℗ ⛱ ♿ (toilets) shop ⊗ (ex guide dogs) 🚌 (advance booking preferred) ♨

## CREETOWN
### Creetown Gem Rock Museum
Chain Road Newton Stewart DG8 7HJ
☎ 01671 820357 & 820554 ▤ 01671 820554
**Email:** gem.rock@btinternet.com
**Web:** www.gemrock.net
**Dir:** *follow signs from A75 at Creetown bypass*
The Gem Rock is the leading independent museum of its kind in the UK, and is renowned worldwide. Crystals, gemstones, minerals, jewellery and fossils, the Gem Rock displays some of the most breathtaking examples of nature's wonders. See the audio-visual 'Fire in the Stones', explore the Crystal Cave, and relax in the Prospector's Study.
**Times:** *Open Etr-Sep, daily 9.30-5.30; Oct-Nov & Feb, Mar-Etr, daily 10-4; Dec, wknds 10-4 or by appointment wkdays. Closed 23 Dec-Jan.
**Fee:** £3.75 (ch £2.25 under 5 free, concessions £3.25). Family ticket £9.75 (2ad+3ch).
**Facilities:** ℗ ℗ (200yds) ⊐ (Homebaking our speciality) ⛱ ▤ 25p ♿ (ideal attraction for wheelchair users, toilets), shop ⊗ (ex guide dogs) 🚌 (call in advance)

## DUMFRIES
### Dumfries Museum & Camera Obscura
The Observatory Rotchell Rd DG2 7SW
☎ 01387 253374 ▤ 01387 265081
**Email:** dumfriesmuseum@dumgal.gov.uk
**Web:** www.dumgal.gov.uk/museums
**Dir:** *A75 from S Carlisle or SW from Castle Douglas, museum in Maxwellton area of Dumfries*
Situated in and around the 18th-century windmill tower, the museum's collections were started over 150 years ago and exhibitions trace the history of the people and landscape of Dumfries & Galloway. The Camera Obscura is to be found on the top floor of the windmill tower.
**Times:** *Open all year, Apr-Sep Mon-Sat 10-5, Sun, 2-5; Oct-Mar, Tue-Sat 10-1 & 2-5.
**Fee:** *Free except Camera Obscura £1.90 (concs 95p)
**Facilities:** ℗ ℗ (50yds - discs needed to park - ask at museum) ♿ (parking available, toilets) shop 🚌 ♨

## DUMFRIES
### Robert Burns Centre

Mill Road DG2 7BE
☎ 01387 264808 ▤ 01387 265081
**Email:** dumfriesmuseum@dumgal.gov.uk
**Web:** www.dumgal.gov.uk/museums
**Dir:** *on Westbank of River Nith*

This award-winning centre explores the connections between Robert Burns and the town of Dumfries. Situated in the town's 18th-century watermill, the centre tells the story of Burns' last years spent in the busy streets and lively atmosphere of 1790s Dumfries. In the evening the centre shows feature films in the Film Theatre.
**Times:** *Open all year, Apr-Sep, daily 10-8 (Sun 2-5); Oct-Mar, Tue-Sat 10-1 & 2-5.

**Fee:** *Free admission to museum, audio-visual theatre £1.60 (concessions 80p).
**Facilities:** ❷ ℗ (50yds - parking disc required-ask at museum) ☲ (open Apr-Sep & restricted Oct-Mar) ⧣ ⤒ ▤ No charge ♿ (induction loop hearing system in auditorium, chairlift, toilets) shop 🚌

## KIRKCUDBRIGHT
### Galloway Wildlife Conservation Park

Lochfergus Plantation DG6 4XX
☎ 01557 331645 ▤ 01557 331645
**Email:** j.d.denerley@btinternet.com
**Web:** www.gallowaywildlife.co.uk
**Dir:** *follow brown signs from A75, 1m from Kirkcudbright on B727*

The wild animal conservation centre for southern Scotland, set in 27 acres of mixed woodland. A varied zoological collection of over 150 animals from all over the world. Close animal encounters and bird of prey displays are some of the features giving an insight into wildlife conservation.
**Times:** Open Feb-Nov, daily, 10-6 (last admission 5); Dec-Jan, wkends, 10-4 (last admission 3).

**Fee:** £5 (ch 4-15 £3.50, under 4 free, concessions £4.50)
**Facilities:** ❷ ⤒ ♿ (British sign language, toilets), shop, ⊗ (ex assist dogs) 🚌 (advance booking required)

## NEW ABBEY
### Shambellie House Museum of Costume

DG2 8HQ
☎ 01387 850375 ▤ 01387 850461
**Email:** info@nms.ac.uk
**Web:** www.nms.ac.uk/costume
**Dir:** *7m S of Dumfries, on A710*

Shambellie House is a beautiful Victorian country house set in attractive wooded grounds. You are invited to step back in time and experience Victorian and Edwardian grace and refinement. See period costume from the 1850s to the 1950s displayed in appropriate room settings with accessories, furniture and decorative art. Telephone for details of special events.
**Times:** Open Apr-Oct, daily, 10-5.
**Fee:** *Free £3 (ch free, pen £2)

**Facilities:** ❷ ⤒ ♿ (ramp and w/chair lift at main entrance) shop ⊗ (ex guide/hearing dogs) 🚌

## PORT LOGAN
### Logan Botanic Garden
Stranraer DG9 9ND

☎ 01776 860231 📄 01776 860333

**Email:** logan@rbge.org.uk

**Web:** www.rgbe.org.uk

**Dir:** *on B7065, 14m S of Stranraer*

Logan's exceptionally mild climate allows a colourful array of tender plants to thrive out-of-doors. Amongst the many highlights are tree ferns, cabbage palms, unusual shrubs, climbers and tender perennials found within the setting of the walled, water, terrace and woodland gardens.

**Times:** *Open Mar-Oct, Mar & Oct daily 10-5. Apr-Sep 10-6

**Fee:** *£3.50 (ch £1, concessions £3). Family £8

**Facilities:** 🅿 🍽 (Licensed) 🛗 ♿ (access limited, wheelchairs available for loan, toilets) shop garden centre guided tours audio commentaries 🚫 (ex guide dogs) 🚌

## STRANRAER
### Castle Kennedy Gardens
Stair Estates Rephad DG9 8BX

☎ 01776 702024 & 01581 400225 📄 01776 706248

**Email:** info@castlekennedygardens.co.uk

**Web:** www.castlekennedygardens.co.uk

**Dir:** *5m E of Stranraer on A75, signed at Castle Kennedy Village*

Situated on a peninsula between two lochs, the gardens around the Old Castle were first laid out in the early 18th century. Noted for their rhododendrons and azaleas (at their best May and early Jun) and walled kitchen garden with fine herbaceous borders (best in Aug and Sep). The gardens contain many avenues and walks amid beautiful scenery.

**Times:** Open Etr-Sep, daily 10-5

**Fee:** *£4 (ch £1, pen £3). Party 20+ 10% discount.

**Facilities:** 🅿 🅿 (200mtrs-coach park) ☕ (tea room) ♿ (tearoom to enable access, toilets) shop garden centre 🚫 (ex on a lead) 🚌

## STRANRAER
### Glenwhan Gardens
Dunragit DG9 8PH

☎ 01581 400222 📄 01581 400222

**Email:** tess@glenwhan.freeserve.co.uk

**Web:** www.glenwhangardens.co.uk

**Dir:** *7m E of Stranraer, signed*

Enjoying spectacular views over the Mull of Galloway and Luce Bay, Glenwhan is a beautiful 12-acre garden set on a hillside. There are two lakes filled with rare species, alpines, scree plants, heathers, conifers, roses, woodland walks to explore and fascinating garden sculpture.

**Times:** *Open Apr-Sep, daily 10-5

**Fee:** *£4 (ch £2, concessions £3). Family £9. Season £10

**Facilities:** 🅿 🅿 ⛽ ♿ (wheelchairs provided, toilets) shop garden centre 🚌 (must be booked in advance) 🚫

## THORNHILL
### Drumlanrig Castle, Gardens & Country Park
DG3 4AQ
☎ 01848 331555 📄 01848 331682
**Email:** bre@drumlanrigcastle.org.uk
**Web:** www.drumlanrig.com
**Dir:** *4m N of Thornhill off A76*

This unusual pink sandstone castle was built in the late 17th century in Renaissance style. It contains a outstanding collection of fine art. There is also French furniture, as well as silver and relics of 'Bonnie' Prince Charlie. The old stable block has a craft centre with resident craft workers, and the grounds offer an extensive garden plant centre, working forge, mountain bike hire and woodland walks. For details of special events phone 01848 331555.

**Times:** *Open early May-late Aug, Castle open daily. Guided tours and restricted route may operate at various times, please verify before visiting.
**Fee:** *£7 (ch £4 & pen £6). Grounds only £4. Party 20+ £5 each.
**Facilities:** 🅿 ℗ (400yds - no parking without ticket) 🍽 (Licensed) 🚻 ♿ (lift for wheelchair users, toilets) shop, garden centre, guided tours ⊗ (ex in park on lead) 🚌 (list of names addresss required)

---

## WANLOCKHEAD
### Museum of Scottish Lead Mining
Biggar ML12 6UT
☎ 01659 74387 📄 01659 74481
**Email:** miningmuseum@hotmail.com
**Web:** www.leadminingmuseum.co.uk
**Dir:** *signed from M74 and A76*

Wanlockhead is Scotland's highest village, set in the beautiful Lowther Hills. Visitors can see miners' cottages, the miners' library as well as the 18th-century lead mine. Visitors can also pan for gold.
**Times:** *Open Apr-2 Nov, daily 10.30-4.30; Jul & Aug 10-5.
**Fee:** *£5 (ch £3.50, concessions £3.75). Family ticket £13.50
**Facilities:** 🅿 ℗ (300yds) 🍽 (Licensed) 🚻 📷 charges vary ♿ (induction loops, toilets), shop, guided tours, audio commentaries ⊗ (ex guide dogs) 🚌 (pre-booking required, max 50 people)

---

## GALSTON
### Loudoun Castle Family Theme Park
KA4 8PE
☎ 01563 822296 📄 01563 822408
**Email:** loudouncastle@btinternet.com
**Web:** www.loudouncastle.co.uk
**Dir:** *signed from A74M, from A77 and from A71*

Loudoun Castle Theme Park is a great day out for the whole family. Theme park rides, live entertainment and McDougals Farm are just a taster of what's on offer. Look out for the 'The Plough' the biggest chairoplane in the world or the Pirates' Cove for exciting swashbuckling action.
**Times:** *Open Etr-end of Sep. Please phone for further details.
**Fee:** *£10.95 (under 4's free). For further details please phone or check website.
**Facilities:** 🅿 🚻 📷 ♿ (toilets), shop ⊗ (ex guide dogs) 🚌

MILNGAVIE
**Mugdock Country Park**
Craigallian Rd G62 8EL
☎ 0141 956 6100 & 6586
**Email:** rangers@mcp.ndo.co.uk
**Web:** www.mugdock-country-park.org.uk
**Dir:** *N of Glasgow on A81, signed*
This country park incorporates the remains of Mugdock
and Craigend castles, set in beautiful landscapes as well
as an exhibition centre, craft shops, orienteering course
and many walks. Events for all the family include pond
dipping, mini beast studies and orienteering.
**Times:** Open all year, daily.
**Fee:** Free
**Facilities:** 🅿 Ⓟ (0.75m - summer 9-9, winter 9-6)
🚻 🗐 ♿ (mobility equip, audio leaflet, large print media,
toilets), shop, garden centre, guided tours, audio
commentaries (charged) 🚌 (Pre-booked preferred)

ABERLADY
**Myreton Motor Museum**
Longniddry EH32 0PZ
☎ 01875 870288 & 07947 066666 🗎 01368 860199
**Email:** myreton.motor.museum@aberlady.org
**Dir:** *1.5m from A198, 2m from A1*
The museum has on show a large collection, from 1899,
of cars, bicycles, motor cycles and commercials. There is
also a large collection of period advertising, posters and
enamel signs etc.
**Times:** Open, Mar-Nov daily 11-4, Dec-Feb, wknds only
11-3
**Fee:** £6 (ch £3).
**Facilities:** 🅿 🚻 ♿ ⊗ (ex guide dogs) 🚌 ♨

EAST FORTUNE
**Museum of Flight**
East Fortune Airfield EH39 5LF
☎ 01620 897240 🗎 01620 880355
**Email:** info@nms.ac.uk    **Web:** www.nms.ac.uk
**Dir:** *signed from A1 near Haddington. Onto B1347, past
Athelstaneford, 20m E of Edinburgh*
The Museum is situated on one of Britain's best
preserved wartime airfields. There are four hangars, with
more than 50 planes, plus engines, rockets and
memorabilia. Displays include two Spitfires, a Vulcan
bomber, Britain's oldest surviving aeroplane (from 1896),
a Phantom jet fighter, and a Harrier jump-jet. The
Concorde Experience explores the story of this historic
plane through the lives of those who worked or travelled
on it. The Experience is free with admission, but a charge
is made to go onto the plane, pre-booking is essential.
**Times:** Open Apr-Oct, daily, 10-5. Jul-Aug, daily, 10-6.
Nov-Mar, wknds only, 10-4.Open 28-31 Dec, 3-7 Jan,
12-18 Feb. **Fee:** *£5, (ch under 12 free, concessions
£4). NMS members free. For Concorde Boarding Pass;
+£3 ad, +£2 ch & concessions. **Facilities:** 🅿 🚻
♿ (toilets) shop guided tours ⊗ (ex assist dogs) 🚌

## EAST LINTON
### Preston Mill & Phantassie Doocot
EH40 3DS

☎ 01620 860426

**Web:** www.nts.org.uk

**Dir:** *signed from A1*

This attractive mill, with conical, pantiled roof, is the oldest working water-driven meal mill to survive in Scotland, and was last used commercially in 1957. Nearby is the charming Phantassie Doocot (dovecote), built for 500 birds.

**Times:** *Open Apr-Sep, Thu-Mon 12-5, Sun 1-5. Times may change for 2007 please telephone or check website

**Fee:** *£3.50 (concession £2.60) Family ticket £9.50. Groups adult £2.80 (ch/school £1). Admission free to NTS members. For details please phone 0131 243 9387

**Facilities:** ❷ ⊓ ♿ (toilets) shop ⊗ (ex guide dogs) 🚌 (pre-booking required) 😋 ♨

## NORTH BERWICK
### Scottish Seabird Centre
The Harbour EH39 4SS

☎ 01620 890202 🖷 01620 890222

**Email:** info@seabird.org

**Web:** www.seabird.org

**Dir:** *A1 from Edinburgh, then A198 to North Berwick. Brown heritage signs clearly marked from A1*

Get close to nature with a visit to this award-winning centre. With panoramic views over the islands of the Firth of Forth and sand-fringed bays of North Berwick, the area is a haven for wildlife. Use state-of-the-art 'Big Brother' cameras to see wide variety of wildlife action live - including gannet colony, hundreds of puffins, seals and sometimes bottlenose dolphins. Wildlife boat safari with landings on the islands and passenger ferry to Fife (summer). New features include the Environmental Discovery Centre and Migration Tunnel.

**Times:** *Open all year, Apr-Oct 10-6 daily, Nov-Jan 10-4 (Mon-Fri) 10-5.30 (Sat & Sun), Feb-Mar 10-5 (Mon-Fri) 10-5.30 (Sat & Sun). Closed 25 Dec

**Fee:** *£5.95 (ch & concessions £3.95). Family ticket (4 persons) £16.50. Subject to change.

**Facilities:** ❷ ℗ (opposite - disabled parking only) ⊓ 🍴 £4.95 ♿ (1 w/chair, parking on site, walking frame available, toilets) shop, guided tours ⊗ (ex guide dogs) 🚌

## PRESTONPANS
### Prestongrange Museum
Prestongrange

☎ 0131 653 2904 🖷 01620 828201

**Email:** elms@eastlothian.gov.uk

**Web:** www.eastlothian.gov.uk/museums

**Dir:** *on B1348*

The oldest documented coal mining site in Scotland, with 800 years of history, this museum shows a Cornish Beam Engine and on-site evidence of associated industries such as brickmaking and pottery. It is located next to a 16th-century customs' port. There are special Events - weekend events for families and children in July/August.

**Times:** *Open end Mar-mid Oct, daily 11-4.

**Fee:** Free

**Facilities:** ❷ ⊓ 🍴 ♿ (grounds partly accessible, toilets) shop, guided tours, audio commentaries ⊗ (ex guide dogs) 🚌 ♨

FALKIRK / FIFE

BIRKHILL

**Birkhill Fireclay Mine**

EH51 9AQ

☎ 01506 825855 🖹 01506 828766

**Email:** mine@srps.org.uk

**Web:** www.srps.org.uk

**Dir:** *A706 from Linlithgow, A904 from Grangemouth, follow brown signs to Steam Railway & Fireclay Mine. Main access is by train from Bo'ness*

Tour guides will meet you at Birkhill Station and lead you down into the ancient woodland of the beautiful Avon Gorge, and then into the caverns of the Birkhill Fireclay mine. See how the clay was worked, what it was used for and find the 300-million-year-old fossils in the mine's roof.

**Times:** *Open Etr-Oct, wknds only; Jul-Aug, daily.

**Fee:** *Mine & Train £8 (ch £4.50, concessions £6.50) Family ticket (2ad+2ch) £21. Mine only £3 (ch £2, concessions £2.50) Family ticket £8.

**Facilities:** (toilets) guided tours

---

BO'NESS

**Bo'ness & Kinneil Railway**

Bo'ness Station Union Street EH51 9AQ

☎ 01506 825855 🖹 01506 828233

**Email:** railway@srps.org.uk

**Web:** www.srps.org.uk

**Dir:** *A904 from all directions, signed*

Historic railway buildings, including the station and train shed, have been relocated from sites all over Scotland. The Scottish Railway Exhibition tells the story of the development of railways and their impact on the people of Scotland. Take a seven mile return trip by steam train to the tranquil country station at Birkhill. Special events take place throughout the year.

**Times:** *Open Apr-Jun & Sep-Oct, Sat-Sun; Jul-Aug, Tue-Sun; Dec wknds only. Steam trains daily, depart 11, 12.15, 1.45 & 3, diesel departs at 4.15. Ring for details of special events.

**Fee:** *Return fare £5 (ch 3-15 £2.50, concessions £4). Family ticket £13. Ticket for return train fare & tour of Birkhill Fireclay Mine £8 (ch £4.50, concessions £6.50), Family ticket £21.

**Facilities:** (100yds) (ramps to station & adapted carriage, toilets) shop guided tours (pre-booking required)

---

ANSTRUTHER

**Scottish Fisheries Museum**

St Ayles Harbour Head KY10 3AB

☎ 01333 310628 🖹 01333 310628

**Email:** info@scotfishmuseum.org

**Web:** www.scotfishmuseum.org

**Dir:** *A917 through St Monans & Pittenweem*

This award-winning national museum tells the story of Scottish fishing and its people from the earliest times to the present. With 10 galleries, 2 large boatyards, and a restored fisherman's cottage, which contain many fine paintings and photographs, boat models and actual boats, clothing and items of daily life to see, a visit to the museum makes for an exceptional day out.

**Times:** *Open all year, Apr-Sep, Mon-Sat 10-5.30, Sun 11-5; Oct-Mar, Mon-Sat 10-4.30, Sun 12-4.30. Closed 25-26 Dec & 1-2 Jan. (Last admission 1 hr before closing).

**Fee:** *£4.50 (concessions £3.50). Party 12+ £3 (primary ch £1, accompanied ch free, concessions £2)

**Facilities:** (20yds - charge in summer) (ramps throughout to provide full access, toilets) shop guided tours (ex guide dogs) (contact in advance)

## CULROSS
### Culross Palace, Town House & The Study
West Green House KY12 8JH

☎ 01383 880359 📄 01383 882675

**Web:** www.nts.org.uk

**Dir:** *off A985, 3m E of Kincardine Bridge*

A royal burgh, Culross dates from the 16th and 17th centuries and has remained virtually unchanged since. It prospered from the coal and salt trades, and when these declined in the 1700s, Culross stayed as it was. It owes its present appearance to the National Trust for Scotland, which has been gradually restoring it. In the Town House is a visitor centre and exhibition; in the building called The Study can be seen a drawing room with a Norwegian painted ceiling, and The Palace has painted rooms and terraced gardens.

**Times:** *Open Palace, Study & Town House: Good Fri-Sep, daily 12-5. Garden all year 10-6 or sunset if earlier. Times may change for 2007 please telephone or check website

**Fee:** *£5 (concessions £3.75). Family ticket £13.50. Groups adult £4 (ch/school £1). Please book groups in advance. Admission free to NTS members. For other details phone 0131 243 9387

**Facilities:** 🅿 ⓟ ⫞ (tearoom) 🏞 ♿ (toilets) shop ⊗ (ex guide dogs) 🚌 (advance booking) ♨ ♿

## CUPAR
### The Scottish Deer Centre
Bow-of-Fife KY15 4NQ

☎ 01337 810391 📄 01337 810477

**Dir:** *3m W of Cupar on A91*

Guided tours around the Scottish Dear Centre take about 30 minutes and allow you to meet and stroke deer. There are indoor and outdoor adventure play areas for children and other features include regular falconry displays, a viewing platform and a tree top walkway for a different view of the park. European Grey Wolves are fed everyday (except Friday) at 3pm. Contact the centre for further information about visiting.

**Times:** *Open daily, Etr-Oct 10-6, Nov-Etr 10-5.

**Fee:** *£5.50 (ch 3-15 £3.95)

**Facilities:** 🅿 ⫞ (Simple snacks & picnic boxes) 🏞

♿ (special parking bay, loan of wheelchairs, toilets), shop, guided tours ⊗ (ex guide dogs) 🚌

## FALKLAND
### Falkland Palace & Garden
Cupar KY15 7BU

☎ 01337 857397 📄 01337 857980

**Web:** www.nts.org.uk

**Dir:** *off A912, 11m N of Kirkaldy*

The hunting palace of the Stuart monarchs, this fine building, with a French-Renaissance style south wing, stands in the shelter of the Lomond Hills. The beautiful Chapel Royal and King's Bedchamber are the most notable features of Falkland Palace and Garden, and it is also home to the oldest royal tennis court in Britain (1539). The garden has a spectacular delphinium border. Recorded sacred music is played hourly in the Chapel. Please telephone for details of concerts, recitals etc.

**Times:** *Open Mar-Oct, Mon-Sat 10-6, Sun 1-5. Times may change for 2007 please telephone or check website

**Fee:** *£7 (concessions £5.25). Family ticket £19. Groups adult £5.60 (ch/school £1). Garden only £3.50 (concessions £2.60). Family ticket £9.50. Groups adult £2.80 (ch/school £1). Admission free to NTS members. For other details please phone 0131 243 9387

**Facilities:** 🅿 ⓟ (100yds) ♿ shop ⊗ (ex guide dogs) 🚌 (pre-booking required) ♨ ♿

**FIFE**

## KIRKCALDY
### Kirkcaldy Museum & Art Gallery
War Memorial Gardens KY1 1YG
☎ 01592 412860 🖨 01592 412870
**Email:** kirkcaldy.museum@fife.gov.uk
**Web:** www.fifedirect.org.uk/museums
**Dir:** *next to train station*
Set in the town's lovely memorial gardens, the museum
houses a collection of fine and decorative art, including
18th to 21st-century Scottish paintings, among them
the works of William McTaggart and S J Peploe. An
award-winning display 'Changing Places' tells the story
of the social, industrial and natural heritage of the area.
**Times:** *Open all year, Mon-Sat 10.30-5, Sun 2-5.
Closed local hols
**Fee:** *Free

**Facilities:** 🅿 ℗ (station car park) 🍽 (light refreshments
and hot meals) 🚻 ♿ (ramp to main entrance & lift to 1st
floor galleries, toilets), shop 🐕 (ex guide dogs) 🚌
(contact museum in advance) ♻

## NORTH QUEENSFERRY
### Deep Sea World
KY11 1JR
☎ 01383 411880 🖨 01383 410514
**Email:** info@deepseaworld.co.uk
**Web:** www.deepseaworld.com/
**Dir:** *from N, M90 take exit for Inverkeithing. From S
follow signs to Forth Rd Bridge, 1st exit left*
The world's longest underwater tunnel gives you a diver's
eye view of an underwater world. Come face to face with
Sand Tiger sharks, and watch divers hand feed a wide
array of sea life. Visit the Amazon Experience with
ferocious piranhas and the amazing amphibian display
featuring the world's most poisonous frog. Also featuring
the newly opened Seal Sanctuary, dedicated to the
rehabilitation and release of injured and orphaned seal
pups. Please telephone or visit website for details
of events running throughout the year.
**Times:** *Open all year daily, Nov-Mar 10-5, Apr-Oct
10-6 wknds & school hols 10-6
**Fee:** *£8.55 (ch 3-5 £6.30 under 3 free, concessions
£6.75). Family ticket discount available.
**Facilities:** 🅿 ℗ (1m) 🚻 🍽 £2.95 ♿ (ramps & disabled
parking, hearing loop, toilets), shop 🐕 (ex guide dogs)
🚌

## ST ANDREWS
### British Golf Museum
Bruce Embankment KY16 9AB
☎ 01334 460046 & 460053 🖨 01334 460064
**Email:** alisonwood@randa.org
**Web:** www.britishgolfmuseum.co.uk
**Dir:** *opposite Royal & Ancient Golf Club*
Where better to find out about golf than in St Andrews,
the home of golf. Using diverse and exciting interactive
displays, this museum explores the history of British golf
from its origins to the personalities of today. The 18th
Hole is fun for all the family, with dressing up, a mini-
putting green and loads to do!
**Times:** *Open Mar-Oct, Mon-Sat 9.30-5.30, Sun 10-5.
Nov-Mar, Mon-Sun 10-4.
**Fee:** *£5 (ch 6-15 £2.75, concs £4). Family £12.75.

**Facilities:** 🅿 (charged) ℗ (100yds) 🍽 ♿ (toilets), shop
🐕 (ex guide dogs) 🚌

FIFE

## ST ANDREWS
### Castle & Visitor Centre
KY16 9AR

☎ 01334 477196

**Web:** www.historic-scotland.gov.uk

This 13th-century stronghold castle was the scene of the murder of Cardinal Beaton in 1546 and the focal point of the Church in Medieval Scotland. The new visitor centre incorporates an exciting multi-media exhibition describing the history of the castle and nearby cathedral. There's also the chance to view a bottle dungeon and explore a siege mine.

**Times:** *Open all year, Apr-Sep, daily 9.30-6.30; Oct-Mar, daily 9.30-4.30. Closed 25-26 Dec & 1-2 Jan.

**Fee:** *£4 (ch £1.60, concessions £3). Joint ticket with St Andrews Cathedral available £5 (ch £2, concessions £3.75). 10% discount for groups 11+. Please phone for further details and to confirm rates.

**Facilities:** Ⓟ & (toilets) shop ⊗ 🚩 🖼

## ST ANDREWS
### St Andrews Aquarium
The Scores KY16 9AS

☎ 01334 474786 🖹 01334 475985

**Web:** www.standrewsaquarium.co.uk

**Dir:** *signed in town centre*

The continually expanding St Andrews Aquarium is home to shrimps, sharks, eels, octopi, seals and much much more. Special features include the Seahorse Parade, and the Sea Mammal Research Unit, which is committed to the care of sea mammals and their increasingly endangered environment.

**Times:** *Open daily from 10. Please phone for winter Opening

**Fee:** *£5.95 (ch & student £3.95, pen £4.95). Family ticket (2ad+2ch) £17.50

**Facilities:** Ⓟ (charged) Ⓟ 🍴 (Licensed) 🎪 & (toilets) shop ⊗ (ex guide dogs) 🚌

## AVIEMORE
### Strathspey Steam Railway
Aviemore Station Dalfaber Road PH22 1PY

☎ 01479 810725

**Email:** strathtrains@strathspeyrailway.co.uk

**Web:** www.strathspeyrailway.co.uk

**Dir:** *from A9 take B970 for Coylumbridge, on B9152, left after railway bridge, car park 0.25m on left. Other stations: Boat of Garten in village; Broomhill, off A95, 3.5m S of Grantown-on-Spey*

This steam railway covers the ten miles from Aviemore via Boat of Garten to Broomhill. The journey takes about 40 minutes, but allow around two hours for the round trip. Shorter trips are possible and timetables are available from the station and the tourist information centre. Telephone for details of events during the year.

**Times:** Open Etr, 1-9 Apr & Jun-Sep, daily; Apr-May & Oct, Wed-Thu, Sat-Sun & BH Mon.

**Fee:** £9.50 basic round trip (ch £4.75); £25 Family round trip. Day Rover £12 (ch £6) Family £30

**Facilities:** ❶ Ⓟ (0.25m- closed overnight) 🍱 (on train) 🍴 (Licensed) 🎪 & (ramps, toilets) shop 🚌 (pre-booking required)

## BALMACARA
### Balmacara Estate & Lochalsh Woodland Garden
Kyle of Lochalsh IV40 8DN
☎ 01599 566325 ▤ 01599 566359
Email: balmacara@nts.org.uk
Web: www.nts.org.uk
Dir: *3m E of Kyle of Lochalsh, off A87*
The Balmacara Estate comprises some 5,600 acres and seven crofting villages, including Plockton, a conservation area. There are excellent views of Skye, Kintail and Applecross. The main attraction is the Lochalsh Woodland Garden, but the whole area is excellent for walking.
Times: *Open Estate: all year. Woodland garden daily 9-sunset. Balmacara Square Visitor Centre, Apr-Sep, daily, 9-5 (Fri 9-4). Times may change for 2007 please telephone or check website
Fee: *Garden £2 (concessions £1). Visitor Centre £1 (honesty box). Admission free to NTS members. For other details please phone 0131 243 9387
Facilities: ♿ 🚌 ⛲ ♿

## BOAT OF GARTEN
### Loch Garten Osprey Centre
RSPB Reserve Abernethy Forest Forest Lodge
Nethybridge PH25 3EF
☎ 01479 821894 ▤ 01479 821069
Dir: *signed from B970 & A9 at Aviemore, follow 'RSPB Ospreys' signs*
Home of the Loch Garten Osprey site, this reserve holds one of most important remnants of Scots Pine forest in the Highlands. Within its vast acreage, some 30,760 acres, are forest bogs, moorland, mountain top, lochs and crofting land. In addition to the regular pair of nesting ospreys, there are breeding Scottish crossbills, capercaillies, black grouse and many others. The ospreys can be viewed through telescopes and there is a live TV link to the nest. Please telephone for details of special events running throughout the year.
Times: * Osprey Centre open daily, Apr-Aug 10-6.
Fee: *£3 (ch 50p) concessions £2. RSPB members free.
Facilities: ♿ 📖 ♿ (low level viewing slots & optics, toilets) shop, guided tours, audio commentaries ⊘ (ex guide dogs in centre) 🚌 (advance booking)

## CARRBRIDGE
### Landmark Forest Theme Park
PH23 3AJ
☎ 01479 841613 & 0800 731 3446 ▤ 01479 841384
Email: landmarkcentre@btconnect.com
Web: www.landmark-centre.co.uk
Dir: *off A9 between Aviemore & Inverness*
This innovative centre is designed to provide a fun and educational visit for all ages. Microworld takes a close-up look at the incredible microscopic world around us. There is a 70ft forest viewing tower and a treetop trail. There are demonstrations of timber sawing, on a steam-powered sawmill and log hauling by a Clydesdale horse throughout the day. Attractions include a 3-track Watercoaster, a maze and a large covered adventure play area, mini electric cars and remote controlled truck arena. New features include; RopeworX, an aerial highwire obstacle course, and Skydive, a parachute jump simulator.
Times: Open all year, daily, Apr-mid Jul 10-6; mid Jul-mid Aug 10-7; Sep-Oct 10-5.30; Nov-Mar 10-5. Closed 25 Dec and 1 Jan.
Fee: *Apr-Oct: £8.95 (ch £6.90); Multi-visit week, £12.95 (ch £10.90), Year £14.95 (ch £12.90)
Facilities: ♿ Ⓟ (100mtrs) 🍴 (Licensed) ⛱ 📖 10p ♿ (ramps, toilets) shop (charged) 🚌

## CAWDOR
**Cawdor Castle**

Nairn IV12 5RD
☎ 01667 404401 📠 01667 404674
**Email:** info@cawdorcastle.com
**Web:** www.cawdorcastle.com
**Dir:** *on B9090, off A96*

Home of the Thanes of Cawdor since the 14th century, this lovely castle has a drawbridge, an ancient tower built round a tree, and a freshwater well inside the house. There is lots to do and see at Cawdor including three superb gardens, the earliest dating from 1600, a golf course, and Putting Green, nature trails and the Bog Wood. Gardens Weekend takes place in June – guided tours of gardens with the head gardener.
**Times:** Open May-7 Oct, daily 10-5.30.

Last admission 5.
**Fee:** *£7 (ch 5-15 £4.30, pen £6). Family ticket £22 Party 20+ £6.10 each. Gardens, grounds & nature trails only £3.70.
**Facilities:** 🅿 🍴 (Licensed) 🍴 📷 £3.50 & £4.50 ♿ (ramps to restaurants, shops and gardens, toilets) shop ⊗ (ex guide dogs) 🚌

## CULLODEN MOOR
**Culloden Battlefield**

IV2 5EU
☎ 01463 790607 📠 01463 794294
**Email:** culloden@nts.org.uk
**Web:** www.nts.org.uk
**Dir:** *B9006, 5m E of Inverness*

A cairn recalls this last battle fought on mainland Britain, on 16 April 1746, when the Duke of Cumberland's forces routed 'Bonnie' Prince Charles Edward Stuart's army. The battlefield has been restored to its state on the day of the battle, and in summer there are 'living history' enactments. This is a most atmospheric evocation of tragic events. Telephone for details of guided tours.
**Times:** *Open Site: all year, daily. Visitor Centre: Feb-Mar & Nov-Dec, daily 11-4; Apr-Jun & Sep-Oct, daily 9-6; Jul-Aug, daily 9-7. Times may change for 2007 please telephone or check website
**Fee:** *£5 (concessions £3.75) Family ticket £13.50. Group adult £4 (ch/school £1). Please book groups in advance. Admission free to NTS members. For other details please phone 0131 243 9387
**Facilities:** 🅿 🍴 ♿ (wheelchair, induction loop, raised map, toilets) shop ⊗ (ex guide dogs) 🚌 (pre-booking required) 🐾 ♻

## DRUMNADROCHIT
**Official Loch Ness Exhibition Centre, Loch Ness 2000**

IV3 6TU
☎ 01456 450573 & 450218 📠 01456 450770
**Email:** brem@loch-ness-scotland.com
**Web:** www.loch-ness-scotland.com
**Dir:** *on A82, 12m S Inverness*

A fascinating and popular multi-media presentation lasting 30 minutes. Seven themed areas cover the story of the Loch Ness Monster, from the pre-history of Scotland, through the cultural roots of the legend in Highland folklore, and into the 50-year controversy which surrounds it and the 'sightings'. Using the latest technology in computer animation, lasers and multi-media projection systems.

**Times:** *Open all year; Etr-May 9.30-5.30; Jun-Sep 9.30-6 (9-8.30 Jul & Aug); Winter 10-4. (Last admission 30 mins before closing).
**Fee:** *£5.95 (ch £3.50, ch under 7 & disabled free, concessions £4.50). Family ticket £14.95. Group.
**Facilities:** 🅿 🅿 🍴 (Licensed) 🍴 ♿ (parking, toilets) shop, guided tours, audio commentaries ⊗ (ex in grounds/guide dogs) 🚌

DUNBEATH
**Laidhay Croft Museum**
Caithness KW6 6EH
☎ 01593 731244
**Dir:** *1m N of Dunbeath on A9*
The museum gives visitors a glimpse of a long-vanished way of life. The main building is a thatched Caithness longhouse, with the dwelling quarters, byre and stable all under one roof. It dates back some 200 years, and is furnished as it might have been 100 years ago. A collection of early farm tools and machinery is also shown. Near the house is a thatched winnowing barn with its roof supported on three 'Highland couples', or crucks.
**Times:** Open Etr-Oct, daily 9-5
**Fee:** £2 (ch 50p)

**Facilities:** ℗ ☕ (tearoom, homebaking, traditional soups) 📖 Booklets, 60p ♿ (toilets) guided tours 🚌 ⓩ

ELPHIN
**Highland & Rare Breeds Farm**
Nr Ullapool Sutherland IV27 4HH
☎ 01854 666204 📄 01854 666204
**Dir:** *on A835 in Elphin*
There are Highland cattle, traditional 4-horned sheep with coloured fleeces, traditional Scottish ewes and lambs, rare breeds of pigs and goats. Many types of poultry, duck ponds, and a farm walk among the animals. Also on display are farm tools, crofting history, wool crafts and hand-spinning. A visit to the Highland and Rare Breeds Farm provides the opportunity for a very 'hands on' day out where you can 'stroke the goats', 'scratch the pigs' and 'feed the ducks' on the ponds.
**Times:** *Open Jul & Aug only
**Fee:** *£3.95 (ch £2.95, students & pen £3.50)

**Facilities:** ℗ ℗ (0.5 miles) 🪑 ♿ (assistance available, toilets) shop 🚫 🚌

FORT WILLIAM
**West Highland Museum**
Cameron Square PH33 6AJ
☎ 01397 702169 📄 01397 701927
**Email:** info@westhighlandmuseum.org.uk
**Web:** www.westhighlandmuseum.org.uk
**Dir:** *museum next door to tourist office*
A small and fascinating museum with displays that illustrate traditional Highland life and history, with numerous Jacobite relics. One of them is the 'secret portrait' of 'Bonnie Prince Charlie', which looks like meaningless daubs of paint but reveals a portrait when reflected in a metal cylinder.
**Times:** Open all year Jun-Sep, Mon-Sat 10-5 (also Jul-Aug, Sun 2-5); Oct-May, Mon-Sat 10-4.
**Fee:** £3 (ch 50p, concessions £2)

**Facilities:** ℗ (100yds – charge all year) ♿ (toilets) shop, guided tours 🚫 (ex guide dogs) 🚌 (pre-booking preferred) ⓩ

## GLENCOE
### Glencoe & North Lorn Folk Museum
PH49 4HS

☎ 01855 811664

**Email:** glencoemuseum@btconnect.com

**Web:** www.glencoemuseum.com

**Dir:** *turn off A82 at Glencoe x-roads then immediately right into Glencoe village*

Two heather-thatched cottages in the main street of Glencoe now house items connected with the Macdonalds and the Jacobite risings. A variety of local domestic and farming exhibits, dairying and slate-working equipment, costumes and embroidery are also shown.

**Times:** Open Apr-Oct, Mon-Sat 10-5.30.

**Fee:** *£2 (ch free, concessions £1.50).

**Facilities:** ❷ Ⓟ (200yds) 📋 Worksheets free. Booklets 20-50p ♿ shop, guided tours 🚌 ♨

## GLENCOE
### Glencoe Visitor Centre
Ballachulish PA39 4HX

☎ 01855 811307 & 811729 📄 01855 811772

**Dir:** *on A82, 17m S of Fort William*

Glencoe has stunning scenery and some of the most challenging climbs and walks in the Highlands. Red deer, wildcats, eagles and ptarmigan are among the wildlife. It is also known as a place of treachery and infamy. The Macdonalds of Glencoe were hosts to a party of troops who, under government orders, fell upon the men, women and children, in a bloody massacre in 1692. The Visitor Centre tells the story.

**Times:** *Open: Site all year, daily. Visitor Centre Apr-Aug, 9.30-5.30; Mar-Apr & Sep-Oct, daily 10-5; Nov-Feb, Fri-Mon 10-4 (last admission 30 mins before closing). Times may change for 2007 please telephone or check website

**Fee:** *50p (ch & pen 30p). Includes parking. For more details phone 0131 243 9387

**Facilities:** ❷ �🪑 ♿ (induction loop in video programme room, toilets) shop ⊗ (ex guide dogs) 🚌 ♨ ♨

## HELMSDALE
### Timespan
Dunrobin St KW8 6JX

☎ 01431 821327 📄 01431 821058

**Email:** enquiries@timespan.org.uk

**Web:** www.timespan.org.uk

**Dir:** *off A9 in centre of village, by Telford Bridge*

Located in a historic fishing village, this museum explores the social and natural history of the area – from the Vikings to the last witch hunt, and includes re-creations of a typical croft, a smithy and a period shop. The art gallery has changing exhibitions of contemporary fine and applied art by visiting and local artists which provides an opportunity to buy original work. The garden has over 100 varieties of herbs and plants and there is a gift shop, and a café with beautiful views of the Telford Bridge.

**Times:** *Open Apr-Oct, Mon-Sat 10-5, Sun 12-5.

**Fee:** *£4 (ch £2, concessions £3). Family ticket £10.

**Facilities:** ❷ Ⓟ (150 mtrs) ♿ (lift, toilets) shop, guided tours ⊗ (ex guide dogs) 🚌 Pre-booking

**HIGHLAND**

## KINCRAIG
**Highland Wildlife Park**
Kingussie PH21 1NL
☎ 01540 651270 🖷 01540 651236
**Email:** info@highlandwildlifepark.org
**Web:** www.highlandwildlifepark.org
**Dir:** *on B9152, 7m S of Aviemore*
Part of the Royal Zoological Society of Scotland the Highland Wildlife Park offers a unique opportunity to see a range of ancient species such as Przewalski's Horse, wolf and wild boar. As you drive through the main reserve, you can see awe-inspiring European bison grazing alongside wild horses, red deer and Highland cattle plus a wide variety of other species. Then in the walk-round habitats of forest, woodland and moorland prepare for close encounters with animals such as wolves, capercaillie, arctic foxes, wildcats, pine martens, otters and owls. Special events are held every weekend April to October.
**Times:** *Open throughout the year, weather permitting. Apr-Oct, 10-6; Jun-Aug 10-7; Nov-Mar 10-4. (Last entry 2 hours before closing).
**Fee:** *£8 (child £5.50, pen £7).
**Facilities:** 🅿 ⛱ ♿ (toilets) shop ⊗ 🚌

## KINGUSSIE
**Highland Folk Museum**
Duke Street PH21 1JG
☎ 01540 661307 🖷 01540 661631
**Email:** highland.folk@highland.gov.uk
**Web:** www.highlandfolk.com
**Dir:** *12m SW of Aviemore off A9 at Kingussie*
First established in 1935, this was Britain's first open-air museum. For a glimpse of life in a Blackhouse or a look at farming implements and domestic objects and furniture, this museum offers an internationally renowned collection of items. The Museum Store, not accessible to visitors in previous years, now displays in excess of 1,500 objects.
**Times:** *Open Apr-Aug, Mon-Sat 9.30-5; Sep & Oct Mon-Fri, 9.30-4
**Fee:** *£2.50 (ch & pen £1.50)
**Facilities:** 🅿 ⓟ (0.25m) ⛱ ♿ (ramp, door, rails, toilets) shop, guided tours ⊗ (ex guide dogs) 🚌

## NEWTONMORE
**Highland Folk Museum**
Aultlarie Croft PH20 1AY
☎ 01540 661307 🖷 01540 661631
**Email:** highland.folk@highland.gov.uk
**Web:** www.highlandfolk.com
**Dir:** *on A86, follow signs off A9*
An early 18th-century farming township with turf houses has been reconstructed at this award-winning museum. A 1930s school houses old world maps, little wooden desks and a Coates library. Other attractions include a working croft with rare breed animals and tailor's workshop. Vintage buses run throughout the site.
**Times:** *Open Apr-Aug, Mon-Sun 10.30-5.30; Sep Mon-Sun, 11-4.30; Oct Mon-Fri, 11-4.30
**Fee:** *£6 (ch & pen £3.50)
**Facilities:** 🅿 ⛱ ♿ (vintage bus with full disabled access, toilets) shop audio commentaries ⊗ (ex guide dogs) 🚌

## POOLEWE
### Inverewe Garden

Achnasheen IV22 2LG
☎ 01445 781200 🖨 01445 781497
Email: inverewe@nts.org.uk
Web: www.nts.org.uk
Dir: *6m NE of Gairloch, on A832*

The influence of the North Atlantic Drift enables this remarkable garden to grow rare and sub-tropical plants. At its best in early June, but full of beauty from March to October, Inverewe has a backdrop of magnificent mountains and stands to the north of Loch Maree.
**Times:** *Open: Garden all year, Apr-Oct, daily 9.30-9 (or sunset if earlier). Nov-Mar, 9.30-4. Visitor Centre Apr-Sep, daily 9.30-5; Oct, daily 9.30-4. Times may change for 2007 please telephone or check website

**Fee:** *£7 (concessions £5.25) Family ticket £19. Groups adult £5.60 (ch/school £1). Admission free to NTS members. For other details please phone 0131 243 9387
**Facilities:** 🅿 🍴 (Licensed) ♿ (some paths difficult, toilets) shop 🚫 (ex guide dogs) 🚌 (pre-booking required) 💈 ♻

---

## STRATHPEFFER
### Highland Museum of Childhood

The Old Station IV14 9DH
☎ 01997 421031
Email: info@highlandmuseumofchildhood.org.uk
Web: www.highlandmuseumofchildhood.org.uk
Dir: *5m W of Dingwall on A834*

Located in a renovated Victorian railway station of 1885, the museum tells the story of childhood in the Highlands amongst the crofters and townsfolk; a way of life recorded in oral testimony, displays and evocative photographs. An award-winning video, A Century of Highland Childhood is shown. There are also doll and toy collections.
**Times:** Open Apr-Oct, daily 10-5, (Sun 2-5) also Jul & Aug evenings open to 7. Other times by arrangement.

**Fee:** £2 (ch, concessions £1.50). Family ticket £5 (2ad+3ch).
**Facilities:** 🅿 🅿 (500yds) 🪑 📋 ♿ (tape tour with induction loop for partially sighted) shop 🚫 (ex guide dogs) 🚌 (20 people max)

---

## DALKEITH
### Edinburgh Butterfly & Insect World

Dobbies Garden World Lasswade EH18 1AZ
☎ 0131 663 4932 🖨 0131 654 2774
Email: info@edinburgh-butterfly-world.co.uk
Web: www.edinburgh-butterfly-world.co.uk
Dir: *0.5m S of Edinburgh city bypass at Gilmerton junct or Sherrifhall rdbt*

Richly coloured butterflies from all over the world can be seen flying among exotic rainforest plants, trees and flowers. The tropical pools, filled with giant waterlilies and colourful fish, are surrounded by lush vegetation. Insect World has scorpions, leaf cutting ants, beetles, tarantulas and other remarkable creatures including snakes and frogs. There is a unique honeybee display and daily insect handling sessions.

**Times:** Open Summer daily 9.30-5.30; Winter daily 10-5. Closed 25-26 Dec & 1 Jan.
**Fee:** *£5 (ch, concessions & students £3.85). Family ticket £16.50 (2ad+2ch). Party 10+.
**Facilities:** 🅿 🪑 📋 ♿ (toilets) shop, garden centre, guided tours 🚫 (ex guide dogs) 🚌

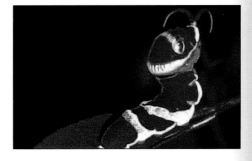

## NEWTONGRANGE
### Scottish Mining Museum
Lady Victoria Colliery EH22 4QN
☎ 0131 663 7519 ▤ 0131 654 0952
**Email:** visitorservices@scottishminingmuseum.com
**Web:** www.scottishminingmuseum.com
**Dir:** *10m S of Edinburgh on A7, signed from bypass*
Based at the Lady Victoria Colliery and offering an outstanding visit to Britains' finest Victorian colliery. Guided tours with miners, magic helmets, exhibitions, theatres, interactive displays and a visit to the coal face. Home to Scotland's largest steam engine.
**Times:** *Open all year, daily Mar-Oct, 10-5. Nov-Feb, daily, 10-4.
**Fee:** *£5.95 (ch & concessions £3.95). Family ticket £17.95. Party 20+ (£4.95, ch £3.50)

**Facilities:** ❷ ℗ (300yds) �🍴 ⋔ 🗊 ♿ (tactile opportunities, interactive, audio tours, toilets) shop, guided tours, audio commentaries
Ⓧ (ex guide dogs) 🚌 (max party 50)

## PENICUIK
### Edinburgh Crystal Visitor Centre
Eastfield EH26 8HB
☎ 01968 675128 ▤ 01968 673622
**Email:** visitorcentre@edinburgh-crystal.co.uk
**Web:** www.edinburgh-crystal.com
**Dir:** *Follow the brown thistle signs from the Edinburgh City Bypass and the A701/703*
Watch skilled craftsmen as they take molten crystal and turn it into intricately decorated glassware. Not only can you talk to the craftsmen themselves but there is also video footage, story boards, artefacts and audio listening posts to help you understand the 300-year-old history of glassmaking.
**Times:** Open Mon-Sat 10-5, Sun 11-5. Closed 25-26 Dec and 1-2 Jan.

**Fee:** Free
**Facilities:** ❷ ℗ (100yds) 🍴 (Licensed) ⋔ ♿ (ramp to first floor, toilets) shop Ⓧ (ex guide dogs) 🚌 (pre-book catering requirements)

## BRODIE CASTLE
### Brodie Castle
Forres IV36 2TE
☎ 01309 641371 ▤ 01309 641600
**Email:** brodiecastle@nts.org.uk
**Web:** www.nts.org.uk
**Dir:** *4.5m W of Forres, off A96*
The Brodie family lived here for hundreds of years before passing the castle to the NTS in 1980. It contains many treasures, including furniture, porcelain and paintings. The extensive grounds include a woodland walk and an adventure playground. Wheelchairs for disabled visitors are available. Please telephone for details of recitals, concerts, open-air theatre etc.
**Times:** *Open Apr & Jul-Aug, daily 12-4; May-Jun & Sep, Sun-Thu 12-4. Grounds all year, daily, 9.30-sunset.

Times may change for 2007 please telephone or check website
**Fee:** *£5 (concessions £3.75) Groups adults £4 (ch/school £1), please book groups in advance. Family ticket £13.50. Garden, grounds & car parking £1. Admission free to NTS members. For other details please phone 0131 243 9387
**Facilities:** ❷ ⋔ ♿ (audio tape & information sheet in Braille, toilets) shop Ⓧ (ex guide dogs) 🚌 (pre-booking required) ♨ ⊠

## ELGIN
### Elgin Museum
1 High Street IV30 1EQ
☎ 01343 543675 ▤ 01343 543675
**Email:** curator@elginmuseum.org.uk
**Web:** www.elginmuseum.org.uk
**Dir:** *E end of High St, follow brown heritage signs*
Scotland's oldest independent museum this award-winning museum is internationally famous for its fossil fish and fossil reptiles, and for its Pictish stones. The museum collection amounts to 36,000 items including a Roman hoard discovered on a local dig. The displays relate to the natural and human history of Moray. The latest exhibition People and Place reflects 1,000 years of Scottish history from the Moray perspective.
**Times:** Open Apr-Oct, Mon-Fri 10-5, Sat 11-4.

**Fee:** £3 (ch £1, pen, students & UB40 £1.50). Family ticket £6.
**Facilities:** ❷ (charged) ℗ (50mtrs - limited time) ▤ ♿ (handrails, case displays at sitting level with large fonts, toilets) shop, guided tours, audio commentaries, ⊗ (ex guide dogs) 🚌 ♨

## FOCHABERS
### Baxters Highland Village
IV32 7LD
☎ 01343 820666 ▤ 01343 821790
**Email:** highland.village@baxters.co.uk
**Web:** www.baxters.com
**Dir:** *1m W of Fochabers on A96*
The Baxters food firm started here over 130 years ago and now sells its products in over 60 countries. Visitors can see the shop where the story began, watch an audio-visual display, and visit five shops. See the great hall, audio-visual theatre and cooking theatre. A food tasting area is open to visitors.
**Times:** *Open all year daily, Jan-Mar 10-5; Apr-Dec 9-5.30.
**Fee:** *Free

**Facilities:** ❷ ℣ (Licensed) ⛱ ♿ (parking facilities, toilets) shop ⊗ (ex guide dogs) 🚌 (pre-booking required)

## FORRES
### Falconer Museum
Tolbooth Street IV36 1PH
☎ 01309 673701 ▤ 01309 673701
**Email:** museums@moray.gov.uk
**Web:** www.moray.gov.uk/museums
**Dir:** *11m W of Elgin, 26m E of Iverness on A96*
Founded by bequests made by two brothers, Alexander and Hugh Falconer. Hugh was a distinguished scientist, friend of Darwin, recipient of many honours and Vice-President of the Royal Society. On display are fossil mammals collected by him, and items relating to his involvement in the study of anthropology. Other displays are on local wildlife, geology, archaeology and history. You can also see the Forres Quincentennial Time Capsule.
**Times:** *Open all year Feb (provisional)-Oct, Mon-Sat 10-5; Nov-Mar, Mon-Thu 11-12.30 & 1-3.30. Closed Good Fri, May Day, Xmas and New Year.
**Fee:** Donations welcome
**Facilities:** ❷ ℗ (100yds - no on-street parking) ▤ ♿ (induction loop system) shop, guided tours, audio commentaries ⊗ (ex guide dogs) 🚌 (prior booking preferred) ♨

**MORAY**

SPEY BAY
**The WDCS Wildlife Centre**
Fochabers IV32 7PJ
☎ 01343 829109 ▤ 01343 829065
Email: enquiries@mfwc.co.uk
Web: www.mfwc.co.uk
Dir: *off A96 onto B9014 at Fochabers, follow road approx 5m to village of Spey Bay. Turn left at Spey Bay Hotel and follow road for 500mtrs*
The centre, owned and operated by the Whale and Dolphin Conservation Society, lies at the mouth of the River Spey and is housed in a former salmon fishing station, built in 1768. There is a free exhibition about the Moray Firth dolphins and the wildlife of Spey Bay. Visitors can browse through a well-stocked gift shop and enjoy refreshments in the cosy tea room.

Times: *Open Apr-Oct 10.30-5. Check for winter opening times
Fee: Free
Facilities: 🅿 Ⓟ (20mtrs) 🏕 🍴 20p ♿ (toilets) shop, guided tours Ⓧ (ex guide dogs) 🚌 (must pre-book)

TOMINTOUL
**Tomintoul Museum**
The Square AB37 9ET
☎ 01309 673701 ▤ 01309 673701
Email: museums@moray.gov.uk/museums
Web: www.moray.gov.uk
Dir: *on A939, 13m E of Grantown*
Situated in one of the highest villages in Britain, the museum features a reconstructed crofter's kitchen and smiddy, with other displays on the local wildlife, the story of Tomintoul, and the local skiing industry.
Times: Open: Mar-May, Mon-Fri, 9.30-12 and 2-4. Jun-Aug, Mon-Sat, 9.30-12 and 2-4.30. Sep, Mon-Sat, 9.30-12 and 2-4. Oct, Mon-Fri, 9.30-12 and 2-4. Closed May day and Good Fri.
Fee: Free Donations welcome.

Facilities: 🅿 Ⓟ (200mtrs) 🏕 🍴 ♿ (induction loop and sound commentaries) shop guided tours audio commentaries Ⓧ (ex guide dogs) 🚌 (pre-booking preferred) 💳

BRODICK
**Brodick Castle, Garden & Country Park**
KA27 8HY
☎ 01770 302202 & 302462 ▤ 01770 302312
Email: brodick@nts.org.uk
Web: www.nts.org.uk
Dir: *Ferry from Ardrossan-Brodick or Lochranza-Kintyre - frequent in summer, limited in winter*
The site has been fortified since Viking times, but the present castle dating from the 13th century was a stronghold of the Dukes of Hamilton. Splendid silver, fine porcelain and paintings acquired by generations of owners can be seen, including many sporting pictures and trophies. There is a magnificent woodland garden, started by the Duchess of Montrose in 1923, world famous for its rhododendrons and azaleas.

Times: *Open Apr-Oct, daily 11-4.30 (closes 3.30 in Oct). Country Park: open all year, daily 9.30-sunset. Times may change for 2007 please telephone or check website
Fee: *£8 (concessions £6) Groups adult £6 (ch/school £2), please book groups in advance. Family ticket £20. Country Park only Apr-Oct £4 (concessions £3) Groups adult £3 (ch/school £2). Family ticket £12. £2. Admission free to NTS members.
Facilities: 🅿 🍴 🏕 ♿ (Braille, wheelchairs, motorised buggy & stairlift, toilets) shop Ⓧ (ex guide dogs) 🚌 (pre-booking required) 🐾 💳

**IRVINE**

## Scottish Maritime Museum

Harbourside KA12 8QE

☎ 01294 278283 📠 01294 313211

Email: smm@tildesley.fsbusiness.co.uk

Web: www.scottishmaritimemuseum.org

Dir: *Follow yellow AA signs from Irvine*

The museum has displays that reflect all aspects of Scottish maritime history. Vessels can be seen afloat in the harbour as well as those exhibited undercover. The museum allows you to experience life in a 1910 shipyard worker's tenement flat. Not to be missed is the Linthouse Engine Shop originally built in 1872, which is being developed and holds a substantial part of the museum's collection in open store.

**Times:** Open Apr-Oct, 10-5

**Fee:** £3 (ch & pen £2). Family ticket £7.

**Facilities:** 🅿 Ⓟ (100yds) 🍴 ♿ (audio tapes for blind, toilets) shop, guided tours Ⓧ (ex guide dogs) 🚌 ♻

---

**LARGS**

## Kelburn Castle and Country Centre

Fairlie KA29 0BE

☎ 01475 568685 📠 01475 568121

Email: admin@kelburncountrycentre.com

Web: www.kelburncountrycentre.com

Dir: *2m S of Largs, on A78*

Historic home of the Earls of Glasgow, Kelburn is famous for its romantic Glen, family gardens, unique trees and spectacular views over the Firth of Clyde. Glen walks, riding and trekking centre, adventure course, activity workshop, Kelburn Story Cartoon Exhibition and a family museum. The Secret Forest at the centre, Scotland's most unusual attraction, is a chance to explore the Giant's Castle, maze of the Green Man and secret grotto. Also included is a Falconry Centre, pottery craft studio and an indoor Adventure Playbarn.

**Times:** Open all year, Etr-end Oct, daily 10-6; Nov-Mar, 11-dusk. Grounds and Sawmill Adventure Playbarn, wknds only

**Fee:** *£7 (concessions £4.50). Family ticket £22.

**Facilities:** 🅿 🍴 (Licensed) 🥢 🍴 ♿ (Ranger service to assist disabled, toilets) shop, guided tours (charged) 🚌

---

**LARGS**

## Vikingar!

Greenock Road KA30 8QL

☎ 01475 689777 📠 01475 689444

Email: cmcnaught@naleisure.co.uk

Web: www.naleisure.co.uk

Dir: *on A78, 0.5m into Largs, opposite RNLI lifeboat station*

A multi-media experience that takes you from the first Viking raids in Scotland to their defeat at the Battle of Largs.

**Times:** Open Apr-Sep, daily 10.30-5.30; Oct & Mar, daily 10.30-3.30; Nov & Feb, wknds only 10.30-3.30. Closed Dec & Jan.

**Fee:** £4.10 (ch 4-15 £2.30, pen £3.10). Family ticket £12.20. Group 10+

**Facilities:** 🅿 🥢 🍴 ♿ (toilets) shop ,guided tours, audio commentaries Ⓧ (ex guide dogs) 🚌 (advance booking essential)

**NORTH AYRSHIRE**

MOTHERWELL
**Motherwell Heritage Centre**
High Rd ML1 3HU
☎ 01698 251000 📄 01698 268867
**Email:** museums@northlan.gov.uk
**Web:** www.nlcmuseums.bravehost.com
**Dir:** *A723 for town centre. Left at top of hill, after pedestrian crossing and just before railway bridge*
This award-winning audio-visual experience, 'Technopolis', traces the history of the area from Roman times to the rise of 19th-century industry and the post-industrial era. There is also a fine viewing tower, an exhibition gallery and family history research facilities. A mixed programme of community events and touring exhibitions occur throughout the year.
**Times:** *Open all year Wed-Sat 10-5 (Thu 10-7), Sun 12-5. Closed Mon & Tue, ex BHs. Local studies library closed Sun
**Fee:** Free
**Facilities:** 🅿 🅟 (50 yds - barrier opens at 10am) 📄 ♿ (lifts, audio info & Braille buttons, toilets) shop, guided tours ⊗ (ex guide dogs) 🚌 ♻

DOUNBY
**Skara Brae**
KW16 3LR
☎ 01856 841815
**Web:** www.historic-scotland.gov.uk
**Dir:** *19m W of Kirkwall on B9056*
Engulfed in drift sand, this remarkable group of well-preserved Stone Age dwellings is the most outstanding survivor of its kind in Britain. Comprising 8 dwellings linked by by low alleyways the buildings and their interiors are amazingly well preserved and show how life was led in Neolithic times. Each house has a central fireplace with a stone bed on either side and stone dresser with shelves for storage.
**Times:** *Open all year, Apr-Sep, daily 9.30-6.30; Oct-Mar, daily 9.30-4.30. Closed 25-26 Dec & 1-2 Jan.
**Fee:** *£6.50 (ch £2.50, concessions £5). Please phone or check website for details.
**Facilities:** 🅿 🍴 🏮 ♿ (toilets) shop ⊗ 🚌 🎒 ♻

HARRAY
**Corrigall & Kirbuster Farm Museums**
KW17 2JR
☎ 01856 771411 & 771268 📄 01856 874615
The museum consists of two Orkney farmhouses with outbuildings. Kirbuster Farm Museum (Birsay has the last surviving example of a 'Firehoose' with its central hearth and stone bed built into the wall. Dating from the mid-18th century the farm is now a working museum and gives a real insight into Orcadian farming life. There is a Victorian garden and for extra entertainment also a putting green, horseshoe pitching, traditional crafts and livestock. Corrigall Farm Museum (Harray) is a rather superior farmhouse with a barn and and a working grain kiln. There are animals here too and a horse gig to bring the life of a 19th-century farmer vividly back to life.
**Times:** *Open Mar-Oct, Mon-Sat 10.30-1 & 2-5, Sun 2-7.
**Fee:** Free
**Facilities:** 🅿 🅟 (at museum) 🏮 📄 ♿ (toilets) shop, guided tours ⊗ (ex guide dogs) 🚌

## KIRKWALL
### Scapa Flow Visitor Centre & Museum
Lyness Hoy
☎ 01856 791300 📄 01856 871560
**Email:** museum@orkney.gov.uk
**Web:** www.orkneyheritage.com
**Dir:** *on A964 to Houton, ferry crossing takes 30 mins, visitors' centre 2 mins from ferry terminal*
Also known as the Lyness Interpretation Centre, this fascinating museum is home to a large collection of military equipment used in the defence of the Orkneys during the First and Second World Wars. There are also guns salvaged from the German ships scuppered in the waters of Scapa Flow during WWII. Visitors arrive at the island after a short trip from the Orkney mainland on the ferry boat.

**Times:** *Open all year: Mon-Fri 9-4.30 (mid May-Oct also Sat, Sun 10.30-3.30)
**Fee:** Free
**Facilities:** 🅿 📋 ♿ (toilets) shop, guided tours, ⊗ (ex guide dogs) 🚌

## KIRKWALL
### The Orkney Museum
Broad St KW15 1DH
☎ 01856 87355 📄 01856 873535
**Email:** museum@orkney.gov.uk
**Web:** www.orkneyheritage.com
**Dir:** *town centre*
Known as Tankerness House this is one of the finest vernacular town houses in Scotland. This 16th-century building now contains a museum of Orkney history, including the islands' fascinating archaeology. In the museum there are Neolithic/Bronze Age galleries and displays that feature the Vikings, Medieval Orkney, Jacobites and smuggling activities as well as temporary and visiting exhibitions. Outside there is a beautiful walled garden with unlimited access.

**Times:** *Open, Oct-Mar Mon-Sat, 10.30-12.30 & 1.30-5, Apr-Sep, 10.30-5 Mon-Sat.
**Fee:** Free
**Facilities:** 🅿 (50yds) 📋 ♿ (toilets) shop ⊗ (ex guide dogs) 🚌

## BLAIR ATHOLL
### Blair Castle
Pitlochry PH18 5TL
☎ 01796 481207 📄 01796 481487
**Email:** office@blair-castle.co.uk
**Web:** www.blair-castle.co.uk
**Dir:** *7m NW of Pitlochry, off A9 at Blair Atholl & follow signs to attraction*
Ancient seat of the Dukes of Atholl and its unique private army, the Atholl Highlanders. The castle dates back to the 13th century but was altered in the 18th, and later given a castellated exterior. There are paintings, furniture, Jacobite relics and Masonic regalia. The extensive grounds include a deer park, and a restored 18th-century walled garden. Events are held throughout the year, including the annual parade of the Atholl Highlanders.

**Times:** *Open all year Nov-end Mar, Tue & Sat 9.30-12.30 (last admission); Apr-end Oct, daily 9.30-4.30 (last admission).
**Fee:** *£6.90 (ch £4.30, pen £5.90). Family ticket £17.50. Party £5.55. Prices to be confirmed
**Facilities:** 🅿 🍽 (Licensed) 🪑 📋 ♿ (scooter, parking) shop, guided tours ⊗ (ex guide dogs) 🚌

KINROSS
**Loch Leven Castle**
Castle Island KY13 7AR
☎ 01786 450000
**Web:** www.historic-scotland.gov.uk
**Dir:** *on an island in Loch Leven accessible by boat from Kinross*
This romantic ruin, built on an island in Loch Levin, was where Mary, Queen of Scots was imprisoned and forced to abdicate in favour of her infant son James VI in 1567. Surrounded by what is known as a 'curtain wall' the ruins still provide a fascinating insight into life in a Scottish castle. The ferry journey across the water is quite short but enough to add an unusual element to the experience and ensure a memorable day out.
**Times:** *Open Apr-Sep, daily 9.30-6.30.

**Fee:** *£4 (ch £1.60, concessions £3). Charge includes ferry trip. Please phone or check website for further details.
**Facilities:** 🅿 🛤 shop ⊗ ⫲ ♿

KINROSS
**RSPB Nature Reserve Vane Farm**
By Loch Leven KY13 9LX
☎ 01577 862355 🖷 01577 862013
**Email:** vane.farm@rspb.org.uk
**Web:** www.rspb.org.uk
**Dir:** *2m E of M90 junct 5, on S shore of Loch Leven, entered off B9097 to Glenrothes*
Well placed beside Loch Leven, with a nature trail and hides overlooking the loch and a woodland trail with stunning panoramic views. Noted for its pink-footed geese, the area also attracts whooper swans, greylag geese and great spotted woodpeckers amongst many others. Details of special events are available from the Visitors' Centre.
**Times:** *Open all year daily, 10-5. Closed 25-26 Dec &

1-2 Jan.
**Fee:** *£3 (ch 50p, concessions £2). Family £6.
**Facilities:** 🅿 ⛶ (coffee shop open 10-4.30) 🛤 ♿ (wheelchair extensions, ramps, telescopes, toilets) shop ⊗ (ex guide dogs) 🚌 (pre-booking required)

PITLOCHRY
**Scottish Hydro Electric Visitor Centre, Dam & Fish Pass**
PH16 5ND
☎ 01796 473152 🖷 01882 634 709
**Dir:** *off A9, 24m N of Perth*
The visitor centre features an exhibition showing how electricity is brought from the power station to the customer, and there is access to the turbine viewing gallery. The salmon ladder viewing chamber allows you to see the fish as they travel upstream to their spawning ground.
**Times:** *Open Apr-Oct, Mon-Fri 10-5.30. Wknd Opening Jul, Aug & BHs
**Fee:** *£3 (accompanied ch free, concessions £2).
**Facilities:** 🅿 Ⓟ (adjacent – no buses or caravans)

♿ (monitor viewing of salmon fish pass, toilets) shop, ⊗ (ex guide dogs) 🚌 ♿

## QUEEN'S VIEW
### Queen's View Visitor Centre
Strathtummel Pitlochry PH16 5NR

☎ 01350 727284 🖷 01350 728635

**mail:** peter.fullarton@forestry.gsi.gov.uk

**Web:** www.forestry.gov.uk

**Dir:** *7m W of Pitlochry on B8019*

Queen Victoria admired the view on a visit here in 1866; is possibly one of the most famous views in Scotland. The area, in the heart of the Tay Forest Park, has a variety of woodlands that visitors can walk or cycle in as well as the stunning view across Loch Tummel to the peak of Schiehallion. This award-winning visitor centre includes an audio-visual film facility, an exhibition, a tearoom and shop.

**Times:** *Open Apr-Nov, daily 10-6.

**Fee:** *Free

**Facilities:** ❷ (charged) ℗ (500mtrs) ⌂ ♿ (toilets) shop 🚌

## SCONE
### Scone Palace
PH2 6BD

☎ 01738 552300 🖷 01738 552588

**Email:** visits@scone-palace.co.uk

**Web:** www.scone-palace.co.uk

**Dir:** *2m NE of Perth on A93*

Scottish kings were crowned at Scone until 1651 and it was the site of the famous coronation Stone of Destiny from the 9th century until the English seized the Stone in 1296. The castellated edifice of the present palace dates from 1803 but incorporates the 16th-century and earlier buildings. The interior houses objets d'art, including French & Scottish furniture, an extensive porcelain collection and paintings. The grounds include a pinetum, the original Douglas Fir, the unique Murray Star Maze, woodland walks and herbaceous plantings. Also the David Douglas Trail.

**Times:** Open Apr-Oct

**Fee:** *Palace & Grounds £7.20 (ch £4.20, concessions £6.20). Family ticket £23. Grounds only £3.80 (ch £2.50, concessions £3.50). Group £6 (ch £4, concessions £5.30)

**Facilities:** ❷ ⑪ (Licensed) ⌂ 🍴 ♿ (stairlift which gives access to all state rooms, toilets) shop, guided tours ⊗ (ex assist dogs & in grounds) 🚌

## WEEM
### Castle Menzies
Aberfeldy PH15 2JD

☎ 01887 820982 🖷 01887 820982

**Email:** castlem@tiscali.co.uk

**Web:** www.menzies.org

**Dir:** *Follow signs from main roads*

Restored seat of the Chiefs of Clan Menzies, and a fine example of a 16th-century Z-plan fortified tower house. Prince Charles Edward Stuart stayed here briefly on his way to Culloden in 1746. The whole of the 16th-century building can be explored, and there's a small clan museum.

**Times:** Open Apr-mid Oct, Mon-Sat 10.30-5, Sun 2-5.

**Fee:** £4 (ch £2, concessions £3.50).

**Facilities:** ❷ ℗ (500yds - limited bus parking space) ⌂ 🍴 ♿ (toilets) shop ⊗ (ex guide dogs) 🚌 (pre-booking prefered, 1 at a time) ♨

**PERTH & KINROSS**

KILBARCHAN
**Weaver's Cottage**
The Cross Johnstone PA10 2JG
☎ 01505 705588
**Email:** aclipson@nts.scot.demon.co.uk
**Web:** www.nts.org.uk
**Dir:** *off A737, 12m SW of Glasgow*
The weaving craft is regularly demonstrated at this delightful 18th-century cottage museum, and there is a collection of weaving equipment and other domestic utensils.
**Times:** *Open Apr-Sep, Fri-Tue, 1-5; morning visits available for pre-booked groups. Times may change for 2007 please telephone or check website
**Fee:** *£3.50 (concessions £2.60) Family ticket £9.50. Groups adult £2.80 (ch/school £1). Please book groups

in advance. Admission free to NTS members. For other details please phone 0131 243 9387
**Facilities:** 🅿 🚫 (ex guide dogs) 🚌 (pre-booking required, am only) 🍽 ♿

LANGBANK
**Finlaystone Country Estate**
PA14 6TJ
☎ 01475 540505 📠 01475 540285
**Email:** info@finlaystone.co.uk
**Web:** www.finlaystone.co.uk
**Dir:** *on A8 W of Langbank, 10m W of Glasgow Airport, follow Thistle signs*
A beautiful country estate with views over the Firth of Clyde and historic formal gardens which are renowned for their natural beauty, woodland walks and play areas. The 'Dolly Mixture' is an international collection of dolls which can be seen in the visitor centre.
**Times:** *Open all year. Woodland & Gardens daily, 10-5.
**Fee:** *Garden & Woods £3.50 (ch & pen £2.50). 'The Dolly Mixture' Doll Museum is free.

**Facilities:** 🅿 ☕ (Apr - Oct daily. Oct – Mar weekends.) 🍴 📖 ♿ (lift to second floor, pathways for wheelchairs, toilets) shop 🚌 (booking essential)

LOCHWINNOCH
**RSPB Lochwinnoch Nature Reserve**
Largs Road PA12 4JF
☎ 01505 842663 📠 01505 843026
**Email:** lochwinnoch@rspb.org.uk
**Web:** www.rspb.org.uk/reserves/lochwinnoch
**Dir:** *on A760, Largs road, opposite Lochwinnoch station, 16m SW of Glasgow*
The reserve, part of Clyde Muirshiel Regional Park and a Site of Special Scientific Interest, comprises two shallow lochs fringed by marsh which in turn is fringed by scrub and woodland. There are two trails with hides and a visitor centre with a viewing area. Please visit website for details of events running throughout the year.
**Times:** *Open all year, daily 10-5. Closed 1-2 Jan & 25-26 Dec.

**Fee:** *Trails £2 (concessions £1, ch 50p). Family ticket £4.
**Facilities:** 🅿 🅿 (at station) 🍴 📖 ♿ (hides are all wheelchair accessible, toilets) shop guided tours 🚫 🚌 (advance booking)

**PAISLEY**
**Coats Observatory**
49 Oakshaw Street West PA1 2DE
☎ 0141 889 2013 🖹 0141 889 9240
**Email:** museums.els@renfrewshire.gov.uk
**Web:** www.renfrewshire.gov.uk
**Dir:** *M8 junct 27, follow signs to town centre until Gordon St, A761. Left onto Causeyside St, left onto New St then left onto High St*
The Observatory, funded by Thomas Coats and designed by John Honeyman, was opened in 1883. It houses a 5-inch telescope under the dome at the top. Weather recording activities have been carried out here continuously since 1884. There is also earthquake-measuring equipment and the Renfrewshire Astronomical Society holds regular meetings here. There are displays on the solar system, earthquakes and the telescope.
**Times:** *Open all year, Tue-Sat 10-5, Sun 2-5. Last entry 15 minutes before closing.
**Fee:** Free
**Facilities:** ℗ (150yds - meters/limited street parking) 🗊 guided tours ⊗ (ex guide dogs) 🚌 max 40 ♿

---

**COLDSTREAM**
**The Hirsel**
Douglas & Angus Estates Estate Office The Hirsel TD12 4LP
☎ 01890 882834 & 882965 🖹 01890 882834
**Email:** rogerdodd@btconnect.com
**Web:** www.hirselcountrypark.co.uk
**Dir:** *0.5m W on A697, on N outskirts of Coldstream*
The seat of the Home family, the grounds of which are open all year. The focal point is the Homestead Museum, craft centre and workshops. From there, nature trails lead around the lake, along the Leet Valley and into woodland noted for its rhododendrons and azaleas.
**Times:** * Garden & Grounds open all year, daylight hours. Museum 10-5. Craft Centre Mon-Fri, 10-5, wknds noon-5.
**Fee:** *£2.50 per car
**Facilities:** ℗ (charged) ⟐ (in season) 🍴 ⟑ 🗊 ♿ (toilets) shop ⊗ 🚌 (prior arrangement) ♿

---

**DUNS**
**Manderston**
TD11 3PP
☎ 01361 883450 & 882636 🖹 01361 882010
**Email:** palmer@manderston.co.uk
**Web:** www.manderston.co.uk
**Dir:** *2m E of Duns on A6105*
This grandest of grand houses gives a fascinating picture of Edwardian life above and below stairs. Completely remodelled for the millionaire racehorse owner Sir James Miller, the architect was told to spare no expense, and so the house boasts the world's only silver staircase. The staterooms are magnificent, and there are fine formal gardens, with a woodland garden and lakeside walks. Manderston has been the setting for a number of films.
**Times:** Open mid May-end Sep, Thu & Sun (also late May & Aug English BH Mons). Gardens open, 11.30-dusk. House open, 1.30-4.15
**Fee:** *House & Gardens £7 (ch £3.50); Gardens only £3.50.
**Facilities:** ℗ ⟐ (tea room) 🗊 £3, shop, guided tours ⊗ (ex guide dogs & on leads) 🚌 (by appointment only) ♿

**SCOTTISH BORDERS**

## INNERLEITHEN
### Robert Smail's Printing Works
7/9 High Street EH44 6HA
☎ 01896 830206
**Email:** smails@nts.org.uk
**Web:** www.nts.org.uk
These buildings contain a Victorian office, a paper store with reconstructed waterwheel, a composing room and a press room. The machinery is in full working order and visitors may view the printer at work and experience typesetting in the composing room.
**Times:** *Open Good Fri-Etr Mon & Jun-Sep, Thu-Mon 12-5, Sun 1-5. Times may change for 2007 please telephone or check website
**Fee:** *£3.50 (concessions £2.60) Family ticket £9.50. Groups adult £2.80 (ch/school £1). Admission free for NTS members. For other details please phone 0131 243 9387
**Facilities:** Ⓟ (300yds) ♿ shop ⊗ (ex guide dogs) 🚌 (pre-booking required) ♻ ♻

## LAUDER
### Thirlestane Castle
TD2 6RU
☎ 01578 722430 📄 01578 722761
**Email:** admin@thirlestanecastle.co.uk
**Web:** www.thirlestanecastle.co.uk
**Dir:** *off A68, S of Lauder*
This fairy-tale castle has been the home of the Maitland family, the Earls of Lauderdale, since the 12th century. Some of the most splendid plasterwork ceilings in Britain may be seen in the 17th-century state rooms. The family nurseries house a sizeable collection of antique toys and dolls. The informal riverside grounds, with their views of the grouse moors, include a woodland walk, picnic tables and adventure playground. Please visit website for details of events running throughout the year.
**Times:** * May-19 Sep, Wed-Fri & Sun. Jul-Aug Sun-Fri. Open from 10.30, last admission 2.30.
**Fee:** *£5.50 (ch £3) Family ticket £15.00.
**Facilities:** Ⓟ Ⓟ 🍽 (light lunches) 🪑 📰 £3.50 ♿ (toilets) shop, guided tours ⊗ (ex guide dogs) 🚌

## MELROSE
### Abbotsford
TD6 9BQ
☎ 01896 752043 📄 01896 752916
**Email:** enquiries@scottsabbotsford.co.uk
**Web:** www.scottsabbotsford.co.uk
**Dir:** *2m W off A6091, on B6360*
Set on the River Tweed, Sir Walter Scott's romantic mansion remains much the same as it was in his day. Inside there are many mementoes and relics of his remarkable life and also his historical collections, armouries and library, with some 9,000 volumes. Scott built the mansion between 1811 and 1822, and lived here until his death ten years after its completion.
**Times:** *Open daily from 3rd Mon in Mar-Oct, Mon-Sat 9.30-5. Mar-May & Oct, Sun 2-5. Jun-Sep, Sun 9.30-5.
**Fee:** *£5 (ch £2.50). Party £3.90 (ch £1.95).
**Facilities:** Ⓟ Ⓟ (200 yds) 🍽 (light lunches/tea & coffee) 🪑♿ (parking at private entrance, ramps at entrance, toilets) shop,guided tours ⊗ (ex guide & hearing dogs) 🚌

## PEEBLES
### Kailzie Gardens
EH45 9HT

☎ 01721 720007 🖺 01721 720007
**Email:** info@kailziegardens.com
**Web:** www.kailziegardens.com
**Dir:** *2.5m SE on B7062*

These extensive grounds, with their fine old trees, provide a burnside walk flanked by bulbs, rhododendrons and azaleas. A walled garden contains herbaceous, shrub rose borders, greenhouses and a formal rose garden. A garden for all seasons - don't miss the snowdrops. A large stocked trout pond and rod hire available, and an 18-hole putting green, plus an open bait pond, ornamental duck pond and osprey viewing centre.
**Times:** *Open 25 Mar-Oct, daily 11-5.30. Grounds close

5.30. Garden open all year.
**Fee:** *mid Mar-Jun £2.50, Jun-Oct £3.50, end Oct-mid Mar £2 honesty box (ch 5-12 80p)
**Facilities:** 🅿 🍴 (Licensed) 🍱 🗒 20p ♿ (ramps in garden, toilets) shop, guided tours 🚌 ♨

## SELKIRK
### Bowhill House & Country Park
TD7 5ET

☎ 01750 22204 🖺 01750 23893
**Email:** bht@buccleuch.com
**Web:** www.heritageontheweb.co.uk
**Dir:** *3m W of Selkirk off A708*

An outstanding collection of pictures, including works by Van Dyck, Canaletto, Reynolds, Gainsborough and Claude Lorraine are displayed here. Memorabilia and relics of people such as Queen Victoria and Sir Walter Scott, and a restored Victorian kitchen add further interest inside the house. Outside, the wooded grounds are perfect for walking. A small theatre provides a full programme of music and drama.
**Times:** * Park open May-Jun 11-5 wknd and BHs only.

Jul gardens daily 11-5, house daily 1-5. Aug Sat-Thu 11-5.
**Fee:** *House & grounds £6 (ch under 5 & wheelchair users free, pen & groups £4). Grounds only £2.
**Facilities:** 🅿 ☕ (Provides light lunches) 🍴 (Licensed) 🍱 🗒 Guidebook £2 ♿ (guided tours for the blind by appointment, toilets) shop, guided tours (charged) ⊗ (ex in park on leads) 🚌

## SELKIRK
### Halliwells House Museum
Halliwells Close Market Place TD7 4BC

☎ 01750 20096 🖺 01750 23282
**Email:** museums@scotborders.gov.uk
**Dir:** *off A7 in town centre*

A row of late 18th-century town cottages converted into a museum. Displays recreate the building's former use as an ironmonger's shop and home and includes an extensive collection of iron tools. There is also an exhibition telling the story of the Royal Burgh of Selkirk. The Robson Gallery hosts a programme of contemporary art and craft exhibitions.
**Times:** *Open Apr-Sep, Mon-Sat 10-5, Sun 10-12; Jul-Aug, Mon-Sat 10-5.30, Sun 10-12; Oct, Mon-Sat 10-4.
**Fee:** *Free

**Facilities:** 🅿 (charged) 🅿 ♿ (lift to first floor, large print, interpretation, toilets) shop ⊗ (ex guide dogs) 🚌 (24hrs notice preferred)

STOBO
**Dawyck Botanic Garden**
Near Peebles EH45 9JU
☎ 01721 760254 ▤ 01721 760214
**Email:** dawyck@rbge.org.uk
**Web:** www.rbge.org.uk
**Dir:** *8m SW of Peebles on B712*
From the landscaped walks of this historic arboretum an impressive collection of mature specimen trees can be seen - some over 40 metres tall and including the unique Dawyck beech-stand. Notable features include the Swiss Bridge, a fine estate chapel and stonework/terracing produced by Italian craftsmen in the 1820s.
**Times:** Open daily Feb-Nov. Feb & Nov 10-4. Mar-Oct 10-5. Apr-Sep 10-6
**Fee:** *£3.50 (ch £1, concessions £3). Family ticket £8

**Facilities:** ❷ ☕ (light refreshments only) 🪑 🗐 ♿ (toilets) shop, garden centre, guided tours ❌ (ex guide dogs) 🚌 (difficult access for large coaches)

TRAQUAIR
**Traquair House**
Innerleithen EH44 6PW
☎ 01896 830323 & 830785 ▤ 01896 830639
**Email:** enquiries@traquair.co.uk
**Web:** www.traquair.co.uk
**Dir:** *at Innerleithen take B709, house in 1m*
Said to be Scotland's oldest inhabited house, dating back to the 12th century, 27 Scottish monarchs have stayed at Traquair House. William the Lion Heart held court here, and the house has associations with Mary, Queen of Scots and the Jacobite risings. The Bear Gates were closed in 1745, not to be reopened until the Stuarts should once again ascend the throne. There is croquet, a maze and woodland walks by the River Tweed, craft workshops and a children's mini adventure playground.

Also a brewery museum and shop and antique shop.
**Times:** *Open Etr-Oct
**Fee:** *Please telephone for admission costs or visit website
**Facilities:** ❷ 🍴 (Licensed) 🪑 🗐 ♿ (toilets) shop, guided tours (charged) 🚌

LERWICK
**Shetland Museum**
Hay's Dock
☎ 01595 695057 ▤ 01595 696729
**Email:** shetland.museum@sic.shetland.gov.uk
**Web:** www.shetland-museum.gov.uk
Rebuilt with the aid of Lottery funding the New Shetland Museum and Archives opens in Spring 2007. Constructed at Hays Dock the new museum has extensive display space, a boat hall – three storeys high – with hanging boats, a lecture theatre and a café and restaurant specialising in local produce. Exhibitions start from the Early Beginnings of Shetland and its people to the present day and the future.
**Times:** Re-launch of museum. Please telephone for details of opening times and admissions.

**Fee:** Free
**Facilities:** ❷ ℗ (30yds) 🍴 (Licensed) 🗐 ♿ (lift, wheelchair available, toilets) shop, guided tours ❌ (ex guide dogs) 🚌 (pre-booking preferred)

## ALLOWAY
**Burns National Heritage Park**
Murdoch's Lone Ayr KA7 4PQ
☎ 01292 443700 📠 01292 441750
Email: info@burnsheritagepark.com
Web: www.burnsheritagepark.com
Dir: *2m S of Ayr*
The birthplace of Robert Burns, Scotland's National Poet
set in the gardens and countryside of Alloway. An
introduction to the life of Robert Burns, with an
audio-visual presentation - a multi-screen 3D experience
describing the Tale of Tam O'Shanter. This attraction
consists of the museum, Burn's Cottage, visitor centre,
tranquil landscaped gardens and historical monuments.
Please telephone for further details.
**Times:** Open all year, Apr-Sep 9.30-5.30, Oct-Mar 10-5.

Closed 25-26 Dec & 1-2 Jan
**Fee:** *£3 (ch & pen £2)
**Facilities:** 🅿 🅟 (200mtrs) 🍽 (Licensed) 🍴 £1.99
♿ (wheelchair available, toilets) shop, guided tours, audio
commentaries (charged) ⊗ (ex guide & hearing dogs) 🚌

## CULZEAN CASTLE
**Culzean Castle & Country Park**
MAYBOLE KA19 8LE
☎ 01655 884455 📠 01655 884503
Email: culzean@nts.org.uk
Web: www.culzeancastle.net
Dir: *4m W of Maybole, off A77*
This 18th-century castle stands on a cliff in spacious
grounds and was designed by Robert Adam for the Earl
of Cassillis. It is noted for its oval staircase, circular
drawing room and plasterwork. The Eisenhower Room
explores the American general's links with Culzean. The
563-acre country park has a wide range of attractions -
shoreline, woodland walks, parkland, an adventure
playground and gardens.
**Times:** *Open Castle: Apr-Oct, daily 10.30-5 (last entry

4). Visitor centre: Apr-Oct, daily 9-5.30; Nov-Mar, wknds
11-4. Country Park: Open all year 9.30-sunset. Times
may change for 2007 please telephone or check website
**Fee:** *£9 (concessions £6.50). Groups adult £9
(concessions £6.50) Family ticket £23. Country Park only
Apr-Oct £5 (concessions £3.75). Family ticket £13.50.
Group adult £4 (ch/school £1) Admission free to NTS
members. For other details please phone 0131 243 93
**Facilities:** 🅿 🍽 (Licensed) 🚻 ♿ (wheelchairs, lift in
castle, Braille guides, toilets) shop garden centre
⊗ (ex castle & guide dogs) 🚌 (pre-booking required)
🐾 ♻

## KIRKOSWALD
**Souter Johnnie's Cottage**
Main Road KA19 8HY
☎ 01655 760603
Email: aclipson@nts.scot.demon.co.uk
Web: www.nts.org.uk
Dir: *on A77, 4m SW of Maybole*
'Souter' means cobbler and the village cobbler who lived
in this 18th-century cottage was the inspiration for
Burns' character Souter Johnnie, in his ballad *Tam
O'Shanter*. The cottage is now a Burns museum and
life-size stone figures of the poet's characters can be
seen in the restored ale-house in the cottage garden.
**Times:** *Open Apr-Sep, Fri-Tue 11.30-5. Times may
change for 2007 please telephone or check website
**Fee:** *£2.50 (concessions £1.90) Family ticket £7.

Groups adult £2 (ch/school £1). Please book in advance
for groups. Admission free to NTS members. For other
details please phone 0131 243 9387
**Facilities:** 🅟 (75yds) ♿ (only one small step into
cottage) ⊗ (ex guide dogs) 🚌 (pre-booking required)
🐾 ♻

## BIGGAR
### Gladstone Court Museum
ML12 6DT

☎ 01899 221050 🖹 01899 221050
**Email:** margaret@bmtrust.freeserve.co.uk
**Web:** www.biggar-net.co.uk
**Dir:** *On A702 40m from Glasgow, 30m from Edinburgh, entrance by 113 High Street*
An old-fashioned village street is portrayed in this museum, which is set out in a century-old coach-house. On display are reconstructed shops, complete with old signs and advertisements. These include a bank, telephone exchange, photographer's booth, a schoolroom and other fascinating glimpses into the recent past. A close encounter with the Victorian age.
**Times:** *Open Etr-Oct, Mon-Sat 11-4.30, Sun 2-4.30.
**Fee:** *£2 (ch £1, pen £1.50). Family ticket £4. Party £1.25 each.
**Facilities:** 🅿 ⓟ (100yds) ♿ shop ⊗ (ex guide dogs) 🚐 ♒

## BIGGAR
### Moat Park Heritage Centre
ML12 6DT

☎ 01899 221050 🖹 01899 221050
**Email:** margaret@bmtrust.co.uk
**Web:** www.biggar-net.co.uk
**Dir:** *On A702, 30m from Edinburgh, 40m from Glasgow*
Using detailed scale models the centre illustrates the history, archaeology and geology of the Upper Clyde and Tweed valleys, showing archaeological sites as they would have been. From early henges and burials sites, Roman forts, medieval castles and a unique model of a Clydesdale defensive farmhouse – known as a bastle house, it is an extraordinary walk through history.
**Times:** *Open all year, Apr-Oct, daily 11.30-4.30, Sun 2-4.30; Nov-Feb, wkdays during office hours. Other times by prior arrangement.
**Fee:** *£2 (ch £1, pen £1.50). Family ticket £4. Party £1.25 each.
**Facilities:** 🅿 ⓟ (100yds) ⛱ 🍴 25p ♿ (upper floor with assistance on request, toilets) shop, guided tours, audio commentaries ⊗ (ex guide dogs) 🚐 ♒

## BLANTYRE
### David Livingstone Centre
165 Station Road G72 9BT

☎ 01698 823140 🖹 01698 821424
**Web:** www.nts.org.uk
**Dir:** *M74 junct 5 onto A725, then A724, follow signs for Blantyre, right at lights. Centre is at foot of hill*
Share the adventurous life of Scotland's greatest explorer, from his childhood in the Blantyre Mills to his explorations in the heart of Africa, dramatically illustrated in the historic tenement where he was born. Various events are planned throughout the season.
**Times:** *Open Apr-24 Dec, Mon-Sat 10-5, Sun 12.30-5. Times may change for 2007 please telephone or check website
**Fee:** *£3.50 (concessions £2.60) Family ticket £9.50. Groups adult £2.80 (ch/school £1). Please book groups in advance. Admission free to NTS members. For other details please phone 0131 243 9387
**Facilities:** 🅿 ⓟ (outside grounds) ⛱ ♿ (toilets) shop ⊗ (ex guide dogs) 🚐 (pre-booking required) 🍴

## EAST KILBRIDE
### Museum of Scottish Country Life
Wester Kittochside Philipshill Road (off Stewartfield Way) G76 9HR

☎ 0131 247 4377 📄 01355 571290

**Email:** info@nms.ac.uk

**Web:** www.nms.ac.uk

**Dir:** *From Glasgow take A749 to East Kilbride. From Edinburgh follow M8 to Glasgow, turn off junct 6 onto A725 to East Kilbride. Kittochside is signed before East Kilbride*

A fascinating museum built on a 170-acre farm and offering an insight into the working lives of people in rural Scotland. The museum runs a programme of events throughout the year, demonstrating its working collection and contrasting modern and traditional farming methods.

**Times:** *Open daily 10-5. Closed 25-26 Dec & 1-2 Jan

**Fee:** *£4.50 (ch under 18 free, concessions £3) NMS and NTS members free. Charge for some events.

**Facilities:** 🅿 Ⓟ (locally) 🍴 ♿ (disabled parking, exhibition building is fully accessible, toilets) shop Ⓧ (ex assist dogs) 🚌

## HAMILTON
### Chatelherault Country Park
Ferniegair ML3 7UE

☎ 01698 426213 📄 01698 421532

**Email:** phyllis.crosbie@southlanarkshire.gov.uk

**Web:** www.southlanarkshire.gov.uk

**Dir:** *2.5km SE of Hamilton on A72 Hamilton-Larkhall/Lanark Clyde Valley tourist route*

Designed as a hunting lodge by William Adam in 1732, Chatelherault, built of unusual pink sandstone, has been described as a gem of Scottish architecture. Situated close to the motorway, there is a visitor's centre, shop and adventure playground. Also a herd of white Cadzow cattle.

**Times:** Visitor Centre,Open all year, Mon-Sat 10-5, Sun 12-5. House closed all day Fri & Sat.

**Fee:** Free

**Facilities:** 🅿 ☕ (snacks and drinks) 🍴 ♿ (ramps, parking, large print guide, toilets) shop garden centre guided tours Ⓧ (ex in grounds & guide dogs) 🚌 (prefer pre-booking)

## NEW LANARK
### New Lanark Visitor Centre
Mill 3 New Lanark Mills ML11 9DB

☎ 01555 661345 📄 01555 665738

**Email:** trust@newlanark.org

**Web:** www.newlanark.org

**Dir:** *1m S of Lanark. Signed from all major routes. Less than 1hr from Glasgow M741/A72 and Edinburgh A70.*

Founded in 1785, New Lanark became well known in the early 19th century as a model community managed by enlightened industrialist and educational reformer Robert Owen. Surrounded by woodland and situated close to the Falls of Clyde, this unique world heritage site explores the philosophies of Robert Owen, using theatre, interactive displays, and the 'Millennium Experience', a magical ride through history. Accommodation is also available at the New Lanark Mill Hotel. Please telephone for details of events running throughout the year.

**Times:** Open all year daily. Jun-Aug 10.30-5. Sep-May 11-5. Closed 25 Dec and 1 Jan.

**Fee:** £5.95 (ch, concessions £4.95). Family ticket (2ad+2ch) £17.95. Family ticket (2ad+4ch) £21.95

**Facilities:** 🅿 🍴 📱 £1.75 ♿ (ramps, disabled parking, wheelchairs, toilets) shop, guided tours, audio commentaries Ⓧ (ex guide dogs) 🚌

**STIRLING**

## BLAIR DRUMMOND
**Blair Drummond Safari & Leisure Park**
Stirling FK9 4UR
☎ 01786 841456 & 841396 🖷 01786 841491
**Email:** enquiries@blairdrummond.com
**Web:** www.blairdrummond.com
**Dir:** *M9 junct 10, 4m on A84 towards Callander*
Drive through the wild animal reserves where zebras,
North American bison, antelope, lions, tigers, white rhino
and camels can be seen at close range as well as African
elephants, giraffes and ostriches. Other attractions
include the sea lion show, a ride on the boat safari
through the waterfowl sanctuary and around Chimpanzee
Island, an adventure playground, giant astraglide, and a
lake with pedal boats. There are also opportunities to
experience falconry.

**Times:** *Open 24 Mar-3 Oct, daily 10-5.30. (Last
admission 4.30)
**Fee:** *£9.50 (ch 3-14 £5.50, ch under 3 free). Discount
rates for party 15+.
**Facilities:** 🅿 ⬚ (outdoor snack bar) ⑩ (Licensed) 🎘 🗐
£2.50 ♿ (special menus & waitress service if booked in
advance, toilets) shop, audio commentaries
⊗ (ex assist dogs) 🚌

## KILLIN
**Breadalbane Folklore Centre**
Falls of Dochart FK21 8XE
☎ 01567 820254 🖷 01567 820764
**Email:** info@breadalbanefolklorecentre.com
**Web:** www.breadalbanefolklorecentre.com
**Dir:** *on A85*
Overlooking the beautiful Falls of Dochart, the centre
gives a fascinating insight into the legends of
Breadalbane – Scotland's 'high country'. Here you may
learn of the magical deeds of St Fillan and hear tales of
mystical giants, ancient prophesies, traditional folklore
and clan history. The centre is housed in the historic St
Fillans Mill which features a restored waterwheel. There
is also Tourist Information and a gift shop.
**Times:** *Open Apr-Jun, 10-5, daily. Jul-Aug, 10-5.30,
daily. Sep-Oct, 10-5, daily.
**Fee:** *£2 (ch & pen £1.25, students £1.50).
Family ticket £5.25.
**Facilities:** 🅿 (30mtrs) ♿ shop ⊗ 🚌

## STIRLING
**Old Town Jail**
Saint John Street FK8 1EA
☎ 01786 450050 🖷 01786 471301
**Email:** info@oldtownjail.com
**Web:** www.oldtownjail.com
**Dir:** *follow signs for castle up hill, jail on left at top of
Saint John's St*
Experience life in a Victorian prison, where real history
performances bring the past to life. Come face to face
with Stirling's notorious hangman and you may even
witness an attempted jailbreak. Stunning rooftop
panorama and gift shop. Multi-lingual audio tour.
**Times:** *Open Apr-Sep, daily 9.30-6; Oct & Mar, daily
9.30-6; Nov-Feb, daily 10.30-4.30 (last admission)
**Fee:** *£5-£5.95 (ch £3.20-£3.80, concessions £3.80-
£4.50). Family ticket £13.25-£15.70.
**Facilities:** 🅿 ♿ (toilets) shop audio commentaries
⊗ 🚌

## STIRLING
### Stirling Castle
Upper Castle Hill FK8 1EJ

☎ 01786 450000

**Web:** www.historic-scotland.gov.uk

Sitting on top of a 250ft rock, Stirling Castle has a strategic position on the Firth of Forth. As a result it has been the scene of many events in Scotland's history. James II was born at the castle in 1430. Mary, Queen of Scots spent some years there, and it was James IV's childhood home. Among its finest features are the splendid Renaissance palace built by James V, and the Chapel Royal, rebuilt by James VI.

**Times:** *Open all year, Apr-Sep, daily 9.30-6; Oct-Mar, daily 9.30-5. Closed 25-26.

**Fee:** *£8.50 (ch £3.50, concessions £6.50). Please

phone or check website for further details.

**Facilities:** ℗ (charged) ⦿ (Licensed) ⋒ ♿ (toilets) shop ⊗ 🚌 🎒 ♨

## STIRLING
### The National Wallace Monument
Hillsfoot Road Causewayhead FK9 5LF

☎ 01786 472140 🖷 01786 461322

**Email:** info@nationalwallacemonument.com

**Web:** www.nationalwallacemonument.com

**Dir:** *from A907 follow brown tourist signs*

Meet Scotland's national hero, Sir William Wallace, and join his epic struggle for a free Scotland. Step into Westminster Hall and witness his trial. Climb the 220 ft tower and experience one of the finest views in Scotland. Each August there is a dramatic performance commemorating the life of Sir William Wallace.

**Times:** Open all year Jan-Feb & Nov-Dec, daily 10.30-4; Mar-May & Oct, daily 10-5; Jun, daily 10-6; Jul-Aug, daily 9-6; Sep, daily 9.30-5.30.

**Fee:** *£6.50 (ch £4, concessions £4.90). Family ticket £17.

**Facilities:** ℗ ⋒ 🗐 no charge for educational groups ♿ (limited access) shop, audio commentaries 🚌

## LIVINGSTON
### Almond Valley Heritage Trust
Millfield EH54 7AR

☎ 01506 414957 🖷 01506 497771

**Email:** info@almondvalley.co.uk

**Web:** www.almondvalley.co.uk

**Dir:** *2m from M8 junct 3*

A combination of fun and educational potential ideal for children, Almond Valley has a petting zoo of farm animals, an interactive museum on the shale oil industry, a narrow gauge railway, and tractor rides. Please telephone for details of events running throughout the year.

**Times:** *Open all year, daily 10-5. Closed Dec 25-26, Jan 1-2

**Fee:** *£3 (ch £2). Family (2ad+4ch) £10.

**Facilities:** ℗ ⊑ (light meals and snacks) ⋒ 🗐 ♿ (toilets) shop 🚌 pre-book req. for large parties

STIRLING / WEST LOTHIAN

ARNOL

**Black House Museum**

Isle of Lewis PA86 9DB

☎ 01851 710395

**Web:** www.historic-scotland.gov.uk

**Dir:** *11m NW of Stornoway on A858*

This traditional Hebridean dwelling is now a small museum. These distinctive buildings were built without mortar – the stone walls were plugged with peat or earth. It was roofed with turf then thatch on a timber framework, the thatch tied down with rope or twine which was attached to rocks to weigh it down. With no chimney the central peat fire created smoke which had to find to find its own way out and was mostly absorbed by the roofing materials. The building included a byre under the same roof. This example was built in 1875.

**Times:** *Open all year, Apr-Sep, Mon-Sat 9.30-6.30; Oct-Mar, Mon-Sat 9.30-4.30. Closed 25-26 Dec & 1-2 Jan.

**Fee:** *£4.50 (ch £2, concessions £3.50). Please phone or check website for further details.

**Facilities:** 🅿 ♿ (toilets) shop ⊗ 🚌 🗟 🚫

**River Tay, Dunkeld**

# Wales

Morfa Nefyn, Gwynedd

# 1001 Great Family Days Out

## CAERPHILLY
### Caerphilly Castle
CF8 1JL
☎ 029 2088 3143
Web: www.cadw.wales.gov.uk
Dir: *on A469*
This concentrically planned castle was begun in 1268 by Gilbert de Clare and completed in 1326. It is the largest in Wales, and has extensive land and water defences. A unique feature is the ruined tower – the victim of subsidence – which manages to out-lean even Pisa! The south dam platform, once a tournament-field, now displays replica medieval siege-engines.
Times: *Open Apr-May & Oct, daily 9.30-5; Jun-Sep, daily 9.30-6; Nov-Mar, Mon-Sat 9.30-4, Sun 11-4. Telephone for XmasOpening times.

Fee: *£3.50 (ch 5-15, concessions £3, disabled visitors and assisting companion free). Family ticket (2ad+all ch/grandch under 16) £10.00. Group rates available. Prices quoted apply until 31 Mar 2007.
Facilities: 🅿 ♿ shop ⊗ 🚌 ♻

## CAERPHILLY
### Llancaiach Fawr Manor
Gelligaer Road Nelson CF46 6ER
☎ 01443 412248 📄 01443 412688
Email: llancaiachfawr@caerphilly.gov.uk
Web: www.llancaiachfawr.co.uk
Dir: *M4 junct 32, A470 to Merthyr Tydfil. Towards Ystrad Mynach A472, follow brown heritage signs*
Step back in time to the Civil War period at this fascinating living history museum. The year is 1645 and visitors are invited into the Manor to meet the servants of 'Colonel' Edward Prichard – from the puritanical to the gossipy. Please telephone for details of events running throughout the year.
Times: *Open daily 10-5. Closed Mon, Nov-Feb and 24 Dec-1 Jan.

Fee: *£4.95 (ch £3.50) concessions £3.75. Family ticket £14.
Facilities: 🅿 🍽 (Licensed) ⛱ 📋 ♿ (toilets) shop, guided tours (charged) ⊗ (ex guide dogs) 🚌 (pre-booking essential)

## CWMCARN
### Cwmcarn Forest Drive & Visitor Centre
Nantcarn Rd NP11 7FA
☎ 01495 272001 📄 01495 271403
Email: cwmcarn-vc@caerphilly.gov.uk
Web: www.caerphilly.gov.uk/visiting
Dir: *8m N of Newport on A467, follow brown tourist signs*
A seven-mile scenic drive with spectacular views over the Bristol Channel and surrounding countryside. Facilities include barbecues, picnic and play areas, and forest and mountain walks. There are also a bike trail and downhill trail on site. Special events are held throughout the year, please ring for details.
Times: Open Forest Drive: Mar & Oct 11-5; Apr-Aug 11-7 (11-9 wknds during Jul & Aug); Sep, 11-6; Nov 11-4 (wknds only). Visitor Centre: all year except between

Xmas & New Year.
Fee: Cars & Motorcycles £3, Minibus £6, Coaches £20. Car season ticket £15.
Facilities: 🅿 ⛱ ♿ (toilets) shop 🚌

**CARDIFF**

## Cardiff Castle

Castle Street CF10 3RB

☎ 029 2087 8100 🖹 029 2023 1417

**Email:** cardiffcastle@cardiff.gov.uk

**Web:** www.cardiffcastle.com

**Dir:** *from M4, A48 & A470 follow signs to city centre*

Cardiff Castle is situated in the heart of the city.
Contained within its mighty walls is a history spanning
nearly 2000 years, dating from the coming of the
Romans to the Norman Conquest. Discover spectacular
interiors on your guided tour, and enjoy magnificent views
of the city from the top of the 12th-century Norman
keep. Regular events throughout the year include a teddy
bears picnic, open air theatre, medieval and Roman
re-enactments, and 1940s-style celebrations to mark the

60th anniversary of the gifting of Cardiff Castle by the
5th Marquis of Bute.

**Times:** Open all year, daily (ex 25-26 Dec & 1 Jan)
including guided tours, Mar-Oct, 9.30-6 (last tour 5);
Nov-Feb, 9.30-5.00 (last tour 4). Royal Regiment of
Wales Museum closed Tue.

**Fee:** *Full guided tour, Norman Keep, green and military
museum, £6.95 (ch £4.30, pen £5.40). Family £22.40.
Norman Keep, green and military museum £3 (ch £3.20,
pen £2.70). Family £11.40.

**Facilities:** ℗ (200 yds) 🍴 free for schools (pre booked)
♿ (access to Castle Green, toilets) shop, guided tours,
audio commentaries ⊗ (ex in grounds & guide dogs)
🚌 (pre-booking essential)

---

**CARDIFF**

## Millennium Stadium Tours

Millennium Stadium Westgate Street Gate 3 CF10 1JA

☎ 029 2082 2228 🖹 029 2082 2151

**Email:** mgibbons@wru.co.uk

**Web:** millenniumstadium.com/tours

**Dir:** *A470 to city centre. Westgate St opposite Castle far
end. Turn by Angel Hotel on corner of Westgate Street.*

In the late 1990s this massive stadium was completed as
part of an effort to revitalise Welsh sporting and cultural
events. It replaced Cardiff Arms Park, and now hosts
major music events, exhibitions, and international rugby
and soccer matches. Its capacity of around 75,000 and
its retractable roof make it unique in Europe. The current
home of five controlling bodies; Welsh Rugby, Welsh
Football, English Football Association, Football league

(English) & British Speedway.

**Times:** Open all year, Mon-Sat, 10-5; Sun 10-4

**Fee:** £5.50 (ch up to 16 £3, ch under 5 free,
concessions £3.50). Party 20+ 15% discount.

**Facilities:** ℗ (opposite gate 3) ♿ (lifts, escalators,
disabled parking, toilets) shop, guided tours (charged)
⊗ (ex guide dogs) 🚌

---

**CARDIFF**

## National Museum Cardiff

Cathays Park CF10 3NP

☎ 029 2039 7951 🖹 029 2037 3219

**Email:** post@museumwales.ac.uk

**Web:** www.museumwales.a.uk

**Dir:** *in Civic Centre, 5 mins walk from city centre & 20
mins walk from bus & train station*

This establishment is unique amongst British museums
and galleries in its range of art and science displays. 'The
Evolution of Wales' exhibition takes visitors on a
spectacular 4,600-million year journey, tracing the world
from beginning of time and the development of Wales.
There are displays of Bronze Age gold, early Christian
monuments, Celtic treasures, silver, coins and medals,
ceramics, fossils and minerals. A significant collection of

French Impressionist paintings sits alongside the work of
Welsh artists, past and present in the elegant art
galleries. 2007 is the centenary year of the museum.

**Times:** *Open all year, Tue-Sun 10-5. Closed Mon
(ex BHs) & 24-26 Dec.

**Fee:** *Free Charge may be made for some events.

**Facilities:** ℗ (charged) ℗ (adjacent to museum –
Voucher scheme) 🍴 (Licensed) ♿ (wheelchair available,
Tel 029 2057 3509 for access guide, toilets) shop
⊗ (ex guide dogs) 🚌 (pre-booking required)

## CARDIFF
### Techniquest
Stuart Street CF10 5BW
☎ 029 2047 5475 ▤ 029 2048 2517
**Email:** info@techniquest.org
**Web:** www.techniquest.org
**Dir:** *A4232 to Cardiff Bay*
Located in the heart of the Cardiff Bay, there's always something new to explore at this exciting science discovery centre. Journey into space in the planetarium, enjoy an interactive Science Theatre Show or experience one of the 150 hands-on exhibits. Please visit website for details of events running throughout the year.
**Times:** Open all year, Mon-Fri 9.30-4.30; Sat-Sun & BHs 10.30-5, school hols 9.30-5. Closed Xmas.
**Fee:** £6.90 (ch 5-16 & concessions £4.80). Family ticket £20 (2ad+3ch). Friend season ticket £47. Groups 10+
**Facilities:** Ⓟ (50mtrs – limited parking for disabled visitors) ▤ ♿ (lift, hearing loop, toilets) shop ⊗ (ex guide dogs) 🚌 (pre-book for discounts)

## ST FAGANS
### St Fagans: National History Museum
Cardiff CF5 6XB
☎ 029 2057 3500 ▤ 029 2057 3490
**Email:** post@nmgw.ac.uk
**Web:** www.nmgw.ac.uk
**Dir:** *4m W of Cardiff on A4232. From M4 exit at junct 33 and follow brown signs*
A stroll around the indoor galleries and 100 acres of beautiful grounds will give you a fascinating insight into how people in Wales have lived, worked and spent their leisure hours since Celtic times. You can see people practising the traditional means of earning a living, the animals they kept and at certain times of year, the ways in which they celebrated the seasons.
**Times:** *Open all year daily, 10-5. Closed 24-26 Dec.
**Fee:** Free Charge may apply to some events.
**Facilities:** Ⓞ (charged) 🍽 (Licensed) 🎏 ♿ (wheelchairs, motorised buggy-must pre-book, toilets) shop ⊗ (ex in grounds if on lead) 🚌 (pre-booking required)

## TONGWYNLAIS
### Castell Coch
CF4 7YS
☎ 029 2081 0101
**Web:** www.cadw.wales.gov.uk
**Dir:** *A470 to Tongwynlais junct, then B4262 to castle on top of hill*
Castell Coch is Welsh for red castle, an appropriate name for this fairy-tale building with its red sandstone walls and conical towers. The castle was originally built in the 13th century but fell into ruins, and the present castle is a late-19th-century creation. Inside, the castle is decorated in fantasy style.
**Times:** *Open Apr-May & Oct, daily 9.30-5; Jun-Sep, daily 9.30-6; Nov-Mar, Mon-Sat 9.30-4, Sun 11-4. Telephone for XmasOpening times. During the periods 18-29 Sep 06 & 8 Jan-9 Feb 07 the monument will be closed for essential conservation works.
**Fee:** *£3.50 (ch 5-15, concessions £3, disabled visitors and assisting companion free). Family ticket (2ad+all ch/grandch under 16) £10.00. Group rates available. Please check for revised 2007 season prices
**Facilities:** Ⓞ 🎏 shop ⊗ 🚌 ♿

## CARREG CENNEN CASTLE
**Carreg Cennen Castle**
Llandeilo SA19 6UA
☎ 01558 822291
**Web:** www.cadw.wales.gov.uk
**Dir:** *unclass road from A483 to Trapp village*
A steep path leads up to the castle, which is spectacularly sited on a limestone crag. It was first built as a stronghold of the native Welsh and then rebuilt in the late 13th century. Most remarkable among the impressive remains is a mysterious passage, cut into the side of the cliff and lit by loopholes. The farm at the site has a rare breeds centre.
**Times:** *Open all year, Apr-Oct, daily 9.30-6.30; Nov-Mar, daily, 9.30-4. Telephone for XmasOpening times.
**Fee:** *£3.50 (ch 5-15, concessions £3, disabled visitors & assisting companion free). Family ticket (2ad+all ch/grandch under 16) £10. Group rates available. Prices quoted apply until 31 Mar 2007.
**Facilities:** 🅿 shop 🚫 🚌 ☺

## DRE-FACH FELINDRE
**National Wool Museum**
Llandysul SA44 5UP
☎ 01559 370929 🖷 01559 371592
**Web:** www.museumwales.ac.uk
**Dir:** *16m W of Carmarthen off A484, 4m E of Newcastle Emlyn*
The museum is housed in the former Cambrian Mills and has a comprehensive display tracing the evolution of the industry from its beginnings to the present day. Demonstrations of the fleece to fabric process are given on 19th-century textile machinery.
**Times:** Open Apr-Sep, daily 10-5; Oct-Mar, Tue-Sat 10-5. Closed Xmas.
**Fee:** Free Charge may be made for some events.
**Facilities:** 🅿 🅟 🛆 📱 ♿ (wheelchair access to ground floor & ample seating, toilets) shop 🚫 (ex guide dogs) 🚌 (prior notification essential)

## KIDWELLY
**Kidwelly Castle**
SA17 5BQ
☎ 01554 890104
**Web:** www.cadw.wales.gov.uk
**Dir:** *via A484*
This is an outstanding example of late 13th-century castle design, with its `walls within walls' defensive system. There were later additions made to the building, the chapel dating from about 1400. Of particular interest are two vast circular ovens.
**Times:** *Open Apr-May & Oct, daily 9.30-5; Jun-Sep, daily 9.30-6; Nov-Mar, Mon-Sat 9.30-4, Sun 11-4. Telephone for XmasOpening times.
**Fee:** *£2.90 (ch 5-15, concessions £2.50, disabled visitors & assisting companion free). Family ticket (2ad+all ch/grandch under 16) £8.30. Group rates available. Prices quoted apply until 31 Mar 2007.
**Facilities:** 🅿 ♿ (toilets) shop 🚫 🚌 ☺

## LAUGHARNE
**Laugharne Castle**
King Street SA33 4SA
☎ 01994 427906
**Web:** www.cadw.wales.gov.uk
**Dir:** *on A4066*
Newly opened to the public, picturesque Laugharne Castle stands on a low ridge overlooking the wide Taff Estuary. A medieval fortress converted into an Elizabethan mansion, it suffered a civil war siege and later became the backdrop for elaborate Victorian gardens, now recreated. Laugharne Castle has also inspired two modern writers – Richard Hughes and Dylan Thomas.
**Times:** *Open Apr-Sep, daily 10-5. Closed at all other times.
**Fee:** *£2.90 (ch 5-15, concessions £2.50, disabled visitors & assisting companions free). Family ticket (2ad+all ch/grandch under 16) £8.30. Group rates available. Prices quoted apply until 31 Mar 2007. Please check for revised 2007 season prices
**Facilities:** ℗ (150mtrs) ఈ (toilets) shop ⊗ 🚌 ☺

## LLANARTHNE
**The National Botanic Garden of Wales**
Middleton Hall SA32 8HG
☎ 01558 668768 📄 01558 668933
**Email:** info@gardenofwales.org.uk
**Web:** www.gardenofwales.org.uk
**Dir:** 8m E of Carmarthen on A48, dedicated intersection - signed
Set amongst 568 acres of Parkland in the beautiful Towy Valley in West Wales, just 7 miles from Carmarthen. The Gardens centrepiece is the Great Glasshouse, an amazing tilted glass dome with a six-metre ravine. The Mediterranean landscape enables the visitor to experience the aftermath of an Australian bush fire, pause in an olive grove or wander through Fuchsia collections from Chile. A 220mtr herbaceous board walk forms the spine of the garden and leads to the children's play area and our 360-surround screen cinema to the Old Stables Courtyard. Here the visitor can view art exhibitions, wander in the gift shop or enjoy a meal in the restaurant. Land train tours will take the visitor around the necklace of lakes, which surround the central garden.
**Times:** *Open 30 Mar-25 Oct 10-6, 26 Oct-27 Mar 10-4.30
**Fee:** £7.50 (ch 5-16 £2.50, concessions £5.50). Family £16.50. Carer with wheelchair user/blind visitor free.
**Facilities:** ℗ 🌂 ఈ (Braille interpretation wheelchairs/scooters shuttle svc, toilets) shop, garden centre, guided tours ⊗ (ex assist dogs) 🚌

## LLANDEILO
**Dinefwr Park**
SA19 6RT
☎ 01558 823902 📄 01558 822036
**Email:** dinefwr@nationaltrust.org.uk
**Web:** www.ukindex.co.uk/nationaltrust
**Dir:** *off A40 Carmarthenshire, on W outskirts of Llandeilo*
At the heart of Welsh history for a thousand years, the Park as we know it today took shape in the years after 1775 when the medieval castle, house, gardens, woods and deer park were integrated into one vast and breathtaking landscape. Access to Church Woods and Dinefwr Castle is through the landscaped park.
**Times:** *Open Mar-Oct, daily (ex Tue & Wed) 11-4.30. (Last admission 30 mins before closing)
**Fee:** *Park only £3 (ch £1.50) Family ticket 7.50 Party 15+ £2.60
**Facilities:** ℗ (charged) ℗ (1.5m)📄 20p ఈ (toilets) guided tours ⊗ (ex outer park on lead) 🚌 (prebooked) ❧

## LLANELLI

### National Wetland Centre Wales

Penclacwydd Llwynhendy SA14 9SH

☎ 01554 741087 📄 01554 741087

**Email:** info.llaneli@wwt.org.uk

**Web:** www.wwt.org.uk

**Dir:** *3m E of Llanelli, off A484*

A wide variety of wild birds, including oystercatchers, redshanks, curlews, little egrets and occasionally ospreys, can be seen here during the right season. The grounds are beautifully landscaped, and include CCTV transmitting pictures of wild birds on the reserve, a wetland craft area and a flock of colourful Caribbean Flamingos. There is also a Discovery Centre and outdoor activities for visitors to take part in. Facilities for the disabled include easy access on level paths, special viewing areas and wheelchair loan.

**Times:** *Open summer 9.30-5; winter 9.30-4.30. Closed 24-25 Dec.

**Fee:** *£5.50 (ch £3.50, pen £4.50). Family £14.50.

**Facilities:** 🅿 🍴 ⛱ ♿ (toilets) shop ⊗ (ex guide/hearing dogs) 🚌 (pre-booking required)

## LLANGATHEN

### Aberglasney Gardens

SA32 8QH

☎ 01558 668998 📄 01558 668998

**Email:** info@aberglasney.org.uk

**Web:** www.aberglasney.org

**Dir:** *4m W of Llandeilo, follow signs from A40*

Aberglasney is a 10-acre restoration project, containing a variety of rare and unusual plants, providing interest throughout the seasons. At its heart is a unique and fully restored Elizabethan/Jacobean cloister and parapet walk. Please telephone for details of events running throughout the year.

**Times:** *Open all year, Apr-Oct, daily 10-6 (last entry 5); Nov-Mar, daily 10.30-4. Closed 25 Dec

**Fee:** *£6 (ch £3, pen £5). Party 10+ £5.50 (ch £3, pen £4.50).

**Facilities:** 🅿 ⛱ ♿ (most areas accessible, wheelchairs available, parking, toilets) shop, garden centre, guided tours ⊗ (ex guide dogs) 🚌 (max 2 in am, 2 in pm)

## PUMSAINT

### Dolaucothi Gold Mines

Llandwrda SA19 8RR

☎ 01558 650177 📄 01588 650707

**Email:** dolaucothi@nationaltrust.org.uk

**Web:** www.nationaltrust.org.uk

**Dir:** *on A482, signed both directions*

Here is an opportunity to spend a day exploring the gold mines and to wear a miner's helmet and lamp while touring the underground workings. The information centre and a walk along the Miners' Way disclose the secrets of 2,000 years of gold mining. This is the only place in Britain where the Romans mined gold.

**Times:** *Open end Mar-end Oct, daily 10-5.

**Fee:** *£2.60 (ch £1.30) Family ticket £6.50. NT members free. Guided underground tours £3.60 (ch £1.80) Family ticket £9. NT members: £2.60 (ch £1.30). Family ticket £6.50.

**Facilities:** 🅿 ⛱ ♿ (toilets) shop 🚌 (book in advance) 🌿

**CEREDIGION**

## ABERAERON
### Llanerchaeron
Llanerchaeron Ciliau Aeron SA48 8DG
☎ 01545 570200 📠 01545 571759
**Email:** llanerchaeron@nationaltrust.org.uk
**Web:** www.nationaltrust.org.uk
**Dir:** *2.5m E of Aberaeron off A482*
Llanerchaeron, a few miles inland from Aberaeron on the Cardigan Bay coast, is centred round a Regency Villa designed by John Nash. The self sufficient country estate, villa, service courtyard, grounds, working organic farm and outbuildings remain virtually unaltered. The 18th century estate features; The Walled Garden and farm complex, mature woodland and ornamental lake, vast parkland and farmland containing Llanwennog sheep and Welsh Black Cattle. Produce and plants from the walled gardens are sold in the visitor building. Please telephone for details of events running throughout the year.
**Times:** Open late Mar-late Oct, Wed-Sun & BH Mons 11-5. (Last admission 1hr before closing). Park open all year dawn to dusk.
**Fee:** *£5.20 (ch £2.60). Family ticket £12.60 (2ad+2ch). Special group rates available
**Facilities:** 🅿 🍴 📋 Free-£3 ♿ (ramp access to villa, wheelchair, Braille guide, toilets) shop  guided tours (charged) 🚫 (except guide dogs) 🚌 Pre booked coaches only 🐾 ♨

## CENARTH
### The National Coracle Centre
Cenarth Falls Newcastle Emlyn SA38 9JL
☎ 01239 710980
**Email:** martinfowler.coraclecentre@virgin.net
**Web:** www.coracle-centre.co.uk
**Dir:** *on A484 between Carmarthen and Cardigan, centre of Cenarth village, beside bridge and river*
Situated by the beautiful Cenarth Falls, this fascinating museum has a unique collection from all over the world, including Tibet, India, Iraq, Vietnam, and North America. Cenarth has long been a centre for coracle fishing, coracle rides are often available in village during summer holiday. Look out for the salmon leap by the flour mill.
**Times:** *Open Etr-Oct, daily 10.30-5.30. All other times by appointment.
**Fee:** *£3 (ch £1, concessions £2.50). Party rates 12+.
**Facilities:** 🅿 🅿 (100yds – on site for disabled only) 📋 £3 ♿ (top floor of mill inaccessible for disabled) shop, guided tours (charged) 🚌

## EGLWYSFACH
### RSPB Nature Reserve
Visitor Centre Cae'r Berllan Machynlleth SY20 8TA
☎ 01654 700222 📠 01654 700333
**Email:** ynyshir@rspb.org.uk
**Web:** www.rspb.co.uk
**Dir:** *6m S of Machynlleth on A487 in Eglwys-Fach. Signed from main road*
The mixture of different habitats is home to an abundance of birds and wildlife. The saltmarshes in winter support the only regular wintering flock of Greenland white-fronted geese in England and Wales in addition to peregrines, hen harriets and merlins. The sessile oak woodland is home to pied flycatchers, wood warblers, redstarts in the summer but woodpeckers, nut hatches, red kites, sparrow hawks and buzzards are here all year round. Otters, polecats, 30 butterfly and 15 dragonfly species are also present. Guided walks and children's activities. Please telephone for details of events running throughout the year.
**Times:** *Open daily, 9am-9pm (or sunset if earlier). Visitor Centre: Apr-Oct 9-5 daily; Nov-Mar 10-4 (Wed-Sun)
**Fee:** *£3.50 (ch £1, concessions £2.50) Family £7 RSPB members free.
**Facilities:** 🅿 🅿 (in Cadw carpark coaches must park in dedicated area) 🍴 📋 Free for under 10's ♿ (can take car to viewpoint) shop, guided tours 🚫 (ex guide dogs) 🚌 (advance booking essential)

## FELINWYNT
### Felinwynt Rainforest Centre
Cardigan SA43 1RT
☎ 01239 810882 & 810250 🖹 01239 810465
**Email:** dandjdevereux@btinternet.com
**Web:** www.butterflycentre.co.uk
**Dir:** *from A487 Blaenannerch Airfield turning, onto B4333. Signed 6m N of Cardigan*
A chance to wander amongst free-flying exotic butterflies accompanied by the recorded wildlife sounds of the Peruvian Amazon. A waterfall, ponds and streams contribute to a humid tropical atmosphere and provide a habitat for fish and native amphibians. See the exhibition of rainforests of Peru and around the world. Free paper and crayons to borrow for children.
**Times:** Open daily, 4 Apr-27 Oct

**Fee:** *£3.95 (ch 4-14 £1.95, pen £3.75)
**Facilities:** 🅿 🖵 (light meals, refreshments) ⏸ 🗐 50p 🚻 (toilets) shop, guided tours ⊗ (ex guide dogs) 🚌 (pre-booking required)

## BETWS-Y-COED
### Conwy Valley Railway Museum
Old Goods Yard LL24 0AL
☎ 01690 710568 🖹 01690 710132
**Dir:** *signed from A5 into Old Church Rd, adjacent to train station*
The two large museum buildings have displays on both the narrow and standard-gauge railways of North Wales, including railway stock and other memorabilia. There are working model railway layouts, a steam-hauled miniature railway in the grounds, which cover over four acres, and a 15inch-gauge tramway to the woods. The latest addition is the quarter-size steam 'Britannia' loco that is now on display. For children there are mini-dodgems, Postman Pat, school bus and Toby Tram.
**Times:** *Open all year daily, 10-5.30. Closed Xmas

**Fee:** *£1.50 (ch & pen 80p). Family ticket £4.00. Steam train ride £1.50. Tram ride £1.00.
**Facilities:** 🅿 🅟 (150 yards) 🖵 (buffet coach) ⏸ 🚻 (ramps & clearances for wheelchairs, toilets) shop, audio commentaries 🚌

## COLWYN BAY
### Welsh Mountain Zoo
Old Highway LL28 5UY
☎ 01492 532938 🖹 01492 530498
**Email:** info@welshmountainzoo.org
**Web:** www.welshmountainzoo.org
**Dir:** *A55 junct 20 signed Rhos-on-Sea. Zoo signed*
Set high above Colwyn Bay with panoramic views and breath-taking scenery, this caring conservation zoo is set among beautiful gardens. Among the animals are many rare and endangered species, and there are daily shows which include Penguins Playtime, Chimp Encounter, Sealion Feeding and Birds of Prey.
**Times:** Open all year, Mar-Oct, daily 9.30-6; Nov-Feb, daily 9.30-5. Closed 25 Dec.
**Fee:** *£7.75 (ch & students £5.50, pen £6.60). Family

ticket (2ad+2ch) £23.40
**Facilities:** 🅿 🍽 (Licensed) ⏸ 🗐 🚻 (toilets) shop ⊗ (ex car park area) 🚌

**CONWY**

## Smallest House

The Quay LL32 8BB

☎ 01492 593484

**Dir:** *leave A55 at Conwy sign, through town, at bottom of High St for the quay, turn left*

For a tiny place, this is a major tourist attraction. The *Guinness Book of Records* lists this as the smallest house in Britain. Just 6ft wide by 10ft high, this tiny terraced house on the quayside is furnished in the style of a mid-Victorian Welsh cottage. Not surprisingly, there is no internal sanitation, the lavatory is outside in the old-fashioned way.

**Times:** *Open Apr-May & Oct 10-5; Jun & Sep, 10-6, first half Jul 10-6 rest of Jul & Aug 10-9

**Fee:** £1 (ch under 16 50p, under 5 free).

**Facilities:** Ⓟ (100yds) 🗎 ♿ shop, guided tours, audio commentaries 🚌 ♿

**DOLWYDDELAN**

## Dolwyddelan Castle

LL25 0EJ

☎ 01690 750366

**Web:** www.cadw.wales.gov.uk

**Dir:** *on A470 Blaenau Ffestiniog to Betws-y-Coed*

The castle is reputed to be the birthplace of Llywelyn the Great. It was captured in 1283 by Edward I, who immediately began strengthening it for his own purposes. A restored keep of around 1200, and a 13th-century curtain wall can be seen. An exhibition on the castles of the Welsh Princes is located in the keep.

**Times:** *Open all year, Apr-Sep, Mon-Sat 10-6 & Sun 11-4; Oct-Mar, Mon-Sat 10-4, Sun 11-4. On occasions the site may be open but unstaffed with no admission charge. Phone for Xmas opening hours.

**Fee:** *£2.50 (ch 5-15, concessions £2, disabled visitors & assisting companion free). Family ticket (2ad+all ch/grandch under 16) £7. Group rates available. Prices quoted apply until 31 Mar 2007.

**Facilities:** Ⓟ Ⓧ 🚌 ♿

**LLANDUDNO**

## Great Orme Bronze Age Copper Mines

Pyliau Road Great Orme LL30 2XG

☎ 01492 870447

**Email:** gomines@greatorme.freeserve.co.uk

**Web:** www.greatormemines.info

**Dir:** *Follow 'copper mine' signs from Llandudno Promenade*

Browse in the visitor centre with a model of a Bronze Age village depicting life in Bronze Age times. Take a look at some original 4,000 year old Bronze Age artefacts and a selection of Bronze Age mining tools. After watching two short films take a helmet and make your way down to the mines. Walking through tunnels mined nearly 4,000 years ago look into some of the smaller tunnels and get a feel for the conditions our prehistoric ancestors faced in their search for valuable copper ores. Excavation on the surface will continue for decades and one of the team is usually available to answer visitors questions as they walk around the site and view the prehistoric landscape being uncovered.

**Times:** Open Mar-Oct, daily 10-5.

**Fee:** *£5 (ch £3.50, students £4.50). Family ticket £15.

**Facilities:** Ⓟ 🍴 🗎 £2 ♿ (toilets) shop, guided tours

CONWY

## LANDUDNO JUNCTION
### RSPB Nature Reserve Conwy
LL31 9XZ
☎ 01492 584091
**Email:** alan.davies@rspb.org.uk
**Web:** www.rspb.org.uk
**Dir:** *off A55, signed*

The visitor centre has a viewing area which overlooks the estuary, Conwy Castle and Mount Snowden. There are several coastal lagoons and grasslands along the estuary, that provide a home or just a stop-over for more than 200 species of birds. There's a nature trail and four hides for viewing the birds. Lapwings and shelduck, amongst many others, are regularly seen. Phone for details of events.
**Times:** *Open all year, daily, 10-5 (or dusk whichever is earlier). Closed 25 Dec
**Fee:** *£2.50 (ch £1, concessions £1.50), Family £5
**Facilities:** ❶ ⴲ 🖵 ♿ (use of wheelchair, toilets) shop, guided tours (charged) 🚫 (ex guide dogs) 🚌 (advance booking)

## TAL-Y-CAFN
### Bodnant Garden
Nr Colwyn Bay LL28 5RE
☎ 01492 650460 🖨 01492 650448
**Email:** ann.harvey@nationaltrust.org.uk
**Web:** www.bodnantgarden.co.uk
**Dir:** *8m S of Llandudno & Colwyn Bay off A470. Signposted from the A55 exit at J19*

Set above the River Conwy with beautiful views over Snowdonia, this garden is a delight. Five Italian style terraces were constructed below the house - on the lowest terrace is a canal pool with an open-air yew hedge stage and a reconstructed Pin Mill. The garden is renowned for its collections of magnolias, camellias, rhododendrons and azaleas and the famous Laburnum Arch, and the colourful displays in summer and autumn are a spectacular sight. Contact for details of open-air theatre.
**Times:** Open 10 Mar-4 Nov, daily 10-5 (last admission 30 mins before closing)
**Fee:** £6.50 (ch £3.25) Party of 20+ £5.50
**Facilities:** ❶ ♿ (ramps to gardens, wheelchairs & Braille guides, toilets) shop garden centre 🚫 (ex assist dogs) 🚌 🌿

## TREFRIW
### Trefriw Woollen Mills Ltd
Main Road Conway Valley LL27 0NQ
☎ 01492 640462
**Email:** info@t-w-m.co.uk
**Web:** www.t-w-m.co.uk
**Dir:** *on B5106 in centre of Trefriw, 5m N of Betws-y-Coed*

Established in 1859, the mill is situated beside the fast-flowing Afon Crafnant, which drives two hydro-electric turbines to power the looms. All the machinery of woollen manufacture can be seen here: blending, carding, spinning, dyeing, warping and weaving. In the Weaver's Garden, there are plants traditionally used in the textile industry, mainly for dyeing. Hand-spinning demonstrations.
**Times:** Mill MuseumOpen Etr-Oct, Mon-Fri 10-1 & 2-5. Weaving demonstrations & turbine house: Open all year, Mon-Fri 10-1 & 2-5. Handspinning & weaver's garden Jun-Sep Tue-Thu, Jul-Aug Mon-Fri 10-5
**Fee:** Free no school parties
**Facilities:** ❶ (35yds) 🖵 ♿ (access to shop, cafe, weaving & turbine house) shop 🚫 (ex assist dogs & on lead) 🚌 (by appointment)

**CONWY**

## BODELWYDDAN
**Bodelwyddan Castle**
LL18 5YA
☎ 01745 584060 📠 01745 584563
**Email:** enquiries@bodelwyddan-castle.co.uk
**Web:** www.bodelwyddan-castle.co.uk
**Dir:** *just off A55, near St Asaph, follow brown signs*
Bodelwyddan Castle houses over 100 portraits from the National Portrait Gallery's 19th-century collection. The portraits hang in beautifully refurbished rooms and are complemented by sculpture and period furnishings. Interactive displays show how portraits were produced and used in the Victorian era. The Castle Gallery hosts a programme of temporary exhibitions and events. The castle is set within 200 acres of woodland.
**Times:** *Open Apr-Sep, daily 10.30-5. Oct-Apr, 10.30-4.

Closed Mon & Fri
**Fee:** *£4.50 (ch £2, concessions £4). Family ticket (4 people) £12.
**Facilities:** 🅿 🅿 ⛱ ♿ (lift to first floor, Braille & audio guides, toilets) shop ⊗ (ex guide dogs) 🚌 (please telephone in advance)

## CORWEN
**Ewe-Phoria Sheepdog Centre**
Glanrafon Llangwm LL21 0PE
☎ 01490 460369
**Email:** info@ewe-phoria.co.uk
**Web:** www.ewe-phoria.co.uk
**Dir:** *off A5 to Llangwm, follow signs*
Ewe-Phoria is an Agri-Theatre and Sheepdog Centre that details the life and work of the shepherd on a traditional Welsh farm. The Agri-Theatre has unusual living displays of sheep with accompanying lectures on their history and breed and twice daily there are displays which put the sheepdogs through their paces. When you have exhausted all there is to see – there is an excellent tearoom in a converted barn
**Times:** *Open Etr-end Oct, Tue-Fri & Sun. Closed Sat &

Mon ex BHs
**Fee:** £4.75 (ch £3.50, concessions £4.20)
**Facilities:** 🅿 ⛱ ♿ (toilets) shop ⊗ (ex guide dogs) 🚌 ♿

## CORWEN
**Pen-Y-Bryn Farm Park**
LL21 9PB
☎ 01490 420244 📠 01490 420244
**Email:** islwynhawkeye@hotmail.co.uk
**Web:** www.pybfarmpark.co.uk
**Dir:** *off A5 onto B5105. 5m from Cerrigydrudion*
Pen-y-Bryn Park is primarily a falconry centre with a number of trained birds of prey. There are regular shows of display flights when members of the audience are invited to put on the gauntlet and become part of the show. There are also training sessions for the more interested. Pen-y-Bryn Park also has a petting zoo, and 'Solo', its very own llama.
**Times:** *Open Etr-Sep, Tue-Sun & BHs, 10-5
**Fee:** *£3.25 (ch, pen £2.75) Family ticket £13.25

**Facilities:** 🅿 ⛱ ♿ (toilets) shop, garden centre 🚌 prior notice required ♿

## LLANGOLLEN
### Horse Drawn Boats Centre

The Wharf Wharf Hill LL20 8TA
☎ 01978 860702 & 01691 690322 🗒 01978 860702
Email: bill@horsedrawnboats.co.uk
Web: www.horsedrawnboats.co.uk
Dir: *A5 onto Llangollen High St, across river bridge to T-junct. Wharf opposite*

Take a horsedrawn boat trip along the beautiful Vale of Llangollen. Visit the canal museum, inside the motor museum, approx 1m along the towpath from the wharf, which illustrates the heyday of canals in Britain. The displays include working and static models, photographs, murals and slides. There is also a narrowboat trip that crosses Pontcysyllte Aqueduct, the largest navigable aqueduct in the world. Full bar on board, commentary throughout.

**Times:** Open mid Mar-Etr, wknds. Etr-end Oct, daily, 10-5.
**Fee:** *Horse Drawn Boat Trip from £4.50 (ch £2.50). Family ticket £12. Narrowboat Trip £9 (ch £7).
**Facilities:** ℗ (400yds) 🎫 £6 ♿ (alighting/pick-up point available, toilets) shop, audio commentaries 🚌

## LLANGOLLEN
### Llangollen Railway

Abbey Road LL20 8SN
☎ 01978 860979 & 860951 (timetable)
🗒 01978 869247
Email: office@llangollen-railway.co.uk
Web: www.llangollen-railway.co.uk
Dir: *Llangollen Station - off A5 at intersection with A539, cross river bridge. Station on left at T-junct. Carrog Station - from A5 at Llidiart-y-Parc take B5437, station on right downhill after crossing railway bridge*

Heritage Railway featuring steam and classic diesel services along the picturesque Dee Valley. The journey consists of a 15-mile roundtrip between Llangollen and Carrog. A special coach for the disabled is available on some services. Please contact for more information.

**Times:** *Open wknds, reduced services off peak, daily services Apr-Oct.
**Fee:** *2nd class return fare for full journey £8 (ch 3-16 £4, pen £6) Family ticket £18 (2ad+2ch)
**Facilities:** ℗ (400yds – free parking at Carrog Station) ☕ (at Llangollen Station) ♿ (coach for disabled – some trains, notice required, toilets) shop 🚌 (pre-book)

## LLANGOLLEN
### Plas Newydd

Hill Street LL20 8AW
☎ 01978 861314 🗒 01824 708258
Email: rose.mcmahon@denbighshire.gov.uk
Dir: *follow brown heritage signs from A5*

The 'Ladies of Llangollen', Lady Eleanor Butler and Sarah Ponsonby, lived here from 1780 to 1831. Having set up home in a relatively isolated area of Wales they were frequently visited by the leading thinlres and artists of the day. The original stained-glass windows, carved panels, and domestic miscellany of two lives are exhibited along with prints, pictures and letters.

**Times:** *Open Apr-Oct, daily, 10-5.
**Fee:** *£3 (ch & pen £2). Family £8.
**Facilities:** 🅿 ℗ (0.5m) 🪑 ♿ (virtual, signed & touch tours, toilets) shop, audio commentaries 🚫 (ex guide dogs or in grounds) 🚌

HOLYWELL
**Greenfield Valley Heritage Park**
Greenfield Road CH8 7GH
☎ 01352 714172 🖷 01352 714791
**Email:** info@greenfieldvalley.com
**Web:** www.greenfieldvalley.com
This fascinating park covers one and a half miles of
woodlands, reservoirs, ancient monuments and industrial
history. Among the multitude of sights are a footpath that
was once a railway line, the remnants of a number of
mills relating to the copper industry, an environment
centre, the shrine of St Winefride's Well, and Basingwerk
Abbey.
**Times:** * ParkOpen all year. Museum & farm Apr-Oct, 10-
4.30.
**Fee:** *Museum & farm £2.75 (ch £1.65, concessions

£2.20). Park free.
**Facilities:** 🅿 🚻 ♿ (ramps to enter buildings, toilets)
shop 🚌 ♨

BANGOR
**Penrhyn Castle**
LL57 4HN
☎ 01248 353084 🖷 01248 371281
**Email:** penrhyncastle@nationaltrust.org.uk
**Web:** www.nationaltrust.org.uk
**Dir:** 1m E of Bangor, off A5122 at Llandegai
A massive 19th-century castle built on the profits of
Jamaican sugar and Welsh slate, crammed with
fascinating artefacts such as a one-ton slate bed made
for Queen Victoria and a grand staircase that took ten
years to build. Also houses a doll museum, two railway
museums and one of the finest collections of Old Master
paintings in Wales. Regular programme of events
throughout the season.
**Times:** *Open 25 Mar-29 Oct, daily (ex Tue) Castle 12-5.

Grounds and stableblock exhibitions 11-5 (Jul & Aug
10-5.30). (Last admission 4.30). Last audio tour 4.
**Fee:** *All inclusive ticket: £8 (ch £7). Family ticket £20.
Party 15+ £6.50 each. Grounds & stable block only
£5.40 (ch £2.70).
**Facilities:** 🅿 🍽 (Licensed) 🚻 📦 ♿ (wheelchairs & golf
buggies pre bookable, toilets) shop, guided tours, audio
commentaries (charged) 🚌 (advance booking) 🐾 ♨

BEDDGELERT
**Sygun Copper Mine**
Caernarfon LL55 4NE
☎ 01766 890595 & 510101 🖷 01766 890595
**Email:** sygunmine@hotmail.com
**Web:** www.syguncoppermine.co.uk
**Dir:** 1m E of Beddgelert on A498
Spectacular audio-visual underground experience where
visitors can explore the workings of this 19th-century
coppermine and see the magnificent stalactite and
stalagmite formations. Other activities include archery,
panning for gold, metal detecting and coin making.
Marvel at the fantastic coin collection from Julius Caesar
to Queen Elizabeth II, and visit the Time-Line Museum
with Bronze Age and Roman artefacts.
**Times:** Apr-late Oct, 9.30-5. SpecialOpening 10-4, 26

Dec-1 Jan and Feb half term.
**Fee:** £7.95 (ch £5.95, pen £6.95). Family £26.
**Facilities:** 🅿 🅿 (250mtrs) 🚻 ♿ (wide access, toilets)
shop, audio commentaries 🚌

## BLAENAU FFESTINIOG
### Llechwedd Slate Caverns

LL41 3NB

☎ 01766 830306 🖨 01766 831260

**Email:** quarrytours@aol.com

**Web:** www.llechwedd-slate-caverns.co.uk

**Dir:** *beside A470, 1m from Blaenau Ffestiniog*

The Miners' Underground Tramway carries visitors into areas where early conditions have been recreated, while the Deep Mine is reached by an incline railway and has an unusual audio-visual presentation. Free surface attractions include several exhibitions and museums, slate mill and the Victorian village which has Victorian shops, bank, Miners Arms pub, lock-up and working smithy.

**Times:** *Open all year, daily from 10. Last tour 5.15 (Oct-Feb 4.15). Closed 25-26 Dec & 1 Jan

**Fee:** *Single Tour £8.25 (ch £6.25, pen £7). Reductions for both tours

**Facilities:** 🅿 🍴 (Licensed) ♿ (toilets) shop ⊗ (ex on surface) 🚌

## CAERNARFON
### Caernarfon Castle

LL55 2AY

☎ 01286 677617

**Web:** www.cadw.wales.gov.uk

Edward I began building the castle and extensive town walls in 1283 after defeating the last independent ruler of Wales. Completed in 1328, it has unusual polygonal towers, notably the 10-sided Eagle Tower. There is a theory that these features were copied from the walls of Constantinople, to reflect a tradition that Constantine was born nearby. Edward I's son and heir was born and presented to the Welsh people here, setting a precedent that was followed in 1969, when Prince Charles was invested as Prince of Wales.

**Times:** *Open Apr-May & Oct, daily 9.30-5; Jun-Sep, daily 9.30-6; Nov-Mar, Mon-Sat 9.30-4, Sun 11-4. Telephone for XmasOpening times.

**Fee:** *£4.90 (ch 5-15, pen & students £4.50, disabled visitors & assisting compainion free). Family ticket (2 ad & all ch/grandch under 16) £15. Group rates available. Prices quoted apply until 31 Mar 2007.

**Facilities:** 🅿 shop ⊗ 🚌 ♿

## CAERNARFON
### Welsh Highland Railway

St. Helen's Road LL55 2YD

☎ 01286 677018 & 01766 516000 🖨 01286 677018

**Email:** enquiries@festrail.co.uk

**Web:** www.festrail.co.uk

**Dir:** *SW of Caernarfon Castle beside harbour. Follow brown signs*

A Millennium funded project to restore the old railway line from Caernarfon to Porthmadog. Experience the stunning scenery of Snowdonia National Park as the narrow gauge, steam and diesel trains travel between Caernarfon and Rhyd Ddu at the foot of Snowdon.

**Times:** Open Etr-end Oct, limited service in Winter

**Fee:** *£16 ad return

**Facilities:** 🅿 (charged) Ⓟ (10mins walk - no parking at Dinas or Rhyd Ddu Stn's) 🍴 £3 ♿ (prior booking advisable, toilets) shop ⊗ (ex in 3rd class) 🚌 booking required

STEAM ~ SCENERY ~ SNOWDONIA

**GWYNEDD**

## FAIRBOURNE
**Fairbourne Railway**
Beach Road LL38 2EX
☎ 01341 250362 ▤ 01341 250240
**Email:** enquiries@fairbourne-railway.co.uk
**Web:** www.fairbournerailway.com
**Dir:** *on A493 follow signs for Fairbourne, main terminus is just past level crossing on left*
One of the most unusual of the 'little trains' of Wales; built in 1890 as a horse-drawn railway to carry building materials it was later converted to steam, and now covers two-and-a-half miles of coastline. Its route passes one of the loveliest beaches in Wales, with views of the beautiful Mawddach Estuary.
**Times:** Open Feb half term (ex Fri). Apr-23 Sep (closed most Fri ex late Jul & all of Aug). Oct wknds & 20-28 Oct (ex Fri).
**Fee:** *Return £6.90 (ch £3.90, pen £5.80). Family £17.50 (2ad+3ch)
**Facilities:** ⓟ (30 mtrs) ☕ (in high season) ♿ (toilets) shop 🚌

## GROESLON
**Inigo Jones Slateworks**
Caernarfon LL54 7UE
☎ 01286 830242 ▤ 01286 831247
**Email:** slate@inigojones.co.uk
**Web:** www.inigojones.co.uk
**Dir:** *on A487, 6m S of Caernarfon towards Porthmadog*
Inigo Jones was established in 1861 primarily to make school writing slates. Today the company uses the same material to make architectural, monumental and craft products. A self-guided audio/video tour takes visitors round the slate workshops, and displays the various processes used in the extraction and working of Welsh slate.
**Times:** *Open all year, daily 9-5. Closed 25-26 Dec & 1 Jan.
**Fee:** *£4 (ch & pen £3.50).
**Facilities:** ⓟ ⛽ ▤ £2.50 ♿ (toilets) shop, guided tours (charged), audio commentaries (charged) 🚫 (ex guide dogs) 🚌 (50 people max)

## HARLECH
**Harlech Castle**
LL46 2YH
☎ 01766 780552
**Web:** www.cadw.wales.gov.uk
**Dir:** *from A496*
Harlech Castle was built in 1283-89 by Edward I, with a sheer drop to the sea on one side. Owain Glyndwr starved the castle into submission in 1404 and made it his court and campaigning base. Later, the defence of the castle in the Wars of the Roses inspired the song Men of Harlech. Today the sea has slipped away, and the castle's great walls and round towers stand above the dunes.
**Times:** *Open Apr-May & Oct, daily 9.30-5; Jun-Sep, daily 9.30-6; Nov-Mar, Mon-Sat 9.30-4, Sun 11-4. Telephone for XmasOpening times.
**Fee:** *£3.50 (ch 5-15, concessions £3, disabled visitors & assisting companion free). Family ticket (2ad+all ch/grandch under 16) £10. Group rates available. Prices quoted apply until 31 Mar 2007.
**Facilities:** ⓟ ♿ (disabled spaces in car park) shop 🚫 🚌 ☺

## LLANBERIS
### Llanberis Lake Railway
Padarn Country Park LL55 4TY
☎ 01286 870549 📠 01286 870549
**Email:** info@lake-railway.co.uk
**Web:** www.lake-railway.co.uk
**Dir:** *off A4086 at Llanberis*
Steam locomotives dating from 1889 to 1948 carry passengers on a five-mile return journey along the shore of Lake Padarn. Passengers are treated to some spectacular views of Snowdon and other mountains. The terminal station is adjacent to the Welsh Slate Museum, in the Padarn Country Park. The railway was formerly used to carry slate.
**Times:** *Open mid Mar-late Oct, Sun-Fri, 11-4 (Sat in Jun-Aug) 10.30-4.30 in peak season. Nov-Feb, send for free timetable or check website.
**Fee:** *£6 (ch £4). Family ticket available. Reduced rates for groups.
**Facilities:** 🅿 (charged) 🅿 (0.25m) 🍴 🗐 £2 ♿ (disabled carriage available, toilets) shop 🚌

## LLANBERIS
### Snowdon Mountain Railway
Caernarfon LL55 4TY
☎ 0870 4580033 📠 01286 872518
**Email:** info@snowdonrailway.co.uk
**Web:** www.snowdonrailway.co.uk
**Dir:** *on A4086, Caernarfon to Capel Curig road. 7.5m from Caernarfon*
The journey of just over four-and-a-half miles takes passengers more than 3,000ft up to the summit of Snowdon; breathtaking views include, on a clear day, the Isle of Man and the Wicklow Mountains in Ireland. The round trip to the summit and back takes two and a half hours including a half hour at the summit.
**Times:** *Open 15 Mar-5 Nov, daily from 9 (weather permitting).
**Fee:** Return £21 (ch £14). Early bird discount on 9am train, pre-booking only
**Facilities:** 🅿 (charged) 🅿 (behind station 50m) ♿ (some carriages suitable for wheelchairs – must notify, toilets) shop, audio commentaries 🚫 (ex assist dogs) 🚌 (pre-booking essential to get discount)

## LLANBERIS
### Welsh Slate Museum
Gilfach Ddu Padarn Country Park LL55 4TY
☎ 01286 870630 📠 01286 871906
**Email:** slate@museumwales.ac.uk
**Web:** www.museumwales.ac.uk
**Dir:** *0.25m off A4086. Museum within Padarn Country Park*
Set among the towering quarries at Llanberis, the Welsh Slate Museum is a living, working site located in the original workshops of Dinorwig Quarry, which once employed 15,000 men and boys. You can see the foundry, smithy, workshops and mess room which make up the old quarry, and view original machinery, much of which is still in working order.
**Times:** *Open Etr-Oct, daily 10-5; Nov-Etr, Sun-Fri 10-4.
**Fee:** Free Some events may incur a charge
**Facilities:** 🅿 (charged) 🅿 (800yds) 🍴 ♿ (all parts accessible except patten loft, toilets) shop 🚫 (ex guide dogs) 🚌 (pre-booking advisable)

**GWYNEDD**

**GWYNEDD**

## LLANUWCHLLYN
### Bala Lake Railway
The Station Bala LL23 7DD
☎ 01678 540666 🖹 01678 540535
**Web:** www.bala-lake-railway.co.uk
**Dir:** *off A494 Bala to Dolgellau road*
Steam locomotives which once worked in the slate quarries of North Wales now haul passenger coaches for four-and-a-half miles from Llanuwchllyn Station along the lake to Bala. The railway has one of the few remaining double-twist lever-locking framed GWR signal boxes, installed in 1896. Some of the coaches are open and some closed, so passengers can enjoy the beautiful views of the lake and mountains in all weathers.
**Times:** Open Etr-last wknd in Sep, daily. (Closed certain Mon & Fri, telephone for details).

**Fee:** *£7 return (pen £6.50). Family ticket (2ad+2ch) £17.
**Facilities:** 🅿 ℗ (0.75m – limited parking at Bala Station) 🍴 (no cooked meals) 🚻 ♿ (wheelchairs can be taken on train) shop 🚌 (24hr notice preferred) ✉

## LLANYSTUMDWY
### Lloyd George Museum & Highgate Cottage
Criccieth LL52 0SH
☎ 01766 522071 🖹 01766 522071
**Email:** amgueddfeydd-museums@gwynedd.gov.uk
**Web:** www.gwynedd.gov.uk/museums
**Dir:** *on A497 between Pwllheli & Criccieth*
Explore the life and times of David Lloyd George in this museum. His boyhood home is recreated as it would have been when he lived there between 1864 and 1880, along with his Uncle Lloyd's shoemaking workshop.
**Times:** *Open Etr, daily 10.30-5; Apr-May, Mon-Fri 10.30-5 (open Sat in Jun); Jul-Sep daily 10.30-5; Oct, Mon-Fri, 11-4.Open BHs; Other times by appointment, telephone 01286 679098 for details.
**Fee:** *£3 (ch & pen £2). Family ticket £7.

**Facilities:** 🅿 ℗ (100yds) 🚻 📷 ♿ (induction loop in audio visual theatre, shop & cottage, toilets) shop ⊗ (ex guide dogs) 🚌 (pre-booking advised)

## PORTHMADOG
### Ffestiniog Railway
Harbour Station LL49 9NF
☎ 01766 516000 🖹 01766 516006
**Email:** enquiries@festrail.co.uk
**Web:** www.festrail.co.uk
**Dir:** *SE end of town beside the harbour, on A487*
A narrow gauge steam railway running for 13.5 miles through Snowdonia National Park, with breathtaking views and superb scenery. Buffet service on all trains including licensed bar (in corridor carriages). Please telephone for details of special events. The company also runs the Welsh Highland Railway Caernarfon, which will eventually link up with the Ffestiniog Railway.
**Times:** Open daily late Mar-late Oct. Limited Winter service mid wk trains Nov & early Dec. Santa specials in Dec.Open Feb half term.

**Fee:** *Full distance return £16 (pen £12.80). Other fares available.
**Facilities:** 🅿 (charged) ℗ (200 yards - Limited parking at other Stations) 🍴 (Licensed) 🚻 ♿ (Wheelchair ramps, trains mostly accessible, toilets) shop, audio commentaries (charged) ⊗ (ex 3rd class) 🚌 (Prior booking required)

PORTMEIRION
**Portmeirion**
LL48 6ET
☎ 01766 770000 🖹 01766 771331
**Email:** info@portmeirion-village.com
**Web:** www.portmeirion-village.com
**Dir:** *off A487 at Minffordd*
Welsh architect Sir Clough Williams Ellis built his airy-tale, Italianate village on a rocky, tree-clad peninsula on the shores of Cardigan Bay. A bell-tower, castle and lighthouse mingle with a watch-tower, grottoes and cobbled squares among pastel-shaded picturesque cottages let as holiday accommodation. The 60-acre Gwyllt Gardens include miles of dense woodland paths and are famous for their fine displays of rhododendrons, azaleas, hydrangeas and sub-tropical flora. There is a mile of sandy beach and a playground for children. The village is probably best known as the major location for 1960s cult TV show, The Prisoner.
**Times:** *Open all year, daily 9.30-5.30.
**Fee:** *£6.50 (ch £4, pen £5).
**Facilities:** 🅟 🍽 (Licensed) ⛩ 🗐 £3.50 ♿ (w/chair available, disabled parking, toilets) shop, guided tours, audio commentaries 🚫 (ex guide dogs) 🚌

---

TYWYN
**Talyllyn Railway**
Wharf Station LL36 9EY
☎ 01654 710472 🖹 01654 711755
**Email:** enquiries@talyllyn.co.uk
**Web:** www.talyllyn.co.uk
**Dir:** *A493 Machynlleth to Dolgellau for Tywyn station, B4405 for Abergynolwyn*
The oldest 27in-gauge railway in the world, built in 1865 to run from Tywyn on Cardigan Bay to Abergynolwyn slate mine some seven miles inland. The railway climbs the steep sides of the Fathew Valley and with stops on the way at Dolgoch Falls and the Nant Gwernol forest. The return trip takes 2.5 hours. All scheduled passenger trains are steam hauled.
**Times:** *Open Sun mid Feb-Mar; Apr-early Nov & 26 Dec-1 Jan daily. Ring for timetable.
**Fee:** *£11Day Rover (ch accompanied £2). Intermediate fares available.
**Facilities:** 🅟 (charged) Ⓟ (0.5m) ☕ (self service) ⛩ 🗐 various ♿ (prior notice useful, wheelchair ramps into carriages, toilets) shop 🚌 (prior booking advisable)

---

Y FELINHELI
**Greenwood Forest Park**
LL56 4QN
☎ 01248 670076 🖹 01248 670069
**Email:** info@greenwoodforestpark.co.uk
**Web:** www.greenwoodforestpark.co.uk
**Dir:** *A55 junct 11, follow Llanberis signs onto A4244, signed from next rdbt. Located between Bangor and Caernafen*
This forest park provides a wide range of exciting activities for the whole family. Try the Great Green Run - the longest slide in Wales, shoot a real longbow, build dens in the woods and saw a log. Ride the Green Dragon, the world's first people-powered family rollercoaster. Try the Jungle Boat Adventure and explore the rainforest. There are large interactive exhibitions in the oak-framed great hall and the Forest Theatre stages events and shows during school holiday periods. The Toddlers Village is ideal for young children. New attractions include the Treetop Towers, and the Crocodile Maze.
**Times:** Open daily mid Mar-late Oct 10-5.30 (Sep & Oct 10-5).
**Fee:** *Seasonal. £5.95-£8.50 (ch £4.95-£7.75, pen £5.30-£7.50, disabled 20% discount). Family ticket (2ad+2ch) £19.50-£29.
**Facilities:** 🅟 ⛩ 🗐 ♿ (grounds mostly accessible, parking, toilets) shop, guided tours (charged) 🚫 (ex on leads) 🚌 booking essential

## BEAUMARIS
**Beaumaris Castle**
LL58 8AP
☎ 01248 810361
**Web:** www.cadw.wales.gov.uk
Beaumaris was built by Edward I and took from 1295 to 1312 to complete. In later centuries it was plundered for its lead, timber and stone. Despite this it remains one of the most impressive and complete castles built by Edward I. It has a perfectly symmetrical, concentric plan, with a square inner bailey and curtain walls, round corner towers and D-shaped towers in between. There are also two great gatehouses, but these were never finished.
**Times:** *Open Apr-May & Oct, daily 9.30-5; Jun-Sep, daily 9.30-6; Nov-Mar, Mon-Sat 9.30-4, Sun 11-4. Telephone for XmasOpening times.
**Fee:** *£3.50 (ch 5-15, concessions £3, disabled visitors and assisting companion free). Family ticket (2ad+all ch/grandch under 16) £10. Group rates available. Prices quoted apply until 31 Mar 2007.
**Facilities:** ℗ ♿ shop ⊗ 🚌 ☺

## BEAUMARIS
**Museum of Childhood Memories**
1 Castle Street LL58 8AP
☎ 01248 712498
**Web:** www.aboutbritain.com/
museumofchildhoodmemories.htm
**Dir:** *turn off A55 onto A545 opposite Beaumaris Castle*
The museum illustrates the life and interests of children and families over 150 years. There are around 2,000 items in the museum's collection including money boxes, dolls, educational toys and games, early clockwork trains, cars and aeroplanes, push toys and cycles.
**Times:** *Open daily 10.30-5.30, Sun 12-5. (Last admission 4.30, Sun 4). Closed Nov-2nd wk Mar
**Fee:** *£4 (ch £2.25, concessions £3.25). Family ticket £11. Free entry for wheelchair users.
**Facilities:** ℗ (50yds) 🍴 ♿ shop ⊗ (ex guide dogs) 🚌 (max 50 people at one time) ☺

## BRYNSIENCYN
**Anglesey Sea Zoo**
LL61 6TQ
☎ 01248 430411 📠 01248 430213
**Email:** info@angleseyseazoo.co.uk
**Web:** www.angleseyseazoo.co.uk
**Dir:** *1st turning off Britannia Bridge onto Anglesey then follow Lobster signs along A4080 to zoo*
Nestling by the Menai Straits, this all-weather undercover attraction contains a shipwreck bristling with conger eels, a lobster hatchery, a seahorse nursery, crashing waves and the enchanting fish forest.
**Times:** *Open Feb half term-late Oct half term. Check website or telephone for times.
**Fee:** *£5.95 (ch & student £4.95, pen & UB40 £5.50). Family ticket £14.95-£21.95. Party 10+. + £1 for high season. Please telephone to confirm 2007 prices.
**Facilities:** ℗ ℗ 🍴 (Licensed) 🪑 🍴 ♿ (2 wheelchairs available, Braille tour notes, toilets) shop, guided tours (charged) ⊗ (ex guide dogs) 🚌 (pre-booking preferred)

## BRYNSIENCYN
### Foel Farm Park
Foel Farm LL61 6TQ
☎ 01248 430646 📄 01248 430066
**Email:** foelfarm@btinternet.com
**Web:** www.foelfarm.co.uk
**Dir:** *left off Britannia Bridge A55 onto A5/A4080 to Llanfairpwllgwyngyll, left on A4080 to Brynsiencyn & follow signs*
Children will love this friendly farm experience, where they can meet animals big and small, and take tractor and trailer rides. The park also contains a luxury handmade chocolate business, a bistro and bar, as well as a tea room and gift shop.
**Times:** *Open daily Mar-Oct 10.30-5.30; Also wknds Nov-Feb 10.30-4.30. AlsoOpen Feb half term.
**Fee:** *£4.75 (ch 4-16 £3.75, pen & students £4.25).
**Facilities:** 🅿 ⚲ & (toilets) shop ⊗ (ex guide dogs) 🚌 (advanced booking required)

## HOLYHEAD
### RSPB Nature Reserve South Stack Cliffs
Plas Nico South Stack LL65 1YH
☎ 01407 764973 📄 01407 764973
**Web:** www.rspb.org.uk/reserves/southstack
**Dir:** *A5 or A55 to Holyhead then follow brown heritage signs*
South Stack Cliffs is an expanse of heathland with dramatic sea cliffs and a tremendous view. In summer breeding seabirds, including puffins, can be seen from the Information Centre at Ellins Tower where telescopes are provided and staff are on hand to help.
**Times:** *Open: Information Centre daily, Etr-Sep, 10-5.30. ReserveOpen daily at all times.
**Fee:** *Free Free entry to Reserve & Ellins Tower Information Centre
**Facilities:** 🅿 Ⓟ (500m) & (toilets) guided tours 🚌 (pre-booking required) ♨

## MERTHYR TYDFIL
### Brecon Mountain Railway
Pant Station Dowlais CF48 2UP
☎ 01685 722988 📄 01685 384854
**Web:** www.breconmountainrailway.co.uk
**Dir:** *follow Mountain Railway signs from A470 or A465 N of Merthyr Tydfil*
Opened in 1980, this narrow-gauge railway follows part of an old British Rail route which closed in 1964 when the iron industry in South Wales fell into decline. The present route starts at Pant Station and continues for 3.5 miles through the beautiful scenery of the Brecon Beacons National Park, as far as Taf Fechan reservoir. The train is pulled by a vintage steam locomotive and is one of the most popular railways in Wales.
**Times:** *Opening times on application to The Brecon Mountain Railway, Pant Station, Merthyr Tydfil.
**Fee:** *Fares are under review, please ring for details.
**Facilities:** 🅿 🍴 (Licensed) ⚲ 🎁 & (adapted carriage, toilets) shop 🚌

## MERTHYR TYDFIL
**Cyfarthfa Castle Museum & Art Gallery**
Cyfarthfa Park CF47 8RE
☎ 01685 723112 🖹 01685 723112
**Email:** museum@merthyr.gov.uk
**Web:** www.museums.merthyr.gov.uk
**Dir:** *off A470, N towards Brecon, follow brown heritage signs*
Set in wooded parkland beside a beautiful lake, this imposing Gothic mansion now houses a superb museum and art gallery. Providing a fascinating glimpse into 3,000 years of history, the museum displays wonderful collections of fine art, social history and objects from around the world in a Regency setting.
**Times:** Open Apr-Sep, daily, 10-5.30; Oct-Mar, Tue-Fri 10-4, Sat-Sun 12-4. Closed between Xmas & New Year

**Fee:** Free
**Facilities:** ❷ ⓟ (300yds – restricted during some special events) ⊓ 📑 £2.50 ♿ (stair lift & wheelchair available, toilets) shop, guided tours ⊗ (ex guide dogs) 🚍 (pre-booking required) ♨

## CALDICOT
**Caldicot Castle & Country Park**
Church Rd NP26 4HU
☎ 01291 420241 🖹 01291 435094
**Email:** caldicotcastle@monmouthshire.gov.uk
**Web:** www.caldicotcastle.co.uk
**Dir:** *M4 junct 23A onto B4245. From M48 junct 2 follow A48 & B4245. Signed from B4245*
Caldicot Castle's well-preserved fortifications were founded by the Normans and fully developed by the late 14th century. Restored as a family home by a wealthy Victorian, the castle offers the chance to explore medieval walls and towers in a setting of tranquil gardens and wooded country parkland, plus the opportunity to play giant chess or draughts.
**Times:** Open Apr-Sep, daily, 11-5.

**Fee:** *£3.75 (ch, pen, student & disabled £2.50). Family (2ad+3ch) £12. Party 10+.
**Facilities:** ❷ ⓟ (100yds) ⊓ 📑 ♿ (taped tour, level trails, induction loop, access guide, toilets) shop, guided tours, audio commentaries 🚍 (pre-booking preferred)

## CHEPSTOW
**Chepstow Castle**
NP6 5EZ
☎ 01291 624065
**Web:** www.cadw.wales.gov.uk
Built by William FitzOsbern, Chepstow is the first recorded Norman stone castle. It stands in a strategic spot beside the Wye. The castle was strengthened in the following centuries, but was not besieged (as far as is known) until the Civil War, when it was twice lost to the Parliamentarians. The remains of the domestic rooms and the massive gatehouse with its portcullis grooves and ancient gates are still impressive, as are the walls and towers.
**Times:** *Open Apr-May & Oct, daily 9.30-5; Jun-Sep, daily 9.30-6; Nov-Mar, Mon-Sat 9.30-4, Sun 11-4.

Telephone for XmasOpening times.
**Fee:** *£3.50 (ch 5-15, concessions £3, disabled visitors and assisting companion free). Family ticket (2ad+all ch/grandch under 16) £10. Group rates available. Prices quoted apply until 31 Mar 2007.
**Facilities:** ❷ ♿ shop ⊗ 🚍 ☼

## ABERDULAIS
### Aberdulais Falls

Neath SA10 8EU

☎ 01639 636674 📄 01639 645069

**Email:** aberdulais@nationaltrust.org.uk

**Web:** www.ukindex.co.uk/nationaltrust

**Dir:** *from M4 junct 43, take A465 signed Vale of Neath. Onto A4109, Falls next to Dulais Rock Pub*

For over 300 years this famous waterfall has provided energy to drive the wheels of industry. The Turbine House allows visitors access to the top of the falls, with views of the power equipment, fish pass and displays. Please contact for details of special events.

**Times:** Open 2-25 Mar, Fri-Sun, 11-4. 26 Mar-2 Nov, Mon-Fri, 10-5. 31 Mar-4 Nov, Sat-Sun, 11-6. WinterOpening times 12 Jan-23 Mar

**Fee:** *£3.20 (ch £1.60) Family ticket £8. Parties 15+ £2.40 (ch £1.20)

**Facilities:** 🅿 ℗ (200yds) 🍴 📄 £1.50 ♿ (lifts for disabled to view falls, toilets) shop, guided tours ,audio commentaries 🚌 (advance booking) 🌿

## CRYNANT
### Cefn Coed Colliery Museum

Neath SA10 8SN

☎ 01639 750556 📄 01639 750556

**Dir:** *1m S of Crynant, on A4109*

The museum is on the site of a former working colliery, and tells the story of mining in the Dulais Valley. A steam-winding engine has been kept and is now operated by electricity, and there is also a simulated underground mining gallery, boilerhouse, compressor house, and exhibition area. Outdoor exhibits include a stationary colliery locomotive. Exhibitions relating to the coal mining industry are held on a regular basis and give a fascinating insight into the the lives of the miners, the conditions in which they worked and how the seams of coal were extracted.

**Times:** *Open Apr-Oct,daily 10.30-5; Nov-Mar, groups welcome by prior arrangement.

**Fee:** Free

**Facilities:** 🅿 🍴 📄 ♿ (toilets) shop, guided tours 🚌

## CYNONVILLE
### South Wales Miners Museum

Afan Argoed Country Park SA13 3HG

☎ 01639 850564 📄 01639 850446

**Email:** aandmboast@btinternet.com

**Web:** www.southwalesminersmuseum.co.uk

**Dir:** *M4 junct 40 onto A4107, 6m NE of Port Talbot*

The picturesquely placed museum gives a vivid picture of mining life, with coal faces, pit gear and miners' equipment. Guided tours of the museum on request. The country park has forest walks and picnic areas, and a visitor centre.

**Times:** *Open all year daily, Apr-Sep 10.30-5 (Sat & Sun 10.30-6); Oct-Feb 10.30-4 (Sat & Sun 10.30-5). Closed Xmas week.

**Fee:** *£1.20 (ch & pen 60p). Concessionary rate for advance bookings.

**Facilities:** 🅿 (charged) 🍴 🍴 ♿ (mechanical & manual wheelchairs on request, toilets) shop guided tours 🚫 (ex guide dogs) 🚌

## NEATH
### Gnoll Estate Country Park
SA11 3BS
☎ 01639 635808 🖹 01639 635694
**Email:** e.ford@npt.gov.uk
**Web:** www.neath-porttalbot.gov.uk
**Dir:** *follow brown heritage signs from town centre*
The extensively landscaped Gnoll Estate offers tranquil woodland walks, picnic areas, stunning views, children's play areas, adventure playground, 9-hole golf course, and coarse fishing. Varied programme of events and school holiday activities.
**Times:** *Open all year - Vistor centre, daily from 10. Closed 24 Dec-2 Jan
**Fee:** *Pitch & Putt £3.80 (ch £ 1.90) Fishing permit £4.20 (ch £2.55)

**Facilities:** 🅿 🍴 ♿ (wheelchair & scooter for hire, designated parking, toilets) shop, guided tours 🚫 (ex guide dogs) 🚌 (advance notice required) 📧

## CAERLEON
### National Roman Legion Museum
High Street Gwent NP18 1AE
☎ 01633 423134 🖹 01633 422869
**Email:** roman@museumwales.ac.uk
**Web:** www.museumwales.ac.uk
**Dir:** *close to Newport, 20 min from M4, follow signs from Cardiff & Bristol*
The museum illustrates the history of Roman Caerleon and the daily life of its garrison. On display are arms, armour and equipment, with a collection of engraved gemstones, a labyrinth mosaic and finds from the legionary base at Usk. Please telephone for details of children's holiday activities.
**Times:** *Open all year: Mon-Sat 10-5, Sun 2-5.
**Fee:** Free Charge may apply to some events.

**Facilities:** 🅿 (100yds) 🍴 ♿ (toilets) shop 🚫 (ex guide dogs) 🚌 (advance booking essential)

## NEWPORT
### Tredegar House & Park
NP10 8YW
☎ 01633 815880 🖹 01633 815895
**Email:** tredegar.house@newport.gov.uk
**Web:** www.newport.gov.uk
**Dir:** *2m W of Newport, signed from A48 & M4 junct 28*
Tredegar House is a fine example of restoration and reflects the rise and fall of the Morgan family through 5 centuries. The house and gardens are set in a 90 acre landscaped park and feature formal gardens, self guided trails, craft workshops and boating.
**Times:** *Open Etr-late Sep, Wed-Sun 11.30-4.
**Fee:** *House tour £5.40 (ch free, concessions £3.95).
**Facilities:** 🅿 ☕ (tea rooms) 🍴 🍽 Free-£2 ♿ (wheelchairs for loan, toilets) shop, guided tours

🚫 (ex guide dogs) 🚌 (tours need to be pre-booked)

## CAREW
### Carew Castle & Tidal Mill
Nr Tenby SA70 8SL

☎ 01646 651782 📄 01646 651782

**Email:** enquiries@carewcastle.com

**Web:** www.carewcastle.com

**Dir:** *on A4075, just off A477 Pembroke to Kilgetty road*

This magnificent Norman castle has royal links with Henry Tudor and was the setting for the Great Tournament of 1507. The castle is set in a stunning position overlooking a 23 acre millpond and shows the development from a Norman castle to an Elizabethan fortified house. Nearby is the Carew Cross (Cadw), an impressive 13ft Celtic cross dating from the 11th century. Carew Mill is one of only four restored tidal mills in Britain, with records dating back to 1558. There is a medieval bridge and a delightful picnic area linked by a circular walk.

**Times:** Open Apr-1 Nov

**Fee:** *£3 (concessions £2). Family ticket £8.

**Facilities:** ❷ Ⓟ (30yds) ⊼ 🍴 from 10p ♿ (toilets) shop, guided tours, audio commentaries (charged) 🚌

## FISHGUARD
### OceanLab
The Parrog Goodwick SA64 0DE

☎ 01348 874737 📄 01348 872528

**Email:** fishguardharbour-tic@pembrokeshire.gov.uk

**Web:** www.ocean-lab.co.uk

**Dir:** *A40 to Fishguard, turn at by-pass, follow signs for Stenaline ferry terminal, pass 2 garages, turn right at rdbt & follow signs to attraction*

Overlooking the Pembrokeshire coastline, OceanLab is a multifunctional centre, which aims to provide a fun-filled experience for the family. There is also a hands on ocean quest exhibition, a soft play area and a cybercafé where visitors can surf the internet. New exhibition, 'Ollie the Octopus's Garden', with hands on displays and activities.

**Times:** Open Apr-Oct 9.30-5, Nov-Mar 10-4.

**Fee:** *Telephone for details

**Facilities:** ❷ Ⓟ (100yds) ⊡ (light lunches and refreshments) ⊼ 🍴 £3.25 ♿ (lift, flat even ground, low counter, toilets) shop ⊗ (ex guide dogs) 🚌

## NARBERTH
### Oakwood Park
Canaston Bridge SA67 8DE

☎ 01834 861889 📄 01834 891380

**Email:** info@oakwoodthemepark.co.uk

**Web:** www.oakwoodthemepark.co.uk

**Dir:** *M4 W junct 49, take A48 to Carmarthen, signed*

Wales' premier theme park, featuring the world's No. 1 wooden roller coaster Megafobia, the 50m-high sky coaster Vertigo, shot n' drop tower coaster The Bounce, and Snake River Falls. For young children there is KidzWorld featuring The Wacky Factory, The Lost Kingdom, Techniquest and Playtown. In summer there are firework displays and live shows at night.

**Times:** *Open 24 Mar-25 Sep daily, from 10 (closing times vary)

**Fee:** *£13.75 (under 2's free, ch 3-9 £12.75, pen £8.85 & disabled £9.75). Family ticket (4) £49, family ticket (6) £70. Party 20+ tickets available £11.75

**Facilities:** ❷ 🍴 ⊼ 🍴 ♿ (wheelchair hire, special access to some rides, toilets) shop ⊗ (ex guide dogs) 🚌

## PEMBROKE
### Pembroke Castle
SA71 4LA

☎ 01646 681510 & 684585 ▤ 01646 622260
**Email:** info@pembrokecastle.co.uk
**Web:** www.pembrokecastle.co.uk
**Dir:** *W end of main street*

This magnificent castle commands stunning views over the Milford estuary. Discover its rich medieval history, and that of Henry VII, the first Tudor king, through a variety of exhibitions. There are lively guided tours and events each Sunday in July and August. Before leaving, pop into the Brass Rubbing Centre and make your own special souvenir. Special Events: 1st week in Sep 'Pembroke Festival'. Please telephone for details.
**Times:** Open all year, daily, Apr-Sep 9.30-6; Mar & Oct 10-5; Nov-Feb, 10-4. Closed 24-26 Dec & 1 Jan.
**Fee:** £3.50 (ch under 16 & pen £2.50, ch under 5 & wheelchairs users free). Family ticket £10.
**Facilities:** ⓟ (100yds) ⏏ (Apr-Oct) ⌷ ▤ & (induction loop, handrails, portable ramp, toilets) shop, guided tours. (charged) 🚌

## SCOLTON
### Scolton Visitor Centre
Haverfordwest SA62 5QL

☎ 01437 731328 (Museum) & 731457 (Park)
▤ 01437 731743

**Dir:** *5m N of Haverfordwest, on B4329*

Scolton Manor Museum is situated in Scolton Country Park. The early Victorian mansion, refurbished stables and the exhibition hall illustrate the history and natural history of Pembrokeshire. There are new displays in the house and stables, plus a 'Pembrokeshire Railways' exhibition. The 60-acre grounds, partly a nature reserve, have fine specimen trees and shrubs. Environmentally friendly Visitor Centre, alternative energy and woodland displays, guided walks and children's play areas.
**Times:** *Open Museum Apr-Oct, Tue-Sun & BHs 10.30-1 & 1.30-5.30; Country Park all year, Etr-Sep 10-7, Oct-Etr 10-6. Closed 25-26 Dec.
**Fee:** *Museum: £2 (ch £1, concessions £1.50). Country Park car park £1 all day.
**Facilities:** ⓟ (charged) ⓟ (100mtrs – no parking outside museum) ⏏ (Open in summmer, otherwise ring first) ⌷ & (disabled parking area near house, toilets) shop ⊗ (ex guide dogs & in grounds) 🚌 (pre-booking preferred) ▦

## ST FLORENCE
### Manor House Wildlife & Leisure Park
Ivy Tower TENBY SA70 8RJ

☎ 01646 651201 ▤ 01646 651201

**Dir:** *on B4318 between Tenby & St Florence*

The park is set in 35 acres of delightful wooded grounds and award-winning gardens. The wildlife includes exotic birds, reptiles and fish. Also here are a pets' corner, a children's playground with free rides on an astraglide slide, and roundabouts. Other attractions include a natural history museum, a go-kart track, model railway exhibition. Daily falconry displays. Telephone for details of displays and animal feeding times.
**Times:** *Open Etr-end Sep, daily 10-6. Please telephone for late opening Jul & Aug.
**Fee:** *£4.50 (ch £3.50, pen £4, disabled/helpers £2.50) Family ticket £14.50 (2ad + 2ch). Party 20+.
**Facilities:** ⓟ ⏏ (self service) ⌷ & (toilets) shop ⊗ 🚌

## ABERCRAF
### Dan-Yr-Ogof The National Showcaves Centre for Wales

SA9 1GJ

☎ 01639 730284 & 730801 🖨 01639 730293

**Email:** info@showcaves.co.uk

**Web:** www.showcaves.co.uk

**Dir:** *M4 junct 45, midway between Swansea & Brecon on A4067, follow brown tourist signs for Dan-Yr-Ogof*

This award-winning attraction includes three separate caves, dinosaur park, Iron Age Farm, museum, shire horse centre and covered children's play area. The caves, considered to be amongst the most spectacular in Northern Europe, were discovered by the Morgan brothers in 1912. The awe-inspiring Cathedral Cave is enhanced by dramatic music and lighting and has an exhibit to the people that once made these caves their home and burial place – 42 human skeletons were discovered in Bone Cave. Overall, the caves are extraordinary in their lakes, stalagtites and stalagmites.

**Times:** Open Apr-Oct, daily from 10 (last admission 3).

**Fee:** £10 (ch 4-16 £6). Group rates 15+.

**Facilities:** 🅿 🍴 📷 ♿ (toilets) shop, audio commentaries (charged) 🚫 (ex assist dogs) 🚌

## BERRIEW
### Glansevern Hall Gardens

Glansevern Welshpool SY21 8AH

☎ 01686 640644 🖨 01686 640829

**Web:** www.glansevern.co.uk

**Dir:** *signed on A483 between Welshpool and Newtown*

Built in the Greek Revival style for Arthur Davies Owen, who chose a romantically positioned site on the banks of the River Severn. The current owners have developed the gardens, respecting the plantings and features of the past, and added a vast collection of new and interesting species. There are many fine and unusual trees, a lakeside walk, walled garden, water gardens and a rock garden with grotto.

**Times:** *Open May-Sep, BH Mon,Thu-Sat 12-5. Parties other dates by arrangement.

**Fee:** *£3.50 (pen £3, ch under 15 free).

**Facilities:** 🅿 ☕ (waitress service) 🍴 📷 ♿ (most areas accessible, toilets) shop, guided tours 🚫 (ex on lead) 🚌 (pre-booking preferred) 🈂

## LLANFAIR CAEREINION
### Welshpool & Llanfair Light Railway

Welshpool SY21 0SF

☎ 01938 810441 🖨 01938 810861

**Email:** info@wllr.org.uk

**Web:** www.wllr.org.uk

**Dir:** *beside A458, Shrewsbury-Dolgellau road*

The Llanfair Railway is one of the Great Little Trains of Wales. It offers a 16-mile round trip through glorious scenery by narrrow-gauge steam train. The line is home to a collection of engines and coaches from all round the world. Please ring for details of special events.

**Times:** *Open Etr-late Oct wknds, daily during holiday periods, phone for timetable enquiries.

**Fee:** *£9.90 return (ch £1, pen £8.90).

**Facilities:** 🅿 🅿 (0.5m) ☕ (available at Llanfair station) 🍴 📷 ♿ (three coachs adapted for wheelchairs, toilets) shop 🚌 (prior booking for reserved seating)

**POWYS**

## MACHYNLLETH
### King Arthur's Labyrinth

King Arthur's Labyrinth Corris SY20 9RF

☎ 01654 761584 📄 01654 761575

**Email:** king.arthurs.labyrinth@corris-wales.co.uk

**Web:** www.kingarthurslabyrinth.com

**Dir:** *on A487 between Machynlleth and Dolgellau*

Easily found on the A487, King Arthur's Labyrinth is a subterranean experience not to be missed. Suitably kitted-up there is a boat ride through the great waterfall and into the labyrinth of tunnels and caverns carved into the ancient rocks of Wales. Tales of King Arthur and other legends are re-told as you travel through this underground terrain. Above ground there is an ehibition dedicated to the slate mining at Corris as well as a wide range of crafts studios and shops, including toymakers, woodworking, candlemaking, jewellers and leathercrafts. There is plenty to do and an excellent café and restaurant which also sells local products and delicasies.

**Times:** Open 31 Mar-4 Nov, daily, 10-5.

**Fee:** *£5.15 (ch £3.60, pen £4.60).

**Facilities:** 🅿 🍴 (hot and cold meals, refreshments) 🪑 📄 ♿ (toilets) shop, guided tours (charged) 🚫 (ex guide dogs) 🚌 prior booking for Labyrinth

## RHAYADER
### Gilfach Nature Discovery Centre and Reserve

St Harmon LD6 5LF

☎ 01597 870301 & 823298 📄 01597 823274

**Email:** info@radnorshirewildlifetrust.org.uk

**Web:** www.radnorshirewildlifetrust.org.uk

**Dir:** *off A470, 3m N of Rhayader*

Situated in the Cambrian Mountains, Gilfach is locally unique due to its wide variety of habitats; high moorland to enclosed meadow, oak woodland to rocky upland river. The reserve therefore supports a tremendous abundance of plants and animals within a relatively small area. This richness of wildlife has adapted to living in the various habitats created over the centuries through the practice of traditional farming. Visitors can take a number of planned walks including the Nature Trail, the Monks Trod Trail, and the Oakwood Path. The Nature Discovery Centre offers the opportunity to learn about the various habitats and wildlife featuring footage from cameras in nestboxes, games and quizzes. Special Events: Childrens activities every Thursday in July and August.

**Times:** *Open Reserve all year. Centre Apr-Jun & Sep-Oct Fri-Mon 10-4.30; Jul-Aug daily 10-4.30

**Fee:** *Donations

**Facilities:** 🅿 🍴 (hot and cold drinks, snacks) 🪑 📄 25p ♿ (wheelchair access path to viewpoint, toilets) shop, guided tours (charged) 🚫 (ex on lead) 🚌 ♻

## TREHAFOD
### Rhondda Heritage Park

Lewis Merthyr Colliery Coed Cae Road CF37 7NP

☎ 01443 682036 📄 01443 687420

**Email:** reception@rhonddaheritagepark.com

**Web:** www.rhonddaheritagepark.com

**Dir:** *between Pontypridd & Porth, off A470, follow brown heritage signs from M4 junct 32*

Based at the Lewis Merthyr Colliery, the Heritage Park is a fascinating 'living history' attraction. You can take the Cage Ride to 'Pit Bottom' and explore the underground workings of a 1950s pit, guided by men who were miners themselves. There are children's activities, an art gallery and a museum illustrating living conditions in the Rhondda Valley. Special events throughout the year, phone for details.

**Times:** Open all year, daily 10-6. Closed Mon from Oct-Etr. (Last admission 4). Closed 25 Dec-early Jan.

**Fee:** £5.60 (ch £4.30, pen £4.95). Family(4) ticket from £16.50, (6) £21.

**Facilities:** 🅿 🍴 (Licensed) 🪑 📄 ♿ (wheelchair available, accessible parking, lifts, toilets) shop, guided tours ,audio commentaries 🚫 (ex guide dogs) 🚌

## PARKMILL
### Gower Heritage Centre
Felin Ddwr SA3 2EH

☎ 01792 371206 📠 01792 371471

**Email:** info@gowerheritagecentre.co.uk

**Web:** www.gowerheritagecentre.co.uk

**Dir:** *follow signs for South Gower on A4118 W from Swansea. W side of Parkmill village*

Based around a 12th-century water-powered cornmill, the site also contains a number of craft workshops, two play areas, animals, a museum and a miller's cottage, all set in attractive countryside in an Area of Outstanding Natural Beauty.

**Times:** *Open daily, Mar-Oct 10-5.30; Nov-Feb 10-4.30. Closed 25 Dec.

**Fee:** *£3.95 (ch under 5 free, concessions £2.80).

Family ticket £12.50.

**Facilities:** 🅿 Ⓟ (100yds - no overnight parking) 🍴 📷 ♿ (ramp entrance access, toilets) shop guided tours 🚌 (pre-booking advised)

## SWANSEA
### Plantasia
Parc Tawe SA1 2AL

☎ 01792 474555 📠 01792 652588

**Email:** swansea.plantasia@swansea.gov.uk

**Web:** www.plantasia.org

**Dir:** *M4 junct 42, follow A483 into Swansea, follow car park signs for attraction*

A unique, giant hot house garden located in the city centre, Plantasia houses a huge variety of unusual and exotic plants of great interest including several species that are extinct in the wild. Also visit the Butterfly House and see a variety of species fly freely and observe various stages of butterfly development.

**Times:** *Open Tue-Sun 10-5 (BH Mons & all Mons Jun-Aug)

**Fee:** *£3 (concessions £2.10)

**Facilities:** 🅿 Ⓟ (3hr short stay car park) ♿ (toilets) shop ⊗ (ex guide dogs) 🚌

## SWANSEA
### Swansea Museum
Victoria Road Maritime Quarter SA1 1SN

☎ 01792 653763 📠 01792 652585

**Email:** swansea.museum@swansea.gov.uk

**Web:** www.swanseaheritage.co.uk

**Dir:** *M4 junct 42, on main road into city centre*

This is the oldest museum in Wales, showing the history of Swansea from the earliest times until today. The museum has a Tramshed and floating boats to explore (summer only) and exhibits that record Swansea's maritime history. There is a continuous programme of temporary exhibitions and events all year around.

**Times:** *Open all year, Tue-Sun 10-5 (last admission 4.45). Closed Mon except BH Mon, 25-26 Dec & 1 Jan.

**Fee:** *Free

**Facilities:** Ⓟ (50yds - on street) 📷 ♿ (toilets) shop ⊗ (ex guide dogs) 🚌 (prior notification preferred)

**SWANSEA**

**TORFAEN**

### BLAENAVON
**Big Pit National Mining Museum of Wales**
Torfaen NP4 9XP
☎ 01495 790311 📄 01495 792618
**Email:** bigpit@nmgw.ac.uk
**Web:** www.nmgw.ac.uk/bigpit
**Dir:** *M4 junct 25/26, follow signs on A4042 & A4043 to Pontypool & Blaenavon. Signed off A465*
The Real Underground Experience! Big Pit is the UK's leading mining museum that actually takes you 300 feet-down the mineshaft. It is a real colliery and was the place of work for hundreds of men, woman and children for over 200 years. The exhibits in the colliery buildings not only dislay the daily struggle to extract the precious mineral that stoked furnaces and lit household fires across the world they also explore modern mining meth-ods with interactive exhibits.
**Times:** *Open mid Feb-late Nov, daily 9.30-5, telephone to confirm
**Fee:** *Free
**Facilities:** ❶ ♿ (underground tours by prior arrangement, toilets) shop 🚌 (pre-booking required) ⊗

### BLAENAVON
**Blaenavon Ironworks**
North Street
☎ 01495 792615
**Web:** www.cadw.wales.gov.uk
The Blaenavon Ironworks were a milestone in the history of the Industrial Revolution. Constructed in 1788-99, they were the first purpose-built, multi-furnace ironworks in Wales. By 1796, Blaenavon was the second largest ironworks in Wales, eventually closing down in 1904.
**Times:** *Open Apr-Oct, Mon-Fri 9.30-4.30, Sat 10-5, Sun 10-4.30. For details of opening outside this period, telephone Torfaen County Borough Council on 01633 648081.
**Fee:** *£2.50 (ch 5-16, concessions £2, disabled visitors & assisting companion free). Family ticket (2ad+all ch/grandch under 16) £7. Group discounts available. Prices quoted apply until 31 Mar 2007. Please check for revised 2007 prices.
**Facilities:** ❶ ⊗ 🚌 ⟳

### CWMBRAN
**Greenmeadow Community Farm**
Greenforge Way NP44 5AJ
☎ 01633 862202 📄 01633 489332
**Email:** greenmeadow_community_farm@compuserve.com
**Dir:** *M4 junct 26. Follow signs for Cwmbran then brown signs*
This is one of Wales' leading tourist attractions - a community farm that was built during the 1980s on land threatened by developers. There are milking demonstrations, tractor and trailer rides, a dragon adventure play area, a farm trail, a nature trail and lots more. Please telephone for details of special events running throughout the year.
**Times:** *Open daily Summer 10-6, Winter 10-4. Closed 23 Dec-1 Feb.
**Fee:** *£4.50 (ch £3.50) Family (2ad+3ch) £16
**Facilities:** ❶ Ⓟ (300yds) ☕ (hot and cold snacks) 🍴 📋 ♿ (tractor & trailer rides for wheelchair users, toilets) shop 🚌 (Prior notification preferred)

## BARRY
**Welsh Hawking Centre**

Weycock Road CF62 3AA

☎ 01446 734687 ▤ 01446 739620

*Dir:* on A4226

There are over 200 birds of prey here, including eagles, hawks, owls, buzzards and falcons. They can be seen and photographed in their hom in the mews and also in some of the breeding aviaries. There is a programme of flying demonstrations held at regular intervals during the day. For those looking a little closer to the ground there are a variety of tame and friendly animals, such as pigs, lambs and rabbits which can be fed and petted, these are particular favurites with younger visitors.

**Times:** *Open late Mar-late Sep, daily 10.30-5 (1hr before dusk in winter)

**Fee:** *£5 (ch & pen £3).

**Facilities:** 🅿 ⊑ (summer only) ⊓ ▤ 50p ♿ (toilets) shop ⊗ 🚌 ⊑

## PENARTH
**Cosmeston Lakes Country Park & Medieval Village**

Lavernock Road CF64 5UY

☎ 029 2070 1678 ▤ 029 2070 8686

**Email:** NColes@valeofglamorgan.gov.uk

**Web:** www.valeofglamorgan.gov.uk

*Dir:* on B4267 between Barry and Penarth

Deserted during the plagues and famines of the 14th century, the original village was rediscovered through archaeological excavations. The buildings have been faithfully reconstructed on the excavated remains, creating a living museum of medieval village life. Special events throughout the year include re-enactments and Living History.

**Times:** *Open all year, daily 11-5 in Summer, 11-4 in Winter. Closed 25 Dec. Country parkOpen at all times.

**Fee:** *Entry to Village £3.50, (concessions £2) Family ticket £8. Entry to Country Park free.

**Facilities:** 🅿 ⫟ ⊓ ♿ (access ramps & wheelchair hire, toilets) shop, guided tours, audio commentaries (charged) 🚌 ⓩ

## CHIRK
**Chirk Castle**

LL14 5AF

☎ 01691 777701 ▤ 01691 774706

**Email:** chirkcastle@nationaltrust.org.uk

*Dir:* 8m S of Wrexham, signed off A483

Chirk Castle is one of a chain of late 13th-century Marcher castles. Its high walls and drum towers have hardly changed, but the inside shows the varied tastes of 700 years of occupation. One of the least altered parts is Adam's Tower. Many of the medieval-looking decorations were created by Pugin in the 19th century. Varied furnishings include fine tapestries. In the garden there are beautiful views that take in seven counties.

**Times:** Open 24 Mar-4 Nov, Wed-Sun & BH Mon, Tue-Sun in Jul-Aug, 12-5 (castle), 10-6 (gardens); Oct, Wed-Sun 12-4 (castle), 11-5 (gardens). (Last admission 30 mins before closing).

**Fee:** £7.40 (ch £3.70). Family ticket £18.50. Party. Garden only £4.70 (ch £2.40) Family ticket £11.80

**Facilities:** 🅿 ⫟ (Licensed) ⊓ ▤ £4 ♿ (stairclimber, hearing loop, coach from car park, toilets) shop, guided tours ⊗ (ex guide dogs & estate walks) 🚌 🌿

# Ireland

Custom House on the River Liffey, Dublin

## BELFAST
### Belfast Zoological Gardens
Antrim Road BT36 7PN
☎ 028 9077 6277 🖷 028 9037 0578
**Email:** blackrhonda@belfastcity.gov.uk
**Web:** www.belfastzoo.co.uk
**Dir:** *M2 junct 4 signed to Glengormley. Follow signs off rdbt to Zoo*
The 50-acre zoo has a dramatic setting on the face of Cave Hill, enjoying spectacular views. Attractions include the award-winning primate house (gorillas and chimpanzees), penguin enclosure, free-flight aviary, African enclosure, and underwater viewing of sealions and penguins. There are also red pandas, free-ranging lemurs, a group of very rare spectacled bears, Barbary lions, maned wolves, and barn owls.

**Times:** *Open all year, daily Apr-Sep 10-5; Oct-Mar 10-2.30. Closed 25 & 26 Dec.
**Fee:** Summer: £7.50 (ch £4), Winter: £6.30 (ch £3.20, ch under 4, pen and disabled free)
**Facilities:** 🅿 Ⓟ (0.5 miles) 🍴 (Licensed) 🛒 📖 Worksheets for educational groups ♿ (free admission & reserved parking, toilets) shop ⊗ (ex guide dogs) 🚌

## BALLYMENA
### Ecos Millennium Environmental Centre
Ecos Centre Kernohams Lane Broughshane Road BT43 7QA
☎ 028 2566 4400 🖷 028 2563 8984
**Email:** info@ecoscentre.com
**Web:** www.ecoscentre.com
**Dir:** *follow signs from M2 bypass at Ballymena*
At the Ecos Centre visitors can enjoy a fun day out on the Ecos Island free of charge where there is a wide range of fun activities for all including electric bikes, remote control boats, toy tractors and diggers' sand pit, BBQs and picnicking facilities, duck feeding, play park and much more. The visitor centre is packed with fun with lots of information on the environment and renewable energy technologies and children's quizzes. This is all set in a 150-acre park and nature reserve where visitors can follow any of the picturesque walking trails along the riverside, and through developing woodlands.
**Times:** *Open all year. Please phone for opening dates. Closed 24 Dec-1 Jan
**Fee:** Free
**Facilities:** 🅿 ☕ (Open Easter/Jun/Jul & Aug) 🛒 📖 ♿ (toilets) shop, garden centre, audio commentaries ⊗ (ex guide dogs) 🚌

## GIANT'S CAUSEWAY
### Giant's Causeway Centre
44 Causeway Road Bushmills BT57 8SU
☎ 028 2073 1855 🖷 028 2073 2537
**Email:** causewaytic@hotmail.com
**Web:** www.northantrim.com
**Dir:** *2m N of Bushmills on B146*
This dramatic rock formation is undoubtedly one of the wonders of the natural world. The Centre provides an exhibition and audio-visual show, and Ulsterbus provides a minibus service to the stones and there are guided walks, and special facilities for the disabled.
**Times:** *Open all year, daily from 10 (closes 7 Jul & Aug). Closed 1 wk Xmas.
**Fee:** *Audio-visual show £1 (ch 50p). Family ticket £2.50 (2ad+2ch under 15). Group rate 80p (ch 40p). Car park charge £5 per car; £7.50 minibus.
**Facilities:** 🅿 (charged) 🍴 🛒 ♿ (mini bus transport with wheelchair hoist, reserved parking, toilets) shop ⊗ (ex guide dogs) 🚌 (recommend advance bookings)

## ARMAGH
### Palace Stables Heritage Centre
The Palace Demesne BT60 4EL
☎ 028 3752 1801 ▤ 028 3751 0180
**Email:** stables@armagh.gov.uk
**Web:** www.visitarmagh.com
**Dir:** *off Friary Rd beside council offices*
This picturesque Georgian building, set around a cobbled
courtyard, has been lovingly restored and now houses a
heritage centre. The building was home to the
Archbishops of the Church of Ireland from 1770 up to
the 1975. A daily Georgian interpretation is provided by
authentic costumed characters. The centre also features
a chapel, gardens, a Victorian conservatory, the ruins of a
Franciscan Friary, and an ice house.
**Times:** Open all year, Jul-Aug, Mon-Sat 10-5.30, Sun 1-
5.30; Sep-Apr, Mon-Sat 10-5, Sun 2-5.
(Last tour 1hr before closing)
**Fee:** £4.50 (pen £3.50). Family £11
**Facilities:** 🅿 Ⓟ (200yds) 🍽 (Licensed) ⌓
♿ (ramps & lift in stables, toilets) shop
🚌 (pre-booking required)

## DOWNPATRICK
### The St Patrick Centre
St Patrick Visitor Centre Market Street BT30 6LZ
☎ 028 4461 9000 ▤ 028 4461 9111
**Email:** director@saintpatrickcentre.com
**Web:** www.saintpatrickcentre.com
**Dir:** *A7 from Belfast, follow brown heritage signs*
This 21st-century multimedia, interactive, audio-visual
feast is dedicated to the fascinating story of Ireland's
Patron Saint Patrick, who brought Christianity to Ireland
in the 5th century. The Centre is located beside the
saint's grave, in the heart of St. Patrick's country, forty
minutes from Belfast and two hours from Dublin.
**Times:** Open all year Oct-Mar, Mon-Sat, 10-5 & St
Patricks Day 9.30-7; Apr-May & Sep, Mon-Sat 9.30-
5.30, Sun 1-5.30 (morning opening on request), Jun-Aug
Mon-Sat 9.30-6, Sun 10-6. (Last admission 1.5 hrs
before closing).
**Fee:** *£4.90 (ch £2.50, concessions £3.30) family ticket
(2ad+2ch) £11.70. Groups 25+, £3.25 (ch £2.20,
concessions £2.65)
**Facilities:** 🅿 Ⓟ (50mtrs) 🍱 (Open 10-4pm, Mon-Sat)
▤ ♿ (lifts & wheelchairs available, toilets) shop,
garden centre, guided tours, audio commentaries
🚫 (ex guide dogs) 🚌 (booking essential)

## HOLYWOOD
### Ulster Folk and Transport Museum
Cultra BT18 0EU
☎ 02890 428428 ▤ 01232 428728
**Email:** uftm.info@magni.org.uk
**Web:** www.uftm.org.uk
**Dir:** *12m outside Belfast on A2, past Holywood on main
road to Bangor*
Voted Northern Ireland's Best Visitor Attraction and Irish
Museum of the Year, this attraction illustrates the way of
life and traditions of Northern Ireland. The galleries of the
Transport Museum display collections of horse drawn
carts, cars, steam locomotives and the history of ship
and aircraft building. Please telephone for details of
special events running throughout the year.
**Times:** Open all year Mar-Jun, Mon-Fri 10-5, Sat 10-6,
Sun 11-6; Jul-Sep, Mon-Sat 10-6, Sun 11-6; Oct-Feb,
Mon-Fri 10-4, Sat 10-5, Sun 11-5.
**Fee:** Folk Museum: £7 (ch 5-16 and concessions £4,
under 5 free) Family ticket (2ad + 3ch) £19. Disabled
visitors free. Transport Museum: as Folk Museum.
Combined ticket £6.50 (ch 5-16 and concessions £4)
Family ticket £19.
**Facilities:** 🅿 ⌓ ▤ ♿ (toilets) shop, guided tours
(charged) 🚌

## LISCANNOR
### Cliffs of Moher Visitor Centre
☎ 065 7081 565 📄 061 361020
Email: reservations@shannondev.ie
Web: www.cliffsofmoher.ie
Dir: *6m NW of Lahinch*

The Cliffs of Moher stand as a giant natural rampart against the aggressive might of the Atlantic Ocean, rising in places to 700ft, and stretch for almost 5 miles. O'Brien's Tower was built in the early 19th century as a viewing point for tourists on the highest point. 'Atlantic Edge' is the new and exciting state-of-the-art interpretation centre in an underground cave with four themed areas: Ocean, Rock, Nature and Man. Also includes 'The Ledge', a virtual reality cliff adventure.

**Times:** Open Visitor Centre all year. Oct-Apr 9.30-5.30. May-Sep 8.30am-9pm
**Fee:** O'Briens Tower €4 (ch€2.50).Family €11.98. Facillities charge per vehicle. Car €8. Separate charge for Buses and Coaches – see website.
**Facilities:** 🅿 (charged) 🍴 (Licensed) 🚻 ▯ ♿ (induction loops at reception & audio visual theatre, toilets) shop, guided tours ⊗ (ex guide dogs in grounds) 🚌 Must be prebooked

## BALLYVAUGHAN
### Aillwee Cave
☎ 065 707 7036 📄 065 707 7107
Email: barbara@aillweecave.ie
Web: www.aillweecave.ie
Dir: *3m S of Ballyvaughan. Signed from Galway and Ennis*

An underground network of caves beneath the world famous Burren. Guided tours take you through large caverns, over bridged chasms and alongside thunderous waterfalls. There is a craftshop, a dairy where cheese is made, a speciality food shop and a tearoom. Santa uses the cave as a workshop around Christmas time, while Easter sees a massive egg hunt in the woods. In addition, a garden shop has opened here in the last year. Special Events: Santa's Workshop, appointments necessary.

**Times:** Open all year from 10. Dec by appointment only.
**Fee:** €12 (ch €5.50 pen €9). Family ticket €29-€35
**Facilities:** 🅿 ☕ (tea rooms, light lunches) 🍴 (Licensed) 🚻 ▯ £3 ♿ (toilets) shop, garden centre, guided tours ⊗ (ex guide dogs) 🚌 (pre-booking required)

## CARRIGTWOHILL
### Fota Wildlife Park
Fota Estate
☎ 021 4812678 📄 021 4812744
Email: info@fotawildlife.ie
Web: www.fotawildlife.ie
Dir: *16km E of Cork. From N25 Cork to Waterford road take Cobh road*

Established with the primary aim of conservation, Fota has more than 90 species of exotic wildlife in open, natural surroundings. Many of the animals wander freely around the park. Giraffes, zebras, ostriches, antelope, cheetahs and a wide array of waterfowl are among the species here.
**Times:** *Open 17 Mar-Oct, daily, 10-6 (Sun 11-6) (last admission 5); Nov-17 Mar 10-4.30 (Sun 11-4.30).*

(Last admission 3.30).
**Fee:** €11.50 (ch, concessions €7, ch under 3 free). Family day ticket €45.
**Facilities:** 🅿 (charged) 🍴 🚻 ▯ €2 ♿ (ramps where required, toilets) shop, guided tours, audio commentaries ⊗ 🚌 (min 20 people for group discount)

## COBH
### The Queentown Story

Cobh Railway Station
☎ 021 4813591 📠 021 4813595
**email:** info@cobhheritage.com
**Web:** www.cobhheritage.com
**Dir:** *off N25, follow signs for Cobh. Attraction at Deepwater Quay, adjacent to train station*

A dramatic exhibition of the origins, history and legends of Cobh. Between 1848 and 1950 over 3 million Irish people were deported from Cobh on convict ships. Visitors can explore the conditions onboard these vessels and learn about the harbour's connections with the *Lusitania* and the *Titanic*.
**Times:** Open May-Nov, 10-6 (last admission 5). Nov-May, 10-5 (last admission 4)

**Fee:** *€6 (ch & student u18 €3, pen €5). Family ticket €16.50
**Facilities:** 🅿 Ⓟ (2min walk – 2 hour parking outside) 🍴 ♿ (fully wheelchair accessible, wide access, toilets) shop, guided tours ⊗ (ex guide dogs) 🚌

## CORK
### Cork City Gaol

Convent Avenue Sundays Well
☎ 021 4305022 📠 021 4307230
**email:** corkgaol@indigo.ie
**Web:** www.corkcitygaol.com
**Dir:** *2km NW from Patrick St off Sundays Well Rd*

A restored 19th-century prison building. The furnished cells, life-like characters and sound effects combine to allow visitors to experience day-to-day life for prisoners and gaoler. There is an audio-visual presentation of the social history of Cork City. A permanent exhibition, the Radio Museum Experience, is located in the restored 1920s broadcasting studio, home to Cork's first radio station, 6CK.
**Times:** *Open all year Mar-Oct, daily 9.30-6; Nov-Feb, daily 10-5. (Last admission 1hr before closing). Closed 23-28 Dec.
**Fee:** *€6 (ch €3.50, concessions €5) Family ticket €18
**Facilities:** 🅿 Ⓟ (2km-2hrs free) ⌷ (High season 11-4) 🍴 🗐 ♿ (not 1st & 2nd flr, customer care policy – individual attention, toilets) shop, guided tours, audio commentaries ⊗ (ex guide dogs) 🚌 ♿

## BALLYSHANNON
### The Water Wheels

Abbey Assaroe
☎ 071 9851580
**Dir:** *cross Abbey River on Rossnowlagh Rd, next turning left & follow signs*

Abbey Assaroe was founded by Cistercian Monks from Boyle Abbey in the late 12th century. They excelled in water engineering and canalised the river to turn water wheels for mechanical power. Of the two restored 12th-century mills, one is used as a coffee shop and restaurant; the other houses a small museum related to the history of the Cistercians. There are interesting walks in the vicinity.
**Times:** Open May-Oct, daily 10.30-6.30
**Fee:** *Free

**Facilities:** 🅿 Ⓟ (200mtrs - narrow road) 🍴 (Licensed) 🍴 🗐 ♿ (toilets) shop, garden centre 🚌 40/50 people ♿

## LIFFORD
**The Old Courthouse**
Visitor Centre The Diamond
☎ 091 41733 🖹 091 41228
**Email:** info@liffordoldcourthouse.com
**Web:** www.liffordoldcourthouse.com
This is one of the oldest courthouse and jails in Ireland and provides an insight into legal history and some of the terrible conditions endured by prisoners in the 18th century. The Visitor Centre holds re-enactments of the famous trials for treason and murder held in this historic building.
**Times:** Open all year, Mon-Fri, 10-5 & Sun 12.30-5 (last tour 4). Closed Sat & BHs.
**Fee:** €6 (ch €3, concessions €4)

**Facilities:** Ⓟ (100mtrs) ☕ (Mon-Fri 10-3) 🛋 📋 ♿ (toilets) shop, guided tours, audio commentaries, ⊗ (ex assist dogs) 🚌

## DUBLIN
**Dublin Zoo**
Phoenix Park
☎ 01 4748900 🖹 01 6771660
**Email:** info@dublinzoo.ie
**Web:** www.dublinzoo.ie
**Dir:** *10mins bus ride from city centre*
Dublin Zoo first opened to the public in 1830, making it one of the oldest zoos in the world and has consistently been Ireland's favourite attraction. The new 'African Plains' is the biggest single development undertaken by the zoo. This 30-acre development has doubled the size of the zoo and provides spacious new areas for African species. Dublin Zoo is a modern zoo with conservation, education & study as its mission. The majority of the animals here have been born and bred in zoos and are part of global breeding programmes to ensure their continued survival.
**Times:** *Open Mar-Oct, Mon-Sat 9.30-6, Sun 10.30-6; Nov-Feb, daily 10.30-dusk.
**Fee:** *€10.10 (ch & pen €6.30, ch under 3 free, students & unwaged €7.70). Family tickets from €29.40
**Facilities:** ❷ Ⓟ (in park around zoo) 🍴 (Licensed) 🛋 ♿ (wheelchairs available, toilets) shop ⊗ 🚌

## CASTLEISLAND
**Crag Cave**
☎ 066 7141244 🖹 066 7142352
**Email:** info@cragcave.com
**Web:** www.cragcave.com
**Dir:** 1m N, signed off N21
Crag Cave is one of the longest surveyed cave systems in Ireland, with a total length of 3.81km. It is a spectacular world, where pale forests of stalagmites and stalactites, thousands of years old, throw eerie shadows around vast echoing caverns complemented by dramatic sound and lighting effects. Now features new indoor and outdoor soft play areas, which are priced seperately. Tours of the caves last about 30 minutes.
**Times:** *Open mid Mar-1 Nov, daily 10-6 (Jul-Aug 6.30). (Last tour 30 mins before closing time). Dec-Feb, telephone for times.
**Fee:** *€9 (ch €5, concessions €7.50). Family ticket (2ad+2ch) €25 (2ad+4ch) €30
**Facilities:** ❷ Ⓟ 🍴 (Licensed) 🛋 📋 ♿ (ramp to visitor centre, toilets) shop, guided tours (charged) ⊗ (ex guide dogs) 🚌 (pre-booking advisable)

## VALENCIA ISLAND
### The Skellig Experience
☎ 066 9476306 📠 066 9476351
Email: info@skelligexperience.com
Web: www.skelligexperience.com
Dir: *Ring of Kerry road, signed after Cahersiveen then Valentia bridge, or ferry from Rena Rd Point*

The Skellig Rocks are renowned for their scenery, sea bird colonies, lighthouses, Early Christian monastic architecture and rich underwater life. The two islands - Skellig Michael and Small Skellig - stand like fairytale castles in the Atlantic Ocean, rising to 218 metres and their steep cliffs plunging 50 metres below the sea. The Heritage Centre, (on Valentia Island, reached from the mainland via a bridge), tells the story of the Skellig Islands in an exciting multimedia exhibition. Cruises around Valentia Habour are also available.

**Times:** *Open May-Jun 10-6; Jul-Aug 10-7; Sep 10-6. Mar, Apr & Oct-Nov 10-5
**Fee:** *€5 (ch €3, concessions €4). Family ticket €14.
**Facilities:** 🅿 🍴 £3.50 ♿ (toilets) shop, guided tours 🚫 (ex guide dogs) 🚌

## KILDARE
### Irish National Stud, Gardens & Horse Museum
Irish National Stud Tully
☎ 045 521617 📠 045 522964
Email: stud@irish-national-stud.ie
Web: www.irish-national-stud.ie
Dir: *off N7, junct 13 then R415 towards Nurney & Kildare. Attraction well signed from rdbt*

Situated in the grounds of the Irish National Stud, the gardens were established by Lord Wavertree between 1906 and 1910, and symbolise 'The Life of Man'. You can also visit the Horse Museum which includes the skeleton of the racehorse Arkle, winner of major races in the 1960s. The Millennium Garden of St Fiachra has 4 acres of woodland and lakeside walks and features a Waterford Crystal garden and limestone monastic cells.

**Times:** *Open 12 Feb-1 Nov, daily 9.30-6 (last admission 5).
**Fee:** €10 (pen & students €8). Family ticket €25
**Facilities:** 🅿 🍴 (Licensed) 🪑 🍴 ♿ (all parts of stud accessible, only small part of gardens, toilets) shop, guided tours 🚌 (pre-booking preferred)

## BIRR
### Birr Castle Demesne
☎ 057 9120 336 📠 05791 21583
Email: mail@birrcastle.com
Web: www.birrcastle.com
Dir: *in town sq take exit beside Bank of Ireland and bear right. Turn left, entrance on right, car park on left*

A large landscaped park with a lake, rivers and waterfalls, with important plant collections including magnolias, maples, limes and oaks. The Demesne is particularly colourful in the spring and autumn, and is noted for its formal gardens, containing the tallest box hedges in the world. It is also home to the Great Birr Telescope, built in 1844, and Ireland's Historic Science Centre, a series of galleries focusing on Ireland's scientific past.

**Times:** *Open all year, Mar-Oct 9-6, Nov-Mar 10-5
**Fee:** *€8.50 (ch €4.50, concessions €6.50). Family ticket (2ad+2ch) €24.
**Facilities:** 🅿 🅿 (in town) 🪑 (open in Summer) 🪑 🍴 £1.50 ♿ (toilets) shop, guided tours 🚌

CO ROSCOMMON / CO WEXFORD

STROKESTOWN
**Strokestown Park House Garden & Famine Museum**
Strokestown Park
☎ 071 9633013 🖷 071 9633712
**Email:** info@strokestownpark.ie
**Web:** www.strokestownpark.ie
**Dir:** *23km from Longford on N5*
A fine example of an early 18th-century gentleman farmer's country estate. Built in Palladian style the house reflects perfectly the confidence of the newly emergent ruling class. The pleasure garden has also been restored, and the Famine Museum, located in the stable yard, commemorates the Great Irish Famine of the 1840s.
**Times:** *Open 17 Mar-Oct, daily.
**Fee:** *€13 (ch €6, concessions €11.50). Family ticket €28.50. Group 20+ €10.50 each
**Facilities:** 🅿 🅟 (5 mins walk) 🍽 (Licensed) ⚌ 🗐 ♿ (toilets) shop garden centre guided tours audio commentaries (charged) 🚫 (ex guide dogs & in grounds) 🚌

FERRYCARRIG
**The Irish National Heritage Park**
☎ 053 912 0733 🖷 053 912 0911
**Email:** info@inhp.com
**Web:** www.inhp.com
**Dir:** *3m from Wexford, on N11*
Sixteen historical sites set in a magnificent 35-acre mature forest explaining Ireland's history from the Stone and Bronze Ages, through the Celtic period and concluding with the Vikings and Normans. Among the exhibits are a reconstructed Mesolithic camp, a Viking boatyard with two full size ships and a Norman motte and bailey. Please visit website for details of events running throughout the year.
**Times:** Open daily Oct-Apr, 9.30-5.30. Apr-Oct, 9.30-6.30.
**Fee:** €7.50 (concessions €6). Family (2 ad & upto 3 ch) €19. Group rates available on request.
**Facilities:** 🅿 🍽 (Licensed) ⚌ 🗐 Free-€1 ♿ (toilets) shop, guided tours, audio commentaries 🚫 (ex guide dogs) 🚌 (pre-booking preferred)

NEW ROSS
**Dunbrody Abbey Visitors Centre**
Dunbrody Abbey Campile
☎ 051 88603
**Email:** patrickbelfast@aol.com
**Web:** www.dunbrodyabbey.com
**Dir:** *10m from New Ross at base of Hook Peninsular*
The visitor centre is based around the Abbey itself and Dunbrody Castle. The abbey was founded in 1170 as a Cistercian monastery. There is an intriguing yew hedge maze with 1,550 yew trees and a museum. In addition there is a golf pitch-and-putt course, a local craft centre and Dunbrody Abbey Cookery School.
**Times:** *Open May-Sep 10-6.
**Fee:** *Abbey €2, Family ticket €5. Maze/Golf €4, (ch €2). Family €10.
**Facilities:** 🅿 🍽 ⚌ 🗐 ♿ shop, garden centre, guided tours 🚌 (must book for guided tour) 🚭

ENNISKERRY
## Powerscourt Gardens & House Exhibition
Powerscourt Estate
☎ 01 2046000 📠 01 2046900
Web: www.powerscourt.ie
Dir: *From Dublin city centre take N11 S, after 12m take exit left to Bray S, Enniskerry. Left at rdbt, over flyover, rejoin N11 N. Take 1st left for Enniskerry Village entrance 500mtrs*

In the foothills of the Wicklow Mountains, these gardens were begun by Richard Wingfield in the 1740s, and are a blend of formal plantings, sweeping terraces, statuary and ornamental lakes together with secret hollows, rambling walks and walled gardens. The gardens cover a massive 20 hectares and contain more than two hundred varieties of tree and shrub. The house itself incorporates an exhibition which traces the history of the estate, and tells the story of the disastrous fire of 1974 which gutted the house. The grounds also contain Powerscourt Waterfall, Ireland's highest at 398ft.

**Times:** Open Gardens & House Exhibition daily 9.30-5.30 (Gardens close at dusk in winter). Waterfall open daily, May-Aug 9.30-7, Mar-Oct, 10.30-5.30, Nov-Feb, 10.30-4. Closed 2 weeks before Christmas.

**Fee:** Gardens & House Exhibition €9 (ch under 16 €5 ch under 5 free, students €7.50). Gardens only €7.50 (ch under 16 €4.50 ch under 5 free, students €6.50). Waterfall €5 (ch under 16 €3.50 ch under 2 free, students €4.50).

**Facilities:** 🅿 Ⓟ (no parking at front of house) 🍽 (self service) 🍴 (Licensed) 🎏 📖 Free-€2 ♿ (lift to first floor, 2 wheelchairs available, toilets) shop, garden centre 🚌

**Ha'penny Bridge in Dublin**

**CO WICKLOW**

NOTES

**NOTES**